Nexus of Empire

UNIVERSITY PRESS OF FLORIDA

Florida A&M University, Tallahassee
Florida Atlantic University, Boca Raton
Florida Gulf Coast University, Ft. Myers
Florida International University, Miami
Florida State University, Tallahassee
New College of Florida, Sarasota
University of Central Florida, Orlando
University of Florida, Gainesville
University of North Florida, Jacksonville
University of South Florida, Tampa
University of West Florida, Pensacola

Nexus of Empire

Negotiating Loyalty and Identity in
the Revolutionary Borderlands, 1760s–1820s

EDITED BY
GENE ALLEN SMITH AND SYLVIA L. HILTON

University Press of Florida
Gainesville/Tallahassee/Tampa/Boca Raton
Pensacola/Orlando/Miami/Jacksonville/Ft. Myers/Sarasota

Copyright 2010 by Gene Allen Smith and Sylvia L. Hilton
Printed in the United States of America.
All rights reserved

First cloth printing, 2010
First paperback printing, 2011

Library of Congress Cataloging-in-Publication Data
Nexus of empire: negotiating loyalty and identity in the revolutionary
borderlands, 1760s–1820s/edited by Gene Allen Smith and Sylvia L. Hilton.
p. cm.
Includes index.
ISBN 978-0-8130-3399-0 (alk. paper); ISBN 978-0-8130-3727-1 (pbk.)
1. Gulf Coast (U.S.)—History—18th century. 2. Gulf Coast (U.S.)—
History—19th century. 3. Identity (Psychology)—Gulf Coast
(U.S.)—History—18th century. 4. Identity (Psychology)—Gulf Coast
(U.S.)—History—19th century. 5. Group identity—Gulf Coast (U.S.)—
History—18th century. 6. Group identity—Gulf Coast (U.S.)—History—
19th century. 7. Loyalty—Social aspects—Gulf Coast (U.S.)—History—18th
century. 8. Loyalty—Social aspects—Gulf Coast (U.S.)—History—19th
century. 9. Social change—Gulf Coast (U.S.)—History. 10. Nationalism—
Gulf Coast (U.S.)—History. I. Smith, Gene A., 1963– II. Hilton, Sylvia L.
F296.N49 2010
976.'0439–dc22   2009026486

The University Press of Florida is the scholarly publishing agency for the
State University System of Florida, comprising Florida A&M University,
Florida Atlantic University, Florida Gulf Coast University, Florida International University, Florida State University, New College of Florida, University of Central Florida, University of Florida, University of North Florida,
University of South Florida, and University of West Florida.

University Press of Florida
15 Northwest 15th Street
Gainesville, FL 32611-2079
http://www.upf.com

Contents

List of Illustrations, Maps, and Tables   vii

Part I. Changing Flags and Political Uncertainty

Introduction   3
   Gene Allen Smith and Sylvia L. Hilton

1. Loyalty and Patriotism on North American Frontiers: Being and Becoming Spanish in the Mississippi Valley, 1776–1803   8
   Sylvia L. Hilton

Part II. Dilemmas Among Native Americans and Free Blacks

2. "Like to Have Made a War among Ourselves": The Creek Indians and the Coming of the War of the Revolution   39
   Kathryn E. Holland Braund

3. Louis LeClerc De Milford, a.k.a. General François Tastanegy: An Eighteenth-Century French Adventurer among the Creeks   63
   Gilbert C. Din

4. Marie Thérèze dit Coincoin: A Free Black Woman on the Louisiana-Texas Frontier   89
   H. Sophie Burton

5. To Strike a Balance: New Orleans' Free Colored Community and the Diplomacy of William Charles Cole Claiborne   113
   Erin M. Greenwald

6. Dehahuit: An Indian Diplomat on the Louisiana-Texas Frontier, 1804–1815   140
   F. Todd Smith

Part III. Building Fortunes through Family Connections and Local Community

7. The Nature of Loyalty: Antonio Gil Ibarvo and the East Texas Frontier 163
   J. Edward Townes

8. Philip Livingston, Chameleon "Premier" of West Florida 183
   Robin F. A. Fabel

9. Oliver Pollock and the Creation of an American Identity in Spanish Colonial Louisiana 198
   Light Townsend Cummins

10. Bordermakers and Landed Women: The Rouquier Sisters of Colonial Natchitoches 219
    Betje Black Klier and Diane M. T. North

11. Daniel Clark: Merchant Prince of New Orleans 241
    Elizabeth Urban Alexander

Part IV. Personal Ambition in Government and Military Service

12. William Dunbar, William Claiborne, and Daniel Clark: Intersections of Loyalty and National Identity on the Florida Frontier 271
    Andrew McMichael

13. "Motivated Only by the Love of Humanity": Arsène Lacarrière Latour and the Struggle for the Southwest 298
    Gene Allen Smith

14. Soldier, Expansionist, Politician: Eleazer Wheelock Ripley and the Dance of Ambition in the Early Republic 321
    Samuel Watson

    Conclusion 347
    Gene Allen Smith and Sylvia L. Hilton

Contributors 355

Index 395

Illustrations, Maps, and Tables

Illustrations

Figure 5.1. William Charles Cole Claiborne, ca. 1805, by Ambrose Duval 115
Figure 8.1. Philip Peter Livingston by Pompeo Girolami Batoni (1708–87) 185
Figure 10.1 The Prudhomme-Rouquier House 221
Figure 13.1. Major General Andrew Jackson 300
Figure 13.2. Portrait of Géraud-Calixte Jean-Baptiste Arsène Lacarrière Latour 301
Figure 13.3. Map showing the landing of the British army 306

Maps

Map I.1. The Gulf Coast borderlands, 1763–83 5
Map 2.1. The Creek towns and their boundaries, ca. 1773 40
Map 3.1. Louis LeClerc De Milford's Gulf world 64
Map 6.1. The nineteenth-century Louisiana-Texas border 141
Map 7.1. The eighteenth-century Louisiana-Texas border 164
Map 9.1. Eighteenth-century Spanish Louisiana 199
Map 13.1. The early nineteenth-century southwestern borderlands 309
Map C.1. The Gulf Coast borderlands, 1783–1821 349

Tables

Table 4.1. Natchitoches Population, 1766–1810 93
Table 4.2. Proportion of *Libres* in the Total, Free, and Nonwhite Populations, Natchitoches, 1766–1810 94
Table 4.3. Increase in Natchitoches Manumissions, 1774–1803 95
Table 4.4. Age Category and Phenotype of Slave by Type of Manumission, Natchitoches, 1774–1803 96
Table 4.5. Phenotype and Sex of Slave by Type of Manumission, Natchitoches, 1774–1803 97
Table 4.6. Owner's Phenotype and Sex by Type of Manumission, Natchitoches, 1774–1803 102

PART I

Changing Flags and Political Uncertainty

Introduction

GENE ALLEN SMITH AND SYLVIA L. HILTON

During the fall of 1806 John Shaw, a captain in the U.S. navy who was commanding the naval station at New Orleans, informed the American government that the political loyalty of Louisiana remained uncertain. He had good reasons for his fears. Discontent prevailed among the multiethnic and multicultural inhabitants of the Louisiana Purchase territory because of the arbitrary manner in which their homeland had been sold to the United States and worries about the management of their full incorporation into the American union. Aaron Burr's activities also suggested the influence of separatism and filibusterism as ongoing threats on the western frontier. In addition, the Spanish government, protesting Jeffersonian efforts to extend the limits of the Louisiana territory both east and west, had mobilized military forces and had taken other defense measures in the Floridas, Texas, and in the Caribbean. These considerations convinced Shaw that a single action might decide the political fate of the entire region. He warned that a successful military strike could permit either Burr or the Spaniards to march into New Orleans and find "numerous . . . followers of a victorious flag."[1] Neither possibility played out. But in reminding the administration that no government could count on the unswerving loyalty of the inhabitants of the Gulf Coast, Shaw was repeating an observation pointed out by many local authorities before him. In fact, the fears articulated by Shaw about potential disaffection permeated the Gulf borderlands throughout the late eighteenth century and the early nineteenth (1763–1821). Indeed, although it may seem foolhardy today, during their campaign against New Orleans in the fall of 1814, British commanders still fondled the hope that the region's multiethnic population would rise and help throw off the yoke of American occupation.

For much of the seventeenth and eighteenth centuries, Great Britain and France had been locked in a power struggle that involved competitive colonial expansion worldwide. Although French sovereignty in North America came to an abrupt end in 1763, American historiography has tended to emphasize the Anglo-French rivalry in the St. Lawrence and Ohio River Valleys and the Great Lakes region as determining the development of North America and, by extension, of the United States. Scholars such as Richard White, Stephen Aron, Andrew Cayton, Fredrika Teute, and Jeremy Adelman have analyzed in colorful and intellectually stimulating terms the specific colonial rivalries that emerged on the northern and northwestern frontiers and that shaped the United States well into the nineteenth century. By contrast, the southern territories strung along the Gulf Coast have attracted less attention and have even been considered to be of minor importance, except in the eyes of a dedicated minority of historians of the South and the Spanish borderlands.[2] This seems amazing when one considers that this Gulf nexus of empire—which, between 1763 and 1821, stretched from the Floridas across to Texas—presented myriad opportunities for demographic, economic, social, cultural, and political interaction, as not two but *three* European imperial metropolises—England, France, and Spain—struggled with one another, and, after 1776, with the United States, as well as with numerous Native American peoples and maroon communities, in their attempts to strengthen and expand their own spheres of political and social control (map I.1). As Colin Bonwick has pointed out in his criticism of historiographical assumptions about the initial development of the United States, "one major impediment clouding our understanding of the early republic is the map of modern America."[3]

The American War for Independence reshaped the geopolitical boundaries of North America and introduced a new competitor struggling for strategic advantage and economic resources. The emergence of the United States as an independent power in North America pitted old regime European imperialism against the new American republicanism and nationalism. Between 1783 and 1821 the old colonial powers—Britain in the North and Spain in the South— reshaped their colonial policies and expectations in North America, partly in response to the consolidation and expansionism of the United States. At the same time, the French Revolution articulated and disseminated throughout the Atlantic world powerful ideas regarding the relationship between individuals and their governments, and the relation of both to the idea of the nation. For a brief period between 1800 and 1803, both the British and the Americans were alarmed by the prospect that France might regain its status as a North American colonial power by virtue of the Spanish cession of the trans-Mississippian territory back into French hands. Napoleon's snap decision to sell that vast piece of real estate to the United States solved that particular problem. Yet the political fate of the lower Mississippi and the Floridas would not be definitively settled until Andrew Jackson's defeat of the Creek Indians at Horseshoe Bend, his successful defense of New Orleans against the British

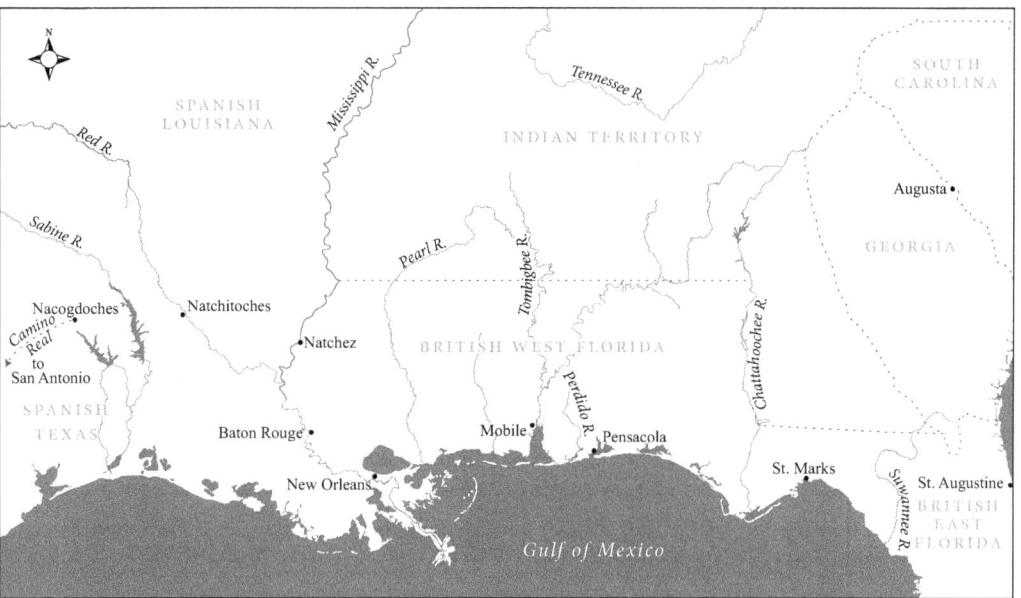

Map I.1. The Gulf Coast borderlands, 1763–83. Map by Tracy Ellen Smith, www.cdrtexas.com.

at the end of the War of 1812, and the U.S. acquisition of the Floridas by virtue of the Adams-Onís (or Transcontinental) Treaty, which was ratified in 1821. By contrast, Spanish diplomacy managed to keep Texas within New Spain's northern frontier, thus placing that westernmost part of the Gulf borderlands beyond the immediate grasp of the United States, although the proclamation of Mexican independence in that same year of 1821 put Texas beyond Spanish imperial control, too.

Consequently, during the tumultuous revolutionary period from 1763 to 1821, a number of flags flew above the Floridas, the Mississippi Valley, and Texas, leaving the inhabitants of the region to wonder whose colors might be hoisted next. As long as the region remained in political flux, the complexities of immigration patterns, social customs, economic transactions, cultural systems, and government regimes permitted, indeed encouraged, a startling fluidity of personal identities and loyalties. Among these, the negotiation of national identity and allegiance was, therefore, only one expression of the adaptability of the inhabitants of the Gulf borderlands during the almost sixty years of changing flags and political uncertainty.

In effect, individuals—by choice or by necessity—often showed themselves both able and willing to modify their identities and loyalties. Nationality was only one of the components of a personal sense of identity, and individuals might consider changing it voluntarily for many different reasons, usually connected with expectations of personal gain or self-interest of some sort. However, for governments and communities, national identity and membership remained matters of fundamental collective interest because they represented a means of regulating access to land property rights and other economic resources, and of ensuring collective security, shared values, participation in certain politically controlled advantages, and, above all, solidarity in the event of military hostilities. While individuals might link patriotic sentiments to their sense of national identity, and governing elites might instrumentalize such sentiments to strengthen the internal cohesion of the nation-state, loyalty remained a much more rational and practical matter. It was measured strictly in terms of a commitment that must be declared in terms understood to be morally and legally binding, and that must be duly fulfilled, especially in times of national danger or need, by service and attention to the common defense. Loyalty, then, became the practical side of national identity, or the rational expression of patriotic solidarity.

The essays in this volume are based on original research with a view to exploring the concepts of loyalty and personal identity. Their mainly biographical approach is appropriate for this purpose because it offers concrete examples of the ways in which a number of historical figures of different sexes, ethnicities, and socioeconomic backgrounds adjusted to the changing geopolitical situation within this important nexus of empire. The essays make no pretense of covering all the possible angles that individual lives and theoretical approaches might suggest. Ultimately, they aim simply to illustrate by example that individuals could and did make significant and sometimes difficult decisions about their own identities and related loyalties, although social constraints meant that not all individuals enjoyed the same range of options. Their choices seem to have been most often motivated by kinship and/or friendship networks as well as by daily survival and economic considerations. Issues of national identity and allegiance sometimes came to the fore, but they do not seem to have been paramount concerns for individuals as they went about their daily lives in these Gulf borderlands where nations and empires played out their own dramas. Jeanne Chase reminds us that historiography is a reflection of present experience, and that in the early twenty-first century many individuals experience "encounters across porous boundaries, multiple identities as assets in the global economy, personal allegiances redefined and contested."[4] Looking back two hundred years, the world has changed but the social survival skills of individuals do not look so different.

Notes

1. John Shaw to the Secretary of the Navy, Oct. 31, 1806, Letters Received by the Secretary of the Navy from Commanders, 1804–86, RG 45, M147, National Archives, Washington, D.C.

2. But see, for example, Thomas D. Clark and John D. W. Guice, *The Old Southwest, 1795–1830: Frontiers in Conflict* (Albuquerque: University of New Mexico Press, 1989; repr., Norman: University of Oklahoma Press, 1996); and Patrick G. Williams, S. Charles Bolton, and Jeannie M. Whayne, eds., *A Whole Country in Commotion: The Louisiana Purchase and the American Southwest* (Fayetteville: University of Arkansas Press, 2005).

3. Colin C. Bonwick, "American Nationalism, American Citizenship, and the Limits of Authority, 1776–1800," in Cornelis A. van Minnen and Sylvia L. Hilton, eds., *Federalism, Citizenship, and Collective Identities in U.S. History* (Amsterdam: VU University Press, 2000), 29.

4. Jeanne Chase, "Porous Boundaries and Shifting Borderlands: The American Experience in a New World Order," in Louis P. Masur, ed., *The Challenge of American History* (Baltimore: Johns Hopkins University Press, 1999), 55.

1

Loyalty and Patriotism on North American Frontiers

Being and Becoming Spanish in the Mississippi Valley, 1776–1803

SYLVIA L. HILTON

> We, the undersigned, freely and spontaneously, ... in recognition of the generous protection which has been granted us by the Spanish Government, desirous of living in this province, and with permission granted by the Governor, ... do pledge our word of honor and promise by all means which serve to keep faith among men, ... not to offend, directly or indirectly, nor to conspire against the Spanish nation; but on the contrary, to defend and assist it to the best of our ability, might and means; revealing to its leaders any plot, conspiracy or enterprise which might be directed against it, of which we may have news, subjecting ourselves completely to the Spanish laws, ... obeying them all with the same exactness and loyalty of His Catholic Majesty's other vassals, in which character and class henceforth we shall be considered.[1]

This is the text of a pledge of allegiance to the Spanish Crown, dated January 1787. All foreign immigrants in West Florida and "Luisiana" were required to give similar pledges. The historiography on late eighteenth-century immigration into these Spanish colonies is considerable and offers insights into many aspects of international migrations, foreign relations, and frontier life during this period.[2] A few authors mention the government's constant concern regarding the population's loyalty to Spain, but very few dedicate more than a passing comment to this subject. It merits some attention because, in this period, revolutionary movements were changing the ways in which people perceived the political relations between individuals, local communities, and state governments. In discussing Spain's policies in Luisiana and the Floridas, Arthur P. Whitaker remarked that "the super-subtlety of the Spanish mind appears in these measures," but he did not inquire further into the "conceptions that lay at the basis of this policy."[3] This chapter aims to explore what these pledges and other documentation generated by the colonization projects can tell us about concepts of loyalty and patriotism on this fast-changing frontier of the Spanish empire.[4]

Spanish Luisiana and West Florida: A Multiethnic Frontier

Even without considering the Native American peoples or those of African descent, the multiethnic character of the population was remarkable. Francophone settlers included the Louisianan Creoles, two waves of displaced Acadians, French Canadians, and after 1789, refugees from the French West Indies. British rule in the Floridas created English-speaking communities after 1763. Soon, a few Scottish and Irish merchants were allowed to set up shop in the vicinity of New Orleans. The liberal land ordinance issued by Governor Alejandro O'Reilly in 1770 attracted hundreds of American immigrants into Spanish Luisiana. After the U.S. War of Independence, many Loyalists stayed in West Florida, as did merchants such as the Indian traders William Panton and John Leslie. Numerous westering Anglo-Americans from the Atlantic states, and Irish priests recruited by the Spanish government, increased the Anglophone contingent. Settlers of German, Dutch, Flemish, and other ethnic origins came in small numbers at different times, sometimes straight from Europe, but often from the United States. The European and American "Spaniards" represented a relatively small percentage of the population.

The Spanish government was largely responsible for increasing the multiethnic character of the population in these colonies. Unprecedented immigration and colonization policies were developed in the 1780s that contemplated the admission of foreign settlers, including non-Catholic Anglo-Americans. This striking departure from the norm was pragmatically justified by local authorities, Prime Minister Floridablanca, his successor Manuel Godoy, and other Spanish officials and government advisors, on the grounds that the demographic growth of these colonies was essential for both frontier defense and economic development.[5] Imperial strategy assigned defensive functions to all of the North American colonies, but the special value of the Floridas and Luisiana hinged on their dual role in the protection of the sea lanes of the Mexican Gulf and Spanish possessions in the Caribbean, and as the front line against British and U.S. overland expansion toward New Spain and the North Pacific.

In addition to the thousands of people who simply arrived and settled in the Floridas and Luisiana, scores of petitions and proposals were addressed to diverse Spanish authorities in connection with colonization projects.[6] The list of foreign immigrants, promoters, and agents includes the names of many men who played more or less significant roles in the early national history of the United States. Among them were James Wilkinson, George Morgan, George Rogers Clark, John Sevier, and Daniel Boone. The sheer audacity of these colonization policies has led many historians to be condescendingly dismissive of Spanish political intelligence. Isaac Joslin Cox opined that "these Spaniards were playing with fire, and they ought to have known it," failing to grasp that Spain's policymakers did know exactly what they were doing.[7] Francis Philbrick thought that the policy was hatched "in desperation, and with pitiable innocence."[8] Arthur Whitaker remarked that it seemed "foolhardy" and "suicidal," but then decided it was actually "heroic." Conceding that "there was reason in this madness," he recognized the validity of the Spanish rationale regarding the immigrants that "if they could not be trusted, they could at least be watched."[9]

Esteban Rodríguez Miró, the governor of Luisiana, admitted that "at first glance it seems dangerous to settle foreigners in Luisiana," but he argued in 1792 that the danger was no greater than if all the migrants settled on the banks of the Ohio and from there invaded the Spanish colonies. The difference, he thought, was that "once they have emigrated and sworn vassalage, anyone who takes part in a revolution will risk a great deal, and far from gaining glory, will stain his reputation with the ugly epithet of traitor." Miró knew that he was catching at straws. "Circumstances force us to run this risk," was his final pragmatic justification, because he could see no viable alternatives.[10] This bold policy was indeed a calculated risk, born out of extraordinary circumstances. It was not representative of "normal" metropolitan reformism under the Bourbons, but it does illustrate Spanish flexibility in adapting political concepts and government practices to an otherwise unmanageable situation. The levels of tolerance shown by local and metropolitan officials in developing this unusual policy of containment indicate the limits to which the agents of Spanish enlightened despotism might go in practical liberalism when under extreme pressure.

Once the strategic necessity of adopting such a policy was recognized, its articulation became a product of enlightened thought, revealing a highly rationalized approach to sociological understanding and political necessity. Officials thought that geographically mobile individuals were guided by self-interest. If migrants had the opportunity, and if there were no impediments, they were moved by their hopes of personal gain, in which diverse economic, social, cultural, and political considerations might be weighed.[11] This analysis thus contemplated migration as a rational, more or less planned undertaking, opening up the prospect of being able to engage in a negotiation in which the colonists, the promoters, and the Spanish government could attain some of their respective goals, for a price.

Spain's priorities were very clear in the mid-1780s, and broad policy lines emerged quickly. The negotiable details seem to have been prompted in part by the needs and requests of settlers and promoters. In designing and implementing the policy, local authorities had a mental list of preferred categories of immigrants, reflecting diplomatic, economic, social, political, and cultural criteria. They also clearly understood the political risks involved, as they faced the myriad social and cultural problems posed by the increasingly multiethnic communities living under Spanish rule. High on the Spanish wish list were families, bonafide farmers, monarchists, and Catholics. Least esteemed were vagabonds, speculators, Anglo-Americans and Protestants. Skilled and industrious settlers of some means who would contribute to the economic growth of the colonies were most desirable. Governor Carondelet, for example, expressed his hopes for the establishment on the Ouachita River of "useful persons," explaining, "I would not have there any kind of idle people or unfit for agriculture."[12]

Settlers must also be upstanding, law-abiding individuals. Most of the promoters gave assurances in this respect, as did all local authorities when they sought higher government approval of their own initiatives or recommendations. For example, in 1799 each of Daniel Boone's followers promised Charles Dehault Delassus, the lieutenant governor of Saint Louis, that "having no other aim than that of living as a peaceful farmer and subject to the laws of the Government," he would "at all times provide an example of faithfulness and obedience."[13] Good character lent greater credence to the settlers' pledge of fidelity. For the newcomers, the pledge represented a commitment to honor a number of very specific practical obligations, such as residence in the colony, obedience of Spanish laws and government officials, vigilance against threats to Spanish interests and sovereignty, and military service. For the Spanish government, the conditions set out in the loyalty oaths represented the bottom line. Indeed, these active and very public duties lay at the heart of the Spanish concept of loyalty.[14]

Loyalty

Timeless political wisdom advises governments that farmers occupying their own lands provide the best military defense in the event of any hostile intent. On this Mississippi frontier, it was essential for Spain to ensure that colonists would cultivate and reside on their lands and not obtain them for speculative purposes. The loyalty oath itself usually included a statement to this effect. Promoters assured Spanish authorities of the intentions of the prospective colonists to establish their homes within territories under Spanish jurisdiction.[15] "Mere vagabonds" were explicitly excluded from the general approval given in 1788 to Wilkinson's proposal for colonization.[16] Carondelet's distrust of the migrants pouring into the backcountry from the Atlantic coast was based partly on his perception that they were "accustomed to changing their place of residence as easily as they changed their shirts."[17] In 1795, he told the commandant at Ouachita to do everything in his power to keep recent immigrants settled on their land, "and to deter them from the wandering life of hunters, which is entirely opposed to agriculture."[18] If they were given land, emigrants arriving at Natchez from Georgia in 1800 promised "to fix their residence" in Spanish territories.[19]

This requirement connects with larger historiographical issues. Almost everywhere in the Atlantic world, fixed residence or domicile was considered to be a key indicator of personal involvement and good intentions as regards the host or adopted community. Tamar Herzog argues that, in Spanish America as in the English colonies, "domicile could transform aliens into natives," and furthermore, "that membership in local communities defined the relationship linking individuals to the kingdom and that a 'law of domicile' was as important, if not more important than the law of birth (*ius soli*) and descent (*ius sanguinis*)."[20]

Several promoters tried to obtain varying degrees of political autonomy for their settlements.[21] Yet there were no concessions on this point. Carondelet underscored this fact repeatedly: for example, he told Juan Filhiol in 1795 that "Maison Rouge . . . will remain under your command, and subject to the general laws of justice, police, and other rules established";[22] and he reminded Gayoso that the American settlers at Natchez had voluntarily agreed "to live under the laws of Spain."[23] The significance of this insistence on political control becomes more apparent when put in a broader context. The petitions for autonomy clashed with the goals of Bourbon reformism, which was seeking to gradually implant a more legally homogenous and centralized political system.[24]

Enlightened reformism was also working to recuperate Spain's much weakened economic and military power. This goal depended on the conservation of overseas colonial resources, making imperial defense a major concern of the metropolitan government.[25] To this end, everywhere in Spanish America great dependence was placed on the local militia. Consequently, the military defense of Luisiana and the Floridas required the participation of many foreign-born residents, and it was essential to be able to count on these militiamen's loyalty to Spain. Miró and Navarro urged: "We ought not to lose an instant, and populate Luisiana with individuals who will swear a solemn oath to take up arms against any invasion attempted by Kentucky and the other [U.S.] establishments, and this obligation ought to be expressly included in the pledge of fidelity that they must necessarily take."[26]

The loyalty oaths did indeed stress this aspect. The immigrants must promise not only to respond immediately to any official call to arms, but to be actively vigilant against any plot or movement that might threaten Spanish interests, especially invasions from British or U.S. territories. Colonization agents underscored this powerful argument when seeking the royal seal of approval on their plans. Agustín Macarty's proposal of 1787 to bring between two thousand and three thousand Catholic Irishmen from the United States argued that this would greatly increase the number of loyal vassals ready and able to defend Spanish sovereignty.[27] When George Rogers Clark communicated to Ambassador Gardoqui his decision "to offer [himself] to His Majesty the King of Spain with a numerous colony of worthy vassals," he stressed their willingness to give military service. "A garrison will be maintained," he promised, "with a big enough body of troops, which will be formed by the settlers themselves, to prevent a surprise [attack]."[28] The petition of the Prussian William Frederick von Steuben included not only the obligation to form militias, subject to "military service within the province," but the suggestion that a body of regular troops could be created, "subject in everything to the discipline and service of His Catholic Majesty's troops," except in disputes over property and religion.[29] George Morgan, too, offered to recruit as many as three militia companies, with officers elected from among the settlers and receiving their commissions from the king.[30]

In addition to these expressions of what loyalty meant to the interested parties in practical terms, other more theoretical aspects merit some attention. Rarely have historians discussed the significance of the Spanish use of loyalty oaths in a general sense. Jon Kukla strives for balance when he says that the oaths "were a slender reed on which to base the security of the colony and the empire."[31] However, interpretations that see only weakness and/or madness in the very idea of this immigration policy have suggested that insistence on these formal pledges epitomized the hopeless utopianism and naive folly of Spain's rulers. A few authors have dismissed outright the sincerity or validity of the loyalty oaths. James R. Jacobs judged them to be a mere formality, a "meaningless gesture." Francis Philbrick maintained that Miró and Navarro understood Wilkinson's oath of allegiance to have "the significance, legally, of blank paper." More recently, John Thornton Posey gave the act a thoroughly cynical reading, affirming that "the oath of allegiance . . . was simply a perfunctory but necessary means."[32]

Nevertheless, loyalty oaths had long been common practice throughout the Atlantic world.[33] Then as now, loyalty was considered to be an ethical principle. Early modern Spanish usage defined loyalty as "the fidelity with which something is done, in accordance with laws of reason and justice. It is a virtue of the spirit, . . . it entails a commitment that obliges."[34] Formal pledges had a special meaning within the social pact, providing a public formula by which free men expressed their connection with society, their commitment to collective security and well-being, in sum, their intention to keep faith with the community in which they lived. By insisting on this formality, local authorities were demanding proof of a conscious determination. Furthermore, all parties understood that the chief moral and political significance of such pledges lay in their voluntary character. Here may be glimpsed some connection between loyalty oaths and the new concept of volitional allegiance. Spanish officials accepted each immigrant's unilateral adoption of a new allegiance to king and country as an expression of a "natural" freedom of choice.[35] Appreciating the political need to involve each settler's sense of personal responsibility, local authorities were trying to engage the moral value of voluntary individual commitments. Only a few liberal theorists supported the idea of volitional allegiance in the early 1800s, but it certainly figured in transatlantic discussions, gradually gaining ground as a democratic principle.[36]

On first broaching the subject of nationality by choice, James Wilkinson knew that he was treading on delicate terrain. Recognizing that his conduct might seem suspicious, he explained: "I hope that it may not be said of me in justice that I am breaking any law of nature or nations, of conscience or honor, in changing my fidelity from the United States of America to His Catholic Majesty." It was not, he implied, that he scorned such considerations, but he did reject the notion that birthplace patriotism obliged a man "to remain fixed like a vegetable." He argued that an intelligent person could legitimately change his allegiance, if he thought that this would improve his personal well-being and happiness.[37] Most historians accuse Wilkinson of highly questionable, if not treasonable conduct toward the United States.[38] At the same time, the Spaniards are portrayed as "gullible," "naive," and "ingenuous" in their dealings with the infamous adventurer.[39] This was not the case. The Spanish officers distrusted him but nonetheless agreed that it was wise to keep him entertained and make use of him if possible. Indeed, it rather seems that they understood one another perfectly well.[40] In any case, this chapter is not so much concerned with Wilkinson's honorability as with his use of language that was unquestionably that of enlightened public discourse of his day. His arguments regarding volitional allegiance were persuasive because they were familiar in liberal discussions of his day and age.[41] In fact, Miró and Navarro may well have shared the opinions put forward in the proposal of colonization of 1787.[42]

The political value of loyalty oaths was not exhausted by considerations of their voluntary character. The pledges were also posited as rational commitments based on each individual's perception of his own interests and needs.[43] This was the premise upon which the entire immigration program was constructed. Many different philosophies of social and personal identity developed in the eighteenth century, but Roy Porter argues that their overarching theme was the shift from a focus on the immortal soul to the conscious mind (whether romantic or broadly utilitarian versions) as the seat of personality.[44] Spanish officials were aware that all individuals could have loyalties to different groups and codes, and that these might change or clash. Loyalty, in short, was susceptible to individual calculations.

Spaniards were not alone in understanding the negotiability of national loyalties. Many Americans clearly thought that their loyalty could be legitimately transferred to whichever power best protected their interests.[45] When discussing a possible "connection with foreign powers," the Kentuckian John Brown argued that if the Union could protect westerners' rights, "reason and gratitude and justice" demanded their continuing allegiance, but if not, "reason points out the propriety of seeking these where they are to be found."[46] Thus, it may well be that one of the factors that actually encouraged the Spanish immigration policy was, as David J. Weber says, the "obvious indifference or disloyalty of many Angloamerican frontiersmen to their own government."[47] However, it does not follow that Spanish authorities believed that it would be easy to gain the loyalty of such men to Spain. Accordingly, the immigration policy aimed to make an attractive offer that addressed some of the sources of the westerners' dissatisfaction as well as Spanish interests.

For their part, promoters attempted to manipulate Spanish biases and interests. One debate developed around different evaluations of private wealth as a factor that could influence the degree of loyalty that might be expected of foreign immigrants. Men of distinction and fortune sought preferential treatment (meaning, in particular but not only, more economic incentives) in comparison with ordinary immigrants.[48] Wilkinson tried to play on Governor Miró's financial difficulties and other worries, when he suggested that "it will be a fixed rule not to authorize the residence of any individual that does not bring with him visible property or does not present a bonafide guarantee, pledging his loyalty under pain of confiscation, and this oath of fidelity being universally required."[49] Apparently a poor man's pledge was worth nothing. Carondelet agreed. The prospect of losing their personal wealth, he thought, would guarantee the loyalty of wealthy immigrants.[50] At a later stage, Wilkinson tried to dissuade the Spaniards from admitting large numbers of poor westering Americans. "It is an undeniable fact," he declared, "that the emigrants that have come down the Ohio with the intention of settling in Luisiana are generally debtors and fugitives from the law, poor and without principles; such people are not only not worthy vassals, but they ought to be considered as dangerous people against whom protection is necessary."[51] He no doubt realized that the Spanish policy of granting free lands to individual settlers undermined his own plan to profit from the sale of Spanish land. Moreover, despite the scorn he heaped on such migrants, Wilkinson may have worried that grateful colonists might well fulfill Spanish hopes and become loyal defenders of Spain's sovereignty, thwarting his own original separatist plans.

Contradicting Wilkinson's arguments, Steuben struck a warning note regarding the true intentions of propertied migrants. Like many others before and after him, Steuben opined that the first wave of Anglo-American frontiersmen were little better than savages. By contrast, he was powerfully struck that many of the men who showed an interest in the West during the late 1780s occupied positions of public trust and influence, both in civil and military capacities, in the Atlantic states. These adventurers, Steuben thought, deserved closer attention. "The character of those who are planning to emigrate is very different," he warned darkly.[52] The premeditation perceived by Steuben could only mean that such emigrants entertained great economic and/or political ambitions that would be incompatible with loyal service to the Spanish Crown. In sum, he felt that Spain could not trust in the loyalty of influential promoters such as George Morgan, Wilkinson, and their associates. By contrast, he thought that poor emigrants would be more loyal and that it would also be easier to cultivate patriotic sentiments in them.[53]

Spanish authorities tried to conciliate theoretical and practical criteria. If poor immigrants managed to get themselves to the frontier, there was a good chance that they would be accepted as settlers, but early government-sponsored projects to settle Acadians and diverse groups of Spaniards had yielded disappointing results, and the Crown simply could not afford to finance any more such expeditions. Macarty's proposal to bring poor Irish Americans to Luisiana was thus deemed to be too costly by the government in Madrid, which preferred "to promote the establishment of wealthy families which are the truly useful ones."[54] According to the general rules published by O'Reilly (1770), Gayoso (1798), and Morales (1799), the size and river frontage of all the land grants were meant to be similar, but in fact, Miró and other officials gave bigger concessions to wealthy or influential settlers.[55] During the mid-1790s, Gayoso worried that Father Francis Lennan's criticisms and complaints about the foreign settlers might drive away the English-speaking Protestants, who happened to be the wealthiest inhabitants, leaving the Catholic Irishmen, who were notoriously disorderly and intriguing.[56]

Spanish officials understood that neither the loyalty oaths nor gratitude were solid enough as guarantees of individual loyalty. They were especially doubtful regarding the reliability of Anglo-American immigrants. Carondelet was most sensitive about migrants from the United States wanting to settle west of the Mississippi. "I will positively not have any Americans in that post," he told Juan Filhiol, the commandant of the Ouachita district.[57] Nevertheless, he soon contradicted himself when he supported the Dutchman Baron de Bastrop's project to bring five hundred families from Kentucky to the Ouachita area.[58] He may have been under the impression that the intended settlers would be Dutchmen, although those who actually arrived were American, Irish, and German. This project was suspended in June 1797 by the intendant Juan Ventura Morales, ostensibly because of shortage of funds, but possibly too, because Morales distrusted Bastrop.[59] The rebellion of some American residents at Natchez in 1797 further weakened Carondelet's faith in the settlers' loyalty.[60]

One case in particular must have been a disappointment to the governor and his right-hand man in Natchez, Manuel Gayoso. Peter Bryan Bruin, who brought a large group of Catholics to West Florida, had received many favors from Gayoso. Bruin had given proof of his loyalty on earlier occasions but in 1797 he supported the rebels.[61] When Gayoso became governor of Luisiana, he too was reluctant to admit Protestant Americans west of the Mississippi. He stopped any further large-scale immigration from the United States into West Florida, as well as the Bastrop and Maison Rouge projects authorized by his predecessor. Nonetheless, Gayoso treated each case on its own merits, and he did continue to approve petitions from Anglo-Americans in whose loyalty he trusted.[62]

By the year 1800, officials such as Gilberto Leonard (the comptroller general of the Royal Treasury in New Orleans), Juan Filhiol (the former commandant at Fort Miró), and the intendant Ramón López y Angulo agreed that it was unwise to continue welcoming immigrants from the United States.[63] The Spanish ambassador Carlos Martínez de Irujo, too, had come to the conclusion that the loyalty of those immigrants was suspect.[64] Reflecting this growing consensus, a royal decree of July 18, 1802, forbade local authorities to grant or sell any land in Luisiana to citizens of the United States.

Despite such forebodings, there is evidence attesting to the loyalty of foreign residents in Spanish West Florida and Luisiana at different times.[65] "May God keep us Spanish!" wrote one Anglo-American resident in Natchez to a friend in 1785 when Georgia's expansionist ambitions threatened to engulf that district and subject its inhabitants to American taxes.[66] When the French revolutionary Edmond Genêt came to the United States in 1793 with a mission that threatened Spanish domains, more than three hundred Anglo-American militiamen from Natchez answered Governor Carondelet's call for aid in the defense of New Orleans.[67] Some settlers' loyalty was no doubt inspired mainly by fear at the prospect of French rule under the auspices of the revolutionary slave-emancipating Directory. Nonetheless, Carondelet was sufficiently impressed by this strong show of loyalty to support a petition from Natchez residents in 1796, requesting confirmation of their land property titles, in view of rumors that Georgia intended to ignore them after Spain evacuated the region. Indeed, he and Gayoso even went so far as to recommend special treatment for settlers in Natchez who wished to relocate to other Spanish colonies, and a few months later, they recommended another project presented by U.S. promoters.[68]

During the rebellion of 1797, many, if not most, Anglo-American settlers in Natchez remained loyal to Governor Gayoso.[69] When it was over, one commanding officer remarked: "even in the uncertain situation of things, I can with confidence presume to say that I could raise as great a party at present in favor of the Government as could be raised on the opposite side."[70] One eyewitness later told Gayoso: "to a man, the people lament their blindness; . . . Pope, Ellicote and Hutchins, with all that gang, are now execrated as the authors of the public misconduct: tho' really it was not so general as it might appear."[71] After the Spanish evacuation of Natchez, not everyone was equally happy about coming under U.S. rule.[72] John Sevier feared that half of the inhabitants would flock over into Luisiana. "Indeed," he told Andrew Jackson, "they are now doing it daily."[73] Then, as rumors of the Spanish cession of Luisiana to France gained in credibility, many residents of that colony, including some foreigners, requested permission to move to Texas and other Spanish territories.[74] Each request was carefully screened, out of the old concern that such petitioners maintained personal connections in the United States and were too imbued with Anglo-American political culture but, as before, a number of these requests were eventually granted.[75]

During the spring of 1803, the acting U.S. vice-consul in New Orleans, Daniel Clark, doubted the loyalty to Spain of the English-speaking settlers there, but he was equally unsure whether the U.S. government could count on any support from them. Clark's explanation reveals his own understanding of the self-interested and negotiable character of loyalty. He warned that the majority were unreliable, expressing his belief that they would abandon their ties to the Union, "if even very slight advantages were held out" by the French.[76] Eyewitness testimonies regarding local reactions to the sovereignty transfers of 1803–4 vary depending on the sympathies of the observer and the precise moment or scene being described, but manifestations of sorrow clearly existed and may be interpreted, at the very least, as expressions of respect toward the outgoing Spanish authorities.[77] This is not incompatible with other interpretations stressing hostility toward revolutionary France or, indeed, with misgivings or hopefulness regarding U.S. rule. Even the blatantly prejudiced Paul Alliot conceded that, although many inhabitants preferred the United States to France, the numerous royalists of New Orleans would have been happier to remain under Spanish rule.[78]

In 1804, Anglo-American militiamen in the Felicianas and Baton Rouge actively supported Spanish authority against the Kemper brothers, who have been styled as heroic American leaders of a West Florida separatist rebellion.[79] According to Andrew McMichael, the members of the Kemper gang were nothing more than self-serving criminals, notwithstanding the rhetoric of liberty used to justify their activities. "Spanish administration in West Florida engendered a high degree of loyalty on the part of Anglo Americans that only broke down after the Kemper raids."[80] This chapter is not attempting to suggest even remotely that foreign immigrants' loyalty to Spain was unshakable, but rather that the attitudes and actions of settlers in these North American frontiers need not be interpreted in terms of nationalistic prejudices, but as a function of perceived self-interest (which might embrace nontangible as well as material benefits), and the capacity of individuals to adapt to rapidly changing circumstances.

Good Government, Happiness, and Patriotism

Although the settlers' loyalty oaths were a necessary start, local authorities realized that they could not depend on the pledges alone, and that they must try to cultivate Spanish patriotism among the foreign newcomers. They knew it was a difficult task because they understood that patriotic attachments involved both interest and sentiment, reason and passion. Patriotism, like loyalty, could reflect rational choices based on individual and group interests, but it was most strongly defined by its emotional character. Patriotism was inspired by a natural affection toward the land and the social relations that, together, provided the physical and human contexts within which individuals perceived their own identity and interests.[81]

In early modern Spanish texts on social and political relations, love, devotion, and affection were frequently repeated key words. Contrary to the historiographical tendency to dismiss their significance, Tamar Herzog argues that the "discourse of love" was an important part of the construction of collective identities, not only in Spain but also in England, France, and Italy.[82] Accordingly, the inhabitants of West Florida and Luisiana must be encouraged to love the community and, by extension, the "Spanish nation," and the king as its visible head and protector. In the words of Joseph Piernas, a Catalonian promoter of two Luisiana colonization projects: "A man born in a monarchy is subject to many indispensable obligations, the honoring of which springs from a strong and sincere love of the government and his homeland [*patria*]. This love should be the motivating force behind every act of an honorable man and a loyal vassal, and the true lodestar that must guide him in his actions in order to contribute, as much as he can throughout his life, to the general improvement of the state and the particular improvement of the province, city, town or village in which he lives."[83]

Certain kinds of emotional attachment to society were impossible to feel as an act of will.[84] The monarchical sentiments of former British loyalists and French refugees might provide some ideological affinity, and Catholicism certainly gave many foreign immigrants a head start in becoming integrated members of local communities. For that reason, Father Carlos Bourke and Captain Remigio O'Hara stressed in their petition the historical record of loyalty to the Spanish Crown of many Irish Catholics.[85] But, clearly, for many of the inhabitants of West Florida and Luisiana, the generally recognized sources of patriotic sentiments were weak if not entirely lacking. Attempts to define the constituent elements of national identity listed genetic and cultural bonds that only a shared history could provide.[86] Wilkinson spoke of "consanguineity, habits, customs, religion, language and laws."[87] Writing about the American settlers, Las Casas thought that their "mutually-shared language, religion, customs, and ancestors, and the ties which they maintain, will preserve a spirit of brotherhood."[88] Irujo emphasized "the conformity of language, religion, and political opinions."[89]

Nonetheless, local authorities had been reasonably successful in gaining the goodwill of the Luisiana Creole population and non-Hispanic immigrants. Referring to the Anglo-American inhabitants of Galveztown in 1779, Francisco Collell spoke of "the love and kindness which they feel for the Spanish nation."[90] This experience encouraged the local architects of the immigration policy in the belief that they might have one viable option in their bid to foment Spanish patriotism. This was the promotion of individual and collective well-being and happiness through good government. Happiness and gratitude would nourish the indispensable emotional component of patriotism.[91] Such a proposition was in line with Spanish thought about the functions of enlightened government. Since the mid-century, some political economists had been arguing that it was the state's duty to ensure the happiness of all of its inhabitants. By the 1780s a few were even suggesting that individual happiness should be the first priority of the state.[92] This converged with another argument expressed by Wilkinson, who declared that the conventionally recognized ethnic and cultural components of nationality were actually "shackles that everywhere restrain timid, credulous, and ignorant men." True patriotism, he suggested, would develop if individuals could freely choose their nationality, in pursuit of their own best interests and happiness.[93]

These theoretical underpinnings combined with necessity and realism in the plan devised by Miró and Navarro. They recommended that government action should be as wide-ranging as possible. Economic incentives appealing directly to self-interest must include not just generous land grants (given, not sold) and other immediate inducements, but continuing commercial facilities and fiscal privileges (in particular, no direct or property taxes), all of which would excite feelings of gratitude.[94] Equitable Spanish laws would be applied with prudence, guaranteeing personal security and justice for all, in combination with an innovative policy of tolerance toward private differences, which included a carefully crafted compromise establishing a degree of religious tolerance.[95] Madrid's approval of this last concession exemplified the secularizing tendency as well as the pragmatism of Bourbon despotism. Even conceding that the policy was inspired by necessity and restricted to relatively unimportant frontier colonies, the willingness to contemplate cultural diversity, even if only temporarily and in a limited way, was what made this experience so tantalizingly modern.[96]

If such a policy, mindful of the people's happiness, could be maintained, the immigrants would not only honor their loyalty oaths to the king and his government, but would eventually develop a patriotic attachment to Spain. "Having won in this way the affection of the first generation," Miró and Navarro argued, "the next ones will not know any other homeland [*patria*] than this one, it being the job of the governor and the priest to engrave in the tender hearts of the young people the Spanish spirit and patriotism."[97] In short, the West Florida and Luisiana policies were based on the conviction that, given time, good government would eventually inspire in the newcomers love of country and community, of their new *patria* and the "Spanish nation."

Miró criticized Gardoqui's authorization of projects presented by George Morgan and Peter Paulus precisely because their aspirations to self-government defeated the purpose of the Spanish policy.[98] Every immigrant settlement, he insisted, must be accompanied by a small garrison representing

Spanish authority, and a Catholic priest, because this was the only means of "cementing the affections of the new colonists to the Spanish government, and of succeeding in obtaining that the second generation, not having known any other government, will have the affection which birth in the country will engender."[99] Irujo was of the same opinion. He emphasized material well-being but did not ignore other foundations of social satisfaction. He warned that any ill-advised economic measures on the part of the metropolitan government, or unjust and arbitrary acts on the part of the colonial authorities, would frustrate the goal. "In a word," he concluded, "it is essential to put them in such a position that they develop affection toward a government that makes them happy."[100]

By century's end, in view of the growing numbers of immigrants, local authorities became ever more worried about the difficulties involved in creating the "Spanish spirit and patriotism" that Miró and Navarro had hoped to instill in the younger generations. The bishop of New Orleans, Luis de Peñalver, had shared their expectations: "I have always thought that the admission of foreigners into this province is in the understanding that time will incline them toward the nation, and that their children will be Spanish."[101] But the cultural resistance of the diverse ethnic groups was frustrating those hopes. The bishop complained that the government had provided French-speaking and English-speaking priests in order "to offer them some immediate but temporary help," which would ease their integration in the community, but instead they simply continued using those languages in their daily lives, without becoming proficient in Spanish.[102] Peñalver was frankly pessimistic. In his opinion, all classes of inhabitants, natives and foreigners, were disrespectful of the traditional religious, social, and political customs of the Hispanic community. "Their souls are prone to agitation," he lamented, "and tinged with principles of democracy." The presence of so many Anglo-American immigrants greatly aggravated the general immorality and weakened loyalty to Spain. The bishop saw an urgent need for army officers who would set a good example and a governor who would cooperate with him in the correction of spiritual and temporal disorders.[103]

In 1800, Governor Casa Calvo, too, expressed concern about the lack of "national patriotism" among the population generally, a failing that he attributed to "republican" attitudes. Yet, he still recommended the admission of American settlers because he thought that the problem resided not so much in the English-speaking immigrants as in the French Creoles. In his opinion, the Frenchmen made bad regiment officers because they showed no ambition, taking up the military career solely "as a reliable way of ensuring their subsistence and improving their fortunes." Like Peñalver, and Gayoso before him, the governor wanted officers and troops sent from Spain in order to Hispanicize the customs and political culture of New Orleans.[104] He thought that if military and political positions were used to recompense "patriotism, loyalty, and love for the sovereign," the population's patriotic enthusiasm would be stronger.[105]

These complaints were manifestations of more general problems. The influence of secularizing trends, libertarian ideologies, and greater opportunities for individuals to act in accordance with their own perceived self-interest was felt everywhere in the Atlantic world, of which these multiethnic frontier communities of North America were a part. This, however, does not mean that the population at large or the armed forces were disloyal to Spain.[106]

According to Arthur Whitaker, there was no chance that the policies in West Florida and Luisiana might inspire loyalty or patriotism.[107] Whitaker's lead has been followed by many authors, such as Alexander DeConde, who clearly thought the Spaniards were pursuing a futile course when he defined the Americans as "unassimilable, an alien element within an alien culture."[108] By contrast, Jack D. L. Holmes's sympathetic study speculated that "Gayoso might have succeeded in his mission had he received the continued support of the Spanish ministers," and Gilbert Din considers that the policies represented "a wise effort of assimilation . . . [and] Hispanicization." Light Townsend Cummins sums up that Spain's "defensive colonization" policy, combined with the diffusion of social, cultural, economic, and political power among different ethnic and professional groups, created "an historically identifiable colonial complex that clearly rivaled in durability and sophistication those elsewhere in North America."[109]

Both the rationalization and the achievements of these local frontier policies fit in well with larger historiographical interpretations of the revolutionary era and the global aims of enlightened Spanish reformism. Like other European monarchs, the Spanish Bourbons and their ministers were aiming to construct a more rationally organized and legally unified Spanish state under an authoritarian monarchy. Their plan involved replacing the multiple *natural* patriotisms, based on local and regional communities and homelands that made up the traditional composite Hispanic monarchy of the Hapsburgs, with a more abstract Spanish national-imperial *political* patriotism designed to invigorate a new unitary monarchy akin to a modern integrated nation-state.[110]

The immigration policy in West Florida and Luisiana gives specific content and special meaning to this interpretation of Bourbon efforts to reinvent the Hispanic monarchy in the quest for modernity. This particular frontier version of the "new" Spanish national patriotism would not depend solely on family ties or biological lineage, birthplace, residence, local and ethnic identities, common history, language, religion, and other cultural commonalities. Such elements would certainly remain of central importance, but the idea of a modern Spanish *political* community would also contemplate benefits that could be more easily rationalized and seemed better adapted to include individuals and groups of different origins and cultures. Cultural differences might be tolerated as long as political unity was maintained.[111]

The role of the king as protector of his subjects had been one of the pillars of the traditional relationship between vassals and their lord or sovereign, and it remained of central importance. All settlers and promoters pledged their loyalty in recognition of the benefits gained from the king's protection and benevolent rule.[112] In addition, promoters or local officials who were trying to persuade the metropolitan government to admit French, Irish, or German immigrants stressed these people's love of monarchy in an abstract sense, implying not only their aversion to republicanism but their predisposition to love the Spanish sovereign.[113]

Furthermore, John Elliott explains that throughout the empire reigned "the conviction that the well-being of the community depended on the proper functioning of a contractual relationship between the ruler and the ruled." This resulted in "a culture of loyalty that permitted resistance within certain understood limits" and required "a continuous process of negotiation between the monarch and his subjects."[114] This open "bargaining and transacting" became especially remarkable after 1790. In the words of Jeremy Adelman, "Iberian colonists began expressing new concepts of interests, and even rights, within the framework of empires that struggled to cope with the spreading effects of revolution. Colonial elites began to push at the edges of what was permissible under the old regimes by marshaling expressions of loyalty to the monarchy that included some basic rights for his subjects."[115]

One fundamental aspect of this contractual relationship revolved around the process by which individuals came to be considered as members of a local community and of the Hispanic monarchy. Hitherto, as Tamar Herzog shows, it had been largely the prerogative of local communities themselves to give or withhold recognition and the enjoyment of privileges. Membership of a local community might change over time, but "people who were integrated in the community and were willing to comply with its duties were indeed natives, independent of their place of birth or descent." Members of local communities were then considered members of the nation by extension, not by law or government acts. Local communities consistently resisted royal attempts to impose formal rules regarding which individuals or groups belonged to the community and which did not. In Tamar Herzog's view, this resistance explains "the inability of royal interests to recast Spain as a community of allegiance."[116]

Thus, the immigration policy in West Florida and Luisiana was an example of interference by the local representatives of the metropolitan government in time-honored customs regarding control of membership of local communities. They, and not the local elites, dictated who would be admitted to the colonies, and on what terms. Foreign immigrants might not be accepted as fully integrated members by the local communities and therefore were not naturalized Spaniards, but they did enjoy considerable advantages by royal concession in exchange for their loyalty to the Crown. It is difficult to say if this policy created widespread discontent, given the peculiar characteristics of West Florida and Luisiana, where the community at large and the local elites were already multiethnic and multicultural. The Spanish authorities seem to have worked well with the Francophone and Anglophone planter and merchant elites, who possibly supported the immigration policy, believing that it would enhance their own economic opportunities. Yet there is some evidence of local resentment against privileged foreign newcomers, and in particular against the firm of Panton and Leslie, which used its Indian trade concession to gain advantages in other mercantile activities. Rival merchants were "hopelessly handicapped" in the general import-export trade because they had to pay duties that Panton and Leslie evaded.[117] Protesting his own "patriotic spirit," the Luisiana intendant Martín Navarro defended Panton and Leslie, asking, "Are they not considered and established in the category of Spaniards by the oath of fidelity that they have given to the government?"[118] One complaint against the company in 1794 requested royal protection, arguing that it was "impossible and improper that a sovereign should prefer foreigners, and grant them more privileges than those of his vassals and members of this community (*vecinos*)," adding that "Panton, Leslie ... are not members of the community." This complaint makes it clear that the problem was not Panton and Leslie's British origin, but their unfair advantage, since it cites among those aggrieved "another member of the community who has lived here since the British period, and is very recommendable by virtue of his intelligence and love of the Province."[119] In 1800, the intendant Ramón López y Angulo expressed bitter criticisms of Panton and Leslie and local authorities whom he accused of consorting with foreign opportunists against the national interest.[120] His diatribes were no doubt fueled by his own strident patriotism, but it is also possible that he was instigated by local discontents. It is difficult to say how far these protests represented a wider resentment against metropolitan government policies within this particular community.[121] Discontented merchants may have been merely instrumentalizing patriotic discourses, but the fact remains that the Spanish Crown was indeed granting privileges that interfered with the local community's control of its own membership.[122]

Conclusion

All of those involved in the discussion of the Spanish colonization policy in West Florida and Luisiana used arguments referring to concepts of loyalty and patriotism. Loyalty was clearly considered to be a conscious, rational, and voluntary commitment, publicly made, and of immediate and sustained practical, political, and military application. Government authorities demanded and immigrants proffered loyalty in these terms, but they were aware that loyalty, as a function of perceived personal and group interests, could change or create conflictive situations. Spanish officials also understood the political value of patriotism. They assumed that it sprang largely from emotional engagement, expressed as love of the community, both local and national. They thought that national identity was shaped by specific genetic and cultural characteristics, and consequently recognized that immigrants could not be expected to feel spontaneously the same kind of patriotic sentiments that native-born countrymen might feel. Nonetheless, most discussants considered that patriotism could and, indeed, should be cultivated. Central to the theoretical fundament of Spanish policies in these provinces was the notion that "good government" could work in harmony with individual self-interest to foment the common well-being and "happiness," and in this way, given time, it could also encourage the development of a strong affective attachment to the Spanish nation and its visible head, the king.

Notes

1. Loyalty oath, Natchez, Jan. 4, 1787, in Jack D. L. Holmes, *Gayoso: The Life of a Spanish Governor in the Mississippi Valley, 1789–1799* (Baton Rouge: Louisiana State University Press, 1965), 20. Other versions: several dated 1769, in Henry P. Dart, ed., "The Oath of Allegiance to Spain," *Louisiana Historical Quarterly* 4, no. 2 (1921): 205–15; pledge dated Jan. 12, 1790, in Archivo General de Indias, Seville (hereafter AGI), Papeles de Cuba (hereafter PC), leg. 2362; pledge in Esteban Miró to Charles de Grandpré, Feb. 20, 1787, in Charles Gayarré, *History of Louisiana: The Spanish Domination* (1854; repr., Baton Rouge: Claitor's, 1974), 3: 202–3; same dated Nov. 30, 1789, in Louis Houck, ed., *The Spanish Regime in Missouri: A Collection of Papers and Documents Relating to Upper Louisiana* (Chicago: R. R. Donnelley and Sons, 1909), 1: 319, and others dated 1795 and 1796, at 320–21. See also Miró, "Proclamation on Immigration into West Florida and Louisiana," April 20, 1789, in Lawrence Kinnaird, ed., *Spain in the Mississippi Valley, 1763–1794* (Washington, D.C.: U.S.G.P.O. for the American Historical Association, 1946–49), 3: 269–71; pledge dated 1797, in James A. Robertson, ed.,

Louisiana under the Rule of Spain, France, and the United States, 1785–1807 (1910–11; repr., Freeport, N.Y.: Books for Libraries Press, 1969), 1: 162–64.

2. Lack of space precludes citing here all the relevant historiography. The Spanish spelling "Luisiana" is used in this essay as a reminder of the vast, if imprecise, extension of that colony.

3. Arthur P. Whitaker, ed., *Documents Relating to the Commercial Policy of Spain in the Floridas, with Incidental Reference to Louisiana* (Deland: Florida State Historical Society, 1931), xxii.

4. The author gratefully acknowledges financial support from the Spanish Ministry of Education and Science for research project HUM2006–11365/HIST. Thanks also to Rafe Blaufarb, David Narrett, and other evaluators for their helpful comments.

5. See, for example, Martín Navarro, "Reflexiones políticas sobre el estado actual de la Provincia de la Luisiana, Año 1782," in Manuel Serrano y Sanz, ed., *Documentos históricos de la Florida y la Luisiana, siglos XVI al XVIII* (Madrid: Victoriano Suárez, 1912), 361–79; Miró to Conde de Campo de Alange, "Descripción de la Luisiana," Madrid, Aug. 11, 1792, in Jack D. L. Holmes, ed., *Documentos inéditos para la historia de la Luisiana, 1792–1810* (Madrid: José Porrúa Turanzas, 1963), 26–27. Pontalba's memoir, Sept. 15, 1800, in Gayarré, *History of Louisiana*, 3: 410–45.

6. Holmes, *Documentos inéditos*, 134, counted more than a hundred such projects.

7. Isaac Joslin Cox, *The West Florida Controversy, 1798–1813: A Study in American Diplomacy* (Baltimore: Johns Hopkins University Press, 1918), 23.

8. Francis S. Philbrick, *The Rise of the West, 1754–1830* (New York: Harper and Row, 1965), 179.

9. Arthur P. Whitaker, *The Spanish-American Frontier, 1787–1795: The Westward Movement and the Spanish Retreat in the Mississippi Valley* (1927; repr., Lincoln: University of Nebraska Press, 1969), 102–5.

10. Miró to Campo de Alange, "Descripción de la Luisiana," Madrid, Aug. 11, 1792, in Holmes, *Documentos inéditos*, 26–27.

11. For late eighteenth-century Spanish views on Anglo-American migrations, see Sylvia L. Hilton, "Movilidad y expansión en la construcción política de los Estados Unidos: 'Estos errantes colonos' en las fronteras españolas del Misisipí (1776–1803)," *Revista Complutense de Historia de América* 28 (2002): 63–96.

12. Carondelet to Juan Filhiol, New Orleans, April 2, 1795; see also Carondelet, Francisco Rendón, José de Orue, and Marquis de Maison Rouge, Contract, New Orleans, March 17, 1795; both in Jennie O'Kelly Mitchell and Robert Dabney Calhoun, "The Marquis de Maison Rouge, the Baron de Bastrop, and Colonel Abraham Morhouse— Three Ouachita Valley Soldiers of Fortune: The Maison Rouge and Bastrop Spanish Land 'Grants,'" *Louisiana Historical Quarterly* 20, no. 2 (1937): 291–368.

13. Associate of M. Daniel Boone: Robert Hall, land concession, Jan. 26, 1798 [*sic*: 1799], Draper Manuscripts, State Historical Society of Wisconsin, Madison, in John Mack Faragher, *Daniel Boone: The Life and Legend of an American Pioneer* (New York: Henry Holt, 1992), 279.

14. Actions or behavior proving loyalty gave the standards by which Spanish communities traditionally judged the status of foreigners. See Tamar Herzog, *Defining*

Nations: Immigrants and Citizens in Early Modern Spain and Spanish America (New Haven, Conn.: Yale University Press, 2003), 66, and "Los americanos frente a la Monarquía: El criollismo y la naturaleza española," in A. Álvarez-Ossorio and B. J. García, eds., *La monarquía de las naciones: Patria, nación y naturaleza en la Monarquía de España* (Madrid: Fundación Carlos Amberes, 2004), 83.

15. See, for example, Pedro Wouves d'Argès to Floridablanca, Paris, Aug. 1, 1787, Archivo Histórico Nacional, Madrid (hereafter AHN), Estado, leg. 3889; also Diego [James] White to José de Ezpeleta, Havana, Dec. 24, 1788, in José Navarro and Fernando Solano, *¿Conspiración española? 1787-1789: Contribución al estudio de las primeras relaciones históricas entre España y los Estados Unidos de América* (Zaragoza: Excma. Dip. Provincial de Zaragoza, 1949), 225-29, 271-74.

16. The Supreme Council of State, Madrid, Nov. 20, 1788, in William R. Shepherd, ed., "Papers Bearing on James Wilkinson's Relations with Spain, 1787-1789," *American Historical Review* 9, no. 4 (1904): 749.

17. Carondelet to Floridablanca, New Orleans, Feb. 25, 1792, in Serrano y Sanz, *Documentos históricos*, 402-5.

18. Carondelet to Juan Filhiol, New Orleans, June 17, 1795, in Mitchell and Calhoun, "The Marquis," 308-9.

19. Casa Calvo to Mariano Luis de Urquijo, New Orleans, Oct. 8, 1800, AHN, Estado, leg. 3889 bis.

20. Herzog, *Defining Nations*, quotes at 197 and 11. For early U.S. norms, see James H. Kettner, *The Development of American Citizenship, 1608-1870* (Chapel Hill: University of North Carolina Press, 1978), 214-19, 246.

21. See, for example, Jorge Rogers Clark to Diego Gardoqui, Caídas del Ohio, March 15, 1788; Barón de Steuben, Plan de proyecto fundado en los hechos y discursos antecedentes, n.d., sent with Gardoqui to Floridablanca, Oct. 24, 1788; and George Morgan to Diego de Gardoqui, "Colonel Morgan's Plan to Establish a Colony of Settlers in the Mississippi," Prospect, N.J., Sept. 1788, all in Navarro and Solano, *¿Conspiración española?*, 231-48.

22. Carondelet to Juan Filhiol, New Orleans, June 17, 1795, in Mitchell and Calhoun, "The Marquis," 308-9.

23. Carondelet to Manuel Gayoso, New Orleans, July 1, 1797, in Juan J. Andreu, "Las consecuencias del Tratado de San Lorenzo," in José A. Armillas, ed., *Congreso Internacional de Historia de América, 7º: 1996* (Zaragoza: Diputación General de Aragón, 1998), 4: 870.

24. See note 110.

25. John H. Elliott, *Empires of the Atlantic World: Britain and Spain in America, 1492-1830* (New Haven, Conn.: Yale University Press, 2006), 366; Jeremy Adelman, *Sovereignty and Revolution in the Iberian Atlantic* (Princeton, N.J.: Princeton University Press, 2006), 54; Guillermo Céspedes, "La independencia de las colonias inglesas y su proclamación en la América virreinal," in Gonzalo Anes et al., *La Ilustración española en la independencia de los Estados Unidos: Benjamin Franklin* (Madrid: Marcial Pons, 2007), 125-42.

26. Esteban Miró and Martín Navarro to Antonio Valdés, New Orleans, Sept. 25, 1787, in Navarro and Solano, ¿Conspiración española?, 207–14.

27. Agustín de Macarty, "Proposal for Colonization in Luisiana," Aug. 14, 1787, in Fernando Solano, "La colonización irlandesa de la Luisiana española: Dos proyectos de inmigración," Estudios 80–81 (1981): 201.

28. Clark to Gardoqui, Caídas del Ohio, March 15, 1788, in Navarro and Solano, ¿Conspiración española?, 231–32.

29. Baron von Steuben to Diego de Gardoqui, "Plan of a Project Based on the Foregoing Facts and Discourses," n.p., n.d. [New York, March 16, 1788], in Navarro and Solano, ¿Conspiración española?, 233–40.

30. Morgan to Gardoqui, Prospect, N.J., Sept. 1788, in Navarro and Solano, ¿Conspiración española?, 241–48. For other examples, see White to Ezpeleta, Havana, Dec. 24, 1788, in Navarro and Solano, ¿Conspiración española?, 271–74; José de Jáudenes to Manuel Godoy, Philadelphia, Dec. 1, 1795, enclosing Mr. [Pierce] Butler's Memorial, Nov. 30, 1795, in Gilbert C. Din, "Spain's Immigration Policy in Louisiana and the American Penetration, 1792–1803" (1973), in *The Louisiana Purchase Bicentennial Series in Louisiana History*, vol. 2, *The Spanish Presence in Louisiana, 1763–1803* (Lafayette: University of Southwestern Louisiana, 1996), 340; and Juan José Andreu, "Los últimos proyectos inmigratorios en la Luisiana española," *Cruz Ansata* 6 (1983): 36–38.

31. Jon Kukla, *A Wilderness So Immense: The Louisiana Purchase and the Destiny of America* (New York: Alfred A. Knopf, 2003), 133.

32. James Ripley Jacobs, *Tarnished Warrior: Major General James Wilkinson* (New York: Macmillan, 1938), 81; Philbrick, *The Rise of the West*, 178; John Thornton Posey, "Rascality Revisited: In Defense of General James Wilkinson," *Filson Club History Quarterly* 74, no. 4 (2000): 325.

33. See, for example, Kettner, *The Development of American Citizenship*, 214–19.

34. Real Academia Española, *Diccionario de la Lengua Castellana* (Madrid: Francisco del Hierro, 1726–39), 2: 373. Similarly, "Fidelity" at 2: 745. See also Sebastián de Cobarruvias, *Tesoro de la Lengua Castellana o Española* (1611; repr., Madrid: Ediciones Turner, 1979), 755, 592.

35. This might be seen as an extension of one of Tamar Herzog's arguments about membership of local communities: "Eighteenth-century Spaniards consistently asserted that both citizenship and nativeness were categories based on natural law," and individuals had a "'natural liberty' to change their adhesion from one community to another." Herzog, *Defining Nations*, 166. See also Herzog, "Los americanos frente a la Monarquía," 85–86.

36. See, for example, [George Hay, or John F. Dumouline?], *An Essay on Naturalization and Allegiance* (Washington City [Washington, D.C.]: Daniel Rapine, 1816), 15: "while the doctrine of unalienable allegiance is . . . utterly repulsive to human reason, the principle of naturalization is one conformable to the law and policy of nations, practiced by every state, and alone concordant to the rational principles of the human breast." For U.S. debates, see Kettner, *The Development of American Citizenship*, especially 173–209, 268–81.

37. James Wilkinson to Esteban Miró and Martín Navarro, New Orleans, Aug. 22, 1787, in Navarro and Solano, ¿Conspiración española?, 185–86, and in William C. Shepherd, "Wilkinson and the Beginnings of the Spanish Conspiracy," *American Historical Review* 9, no. 3 (1904): 490–506.

38. See, for example, James Alton James, *The Life of George Rogers Clark* (Chicago: University of Chicago Press, 1928), 374, citing Frederick Jackson Turner; Ray Allen Billington, *Westward Expansion: A History of the American Frontier* (1949; repr., New York: Macmillan, 1974), 226; Robert V. Remini, *Andrew Jackson*, vol. 1, *The Course of American Empire, 1767–1821* (1977; repr., Baltimore: Johns Hopkins University Press, 1998), 146; and many others cited in Posey, "Rascality Revisited," 351 and 311. Cox, *The West Florida Controversy*, 34, incredibly accuses Carondelet of "tampering with the loyalty of the American commander" in 1796–97.

39. Arthur P. Whitaker, ed., "Harry Innes and the Spanish Intrigue, 1794–1795," *Mississippi Valley Historical Review* 15, no. 2 (1928): 236; Billington, *Westward Expansion*, 226; Posey, "Rascality Revisited," 316, 321, 340.

40. See, for example, Miró to Luis de las Casas, New Orleans, Oct. 7, 1790, in Caroline Maude Burson, *The Stewardship of Don Esteban Miró, 1782–1792* (New Orleans: American Printing Co., 1940), 166; Gayoso to Floridablanca, New Orleans, Jan. 7, 1792, in Holmes, *Documentos inéditos*, 39; Carondelet to Floridablanca, New Orleans, Feb. 25, 1792, in Serrano y Sanz, *Documentos históricos*, 402–5. See also Philbrick, *The Rise of the West*, 183; Kukla, *A Wilderness So Immense*, 133; and Charles A. Weeks, *Paths to a Middle Ground: The Diplomacy of Natchez, Boukfouka, Nogales, and San Fernando de las Barrancas, 1791–1795* (Tuscaloosa: University of Alabama Press, 2005), 51.

41. When Posey, "Rascality Revisited," 315, calls Wilkinson's discourse on expatriation "the rationalizing mantra of his ilk," one wonders if he included the Virginian politicians who approved the citizenship statute of 1779, which affirmed that every man has a "natural right of expatriating himself," and upheld "that natural right which all men have of relinquishing the country in which birth or other accident may have thrown them, and of seeking subsistence and happiness wheresoever they may be able or may hope to find them." See similar arguments by T. C. of Northumberland in the *Philadelphia Aurora*, 1799, in Kettner, *The Development of American Citizenship*, 268 and 273.

42. Whitaker, *The Spanish-American Frontier*, 98, thought that the Memorial of 1787 "was doubtless the joint product of their three minds." Gilbert C. Din, "The Immigration Policy of Governor Esteban Miró in Spanish Louisiana" (1969), in *The Louisiana Purchase Bicentennial Series in Louisiana History*, 2: 317–33, and "Proposals and Plans for Colonization in Spanish Louisiana, 1787–1790," *Louisiana History* 11, no. 3 (1970): 197–213, maintains that the project was mainly the work of the Spaniards. Kukla, *A Wilderness So Immense*, 127–28, concurs.

43. Individual "life goals" or "life expectations," in the terminology of the political scientist Morton Grodzins in "The Basis of National Loyalty" (1951), in Geraint N. D. Evans, ed., *Allegiance in America: The Case of the Loyalists* (Reading: Addison-Wesley, 1969), 176–80.

44. Roy Porter, *Flesh in the Age of Reason* (London and New York: Allen Lane, 2003).

45. See, for example, Remini, *Andrew Jackson*, 1: 145–46; Andrew R. L. Cayton, "'Separate Interests' and the Nation-State: The Washington Administration and the Origins of Regionalism in the Trans-Appalachian West," *Journal of American History* 79 (1992): 39–67; Peter J. Kastor, "'Equitable Rights and Privileges': Divided Loyalties in Washington County, Virginia, during the Franklin Separatist Crisis," *Virginia Magazine of History and Biography* 105 (1997): 193–226; James E. Lewis Jr., *The American Union and the Problem of Neighborhood: The United States and the Collapse of the Spanish Empire, 1783–1829* (Chapel Hill: University of North Carolina Press, 1998), 10–32; Peter S. Onuf, *Jefferson's Empire: The Language of American Nationhood* (Charlottesville : University Press of Virginia, 2000), 73–74, 77.

46. John Brown to James Breckinridge, Aug. 5, 1788, in Patricia Watlington, "John Brown and the Spanish Conspiracy," *Virginia Magazine of History and Biography* 75, no. 1 (1967): 52–68.

47. David J. Weber, *The Spanish Frontier in North America* (New Haven, Conn.: Yale University Press, 1992), 282.

48. See, for example, Wilkinson to Miró and Navarro, New Orleans, Aug. 22, 1787, in Navarro and Solano, *¿Conspiración española?*, 185–86; Morgan to Gardoqui, Prospect, N.J., Sept. 1788, in Navarro and Solano, *¿Conspiración española?*, 241–48; Wilkinson to Miró, New Orleans, Sept. 17, 1789, and Sept. 18, 1789, in Shepherd, "Papers," 756–57 and 764–66.

49. Wilkinson to Miró and Navarro, "Memorial," New Orleans, Sept. 5, 1787, in Navarro and Solano, *¿Conspiración española?*, 187–202, and in Shepherd, "Wilkinson and the Beginnings of the Spanish Conspiracy," 498–503.

50. Carondelet to Floridablanca, New Orleans, Feb. 5, 1792, in Serrano y Sanz, *Documentos históricos*, 402–5.

51. Wilkinson to Miró, "New Suggestions on the Proposals of His Memorial," Lexington, Ky., Feb. 12, 1789, in Navarro and Solano, *¿Conspiración española?*, 249–59.

52. On this distinction made by Steuben, see John Mack Faragher and Carol Sheriff, "The Expanding Nation: Pioneers or Planners?" in Francis G. Couvares, Martha Saxton, Gerald N. Grob and George A. Billias, eds., *Interpretations of American History: Patterns and Perspectives* (New York: Free Press, 2000), 216–34.

53. Steuben to Gardoqui, "Plan of a Project," [March 16, 1788], in Navarro and Solano, *¿Conspiración española?*, 233–40.

54. Royal Order, May 14, 1789, AHN, Estado, leg. 3888.

55. See, for example, Miró to the Commandant at Saint Louis, New Orleans, July 1789, in Ada Paris Klein, ed., "The Missouri Reader: Ownership of the Land under France, Spain, and the United States," *Missouri Historical Review* 44, no. 3 (1950): 274–94, at 281.

56. Gayoso to Godoy, March 31, 1795, in Jack D. L. Holmes, "Irish Priests in Spanish Natchez," *Journal of Mississippi History* 29, no. 3 (1967): 176–79.

57. Carondelet to Juan Filhiol, New Orleans, March 6, 1797, in Mitchell and Calhoun, "The Marquis," 321.

58. Carondelet and Andrés López Armesto to Juan Filhiol, New Orleans, June 21, 1796, and Carondelet to Morales, June 11, 1797, in Mitchell and Calhoun, "The Marquis," 372 and 384. Bastrop's proposal is in "Memorial of the Baron de Bastrop, New Orleans, March 14, 1795," sent by Carondelet to Francisco Rendón, New Orleans, March 16, 1795, AGI, PC, leg. 2364.

59. "Testimony of David Stuart," in *Cities of Philadelphia and New Orleans v. the United States*, 1846; Mitchell and Calhoun, "The Marquis," 372–88.

60. Carondelet to Gayoso, New Orleans, July 1, 1797, AHN, Estado, leg. 3900, in Andreu, "Las consecuencias," 870.

61. Arthur P. Whitaker, *The Mississippi Question 1795–1803: A Study in Trade, Politics, and Diplomacy* (1934; repr., Gloucester, Mass.: Peter Smith, 1962), 63 and 281. Jack D. L. Holmes, "Some Irish Officers in Spanish Louisiana," *The Irish Sword* 6, no. 25 (1964): 246. See also William S. Coker, "The Bruins and the Formulation of Spanish Immigration Policy in the Old Southwest, 1787–88," in Francis McDermott, ed., *The Spanish in the Mississippi Valley, 1762–1804* (Urbana: University of Illinois Press, 1974), 61–71.

62. Andreu, "Los últimos proyectos," 45–46; Holmes, *Gayoso*, 196, 219, 226–29, 242–43.

63. Whitaker, *The Mississippi Question*, 156–57; Mitchell and Calhoun, "The Marquis," 388–89.

64. Carlos Martínez de Irujo to Pedro Cevallos, Mont Plaisant, July 24, 1802, AHN, Estado, leg. 5630.

65. See, for example, Whitaker, *The Mississippi Question*, 62 and 155; Holmes, *Gayoso*, 170–71, 253–55; Light Townsend Cummins, "An Enduring Community: Anglo-American Settlers at Colonial Natchez and in the Felicianas, 1774–1810" (1993), in *The Louisiana Purchase Bicentennial Series in Louisiana History*, vol. 10, *A Refuge for All Ages: Immigration in Louisiana History* (Lafayette: University of Southwestern Louisiana, 1996), 246–50.

66. John Gordon to George Profit, Natchez, June 25, 1785, in Martin Ridge and Ray Allen Billington, eds., *America's Frontier Story: A Documentary History of Westward Expansion* (New York: Holt, Rinehart, and Winston, 1969), 218–19.

67. Carondelet to Grand-Pré, New Orleans, June 4, 1795, in Holmes, *Documentos inéditos*, 320; Andreu, "Los últimos proyectos," 40; Holmes, *Gayoso*, 170–71; Gilbert C. Din, *Spaniards, Planters, and Slaves: The Spanish Regulation of Slavery in Louisiana, 1763–1803* (College Station: Texas A & M University Press, 1999), 152. On the Genêt threat, older historiography is still useful, but see Harry Ammon, *The Genêt Mission* (New York: W. W. Norton, 1973); and José Antonio Armillas, "Ecos de la Revolución Francesa en los Estados Unidos de Norteamérica," *Estudios del Departamento de Historia Moderna* (1971–72): 75–95.

68. Gayoso to Carondelet, Natchez, June 2, 1796; Carondelet to Príncipe de la Paz, New Orleans, June 12, 1796, and Nov. 1, 1796, in Andreu, "Los últimos proyectos," 40–41. Also Cox, *The West Florida Controversy*, 58–59.

69. See Franklin L. Riley, "Transition from Spanish to American Rule in Mississippi," *Publications of the Mississippi Historical Society* 3 (1900): 261–311; Glenn R. Conrad, "The Indefatigable Dr. James White," *Southern Studies* 6, no. 3 (1995): 33; Holmes, *Documentos inéditos*, 309, and *Gayoso*, 174–95.

70. Stephen Minor to Manuel Gayoso, Natchez, Nov. 4, 1797, in Holmes, *Gayoso*, 197.

71. James White to Manuel Gayoso, Natchez, Oct. 4, 1798, in Holmes, *Documentos inéditos*, 332. Holmes points out that White was a close friend of Gayoso, who by that time was the governor of Luisiana.

72. Holmes, *Gayoso*, 195–96.

73. John Sevier to Andrew Jackson, Nov. 26, 1797, in Remini, *Andrew Jackson*, 1: 440. Also Archibald Henderson, "The Spanish Conspiracy in Tennessee," *Tennessee Historical Magazine* 3, no. 4 (1917): 229–49.

74. Carlos DeHault DeLassus, Journal, in Louis Houck, *A History of Missouri* (Chicago: R. R. Donnelley, 1908), 2: 367; *Official Letter Books of W. C. C. Claiborne, 1801–1816*, ed. Dunbar Rowland (Jackson, Miss.: State Department of Archives and History, 1917), 1: 47.

75. For example, both Casa Calvo and Manuel Salcedo vouched for Bastrop's loyalty. Mitchell and Calhoun, "The Marquis," 402–3. Conrad, "The Indefatigable Dr. James White," 33–34, discusses White's petition.

76. Daniel Clark to James Madison, New Orleans, April 27, 1803, in Lewis, *The American Union*, 26.

77. See, for example, Daniel Clark to James Madison, New Orleans, Dec. 3, 1803, in Whitaker, *The Mississippi Question*, 251; C. Robin, *Voyages dans l'Intérieur de la Louisiane* (Paris: F. Buisson, 1807), 2: 138–39; Juan La Vallée to Casa Calvo and Manuel Salcedo, New Madrid, March 29, 1804, in Houck, *A History of Missouri*, 2: 363; and Gayarré, *History of Louisiana*, 3: 582, 588–90, 620. Also Alexander DeConde, *This Affair of Louisiana* (New York: Charles Scribner's Sons, 1976), 196–208.

78. Paul Alliot, "Historical and Political Reflections on Louisiana," in Robertson, *Louisiana*, 1: 55. Also Pierre-Louis Berquin-Duvallon, *Vue de la Colonie Espagnole du Mississipi ou des Provinces de la Louisiane et Floride Occidentale, en l'année 1802* (Paris: L'Imprimerie Expéditive, 1803), in ibid., 1: 176.

79. Stanley Clisby Arthur, *The Story of the West Florida Rebellion* (St. Francisville, La.: St. Francisville Democrat), 1935.

80. Andrew McMichael, "The Kemper 'Rebellion': Filibustering and Resident Anglo-American Loyalty in Spanish West Florida," *Louisiana History* 43 (2002): 135 and 159. See also Andrew McMichael, *Atlantic Loyalties: Americans in Spanish West Florida, 1785–1810* (Athens: University of Georgia Press, 2008), 100–102.

81. Spaniards were not alone in this conception. On the rational and emotional sources of early U.S. nationalism, see, for example, James Madison, "Foreign Influence," *Aurora* (Philadelphia), Jan. 23, 1799, in William T. Hutchinson et al., eds., *The Papers of James Madison: Congressional Series* (Chicago: University of Chicago; and Charlottesville: University Press of Virginia, 1959–91), 17: 214–20; Onuf, *Jefferson's Empire*, 77, 91; T. H. Breen, "Ideology and Nationalism on the Eve of the American

Revolution: Revisions *Once More* in Need of Revising," *Journal of American History* 84, no. 1 (1997): 13–39.

82. Herzog, *Defining Nations*, 167, 198, and "Los americanos frente a la Monarquía," 82–83.

83. Joseph Piernas to Carondelet, "Project," New Orleans, April 24, 1795, in Holmes, *Documentos inéditos*, 144–70, at 148. English translation in Jack D. L. Holmes, ed., "Joseph Piernas and a Proposed Settlement on the Calcasieu River, 1795," *McNeese Review* (McNeese State College, Lake Charles, La.), 13 (1962): 59–80. See also Din, "Spain's Immigration Policy," 339.

84. Herzog, *Defining Nations*, 167.

85. Bourke and O'Hara to the king, April 22, 1801, AHN, Estado, leg. 5537, exp. 15. Bourke had served as a priest in Baton Rouge and O'Hara was a veteran of the Hibernia Regiment. The two men claimed to be relatives.

86. On this subject, see, for example, Anthony D. Smith, *The Ethnic Origins of Nations* (Oxford: Blackwell, 1986); or Simon Schama, *Citizens: A Chronicle of the French Revolution* (Harmondsworth: Penguin Books, 1989), chap. entitled "The Cultural Construction of a Citizen."

87. Wilkinson to Miró, "New Suggestions," Feb. 12, 1789, in Navarro and Solano, *¿Conspiración española?*, 249–59.

88. Luis de las Casas to Campo de Alange, Havana, Feb. 17, 1791, cited in Holmes, *Gayoso*, 195–96.

89. Irujo to Cevallos, Mont Plaisant, July 24, 1802, AHN, Estado, leg. 5630.

90. Francisco Collell to Bernardo de Gálvez, Galveztown, Jan. 15, 1779, in Lawrence Kinnaird, "American Penetration into Spanish Louisiana", in [George P. Hammond, ed.], *New Spain and the Anglo-American West: Historical Contributions Presented to Herbert Eugene Bolton* (1932; repr., New York: Kraus, 1969), 2: 229.

91. Philbrick, *The Rise of the West*, 175, may represent many historians who find such a proposition unbelievable, at least regarding immigrants from the United States.

92. Manuel Herrera Gómez, *Demografía e Ilustración en España* (Granada: Universidad de Granada, 1999), 88–96, citing Teodoro de Argumosa, J. de Nuix de Perpiñá, Francisco Cabarrús, and Gaspar M. de Jovellanos.

93. Wilkinson to Miró, "New Suggestions," Feb. 12, 1789, in Navarro and Solano, *¿Conspiración española?*, 249–59.

94. Din, "Proposals and Plans," 208.

95. Local Spanish authorities tried to maintain the policy of religious toleration, but a few Protestants caused disputes by deliberately infringing the rules, which were well known to all immigrants. See Glenn R. Conrad, "Some Observations on Anglo-Saxon Settlers in Colonial Attakapas" (1984), in *The Louisiana Purchase Bicentennial Series in Louisiana History* 10: 236, and "Friend or Foe? Religious Exiles at the Opelousas Post in the American Revolution" (1977), ibid., 227–30. See also Jack D. L. Holmes, "Spanish Religious Policy in West Florida: Enlightened or Expedient?" *Journal of Church and State* 15, no. 2 (1973): 259–69.

96. This does not mean that we are disputing the central importance of Catholicism in the cultural identity of the Hispanic monarchy, which is stressed, for example,

by Luis Navarro García, "Poblamiento y colonización estratégica en el siglo XVIII indiano," *Temas Americanistas* 11 (1994): 15–21; and Herzog, *Defining Nations*, 121.

97. Miró and Navarro to Valdés, New Orleans, Sept. 25, 1787, in Navarro and Solano, *¿Conspiración española?*, 207–14. Similar text in Miró to Campo de Alange, "Descripción de la Luisiana," Madrid, Aug. 11, 1792, in Holmes, *Documentos inéditos*, 26–27. See also Pontalba's memoir, Sept. 15, 1800, in Gayarré, *History of Louisiana*, 3: 410–45.

98. Din, "Proposals and Plans," 207–9.

99. Esteban Miró to Antonio Valdés, New Orleans, May 20, 1789, in Houck, *The Spanish Regime*, 1: 277.

100. Irujo to the Prince of the Peace, Philadelphia, July 20, 1797, n. 73, AHN, Estado, leg. 5630.

101. Luis de Peñalver to Carondelet, New Orleans, Nov. 1, 1795, AGI, SD, leg. 2673.

102. Ibid.

103. Peñalver's letter, July 30, 1799, in Gayarré, *History of Louisiana*, 3: 407–9. See also Joseph Antonio Caballero to Antonio Cornel, San Lorenzo, Nov. 13, 1799, summarizing same, in Robertson, *Louisiana*, 1: 355–57; Whitaker, *The Mississippi Question*, 161–62; and Carmen Cebrián González, "La Iglesia en la Luisiana española," in *Iglesia, religión y sociedad en la historia latinoamericana, 1492–1945* (Szeged: Jozsef Attila University, 1989), 1: 269.

104. Casa Calvo to Urquijo, New Orleans, Oct. 8, 1800, AHN, Estado, leg. 3889 bis. Carondelet and Gayoso had also complained about the poor moral fiber of cadets and some officers. See Gilbert C. Din, "'For Defense of Country and the Glory of Arms': Army Officers in Spanish Louisiana, 1766–1803," *Louisiana History* 43, no. 1 (2002): 19.

105. Casa Calvo to Urquijo, New Orleans, Oct. 8, 1800, AHN, Estado, leg. 3889 bis.

106. Din, "For Defense of Country," 40, and "Spanish Control over a Multiethnic Society: Louisiana, 1763–1803," in Jesús F. De la Teja and Ross Frank, eds., *Choice, Persuasion, and Coercion: Social Control on Spain's North American Frontiers* (Albuquerque: University of New Mexico Press, 2005), 52. See also Jack D. L. Holmes, *Honor and Fidelity: The Louisiana Infantry Regiment and the Louisiana Militia Companies, 1766–1821* (Birmingham, Ala.: Louisiana Collection Series [books and documents on colonial Louisiana], 1, 1965).

107. Whitaker, *The Mississippi Question*, 61.

108. DeConde, *This Affair of Louisiana*, 66.

109. Holmes, *Gayoso*, 272; Din, "The Immigration Policy," 330; Light Townsend Cummins, "'In Territories So Extensive and Fertile': Spanish and English-Speaking Peoples in Louisiana before the Purchase," in Paul Hoffman, ed., *The Louisiana Purchase and Its Peoples: Perspectives from the New Orleans Conference* (Lafayette: Louisiana Historical Association and University of Louisiana, 2004), 117.

110. See, for example, Guillermo Céspedes, *América Hispánica (1492–1898)* (Barcelona: Labor, 1983), 319, 336; Adelman, *Sovereignty and Revolution*, 176; Elliott, *Empires of the Atlantic World*, 308, 319–23, 376; Javier M. Donézar, "De las naciones-

patrias a la 'nación-patria': Del Antiguo al Nuevo Régimen," in A. Álvarez-Ossorio and B. J. García, eds., *La monarquía de las naciones*, 93–120; Richard L. Kagan and Geoffrey Parker, Introduction to Kagan and Parker, eds., *Spain, Europe, and the Atlantic World: Essays in Honour of John H. Elliott* (Cambridge: Cambridge University Press, 1995), 19; I. A. A. Thompson, "Castile, Spain and the Monarchy: The Political Community from *Patria Natural* to *Patria Nacional*," in ibid., 125–60.

111. It could be seen as a new variation on an old challenge. Adelman, *Sovereignty and Revolution*, 9, points out that the Hispanic monarchy traditionally "sheltered multiple identities under a single roof."

112. See, for example, loyalty oath, Natchez, Jan. 4, 1787, in Holmes, *Gayoso*; Wouves d'Argès to Floridablanca, Aug. 1, 1787, AHN, Estado, leg. 3889; White to Ezpeleta, Havana, Dec. 24, 1788, in Navarro and Solano, *¿Conspiración española?*, 271–74; Wilkinson to Miró and Navarro, "Memoria," New Orleans, Sept. 5, 1787, in Navarro and Solano, *¿Conspiración española?*, 187–202; Jáudenes to Godoy, Philadelphia, Dec. 1, 1795, n. 320, enclosing Mr. Pierce Butler's Memorial, Nov. 30, 1795, in Din, "Spain's Immigration Policy," 340; and Andreu, "Los últimos proyectos," 36–38.

113. See, for example, Piernas to Carondelet, "Project," New Orleans, April 24, 1795, in Holmes, *Documentos inéditos*, 144–70. See also Din, "Spain's Immigration Policy," 339.

114. Elliott, *Empires of the Atlantic World*, 131, 133.

115. Adelman, *Sovereignty and Revolution*, quotes at 10 and 101–2.

116. Herzog, *Defining Nations*, 5–6, 11, 15, 66, 180, 196, quotes at 9, 199.

117. Whitaker, *Documents Relating to the Commercial Policy*, xxxvii.

118. Martín Navarro to the Marquis of Sonora, New Orleans, Feb. 12, 1787, AHN, Estado, leg. 3885 bis.

119. "Petition of several inhabitants of St. Augustine regarding trade in East Florida," St. Augustine, Nov. 27, 1794, forwarded by José de Ortega, a royal treasury official in East Florida, in Whitaker, *Documents Relating to the Commercial Policy*, xxxvi, and 184–99, quotes at 190, 198.

120. See, for example, letters from Ramón de López y Angulo to Casa Calvo, New Orleans, Feb. 14, 1800; to Mariano Luis de Urquijo, New Orleans, Sept. 25, 1800; to the secretary of state, New Orleans, Nov. 20, 1800, reserved, numbers 3, 4, 5, AHN, Estado, leg. 3888, documents 96, 101, 104, 108, 108 bis, 110, 112.

121. Herzog, *Defining Nations*, 82, sees a growing general protest against "integrated" foreign merchants who did not fully assume Spanish "nativeness."

122. The dynamics of the relationships between different merchant groups in the context of local and imperial politics lies beyond the scope of this chapter, but see relevant comments in Herzog, *Defining Nations*, 180, and Light Townsend Cummins, "Anglo Merchants and Capital Migration in Spanish Colonial New Orleans, 1763–1803," *Gulf Coast Historical Review* 4 (1988): 378.

PART II

Dilemmas Among Native Americans and Free Blacks

2

"Like to Have Made a War among Ourselves"

The Creek Indians and the Coming of the War of the Revolution

KATHRYN E. HOLLAND BRAUND

In September 1777, the Creek people nearly went to war—among themselves. Their strife was the result of contested loyalties that grew out of the troubles between the British Crown, their ally and trade partner since 1685, and their personal and business associates in Georgia and South Carolina who were rebelling against their king. The British and their colonial subjects did not avoid open warfare. The Creeks did. This chapter examines the experiences of the Creek Indians and a cluster of determined men—ostensibly "friends and brothers"—who found themselves locked in a bitter contest for the loyalty of the Creek people in the opening years of the Revolutionary War in America.

The Creeks were a diverse confederation of allied tribes living in sixty-odd towns divided among two main geographical divisions: the Upper and Lower Towns. A third group, living in relative isolation in the Florida peninsula, was known as Seminoles. The Creeks claimed territory that encompassed most of the modern states of Alabama, Georgia, and Florida and might rightly be considered the most powerful Indian nation in the Southeast (map 2.1).

Creek diplomacy was handled by headmen from leading towns whose prestige rested on their charisma and clan connections. The most prominent were recognized by the British as "medal chiefs," and received special recognition from the king. These "medal chiefs" were far from puppets, and were nominated by the Creeks themselves. There was no "national" council, but town headmen met with some regularity at regional meetings to discuss issues and plot policy, mostly related to protecting Creek lands from white encroachment and adjusting matters relating to trade. The Lower Creeks, who held primary claim on lands to the east, took the lead in negotiations on issues relating to Georgia and East Florida, including boundaries. Upper Creek towns took the lead in dealings with West Florida. Even so, the Upper and Lower Creek towns, or "nations" as they were commonly called, made it

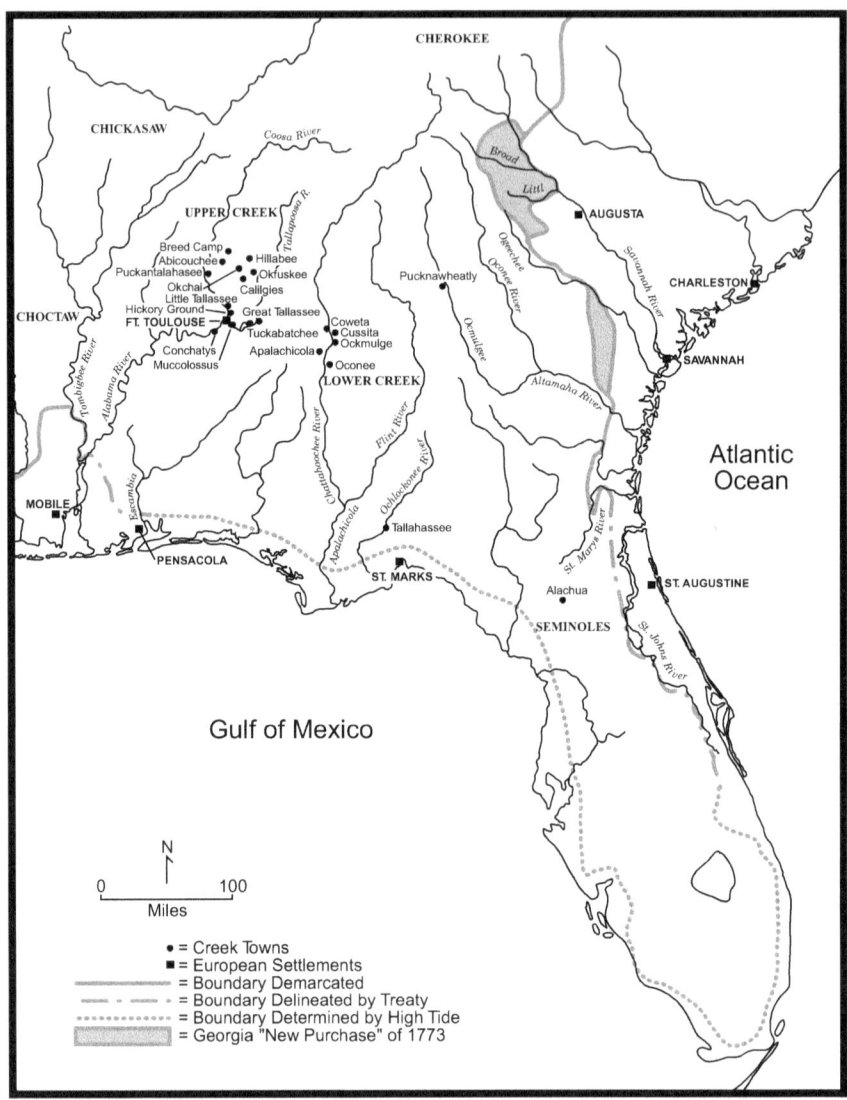

Map 2.1. The Creek towns and their boundaries, ca. 1773. Boundary based on the work of Louis De Vorsey Jr. Map by Sarah Mattics, Center for Archeological Studies, University of South Alabama.

clear that they were "one People." The system was held together by persuasion and consensus and great efforts were made to reconcile diverse points of view. By the eve of the American Revolution, the Creek towns had evolved into a powerful political entity with a long tradition of self-government and their sovereignty extended over a vast territory with marked boundaries recognized under international law.[1]

Long before the official break with Great Britain on July 4, 1776, American rebels and British functionaries had purposefully set about pursuing southeastern Indian loyalty. In January 1776, John Stuart, the superintendent of Indian Affairs for Britain's Southern Department, had learned that commissioners appointed by the Continental Congress to direct Indian affairs had met in North Carolina and had planned spring meetings with the Creek and Cherokee Indians. Stuart, who had held the office since 1762, had developed a notable rapport with many influential headmen in both tribes. His efforts to impose fair trade regulations, establish mutually agreeable exchange rates for the deerskin trade and to negotiate defensible—and marked—borders between the southern tribes and the British colonies had also established his reputation for honesty and fair dealing. Since his appointment, he had cultivated personal friendships with many influential headmen, including Emisteseguo of the Little Tallassee, who in turn considered Stuart's word superior to that of ordinary traders and settlers. As those in rebellion stepped up their efforts among the southern Indians, Stuart assumed that his influence among the Indians would be "superior to theirs," stating, "I shall employ it all in Counteracting them."[2]

Stuart's influence among the Indians was precisely what his rebellious South Carolina neighbors feared. The "liberty men" were convinced that Stuart was organizing the Cherokee to attack the frontier.[3] Their speculations were justified, for Stuart's instructions to his deputy revealed an incredible effort to get arms to the Cherokee through West Florida, far removed from the normal trading paths.[4] With the "liberty men" hot on his heels, Stuart had fled his home in late May for St. Augustine.[5] With Stuart out of the way, South Carolina and ultimately the Continental Congress appointed new commissioners—the longtime Creek traders George Galphin and Robert Rae—and Lower Creek Indians learned it had been "determined that he [Stuart] should die."[6]

Indeed, the key element of rebel strategy was the apprehension of John Stuart and his agents in order to end their influence among the Indians. Among the Upper Creeks, Robert Rae and his trading partner procured handcuffs and attempted to capture David Taitt, Stuart's commissary among the Upper Creeks.[7] Other reports placed hired assassins on their way to the Cherokee towns to dispose of the Cherokee deputy Alexander Cameron in addition to a posse that would be sent "to take away the king's friends" among the traders.[8] The tumult quickly disrupted the normally staid councils of the Creek towns: at Coweta, other headmen "reprimanded" a chief loyal to Galphin who insulted Taitt, while at a council called by the Upper Creek towns, rebel "committee agents" were not allowed to sit "among" the headmen.[9]

Galphin and Rae, the new rebel commissioners, were major suppliers to the Lower and Upper Creek towns respectively. Like Stuart, they realized that peaceful relations with the tribes would likely hinge on the ability of either side to supply needed trade goods: weapons and ammunition, blankets, cloth and clothing and other manufactured goods upon which the economy of the Indians had come to depend.[10] Due to colonial non-importation policies, both sides faced supply troubles. With traditional trade centers in Georgia and South Carolina largely controlled by rebels, Stuart actively worked to relocate experienced merchants and traders to safe territory in loyalist-dominated West Florida.[11]

Galphin and Rae faced more complex problems. In November 1775, the Continental Congress had suspended all exports to Great Britain, including deerskins. Galphin summed up the dilemma that he and his commissioner colleagues faced: "it is the Trade with them that keeps them [Indians] in our Interest, they have great encouragement to go to the Florida's to be suply'd, but the Lower Towns will never go if we can suply them here, & the Uper Towns will do us no hurt without the Consent of the lower Towns there are the best part of the Uper Towns suply'd from West Florida & if the Trade is stop'd from them here they will go all to Florida, & then we may Expect an Indian War." Galphin believed that if an American supply could be established "it is not in the power of Mr. Stewart & all his Agents to set them upon us."[12] But, non-importation had stopped the flow of munitions to the frontier, making an American supply of goods a virtual impossibility.

Galphin, one of the most highly regarded and well-respected of the southern traders, summed it up eloquently but not entirely accurately. True, the Creek economy depended on the trade for necessities such as cloth and clothing as well as arms and ammunition for hunting and defense. But as Galphin and Stuart both learned, trade was only one part of the complicated equation that involved clan responsibility, commitments of honor, and underlying belief about which side could be trusted in regard to Creek self-interest. For their part, most Creeks felt keenly that neutrality remained the best option in the Anglo-American family feud. As early as the fall of 1775, as machinations increased and Stuart and Galphin pressed them to commit to one side or the other, the Lower Creeks "all as one" sent word that they viewed their neighbors as "one people" and wished them to mend their feud.[13] The king's strength was clearly among the Upper Towns, and Galphin estimated that "about half" of the Upper Creek towns were sympathetic to Stuart and their headmen were attempting to "bringe the rest of the nattion to there way of thinking."[14]

In the wake of events in Massachusetts and the employment of Stockbridge Indians around Boston by Americans, Stuart received orders from Thomas Gage, the British commander in chief, "to employ the Indians in the Southern

District in distressing the Rebels by all means in their Power when occasion offers."[15] Thus, Stuart and his deputies, particularly the Creek commissary David Taitt, earnestly set to work cementing the loyalty of the Creeks and preparing them to assist the king in the war against his rebellious subjects should the need arise. And this meant ending rebel influence among the Creeks.

In contrast, Galphin began working assiduously to keep the Creeks neutral. He feared that should Stuart succeed and the Creeks go to war, Americans would then launch counterstrikes into the heart of the Creek nation and lay waste to the Indian towns, putting his Indian friends and relatives in grave danger. Galphin once had a Creek wife, and their two sons, George and John, would work among his Lower Creek kinsmen to support the neutrality position.[16] Galphin had accumulated sizeable land holdings in both South Carolina and Georgia and had enormous stocks of cattle and horses and slaves. During his years in the trade, he had been an interpreter and advisor for the Lower Creek headmen and he was widely respected by his Creek customers as well as by the governments of South Carolina and Georgia. He claimed, "[I] allwise made it a rule to tell them the Truth, which is the reason they always put so much Confidence in what I say." According to Galphin, "[My] influence among the Lower Creeks was so great, that it was not in the power of any Man to set them upon us if I oposed them."[17]

Galphin and Stuart had been allies in the past in the regulation of the deerskin trade, but even before the war the same tensions that led Americans to resent and then resist the king's authority had strained the two men's relationship. The New Purchase Cession of 1773 caused the breach. Galphin had worked hard to achieve Creek consent to the deal, which had transferred some 2.5 million acres of land directly to Georgia in return for the cancellation of the Creek debt. But the cession had created deep divisions among the Creeks and the bitterness had culminated in a series of murders of settlers on the newly ceded lands. John Stuart and Georgia's governor quickly settled those differences, but Stuart blamed the troubles on Galphin and other traders who had used their influence among the Creeks and had subverted his authority. Galphin rightly sensed the superintendent's animosity and believed that part of Stuart's attempts to shift the trade to West Florida lay in his effort to undermine the economic and political clout of the old-line traders from Augusta.[18]

Thus, Galphin could easily predict what John Stuart and his Creek commissary, David Taitt, had in mind. First, they would lay blame for the lack of trade goods from Georgia on the Americans and then work to reestablish a new trade pattern through West Florida that would tie the Creeks to the British interest. Then, ostensibly to prove his concern for Indian welfare, Stuart would patch up a bitter war between the Creek and Choctaw Indians that had been devastating to both tribes since it began in 1763. And once that had been completed, Galphin could foresee with dread British-armed warriors, potentially numbering ten thousand to twelve thousand, employed against Georgia and South Carolina. But Galphin hoped, "As long as we can keep the Creeks our Frinds they will be a Barrier between us & all the other Indians."[19] Galphin's hope was Stuart's fear, for the British rightly guessed that they would need all weapons at their disposal to subdue the rebellion.

The British did not bother to factor the best interests of their Indian allies into their plans. Indeed, the Creeks themselves did not agree on their own best interest. And as tensions increased, loyalty to old friends and allies resulted in growing divisions among the Creeks. Since the 1760s, the impressive coterie of headmen and warriors, acting in the official capacities as town micos, head warriors, speakers, and second men, had worked closely with Stuart, the various colonial governors, and traders to maintain peace and trade, and they valued the Creek-British alliance. And though they were used to witnessing challenges to imperial authority by traders and bickering among royal officials, the spectacle of the superintendent on the run and the British colonists turning against each other shocked the entire generation of Creek leaders who had came to power under British hegemony.

Emisteseguo of the Little Tallassee quickly emerged as Stuart's primary ally among the Upper Creeks. He had first entered the diplomatic scene in 1763 as the representative of the Upper Creek towns at the Congress of Augusta. A recognized speaker, noted warrior, and member of the Tyger clan, he had been designated as one of five "great medal chiefs" at the Congress of Pensacola in 1765. His loyalty to Stuart—and the Crown—was unshakable.[20] The Americans, working through George Galphin's longtime partner John Rae and his brother, Robert, turned to Handsome Fellow (Hobbythacco) of the Okfuskee. Like Emisteseguo, Handsome Fellow was a head warrior in his town and had played a leading role in Creek diplomacy for more than two decades. More an outsider than Emisteseguo, and seldom called upon after 1763 to speak for the Upper Towns, Handsome Fellow was still a prominent and powerful Creek from one of the most populous and powerful Upper Creek Towns. In some way, his stance was directed by loyalty to his longtime traders, whose business connection to Okfuskee reached back decades. At the same time, Handsome Fellow had long harbored anti-British bias and had never been particularly friendly with the British Indian establishment, and he has largely been viewed by historians as a personal rival of Emisteseguo.[21]

In early 1776, the primary concern of all Creeks remained the continued lack of trade goods and supplies. By the end of March, both the Upper and

Lower Creek towns had agreed to Stuart's re-routed trade path, which was designed to supply the Creek towns as well as the Cherokee. While the path leading from Pensacola to the Creek towns had been in frequent use since the end of the Seven Years' War, the long trail leading north from the Upper Creek towns to the Cherokee town of Chota had never been used as a trade path. Essentially, Stuart sought to re-route the entire southeastern deerskin trade through the loyal colony of West Florida.

The Creeks made their views known to both sides through "talks" delivered by appointed speakers that were transcribed by their interpreters and then dispatched to various recipients. Speaking for the Upper Towns, Emisteseguo made it clear that their support for the British was largely due to resentment over the New Purchase Cession and repeated encroachments on Creek land. He implored the Georgians to remain loyal to the king and warned them that the Creeks would view Britain's enemies as their own.[22]

The Lower Towns did not instruct their spokesman to embrace the British view with such vigor, but they did agree to support a new trade path from Pensacola through the Upper Creek nation, since "both [of their] former Trading Paths are shut up and no more Goods can come to Augusta." But their concern over the growing turmoil in their midst was clearly evident. Speaking to their traders as well as Stuart, they lectured their "Eldest Brothers," imploring them to drop "their Disputes and not spoil one another."[23] The talk from the Lower Creek headmen and warriors was very clear: "we don't want to Concearn in the matter but leave you to settle the matter yourselves and will be glad to hear the difference settled and all at peace again."[24]

A frustrated Galphin could merely observe that Stuart "Sertenly is yousing all his Interest to bringe over the Indians but not in his publice talkes."[25] Galphin correctly suspected that Stuart and his agents engaged in quiet talks with leading men to gain their support, while at the same time made public talks of peace. In early 1776, with East Florida facing a potential invasion by rebels from Georgia and South Carolina, Governor Patrick Tonyn called for Stuart and Taitt to drop the pretense and demand assistance from Britain's Creek allies. The governor put David Taitt on notice: the "Creeks ought to be prepared to give us all their assistance," he claimed.

Tonyn was especially irritated that the "Seminolies," or expat Creeks who settled in East Florida, would not promise to defend his colony, even though they were well supplied with British goods out of St. Augustine. Though their towns were primarily around the lush Alachua savannah near modern Gainesville, Florida, miles from the leading Lower Creek towns on the Chattahoochee, they deferred to Lower Creek authority, especially in matters of diplomacy, and would not budge from the neutralist position.[26] Tonyn charged Taitt, the Creek agent, with convincing the Lower Creeks to abandon their neutralist position in order to free the Seminoles for action.[27]

Meanwhile, Stuart and his agents, Taitt and William McIntosh, continued to propound the loyalist argument to the Creeks, which largely involved promises of trade and respect for Creek boundaries.[28] By May 1776, Taitt reported success among the Upper Creek towns and he declared them "disposed to a man . . . to act in favour of Government" and claimed to have "people at a Call" and ready to march against the Georgia frontier as soon as ammunition was available. He admitted less confidence in the Lower Creeks.[29]

To counter the British effort, the Americans worked to convince Creeks that the best course was to "lye quiet and not to take any part or either side." They also sent messages to Stuart's interpreter among the Lower Creeks and loyal traders with a plaintive message: "I hope you'll never be an Insterment of bringing down a Savage nation against your country," wrote Robert Rae to the interpreter Samuel Thomas.[30] In the end, it was not the neutrality talk that swayed the Lower Creeks, but a rejection of "Tate's bad talks in his Advising them all to spill their brothers (the White people's) blood." The Cussita King "considered Stuart as out of his senses to ask such a thing."[31]

Thus, by May 1776, the American commissioners had achieved their goal, and nearly two hundred leading headmen and warriors from both the Upper and Lower Towns responded to an invitation to visit Augusta and hear a talk sent by the Continental Congress detailing the success of American armies in Boston and Quebec. The attendees reveal deep divisions among the Creeks, for pro-British headmen, including Emisteseguo, did not attend, while those with the closest ties to Galphin and Rae, including Handsome Fellow of the Okfuskee, and the two most important Lower Creeks, Escochabey of Coweta and Captain Allick of Cussita, were there in force. Their motives for rejecting Taitt's advice and meeting with the Americans can only be surmised, but certainly the close personal bond of the Okfuskee leader to Robert Rae and the influence of Galphin among the Coweta and Cussita headmen cannot be understated. Indeed, it was a main theme of the conference: "Tate will tell you lies; do not believe him. . . . You have long known Messrs. Galphin and Rae. They have spoke the language of Truth to you upon all Occasions and will not decieve you now."[32] The Americans denied they had stopped the trade to reduce the Creeks to poverty and instead blamed the lack of goods on the British king whose aim was to impoverish the colonists. The Georgians promised that soon Americans would prevail against the king's armies and supply the Creeks. The Americans blamed Stuart and his men for the divisions and confusion and were pointed in their advice to the Creeks: "you had best send Taitt out of the nation . . . You must neither Join the Kings Troops nor us."³³

The American position was soon undermined when Thomas Fee, a Georgia outlaw who had previously killed an unarmed Indian in Augusta, struck again and murdered a Coweta warrior named Mad Turkey. The Georgia Council of Safety promptly ordered Fee's arrest, but the hate crime, along with the erection of two new forts on the recently ceded lands, bred distrust and angered the Creeks.³⁴ Coweta's two leading headmen, Ishenpoaphe and Escochabey, abandoned Galphin, and Cowetas killed an Ogeechee River settler in retaliation for the Creek death. Cowetas also sent word to the Seminoles that assisting Tonyn now met with their approval and by July 1776, the Cowkeeper of Latchoway, a "great medal" Seminole chief, was leading cattle rustling raids against Georgia in order to supply food to the growing loyalist population of East Florida.³⁵

But just as the sentiment seemed to shift in Britain's favor, horrific news from the north sent Creek destiny flying in another direction. That news was the destruction of the Cherokee country as a result of the war that tribe launched against their American neighbors in July 1776.³⁶ It was in the wake of the Cherokee war that the Coweta took revenge for the Creek warrior murdered by Fee in August. It was not a propitious time to strike Georgia, and Galphin seized the opportunity to warn the Creeks about the growing peril they faced by this seeming cooperation with the British plans to attack the frontier. To the Coweta, he sent a bleak report about the outcome of the Cherokee offensive, noting that "their Towns is all burn'd their Corn cut down & themselves drove into the Woods."³⁷ To Timothy Barnard, an old trader of his employ still among the Creeks, he mused that "the Majority of the [Georgia] people wants a Creek War for I suppose in a few months they could raise 5 or 6000 men to go against them."³⁸

A chorus of other American voices joined Galphin's, hoping to head off a devastating Creek war. The official Georgia notice came through Jonathan Bryan, a man of wealth and power who plainly told the Lower Creeks that any attack on Georgia would "end in your own distruction and Ruin." The Georgia messenger stressed that the Cherokee debacle was "brought on themselves by believing the Lying Talks given them by Mr. Stuart and his Men."³⁹ In September, as the Lower Creeks continued to assist East Florida against American attacks, Galphin sent a headman to the Lower Towns with specific instructions to "call home all their young warriors" from East Florida or risk provoking an attack from Georgia.⁴⁰ Lower Creeks took the cue.

The situation was different among the Upper Towns, where Alexander

Cameron, the British agent to the Cherokee, and Cherokees fleeing the Americans took refuge. As Cherokee resentment of encroachment and invasion festered, Emisteseguo decided to raise the "red stick" against the "Virginians" as the Creeks termed all those on the frontiers. Emisteseguo noted, "I have sat quietly a long time without joining either party, but the Virginians are now come very near my nation and I do not want them to come any nearer."[41]

Creek willingness to send warriors to assist the Cherokees was a direct result of another action by Stuart. In October 1776, he had, as Galphin predicted, orchestrated a peace between the Creeks and Choctaws with the specific aim of freeing up both tribes to assist in his own war efforts. The burden of the long-running Choctaw war removed, the Creeks promised to send aid to the Cherokees. John Stuart's logic was compelling as he urged them to unite against the common threat from the colonies rather than allowing each "nation to be cut off and their country to be possessed by Rebells."[42] In addition to assisting the Cherokees, the end of the Creek-Choctaw War allowed the Choctaws to aid in the defense of the Mississippi River and West Florida, while East Florida could also expect more support from the Lower Creeks.[43]

Many Lower Creeks took a different point of view—no doubt in light of the knowledge that any retaliation from Georgia would be aimed at their towns. Thus, while more than one thousand Upper Creeks traveled to Pensacola to reaffirm their allegiance to the British Empire, a dozen Cussita Indians visited Galphin's South Carolina plantation.[44] Galphin liberally passed out trade goods procured from the French West Indies and reassured the Lower Towns' representatives that the trade would resume in the near future. As this favorable news began to sway Creek opinions, pro-British Creeks attacked a party of Georgia rangers, killing four and wounding two others in a clear attempt to thwart Galphin's progress. Galphin could not deliver on his promise of goods and as British goods arrived from Pensacola, the pro-British party among the Lower Towns gained ground.[45] But by the end of 1776, a tough peace talk arrived from Georgia with graphic accounts of the Cherokee defeat, the success of American armies in the north, and news that three Creeks who had killed a man on the frontier had been taken prisoner and placed in irons. General Lachlan McIntosh sent word to the Creeks that those he described as "our warriors" wished to kill them immediately, but the "wise men" of Georgia, mindful of the laws of retaliation, would hold them as prisoners until the Creek headmen came to Savannah to take care of that business themselves. Once that was accomplished, McIntosh assured the Creeks that Georgia would make a "firm peace . . . that will last as long as the sun shines or the waters Run."[46] Stuart intercepted the talk and read it to a select group of headmen who visited with him at Pensacola. These men were not moved, at least according to Stuart.[47]

Indeed, by early January, Stuart believed that Emisteseguo and an army of between three and four hundred Creek warriors were "seriously engaged" in an effort to render aid to the Cherokee, while another party "under the direction of a person of confidence" moved toward St. Augustine to assist Tonyn and would be "joined by about 250 Seminollies."[48] More importantly, at least from the Creek perspective, a trade caravan, mainly weapons, arrived from Pensacola for distribution to the Indians.[49] Some of the goods were to have continued on to the Cherokees, but as rumors flew that Georgians were sending their own army out to stop that traffic, Emisteseguo advised Taitt to halt the traders until they could be escorted. Meanwhile, Emisteseguo, with a much smaller contingent of warriors than Stuart envisioned, proceeded to the Cherokee towns.[50]

As John Stuart and George Galphin struggled to gain an upper hand of credibility among the Creeks, each faced problems. Galphin's talks and letters were routinely relayed to Stuart by loyal traders.[51] In return, Stuart had to battle the "plague and trouble" of rebel "spies" among traders and packhorsemen whose anti-British propaganda, paired with exaggerated and overly optimistic stories of American success, undercut his message.[52]

As the stakes grew, Galphin sent peace emblems to the Creeks, urged them to pull back from an all-out commitment to the king's cause, and pushed them to drive Stuart's agent provocateurs—Taitt, Cameron, and McIntosh—from their midst.[53] Creek headmen from across the nation assembled to debate the issue, and in the end, thirty-seven towns declared that they had "thrown away" Stuart's bad talk and accepted Galphin's "good" talk. Cussita, a Lower Creek war town, took the lead in organizing the meeting, and the response was laden with symbolic gestures of peace, including a white crane skin delivered by the Old Tallassee King, the headman of a leading Tallapoosa white (peace) town, and the headman of an Abeika town, the mico of Okfuskee. In his speech, the Old Tallassee King alluded to the fact that Cussita's interest was paramount in the issue, as Lower Creek views had traditionally taken precedence when matters involved Georgia. Although the towns initially agreed "to turn Tate in six days out of the nation," more prudent heads demanded reconsideration and in the end the towns agreed to drive Taitt out if the Americans could assure them of a viable trade. The Okfuskee mico proposed that since men had been killed on both sides, "we must let it all drop and say no more about it." He also informed Galphin that to ensure Upper Creek compliance there should be "three traders if the cargoes be ever so small" with American goods coming first to neutral towns of Cussitaws, Okfuskee, and Okchai—towns that Taitt had taken particular care to supply by loyal traders.

While embracing the prospect of peace with the Americans, the Upper

Creeks remained realists and refused to cut the British trade from Pensacola.[54] Although the records are scanty, it seems clear that the Little Tallassee, Coosada, and the Muccolossus—towns representing the three great divisions among the Upper Creeks—actively lobbied for aggressive support of the British cause, while Tallassee and Okfuskee posited the neutralist position.[55] When the devastated Cherokees sued for peace in the spring, the neutralist position gained ground and by June 1777 substantial numbers of headmen had accepted George Galphin's invitation to attend more peace talks on the Ogeechee River. Galphin's friendly overtures, combined with explicit threats that Americans could use an invasion route from the Cherokee towns, had done the trick.

Indeed, rebel rumors that the French and Spanish had joined the colonists and would soon blockade the British ports in Pensacola and St. Augustine resulted in Creek anxiety over the British supply line. The rumors fed on fact, and as British trade dried up, Taitt reported that the Creeks were "so greatly distressed for provisions that we do not know what to do." The one trade commodity getting through was also the most lucrative—rum. Taitt reported that "all our Indians are so totally debauched with liquor from West Florida that they are seldom a day sober."[56] Somber Creek headmen, hoping to thwart the traffic, accosted trading caravans and destroyed the cargo.[57] The inability of the British to supply their allies or control the rum trade was a blow to their cause.

The meeting at Galphin's cowpens on the Ogeechee River took place in mid-June 1777.[58] The contingent included not only leading men from Cussita, but the Upper Creek headmen Handsome Fellow (Okfuskee) and the Old Tallassee King (Tallassee). Pro-British Coweta and Tuckabatchee headmen attempted to stop the Old Tallassee King, but their efforts failed. Frustrated, Taitt attempted to raise a war party "against the settlements" to scotch the peace talks. Aware that such actions would mean an invasion from Georgia, the Cowetas proposed building a fort at first word of "marching on the rebels." Taitt could only promise assistance but noted warily to John Stuart that "forts without provisions and ammunition are of little use." And Taitt could offer neither. Meanwhile, bent on removing "bad men" from among the Creek towns, Taitt actively worked to have traders who trafficked in liquor or who professed rebel sentiments detained and removed from the towns.[59]

As Taitt's increasingly futile efforts proceeded, Galphin was forced to confess to the assembled Creeks, which he estimated at "between 4 & 500," that he had no trade goods, but would have them "in Abundance" soon from the French. But he told the Creeks that he would not send the goods unless the Creeks could promise the American traders "Security both to their person and property from Tate, McIntosh, or other Enemies of the State, you made us a promise of driving those Emissaries from your Nation if we would Supply you with Goods."⁶⁰ The assembled headmen claimed the authority to speak for the Upper Creeks and in return could only note their dependence on foreign trade and their unwillingness to completely sever ties to the British supply line.⁶¹

As Galphin's talks proceeded, loyalist Creeks raided the frontier and suffered for it. The war parties came from both Upper Creeks (Tuckabatchee, Savannah, Coosada, Okchai, Tuskegee) and Lower Creek Coweta, which lost the nephew of Ishenpoaphe, its leading man, as well as two others severely wounded by Georgia guns.⁶² Galphin, assured that these were "Runagading Indians" numbering no more than "30 or 40," maintained a sanguine view and took the word of the Creeks visiting his cowpens that they would be called off by the conferees upon their return home. Still, Galphin had real worries. To Laurens, he put it plainly: "there is numbers of bad people in Georgia that wants a Creek war Some on aCount of geting thier Lands. . . . Some of those villians has thretned to Shute me . . . the Say if I was put out of the way they wood Sone have a Creeke warr . . . if it was not for these Damed villians upon the frontier I should tacke a plasure in Serving my Contrey."⁶³

Galphin had nothing to offer the Creeks but rum and he distributed it with abandon. William McIntosh reported to John Stuart that the conferees returned home so befuddled with drink that he could not obtain reliable intelligence about the meeting. What he did manage to discern was a plan to call all the towns together and demand the ouster of the British agents. The rumblings were made credible when a Cussita warrior attempted to scalp McIntosh, but "mist his Aim."⁶⁴

Even as neutralist chiefs plotted the removal of the British, Stuart received word from General William Howe to prepare the Indians for a coming campaign against Georgia.⁶⁵ Stuart set to work to procure "a Book of manual Exercise" and a drum so Cameron could properly train the Loyalist traders, packhorsemen, and Indians. For their part, loyal Creeks pledged that they would hit the Georgia frontier after the Busk, their annual harvest celebration, which was usually held in late August.⁶⁶ Late in July, Stuart sent "a troop of twenty-five light horse" loyalist refugees to assist in the planned hostilities against Georgia, as well as "a very considerable supply of Arms ammunition and other goods."⁶⁷ The plan called for a two-pronged assault against Georgia, with the Creeks attacking the frontier as Howe was "reducing the Lower part of the Province."⁶⁸

Taitt was eager to strike before Creek enthusiasm for the plan waned, but the attack was delayed by a number of factors, including a lack of food and materiel. But the primary reason for hesitation was that Handsome Fellow of the Okfuskee was visiting Charleston as a guest of Galphin. Fearing for his life should the Creek onslaught begin before his return, his town threatened to attack British Mobile and Pensacola if the loyalist Creeks proceeded with their plan of attack.[69] Meanwhile, Galphin's emissaries freely visited the Upper Towns and were guarded by Indian escorts on their journeys.[70]

Galphin's Charleston tour with Handsome Fellow, accompanied by five other headmen and a sizeable entourage, came off flawlessly. The party arrived on July 9, and was treated to scenes of American military might, including a visit to the arsenal, a ship in the harbor, the harbor forts that had previously fended off British attacks, and a parade by the local military establishment. Handsome Fellow presented the Americans with symbols of peace: the eagle tail standard and a ceremonial rattle to be forwarded to the American Congress. The great chief concluded a peace oration by flinging onto a table the commissions he had received from previous royal governors. John Rutledge promptly produced a new American commission. Rutledge and the others present were convinced that peace was a certainty if a trade could be established, unless Georgians started a war.[71] Galphin later reported that he "youle^d all the influence^s I ha^d with them," and then demanded as the price of peace the ouster of royal agents who fomented war talk against the Americans.[72]

The peace hopes generated by the conference were indeed soon "spoiled" by Georgia, after provocation by Coweta warriors, who attacked a frontier stockade and made off with a number of horses. Incensed Georgians pursued, killing one Creek and seriously wounding another. The Creeks "pretended to fly, but wheeling round unperceived by the Rebels, they placed themselves in ambush near the Road by which the Enemy were to return, and attacked them unexpedly." Initial reports placed the American dead at twenty, but later intelligence revealed more moderate numbers of killed (four) as well as wounded. Notable among the dead was Captain Thomas Dooly of the 3rd Georgia Continental Battalion. Pro-loyalist Coweta warriors continued their attacks along the frontier, burning houses, stealing horses, and taking prisoners, and in the process killed more Georgians as well as the neutralists' goal to maintain friendship with Georgia.[73]

Captain Dooly's brother John, himself a captain in the 12th Troop of Rangers, promptly demanded the arrest of Handsome Fellow and the nine Creek delegates, who were still with Galphin at his home in Silver Bluff, South Carolina, waiting for packhorses to be fitted out with goods before returning home. Colonel Samuel Elbert, in command of Georgia's forces, just as promptly refused, whereupon Dooly and a group of like-minded enlistees proceeded to Silver Bluff. According to American reports, Dooly and his comrades "forciby took the ten Deputies out of this State, & carried them into Georgia at Augusta where they are kept Close prisoners." South Carolinians correctly noted that the action was "a great Insult offered to this State, under whose protection, & the Laws of nations, they were as Ambassadors from the Creeks It is also an Insult to the United States, as they were taken by force of arms from the Continental Commissioner of Indian Affairs."[74]

Galphin and Rae, attempting damage control, blamed the uproar on Emisteseguo and the activities of pro-British Creeks, telling the Indians they were detained for their own protection. Ultimately, Galphin secured the release of the hostages, who made the trip back across the Savannah River to Silver Bluff, where he finished fitting them out for the trip home. By the end of August, he had sent them on their way under the protection of a company of continental troops. Within ten miles of Silver Bluff, the party was ambushed by loyalists under the command of Sam Moore. One of the group mistaken for Galphin was purposely shot and killed, but the Creeks escaped unharmed. Their plans to oust the king's agents suffered a temporary setback when Handsome Fellow died on the path before reaching home.[75] Stuart, elated, reported home that Handsome Fellow's death has "again spoilt Galphin's path, and made it as crooked as Ever and the whole nation is now unannimous for War."[76]

But Stuart was badly mistaken. The Creek towns were even more sorely divided. As the neutralists regrouped, Taitt and Cameron prepared for an all-out assault on Georgia. Taitt was convinced that the Upper Creeks were "entirely unanimous" in their support of the effort. Loyal traders volunteered to head Indian war parties, and together with loyalist refugees Taitt's force came to 200 white men, as well as traders and warriors from the Lower Towns. In East Florida, the assistant commissary prepared Seminole warriors to strike from the south, while Alexander Cameron and about 150 exiled Cherokees, with their traders, also planned to participate in the effort.[77] No doubt, the arrival of a large shipment of goods (reports say 100 horse loads) from Stuart bolstered the show of loyalty.[78] Taitt selected September 21 as the date to set out for Georgia.

Meanwhile, Stuart deployed a new agent to assist Taitt: Alexander McGillivray. He was the son of a Creek woman and Lachlan McGillivray, a wealthy Georgia loyalist and friend of George Galphin. The young McGillivray was the unique product of allied cultures and he was well prepared for life in both, and in the coming days he called upon his British education and his Creek clan connections. His first real assignment came when Taitt sent him to Okfuskee to counteract a recent visit by Daniel McMurphy, Galphin's agent. In fact, McMurphy's message was that the Americans would not supply goods until the British commissaries were driven out of the nation or killed. As McGillivray neared Okfuskee, small parties of warriors passed him heading south toward the Creek towns on the Tallapoosa River. The armed men refused to answer questions about their purpose or destination, other than a rather unbelievable story that they were headed to pick leaves for black drink. By the time he arrived at the town of Calidgee, McGillivray had sent a runner with a warning to Ocheubofau (the Hickory Ground) and the Little Tallassee, the Creek towns some twenty-five miles away where David Taitt, Alexander Cameron, and the Creek interpreter Jacob Moniac were stationed. As McGillivray dispatched his runner, a number of leading Okfukee headmen and 120 men arrived, and they confirmed McGillivray's suspicion that they were indeed intent on the ouster or death of all of Britain's "beloved men" among the Creeks. Through force of rhetoric, McGillivray convinced them that the result of their action would not be neutrality but a civil war that would devastate the already divided Creeks. In turn, the Okfuskee headmen insisted that the Anglo-Creek assault plan be "Intirely dropt & laid aside" before they promised to abandon their attack on the commissaries. Although McGillivray's heated "wranglings" convinced these Abeika Creeks to abandon their mission, other parties of Creeks from the Tallapoosa towns proceeded on their mission. McGillivray's runner reached the British agents "about three in the morning," arriving only minutes ahead of the war parties. Cameron and Taitt, forewarned, fled on horseback, narrowly avoiding capture. According to Cussita reports, Taitt "jumpt upon an Indians horse that was tied in his yard and rode off without vicutals" as his attackers approached, while American officials somewhat sourly noted that Cameron "got of his shirt upon an Indian horse." Having missed their main targets, the warriors plundered Cameron's supply store as well as the stores of all the resident traders still loyal to the Crown, and in one case they destroyed a trader's cattle and horses. Refugee Cherokees, who had planned to join the British assault against the Georgia backcounty, were also targeted and fled with Cameron and Taitt to Pensacola via the Choctaw towns—as did Emisteseguo.[79]

The attacks were part of a carefully orchestrated plan, coordinated by the ancient Creek tradition of "broken days" that also included a simultaneous attack on the Lower Creek commissary William McIntosh, whose headquarters were at Coweta. McIntosh had had the foresight to procure guards, whom he had paid with British rum, and managed to survive the initial assault because the attackers would not risk harming his loyal guards. And after several days, his Coweta and Chehaw guardians were able to escort him safely to Pensacola. When the loyalists evacuated, women from Cussita "went over to their Houses and pulled them down" and looted the commissary's store.[80]

The concerted attacks against the British emissaries and their war plans effectively stopped the assault against the Georgia frontier, but did not end the division in Creek opinion about the proper course of action. As the headman of Cussita noted in a report to George Galphin, the Creeks "had like to have made a War among ourselves." Civil war had been a real possibility, and the Creek warriors involved in the three-pronged attack against the British commissaries, the Cherokee, and Emisteseguo, certainly realized how dangerously close they came to the brink. Thus, in the stand-off at Coweta, even incendiary rum was not enough to drive Creek warriors to attack their own, and McIntosh slipped away unharmed. The same observation is even more appropriate in the case of Emisteseguo, for as the neutralists reported to the Americans, the headman had "some of his Friends to interfere for him to Come Back & promise to Give out no bad Talks."[81] McGillivray's timely warning can justly be credited with heading off internecine warfare in the Upper Creek towns, for had Emisteseguo been slain, clan retaliation for his death would have launched a dangerous game of retribution and counterstrike. The death of commissaries, with no Creek clan to protect them, would also have provoked counterstrikes by pro-British Creeks.

The ultimate aim of the neutralists' plot, there can be no doubt, was to stop the planned attack against Georgia and South Carolina by driving out the British planners. An added benefit was the acquisition of sorely needed trade goods from the plunder of the stores. In that respect, Alexander McGillivray joined the spoils game and took control of all of the goods that remained in Taitt's store—spared no doubt by the quick thinking of his own clan. With his large and powerful Wind clan to protect him, McGillivray became the leading pro-British spokesman among the Upper Creeks and the event marked the beginning of his rise to power.[82]

As the furor died down, the neutralists leaders of Cussita, Tallassee, and Okfuskee "apointed a Day to put up the Liberty Coulours" and asserted that there were only "four towns in the Nation that Stand up for the Commissarys." Meanwhile, they waited on supplies of goods from Georgia as their due for driving out the king's men.[83] Though his plan to maintain Creek loyalty was ostensibly a success, Galphin found no reason to celebrate success as rumors soon reached him that the British had put a bounty of five hundred pounds sterling on his head. He noted sullenly that "there is numbers in Georgia wants a Creek war and has thretan[d] to kill me for keeping the Indians peasable." Nonetheless, he made plans to oversee a shipment of goods to their towns—if he could get them—and mused, "we want nothing know but Seply of goods to keep the Creeks and all their allies at pease with us."[84] At pro-British Little Tallassee, young McGillivray, with strong clan support, speaking for both his town and the Crown, chastised his fellow Creeks for the disrespect paid to their old allies and promised to work "to restore harmony & put an end to these confusions."[85]

By the end of October, Lower Creek headmen again renounced any part in the war between the Crown and the colonies. The Cussita King proclaimed that all the Creek towns were "determined to sit neutral" and made clear the reason for the ouster of the royal commissaries: "We have heard the Talks from the other Party and they say Nothing but peace."[86] In mid-October, Stuart dispatched emissaries into the towns to soothe relations, and they quickly found themselves surrounded by "upwards of 300 armed Indians all painted Black" who took them prisoner and released them only after they declared that they had "no Intentions to say any Thing but what was peaceable & reasonable."[87]

Thus, as David Corkran has written, "for the moment, the neutralist faction had triumphed."[88] Both John Stuart and George Galphin had expected the Creeks to be driven by a desire for trade goods as each attempted to manipulate the actions of their friends and allies. But trade was only one part of the complicated equation that involved clan responsibility, commitments of honor, and underlying belief about which side could be trusted in regard to Creek self-interest. There is no doubt that personal friendship and personal loyalty—and family connections—motivated many on both sides. And there seems no doubt that the staunchest allies of the British, namely Emisteseguo and Alexander McGillivray, were firmly convinced that maintaining British authority over rowdy settlers was in the Creeks' best interest. But Upper and Lower Creeks frequently held differing views based on what constituted their own best interests. Upper Creeks, traditionally the most fierce in offering resistance to land cessions—no matter that Lower Creeks took precedence in affairs involving lands bordering Georgia—exhibited more suspicion of Americans on that count than did Lower Creeks. For their part, Lower Creek towns were always most sensitive to threats of invasion from the east and realized that any retaliatory military action against the Creeks would put them in immediate peril. And to complicate matters, not all Upper and Lower Creeks shared uniform points of view on any of these matters. But all Creeks realized the necessity of a steady trade in European manufactures, particularly guns and ammunition during troubling times and neutrality seems to have been the dominant sentiment. Moreover, it is obvious that even when divided, the Creek people viewed themselves "as one" and knew that others would hold all responsible for the acts of any faction. During the fall of 1777, those who favored peace precipitated a disastrous civil war far more dangerous than any invasion by Georgians as they attempted to drive out those who supported the British position.

Though an internal conflict was averted in 1777 due to the timely warnings by Alexander McGillivray, this crisis would not be the last in the escalating struggle of colonies against Crown. As all would soon learn, talks that were "peaceable & reasonable" would be absent from the Creek country—indeed from the entire southern backcountry—for years to come. Even as the Creek peace tokens (Handsome Fellow's eagle tail and rattle) made their way north to the Continental Congress, events far from the control of the Creek headmen brought new troubles.[89] Within a year, the British captured Savannah. David Taitt returned to the Creek towns, and Emisteseguo and Alexander McGillivray—aided by British goods—surmounted neutralists' opposition to war and sent Creek warriors against the Americans. When the British gained control of Georgia, Upper Creek support for the war effort reached an all-time high, but neutralist opposition to these activities continued to the end, although the arrest of George Galphin in 1780 and the death of Handsome Fellow earlier deprived the anti-war faction of two strong guiding lights. Creek fealty to Britain in fighting on the Georgia frontier and in the defense of Pensacola counted for nothing in the end. After losing their colonies by force, the British simply abandoned their Creek friends. The bitter legacy of loyalty to Britain was a divided Creek nation that would be forced to pay for the blood they spilled in Britain's cause with cessions of Creek land to Georgia after 1783.

Notes

1. Kathryn E. Holland Braund, "'Like a Stone Wall Never to Be Broke': The British-Indian Boundary Line with the Creek Indians, 1763–1773," in Joseph P. Ward, ed., *Britain and the American South from Colonialism to Rock and Roll* (Jackson: University of Mississippi Press, 2003), 53–79. Quotation is from William L. Saunders, ed., *The Colonial Records of North Carolina*, 16 vols. (Raleigh: Josephus Daniels, 1886–90), 11: 167. See Steven C. Hahn, *The Invention of the Creek Nation, 1670–1763* (Lincoln: University of Nebraska Press, 2004) for an examination of the evolution of the Creek nation.

2. John Stuart to the earl of Dartmouth, Jan. 6, 1776, Great Britain, Public Record Office (National Archives) Colonial Office, America and West Indies, Indian Affairs, Class 5, vol. 77, fol. 40. (Class 5 material will hereafter be cited using the following form: C05/vol. number, fol. number.) The meeting was held Nov. 13, 1775. See *The Papers of Henry Laurens*, ed. by Philip M. Hamer et al., 16 vols. (Columbia: South Carolina Historical Society Press, 1968–2002), 10: 437n.; hereafter cited as *LP*. The standard work on the Creek nation during the American Revolution is David H. Corkran, *The Creek Frontier, 1540–1783* (Norman: University of Oklahoma Press, 1967). See also James H. O'Donnel II, *Southern Indians in the American Revolution* (Knoxville: University of Tennessee Press, 1973).

3. For the situation in South Carolina, see Russell J. Snapp, *John Stuart and the Struggle for Empire on the Southern Frontier* (Baton Rouge: Louisiana State Press, 1996), 159.

4. Henry Stuart to John Stuart, Aug. 25, 1776, C05/77, fol. 169.

5. Snapp, *John Stuart*, 160–61.

6. "Substance of a Message Sent by George Galphin into the Creek Nation," in John Stuart to Dartmouth, Sept. 17, 1775, C05/76, fol. 175.

7. John Stuart to Sir Henry Clinton, March 15, 1776, C05/77, fol. 107 (also in K. G. Davies, *Documents of the American Revolution, 1770–1783*, 20 vols. (Dublin: Irish University Press, 1976) 12: 78. hereafter cited as *DAR*. According to Stuart, Rae was dispatched by the Georgia congress.

8. *DAR*, 12: 194, 197.

9. John Stuart to the earl of Dartmouth, Oct. 25, 1775, C05/76, fol. 183; *DAR*, 11: 167.

10. John Stuart to earl of Dartmouth, Jan. 19, 1776, C05/77, fol. 38. For information on the deerskin trade, see Kathryn E. Holland Braund, *Deerskins and Duffels: The Creek Indians, Anglo-America, and the Deerskin Trade, 1685–1815* (Lincoln: University of Nebraska Press, 1993).

11. John Stuart to the earl of Dartmouth, Jan. 19, 1776, C05/77, fol. 38.

12. George Galphin to Henry Laurens, Feb. 7, 1776, in *LP*, 11: 94. Council of Safety to George Galphin, Feb. 14, 1776, *LP*, 11: 102.

13. Lower Creeks to John Stuart, Sept. 29, 1775, C05/77, fol. 58. The talk was signed by Simpoyaufy of the Cowitaws, Blue Salt King of the Cussitaws, Pumpkin King of Osichess, the king of the Chihaws, and the Long Warrior of the Chihaws.

14. George Galphin to Council of Safety, Oct. 15, 1775, *LP*, 10: 467.

15. John Stuart to David Taitt, 15 Dec. 15, 1775, C05/77, fol. 39.

16. "Will of George Galphin," *Richmond County History* 13 (1981): 19–27. David Taitt to John Stuart, July 7, 1776, *DAR*, 12: 160; George Galphin to Council of Safety, Oct. 15, 1775, *LP*, 10: 467. John Stuart to the earl of Dartmouth, Oct. 25, 1775, C05/76, fol. 183.

17. George Galphin to Henry Laurens, Feb. 7, 1776, in *LP*, 11: 94–5.

18. Ibid., 11: 95–96. For details on the New Purchase Cession, see Braund, *Deerskins and Duffels*, 150–53; and Corkran, *The Creek Frontier*, 281–87. Galphin's main base was in Silver Bluff, South Carolina, just across the Savannah River from Augusta. See Edward J. Cashin, ed., *Colonial Augusta: "Key of the Indian Countrey"* (Macon, Ga.: Mercer University Press, 1986); and Braund, *Deerskins and Duffels*, chap. 3. For the tensions between Stuart and those he sought to regulate, see Snapp, *John Stuart*.

19. George Galphin to Henry Laurens, Feb. 7, 1776, in *LP*, 11: 95–96.

20. Talk of Emisteseguo to Superintendent John Stuart, Sept. 20, 1775, C05/77, fol. 56 (copy also in Henry Clinton Papers, William L. Clements Library, Ann Arbor, Mich.). A published version is in Alden T. Vaughan, ed., *Early American Indian Documents: Treaties and Laws, 1607–1789*, vol. 12, *Georgia and Florida Treaties, 1763–1776*, ed. John T. Juricek (Bethesda, Md.: University Publications of America, 2002), 174; hereafter cited as Juricek, *Georgia and Florida Treaties*. John Stuart to David Taitt, Dec. 15, 1775,

C05/77, fol. 39; John Stuart to Henry Stuart, Oct. 24, 1775, C05/76, fol. 189 (See *DAR*, 11: 163).

21. Corkran, *The Creek Frontier*, 296; Joshua Piker, *Okfuskee: A Creek Indian Town in Colonial America* (Cambridge, Mass.: Harvard University Press, 2004).

22. Emisteseguo to Superintendent Stuart, March 2, 1776, C05/77, fol. 132.

23. A Talk from the Headmen and Warriors of the Lower Creek Nation in Answer to a Message from the Honbl. John Stuart, December 1775; at the Cussitas, March 23, 1776, C05/77, fol. 130.

24. Talk by Lower Creeks to John Stuart, Sept. 29, 1775, C05/77, fol. 58.

25. George Galphin to Henry Laurens, March 13, 1776, in *LP*, 11: 157.

26. Patrick Tonyn to David Taitt, March 30, 1776, in Juricek, *Georgia and Florida Treaties*, 501.

27. David Taitt to Patrick Tonyn, May 3, 1776; Juricek, *Georgia and Florida Treaties*, 503.

28. John Stuart to Lord George Germain, Oct. 26, 1776, *DAR*, 12: 240.

29. Thomas Brown to Governor Tonyn, May 2, 1776; Juricek, *Georgia and Florida Treaties*, 502–3 (first quotation); Alexander Cameron to John Stuart, May 7, 1776, C05/77, fol. 139 (second quotation). Talk delivered by Hamilton and interpreted by Samuel Forest to the Creek Indians, in Stuart's letter of Aug. 23, 1776, C05/77, fol. 200. See also Alexander Cameron to John Stuart, May 7, 1776, C05/77, fol. 139.

30. Copy of a letter from Robert Rae to Samuel Thomas, May 3, 1776, in Mr. Stuart's letter of Aug. 23, 1776, C05/77, fol. 137. Thomas was a trader at Cussita and became an official Lower Creek interpreter after the resignation of Stephen Forrester in 1772. See David Taitt to John Stuart, Sept. 21, 1772, C05/74, fol. 28.

31. "Journal of a Conference Between the American Commissioners and the Creeks at Augusta," May 16–19, 1776, in Juricek, *Georgia and Florida Treaties*, 185 (first quotation) and 190 (second quotation).

32. Ibid., 187.

33. Talk delivered by Hamilton and interpreted by Samuel Forest to the Creek Indians, in Stuart's letter to Lord George Germain of Aug. 23, 1776, C05/77, fol. 200.

34. "Journal of a Conference Between the American Commissioners and the Creeks at Augusta," May 16–19, 1776, in Juricek, *Georgia and Florida Treaties*, 183–90.

35. Corkran, *The Creek Frontier*, 298; Patrick Tonyn to Lord George Germain, Oct. 30, 1776, *DAR*, 12: 243.

36. John Stuart to Lord George Germain, Aug. 23, 1776, C05/77, fol. 126.

37. Copy of a talk from George Galphin to the Creek Indians, in John Stuart's letter of Oct. 26, 1776, C05/78, fol. 41.

38. Copy of a letter from George Galphin to Timothy Barnard, Aug. 18, 1776, C05/78, fol. 51; John Stuart to Lord George Germain, Aug. 23, 1776, C05/77, fol. 126; Henry Stuart to John Stuart, Aug. 25, 1776, C05/77, fol. 169.

39. Talk by Jonathan Bryan to the Lower Creeks, Sept. 1, 1776, C05/78, fol. 26.

40. Samuel Thomas to John Stuart, Sept. 19, 1776, C05/78, fol. 30.

41. Emisteseguo to John Stuart, Nov. 19, 1776, *DAR*, 12: 250 (first quote) and 251 (second quote).

42. John Stuart to Lord George Germain, Oct. 26, 1776, C05/78, fol. 15.

43. Lord George Germaine to John Stuart, Feb. 7, 1777, *DAR*, 14: 36; see also John Stuart to Lord George Germain, Nov. 24, 1776, C05/78, fol. 71 (*DAR*, 12: 253–54).

44. John Stuart to Lord George Germain, Nov. 24, 1776, C05/78, fol. 71 (*DAR*, 12: 253–54).

45. John Stuart to Lord George Germain, March 10, 1777 (*DAR*, 14: 49).

46. Talk from General McIntosh to the Creek Nation, Dec. 23, 1776, C05/78, fol. 109. A published version appears in Lilla M. Hawes, ed., "The Papers of Lachlan McIntosh, 1774–1779," in *Collections of the Georgia Historical Society* (Savannah: Georgia Historical Society, 1957), 12: 59–60.

47. John Stuart to Lord George Germain, March 10, 1777, C05/78, fol. 105 (*DAR*, 14: 50).

48. John Stuart to Lord George Germain, March 10, 1777, *DAR*, 14: 49. The "person of confidence" was Joseph Cornell. David Taitt to John Stuart, Feb. 19, 1777, C05/78, fol. 107.

49. Talk from Cussita Town, Feb. 6, 1777, C05/78, fol. 111.

50. David Taitt to John Stuart, Feb. 19, 1777, C05/78, fol. 107.

51. For example, see "Substance of a Message Sent by George Galphin into the Creek Nation," in John Stuart's letter of Sept. 17, 1775, C05/76, fol. 175.

52. John Stuart to General Sir William Howe, April 13, 1777, *DAR*, 14: 68.

53. Ibid.; "A Talk from Indians to Geo. Golphin [sic], one of the Commissioners of Indian Affairs," April 21, 1777, American Philosophical Society, B: F85, vol. 71, fol. 12f.

54. "A Talk from Indians to Geo. Golphin [sic], one of the Commissioners of Indian Affairs," April 21, 1777, American Philosophical Society, B: F85, vol. 71, fol. 12f. David Taitt to John Stuart, April 13, 1777, C05/79, fol. 156.

55. David Taitt to John Stuart, April 13, 1777, C05/79, fol. 156. For "A List of Sundry Articles to be delivered at Pensacola in February next by Mr. James Pinman, merchant," see C05/77, fol. 60.

56. David Taitt to Thomas Brown, May 23, 1777, *DAR*, 14: 95.

57. Gregory A. Waselkov and Kathryn E. Holland Braund, eds., *William Bartram on the Southeastern Indians* (Lincoln: University of Nebraska Press, 1995), 116.

58. Robert Scott Davis, "George Galphin and the Creek Congress of 1777," in *Proceedings of the Georgia Association of Historians* (Marietta: GAH, 1983), 13–29. John Stuart to Prevost, July 24, 1777, C05/78, fol. 205.

59. David Taitt to John Stuart, May 23, 1777, *DAR*, 14: 95.

60. George Galphin to Henry Laurens, July 20, 1777, *LP*, 11: 402 (first quote); Alden T. Vaughan, ed., *Early American Indian Documents: Treaties and Laws, 1607–1789*, vol. 18, *Revolution and Confederation* (Bethesda, Md.: University Publications of America, 2002), 221–22 (other quotations).

61. Vaughan, *Early American Indian Documents*, 18: 223–24.

62. David Taitt to John Stuart, June 5, 1777, C05/78, fol. 157. See also John Stuart to Brig.-Gen. Augustine Prevost, July 24, 1777, *DAR*, 14: 147–50.

63. George Galphin to Henry Laurens, July 20, 1777, *LP*, 11: 402–3.

64. William McIntosh to Alex Cameron, July 6, 1777, C05/78, fol. 193. David Taitt to John Stuart, Aug. 13, 1777, C05/78, fol. 211.

65. John Stuart to David Taitt, July 14, 1777, C05/78, fol. 203.

66. John Stuart to Alex Cameron, July 11, 1777, C05/78, fol. 195.

67. John Stuart to Prevost, July 24, 1777, C05/78, fol. 205; John Stuart to Brig.-Gen. Augustine Prevost, July 24, 1777, *DAR*, 14: 149.

68. Extract of a letter from David Taitt, Aug. 3, 1777, C05/78, fol. 209; David Taitt to John Stuart, Aug. 13, 1777, C05/78, fol. 211.

69. Extract of a letter from David Taitt, Aug. 3, 1777, C05/78, fol. 209.

70. Ibid. John Stuart to Lord George Germain, Aug. 22, 1777, *DAR*, 13: 169.

71. John Rutledge to Henry Laurens, Aug. 8, 1777, *LP*, 11: 435. The others were William Henry Lyttelton of South Carolina, and John Reynolds and Henry Ellis of Georgia. Henry Laurens to George Galphin, Sept. 16, 1777, *LP*, 11: 522–23.

72. George Galphin to Col. Lawrence, Oct. 13, 1777, *LP*, 11: 553.

73. Stuart to Lord George Germain, Aug. 22, 1777, C05/78, fol. 186. Davis, "George Galphin," 18–20.

74. John Lewis Gervais to Henry Laurens, Aug. 16, 1777, *LP*, 11: 461.

75. Davis, "George Galphin," 22–23. Hawes, "The Papers of Lachlan McIntosh, 1774–1779," 12: 78. "Order Book of Samuel Elbert, Colonel and Brigadier General in the Continental Army, October 1776, to November, 1778," in *Collections of the Georgia Historical Society*, vol. 5, part 2 (Savannah: Morning News Print, 1902), 54.

76. John Stuart to William Knox, Aug. 26, 1777, C05/78, fol. 220.

77. John Stuart to Lord George Germain, Oct. 6, 1777, *DAR*, 14: 192–94.

78. Ibid., 14: 193. John Gervais to John Laurens, Oct. 27, 1777, John Lewis Gervais Papers, South Carolina Historical Society.

79. Alexander McGillivray to John Stuart, Sept. 21, 1777, C05/79, fol. 33. David Taitt provided the dates and times: David Taitt to Lord George Germain, Aug. 6, 1779, C05/80, fol. 234 (*DAR*, 17: 181). "A Talk from the head men of the Upper and Lower Creeks given by Nea Micko and Neaclucko two of the headmen of the Cussitaws to George Galphin Esq. one of the commissioners of Indian Affairs, 13 October 1777," in *The Papers of Henry Laurens in the South Carolina Historical Society with Introduction by Philip M. Hamer*, 19 reels (Charleston: South Carolina Historical Society; reproduced by Micro Photo, 1966), reel 17, hereafter cited as "Talk from the head men of the Upper and Lower Creeks," Galphin Papers; John Lewis Gervais to John Laurens, Oct. 27, 1777, Gervais Papers.

80. "Talk from the head men of the Upper and Lower Creeks," Galphin Papers (all quotations). When McIntosh learned of the plot, he dispatched a warning to Taitt.

81. "Talk from the head men of the Upper and Lower Creeks," Galphin Papers (all quotations). John Stuart to Lord George Germain, Oct. 6, 1777, *DAR*, 14: 192–94.

82. Alexander McGillivray to John Stuart, Sept. 21, 1777, C05/79, fol. 33. David

Taitt soon struck a more personal alliance with McGillivray's sister Sehoy. The union produced a son, Davy Tate, born between 1778 and 1780.

83. "Talk from the head men of the Upper and Lower Creeks," Galphin Papers. See also Alexander McGillivray to John Stuart, Sept. 21, 1777, C05/79, fol. 33–34.

84. George Galphin to Col. Lawrence, Oct. 13, 1777, *LP*, 11: 552–53.

85. Alexander McGillivray to John Stuart, Sept. 21, 1777, C05/79, fol. 33.

86. Talk from the Head Men and Warriors of the Lower Creek Nation to John Stuart, Cussitaw King Speaker, Cussitaws, Oct. 19, 1777, PR030/55/6, fol. 169.

87. David Holms and Thomas Scott to John Stuart, Cussitaws, Oct. 19, 1777, PR030/55/6, fol. 168.

88. Corkran, *The Creek Frontier*, 308.

89. Henry Laurens to James Duane, 24 December 1777, *LP*, 12: 197.

3

Louis LeClerc De Milford, a.k.a. General François Tastanegy

An Eighteenth-Century French Adventurer among the Creeks

GILBERT C. DIN

Louis LeClerc de Milford has long presented a dilemma to historians who study the eighteenth century.[1] Despite its copious inaccuracies and self-promoting assertions, his French memoir of 1802, which detailed his sojourn among the Creek Indians, provided the only information about him.[2] Two commercial translations in the 1950s finally made the memoir available to American readers and, in the first, the editor and historian John Francis McDermott contributed an introduction that brought fresh insights to Milford's obscure life and personality.[3] Scholars, however, have debated the significance of his controversial memoir and his role in the Southeast.[4]

His arrival in 1785 in the Creek homeland (largely today's Alabama, western Georgia, and the Florida panhandle) occurred at a time of turmoil (map 3.1). Indians then battled the relentless American advance initiated by speculators and settlers seeking cheap frontier lands. During a ten-year stay, Milford's aspirations for power developed gradually. While possessing ability, he largely emulated others in grasping at authority and influence. Milford served in several capacities, first as an ordinary Creek brave before his French army training in tactics enabled his rise to leadership among the tribe's warriors. His success later led him to crave his deceased brother-in-law's position as head of the Creek confederation, but rival chiefs denied him that office. Switching loyalties, Milford temporarily functioned as a Spanish agent among the Creeks. In the mid-1790s, when France sought to resurrect its North American empire and revolutionaries sprouted up to seize adjacent Spanish-held lands, his loyalty changed again. He returned to Europe in 1795 to convince the French government to recover Creek lands. He envisioned himself becoming the French commissioner in charge of the native confederation.

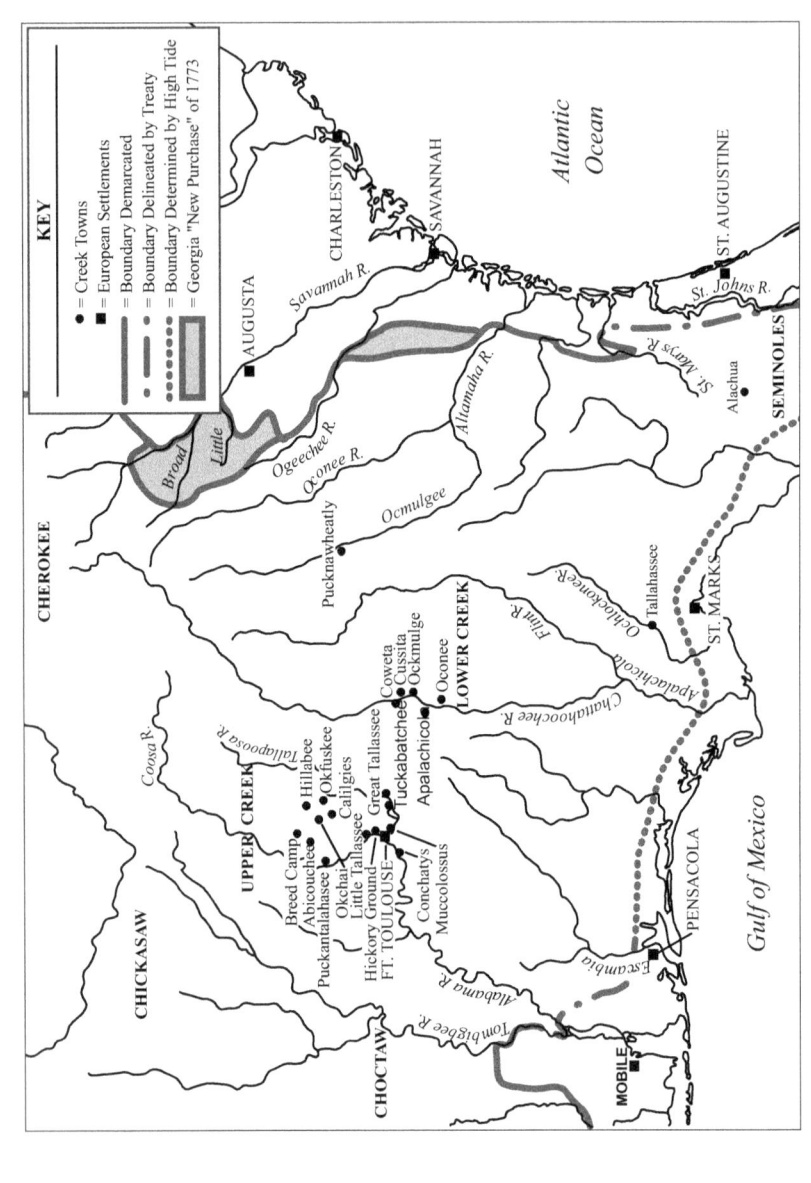

Map 3.1. Louis LeClerc De Milford's Gulf world. Map by Tracy Ellen Smith, www.cdrtexas.com.

In France, Milford relied on memory to compose his narrative to win a coveted government post, but with unabashed ego he inflated his role and influence among the natives. To conceal presumably compromising years in his life, he contrived to convince readers that he spent two decades among the Creeks by placing his arrival in 1775. Spanish officials such as Col. Arturo O'Neill, the commandant at Pensacola, Juan Nepomuceno de Quesada, the governor of East Florida, and Lieutenant Colonel Enrique White, the interim commandant at Pensacola, all correctly dissented and situated his appearance in the tribe at no sooner than 1785.[5]

In addition, his memoir displayed greater familiarity with the Old Southwest between 1785 and 1795 than between 1775 and 1785, when he often erred in dates and events. For example, he asserted that he departed the Creek nation on February 1, 1781, with a large retinue of warriors on an eighteen-month journey, claiming reluctance to assist the pro-British Creeks against the French-backed Americans struggling for independence. At Mobile, he was unaware that General Bernardo de Gálvez had conquered it from Great Britain the previous spring, or that Spanish soldiers thwarted a British attack on Mobile Bay's eastern shore shortly before. He misidentified the Mobile commandant as Captain Pierre Favrot, who governed from 1784 to 1787, and not in 1781, when Lieutenant Colonel José de Ezpeleta held sway.[6]

Only two Spanish governors, who ruled over both Louisiana and West Florida, merited his attention: Esteban Miró (1782–91) and his successor, Francisco Luis Héctor, Barón de Carondelet (1791–97).[7] Milford attempted to display his knowledge of Louisiana through his journey up the Mississippi River in 1781–82, when he attested visiting New Madrid—a singular achievement inasmuch as the town was founded in 1789. He also bungled when he called its inhabitants Acadians, who settled only in lower Louisiana, and not Americans, who established the town under George Morgan.[8]

Putting aside Milford's gaffes and deception, the focus here centers on his activities as a warrior leader, Spanish agent, and advocate for France's recovery of greater Louisiana. Only a modest portion of these activities are recounted in part 1 of his memoir and, alas, often inaccurately. His ethnographic discussion of the Creeks, found mostly in part 2, is omitted here.[9]

Evidence of Milford's origins remains scant beyond his birth on February 2, 1752, at the village of Thin-le-Moutier, in the Ardennes in northeastern France. The son of a military family, he entered the Lorraine Infantry Regiment as a cadet around 1764. Christened Jean-Antoine LeClerc, he adopted the pseudonym Louis Milford, either when after fifteen years in uniform he deserted or when he left France. Christian Buchet asserts that Milford was barely literate and dictated his memoir and letters, in my opinion a caustic judgment. Buchet never saw Milford's correspondence with Spanish officials in the 1790s, and his other writings, despite exaggerations and mendacity, reflect a perceptive mind.[10] His life between 1779 and 1785 remains shrouded in mystery, and he departed France following the American Revolution, not in 1775 as he wrote. He alleged that a duel in which he killed a court retainer compelled his departure, but this story reeks of contrived melodrama. After reaching North America where American society alienated and aborigines intrigued him, he drifted southwestward into the anonymity of the Creek homeland. By 1785, he had met and formed a bond with Alexander McGillivray, the head of the Creek confederation and the son of the former Scottish trader Lachlan McGillivray.[11]

Perhaps two years later, Milford married Alexander's sister, Jeanette McGillivray. Although the marriage soured after several years, it produced at least one child.[12] Milford's memoir totally ignored his offspring and shed scant light on his wife, except to recount the first time he saw her. She then must have been in her late teens or early twenties and, like her brother, was only a quarter Creek. He described her as "one of the prettiest girls in town" and finely clad in beautiful clothes, silver jewelry, and multi-colored hair ribbons.[13]

Milford's proficiency in martial arts permitted him to settle down among the Creeks as a warrior, and he quickly emerged as a skilled native tactician and formidable tribal asset.[14] As such, he emulated the Creeks and fought naked, except for terrifying war paint designed to "shock and awe" the enemy. After two years of border conflict, he rose to Little War Chief and, after five years, to Tastanegy, or Great War Chief, of all the towns of the Creek confederation, according to his own immodest admission.[15] With his penchant for self-aggrandizement, he employed the name General François Tastanegy among the Creeks. "François" symbolized his vestigial tie to France, although his loyalty had shifted to the Creeks.

Information on the Frenchman's early years among the natives, when his forays into battle occurred, is meager. During this time, the Fat and the Tame *miccos* (chiefs or kings) sought to alienate Creek lands to the Georgians in several bogus treaties that other tribal chiefs rejected. Milford also mentioned efforts at unity among the Southeastern natives and attempts by the American government to extract land from them.[16]

In late 1787, Milford escorted McGillivray to the Apalache district in eastern West Florida. William Panton, of the British trading firm Panton, Leslie and Company, which enjoyed a trading monopoly in both East and West Florida, also journeyed to his store on the Wakulla River, four miles above Fort San Marcos de Apalache. In October, the Scottish merchant learned of the death of the store's manager, Charles McLatchy, and both McGillivray and Panton wanted to ensure that the trading post, which was easily accessible to many Seminoles and Lower Creeks, remained open.[17]

About 1789, McGillivray entertained the American immigrants Colonel Moses Kirkland, his son, and several others, who trekked through Creek lands to settle on Spanish soil. Led by a guide the chief provided, the travelers and two slaves journeyed down to Spanish Pensacola. On the road, they encountered three vicious thieves: a Hillabee Indian known as Istillicha ("Manslayer"); "Cat" or "Catt," another native; and the cutthroat Bob, a black slave. They soon murdered the whites for their bags of silver coins. The criminal trio returned to the Creek country with three slaves, one of whom was McGillivray's guide, and their "coup" quickly became common knowledge. An enraged McGillivray dispatched warriors to arrest them, but they captured only Cat. The chief ordered Milford to string up the culprit at the spot of the murders. He did this, but when the dangling Cat took too long to strangle, Milford dispatched him with a pistol shot.[18]

By May 1789, McGillivray acknowledged Tastanegy as the Creek military leader: "I have again given the Martial's Staff to Milford who set out yesterday to join a large [war] party."[19] The Frenchman had proved his mastery in native warfare and fulfilling McGillivray's commissions, but serious problems then plagued the Creeks and involved him. British merchants in Nassau intrigued to recover trade lost in East and West Florida when England ceded them to Spain in 1783. William Augustus Bowles, an adopted Creek and an agent for Miller, Bonnamy and Company, and the governor of the British Bahamas, the Earl of Dunmore, figured prominently in this illegal trafficking that subverted Spanish domination of the natives. Bowles's ambitions soon aspired to the director generalship, a title and position he invented, of the Creek nation through becoming its sole arms provisioner and at irresistibly low prices.[20]

Arms had become indispensable to Creeks because of American encroachment on their lands. Speculators and frontiersmen insisted on the boundary stipulated in the peace treaty of 1783 between the United States and Great Britain that embraced most Creek lands. That accord, however, ignored the Spanish conquest and occupation of British West Florida in the war and the British cession of both Floridas to Spain. Cognizant that territorial retention ultimately rested upon its indigenous inhabitants, Spain courted them. At the congress of Pensacola in 1784, Spanish officials agreed to furnish Creeks arms to defend themselves and their lands. But three years later, fearful that providing weapons might precipitate a war with the United States, Spain severely curtailed their flow. McGillivray dissented since his people were already at war, and he felt compelled to obtain arms wherever possible, even from Bowles.[21]

In 1787, Milford, who years later became a rival of Bowles, accompanied

McGillivray to a meeting to discuss trade with Nassau. The chief welcomed the prospect of British arms and gifts.[22] On Bowles's return to Nassau, his intrigues swelled as he fancied ousting the Panton Company from its trading monopoly, McGillivray from Creek leadership, and the Spaniards from both Floridas. To achieve these ends, in 1788 Bowles and Dunmore enlisted the only white recruits available—a motley rabble of jailbirds, deserters, and ne'er-do-wells anxious to escape incarceration or improve their lot in Indian territory. This ill-conceived and poorly directed filibustering expedition turned into a tragic-comical disaster. While foiled in his plan to pillage a Panton store, Bowles alarmed the Spaniards and McGillivray. The chief sent Milford to interview the adventurer at a Lower Creek town after his expedition disintegrated. Milford concluded that he was a disreputable man and reportedly ordered him to leave in three days or lose his ears.[23]

He left but quickly returned on a third trip. The agile and silver-tongued orator assured the gift-hungry natives that he expected a Nassau ship loaded with presents. At a council meeting, Bowles's impassioned speech belittling McGillivray won the adherence of only Seminoles and some Lower Creeks. He soon boasted that this remnant "elected" him director general of the Creek nation. He planned the creation of a "sovereign" Indian state under his tutelage, promised inexpensive British goods, and selected five Anglo-mestizos for a trip to England to win essential government help. Hearing about these activities, McGillivray assigned Milford to join the intruder on the Flint River, in today's southwestern Georgia, and wait for an arms-laden vessel. There Milford learned from John Richmond, the secretary of the Miller Company, that Bowles intended to supplant Panton in trade. On learning this, Milford rushed to inform McGillivray in late January 1789. Rather than pounce on Bowles immediately, the Creek leader still dreamed of confiscating his weapons, but the awaited ship brought little.[24] The adventurer soon left unimpeded for Nassau and England.

Milford's activities continued. At a meeting in May 1789, the Lower Creeks agreed to raid intrusive Georgians on the Ogeechee River, and Milford possibly participated in the foray. In June, he arrived at Pensacola to pick up arms and munitions from the Spaniards, who had resumed supplying the Creeks.[25] Milford surfaced again later in the summer of 1789, when Romain, an itinerant slaver, entered Creek territory, seeking to buy black slaves for resale in New Orleans. He soon ran into Milford, who, recognizing Romain's mischievous intentions to steal or defraud, threatened to send him in chains to New Orleans. The slaver hurriedly retired to safer parts.[26]

In the spring of 1790, after McGillivray departed for New York, where he negotiated a much despised treaty ceding land to the United States, Milford traveled down to Pensacola to collect fusils and munitions for Creek warriors. O'Neill, the commandant at Pensacola, abhorred the visit because it meant feeding Indians and depleting his limited food stores. More important, Milford revealed a character flaw when he lost his temper, a defect McGillivray had recognized, and broke his pledge to conduct himself properly. Upon whom the egotistical Frenchman vented his rage is unknown. A disgruntled Panton felt compelled to bare Milford's indiscretion to McGillivray. In replying, the chief expressed regret over "the very unruly & Improper Conduct of Milfort; when he was in Pens[aco]la on the Business I sent him for. Knowing something of his rashness of temper I always Strictly Charged him to Conduct himself in a Manner that Might not give any room for Censure either on his own account or mine, & on which Subject I have been very free with him & he Shall no more be in a Situation which Shall give Your Excellency any future umbrage."[27] Despite his wretched conduct, the Frenchman remained the chief warrior.

Conditions in the Creek nation, however, changed in September 1791, when Bowles returned from England in another attempt to trade with the Creeks and attain their leadership. For several months, Bowles wandered unfettered among friendly Seminole and Lower Creek towns, issuing decrees for the formation of his Indian state of Muskogee and trade regulations. McGillivray and Milford purposely abstained from provoking intra-tribal clashes while the Spaniards lacked the manpower to pursue the adventurer into the native heartland. But when Indian allies abetted him in sacking Panton's store on the Wakulla River, on January 16, 1792, the Spaniards vowed to apprehend the criminal, and they soon succeeded.[28]

Before Bowles's capture, Panton recruited Milford at Pensacola on February 25 to lead an expedition to disperse the adventurer's native supporters in the Apalache district. Panton furnished Milford with a talk to encourage Lower Creek warriors to fight Bowles's followers. Milford reached the native towns in early March and persuasively harangued the Lower Creeks, who flocked to join. By March 11, he had recruited nearly four hundred braves. Upon reaching the Flint River, Milford heard that the Spaniards had apprehended Bowles at Fort San Marcos.[29]

Nevertheless, two hundred natives under the adventurer's subordinate, George Wellbank, still hovered near the mouth of the Ochlockonee River, where Bowles had built crude warehouses for goods from Nassau. Perceiving the innocuousness of these natives, Milford dismissed the bulk of his warriors and proceeded to the Indian camps. Both he and his opponents refrained from combat and that led to lengthy parlays before most insurgents disbanded. Milford then pushed on to Panton's Wakulla store, which Wellbank still held, where more talks ensued. Milford finally convinced Wellbank to surrender the ransacked store. Panton praised Milford's scramble to disperse the last hostile natives in Apalache. Robert Leslie, who had witnessed the looting of the Wakulla store, greatly appreciated the Frenchman's prompt and effective work and considered him deserving of a gratuity of five hundred dollars.[30]

Following his work in Apalache, Milford sailed to Pensacola in late March 1792. Although he did not explain his reasons, his recent exploit was the last known occasion during which he personally led Indian warriors. Gripped by ambition, he now aspired to a more prestigious position in Creek society. He arrived at Pensacola on April 2, and waited until White, the acting commandant, obtained the governor's permission for him to proceed to New Orleans. Perhaps he considered his recent work against a menacing adversary worthy of a post in the Spanish government, especially now that he had broken ties to McGillivray.[31]

What precipitated the break is unknown. Possibly it resulted from, or led to, Milford's quest for greater power within the tribe. The rupture conceivably originated the year before, when Milford separated from his wife. Soon even Governor Quesada of East Florida learned that in the spring of 1792, Milford had severed his marriage and connection to McGillivray and intended to return to Europe.[32]

Abandoning the Creek nation did not yet figure in Milford's plans, however. He arrived in New Orleans on May 1, 1792, favorably impressed Carondelet, the governor, and obtained a Spanish post at the Creeks. Nevertheless, by September Carondelet had retracted his initial positive impression after McGillivray voiced reservations. In the summer of 1792, the chief had reached New Orleans, where he abrogated his New York agreement through a new Spanish treaty on July 6 that gained protection and arms. McGillivray's misgivings about Milford obliged Carondelet to hem and haw about what he had told the Frenchman, and he admitted derisively that he limited Milford's employment exclusively to military "expeditions that require more handwork than headwork." Carondelet later deceptively denied that his offer of five hundred pesos implied a salary, but his disclaimer rang hollow. He still found Milford irritating because of his "arrogance toward [D]on Pedro Olivier [the Spanish commissary to the Creeks] to whom he is by no means obedient," or so O'Neill had disclosed. Wrote Carondelet to McGillivray, "[That fact] displeased me exceedingly and dissuaded me from employing him in the future."[33] Despite his assertion, it lacked truth because Milford's compliance was necessary only in government service, and he retained his job.

As his loyalty shifted from the Creeks to the Spaniards, Milford envisioned himself as a quasi-agent or assistant commissary, since the governor had designated him to aid Olivier in his duties. By the summer or early fall of 1792, he had returned to the Upper Creeks to report on conditions, remit messages, and preach devotion to Spain. It marked a new era in Milford's final two and a half years with the tribe. His service to the Creeks ended not long after Alexander McGillivray's death on February 17, 1793. Although the chief's demise saddened Milford, he relished the opportunity it created. Foremost, he yearned to replace his dead brother-in-law as head of the Creeks and, failing in that, become the Spanish commissary to the tribe. His first plan misfired completely because, similar to Bowles, many chiefs resented him as an outsider. But he achieved the second on an ad interim basis, when Olivier, whom Carondelet had appointed commissary in 1792, left the post.[34]

McGillivray had indicated to Panton a "brother" as his successor, and the historian Caughey assumed he meant his "brother-in-law" Milford. In all probability, however, the chief implied an Indian relation.[35] But even had the Creek chief chosen Milford, his prospects as tribal head were dim since he had not endeared himself to many leaders, Creek society was matrilineal, and ambitious chiefs resisted vesting authority in McGillivray's lineage. The absence of a powerful leader comparable to the deceased chief soon shattered unity within the already fragile confederation.

At the time of McGillivray's death, Milford was planning a major attack on the Chickasaws with twelve hundred Creek warriors. Although the army departed on May 16, four days later Milford received the governor's order of March 25 to abort the assault, and he sent an express messenger to recall the warriors.[36] Despite personal disagreements, both Milford and Olivier cooperated in halting the operation.

In April 1793, Milford reported on the Great Council held early that month. He relayed Carondelet's admonition to the chiefs to avoid disputes with Americans and not to participate in marking boundaries, a subject that Spain and the United States were then negotiating. Spain planned no interference in the Creek-Choctaw war, but it counseled friendship among natives, good treatment of Spanish subjects, and defense of Indian lands against common enemies. Carondelet noted American efforts to gain a sizable Creek following by distributing corn at the St. Marys River in southern Georgia and reminded the tribe of the closer help available from Pensacola.[37]

On May 20, 1793, Milford received letters from Governor Carondelet, who instructed him to send the new Creek leader to Pensacola, where Olivier awaited to arrange a Creek-Chickasaw peace agreement. The meeting, however, never occurred. Unwisely, Carondelet also solicited the arrest of James Seagrove, the American commissioner to the Southeastern Indians, which Milford mentioned to Mad Dog, the most prominent Creek leader to emerge on McGillivray's death. He and two other chiefs promised to arrest Seagrove if he appeared in Tuckabatche. The likelihood of Mad Dog complying, however, was negligible since he was pro-American, and Seagrove had left for the Cherokees. Other Spanish officials shied away from fulfilling such a reckless order.[38]

Meanwhile, trouble on the Georgia frontier persisted. Lower Creeks from a Chehaw village killed Robert Seagrove, the brother of James, and five others and burned Seagrove's store at the St. Marys River.[39] The attack ignited more fighting. An American retaliatory assault on the Flint River destroyed the Little Chia (Chehaw) village and stole black slaves. About the same time, warriors from the Upper Creek Coullymy (or Cooloome) town raided on the Oconee River in central Georgia, killing several people. These attacks, Milford opined, presaged the inevitability of warfare.[40] John Galphin, a Lower Creek mestizo and an accomplice of Bowles, robbed two Spanish subjects near the St. Marys River of their livestock and slaves. An angry Milford contemptuously accused Galphin of vile deeds, and a principal Creek chief granted everybody license to eradicate the responsible outlaw band, but it did not happen.[41]

In the midst of this turmoil, Milford passionately resented people who behaved improperly toward him. His most ardent critic, O'Neill, disdained him. O'Neill had neither divulged to Milford his ability to draw Indian supplies at Pensacola nor given him any.[42] Ignoring this sordid treatment, Milford boasted that he had restored the three largest Creek towns to Spanish devotion and rewarded fifteen chiefs who rejected the American offer to draw a line of demarcation. He admitted to the governor, "I know that I have several enemies who are trying to make my conduct seem to you as black as it is white, but I also know that you have too much intelligence not to see their malice. It is true that I did not show great friendship for Mr. Olivier last year, but I had reasons." He blamed McGillivray's "disposition" for the mistrust between them since McGillivray feared Milford's power as general of the Creek warriors. With the chief's passing, these concerns dissipated. Having spent a year without emolument, Milford solicited his salary, plus 150 pesos expended to fulfill his duties. He also awaited convocation of the important Creek council at Tuckabatche in June 1793 to determine leadership.[43]

Prior to its gathering, Milford met with Olivier, but ruffled feelings persisted. Milford believed that the commissary, who declined to forward his letters to the governor, behaved "conceited and cool." He therefore arranged to send his correspondence to New Orleans by a special courier, who ran into a roadblock on reaching Pensacola. White, now proprietary commandant and imbued with O'Neill's prejudice toward Milford, disapproved the travel expenditure and entrusted delivery of Milford's letters to a ship captain.[44]

Milford had been waiting for the Creek council to determine his position within the tribe. He radiated optimism, but Olivier attended the meeting and related its proceedings to the governor. On June 11, 1793, the Creek chiefs declined to confer McGillivray's former post on Milford. The commissary disclosed telling information about him:

> I have heard that he has written to Your Lordship that [the chiefs] had already elected him, but this never existed anywhere except in his head. This was the cause of some debates between him and me, during which I have been under the necessity of telling him Your Lordship's intentions in this matter and my way of thinking, in order to make him understand the independence which the commissaries of His Majesty ought to preserve in this nation. It seems that he believed that he was already authorized to conduct himself as a little sovereign. This came to the attention of the Indians, and I believe was the reason why they expressed themselves plainly to me in the assembly, telling me clearly that they respected Mr. Milford as a man who had lived among them many years and who had been employed by McGillivray on some commissions with the Indians in which he merited the title or name of *Tostanaky* [sic], which signifies warrior. They said that they regarded him in that light, and would allow him to remain among them as long as he wished. They stated that they had been told he was employed by the [Spanish] government, which was very good, and, if Your Lordship desired to give him a commission, they would attend to whatever he told them conducive to the good of the nation.[45]

Although Creek leaders declined to confer authority on Milford, his usefulness to the Spaniards remained. The governor's earlier bluster about not hiring Milford withered when he ordered payment of his salary. In June 1793, he indirectly instructed White to give Milford 650 pesos for his labor and expenses. An unduly meticulous and hostile White, eager to avoid the disbursement, noticed the absence of a formal order. He maliciously sealed the letter the governor had sent him open to read and forwarded it to Milford without the funds.[46] The next month, an angry Carondelet, who had expected White to act without an express command, pointedly instructed him to pay Milford.[47]

In August 1793, as Olivier had orders to encourage unity and resistance to the United States at an assembly of tribes, Milford attained authority as the Spanish agent at the Creeks for about nine months. That same month, he entrusted a letter, probably a recommendation, to the grand chief of the important village of Kasihta, who took a party to Pensacola for ammunition.[48]

It was needed as clashes along the frontier continued. Milford kept White and the governor informed of events. On August 27, Upper and Lower Creek chiefs agreed to send four parties to attack Georgia settlements. Olivier, however, dissuaded them with threats of abandonment. In September, a Georgia cavalry detachment burned the small Creek village of Hothlitiaga, forty-five miles from the principal Lower Creek town of Coweta. Soldiers killed, wounded, and carried off eight Indian captives. With attacks on both sides escalating, White feared a general war and requested more gunpowder. Later that month and in early October, inhabitants from Creek towns descended on Pensacola for arms and munitions following their harvests and festivals. Indians raged at and threatened Seagrove's life since he was then at Ocfuskee proclaiming peace.[49]

Galphin also notified Panton about the assembly of Creek chiefs on October 15. Their talk centered on the previous month's American raid on Hothlitiaga. The chiefs differed on what to do since some attributed to Milford encouragement for immediate retaliation while Galphin allegedly promoted a peaceful recovery of the captives. The latter's statement, however, is suspicious because he was not Milford's friend. The chiefs eventually requested the Georgians to release the prisoners. American claims to Creek hunting grounds in Georgia and denial of access to them also agitated the natives.[50]

On October 19, 1793, Milford, sick at Cloaly, reported his version of the assembly at Tuckabatche. Joseph Cornell, the uncle of Milford's representative at the meeting, delivered an anti-Spanish speech. In return for the prisoners, he proposed Creek acceptance of the six natives killed in the American raid on Hothlitiaga to offset the white deaths perpetrated on the St. Marys. He further promised abandonment of the Spaniards. The speech, however, garnered only one adherent, the pro-American White Lieutenant, while the dominant dissenting chiefs openly laughed at the proposition. Despite the absence of approval, Cornell and White Lieutenant informed Seagrove that, in return for the eight captives, they offered the renewal of peace, Creek abandonment of Spain, and the Americans as the tribe's only white friends. While elucidating on the inner workings of the council, Milford vented anger at the burdens he bore. White at Pensacola diminished Milford's status among the natives by disregarding his letters recommending Creek towns to receive powder and shot. Milford's resentment welled up at the Indians who had begun calling him Apatana Ajoo (Mad Frog), no doubt for his temper, and at the interpreter Antonio Garzón for depreciatory jokes.[51]

In addition, Olivier alluded to his troubles with Milford, although he had not lost confidence in him. The former commissary had been building a house, and Milford later bemoaned that Olivier had defrauded him of such a property. He neglected to provide details, but he had a house and a servant at Cloaly.[52]

Carondelet had informed Milford in the spring of 1793 about his attempts to unite the Creeks, Chickasaws, Choctaws, and Cherokees into a confederation for their mutual protection. Divisive inter-tribal warfare, however, needed resolution first, and the Creeks created problems with their other priorities.[53] Despite obstacles, the Spaniards succeeded in convoking a meeting at the Yazoo River. On October 28, the tribes signed the Treaty of Nogales, a defensive alliance designed to protect their dominions within Louisiana and West Florida. The tribes also wanted Spain to procure permanent boundaries for them to prevent the further loss of land. Milford did not attend the assembly.[54]

Peace, however, proved elusive. Farther east, the Georgians and Tennesseans, on the one side, and the Creeks and Cherokees, on the other, waged war. At the same time, animosity persisted between the Creeks and Chickasaws. On December 17, Milford reported a minor Creek meeting at Tuckabatche, where natives from eleven towns heard Seagrove's blandishments for them to obtain American goods at Rock Landing. Milford related that the Americans had distributed presents liberally to win over the natives and advised the Spaniards to counteract them with similar generosity.[55]

Seeking to emphasize his importance, Milford tried to diminish Olivier's prestige through his alleged sniveling before Seagrove and many natives. The American had ridiculed the Spanish commissary, and an angered Milford crowed that he would not have tolerated such insolence. This incident possibly never occurred. Milford feared that Seagrove might generate much trouble for the Spaniards. Perhaps for this reason, Milford advocated Lower Creek hostilities against the Georgians in the spring to commit the natives to Spanish interests; some Creeks were then disparaging the Spaniards. Speaking in their Muskogean language, Milford recounted, "I scolded them and shut them up, and I reproached them for their conduct towards the Spaniards, and they agreed that they were wrong." Finally, Milford arranged to send representatives from Creek towns down to Pensacola for their annual gifts.[56]

In March 1794, Milford encountered more quandaries in fulfilling his duties. He no longer trusted Creeks to carry mail and requested a white letter-carrier. The chief of Kasihta had pricked his ire when he collected letters for Milford at Pensacola and then declined to deliver them. The chief, Milford observed, was a crony of the "thorough-going rascal" and American adherent Mad Dog, who had threatened him over responsibility for informing the towns that gifts had arrived for them at Pensacola, a privilege that conferred status. Milford advocated haranguing the Creek leaders at a congress to reject subversive American advice. He noted that the Creeks were badly divided and verged on intra-tribal war. He claimed that he had received death threats from Mad Dog and urged vengeance should he be assassinated. As part of Carondelet's plan to resist a threatened invasion from Kentucky, the governor declared that he had sent two hundred Creek warriors for Milford to lead to the Mississippi. But illness and other chores in the Creek country prevented him from going.[57]

Although Milford tried speaking to the council on two days, the pro-American faction stirred up clamors that interfered. In contrast, Seagrove spoke on several days, denigrating the Spaniards, condemning their exorbitant prices that impoverished Creeks, and predicting the American opening of the Mississippi. Moreover, the inconsistent Seagrove suggested, on the one hand, that Louisiana's French Creoles and American residents would rise up to welcome the revolutionary and backwoods invaders who detested Spanish control of the Mississippi River, while he dismissed the invaders, on the other hand, as a figment of Carondelet's fertile imagination. Suspicious of Creoles, Milford advocated not employing them in key posts and assured that once the invaders recognized the impossibility of inciting an uprising in Louisiana, they would abandon their efforts. Seagrove, he charged, had bribed many Indians and gained the adherence of most whites in the Creek nation.[58]

Milford's temporary post as commissary ended when Lieutenant Luis de Villiers arrived at Cloaly on April 10, 1794. Despite the loss of the coveted position, Milford boasted that his tenure had prevented Upper and Lower Creeks from inflicting harm. To demonstrate his diligence as temporary commissary, he sent Carondelet the diary he composed of the Tuckabatche assembly held in March.[59]

Despite being replaced, Milford still provided a service among the Creeks. In early June, Capt. Juan de la Villebeuvre, a Spanish commissary at the Chickasaws, grumbled that Villiers had not informed him about Seagrove or the Creek thefts of Chickasaw horses. The lost steeds angered the chiefs, who advocated war in retaliation. De la Villebeuvre advised the governor, "I recommended that [Villiers] make friends with the Parisian [Milford], who is quite familiar with these nations and can give them only good advice."[60]

Milford, nevertheless, had Creek adversaries. In early June 1794, the pro-American chiefs of Ocfuskee and Tuckabatche informed the Pensacola commandant that if Milford returned they would eliminate him. Mad Dog and his adherents also intimidated Spanish employees and had murdered one. White suspected Milford's loyalty and feared his knowledge of Pensacola's military defects.[61]

Creeks from most towns eventually trekked to Pensacola for their annual gifts in 1794. They included a large party of 122 Broken Arrow Creeks, headed by Chief Small Prince, whom Milford had encouraged to go. When Milford arrived at Pensacola, he quickly noticed discrepancies between his list of towns to receive gifts and the governor's. Milford reported the errors to White, who perceived them as trickery to finagle more gifts for his loyal Indians. The Pensacola commandant further worried about a protracted Indian visit, and he scorned the inordinate expense to feed them, as Milford advocated, until the governor decided on their gifts. White never disguised his contempt for Milford or for providing for Indians. In June, he groaned that they, along "with the impertinency of Milford," gave him "much to do." Meanwhile, the new commissary to the Creeks, Villiers, griped about his profound displeasure with his post and yearned to quit.[62] Despite White's carping, Milford had performed reasonably well as commissary in the governor's estimation.

If criticism of Milford persisted at Pensacola and among some Creeks, it did not affect Carondelet. Upon receiving White's nitpicking letters, the governor praised his agent's work in calming the Upper Creeks during the invasion dangers of Citizen Edmond Genêt and George Rogers Clark, who were recruiting volunteers in Kentucky and Georgia to attack Louisiana and East Florida since Spain and France were at war in Europe (and elsewhere). The U.S. Congress's Neutrality Act of 1794 specifically disallowed hostile activities on American soil and support for them gradually dissipated.[63] Carondelet deemed Milford's trip to New Orleans, possibly to press for his salary, unnecessary. He instructed White, "As [D]on Luis Milford has continued his service in the Tallapoosa (Creek) Nation during the critical circumstances of invasion, that this province was threatened upriver and by Georgians, he succeeded in quieting the confused and distracted spirits of the [Creeks], I have decided to reward him for his merit with a payment of five hundred pesos in the same terms that I ordered a release of another similar amount by that royal treasury office in my official letter of May 28 last year."[64]

As late as September 1794, Carondelet still worried about a Franco-American invasion. He notified White the moment he knew that Elijah Clarke's army of Georgia revolutionaries had crossed the Oconee River to deluge the Creeks with arms and munitions. The governor further instructed using Milford, despite "his fickleness," to energize the Indians and their chiefs against Clarke.[65]

Soon potential hostile activities with Georgia subsided and Milford's duties diminished, which led him to consider other venues. White Lieutenant of Ocfuskee, no impartial observer, issued perhaps the last recorded Creek reference to Milford. On November 14, 1794, he alerted Governor Carondelet of his change of heart because of the recent threat of invasion. He now angrily condemned Seagrove as a "Lyar and his heart is crooked and his Tongue is forked, for in so treacherous a manner to attempt our ruin." The chief sought protection of Creek lands with the sword, and he insisted upon an able agent, comparable to Olivier, to advance the best interests of both the governor and the tribe. He added, "[A]s for Mr. Millford [sic], and the man you sent last to us [Villiers] they are no Body & their hearts & Tongues are not straight."[66]

Whether White Lieutenant's talk represented Creek opinion is unknown since he had espoused the American position. After breaking with his former confidant and protector, McGillivray, Milford's status within the Creek nation waned. His employment by Carondelet from 1792 through 1794, however, propped up native respect for him to a degree.

In his memoir, Milford recounted that loyalty to France inspired him to tender his resignation as soon as he learned of its hostilities with Spain (1793–95) and that Carondelet forced him to wait eighteen months before granting him a passport. This was far from the truth as he had served the Spaniards dutifully during this time. More probably, revolutionary French activity in Kentucky and Georgia gradually awakened realization that France's recovery of the Creek homeland might bolster his ambitions. With Milford's service to Spain declining by late 1794 and, in response to his request for a passport, on February 17, 1795, Carondelet dispatched the document and an order to pay him three hundred pesos for his salary through 1794. By the end of the month, the Pensacola commandant had complied.[67]

Milford had already planned his journey. On March 9, 1795, White in Pensacola noted, "Yesterday afternoon, the renowned Milford took leave from me for Mobile, where he is to board a brigantine, hired by the Panton Company, for Charleston, and travel from there to London."[68] Nothing tied him to the Southeast any longer, neither wife nor offspring; his former spouse soon married Ben Crook, a white trader at Little Tallassee, and died four years later. Instead of continuing on Panton's ship, at Charleston Milford journeyed to Philadelphia to see the French minister Jean Antoine Joseph Fauchet, an avid expansionist, who provided a passport and passage to France. Before sailing, Milford notified his friend Panton that Fauchet had assured him that Spain had offered to cede Louisiana and both Floridas to France, and Milford became determined to persuade the highest French authorities to recoup lost territories in North America. By July 27, 1795, he was in Paris.[69]

France had undergone a historic transformation since his departure a decade or more before. Disaffected subjects had risen up in revolution in 1789 and overthrown the effete monarchy. Perhaps with it, memory of Milford's desertion from the royal army vanished. The fervor of the revolution's radical republican leadership faded after several years with the takeover of the moderate Directory. By 1795, it was attempting to recover Louisiana, which heartened Milford. He, however, wanted the inclusion of Creek lands. He proposed that as Tastanegy of the Creeks he would control tribal policies, a power he had never possessed under the Creeks or Spaniards. He exuded confidence in his ability to persuade the Southeastern Indians to accept French suzerainty. On February 26, 1796, Charles Delacroix de Constant, the minister of foreign affairs, gave Milford an enthusiastic welcome. In short order, Milford pledged to rally twenty thousand Creek warriors to French service. The government embraced his plan and conferred on him the army rank and pay of general of brigade on April 19, 1796. But until conditions converged to recover those lands, Milford had to wait. The government dispatched, or already had, agents in North America such as Gen. George Victor Collot and Robert Fulton.[70]

Since realization of his plans proceeded sluggishly, in 1798 Milford hoped to inject momentum through a discourse on reasons for the reclamation of the Creek homeland. Recovery of their territory would halt the expansion of the United States and provide France with raw materials and foodstuffs. Defense of Louisiana and the Southeast, he argued, required only ten thousand soldiers. Furthermore, the population would grow with the addition of French deportees and western Americans attracted by the region's fertile lands.[71]

Spain, however, still held Louisiana. Fortunately in Madrid, Manuel Godoy, the head of government, had developed a negative attitude toward the colony as he sought to reduce overseas expenditures and international tension. He succeeded in part through the Treaty of San Lorenzo in 1795, which granted the United States the boundary it wanted in West Florida and opened the Mississippi River to American shipping. This, nevertheless, did not resolve all problems. In late 1799, the Directory gave way to the Consulate, which Napoleon Bonaparte dominated as First Consul. After French prodding, Godoy agreed in 1800 to surrender the territory Spain had received in 1763.[72]

Almost simultaneously, however, Bonaparte terminated Milford's army rank and pay. Despite the contretemps, France's recovery of Louisiana revived Milford's aspirations. In 1802, the Spanish court assented to the colony's transfer upon France taking possession. At this time, Milford penned his memoir, detailing his experience among, and extensive knowledge of, the Southeastern natives. He rushed publication to earn passage on the expedition Bonaparte prepared in Holland under General Claude Perrin Victor to assume control of Louisiana. But his literary effort proved fruitless. On July 24, 1802, he wrote to Bonaparte, requesting employment in the colony. The star-crossed adventurer never received a reply since the French ruler shunned him. The next year, as Bonaparte's dream of an overseas empire crumbled with his failure to subdue

Haiti's defiant slaves and renewed warfare in Europe, he judged whatever legal tender Louisiana's sale to the United States reaped more valuable.[73]

This effectively quashed Milford's yearnings for a return to the Creeks. It was a felicitous decision because the likelihood of him governing them or raising twenty thousand warriors, a grossly inflated figure that exceeded the total Creek population, bordered on zero. In May 1803, about the time he left Paris for the countryside, he received a pension as a discharged army officer.[74]

Milford lived on in France for another seventeen years, during which time news about him occasionally surfaced. In vain he repeatedly requested restoration of his general's rank. Even an entreaty for a colonial post failed to elicit a positive response. In January 1814, he boasted that at the age of sixty-one he still possessed the physical stamina to endure rugged military campaigns. His appeals all fell on deaf ears. Furthermore, the ministry of war disavowed knowledge of his service among the Creeks and his Cross of St. Louis, allegedly awarded by Louis XV for bravery in the Mediterranean when he was twenty-one.[75]

Milford's personal life at this time underwent periodic upheavals. He initially resided in Paris for several years. In 1798, the city police, while presumably tolerant of the general's addiction to the fleshpots of Paris, reported to the ministry of war that his dissolute lifestyle had resulted in one or more clashes with the law. His promiscuity raises an eyebrow at his memoir's puritanical assertion of his continence during his first two years among the Creeks, and this in a society where young women enjoyed sexual freedom before marriage.[76]

Perhaps he curbed his licentiousness in the next few years when he returned to the Ardennes and married Marie-Anne Bega, with whom he had a child. He again emerged from obscurity when the Napoleonic Wars neared their conclusion with allied armies invading France. Milford received command of volunteers organized to prey on enemy roads. Instead, the general harassed his men so much they disbanded. Later, on March 15, 1814, a party of uhlans or Cossacks assaulted the old warrior's house. Armed with three double-barreled shotguns, Milford held his attackers at bay and gunned down a large number of the enemy. Three years later, his baser instincts emerged again when his wife charged him with abuse so flagrant that he had driven her from their home. Milford fought these accusations in court with allegations denigrating Marie-Anne's character. She, however, refuted his desperate charges and obtained a legal separation and an allotment of five hundred francs for her and their child's sustenance. Following this reversal of fortune, Milford moved to Villevallier in Yonné. There final news about the long-retired general came on July 16, 1820, when, at 5:00 a.m. and at the age of sixty-eight, his heart stopped beating.[77]

Although slowly, the real Milford has finally begun to emerge from the murky past, much of it spawned by his own controversial memoir. A careful examination of his life, stripped of embellishments and distortions, proves that he was still a remarkable and colorful figure. While many differences separated him from the much heralded Bowles, who strode across the same stage and similarly strove for leadership of the Creeks, Milford importantly never possessed the finances, arms suppliers, or limited government assistance that Bowles enjoyed. These were powerful advantages in the quest to control the Creeks, given American pressure on tribal lands. On a positive note, Milford's personal courage in combat, command of indigenous warriors, and description of Creek customs raise him head and shoulders above Bowles. Furthermore, Milford acted within the political and cultural norms during his time in Creek lands and in Spanish employment, unlike the swashbuckler Bowles, who filibustered, pillaged, and colluded with a foreign government and a tribal minority mesmerized by gifts and munitions to foist himself upon the Creeks as their savior.[78] Only upon returning to France did Milford propose to impose new European masters upon them. Persuasion constituted his sole faculty to influence the Creeks, and behavioral quirks severely undermined that ability. His personal failings also bred enemies and destroyed his two marriages. Despite deficiencies in the talents needed to match his ambitions, Milford stands out as a little known but noteworthy personality on the Southeastern Borderlands at the close of the eighteenth century.

Notes

1. Louis LeClerc de Milford's name is in dispute. In North America, he used the French "Milford," but other people repeatedly spelled it "Milfort," as does the Library of Congress, no doubt influenced by his memoir of 1802, which bore this spelling. I, however, employ his name as he wrote it in the 1790s.

2. G[énér]al Milfort, *Mémoirs, ou, Coup-d'oeil rapide sur mes différents voyages et mon séjourn dans la nation Crëck* (Paris: Giguet et Michaud, 1802).

3. Louis LeClerc de Milford, *Milford's Memoir, or A Cursory Glance at My Different Travels and My Sojourn in the Creek Nation*, ed. John Francis McDermott, trans. Geraldine de Courcy (Chicago: Lakeside Press, 1956); and General Milfort, *Memoirs, or A Quick Glance at My Various Travels and My Sojourn in the Creek Nation*, ed. and trans. Ben C. McCary (Kennesaw, Ga.: Continental Book Company, 1959).

4. John Walton Caughey, *McGillivray of the Creeks* (Norman: University of Oklahoma Press, 1938); Lawrence Kinnaird, ed., *Spain in the Mississippi Valley, 1765–1794*, American Historical Association Annual Report for 1945, 3 parts (Washington, D.C.: United States Government Printing Office, 1949), hereafter abbreviated as Kinnaird, *SMV*; and various publications by Arthur Preston Whitaker cited below. Historians have sometimes condemned Milford's memoir while ethnologists and anthropolo-

gists have generally praised it. Frederick Jackson Turner, "The Policy of France toward the Mississippi Valley in the Period of Washington and Adams," *American Historical Review* 10 (January 1905): 249–79; and Caughey, *McGillivray*, 218–19n., were critical. The introduction by McDermott in Louis LeClerc de Milford, *Milford's Memoir: Or, a Cursory Glance at My Different Travels and My Sojourn in the Creek Nation* (Santa Barbara: Narrative Press, 2000) (all subsequent citations to Milford will be to this reprint); John R. Swanton, "Social Organization and Social Usages of the Indians of the Creek Confederacy," *Forty-Second Annual Report of the Bureau of American Ethnology* (New York: Bureau of American Ethnology, 1970), 429; and E. Wilson Lyon, ed., "Milfort's Plan for a Franco-Creek Alliance and the Retrocession of Louisiana," *Journal of Southern History* 4 (February 1938): 77, were more charitable.

5. Caughey, *McGillivray*, 338n.; Milford, *Milford's Memoir*, 8–10, 123–26; Enrique White to Esteban Miró, Pensacola, April 10, 1792, Archivo General de Indias (Seville), Papeles procedentes de la Isla de Cuba, legajo 25 (hereafter abbreviated as AGI, PC, leg.), cited in Arthur Preston Whitaker, "Alexander McGillivray, 1783–1789," *North Carolina Historical Review* 5, no. 2 (April 1928): 182n.

6. Milford, *Milford's Memoir*, 55–56, 56n.; John W. Caughey, *Bernardo de Gálvez in Louisiana, 1776–1783* (Berkeley: University of California Press, 1934), 171–95; Francisco de Borja Medina Rojas, *José de Ezpeleta: Gobernador de la Mobila, 1780–1781* (Seville: Escuela de Estudios Hispano-Americanos, 1980); and Jack D. L. Holmes, "Alabama's Bloodiest Day of the American Revolution: Counterattack at The Village, January 7, 1781," *Alabama Historical Review* 29 (July 1976): 208–19.

7. Joseph G. Dawson, III, ed., *The Louisiana Governors: From Iberville to Edwards* (Baton Rouge: Louisiana State University Press, 1990), 61–64, 64–69; Caroline Maude Burson, *The Stewardship of Don Esteban Miró, 1782–1792* (New Orleans: American Printing Company, 1940); and Thomas M. Fiehrer, "The Baron de Carondelet as Agent of Bourbon Reform: A Study of Spanish Colonial Administration in the Years of the French Revolution" (Ph.D. diss., Tulane University, 1977).

8. Milford, *Milford's Memoir*, 84–85; two works by Max Savelle, "The Founding of New Madrid, Missouri," *Mississippi Valley Historical Review* 19 (June 1932): 30–56, and *George Morgan, Colony Builder* (New York: Columbia University Press, 1932); and Fernando Solano Costa, "La Fundación de Nuevo Madrid," *Cuadernos de Historia Jerónimo Zurita* 4–5 (1956): 91–108.

9. Milford, *Milford's Memoir*, 31–119. Among many Creek studies, see Claudio Saunt, *A New Order of Things: Property, Power, and the Transformation of the Creek Indians, 1733–1816* (Cambridge: Cambridge University Press, 1999); Robbie Ethridge, *Creek Country: The Creek Indians and Their World* (Chapel Hill: University of North Carolina Press, 2003); Kathryn E. Holland Braund, *Deerskins and Duffles: Creek Indian Trade with Anglo-America, 1685–1815* (Lincoln: University of Nebraska Press, 1993); and Bonnie G. McEwan, ed., *Indians of the Greater Southeast: Historical Archaeology and Ethnohistory* (Gainesville: University Press of Florida, 2000).

10. Milford, *Milford's Memoir*, 9–10; Christian Buchet, *Chef de guerre chez les Creeks* (Paris: Éditions France-Empire, 1994), 28–29; Lyon, "Milfort's Plan," 72–76. See also

Rafe Blaufarb, *The French Army, 1750–1820: Careers, Talent, Merit* (Manchester, U.K.: Manchester University Press, 2002).

11. On McGillivray, see Caughey, *McGillivray*; Whitaker, "Alexander McGillivray, 1783–1789," 181–203; Whitaker, "Alexander McGillivray, 1789–1793," *North Carolina Historical Review* 5, no. 3 (July 1928): 289–309; and J. H. O'Donnell, "Alexander McGillivray: Training for Leadership, 1777–1783," *Georgia Historical Quarterly* 49, no. 2 (June 1965): 172–86. See also Linda Langley, "The Tribal Identity of Alexander McGillivray: A Review of the Historical and Ethnographic Data," *Louisiana History* 46, no. 2 (Spring 2005): 231–39.

12. Amos J. Wright, Jr., *The McGillivray and McIntosh Traders on the Old Southwest Frontier, 1716–1815* (Montgomery, Ala.: New South Books, 2001), 212, 215–16. See also Charles Hudson, *The Southeastern Indians* ([Knoxville]: University of Tennessee Press, 1976), 196–202; J. F. H. Claiborne, *Life and Times of General Sam Dale* (Spartanburg, S.C.: Reprint Company, 1976), 120–21. Two possible Milford children were Alexander and Polly, or so Leora M. Sutton contends in *Success Beyond Expectations: Panton Leslie Co. of Pensacola* (Pensacola: L. M. Sutton, 1991), 104.

13. Caughey, *McGillivray*, 11; Milford, *Milford's Memoir*, 197; A. Wright, *McGillivray and McIntosh*, 188–89.

14. Milford, *Milford's Memoir*, 44–47.

15. Ibid., 47–51; Hudson, *The Southeastern Indians*, 225.

16. Bogus treaties of the Fat and Tame *miccos* were those of Augusta in 1783, Galphinton in 1785, and Shoulderbone in 1786; Milford, *Milford's Memoir*, 96–103. See also J. Leitch Wright, Jr., "Creek-American Treaty of 1790: Alexander McGillivray and the Diplomacy of the Old Southwest," *Georgia Historical Quarterly* 51 (December 1967): 379–400; Kinnaird, *SMV*, 3: xiv–xv; Reginald Horsman, "The Indian Policy of an 'Empire for Liberty,'" in Frederick E. Hoxie, Ronald Hoffman, and Peter J. Albert, eds., *Native Americans and the Early Republic* (Charlottesville: University Press of Virginia, 1999), 37–61; Reginald Horsman, *Expansion and American Indian Policy, 1783–1812* (1967; repr., Norman: University of Oklahoma Press, 1992), 24–52; and William S. Coker and Thomas D. Watson, *Indian Traders of the Southeastern Spanish Borderlands: Panton, Leslie and Company and John Forbes and Company, 1783–1847* (Pensacola: University Press of Florida, 1986).

17. Milford, *Milford's Memoir*, 189–92; Luis Bertucat to O'Neill, San Marcos de Apalache, Oct. 14 and Nov. 21, 1787, in AGI, PC, leg. 37 and Mississippi Provincial Archives, Spanish Dominion, vol. 3, ff. 194–97, respectively; Coker and Watson, *Indian Traders*, 48. On Fort San Marcos, see Gilbert C. Din, "William Augustus Bowles on the Georgia Frontier: A Reexamination of the Spanish Surrender of Fort San Marcos de Apalache in 1800," *Georgia Historical Quarterly* 88 (Fall 2004): 305–37.

18. Albert James Pickett, *History of Alabama, and Incidentally of Georgia and Mississippi*, 2 vols. in 1 (New York: Arno Press, 1971), 80–82; Thomas Foster, ed., *The Collected Works of Benjamin Hawkins* (Tuscaloosa: University of Alabama Press, 2003), 79–81; Daniel F. Littlefield, Jr., *Africans and Creeks: From the Colonial Period to the Civil War* (Westport, Conn.: Greenwood Press, 1979), 29–30. Milford acknowledged in

1802: "Twelve years ago I had one of the latter savages [of the Cat nation or Owabenaki] hanged for murdering an American colonel and his son." Milford, *Milford's Memoir*, 97.

19. McGillivray to Panton, [Little Tallassee?], May 20, 1789, in D. C. Corbitt, ed., "Papers Relating to the Georgia-Florida Frontier, 1784–1800," *Georgia Historical Quarterly* 21 (September 1937): 287.

20. J. Leitch Wright, Jr., *William Augustus Bowles: Director-General of the Creek Nation* (Athens: University of Georgia Press, 1967); and Arthur Preston Whitaker, *The Mississippi Question, 1795–1803: A Study in Trade, Politics, and Diplomacy* (1934; repr., Gloucester, Mass.: Peter Smith, 1962), 162–75, exaggerate Bowles's accomplishments. See also Elisha P. Douglass, "The Adventurer Bowles," *William and Mary Quarterly* 6 (January 1949): 3–23; Lyle McAlister, "William Augustus Bowles and the State of Muskogee," *Florida Historical Quarterly* 30 (April 1962): 317–28; and David Hart White, "William Augustus Bowles," *Florida Historical Quarterly* 54 (October 1975): 145–55.

21. John W. Caughey, "Alexander McGillivray and the Creek Crisis, 1783–1784," in *New Spain and the Anglo-American West*, 2 vols. (New York: Kraus, 1969), 268–88. See also Thomas A. Bailey, *A Diplomatic History of the American People*, 7th ed. (New York: Appleton-Century-Crofts, 1964), 44–51, 59–60; Arthur Preston Whitaker, *The Spanish-American Frontier: 1783–1795* (1927; repr., Gloucester, Mass.: Peter Smith, 1962), 7–13, 41–43, 61–62.

22. J. Wright, *Bowles*, 27–29; McAlister, "Bowles," 318–19; Lawrence Kinnaird, "The Significance of William Augustus Bowles's Seizure of Panton's Apalachee Store in 1792," *Florida Historical Quarterly* 9 (1931): 160–66.

23. Milford, *Milford's Memoir*, 90–91; J. Wright, *Bowles*, 30–38; McAlister, "Bowles," 318–20. Most historians believe that Cusseta in Spanish documents was really Kasihta.

24. McGillivray to Panton, Little Tallassee, Feb. 1, 1789, in Caughey, *McGillivray*, 215–20; Milford, *Milford's Memoir*, 10–12, 90–91; Helen Hornbeck Tanner, *Zéspedes in East Florida, 1784–1790* (1963; repr., Jacksonville: University Press of Florida, 1989), 194; [Francisco Cruzat] to Miró, no. 65 reserved, March 31, 1789, AGI, PC, leg. 225A; Milford, *Milford's Memoir*, 82–83. Pickett, *History of Alabama*, 411, has a different version of Milford's meeting with Bowles.

25. McGillivray to Panton, Little Tallassee, May 20, 1789, in Corbitt, ed., "Papers Relating to the Georgia-Florida Frontier, 1784–1800," *Georgia Historical Quarterly* 21 (September 1937): 286–87; McGillivray to Francisco Cruzat, [Little Tallassee], July 2, 1789, in Caughey, *McGillivray*, 241.

26. McGillivray to Panton, Little Tallassee, Aug. 10, 1789, in Caughey, *McGillivray*, 249.

27. [O'Neill] to [Miró], [Pensacola], May 6, 1790, AGI, PC, leg. 224A; McGillivray to O'Neill, Little Tallassee, Nov. 2, 1790, in Caughey, *McGillivray*, 286.

28. J. Wright, *Bowles*, 61–70; Kinnaird, "The Significance of Bowles's Seizure of Pan-

ton's Store," 156–92; Jack D. L. Holmes, ed., in *José de Evia y sus reconocimientos del Golfo de México, 1783–1796* (Madrid: Ediciones J. Porrúa Turanzas, 1968), 193–208.

29. [White] to [Carondelet], Pensacola, March 3, 1792, AGI, PC, leg. 225A; Panton to Carondelet, Pensacola, April 12, 1792, in D. C. Corbitt, ed., "Papers Relating to the Georgia-Florida Frontier," *Georgia Historical Quarterly* 22 (1938): 289–90.

30. Panton to Carondelet, Pensacola, April 12, 1792, and Robert Leslie to Panton, Apalache, April, n.d., 1792, both in Corbitt, ed., "Papers Relating to the Georgia-Florida Frontier," *Georgia Historical Quarterly* 22 (1938): 289–90 and 291 respectively; Milford, *Milford's Memoir*, 15–17; O'Neill to Carondelet, Pensacola, May 12, 1792, with attached Francisco Guesy to White, Apalache, May 4, 1792, both in AGI, PC, leg. 225A.

31. White to Carondelet, Pensacola, April 10 and 18, 1792, both in AGI, PC, leg. 25.

32. Caughey, *McGillivray*, 338n; Milford, *Milford's Memoirs*, 113–15; A. Wright, *McGillivray and McIntosh*, 214–15.

33. Carondelet to McGillivray, New Orleans, Feb. 6 and Sept. 14, 1792, both in Caughey, *McGillivray*, 397 and 337–38; Gilbert C. Din, "Father Jean Delvaux and the Natchitoches Revolt of 1795," *Louisiana History* 40, no. 1 (Winter 1999): 5–33.

34. Caughey, *McGillivray*, 53; Olivier to Carondelet, Mongulacha, June 11, 1793, in Kinnaird, *SMV*, 3: 170–71; Milford to Carondelet, Tuckabatche, March 29, 1793, AGI, PC, leg. 208; A. Wright, *McGillivray and McIntosh*, 192; [O'Neill] to [Miró], Pensacola, Dec. 29, 1788, AGI, PC, leg. 225A; Panton to John Leslie, n.p., Aug. 28, 1793, in Caughey, *McGillivray*, 359.

35. Caughey, *McGillivray*, 54; Panton to Carondelet, n.p., late February or early March, 1793, ibid., 355–56; A. Wright, *McGillivray and McIntosh*, 189, 191; Charles A. Weeks, *Paths to a Middle Ground: The Diplomacy of Natchez, Boukfouka, Nogales, and San Fernando de las Barrancas, 1791–1795* (Tuscaloosa: University of Alabama Press, 2005), 106.

36. McGillivray to Carondelet, Nov. 15, 1792, AGI, PC, leg. 205; Caughey, *McGillivray*, 344–49; R. S. Cotterill, *The Southern Indians: The Story of the Civilized Tribes before Removal* (Norman: University of Oklahoma Press, 1954), 102; Coker and Watson, *Indian Traders*, 178–79; Milford to Carondelet, Tuckabatche, May 26, 1793, in Kinnaird, *SMV*, 3: 160–62.

37. Milford to Carondelet, Tuckabatche, April 9, 1793, in D. C. Corbitt and Roberta Corbitt, trans. and eds., "Papers from the Spanish Archives Relating to Tennessee and the Old Southwest," *East Tennessee Historical Society's Publications* 31 (1959): 79–80; Saunt, *A New Order of Things*, 205–6; Paul E. Hoffman, *Florida's Frontiers* (Bloomington: University of Indiana Press, 2002), 414n.

38. Milford to Carondelet, Tuckabatche, May 26, 1793, in Kinnaird, *SMV*, 3: 160–82; A. Wright, *McGillivray and McIntosh*, 191.

39. Panton to Carondelet, Pensacola, April 10, 1793, in Corbitt and Corbitt, "Papers from the Spanish Archives Relating to Tennessee and the Old Southwest," 31 (1959): 80; Cotterill, *The Southern Indians*, 102–3; Panton to Leslie, [Pensacola], Aug. 28, 1793, in Caughey, *McGillivray*, 359; Saunt, *A New Order of Things*, 99.

40. Milford to O'Neill, Tuckabatche, April 31, 1793, in Kinnaird, *SMV*, 3: 154–55.

41. Milford to Carondelet, Tuckabatche, May 26, 1793, in Kinnaird, *SMV*, 3: 161; J. Wright, *Bowles*, 64.

42. Coker and Watson, *Indian Traders*, 111; A. Wright, *McGillivray and McIntosh*, 190.

43. Milford to Carondelet, Tuckabatche, May 26, 1793, in Kinnaird, *SMV*, 3: 160–62. Colonel Enrique White relieved General Arturo O'Neill as commandant at Pensacola on May 15, 1793. White to Carondelet, Pensacola, May 30, 1793, in Kinnaird, *SMV*, 3: 163.

44. Milford to Carondelet, Tuckabatche, May 31, 1793, in Kinnaird, *SMV*, 3: 162–63; White to Carondelet, Pensacola, May 30 and June 11, 1793, in ibid., 3: 163 and 174 respectively.

45. Olivier to Carondelet, Mongulacha, June 11, 1793, in Kinnaird, *SMV*, 3: 170–71. The same document is dated June 14, 1793, in Archivo Histórico Nacional (hereafter AHN), Est., leg. 3899, exped. 1.

46. White to Carondelet, Pensacola, July 4, 1793, in Kinnaird, *SMV*, 3: 178.

47. [White] to [Carondelet], Pensacola, Aug. 8, 1793, AGI, PC, leg. 225A. White reproduced the governor's message in this letter.

48. White to Carondelet, Pensacola, Sept. 2, 1793, in Kinnaird, *SMV*, 3: 203.

49. White to Carondelet, Pensacola, Oct. 10, 1793, in Kinnaird, *SMV*, 3: 216–17; Saunt, *A New Order of Things*, 99; Olivier to White, Wutonká, Oct. 5, 1793, in Kinnaird, *SMV*, 3: 215–16.

50. John Galphin to Panton, Broken Arrow, Oct. 16, 1793, with enclosure, "A Talk of the Grand Council to Georgia," n.p., Oct. 4, 1793, in Kinnaird, *SMV*, 3: 218–20.

51. Milford to [Enrique] White, Cloaly, Oct. 19, 1793, in Kinnaird, *SMV*, 3: 221–22; White to Carondelet, Pensacola, Nov. 11, 1793, in ibid., 3: 229. See also Joshua Aaron Piker, *Okfuskee: A Creek Indian Town in Colonial America* (Cambridge: Cambridge University Press, 2004).

52. White to Carondelet, Pensacola, Oct. 10 and Nov. 11, 1793, in Kinnaird, *SMV*, 3: 217 and 227–29, respectively; Milford to Carondelet, Cloaly, April 14, 1794, in ibid., 3: 266–68.

53. Carondelet to Aranda, no. 20 confidential, New Orleans, Nov. 8, 1792, in vol. 28 (1956): 134–36; Carondelet to Casas, no. 69 confidential, New Orleans, March 19, 1793, in vol. 31 (1959): 66–68; Gayoso to Carondelet, Natchez, April 11, 1793, in vol. 31 (1959): 81–82; Carondelet to Casas, no. 89 confidential, New Orleans, Aug. 3, 1793, in vol. 34 (1962): 97–101, all in D. C. Corbitt and Roberta Corbitt, trans. and eds., "Papers from the Spanish Archives Relating to Tennessee and the Old Southwest," *East Tennessee Historical Society's Publications* 28–36 (1956–62).

54. "Treaty of Nogales," Oct. 28, 1793, in Kinnaird, *SMV*, 3: 223–27; Jack D. L. Holmes, "Spanish Treaties with West Florida Indians, 1784–1802," *Florida Historical Quarterly* 48 (October 1969): 140–54; Lawrence and Lucia B. Kinnaird, "San Fernando de Las Barrancas: Spain's Last Outpost of Empire," *West Tennessee Historical Society Papers* 35 (1981): 28; Weeks, *Paths to a Middle Ground*, 103–25.

55. Milford to Carondelet, Cloaly, Dec. 17, 1793, in Kinnaird, *SMV*, 3: 235-36. See also Daniel M. Smith, "James Seagrove and the Mission to Tuckaubatchee, 1793," *Georgia Historical Quarterly* 44, no. 1 (March 1960): 41-55.

56. Milford to Carondelet, Cloaly, Dec. 23, 1793, in Kinnaird, *SMV*, 3: 243-45.

57. Carondelet to Gayoso, confidential, New Orleans, Feb. 7, 1794, in D. C. Corbitt and Roberta Corbitt, eds. and trans., "Papers from the Spanish Archives Relating to Tennessee and the Old Southwest," *East Tennessee Historical Society's Publications* 37 (1965): 101-2; Carondelet to White, New Orleans, April 9, 1794, AGI, PC, leg. 21.

58. Milford to Carondelet, Cloaly, March 20, 1794, enclosed in Carondelet to the Duque de la Alcudia, no. 31 reserved, AHN, Est., leg. 3899, exped. 1; Milford to Carondelet, Cloaly, March 25, 1794, and Luis de las Casas to the Conde del Campo de Alange, Havana, May 19, 1794, both in Kinnaird, *SMV*, 3: 261-63 and 3: 286-89 respectively; Ernest R. Liljegren, "Jacobinism in Spanish Louisiana, 1792-1797," *Louisiana Historical Quarterly* 22 (1939): 47-97; Carondelet to Juan de la Villebeuvre, New Orleans, April 23, 1794, in Kinnaird, *SMV*, 3: 271-72.

59. Milford to Carondelet, Cloaly, April 14, 1794, in Kinnaird, *SMV*, 3: 266-68. Milford's diary is attached to Milford to Carondelet, Cloaly, March 20, 1794, which is, in turn, enclosed in Carondelet to the Duque de la Alcudia, New Orleans, April 9, 1794, AHN, Est., leg. 3899, exped. 1.

60. De la Villebeuvre to Carondelet, Fort Confederation, June 9, 1794, in Kinnaird, *SMV*, 3: 298.

61. White to Carondelet, Pensacola, June 14 and 16, 1794, both in AGI, PC, leg. 29. In his *Memoir*, 90, Milford displayed his royalist and later Napoleonic sentiments. Carondelet to the Duque de la Alcudia, reserved, nos. 16 and 17, New Orleans, both dated Aug. 30, 1793, in AHN, Est., leg. 3899, exped. 1.

62. White to Carondelet, Pensacola, June 4, 5, 14, and 16, 1794, all in AGI, PC, leg. 29; David Hart White, *Vicente Folch, Governor in Spanish Florida, 1787-1811* (Washington, D.C.: University Press of America, 1981), 19; [Carondelet] to White, reserved, New Orleans, June 26, 1794, AGI, PC, leg. 29.

63. Bailey, *Diplomatic History*, 72, 85; Milford to Carondelet, Cloaly, March 24, 1794, in Kinnaird, *SMV*, 3: 261-63.

64. White to Carondelet, Pensacola, July 2 and Aug. 11, 1794; [Carondelet] to White, New Orleans, July 22, 1794; all in AGI, PC, leg. 29; E. Merton Coulter, "Elijah Clarke's Foreign Intrigue and the Trans-Oconee Republic," *Proceedings of the Mississippi Valley Historical Association* 10 (1919-20): 260-79; Richard K. Murdoch, *The Georgia-Florida Frontier, 1793-1796: Spanish Reaction to French Intrigue and American Designs* (Berkeley: University of California Press, 1951); Charles E. Bennett, *Florida's "French" Revolution, 1793-1795* (Gainesville: University Press of Florida, 1981).

65. Carondelet to White, New Orleans, Sept. 11, 1794, AGI, PC, leg. 30.

66. Taskiniahatkie (White Lieutenant) to Carondelet, Kasihta, Lower Creeks, Nov. 20, 1794, in Kinnaird, *SMV*, 3: 375-77. Compare this letter with "A Talk from the White Lieutenant of the Ocfuskees to His Friend and Brother, and Also His Father the

Governor of New Orleans, Nov. 9, [1793]," in Caughey, *McGillivray*, 360-61. Internal evidence shows that 1794 is correct.

67. White to Carondelet, Pensacola, Feb. 28, 1795, AGI, PC, leg. 31. In Milford, *Milford's Memoir*, 114, he "reproduces" a letter to Carondelet dated Jan. 14, 1795, sending him a passport and a payment of three hundred pesos. Working from memory, Milford erred in the date since the letter was written in February.

68. White to Carondelet, Pensacola, March 9, 1795, AGI, PC, leg. 31.

69. White to Carondelet, Pensacola, Aug. 9, 1795, AGI, PC, leg. 32; A. Wright, *McGillivray and McIntosh*, 214-15; Milford, *Milford's Memoir*, 111-16; Caughey, *McGillivray*, 218-17n; E. Wilson Lyon, *Louisiana in French Diplomacy, 1759-1804* (Norman: University of Oklahoma Press, 1974), 79-91; A. Wright, *McGillivray and McIntosh*, 216; Buchet, *Chef de guerre*, 38.

70. Buchet, *Chef de guerre*, 39-40; "General Collot's Plan for a Reconnaissance of the Ohio and Mississippi Valleys, 1796," trans. Durand Echeverria, *William and Mary Quarterly* 9 (1952): 512-20; George W. Kyte, "A Spy on the Western Waters: The Military Intelligence Mission of General Collot in 1796," *Mississippi Valley Historical Review* 34 (1947): 427-42; and George H. V. Collot, *A Journey in North America* (Florence, Italy: O. Lange, 1926). Isaac Joslin Cox, in *The West Florida Controversy, 1798-1813* (1918; repr., Gloucester, Mass.: Peter Smith, 1967), 39, argued that Milford was a French agent while among the Creeks. He was not.

71. Lyon, "Milfort's Plan," 72-87.

72. Felix Gilbert, gen. ed., *The Norton History of Modern Europe* (New York: Norton, 1971), 827-28; E. Wilson Lyon, *Louisiana in French Diplomacy*, 106-10; Alexander DeConde, *This Affair of Louisiana* (New York: Scribner, 1976), 91-97.

73. Buchet, *Chef de guerre*, 40; Lyon, "Milfort's Plan,": 72-87; DeConde, *This Affair of Louisiana*, 161-75; Bailey, *Diplomatic History*, 80-82, 102-3; J. Wright, *Bowles*, 95-108; Milford, *Milford's Memoir*, 115-19; Ronald Smith, "Napoleon and Louisiana: Failure of the Proposed Expedition to Occupy and Defend Louisiana, 1801-1803," *Louisiana History* 12, no. 1 (Winter 1971): 21-40.

74. Buchet, *Chef de guerre*, 49; Peter H. Wood, "The Changing Population of the Colonial South: An Overview by Race and Region, 1685-1790," in Peter H. Wood, Gregory A. Waselkov, and M. Thomas Hatley, eds., *Powhatan's Mantle: Indians in the Colonial Southeast*,(Lincoln: University of Nebraska Press, 1989), 60; "Pedro Olivier's Population Estimate for the Upper and Lower Creeks of 1793," in Kinnaird, *SMV*, 3: 231-32.

75. Buchet, *Chef de guerre*, 46-48.

76. Ibid., 48; Hudson, *The Southeastern Indians*, 200.

77. Buchet, *Chef de guerre*, 49-52.

78. Bowles returned to West Florida in 1799 and remained there until his capture in 1803. J. Wright, *Bowles*, 124-74; David H. White, "The Spaniards and William Augustus Bowles in Florida, 1799-1803," *Florida Historical Quarterly* 54, no. 2 (October 1975): 145-55; Lawrence Kinnaird and Lucia B. Kinnaird, "War Comes to San Marcos," *Florida Historical Quarterly* 62, no. 1 (July 1983): 25-43.

4

Marie Thérèze dit Coincoin

A Free Black Woman on the Louisiana-Texas Frontier

H. SOPHIE BURTON

Marie Thérèze dit Coincoin[1] was born in Natchitoches, a town located on the Red River in the interior of Louisiana near the province of Texas, in August 1742.[2] Coincoin was the second of twelve children born to François and Marie Françoise, two African-born slaves belonging to the town's commandant, Louis Juchereau de St. Denis. When her master died in 1744, Coincoin along with her siblings and parents, who were all *morenos*, or dark-skinned, continued to live in the commandant's widow's household. Circumstances changed suddenly for Coincoin and her siblings when they lost both of their parents and their female owner in April 1758, probably from an epidemic. All of the slaves in the household suddenly found themselves partitioned among the children and grandchildren of St. Denis and had to live apart for the first time. Coincoin and her siblings went into six lots of one or two slaves, and Coincoin and her brother Jean Baptiste went to Pierre Antoine Juchereau de St. Denis, the youngest son of the former commandant. Coincoin became a mother when she had two *morena* daughters, Marie Louise and Thérèze. Between 1761 and 1766, she and her daughters became the property of her master's youngest sister, Marie des Nieges de St. Denis, the wife of Antoine Manuel Bermúdez y de Soto. Coincoin had a third *morena* daughter, Françoise, and in 1766 a *moreno* son named Jean Joseph.

Now a mother of four, Coincoin's life shifted again in 1767 when she met Claude-Thomas-Pierre Metoyer. Metoyer was a French merchant who had gone to New Orleans with his brother and traveled up the Mississippi and Red Rivers to Natchitoches to see a friend and fellow merchant named Étienne Pavie. Twenty-five-year-old Coincoin and twenty-three-year-old Metoyer became involved with one another, and Metoyer persuaded Marie de St. Denis to lease Coincoin to him as a house slave in return for free room and board as long as she served him. In January 1768, Coincoin gave birth to the first two of ten children who would be born from this French-African alliance when she had twins, who were named Nicolas Augustin and Marie Suzanne. Spanish censuses and parish records categorized these lighter-skinned children as *pardos*. Between 1769 and 1777, Coincoin and Metoyer had four more children, Louis, Pierre, Dominique, and Marie Eulalie. When she was pregnant with Metoyer's seventh child, who would be named Joseph Antoine and would actually be her eleventh child, Coincoin's union with the Frenchman became the target of a Spanish Capuchin priest named Father Louis de Quintanilla, who had recently been assigned to Natchitoches. Objecting to concubinage on moral grounds, Father Quintanilla put pressure on Athanase de Mézières, the commandant of Natchitoches, until he ordered Coincoin to return to Marie de St. Denis's household in late 1777. Early the following year, however, Coincoin returned to live with Metoyer after de Mézières went away on business in the neighboring province of Texas. By the time the protracted litigation on the subject ended, Metoyer had freed Coincoin as a means of quieting Father Quintanilla's continued pressure on authorities to seize and sell her.[3]

In 1778, Coincoin became one of the few *libres*, or free people of color, in Natchitoches when Metoyer, shortly after purchasing her and her youngest son, Joseph Antoine, from Marie de St. Denis, took advantage of Spain's liberal manumission policy in order to declare them both free. Metoyer had already bought four of his mulatto children with Coincoin, and in 1780 Metoyer bought the remaining two of his *pardo* children who still belonged to Marie de St. Denis. After Coincoin's manumission, however, little changed for her in spite of the fact that she was legally free. Coincoin continued to live with Metoyer and to serve as his domestic slave and concubine. In fact, during this time Coincoin gave birth to her last three *pardo* children, Marie Françoise Roselie, Pierre, and François.[4]

By dint of her hard work, Coincoin eventually became the founder and heart of a small group of *libres* in Natchitoches. In 1786, when she was a forty-six-year-old mother of fourteen, Coincoin's life took yet another direction when Metoyer ended their union and living arrangement. Metoyer granted her a tract of land of five arpents (one arpent was equal to slightly less than one acre) fronting on both sides of the Red River. Even though Metoyer also gave her an annual stipend of 120 piastres, the amount was small for a mother with so many children. On January 18, 1787, Coincoin petitioned the Spanish government for the title to her land and received the concession in her name. She grew tobacco and indigo, traded in deerskins and bear oil, and sold medicines made from herbs and roots. Like many other free Natchitoches residents, she petitioned the Spanish government for a larger land grant that she employed as a *vacherie*, or ranch, in 1794. Along with inheriting Metoyer's land along Cane River, some Metoyers *de couleur* (of color) purchased or petitioned the

Spanish government for tracts of fertile land at the Isle Brevelle, beginning in 1795. With her modest economic success, Coincoin had been able to increase the numbers of *libres* in Natchitoches over the years by purchasing and freeing a number of enslaved relatives whom Metoyer had failed to emancipate, including some of her children and her sister Marie Louise dit Mariotte. Most of these *libres* came to settle near Coincoin herself and Metoyer's *pardo* children and grandchildren at Isle Brevelle. In May 1795, for example, Coincoin's eldest son by Metoyer, Nicolas Augustin, received a land grant of 395 acres. Augustin's brothers and other relatives settled on adjacent lands by the late 1790s. Augustin was the first Isle Brevelle *libre* to acquire slaves, and eventually most Metoyers *de couleur* came to own and employ enslaved laborers. Seven years into the American period in 1810, they already owned a total of fifty-eight slaves, and the colony was beginning to flourish economically. In fact, Isle Brevelle plantations came to be comparable to successful white-owned Natchitoches plantations during the nineteenth century. The exact date of Coincoin's death is not certain, but the final records of her transactions were in 1816.[5]

The origins of the large and propertied free black population in Louisiana's antebellum period were in the colonial French and Spanish eras.[6] Only a few *libres* resided in the province from the beginning of French rule (1699–1762), when most denizens of the frontier town of Natchitoches worked in the trade with Indians and neighboring Spaniards of Texas. Increasingly in the Spanish era (in name from 1762 to 1800 but in reality from 1766 to 1803) whites turned to large-scale plantations of tobacco, indigo, and even cotton, importing more and more black slaves as laborers. Just as society was developing a clear plantation hierarchy under Spanish rule, the demographic, economic, cultural, legal, and political circumstances, rather paradoxically, spurred the growth and maintenance of a group of free people of color. Spanish slave laws hastened the ability of a number of enslaved blacks and Indians to move from bonded status to free in Louisiana. Moreover, under Hispanic laws freed people or blacks born free could not be reenslaved and manumission was more easily obtained than under French laws. Under the French Code Noir, manumission was more difficult. Slave holders had to be at least twenty-five years of age to manumit a slave, and manumission required the consent of the Louisiana Superior Council in New Orleans. Moreover, the Code Noir was contradictory on the status of *libres*. While the code stated unequivocally that manumitted slaves held the same rights as French citizens, other parts of the code made it legal to penalize freed slaves in ways that the freeborn never experienced. For example, *libres* had larger fines for infractions than whites and owed perpetual respect to their former owners. In addition, the code even allowed the reenslavement of freed people under certain conditions, and it was illegal for *libres* to inherit property or receive gifts from former owners. When the French Code Noir no longer applied, Spanish Louisiana consequently experienced an increase in the population of *libres*. Free people of color in New Orleans learned to maintain their unique status by distancing themselves from their slave past and identifying with the values of hegemonic white society. Even though they forged an identity separate from whites and slaves, the historian Kimberly Hanger concludes that they "still did not constitute a uniform group whose interests and character were one" even by the end of the Spanish period.[7] Likewise, in Natchitoches, the *libre* population grew as a result of more lenient Hispanic legislation, but Coincoin was still one of the few free people of color in Spanish Natchitoches as the increase of *libres* in the interior posts was neither as dramatic nor as constant as in coastal settlements like New Orleans.[8]

Although the patterns and trends associated with the group of *libres* in Spanish Natchitoches reveal that Spanish laws were more lenient than subsequent American ones, it is clear that Coincoin, like other free people of color in Natchitoches, had to work hard to negotiate many social and cultural obstacles imbedded in a plantation system that was dedicated to the oppression of all people of color. In order to ensure their survival, *libres* tended to lend their tacit support to the slave system, for most free whites saw *libres* as possessing an identity tainted by their former status as slaves and were suspicious of their loyalty to the slave system. As a result, many *libres* found they had to separate themselves from slaves and chose to identify with slaveholders. While Coincoin had a certain degree of agency, she still lived in a society and culture committed to circumscribing her in order to keep black plantation slavery—and the ideal of rigid color lines inherent to that system—in place.[9] Once a slave attained free status, the laws called for the equal treatment of emancipated people of color with other free people, but in practice *libres* such as Coincoin had to contend on a daily level with social and cultural prejudices that bolstered plantation society. Most *libres* in Natchitoches, quite few in number for most of the Spanish period, had white relatives to thank for having obtained a manumission in the first place and continued to rely economically on former owners or whites after their emancipation. Moreover, *libres* tended to reside in scattered households and were closer to whites than to other *libres* or slaves. As a result of these obstacles, *libres* in Natchitoches were only able to develop a sense of communal identity when they attained larger numbers and reached economic independence during the American period.[10]

Growth of the *Libre* Population in Spanish Natchitoches

Though the *libre* population of Louisiana augmented during the Spanish period, the number of free blacks in Natchitoches grew at a much slower and less substantial rate than that of New Orleans. At the beginning of the Spanish regime, only 15 *libres* lived in Natchitoches. This number declined to 7 within the following decade as they probably moved to other parts of Louisiana or Texas. Only in the 1780s did the *libre* population begin to take off when in 1787 their numbers doubled to 14. This trend continued throughout the rest of the period as the numbers grew to 33 in 1795 and then to a highpoint of 48 in 1802 (table 4.1).[11] While the *libres* of Natchitoches increased their population threefold during the Spanish era, the number of free blacks in New Orleans swelled fifteen times from 97 *libres* in 1771 to 1,566 thirty years later.[12]

In addition to having few free people of color in Natchitoches, the *libres* there formed a less significant proportion of the total free population than *libres* in towns of the Gulf Coast. By the late 1780s, *libres* in New Orleans composed 25.7 percent of the free population while they constituted a trifling 2.1 percent of free people in Natchitoches (table 4.2). Although the forty-eight *libres* in Natchitoches had increased their proportion to 5.6 percent of the free population by the end of the Spanish era, *libres* in New Orleans escalated to 30.7 percent of the free population. Moreover, other urban areas along the Gulf Coast were more comparable to the capital than to frontier towns in the interior. In 1787, Mobile's free people of color composed 17.1 percent of the

Table 4.1. Natchitoches Population, 1766–1810

Year	Whites	*Libres*	Slaves	Total
1766	308	15	269	592
1776	592	7	422	1021
1787	647	14	734	1395
1795	728	33	904	1665
1802	804	48	936	1788
1810	1213	181	1476	2870

Source: "1766 French Census of Natchitoches, January 27, 1766," "1787 Census of Natchitoches, August 17, 1787," "1795 Census of Slave Owners at Natchitoches, October 15, 1795," "1801 Census of St. François des Natchitoches, March 15, 1802," in Elizabeth Shown Mills, ed., comp., and trans., *Natchitoches Colonials: Censuses, Military Rolls, and Tax Lists, 1722-1803* (Chicago: Adams Press, 1981), 9–14, 45–62, 111–14, 120 includes a number of original censuses and lists (hereafter cited as *Natchitoches Colonials*); Demézières to Unzaga y Amézaga, February 16, 1776, in Herbert Eugene Bolton, ed., *Athanase de Mézières and the Louisiana-Texas Frontier, 1768–1780* (Cleveland: Arthur H. Clark Co., 1914), 2: 120–21 (hereafter cited as *ADM*); "1810 Census, Natchitoches Parish, Louisiana," in Robert Bruce L. Ardoin, comp., *Louisiana Census Records: Iberville, Natchitoches, Pointe Coupee, and Rapides Parishes, 1810 and 1820* (New Orleans: Polyanthos, 1972), 33–38 (hereafter cited as *Louisiana Census Records*).

Table 4.2. Proportion of *Libres* in the Total, Free, and Nonwhite Populations, Natchitoches, 1766–1810

Year	% of Total Population	N	% of Free Population	N	% of Nonwhite Population	N
1766	2.5	592	4.6	323	5.3	284
1776	0.7	1021	1.2	599	1.7	422
1787	1.0	1395	2.1	661	1.9	748
1795	2.0	1665	4.3	761	3.5	937
1802	2.7	1788	5.6	852	4.9	984
1810	6.3	2870	13.0	1294	10.9	1657

Source: "1766 French Census of Natchitoches, January 27, 1766," "1787 Census of Natchitoches, August 17, 1787," "1795 Census of Slave Owners at Natchitoches, October 15, 1795," "1801 Census of St. François des Natchitoches, March 15, 1802," in *Natchitoches Colonials*, 9–14, 45–62, 111–14, 120; Demézières to Unzaga y Amézaga, February 16, 1776, in *ADM*, 2: 120–21; "1810 Census, Natchitoches Parish, Louisiana," *Louisiana Census Records*, 33–38.

free population, a proportion that jumped to 30 percent by 1805. Likewise, Pensacola saw a tenfold increase of *libres* between 1783 and 1821 in which they came to form 36 percent of the free population.[13]

Manumissions were largely responsible for the growth of the *libre* group in Natchitoches. Most of this increase in *libres* occurred late in the eighteenth century in large part because the population base was not large enough for the numbers to grow through natural means until after 1803, the beginning of the American period. Because children legally had the status of their mother rather than their father, *libres* in Natchitoches had to wait for substantial numbers of *libre* women who were emancipated at a young enough age to have sufficient numbers of free children to augment the population naturally. Therefore, manumissions, rather than births, fueled the initial small number of *libres* during the Spanish period. Though there were 84 total acts of manumission between 1774 and 1803, an overwhelming majority took place only in the last third of the period. In the first third (1774–83), only 7 manumissions (8.3 percent) occurred, and this number increased to 29 (34.5 percent) in the second third. Manumissions took off in the final years as 48 *libres* (57.1 percent) were freed between 1794 and 1803 (table 4.3). Since the *libre* population had finally reached the level at which the numbers could increase naturally, the free black population of Natchitoches increased 277 percent between 1802 and 1810. The 181 free blacks living in the region seven years after the Louisiana Purchase now made up 13 percent of the free population.

Table 4.3. Increase in Natchitoches Manumissions, 1774–1803

1774–83	1784–93	1794–1803
7	29	48

Source: Most manumissions employed in this study are found in Natchitoches Parish Conveyance Records, Microfilm Copy, Mormon Genealogy Society, consulted at the Family History Center in Dallas, Texas (hereinafter cited as NPCR); others are in the Melrose Collection, Cammie G. Henry Research Center, Eugene P. Watson Memorial Library, Northwestern State University, Natchitoches, Louisiana (hereinafter cited as Melrose Collection). This collection is one of several in the center that contain notarial records; a few more manumissions came from the Papeles Procedentes de Cuba (Archivo General de Indias, Seville, Spain) (hereafter cited as AGI, PC).

Types of Manumissions

These same eighty-four manumissions in Natchitoches can be divided into various kinds of acts recorded by a notary, and an analysis of manumissions points to the critical importance of paternalism in the lives of the free people of color in Natchitoches in contrast to many of the *libres* in New Orleans. Under Spanish slave law, a slaveholder could emancipate a slave by a simple notarized act called a *graciosa*. Proprietors employed two variations: an outright *graciosa* or one with conditions in which the slave's emancipation was contingent upon service or the death of the owner. Both kinds of manumission were owner-driven in that slaveholders were the active parties who instigated the manumission. Coincoin of course received her freedom from Metoyer through this type of act. Other Spanish slave laws, however, allowed the bondspeople to employ measures to escape slavery energetically through *coartación*, or self-purchase, or, in certain cases, through a tribunal manumission in which a slave forced his or her freedom from a recalcitrant owner. In contrast to *graciosas*, these latter types of manumissions were slave-driven, allowing bondspeople to take the initiative in gaining their own emancipation. Another kind of manumission was the third party purchase in which an interested third party such as a relative or friend legally bought a slave out of slavery directly. A third party purchase was inherently neither slave-driven nor owner-driven for any concerned person had the right to purchase a bondsperson out of slavery, permitting *libres* and whites an equal chance to free a slave. In spite of the opportunities for slave-driven manumissions, in Natchitoches, seventy-two *libres*, or 85.7 percent of all recipients, received their liberty through owner-driven manumissions that involved the direct aid of whites, who were mostly male. In fact, a consideration of phenotype and age data together with the type of manumission indicates that many enslaved recipients of *graciosas*—with or without conditions—were liberated with the

Table 4.4 Age Category and Phenotype of Slave by Type of Manumission, Natchitoches, 1774–1803

	Graciosa	Conditional	Coartación	Third Party	Tribunal	Total
Age I(1–13)						
Pardo	20	1	0	2	0	23
Moreno	0	0	0	1	0	1
Indio	0	0	0	0	0	0
Grifo	2	0	0	0	0	2
Not Given	1	8	0	0	0	9
Total	23	9	0	3	0	35
Age II(14–49)						
Pardo	9	3	0	1	1	14
Moreno	2	9	1	3	0	15
Indio	1	0	0	0	0	1
Grifo	0	0	0	0	0	0
Not Given	2	4	0	0	0	6
Total	14	16	1	4	1	36
Age III(50+)						
Pardo	0	0	0	0	0	0
Moreno	1	1	5	0	0	7
Indio	0	0	0	0	0	0
Grifo	0	0	0	0	0	0
Not Given	0	1	0	0	0	1
Total	1	2	5	0	0	8

Source: NPCR; Melrose Collection; AGI, PC. The total for this chart is seventy-nine, not eighty-four, because officials failed to note the ages of five manumitted slaves.

assistance of a third party because they were the children of white males (table 4.4).[14]

A statistical analysis of manumitted slaves reveals a strong paternalism in Natchitoches slave society, for most *libres* were female *pardos* who received their manumissions with the help of whites (table 4.5). Of the sixty-eight manumissions that specify phenotype, only three slaves manumitted were of Indian descent. Most manumitted slaves were *pardos* (57.4 percent) while the rest were *morenos* (38.2 percent) as well as slaves whose origins were not given in the documents.[15] Moreover, a majority of manumitted slaves were female (forty-nine females to thirty-five males). A typical beneficiary of manumission was the twenty-six-year-old *parda* Calhiche, whom Jean Baptiste Grappe purchased from Louis Fontenot on April 1, 1796. Grappe then emancipated her twenty days later. New Orleans manumissions differed radically from Natchitoches cases. While manumitted slaves in the capital also tended to be females

Table 4.5. Phenotype and Sex of Slave by Type of Manumission, Natchitoches, 1774–1803

Phenotype	Graciosa	Conditional	Coartación	Third Party	Tribunal	Total
Pardo						
Female	19	3	0	1	1	24
Male	11	2	0	2	0	15
Moreno						
Female	5	3	2	3	0	13
Male	0	7	5	1	0	13
Indio						
Female	1	0	0	0	0	1
Male	0	0	0	0	0	0
Grifo[1]						
Female	1	0	0	0	0	1
Male	1	0	0	0	0	1
Not Given						
Female	2	8	0	0	0	10
Male	2	4	0	0	0	6
Total	42	27	7	7	1	84

Source: NPCR; Melrose Collection; AGI, PC.
[1] A *grifo* was a person of mixed Indian and black parentage.

by a margin of almost two to one, they were more likely to be *morenas* who attained free status through slave-driven manumissions rather than *pardas* who got them through owner-driven manumissions. The self-driven manumission dominated in New Orleans, while in Natchitoches manumissions were much more reliant upon white owners.[16]

Indeed, the owner-driven *graciosa* was the most common kind of manumission in Natchitoches, occurring forty-two times and composing half of all manumissions. In a typical *graciosa*, the owner stipulated that a slave be freed immediately after the act was notarized in exchange for loyal services rendered. Very few slaveholders aided their former slaves after emancipation with cash or gifts; in this regard, Coincoin was an exception for Metoyer gave her land and an annual stipend, and she was also fortunate in that Metoyer freed some, but not all, of her children. Fewer than half of the slaveholders in Natchitoches who granted a *graciosa* did so for only one of their bondspersons during their lifetimes, which meant that most *libres* were in the uneasy position of enjoying their free status while being tormented by the knowledge that most of their loved ones were still enslaved. For instance, the unnamed sixty-six-year-old *morena* slave freed by Marie Anne Rousseau, the Widow Buard, most likely left her children in slavery to the Buard family after Rousseau legally freed her. While Rousseau stipulated in her will that it was "up to her heirs to provide her with food and upkeep, principally from Jean Baptiste Buard, who promises to take care of her," there was no guarantee that elderly freed slaves received the support. Moreover, it is important to remember that such generosity was not the norm, for the majority of owners failed to free slaves or give emancipated slaves any money, land, or other financial aid that would ease the transition to a free life that suddenly called for self-sufficiency.

Most Natchitoches *graciosas* freed *pardos* who obtained free status as children because the owners were freeing relatives or concubines. In this regard, the town fell into the pattern of most slave societies in the Americas in which *graciosas* favored *pardo* children. This pattern occurred in Natchitoches more frequently than in New Orleans, where many more *libres* helped to free their loved ones. In fact, one Natchitoches master, François Grappe, accounted for a little more than half of all of the town's *graciosas* when he emancipated twenty-two of his slaves. Grappe intermittently had been purchasing some of his *pardo* children as well as a few of his *morena* mistresses. After owning some of his offspring and concubines for years, on November 13, 1796, Grappe filed a document with the notary that granted them all their liberty at once, accounting for many of the *libres* that suddenly appear in various town counts in the last decades of the Spanish period.[17]

Twenty-seven slaves, or 32.1 percent of manumitted slaves, were recipients of a *graciosa* with conditions, the other kind of owner-driven manumission, which constituted the second most common type of Natchitoches manumission (see table 4.5). In most of these cases, the *graciosas* were conditional because the proprietors stipulated in their wills that slaves be freed upon the proprietors' deaths. One Natchitoches slaveholder, Pierre Badin, singlehandedly accounted for almost three-fourths of all conditional *graciosas* when he signed a will in which he freed his twenty slaves upon his death, which occurred in 1791. The remainder of *graciosas* with conditions also tended to center around the death of a member of the owner's family. In 1802, two *pardas*, five-year-old Marie Françoise and six- month-old Minette, received their freedom because their proprietor, Charlotte Mercier, specified in her will that they would be freed upon her demise. Mercier also specified that her husband, Joseph Capuran, was to care for Minette until she attained twenty-five years of age. The arrangement was generous for Minette even though her mother, a *parda* named Pauline, remained enslaved and her sister had to fend for herself economically. A few other owners stipulated that their slaves be released upon completion of particular services for specified periods of time. For example,

Metoyer drew up a will in 1801 that allowed for the eventual emancipation of one of Coincoin's daughters, Marie Suzanne, on the condition that she care for his legitimate white son, François Benjamin, who was Marie Suzanne's half brother whom she had nursed as an infant. Metoyer specified that his *parda* daughter care for her half brother as long as his legitimate white wife, Marie Thérèze Buard, lived. Marie Suzanne resided in her father's household and served as a house slave until 1813 when Buard died.[18]

Bondspeople could make use of Spanish laws through the slave-driven manumission of self-purchase in which slaves had the legal right to free themselves after they had agreed with their masters on a purchase price. More enterprising slaves acquired the money to purchase themselves through *coartaciones*, but only seven, or 8.3 percent of slaves, were able to overcome the obstacles of Natchitoches slave society and take advantage of this kind of manumission along the Louisiana-Texas frontier (see table 4.5). Throughout Spanish America, including New Orleans, *morenos* tended to have to use self-purchase to get out of slavery because slaves with a darker phenotype lacked white relatives who might grant them *graciosas* or purchase them and grant them liberty. They had to rely upon themselves or relatives to obtain the money, and all seven Natchitoches slaves to instigate *coartaciones* were *morenos*. Throughout Spanish America, bondspeople who received their freedom through self-purchases tended to be older since they had to wait for years to save the amount of money necessary. Natchitoches was no exception, for all seven slaves who benefitted from *coartación* were also adult *morenos*; six were over fifty, likely including the two "very old" *moreno* slaves Pierrot and Nanette, who in May 1777 instigated their *coartaciones* by paying their owner, Louis de la Chaise, 50 piastres each. They stated in the act that they had acquired the money with the help of their *libre* daughter. Another *morena* who purchased herself out of captivity was thirty-six-year-old Marie Anne Douglas, who paid de Vaugine, the commandant's son, 575 piastres to obtain her liberty.[19]

Finally, seven people, or 8.3 percent of manumitted slaves in Natchitoches, attained free status when relatives or friends directly purchased them out of slavery in a third party purchase. These manumissions only reveal whether they were slave-driven or owner-driven by taking into account whether the buyer was a free person of color or a free white person. When the buyer was white, the third party purchase became an owner-driven manumission. When a former slave was the buyer, however, the third person purchase changed in intent and became a slave-driven manumission as it is clear that a former slave took an active role. Coincoin proved again to be an exception among *libres* by being the only former slave to buy and emancipate other slaves through third party purchases. She undertook four of these purchases of her own children and grandchildren in the 1780s after her own emancipation. In contrast, the remaining three slaves to receive freedom through third party purchase were *pardos* bought by white males buyers who were almost certainly also their fathers. The *pardos* were all children between two and fourteen years of age; in each case they were purchased by a white from another slaveholder and emancipated immediately upon purchase. For instance, on September 29, 1799, Jean Baptiste Rachal paid the Widow LeComte 120 piastres for a two-year-old *pardo*, also named Jean Baptiste, "to become free as granted by the buyer." Indeed, when performed by white owners, third party purchases resembled owner-driven *graciosas* for both involved young *pardos* who received emancipation from white male relatives. In light of the paternalism that dominated Natchitoches manumissions, Coincoin's agency in purchasing her own children and grandchildren was all the more remarkable.[20]

Coincoin was not alone, however, for Françoise was another black woman who also displayed an unusual degree of initiative under great pressure from the white establishment. Slaves could go so far as to go to court to obtain their right to manumission under Spanish law. If a slaveholder refused to allow *coartación* or third party purchase, the slave, a relative, or a friend had the legal right to bring that recalcitrant owner to a court's attention. The tribunal would then arbitrate a sum for the slave and, once the proprietor received payment, could enforce the former slave's right to remain out of the owner's control. In Natchitoches, only one slave, Françoise, Marie Poissot's slave, employed this type of manumission, which required an aggressive pursuance of one's legal rights. Françoise, a twenty-nine-year-old *parda*, received the 500 piastres to purchase her own freedom from her free *pardo* brother Pierre in 1783. When she attempted to purchase her liberty, however, her mistress refused on the grounds that Françoise was worth more. Françoise insisted that she be appraised; Poissot's agent estimated she was worth 1,000 piastres, while she estimated her own worth at 600 piastres. With the help of her free *pardo* brother and *libre* father, Jeannot Mulon, and after extensive negotiations with her acrimonious owner, the court allowed Françoise the right to purchase herself for 600 piastres on August 9, 1784. Thirteen days later, Mulon confirmed his daughter's manumission in the capital, ending the family's two-year legal struggle. Françoise's story parallels the experiences of many New Orleans *libres* who attained free status with the aid of *libre* relatives who provided not only financial resources but psychological support as well. After her emancipation, Françoise worked as the commandant's cook.[21]

Natchitoches owners drove most manumissions. *Graciosas*, which were all owner-driven manumissions whether or not they included conditions, dominated Natchitoches records, numbering 69 of the 84, composing 82.1 percent of manumissions. In New Orleans, only 870 out of 1,921, or 45.3 percent, were *graciosas* with and without conditions. In fact, in the capital, self-purchase and tribunal manumissions that were slave-driven and slave-driven third party purchases were much more common than along the Louisiana-Texas frontier. Third party manumissions in Natchitoches only occurred 8.3 percent of the time while in the capital these acts occurred with 445 slaves, or 23.2 percent of cases. *Coartaciones* in New Orleans took place for 452 individuals, or 23.5 percent of the time, while in Natchitoches it was much more unusual for slaves to purchase themselves, only occurring in 8.3 percent of cases. The tribunal procedure, which required slaves to know and pursue their legal rights aggressively, was employed by only one Natchitoches slave, Françoise, while in the capital, 154 slaves, or 8 percent of manumitted slaves, pursued their owners for the right to self-purchase. While many New Orleans *libres* depended upon one another to attain free status, fewer Natchitoches free people of color—Coincoin and Françoise stand out—were able to overcome the great obstacles presented by the entrenched paternalism and isolation of that Creole plantation slave society.[22]

Life after Slavery

Along the Louisiana-Texas frontier, *libres* struggled to survive financially within the expanding plantation-style economy that was deemphasizing trade-based activities. In contrast, in the capital and other coastal towns, the growth of the free black population owed to the variety of economic opportunities open to slaves in port cities as well as lenient Hispanic slave laws that sanctioned manumissions. Thus, the *libre* population of New Orleans expanded under more independent circumstances than the *libre* population of Natchitoches.

Another major obstacle for Natchitoches *libres* after manumission was that Natchitoches slaveholders who manumitted their bondspeople tended to be whites, rather than fellow *libres* (table 4.6). The majority of kinspeople or relatives who sought to free slaves were white males like Metoyer. While Coincoin clearly showed amazing resilience after Metoyer abandoned her, she continued to rely on Metoyer for most of the advantages she had, such as food, lodging, and money. *Libres* were also more likely to help bondspeople secure their liberty in New Orleans than in Natchitoches, where Coincoin was the only free person of color responsible for manumissions. In contrast, *libres* in New Orleans manumitted 10.9 percent of a total of 209 slaves and came to constitute a well-organized group that actively sought manumissions. Perhaps because the port city provided more opportunities for employment, many free

Table 4.6 Owner's Phenotype and Sex by Type of Manumission, Natchitoches, 1774–1803

Owner's Phenotype and Sex	*Graciosa*	Conditional	*Coartación*	Third Party	Tribunal	Total
White Female	4	3	2	0	0	9
White Male	37	24	5	3	0	69
Libre Female	1	0	0	4	1	6
Libre Male	0	0	0	0	0	0
Total	42	27	7	7	1	84

Source: NPCR; Melrose Collection; AGI, PC.

blacks became financially self-sufficient and began to participate in Spanish society as a corporate group through a free black militia and a fraternal order in the church. In turn, their relative independence from whites made them more capable of emancipating enslaved relatives and friends than *libres* in Natchitoches. Because of the lack of economic opportunities outside of the plantation economy for the few *libres* along the Louisiana-Texas frontier, they continued to depend upon white male slaveholders as a means for recruiting new members, perpetuating a paternalism that circumscribed *libres* even after manumission.[23]

Upon receiving their freedom through manumission, slaves in Natchitoches started their new lives as free people in a town that had few other *libres* with whom to associate. *Libres* in Natchitoches only began to develop an adequate population base and a sense of community after 1793, a late date in comparison with New Orleans. Starting in the 1770s, an average of 44.4 manumissions occurred every year in New Orleans, and this figure increased to 53 and 62.8 in the following two decades. Because more *libres* in the capital began receiving their liberty earlier in the era of Spanish rule, slave-driven manumissions were more common, and *libres* were able to develop a sense of self-sufficient community.[24]

As late as 1787, the fourteen *libres* in Natchitoches were not only few in number but lived far from one another in a settlement already characterized by widely dispersed plantations. Though Coincoin became the matriarch of the *libres* at Isle Brevelle only eight years later, in 1787 she was still only a recently manumitted mother with three free *pardo* children who lived as Metoyer's mistress in his household and was financially dependent upon him. Though two other free people of color lived nearby, they were Pierre, a *moreno*, and Nicolas Piquery, a *pardo*; both were poor and lived alone as bachelors. Because Coincoin and her children had ties to a wealthy planter like Metoyer, they held a higher status and had more stable lives than these two poor *libre* men, but they were more circumscribed than these men with no children. Another free *morena* concubine, Ursule Bernarde, and her three *pardo* children lived on Antoine Guichard's plantation and also rarely interacted with other *libres*.

Aside from poor bachelors and African concubines with *pardo* infants, the remaining *libres* in 1787 were orphaned children who lived in white households. One such child was Marie Agnes Poissot. In 1770, Agnes was born in the household of a white planter, Pierre Derbanne, and was the daughter of his slave, Françoise. When she was six years old, a neighboring planter who was her father, Athanase Poissot, gave Derbanne a seven year old black girl he owned and took Marie Agnes home. Two months later Agnes's grandfather, Remy Poissot, emancipated her, and she eventually went to live with the Rachal family because Athanase Poissot's wife objected to her presence.[25] At the Cane River settlement, members of the LeComte family were raising two orphans, a mestizo named Jacques and a mulatta named Marguerite. Nearby, Pelagie Lecourt or LaCourt, an orphaned quadroon, or child of a mulatta mother and a white father, also lived with a white family. Whether a Natchitoches *libre* was a white man's mistress or child or a bachelor trying to eke out a living, these few free people of color shared little in common aside from a Spanish corporate identity that defined them as *libres*. Moreover, it is quite likely that Coincoin and her *pardo* children—like Ursule Bernarde and hers— stood to jeopardize their already uneasy standing as free people of color in a plantation slave society by associating with blacks, even fellow *libres*, instead of whites. Their dispersion among scattered households, few numbers, and precarious social standing all helped to foster circumstances in which *libres* found it more natural to interact and establish closer ties with whites than with one another.[26]

Continued Dependence upon Whites after Manumission

Because most *libres* in the Spanish period gained their freedom through manumissions that failed to include any financial help to ease their transition to free person, most *libres* had to continue to work hard after emancipation and most often found themselves in the employment of whites as before. Free women of color in particular had more burdens to bear than their male counterparts because they were responsible for feeding and caring for children. Coincoin was more successful than most *libres* as she had help from Metoyer and her emancipated sons and daughters. She was able to undertake a variety of occupations after her residence in a small cabin on a sixty-eight-acre land grant from Metoyer. She cultivated tobacco and indigo and sold bear oil and medicines. In contrast, other *libre* women were less independent. Like most women in Natchitoches, whether free or enslaved, female *libres* tended to perform work that the wider culture associated with motherhood and domesticity; they wet-nursed and cared for white children as well as their own, performed domestic work such as laundry and planting provisions, and nursed the ill or elderly. For instance, Coincoin's *libre* sister, Marie Louise dit Mariotte, signed a contract with the Frenchman Antoine Bergeron in which she agreed to do his laundry for a year in exchange for land.[27]

Libre men also tended to continue working for whites after their emancipation. Jean Lebrun dit Mulon, a *pardo libre* who was also Françoise's father, was fluent in Caddoan, an indigenous language. Creole traders hired him as a translator in the Indian trade, and he came to own land near the Natchitoches Indian village near town. While more successful free people of color accepted cash for payment, most *libres*—like Indians and slaves—were more likely to engage in informal exchanges involving manual labor for goods or foodstuffs. For instance, a *pardo libre* named Regis directed the production of indigo at Jean Baptiste Dartigaux's plantation for one year for 180 piastres and a good horse. One free *moreno* man, Jean Pierre, contracted with Jean Baptiste Ailhaud St. Anne, a French merchant from Dauphiné, for one year as an overseer for 120 piastres. Jean Pierre's duties included directing the slaves as they cleared new land for planting and rowed on Ailhaud St. Anne's boat to New Orleans.[28]

Because Natchitoches *libres* lived and worked in close proximity to whites, *libres* came to see social connections with whites as a more realistic means for obtaining success for both themselves and their children than connections to fellow *libres* or slaves. In fact, *libres* actively sought to reinforce their paternalistic ties to whites by selecting white godparents for their children. Within a hierarchical society, fictive or ritual kinship such as godparenthood (*compadrazgo*), or the selection of godparents for a child's baptism, linked people of lower status to those of higher standing. Through this fictive kinship, those of higher standing and those of lower standing were tied in a client and patron relationship. Most *libre* parents strove to choose godparents of equal or preferably higher status in order to allow their children the possibility of gaining privileges. As Louisiana was not only a slave society but a patriarchal one as well, the godfather was a more important connection for children. In New Orleans, *libre* parents elected a white godfather in 56.5 percent of cases. Nevertheless, a majority still opted to select a free black godmother from the *libre* community 60.1 percent of the time. In the capital, the *libres*' more independent and stable community permitted some *libres* to succeed, and free black parents came to rely upon other *libres* almost as often as whites. In contrast, along the Louisiana-Texas frontier, where whites clearly were the only group of higher standing, *libre* parents tended to select both white godfathers and white godmothers for their offspring in 65.5 percent of cases. The Natchitoches preference for both godmothers and godfathers to be white suggests that *libres* had little practical choice but to acknowledge their dependence upon free whites in order to ensure their children's success.[29]

Echoing the close ties their founding mother Coincoin had with Metoyer, *libres* of Isle Brevelle also chose to adopt dominant white values in their community. They avoided social ties with slaves, which would have put a free black family at risk of being downwardly mobile within plantation society's rigid hierarchy, and sought to contract marital ties only with other *libres* or whites. As the Metoyers *de couleur* began forming a plantation-based colony at Isle Brevelle, more and more Natchitoches-born *libres* married into the community. Metoyers frequently wed the LeComtes *de couleur* mentioned in the census of 1787, many of whom had resided at the upper end of the Rivière aux Cannes settlement just below Isle Brevelle. For example, Dominique Metoyer married Margueritte LeComte in 1795, while six years later Pierre Metoyer wed Marie Perine LeComte. A few other Natchitoches free people of color also established unions with Metoyers; for instance, Agnes Poissot wed Nicolas Augustin Metoyer in 1792, and Joseph Antoine Metoyer married Marie Pelagie LeCour or LaCour. Denizens of Isle Brevelle also attracted *libres* born outside of town, especially in New Orleans. They also guarded their social status by accepting the few white Frenchmen from Haiti who formed alliances with *libre* mistresses and welcoming the *pardo* children of these unions.[30]

Conclusion

In Natchitoches, while Coincoin and the other *libres* under Spanish rule had a certain amount of agency and certainly made the most of whatever legal and social rights they possessed, the dominant plantation culture made certain that birth and ethnicity circumscribed their lives. Paternalism played such an important role in the way that Natchitoches slaves obtained their freedom that after manumission *libres* such as Coincoin frequently remained culturally and economically tied to the whites. In addition, *libres* lacked the numbers for successful group cohesion throughout most of the Spanish era. The Metoyers of color benefited from the advantages of the close ties to their wealthy planter father and the insightful leadership of their *libre* mother, Coincoin. These siblings looked to the free people of European descent to provide a cultural and economic model and were able to set the stage for the Isle Brevelle *libre* community, which attracted more dynamic *libre* individuals as early as the end of the Spanish period. One bright spot was that the expanding numbers of manumissions late in the period did create a population base that allowed subsequent *libres* to form a flourishing community during the American period. While *libres* established plantations in the late Spanish era, it was not until well into the American era that they and their descendants began to succeed as slave-holding planters. Until the nineteenth century, the *libres* of Isle Brevelle and other Natchitoches *libres* were never able to break from their initial reliance on former white owners or fathers—such as had been the case with Metoyer and Coincoin—soon after manumission. Most historians—no doubt with the subsequent American period on their minds—have tended to view the Spanish regime in Louisiana as a boom time for free people of color because of the lenient laws that led to more frequent manumission. However, it is important to keep in mind that the Spanish reign, the French regime before it, and the American dominion after it had more commonalities than differences from the perspective of slaves and people of color. All of these regimes were essentially committed to maintaining a social order with slaves or people of color at the bottom of society. In all cases, powerful white slaveholders continued to define the existence of free people of color based upon their identity as former slaves or members of nonwhite racial groups, giving *libres* no choice but to respond by separating themselves from slaves. Moreover, the paradoxical position of *libres* as former slaves within Natchitoches slave-holding society forced them to be loyal to the slave system in order to succeed economically, which ironically meant becoming slaveholders in their own right. Thus, the strength of the institution of Natchitoches slavery—no matter whether the slave system was Gallic, Hispanic, or English—reveals that *libres*, unable to form a group identity, were pressed into loyalty to the same slave system that oppressed them. While it is laudable to appreciate the successes of Coincoin and her relatives, most Natchitoches *libres* did the best they could within a society that had consciously developed and maintained cultural and legal traditions intended to keep them down.

Notes

1. Coincoin is one of the better-known colonial residents of Natchitoches. For much more information, see Gary B. Mills, *The Forgotten People: Cane River's Creoles of Color* (Baton Rouge: Louisiana State University Press, 1977), 3, 50–60, which discusses Coincoin in great detail. Marie Thérèze Coincoin's "dit" name, or nickname, "Coincoin," was probably a phonetic variation of a name, Ko Kwé, used among a linguistic group in the Gold Coast/Dahomey region of Africa. However, since other phonetically spelled variations of the name in various sources are "Quoinquin" or "KuenKuoin," it is also possible that Marie Thérèze's nickname was the quacking of a duck in French.

2. In his excellent study, Mills traced the nineteenth-century development of the Isle Brevelle plantation community along Cane River, south of Natchitoches. Isle Brevelle was a narrow strip of land about thirty miles long and about four miles wide delineated by a wandering channel known as Cane River, which was part of the Red River until the 1760s when it took a different course. Mills illuminated the family history of the Metoyers *de couleur*. The study's focus was the nineteenth century, when the isle, populated largely by Coincoin's relatives, flourished into a prosperous plantation community that collapsed during the turbulent economic and political conditions during the Civil War and Reconstruction.

3. Elizabeth Shown Mills, "Quintanilla's Crusade, 1775–1783: 'Moral Reform' and Its Consequences on the Natchitoches Frontier," *Louisiana History* 42 (Summer 2001): 277–302, shows that the Capuchin priest Father Louis de Quintanilla attempted yet failed to impose various moral reforms in Natchitoches.

4. After Coincoin's manumission, she had two more children by Metoyer who were born free due to the status of their mother while Metoyer ensured through his will that their five other enslaved children were to be free at his death. In 1786, Metoyer and Coincoin agreed to dissolve their relationship, but as long as Metoyer was still alive, their *pardo* sons and daughters were slaves who lived like free people; upon his death they were to attain legal freedom. Relieved of responsibility to her *pardo* children, Coincoin began purchasing and freeing *moreno* relatives, including the two daughters she had had before Metoyer and two grandchildren.

5. G. Mills, *The Forgotten People*, 66. By the time Louisiana went to the United States in 1803, Coincoin and her relatives had a total of nineteen claims for land based on Pierre Metoyer's donations, land purchases, and Spanish land grants; the author would like to thank Elizabeth Shown Mills for sharing the findings of her unpublished essay, "Which Marie Louise Is 'Mariotte'? Sorting Slaves with Common Names," dated December 10, 2005. Mills shows that Mary Louise dit Mariotte was Coincoin's sister rather than her daughter.

6. Kimberly S. Hanger, *Bounded Lives, Bounded Places: Free Black Society in Colonial New Orleans, 1769–1803* (Durham, N.C.: Duke University Press, 1997), 24, argued that in Louisiana the Crown fostered the increase of a *libre* population to fill middle-sector occupations, defend the colony, and mollify slaves by providing an officially approved means of realizing their desires for liberty. Gilbert C. Din, *Spaniards, Planters, and Slaves: The Spanish Regulation of Slavery in Louisiana, 1763–1803* (College Station: Texas A & M University Press, 1999), 223–24, and Thomas N. Ingersoll, *Mammon and Manon in Early New Orleans: The First Slave Society in the Deep South, 1718–1819* (Knoxville: University of Tennessee Press, 1999), 344, countered that Louisiana's free people of color grew in number because of more lenient laws, not official policy, for the idea of a privileged *libre* class within a slave society was improbable.

7. Hanger, *Bounded Lives, Bounded Places*, 57, examined the *libre* community in the capital of New Orleans, where more than two-thirds of Louisiana's *libres* resided in the Spanish era. She used censuses and manumissions to trace their numerical increase and showed the development of a corporate identity through marriage, fictive

kinship, and participation in free black militias and religious fraternities. A great deal has been published about free blacks in New Orleans: see, for example, Thomas N. Ingersoll, "Free Blacks in a Slave Society: New Orleans, 1718–1812," *William and Mary Quarterly* 48 (1991): 173–200; Paul F. Lachance, "The Formation of a Three-Caste Society: Evidence from Wills in Antebellum New Orleans," *Social Science History* 18 (1994): 211–42; Donald E. Everett, "Emigres and Militiamen: Free Persons of Color in New Orleans, 1803–1815," *Journal of Negro History* 38 (1953): 377–402; Donald E. Everett, "Free Persons of Color in Colonial Louisiana," *Louisiana History* 7 (1966): 21–50; Laura Foner, "The Free People of Color in Louisiana and St. Domingue: A Comparative Portrait of Two Three-Caste Slave Societies," *Journal of Social History* 3 (1970): 406–30.

8. Important social histories of colonial Louisiana include Daniel H. Usner, Jr., *Indians, Settlers, and Slaves in a Frontier Exchange Economy: The Lower Mississippi Valley before 1783* (Chapel Hill: University of North Carolina Press, 1992); Gwendolyn Midlo Hall, *Africans in Colonial Louisiana: The Development of Afro-Creole Culture in the Eighteenth Century* (Baton Rouge: Louisiana State University Press, 1992); and Ingersoll, *Mammon and Manon*, all of which touch upon the free black and Indian population during the French and Spanish eras. See also Virginia Meacham Gould, "In Full Enjoyment of Their Liberty: The Free Women of Color of the Gulf Ports of New Orleans, Mobile, and Pensacola, 1769–1860" (Ph.D. diss., Emory University, 1991); Virginia Meacham Gould, "The Free Creoles of Color of the Antebellum Gulf Ports of Mobile and Pensacola: A Struggle for the Middle Ground," in James H. Dorman, ed., *Creoles of Color of the Gulf South* (Knoxville: University of Tennessee Press, 1996), 28–50; Carl A. Brasseaux, "Creoles of Color in Louisiana's Bayou Country, 1766–1877," in Dorman, *Creoles of Color*, 67–86; Carl A. Brasseaux, Keith P. Fontenot, and Claude F. Oubre, *Creoles of Color in the Bayou Country* (Jackson: University Press of Mississippi, 1994).

9. Peter A. Coclanis, "The Captivity of a Generation," *William and Mary Quarterly* 61 (July 2004): 544–55 is a review article of Ira Berlin, *Generations of Captivity: A History of African-American Slaves* (Cambridge and London: The Belknap Press of Harvard University Press, 2003). Coclanis points out that it does an injustice to *libres* or slaves to exaggerate examples of their agency when their lives were actually circumscribed by a plantation slave system dedicated to servicing the slaveholder. Likewise, to overemphasize the agency of *libres* or slaves under Spanish rule overlooks the fact that the Spanish Bourbons had a commitment to economic development through the consolidation of a slave regime begun under French rule. In this respect, their intentions marked both the French and Spanish colonizers as more similar to future settlers from the United States than dissimilar from the perspective of slaves and people of color.

10. Din, *Spaniards, Planters, and Slaves*, 223–24; Hanger, *Bounded Lives, Bounded Places*, 24; Hanger, "Origins of New Orleans's Free Creoles of Color," in Dorman, *Creoles of Color*, 6.

11. The author would like to thank Virginia (Ginger) Meacham Gould for running the names or nicknames of about one hundred Natchitoches *libres* (obtained from manumissions, notarial documents, parish records, or censuses) through her database of *libres* in Spanish New Orleans. Even though Meacham Gould found no Natchitoches *libres* residing in New Orleans, the findings are inconclusive because of the changeable spelling of names and frequent use of nicknames in colonial Louisiana. It is probable that some Natchitoches *libres* did move to New Orleans or other posts in Louisiana and Texas.

12. Hanger, *Bounded Lives, Bounded Places*, 22.

13. In "Free Creoles of Color of Mobile and Pensacola," 32, and "In Full Enjoyment of Their Liberty," 81–84, Meacham Gould argues that Mobile, where the Spanish period was from 1781 to 1812, saw an increase in the numbers of free people of color comparable to the capital. The port of Pensacola was Spanish from 1783 to 1821 and its free population even exceeded *libre* growth in Mobile. Hanger, *Bounded Lives, Bounded Places*, 22; Meacham Gould, "Free Creoles of Color of Mobile and Pensacola," 34; Brasseaux, "Creoles of Color in Louisiana's Bayou Country," 69.

14. This study divides Natchitoches manumissions into the same categories employed for New Orleans in Hanger, *Bounded Lives, Bounded Places*, 27–28. Meacham Gould, "In Full Enjoyment of Their Liberty," 90, reports that early manumissions are not available for either Mobile or Pensacola, precluding any comparisons between Natchitoches and these coastal settlements. Brasseaux, "Creoles of Color in Louisiana's Bayou Country," 68, mentions that manumissions fueled the growth of the free black population in Attakapas and Opelousas but does not analyze the types since his article aims to provide an overview between 1766 and 1877 rather than focusing on the Spanish era. As a result, his approach eliminates possible comparisons with Natchitoches manumissions.

15. The discrepancy between the large number of manumissions and the much smaller count in censuses is difficult to explain. Possibly, many *libres* died or left town after emancipation, perhaps opting for the better opportunities in the capital. Another incompatibility between censuses and manumissions is that census takers in Natchitoches consistently reported more males than females in town despite manumissions favoring females. Hanger, "Origins of New Orleans's Free Creoles of Color," 5, notes that New Orleans censuses undercounted *libres*, and perhaps Spanish census takers in Natchitoches undercounted free persons of color as well.

16. Liberty Accorded to Calhiche by Jean Baptiste Grappe, April 21, 1796, Natchitoches Parish Conveyance Records, Microfilm Copy, Genealogy Library, The Church of Jesus Christ of Latter Day Saints, Dallas (hereafter NPCR), book 27. Hanger, *Bounded Lives, Bounded Places*, 23, 27, finds that female *libres* in New Orleans outnumbered males two to one because about twice as many females were manumitted while males tended to die young. Meacham Gould, "Free Creoles of Color of Mobile and Pensacola," 34, reports that Mobile's free women of color outnumbered their male counterparts 105 to 100 in 1805, while in Pensacola 151 female *libres* outnumbered 101

male *libres* in 1820. Brasseaux, "Creoles of Color in Louisiana's Bayou Country," 69, notes that of 269 and 380 *libres* in Attakapas and Opelousas, respectively, the censuses failed to differentiate by sex.

17. Will and Testament of Marie Anne Rousseau, November 14, 1791, NPCR, book 21. G. Mills, *The Forgotten People*, 22, 26, 41–44, notes that Metoyer emancipated Coincoin in 1778, but he freed some of his children with conditions. Metoyer waited until 1787 to begin paying an annual stipend of 120 piastres to Coincoin, which he later made conditional. Even after his marriage to a white woman, Metoyer supported his *libre* and enslaved relatives through informal cash payments and land grants. Liberty Accorded to 22 Pardo and Moreno Slaves by François Grappe, November 13, 1796, NPCR, book 27.

18. Will and Testament of Charlotte Mercier, November 10, 1802, Melrose Collection, folder 731; G. Mills, *The Forgotten People*, 44 reports that Marie Suzanne's manumission only took effect in the American period after 1803, which was characteristic of many manumissions written in the Spanish era; Will and Testament of Pierre Badin, October 30, 1791, NPCR, book 21.

19. Self-Purchase, Marie Anne Douglas to Etienne de Vaugine, fils, December 7, 1787, NPCR, book 19; Self-Purchases, Pierrot and Nanette to Louis de la Chaisse de St. Denis, May 30, 1777, NPCR, book 10; see entry number 579 in Elizabeth Shown Mills, *Natchitoches, 1729–1803: Abstracts of the Catholic Church Registers of the French and Spanish Post of St. Jean Baptiste des Natchitoches in Louisiana* (New Orleans: Polyanthos, 1977), in which Manuel Marianne, born November 11, 1754, was the daughter of Nanette and Pierrot, *morenos* belonging to Madame de St. Denis.

20. Meacham Gould, "In Full Enjoyment of Their Liberty," 90–92; Hanger, *Bounded Lives, Bounded Places*, 30; Sale, Slave, Widow LeComte to Jean Baptiste Rachal, September 29, 1799, NPCR, book 30; Sale and Manumission, Slave, Jean Baptiste Buard to Emmanuel Derbanne, November 10, 1798, NPCR, book 30. Derbanne paid 150 piastres for Sylvie, a two-and-a-half-year-old mulatta, whom he freed; Sale and Manumission, Slave, of Antoine, François Grappe to Louis Lamalathie, December 9, 1795, NPCR, book 27. Lamalathie paid 400 piastres for Antoine, a fourteen-year-old *pardo*, before manumitting him.

21. Hanger, *Bounded Lives, Bounded Places*, 27, 30, notes that tribunal manumissions were also rare in New Orleans, composing only 8 percent of manumissions; Meacham Gould, "In Full Enjoyment of Their Liberty," 90–92; Inventory of Goods of Jacques Lambre and Marie Anne Poissot, December 5, 1782, NPCR, book 17; Petition of Jeannot LeBrun dit Mulon to Governor General, April 17, 1784, legajo 197, AGI, PC; Widow Lambre to Commandant, April 28, 1784, legajo 197, AGI, PC; Self-Estimate of Françoise, August 2, 1784, legajo 197, AGI, PC; Françoise's request to go to New Orleans, August 5, 1784, legajo 197, AGI, PC; Françoise's Declaration of Departure to New Orleans, August 7, 1784, legajo 197, AGI, PC; Widow Lambre's Declaration of Manumission of Françoise, August 9, 1784, legajo 197, AGI, PC; Vaugine to Miro, August 20, 1784, legajo 197, AGI, PC; Testimony of Françoise, free mulatta, December 26, 1784, legajo 197, AGI, PC.

22. See Table 1.4 in Hanger, *Bounded Lives, Bounded Freedom*, 27–28, for comparisons with Natchitoches.

23. See Table 1.8 in Hanger, *Bounded Lives, Bounded Places*, 33, for comparisons; E. Mills, *Natchitoches, 1729-1803*; using sources other than the NPCR, Melrose Collection, and AGI, PC, G. Mills, *The Forgotten People*, 38, 64–65 traces a child and a grandchild whom Coincoin successfully freed in Opelousas as well as some relatives Coincoin emancipated in Natchitoches. He also finds that her son, Nicolas Agustin Metoyer, purchased three slaves whom he freed in the late Spanish period; most *libres* owed their freedom to white men rather than white women; only 11.9 percent of Natchitoches slaveholders who emancipated slaves were white women while 19.2 percent of New Orleans slaveholders who manumitted slaves were white women.

24. Hanger, *Bounded Lives, Bounded Places*, 21, charts manumissions in New Orleans, which begin in 1771, by decade.

25. G. Mills, *The Forgotten People*, 81–82; Marie Agnes Poissot eventually married Nicolas Augustin Metoyer, Coincoin's son, in 1792 and resided at Isle Brevelle.

26. "1787 Census of Natchitoches, August 17, 1787," in Elizabeth Shown Mills, ed., *Natchitoches Colonials: Censuses, Military Rolls, and Tax Lists, 1722-1803* (Chicago: Adams Press, 1981), 45–62; Liberty Accorded to Agnes Poissot, parda, by Remy Poissot, March 8, 1775, NPCR, book 8; Liberty Accorded to Agnes Poissot, parda, by Remy Poissot, March 8, 1776, NPCR, book 13, is either a reiteration or a new act of manumission.

27. Contract, Bertrand Mailloche and Marie Louise dit Mariotte, free black woman, October 11, 1794, NPCR, book M; Contract, Antoine Bergeron and Mariotte, free black woman, January 4, 1799, NPCR, book 30; G. Mills, *The Forgotten People*, 28–32, 42; Will and Testament of Marie Conand, August 26, 1799, folder 723, Melrose Collection; Will and Testament of Pierre Metoyer, April 27, 1801, folder 728, Melrose Collection.

28. Since it was unusual for freedmen or slaves to have family names such as Lebrun, he probably was the son of Guillaume Bossier Lebrun, a Frenchman, and an unknown slave mother of African descent; Land Sale, St. Denis to Jeannot Mulon, September 15, 1768, NPCR, book 2; Contract, Mulon and Gerome Matuliche, May 28, 1775, NPCR, book 8. Matuliche hired Mulon as an interpreter as well as a hired man to work on his boats and cure peltries for a year for 500 piastres. Mulon was a valued employee because of his fluency in Caddoan for Matuliche added an unheard of stipulation, allowing Mulon to trade on his own account 100 francs of merchandise; Contract, Jean Pierre and Jean Baptiste Ailhaud St. Anne, December 31, 1787, NPCR, book 20; Contract, Regis and Jean Baptiste Dartigaux, June 24, 1794, NPCR, book 25.

29. G. Mills, *The Forgotten People*, 50–60; Hanger, *Bounded Lives, Bounded Places*, 105, discusses the role of fictive kinship in uniting New Orleans *libres* as do Stephen Gudman and Stuart B. Schwartz, "Cleansing Original Sin: Godparenthood and the Baptism of Slaves in Eighteenth-Century Bahia," in Raymond Smith, ed., *Kinship Ideology and Practice in Latin America* (Chapel Hill: University of North Carolina Press, 1984), 35–58.

30. G. Mills, *The Forgotten People*, 22, 77–78, details the genealogical origins of most *libres* who married Metoyers *de couleur*. Some *libres* from Rivière aux Cannes were probably former Lipan Apache slaves.

5

To Strike a Balance

New Orleans' Free Colored Community and the Diplomacy of William Charles Cole Claiborne

ERIN M. GREENWALD

For contemporary observers, New Orleans in 1803 must have seemed a terribly chaotic place. In the last months of that year, the heterogeneous hodgepodge of peoples that constituted the city's population witnessed firsthand the instability of their provincial outpost at the edge of empire in a remarkable series of public ceremonies on the Place d'Armes, in which the very symbol of empire was hoisted up or down no less than four times.[1] By the time the Americans raised their standard on December 20, the populace was surely suffering from *une crise d'identité* that had no parallel even in Louisiana's own rather tumultuous past. French Creoles, Spanish administrators, African slaves, American traders, Native Americans, and a burgeoning population of free people of color struggled to make sense of their world and of each other. Divided as the population was by religion, politics, race, and language, the prospect of stable governance in the newly American city must have seemed slim. Indeed, as Thomas Jefferson quickly discovered, few qualified candidates displayed any interest in attempting to govern in such a blatantly unstable political environment.[2]

With the 1803 cession of Louisiana from France to the United States, President Jefferson faced the challenging task of selecting a leader capable of integrating a population whose language, political customs, and religion differed greatly from those of the majority of the American populace. The capacity to guide Louisiana's inhabitants toward a political landscape that was more representative of the emerging American model was a fundamental component of Jefferson's expectations for the incoming governor. Yet despite repeated attempts to appoint an experienced leader, Jefferson failed to convince any of his preferred candidates of the political gains to be had from entering what were essentially the uncharted waters of American colonization. Instead, Jefferson granted what he hoped would be an interim appointment as governor of Orleans Territory to twenty-eight-year-old William C. C. Claiborne, who was then serving as the governor of the nearby Mississippi Territory (fig. 5.1).[3] Despite Claiborne's inexperience with international affairs (and his nearly complete ignorance of the French language), he successfully parlayed the experience he gained as a frontier mediator in the Mississippi Territory into the ability to diffuse repeatedly the potentially explosive animosity between incoming American settlers, Louisiana Creoles, and New Orleans's free colored community. In his repeated attempts to strike a balance between the free colored and white populations in New Orleans, Claiborne revealed a chameleon-like ability to adapt his diplomatic prowess to the needs and temperaments of each group.

Born in the midst of revolutionary fervor in Sussex County, Virginia, William Charles Cole Claiborne (1775–1817) grew up listening to his father recount proofs of his dedication to the cause of American independence. According to William's brother Nathaniel, their father "impressed upon their minds an invincible attachment to free government" that served as a guiding principle in William's life.[4] Unable to rely on his family for financial support, William left Virginia for New York at the age of fifteen hoping to secure a clerkship under John Beckley, a fellow Virginian serving as a congressional clerk to the House of Representatives. Successful in his bid for employment, Claiborne settled into his duties as enrollment clerk, "copying bills and resolutions of congress, and drawing original bills for members and committees." When Congress moved from New York to Philadelphia in 1790, Claiborne followed.[5]

In Philadelphia, Claiborne began cultivating the network of powerful associates who would help launch his own political career. Chief among these connections was Thomas Jefferson. Claiborne's oratory skill also caught the attention of John Sevier, who represented the "Territory South of the Ohio River." At Sevier's suggestion, Claiborne undertook formal preparation to practice law. Sevier likely foresaw the need for jurists in the western territory that would soon become Tennessee and viewed Claiborne as a suitable, non-threatening supporter. By 1794 Claiborne was practicing law in Sullivan County. Two years later, the twenty-one-year-old Virginian found himself among those individuals selected to draft the state constitution for Tennessee.[6]

From 1796 until his appointment as governor of the Orleans Territory in 1803, Claiborne moved rapidly through a series of increasingly public roles. It was as Tennessee's sole delegate to the House of Representatives, however, that Claiborne assumed a central role in breaking the deadlock that resulted in the "Revolution of 1800," thereby strengthening his ties to the national gov-

Figure 5.1. William Charles Cole Claiborne, ca. 1805, by Ambrose Duval, courtesy of The Historic New Orleans Collection, accession no. 1975.142.

ernment. With Thomas Jefferson and Aaron Burr tied in electoral votes for the presidency, the responsibility for determining the outcome lay with the House. As a relative newcomer, Claiborne fell outside the delicate political balance that existed between the Republicans and Federalists in the House. Each side sought Claiborne's approbation in hopes of turning the tide in its favor, but Claiborne's loyalty lay with his former Philadelphia mentor, Thomas Jefferson. On February 17, 1801, Jefferson became president of the United States after thirty-five unsuccessful attempts to break the tie. W. C. C. Claiborne remained faithful in his support of Jefferson through all thirty-six ballots.[7]

With Jefferson ensconced in the nation's highest office, Claiborne soon reaped a reward for his faithfulness to the Republicans. A combination of factors led to Claiborne's appointment as governor of the Mississippi Territory in 1801. Although his unwavering loyalty may have won him Jefferson's favor, Claiborne's experience on the Tennessee frontier and Jefferson's desire to turn Mississippi's unstable political landscape to the favor of the Republicans ultimately led to his gubernatorial appointment.[8] Essential to the stability of the Mississippi Territory was the maintenance of stable relations between the territory's diverse Native American population and the ever-increasing number of white settlers. One of Claiborne's primary roles in Mississippi would be to supervise Indian affairs in the territory. Claiborne had experience with the types of problems that stemmed from settler expansion into disputed land holdings prior to his Mississippi appointment, but his direct contact with the Creek and Cherokee in Tennessee had been fairly limited. As Tennessee's delegate to the House of Representatives, Claiborne served on a committee designed to hear settlers' land grievances against the Cherokee in Tennessee and the Creek in Georgia who publicly disputed American land claims. The land dispute ended in October 1798 when the Cherokee agreed to cede the disputed land in the Treaty of Tellico.[9] Over the course of 1799, Claiborne continued to gain experience as chair of the House's Indian Affairs committee whose primary aim was to maintain peaceful relations with local tribes and to impose stringent penalties on persons whose actions "alienated the confidence of the Indians from the government of the United States." Much of the legislation introduced at this time reflected the ever-present concern that Native Americans in the South and Southwest might be enticed into Spanish service, or worse, British service, thereby upsetting the volatile peace in the borderlands.[10]

Claiborne's indirect experience with Native Americans prior to his first territorial appointment did little to prepare him for the complicated battle for land and resources already underway between the Mississippi Choctaw, American settlers, and British land speculators when he arrived in late November 1801.[11] Unsure of how to behave in his capacity as superintendent of Indian Affairs and wary of repeating the missteps of his predecessor, Winthrop Sargent, Claiborne first sought guidance from the federal government. Three weeks after his arrival in the Mississippi Territory, Claiborne wrote to Secretary of State James Madison requesting that the "Powers, duties & Emoluments" of the position be defined. Claiborne knew full well the humiliation Sargent had suffered in "the Indian Department" and wished to ensure that he would not find himself similarly impeded.[12] After experiencing persistent problems of theft in the Natchez area—problems Claiborne attributed to bands of Choctaws—

Claiborne pleaded with Secretary of War Henry Dearborn for someone to outline his duties as superintendent of Indian Affairs.[13]

On April 18, nearly four months after Claiborne's initial inquiry, the governor received Dearborn's much anticipated yet ambiguous response. Saying nothing of Claiborne's power to arbitrate in the face of Indian antagonism, Dearborn stated simply that "all means in our power should be unremittingly pursued for carrying into effect the benevolent views of Congress relative to the Indian Nations." He then highlighted President Jefferson's wish that Claiborne encourage agricultural pursuits and the establishment of trade between the Indians and the settlers to promote friendship and "the introduction of Civilization" to the Indian nations of the Southwest.[14]

Claiborne frequently sought guidance from the federal level prior to entering into uncharted political territory in order to ensure alignment with and acknowledgment from the Jefferson administration. But the administration usually responded with a very rough overview of instructions, choosing to depend on Claiborne to interpret policy through an appropriately local and Republican lens. Despite his incessant calls for advice and the vague instructions he repeatedly received from the Jefferson administration, Claiborne himself determined the most effective way to maintain order among the heterogeneous population while diffusing any potential uprising caused by the American takeover.[15]

Perhaps in an effort to slow the near-constant stream of inquiries from Claiborne as much as to give encouragement to the inexperienced governor, Madison wrote, "We rely much . . . on your patriotic dispositions and prudent counsels which as they develop themselves cannot fail to inspire."[16] Such lenient supervision of a young and relatively inexperienced politician suggests a certain naiveté at the federal level regarding the potentially explosive relationship between white settlers and their more numerous native counterparts in the Mississippi Valley. More significantly perhaps, the administration's laissez-faire attitude toward Claiborne's handling of the Mississippi Territory's native population reveals that later plans for Indian removal remained as yet unformulated in the early years of Jefferson's first term.

In Mississippi, Claiborne preferred calm negotiation to explicit action when faced with questions of conflict between opposing groups of native and non-native inhabitants. It is likely that the dearth of adequate numbers of armed militia as well as "a general want of arms" among those militia active in the territory contributed significantly to Claiborne's tendency to seek peaceful resolution. Claiborne noted the shortage of arms and militia in the Mississippi Territory in his correspondence with both Madison and General James Wilkinson, citing the danger of such an exposed position in a territory "surrounded as it is, by numerous Indian Tribes, and with a population of Negroes, nearly equal to the number of whites."[17]

Claiborne's comportment as superintendent of Indian Affairs while governor of the Mississippi Territory can, in some ways, be seen as a preview of his later dealings with New Orleans's free colored population. Vulnerable to political instability that could spill over into an armed conflict, which Claiborne was ill prepared to meet, he avoided an aggressive response that would have required an organized American military presence to sustain. Instead, Claiborne maintained stability in the territories through diplomatic means. In Mississippi, Claiborne set the political precedent of holding private meetings intended to resolve issues of contention between non-white and white territorial inhabitants. The first formal meeting between Claiborne and a group of local Native Americans took place in April 1802. Acting on complaints from white settlers in the Natchez area who protested the "frequent and oppressive" raids on settler property by Choctaws camped out along the perimeter of the settlement who sustained "themselves principally by depredations upon the Cattle Hogs &c &c of the Citizens," Claiborne called for a formal meeting between himself and several Choctaw at the Government House in Natchez.[18]

The address that Claiborne delivered reflected his desire to appear in touch with his Choctaw guests, a tactic he employed with increasing efficacy as his political career matured. Claiborne's speech, however, failed to conceal a decidedly paternalistic message that placed the Choctaw in a dependent relationship to their white neighbors. Claiborne spoke initially of the friendship that he hoped would flourish among white settlers and local tribes "as long as the Mountains stand, or the Waters Run," but he spoke to those gathered at the Government House in Natchez as he would to dependents. Speaking "with the freedom of a Father," Claiborne urged the Choctaw men to listen well to his advice to leave the settlement and lead productive lives free of debauchery (which would turn them into "Fools & Old Women") and "Idleness."[19]

After enumerating the offences that had sparked a rash of complaints from American settlers on the periphery of Natchez, the governor, in a rather disingenuous profession of his belief in the Choctaw's innocence, affirmed, "I know you would not take anything that was not your own, but I must tell you, that if anything should be missing in this Town or Country hereafter, I will have your Camps searched, and if I discover that any of you have acted improperly, you shall be punished according to the White People's Laws."[20] Behind this thinly veiled threat lay Claiborne's belief that this particular group of Choctaw was in fact guilty of the charges brought forward by the settlers. In a letter to Dearborn, Claiborne described the Choctaw camped in the Natchez vicinity as "very worthless characters" but he differentiated between the wider Choctaw community and this particular group, who were "in a measure disowned by their Nation, & declared by their Chiefs to be a set of Vagabonds, whom they cannot control." This was an important differentiation; for while some may have ignored such a distinction, Claiborne recognized that the callous acts of the few were not necessarily the trademark of all. In fact, Claiborne admitted candidly that American settlers played a destructive role in increasing the likelihood of misconduct among local natives by furnishing them with "Strong Drink" despite the territorial laws that prohibited them from doing so.[21]

While Claiborne's talk with the Indians failed to eliminate the ongoing antagonism between encroaching settlers and the Choctaw, it did curtail Choctaw raids of livestock in the Natchez area. Within weeks, Claiborne reported that "most of those poor Indians who recently supported themselves, by begging and plundering in our settlements have returned to their own Lands."[22] Through peaceful mediation Claiborne prevented an escalation of violence that could have resulted from the continued pilfering of settlers' goods and property. Some historians have characterized Claiborne as weak or indecisive, but Claiborne's political temperament derived more from an acute awareness of the limitations of his power than from any inherent weakness. Because Claiborne lacked in both arms and militiamen, his choices reflected an openness to negotiation that was uncommon among his peers.

After only two years as governor of the Mississippi Territory, Claiborne received word that he was to travel to New Orleans to serve with General James Wilkinson as one of the two American commissioners to officially receive the Louisiana Purchase territory from France.[23] His commission was intended to be a temporary one until Jefferson managed to coax a more qualified candidate into accepting the post. The most important political appointment of William Claiborne's career then—governorship of Orleans Territory—resulted not from any remarkable display of leadership skills on Claiborne's part, but rather from the convenience of his being "on the spot." Thus, the non-French speaker whom Jefferson appointed as an interim official remained governor by default, though Jefferson continued to search for a more suitable candidate until 1807 when it appears he resigned himself to Claiborne's permanency.

Named the Territory of Orleans shortly after its purchase from France, lower Louisiana did not resemble any other American state or territory.[24] Claiborne faced a population in political and cultural flux. The largely Protestant, English-speaking Americans streaming into the territory encountered a bustling, established city inhabited chiefly by French and Spanish-speaking Catholics whose form of government, demeanor, and social customs stood outside of the newcomers' realm of familiarity. One of the greatest obstacles to Jefferson's goal of American assimilation was the existence of a substantial number of free people of color who clamored for recognition of their economic and political rights under American rule. By 1803 Louisiana had been a slave-holding society for nearly a century, but racial classification was not as transparent as in other American states and territories. The territory's population consisted of a heterogeneous mélange where the line between slave and free was not always the same as the line between black and white. By 1790, the city of New Orleans possessed the largest free black population in continental North America. By 1810, the *gens de couleur libres* had reached a stunning 29 percent of the total population of New Orleans, a percentage that had nearly doubled in twenty years.[25]

This intermediate caste of inhabitants possessed economic and political rights equal to those enjoyed by whites under Spanish law. No other free black population in the slave-holding southern states had ever enjoyed such equality under the law. Under Spanish rule, free people of color had full rights to enter into business or personal contracts and recourse to the court system in cases of breach of contract. Spanish law also guaranteed protection of property rights to all of Louisiana's inhabitants regardless of color.[26] While the free colored population enjoyed extensive political and economic equality, however, ordinances regulating their public behavior subjected the free colored population to a socially subordinate status. Laws such as the *tignon* ordinance of 1788, which required all free women of color appearing in public to wrap their hair with a kerchief and prohibited them from wearing silk, jewelry, or feathers, were intended to maintain a social divide between the white and free colored communities.[27] For those in the free colored community who had been manumitted in their lifetime, the law mandated that freed slaves show deference to their former owners and to their owner's offspring.[28] These laws reinforced the social disabilities of the free colored community. By creating mechanisms of subordination, Spanish law sought to ensure that the members of the free colored caste recognized the limitations of their "place" within the social hierarchy.

Aside from social disabilities, access to economic and political participation for free people of color paralleled that of white society. Free people of color held property in the form of both land and chattel, maintained an active participation in the Catholic Church, had recourse against legal injustices in both the civil and criminal courts, and engaged actively in the defense of the colony via service in the colonial militia.[29] In his early observations of Louisiana's populace, Claiborne noted quickly the tensions between New Orleans's free colored population and its white inhabitants. Many whites viewed the free people of color as competitors in the fight to gain economic power. The struggle that ensued shortly after the official transfer on December 20, 1803, left the hard-won position of the free people of color vulnerable to attacks from native white inhabitants, eager to shoulder them aside, and from incoming Americans, who envisioned a strict racial hierarchy with free blacks in an unquestionably subordinate position. For the free colored community then, the first years of American rule represented a pivotal period when their political, economic, and social standing in the territory's hierarchy remained unclear.

Militia service for New Orleans's free men of color represented the first aspect of interracial equality questioned publicly by American elites who vied for power with native white Louisianians in the months following the transfer to the United States. Militia service for blacks in Louisiana began in the 1720s under the French. Slaves in the service of the Company of the Indies, France's commercial agency in Louisiana, participated in military action against the Natchez at Fort Rosalie and later against the Chickasaw.[30] As a reward, military service became one of the most common routes to manumission under the French. From the early 1770s through the 1790s, the Spanish expanded considerably the practice of manumitting slaves. Free black men often entered militia service.[31]

Under the Spanish, militia service elevated the position of free men of color by expanding routes to the fulfillment of civic and patriotic duties. By the late 1770s, the high level of military participation among free men of color led the Spanish governor, Bernardo de Galvez, to form two permanent companies of free colored militia troops. These regiments, like their counterparts throughout colonial Spanish America, were distinguished by color—the *morenos*, or the darker-skinned free men, and the *pardos*, the lighter-skinned free men of color. This division remained in place at the time of the American acquisition.[32] Militiamen were entitled to retirement benefits, tax exemption under the *fuero militar*, and the right to bear arms and wear military uniforms. Moreover, officers enjoyed an elevated position in New Orleans's social hierarchy. Militia service highlighted the difference between enslaved blacks and free men of color. Through participation in the defense of the colony, free men of color sought to align their legal status with that of their white counterparts.

In the early territorial period, New Orleans's free men of color asserted that their military service, in combination with their economic contributions to the colony, should secure them equitable status in the community. This assertion mirrored the claim made by free men of color on the island of Saint Domingue in the early 1790s. Two years after the Declaration of the Rights of Man in France, conflicts in Saint Domingue between whites and the free colored community climaxed when free people of color demanded the extension of the "universal" principles of *liberté, égalité,* and *fraternité* to their caste. Free men of color, in particular, relied on a long-standing history of service in the colonial militia as proof of their civic and economic dedication to the colony and to France.[33] The French National Assembly endorsed the push for equality in 1792 when it granted equal rights to all free men, in France and her colonies, regardless of color. Saint Domingue's colonial establishment, however, refused to act on the National Assembly's mandate. Unable to secure the political, social, and economic equality they had rallied for, a number of free men of color rejected the legitimacy of the colonial regime and secured an unprecedented alliance with the slave population that touched off the Haitian Revolution.[34]

The specter of the Haitian Revolution remained an ominous example for slave-holding societies throughout the Americas. The political climate of Orleans Territory, in particular, reflected a persistent fear that New Orleans's own society, which mirrored closely the three-tiered society of pre-revolutionary Saint Domingue, might witness similar unrest. Any threat, whether real or imagined, to the territory's established racial stratification sent waves of apprehension through the white elite and, subsequently, into the halls of the territorial legislature.

In an effort to curtail the liberties extended to the free colored population under Spanish rule, many whites sought an immediate reduction of the free colored militia. But Governor Claiborne, desperate to secure the territory and unwilling to bear the sole responsibility of defining the role of the free people of color under the American flag, chose to maintain the extant free colored militia companies in New Orleans until he received advice from the federal government. Claiborne's decision angered many native French-speaking Louisianians as well as members of New Orleans's Anglo-American merchant class. They saw Claiborne's actions as weak and indecisive at best, and duplicitous, at worst. In his initial engagements with the free people of color, Claiborne was not dismissive. He proceeded with caution toward establishing a relationship with the free colored community that kept the whole of the population in relative harmony. It is important to note, however, that in his political manipulations of the color line, Claiborne did not act independently of the federal government. In his early contact with the Jefferson administration, the subject of Louisiana's free colored population surfaced often.

President Jefferson first expressed apprehension over Louisiana's sizable non-white population in July 1803. In a series of questions put forth to Claiborne, then governor of the Mississippi Territory, and to Daniel Clark, the U.S. consul in New Orleans, Jefferson requested that each of them ascertain the population of the territory, "distinguishing between Whites and black (but excluding Indians)." He also called for an enumeration of the "free Males" enlisted in the militia. Claiborne responded pointedly that the militia consisted of "many free Mulattoes." Even more explicit, Clark cited figures submitted to the Spanish Court by the former governor, Carondelet, that consisted of two mulatto companies and one Negro company whose combined enlistment numbered three hundred men.[35]

In the months leading to the transfer of power from France to the United States, Claiborne repeatedly expressed concerns over the territory's free colored population. Reflecting on the consequences that resulted from the conflict between white colonists and the sizable free colored population in Saint Domingue, Louisiana's administrators feared an uprising at the time of the transfer. Claiborne and his co-administrator, Wilkinson, recognized that the instability inherent in a changing of the guard could be viewed as an opportunity for civil unrest among factions of the population, including the free people of color, who felt insecure in their future positions under the United States.

In September 1803, three months before the scheduled transfer, Claiborne recommended that Jefferson authorize the deployment of four to five thousand troops to New Orleans. He wrote, "The negroes on the island of Orleans are numerous, and the number of free mulattoes is also considerable;—on the change of Government, it is not impossible, but these people may be disposed to be riotous." A deployment of armed white troops, he assured Jefferson, "would not only discourage any disorderly spirit, but give entire safety to the Province."[36] Daniel Clark, who acted as an informant prior to the transfer, urged Claiborne further to bring "a considerable number of spare arms" with him from the Mississippi Territory in case of opposition to the new American government from the free people of color.[37]

In addition to the fears of New Orleans undergoing the turmoil that led to revolution in Saint Domingue, concerns arose from rumors that members of New Orleans's Free Colored Battalion had sworn allegiance to the Spanish Crown shortly before the transfer of sovereignty to the United States. Prefect Pierre Clement Laussat, the administrator who represented France during the brief period of French control of the territory in 1803, and who lingered in New Orleans until well after the transfer ceremonies, claimed that when Spain's representative, the Marquis de Casa Calvo, arrived from Cuba the Marquis immediately "summoned all the militia officers to come to his lodging and declare by *yea* or *nea* whether they intended to remain in the service of the King of Spain." Casa Calvo, who had difficulty securing many supporters for the Spanish cause, imprisoned members of the two free colored militia units until he procured "a declaration in the *affirmative*" of their allegiance to Spain.[38] A more likely scenario, however, is that Claiborne was unsettled by the existence of a large contingent of free people of color that assumed an active role in New Orleans's civic and economic life. Claiborne, in his experience in Congress and later as governor of the Mississippi Territory, had never before faced such a diverse group of inhabitants—inhabitants separated not only by language and national origin, but by skin tone and varying degrees of personal freedom.

General Wilkinson also appeared uncomfortable with the presence of New Orleans's armed free men of color. Especially "painful and perplexing" to Wilkinson was the specter of the "armed Blacks and Mulattoes, officered and organized" who had participated in the transfer ceremonies.[39] Under the direction of Prefect Laussat, the Free Colored Battalion "appeared on parade" in an official capacity during the "surrender of Louisiana to the United States." Laussat, like the Spanish administrator before him, validated the Free Colored Battalion as a legitimate component of the colonial militia.[40] Despite the peaceful nature of the transfer of Louisiana in December 1803, Wilkinson continued to fear unrest among the blacks and mulattoes of New Orleans and requested that Secretary of War Henry Dearborn immediately send a garrison of five hundred regulars to secure the city.

Just seven days after the transfer ceremonies, Claiborne echoed Wilkinson's uncertainty in a letter to Dearborn. He also sought advice from Secretary of State James Madison, to whom he wrote,

> my principle difficulty arises from two large Companies of people of Colour, who are attached to the Service, and were esteemed a very Serviceable Corps under the Spanish Government. On this particular Corps, I have reflected with much anxiety. To recommission them might be considered as an outrage on the feelings of a part of the Nation, and as opposed to those principles of Policy which the Safety of the Southern States has necessarily established; on the other hand not to be recommissioned would disgust them, and might be productive of future mischief. To disband them would be to raise an armed enemy in the very heart of the Country, and to disarm them would savor too strongly of that desperate System of Government which Seldom Succeeds.[41]

Claiborne understood that armed companies of free blacks ran contrary to the established norms of the slave-holding south. Moreover, Claiborne knew that either course of action—to disband or to recommission the militia—posed a danger. Hesitant to bear the weight of the decision alone, Claiborne delayed any action until instructions reached him from the capital.[42]

The presence of the Free Colored Battalion in New Orleans led President Jefferson to conclude that their existence would be tolerated in the territory only as long as it took to disband them quietly and peacefully. Claiborne, unsure initially of the federal government's stance on the existence of the free colored militia, did not want to ignite a conflict akin to those in Saint Domingue. But before any federal instructions arrived, Claiborne received an address from a group of influential free men of color seeking to immediately establish their allegiance to the new American government.

In the address, fifty-five members of the free colored militia, including its commanding officers, professed their "sincere attachment to the Government of the United States," whose democratic and revolutionary principles they believed would forever assure them their "personal and political freedom." The signers expressed their "fullest confidence in the Justice and Liberality" of the United States "towards *every* Class of Citizens which they have here taken under their Protection." Well aware of their precarious position, these free men of color paid tribute to the founding principles of the United States and sought to secure their own rights, as expressed in the Declaration of Independence, by stressing the applicability of those principles to their caste. This memorial echoed the attempts of Saint Domingue's free people of color to secure their rights under the Declaration of the Rights of Man.[43]

The second portion of the memorial recounted their history of military service and conveyed a desire to continue their exemplary contributions under the United States. They assured Claiborne, "Should we be in like manner honored by the American Government, to which every principle of Interest as well as affection attaches us, permit us to assure your Excellency that we shall offer our services with fidelity and Zeal." The signers highlighted their record, which had "ever been distinguished by a ready attention to the duties required" of them under the Spanish and offered this as proof of their military ability and devotion. After establishing their esteem for the United States, the free men of color closed the memorial by extending an offer to serve the new government "as a Corps of Volunteers agreeable to any arrangement which might be thought expedient."[44]

In typical Claiborne fashion, the governor skirted the issues at hand. He informed the authors of the address that "their Liberty, Property and Religion were safe." Regarding the status of the Free Colored Battalion, Claiborne kept his intentions vague. He said only that he "should not attempt a general reorganization of the Militia" until he "received particular instructions from the President." By placing the decision to maintain or discontinue the militia in the hands of the federal government, Claiborne removed himself from a position of future blame should the decision prove unfavorable.[45]

Claiborne received explicit instructions from Secretary of War Dearborn in late February 1804. Dearborn left the choice to Claiborne of whether "to continue or renew the organization," but he detailed the long-term plan of action envisioned by the federal government. He advised Claiborne "not to increase the Corps, but diminish, if it can be done without giving offence." The federal government wished to gradually weaken the free colored militia, an objective Claiborne moved toward in June 1804 when he ordered the replacement of free colored officers with white officers. After further instruction from Dearborn, Claiborne set in motion a deliberate and controlled plan for the diminishment of the Free Colored Battalion. He appointed two white "gentlemen" to the commanding officer positions of the Free Colored Battalion. In an overt display of diplomacy, Claiborne assigned Michel Fortier, a Francophone Louisianian with military experience who held a position on the Municipal Council, and Lewis Kerr, an Anglophone American and relative of the governor.[46]

While Claiborne likely intended the general populace to view the appointments of Fortier and Kerr as a unifying gesture of native Louisianians and the Anglo-Americans, the displacement of their own officers offended members of the free colored militia. "The Battalion was desirous of being commanded by people of their own color," Claiborne informed Dearborn, but after meeting with "several of the most influential men among them," he claimed that he had smoothed over "every appearance of discontent." This was the first documented meeting between Claiborne and members of the free colored community. Held privately between the governor and prominent free men of color, this encounter set the stage for future closeted discussions.[47]

To Major Fortier, however, Claiborne outlined the long-term goal of diminishing the free colored militia but stressed the necessity of doing so "without giving offence." Claiborne instructed Fortier "to *Muster* no free man of colour who resides without the city or suburbs," and additionally to "avoid *enrolling* any new recruit." Knowing this policy would arouse suspicion among the free men of color, whose initial term of militia service had been compulsory under Spanish rule, Claiborne advised Fortier to encourage the belief that those not enrolled at present would "hereafter be formed into a separate corps." To strengthen the illusion that the Free Colored Battalion represented an important asset to the United States and to further distract its members from discovering the objective of gradual elimination, Claiborne arranged to present the corps with the American standard at a public ceremony in the Place d'Armes.[48]

On June 21, 1804, Governor Claiborne presented the Free Colored Battalion with a standard "made of white silk, Ornamented with fifteen Stripes (alternately red and white)," which "was thankfully received and apparently excited a great share of Sensibility and gratitude." True to his word, Claiborne also presented the all-white Battalion of Orleans Volunteers and the Regiment of City Militia with standards. Significantly, Claiborne bestowed used flags, which he procured from General Wilkinson "in order to avoid the expense of purchasing new ones," upon the white regiments. Claiborne had the standard given to the Free Colored Battalion custom made in New Orleans.[49]

Claiborne came under harsh criticism for publicly presenting the Free Colored Battalion with a stand of colors.[50] For months after the presentation of the standard, he faced ridicule in the press. Chief among his critics was "Louisianian"—a pen name most frequently attributed to Pierre Derbigny—who decried Claiborne's treatment of the Free Colored Battalion, which he insisted "had rendered no services and whose rank in society would entitle it to no distinction." According to "Louisianian," Claiborne had overstepped his authority and severely offended the sentiments of the white militia. The white militiamen, he wrote, had been "neglected" and humiliated "in the extreme" to see "their inferiors treated with a marked attention and distinction to which they were not entitled."[51] Claiborne probably could have foreseen the protests raised by the Creole population, but he could not afford to create conditions similar to those that had sparked Saint Domingue's revolution. Because the governor lacked the military resources to ensure stability, he preferred to err on the side of peaceful relations between the territorial government and the free colored community even if that meant that his relationship with the *anciens habitants* in New Orleans became strained.

By the time the newspaper debates protesting Claiborne's preferential treatment of the Free Colored Battalion and his inadequate handling of illegal immigration from the volatile West Indies appeared in late November, Claiborne had already waded through another political fiasco involving prominent members of both the white and free colored communities of New Orleans. On July 12, 1804, Claiborne wrote to Madison of an event that had contributed to the mounting tensions.[52] Shortly after the governor had recognized the Free Colored Battalion with the custom-made standard, an anonymous free man of color registered his displeasure at being slighted by prominent whites when he attempted to publish a pamphlet calling for a public assembly of free colored males.

The dissatisfaction so publicly manifested by the anonymous free man of color stemmed from a general feeling of resentment within the free colored community that was exacerbated when white citizens failed to extend an invitation to the free colored community to participate in the adoption of a memorial to Congress. Unhappy with the congressional decision that denied immediate statehood to Louisiana, a group of prominent white Americans and Creoles drew up a memorial to Congress that gave a formal shape to their grievances. In this memorial, written in 1804, they addressed their complaints over "the denial of statehood, restrictions on slavery, the introduction of the American legal system, unfair appointments, the governor's excessive powers, and Claiborne's inability to speak the [French] language."[53]

Offended by the exclusion of the free colored community in the memorial's adoption, the author of the pamphlet urged his fellow free men of color to assemble so that they "might consult together as to *their* rights, and the propriety on their part of drafting a memorial to Congress." The author's failure to secure a printer for the piece prevented its widespread circulation but did not curb the outrage of the white community, which perceived the prospect of the proposed meeting of free people of color as "highly reprehensible."[54] Members of the New Orleans Conseil de Ville called for Claiborne's attention to this "provocation," which they believed was intended to "raise the flag of rebellion" through the demand for the freedom of the free colored population to exercise the same rights of citizenship as those enjoyed by whites. The council members stressed the danger of allowing this "seed of insurrection" to grow and resolved to draft a pressing letter to the governor demanding that the threat be crushed immediately.[55] The anonymous author, by publicly challenging the free colored community to unite independently of New Orleans's white citizens, questioned the established social and political hierarchy that required free people of color to remain unseen in matters of public policy. The author had overstepped the boundaries of his caste, an act that heightened whites' distrust of those individuals whose status remained precariously balanced between slave and free.

It is unclear how members of the white community learned of the piece's content and existence. Exiled Saint Domingue printers operated all of the French-language newspaper presses in the city, so it is unlikely that the author would have sought publication through one of the well-known presses.[56] One possible scenario is that a member of the free colored community discussed the malaise created by their exclusion with a member of the white community. This is plausible, for while tension existed between the groups, many lines of communication remained open due to the unseverable economic and familial ties that bound members of each community to the other.[57]

Perhaps more important than how the piece's existence came to be known is the way in which the recently appointed governor diffused the sensitive situation. Claiborne's response revealed much about his developing style of diplomacy and the important security considerations that weighed on his diplomatic policy. Rather than inflame the situation by pursuing harsh measures against the free people of color, Claiborne privately communicated his sympathy and understanding to each side.

Claiborne's first step in alleviating the tensions between the municipality, or the municipal council, and the free colored community was to assure New Orleans's mayor, James Pitot, that he considered "the Late conduct of some of the free people of Colour" unacceptable "and of a nature to create anxiety." He promised Pitot that he would use all means in his power to insure the "preservation of the *peace and safety* of Louisiana" and that "necessary measures would be taken" to prevent disruption of the status quo.[58] Though Claiborne did not specify exactly what measures he would take, he clearly expressed disapproval of behavior deemed intolerable and dangerous to the preservation of stability in the territory.[59] Concurrently, Claiborne conducted a private meeting with "8 or 10 of the influential characters among the free people of Colour" with the intent to diffuse *their* feelings of resentment and anger, while simultaneously providing them a forum to discuss their grievances with the governor. Claiborne showed leaders of the free colored community a respect denied them by the whites who had barred them from participating in their communication with Congress. As a result, the free men of color agreed "to abandon the suggested project, gave the most unqualified assurances, of their friendly pacific disposition, and devoted attachment to the present Government and to good order."[60] Claiborne, in light of this meeting, remained convinced that the loyalty of the free people of color to the American government remained connected to the recognition of their economic and military contributions to the territory.[61]

In his correspondence with James Madison, Claiborne exhibited a keen understanding of the fragility of the relationship between the free people of color and the territory's white population. The mere existence of this intermediate caste of people whose rights and position remained ambiguous created an atmosphere of anxiety among many land-holding whites and territorial officials. The municipality demanded that the free man of color who attempted to publish the call to assembly be punished "with great Severity" and that Claiborne "banish the author from the province," but Claiborne clearly felt that the more reasonable course of action was to seek a peaceful resolution that would not further inflame the tempers of the opposing groups. In a letter expressing his desire for propriety, Claiborne wrote, "In a Country where the Negro population was so great the Less noise that was made about this occurrence the better." Rather than publicly excoriate the piece's author, Claiborne sought to privately discourage the author's inflammatory action. In fact, Claiborne "did not make any exertions to discover the Author of the Letter" for he "thought it best he should not (for the present) be known, for the indignation of the white inhabitants was so roused, that the probability is, violent outrages on his person, would be offered." Claiborne feared that blatant actions against the free people of color would ultimately produce a much-unwanted alliance between the free colored and slave populations.[62]

Claiborne pointed to the example of Saint Domingue, whose bloody revolution resulted in an independent Haitian state, as the principal motivating factor in his decision to resolve the tensions through diplomatic channels rather than violent ones. Acutely aware of the active role played by free men of color in the uprising in Saint Domingue, Claiborne treated the native New Orleans free colored population with caution. He realized that the events that "Spread blood and desolation" in Saint Domingue "originated in a dispute between the white and Mulatto inhabitants, and that the too rigid treatment [by] the former, induced the Latter to seek the support and assistance of the Negroes."[63] Claiborne's recognition of the role played by Saint Domingue's free colored population in the outbreak of the Haitian Revolution remained crucial to the development of his political road map for Louisiana's free people of color. His direct reference to the connection between free mulattoes and slaves in Saint Domingue reflected a deep concern that the events of the Haitian Revolution not be repeated in Louisiana.

The early years of William C. C. Claiborne's tenure as governor of the Territory of Orleans revealed much about the developing style of diplomacy that would shape his policies in Louisiana over the next thirteen years. In addition to the difficult task of overcoming the obvious linguistic and religious differences between Louisiana's predominantly Francophone, Roman Catholic population and that of the primarily Anglo-Protestant United States, the new governor also faced the challenge of manipulating the more subtle differences inherent in the racial fabric of the newly acquired territory. Claiborne's initial response to New Orleans's sizable free colored population revealed a cosmopolitan awareness that fluctuated between cautious apprehension and an unprecedented openness toward the free colored caste.

Governor Claiborne was central to the outcome of the struggle for power that ensued among the increasingly diverse factions within New Orleans's population, despite the temporary nature of his initial appointment. For though Jefferson intended to replace him as soon as a more suitable administrator could be coaxed into taking the position, he remained in power until 1816, when he was elected senator of the state of Louisiana.[64] Claiborne faced a population undergoing drastic changes—political and cultural—that characterized the people's sense of fear and uncertainty. Rather than exacerbate whites' pervading fear of a Louisiana version of the Haitian Revolution, Claiborne struggled incessantly to maintain peace between all of the territory's free inhabitants. Claiborne's successful mediation between Catholics and

Protestants, between French-speakers and English-speakers, and especially between whites and free people of color, suggests that he possessed the rare ability to weigh carefully the potential outcomes of his decisions. Claiborne balanced his struggle to maintain order with the knowledge that any outright attempt to strip free men of color of rights they had enjoyed for nearly half a century might lead to rebellion. What some historians have seen as Claiborne's weakness—his seeming hesitancy to act quickly—was, in fact, a strategy of slow and deliberate change meant both to bring Louisiana into step with Jeffersonian policy and to avoid a large-scale revolt.

Despite the controversy surrounding Claiborne's actions during the early years of territorial rule, he employed all of his diplomatic skill in attempting to stay the course outlined by the federal government. It is ironic that the very people who caused the American administration the most anxiety prior to U.S. possession of the territory were the first to openly support the new government. Even Wilkinson, who had been so alarmed at the presence of armed free people of color at the transfer ceremony, soon amended his initial apprehension. By early 1804, he noted positively the enthusiasm displayed by the free colored militia toward the United States. He indicated to Secretary Dearborn that of all the segments of New Orleans's native population, the free people of color "are most to be relied ... for they have universally mounted the Eagle in their Hats & avow their attachment to the United States."[65]

As a result of the fear of repeating the Saint Domingue scenario, Claiborne publicly treated the free colored population with respect. He attempted to maintain respectful relationships with New Orleans's free people of color as well as with the various factions of the city's white population in order to win their loyalty and to achieve the delicate balance needed to preserve a controlled, peaceful environment. Fully conscious of the role free men of color played in the Haitian Revolution, Claiborne had a tendency to treat New Orleans's free people of color with guarded apprehension. Throughout his tenure as governor, he made continual reference to the necessity of recognizing the efforts of the Free Colored Battalion in an attempt to encourage solidarity with the government of the United States. This recognition was in part superficial, as Claiborne, under the direction of President Jefferson, had by early 1804 begun the quiet and measured reduction of the free colored militia.[66]

Claiborne saw balance and control as key to any diminishment of power enjoyed by the free colored militia; a majority of the newly formed Legislative Council did not share his vision.[67] In an act approved on April 10, 1805, the council omitted any mention of the Free Colored Battalion in the territory's militia law. Because the Free Colored Battalion was not included in the act, it could not participate lawfully in the militia.[68] Claiborne urged the Legislative Council to rethink the exclusion of the Free Colored Battalion. He feared that its omission might touch off an escalation of hostility toward whites.[69] On a more practical level, Claiborne considered the number of active militiamen in the territory to be so low as to be dangerous. Without the support of the free colored militia, the preservation of the territory's defense capabilities would be weakened considerably. He was therefore reluctant to discontinue the military service of the free colored militias prior to having in place a well-conceived replacement strategy.

At the same time, however, Claiborne's repeated failure to veto the bill that left the Free Colored Battalion out of the militia law—the Legislative Council and later the House of Representatives maintained the omission in every session from 1805 to 1811—indicates that he would not sacrifice his own political career in order to defend the civic rights of the free colored community.[70] In light of the negative press campaign against him and the political fiasco involving the anonymous free man of color, Claiborne perhaps felt that further attention to the plight of the free colored militia was politically unwise. Recognizing that a veto of the militia bill would again expose him to harsh criticism that would ultimately be heard by officials at the federal level, Claiborne opted to take the path of least resistance. With the establishment of the Legislative Council and House of Representatives as legislative bodies within the territory, Claiborne no longer had recourse to the closed-door decision-making process that he had relied on in the first years of his tenure. Forced into the public political arena, Claiborne continuously refused to veto the legislature's militia law in what was an act of self-preservation that sought to instill loyalty in the populace while pacifying growing animosity toward the free colored community.

Despite Claiborne's refusal to exercise his veto power, he continued to urge the legislature to rethink its exclusionary militia law. Given the underwhelming state of the territory's unorganized and poorly attended militia, Claiborne feared that the territory would be unable to protect its citizens and property in the event of attack from any number of potential threats—both those fomented from within and without the region's geographic confines. The governor's fears were realized in January 1811. As the new year unfurled, so too did rumors of a large-scale slave uprising on Manuel Andry's plantation, some thirty-five miles upriver from New Orleans. Led by Charles Deslonde, an émigré slave driver of color from Saint Domingue, the insurrectionary force swelled with reinforcements as the rebels moved from Andry's plantation toward New Orleans.[71] Desperate to secure the city and quell the rebellion, Claiborne activated all militia forces in New Orleans, including members of the disbanded free colored unit. A combined force of militia and U.S. troops put down the slave insurrection within days of their deployment.

In the wake of the slave revolt of 1811, Claiborne once again recommended that the legislature undertake a thorough revision of the militia law. He specifically cited the performance of the free colored militiamen during the uprising as proof of their loyalty—a loyalty, at least in part, derived from mutual interests shared by both free colored and white property holders—and submitted testimonials from prominent whites attesting to the militia's recent conduct.[72] But the legislature delayed an overhaul of militia law until 1812, when Louisiana achieved statehood and found itself preparing for an impending war with England. Ultimately, the necessities of war—not Claiborne's repeated urgings—prompted the legislature to pass "an act to organize in a Corps of Militia for the service of the State of Louisiana, as well as for its defense as for its Police, a certain portion of chosen men from among the free men of colour." This act, passed as a part of a larger legislative attempt to strengthen the state's militia law, allowed a limited number of qualified free men of color to serve in the state militia.[73] Militia participation by free men of color continued in Louisiana until 1834, when an increasingly exclusionary legislature introduced a definitive whites-only policy into militia law.[74]

Notes

1. France initially ceded Louisiana to Spain in 1762 via the secret Treaty of Fontainebleu, but Spain did not formally take possession until 1768 and ruled only until early 1803, when France technically regained Louisiana via the secret Treaty of San Ildefonso, which was signed in October 1800. In November 1803, Spain formally returned the colony to France, which had already sold it to the United States; New Orleans witnessed the raising of the Stars and Stripes on Dec. 20, 1803.

2. For the purposes of this chapter, I use the term "Creole" as it was used contemporaneously in New Orleans, meaning white native Louisianians of French and/or Spanish ancestry. For treatment of the debate surrounding the application of this term, see Gwendolyn Midlo Hall, *Africans in Colonial Louisiana: The Development of Afro-Creole Culture in Eighteenth Century Louisiana* (Baton Rouge: Louisiana State University Press, 1992), 157–59; Joseph Hatfield, *William Claiborne: Jeffersonian Centurion in the American Southwest* (Lafayette: University of Southwestern Louisiana, 1976), 129–30.

3. Claiborne was by no means Jefferson's first choice as steward of the Louisiana Territory. Jefferson attempted to convince the Marquis de Lafayette and James Monroe to accept the appointment, but both candidates refused. See Thomas Jefferson to Marquis de Lafayette, Nov. 4, 1803; Marquis de Lafayette to Thomas Jefferson, Feb. 26, 1804 and April 22, 1805, in Gilbert Chinard, ed., *Letters of Lafayette and Jefferson* (Bal-

timore: Johns Hopkins Press, 1929), 225–26; 227–29; 236–37; William Plumer, *William Plumer's Memorandum of Proceedings in the United States Senate, 1803-1807*, ed. Everett Somerville Brown (New York: Macmillan, 1923), 142; Thomas Jefferson to James Monroe, Jan. 8, 1804, in Paul Leicester Ford, ed., *The Works of Thomas Jefferson*, 12 vols. (New York: G. Putnam's Sons, 1905), 10: 62–64, 65–66; Walter Prichard, "Selecting a Governor for the Territory of Orleans," *Louisiana Historical Quarterly* 31, no. 2 (April 1948): 269–393.

4. Nathaniel Herbert Claiborne, *Notes on the War in the South with Biographical Sketches of the Lives of Montgomery, Jackson, the Late Governor Claiborne, and Others* (Richmond: William Ramsay, 1819), 92–93. Nathaniel Claiborne was the governor's youngest brother. Written within two years of Claiborne's death, this laudatory account provides the only known details of his childhood and adolescence. Subsequent accounts of W. C. C. Claiborne's early life have drawn heavily from this commentary.

5. Ibid., 92, 95, 97–99; Hatfield, *William Claiborne*, 5–7.

6. Claiborne, *Notes on the War in the South*, 98–103; Hatfield, *William Claiborne*, 13–16.

7. Hatfield, *William Claiborne*, 39–40; Gerard Toups, "The Provincial, Territorial, and State Administrations of William C. C. Claiborne, Governor of Louisiana 1803–1816" (Ph.D. diss., University of Southwestern Louisiana, 1979), 12.

8. When Jefferson took office, the Territory of Mississippi was under the auspices of Winthrop Sargent, whom Robert Haynes describes as "a fervent federalist from New England." For more on the controversy surrounding Sargent, see Haynes, "Territorial Mississippi, 1798–1817," *Journal of Mississippi History* 64 (Winter 2002): 298–303.

9. "Treaty with the Cherokee, 1798: Treaty of Tellico," April 30, 1802, in Charles J. Kappler, ed., *Indian Affairs: Laws and Treaties*, (Washington: Government Printing Office, 1904), 2: 51–55.

10. Jared Bradley, "William C. C. Claiborne, the Old Southwest, and the Development of American Indian Policy," *Tennessee Historical Quarterly* 33, no. 3 (1975): 266–76; U. S. Congress, *United States Statutes at Large, 6th–12th Congress, 1799–1813, vol. 2 Public Acts*, (Boston: Charles C. Little and James Brown, 1845), 6–7.

11. James Madison to William Claiborne, July 10, 1801; William Claiborne to James Madison, Aug. 2, 1801; Sept. 16, 1801; Oct. 7, 1801; Nov. 24, 1801, in Dunbar Rowland, ed., *Official Letter Books of W. C. C. Claiborne, 1801–1816*, 6 vols. (Jackson, Miss.: State Department of Archives and History, 1917), 1: 1–12.

12. Sargent faced repeated embarrassment in his dealings with local native groups, especially the Choctaw and the Chickasaw, stemming in part from his inability to retain dependable interpreters and his chronic shortage of gifts to distribute. William Claiborne to James Madison, Dec. 12, 1801, in Rowland, *Official Letter Books*, 1: 12–14; Daniel Usner, *American Indians in the Lower Mississippi Valley: Social and Economic Histories* (Lincoln: University of Nebraska Press, 1998), 87–88, 96.

13. William Claiborne to Henry Dearborn, April 8, 1802, in Rowland, *Official Letter Books*, 1: 71–74.

14. Henry Dearborn to William Claiborne, Feb. 23, 1802, in ibid., 84–86; see also Joseph T. Hatfield, "Governor William Claiborne, Indians, and Outlaws in Frontier Mississippi, 1801–1803," *Journal of Mississippi History* 27 (1965): 330–38.

15. Hatfield, *William Claiborne*, 51–52; 55–57; Toups, "The Administrations of William C. C. Claiborne," 14.

16. James Madison to William Claiborne, May 11, 1802, in Clarence E. Carter, ed., *The Territorial Papers of the United States*, 28 vols. (Washington D.C.: U.S. Government Printing Office, 1937), 5: 150–51.

17. William Claiborne to James Madison, Feb. 5, 1802 and April 3, 1802; William Claiborne to James Wilkinson, Jan. 29, 1802, in Rowland, *Official Letter Books*, 1: 40–41, 69–70, 42–43.

18. William Claiborne to John McKee, March 28, 1802, in ibid., 59–60.

19. "Talk to the Indians," April 2, 1802, in ibid., 67–68.

20. Ibid., 68.

21. William Claiborne to Henry Dearborn, April 8, 1802; July 20, 1802, in ibid., 73, 150–51; William D. McCain, ed., *Laws of the Mississippi Territory, May 27, 1800* (Beauvoir Community: Book Farm, 1948), 237–40.

22. William Claiborne to Henry Dearborn, May 14, 1802, in Rowland, *Official Letter Books*, 1: 109.

23. Thomas Jefferson to William Claiborne, July 18, 1803; "Commission of William C. C. Claiborne and James Wilkinson as Agents," in Carter, *Territorial Papers*, 9: 5, 94–95.

24. "An Act for the Organization of Orleans Territory and the Louisiana District," March 26, 1804, in Carter, *Territorial Papers*, 9: 209–14.

25. In 1805, the free people of color in New Orleans numbered 1,566 in a total population of 8,475. This number represented just under 30 percent of the total *free* population for New Orleans. The city's free colored population grew from 3.1 percent of the total population in 1771 to 17.1 percent in 1791. By 1805, New Orleans's free people of color represented 19 percent of the *total* population. Kimberly Hanger, *Bounded Lives, Bounded Places: Free Black Society in Colonial New Orleans, 1769–1803* (Durham, N.C.: Duke University Press, 1997), 18; Matthew Flannery, comp., *New Orleans in 1805: A Directory and Census*, ed. Dolley Madison Heartman and Charles Louis Thompson (New Orleans: The Pelican Gallery, 1936), 107.

26. George Dargo, *Jefferson's Louisiana: Politics and the Clash of Legal Traditions* (Cambridge, Mass.: Harvard University Press, 1975), 7.

27. Laura Foner, "The Free People of Color in Louisiana and St. Domingue: A Comparative Portrait of Two Three-Caste Slave Societies," *Journal of Social History* 3 (Summer 1970): 416–17.

28. Louis Moreau Lislet and Henry Carleton, trans. and ed., *The Laws of Las Siete Partidas: Which Are Still in Force in the State of Louisiana*, (New Orleans: James M'Karaher, 1820), 591–94.

29. Hanger, *Bounded Lives, Bounded Places*, 55–60.

30. Daniel H. Usner, Jr., *Indians, Settlers, and Slaves in a Frontier Exchange Economy: The Lower Mississippi Valley before 1783* (Charlotte: University of North Carolina Press, 1992), 86–87.

31. Roland McConnell, *Negro Troops of Antebellum Louisiana: A History of the Battalion of Free Men of Color* (Baton Rouge: Louisiana State University Press, 1968), 15–16.

32. Ibid., 5–12; 35–48; 16–17. The census of 1805 listed 215 free men of color over the age of sixteen residing within New Orleans's city limits. A report from 1797 on New Orleans's defenses cited 205 free men of color (not including officers) enlisted in the militia divided into one *moreno* unit and two *pardo* units. Flannery, *New Orleans in 1805: A Directory and Census*; "The Defenses of New Orleans in 1797," in McConnell, *Negro Troops*, 29–30 n. 49.

33. Saint Domingue comprised the geographic outline of present-day Haiti. While Saint Domingue's white planters stayed at home, making their patriotic contributions to France via commercial channels, the island's free men of color joined the ranks of the militia and served their country through active military participation. John Garrigus, "Redrawing the Color Line: Gender and the Social Construction of Race in Pre-Revolutionary Haiti," *Journal of Caribbean History* 34 (2000): 41–42; Anton Andereggen, "*Hommes de Couleur* During the French Revolution," *San Jose Studies* 15, no. 3 (1989): 4–13.

34. For more on the role of free people of color in the Haitian Revolution, see C. L. R. James, *The Black Jacobins: Toussaint l'Ouverture and the San Domingo Revolution* (New York: Random House, 1963); Carolyn Fick, *The Making of Haiti: The Saint Domingue Revolution from Below* (Knoxville: University of Tennessee Press, 1991); David Geggus, *Haitian Revolutionary Studies* (Bloomington: Indiana University Press, 2002); and Laurent Dubois, *Avengers of the New World: The Story of the Haitian Revolution* (Cambridge, Mass.: Harvard University Press, 2004).

35. The number given by Clark is likely an underestimate since it was based on a report given by the Spanish governor, the Baron de Carondelet, during his tenure, which spanned from 1792 to 1797. Claiborne estimated the population at thirty-six thousand whites with an equal number of slaves but admitted that his calculation was "not sufficiently authentic, to justify [his] hazarding an Answer in detail." Clark avoided distinguishing between slave and free, stating only that "the population of the Country considerably exceeds 50,000 Souls." Thomas Jefferson to William Claiborne, July 17, 1803; William Claiborne to Thomas Jefferson, Aug. 24, 1803; Daniel Clark to James Madison, Sept. 8, 1803, in Carter, *Territorial Papers*, 9: 3–4, 16–25, 28–47.

36. William Claiborne to Thomas Jefferson, Sept. 29, 1803, in Carter, *Territorial Papers*, 9: 59.

37. Daniel Clark to William Claiborne, Nov. 23, 1803, ibid., 121.

38. Some members of Louisiana's *pardo* and *moreno* militia companies maintained their service to the Spanish by transferring to Pensacola under the command of Luis Dessalles. See Jack D. L. Holmes, *Honor and Fidelity: The Louisiana Infantry Regiment and the Louisiana Militia Companies, 1766–1821* (Birmingham: n.p.), 1965), 57–59;

Pierre Clement Laussat quoted in Charles Gayarré, "The Spanish Domination," in *History of Louisiana* (New Orleans: James A. Gresham, 1879), 3: 595; McConnell, *Negro Troops*, 31.

39. James Wilkinson to Henry Dearborn, Dec. 21, 1803, in Carter, *Territorial Papers*, 9: 139.

40. William Claiborne to Henry Dearborn, June 22, 1804, in Rowland, *Official Letter Books*, 2: 217–19.

41. William Claiborne to James Madison, Dec. 27, 1803, in ibid., 1: 314.

42. William Claiborne to Henry Dearborn, June 22, 1804, in ibid., 2: 217–19.

43. Emphasis added, "Address from the Free People of Color," in Carter, *Territorial Papers*, 9: 174–75. An unofficial delegation of free men of color from Saint Domingue appealed to the French National Assembly for full recognition of their rights as men and as citizens in October 1789. The delegation stressed their civic and economic contributions to the state, focusing specifically on their status as land owners, farmers, and militia men in Saint Domingue; séance du jeudi octobre 22, 1789, *Archives Parlimentaires de 1787 à 1860*, Première série, 1789 à 1799 (Paris: Librarie Administrative de Paul Dupont), 9: 476–8.

44. "Address from the Free People of Color," in Carter, *Territorial Papers,* 9: 174–75.

45. William Claiborne to James Madison, Jan. 17, 1804, in Rowland, *Official Letter Books*, 1: 339–41. Claiborne's assurances echoed those that he offered the wider Francophone population. See *Le Moniteur de la Louisiane*, Dec. 24, 1803, New Orleans Public Library, Louisiana Division.

46. William Claiborne to Henry Dearborn, June 9, 1804, in Rowland, *Official Letter Books*, 2: 199–200; Michel Fortier is also listed as Miguel Fortier.

47. Ibid.

48. William Claiborne to Michel Fortier, June 22, 1804, in ibid., 215–16.

49. William Claiborne to Henry Dearborn, June 22, 1804, in ibid., 217–19; William Claiborne to Thomas Jefferson, May 3, 1804, in Carter, *Territorial Papers*, 9: 239–40.

50. The three-way debate over Claiborne's actions appeared in the *Louisiana Gazette*, Nov. 2, 9, 1804, and Jan. 11, 15, 29, 1805. See also the pamphlet attributed to Pierre Derbigny, *Esquisse de la situation politique et civile de la Louisiana depuis le 30 novembre 1803, jusqu'au 1er octobre 1804, par un Louisianais* (New Orleans: l'Imprimerie du Télégraphe, 1804). On a personal level, the smear campaign in the press could not have come at a worse time for Claiborne. On September 16, his personal secretary, Joseph Briggs, succumbed to yellow fever. Briggs's death was followed by the deaths of Claiborne's first wife, Elizabeth, and their only child, Cornelia Tennessee, on September 26, 1804. The press campaign against Claiborne began less than a month after these personal tragedies. William Claiborne to James Madison, Sept. 27, 1804, in Carter, *Territorial Papers*, 9: 299.

51. *Louisiana Gazette*, Jan. 29, 1805.

52. William Claiborne to James Madison, July 12, 1804, in Rowland, *Official Letter Books*, 2: 244–46.

53. William Claiborne to James Madison, July 1, 1804, in ibid., 233–34; William Claiborne to James Madison, July 13, 1804, in Carter, *Territorial Papers*, 9: 261; U.S. Congress, "The Louisiana Remonstrance," 8th Cong., 2nd sess., *Debates and Proceedings* (Dec. 31, 1804 and Jan. 4, 1805), 1598–1620; Plumer, *William Plumer's Memorandum*, 222–24. See also, Dargo, *Jefferson's Louisiana*, 30–32, 116–20, 190–91; Michael Wohl, "A Man in Shadow: The Life of Daniel Clark" (Ph.D. diss., Tulane University, 1984), 101–7.

54. William Claiborne to James Madison, July 3, 1804, and William Claiborne to James Pitot, July 1, 1804, in Rowland, *Official Letter Books*, 2: 234–36 and 2: 232–33.

55. See the proceedings from the afternoon session, July 7, 1804, New Orleans Conseil de Ville, *Official Proceedings 1803–1829*, vol. 1, microfilm, New Orleans Public Library, Louisiana Division, AB301.

56. Samuel J. Marino, "Early French-Language Newspapers in New Orleans," *Louisiana History* 7 (1966): 310–13.

57. In this instance, there existed one prominent New Orleanian in particular who held positions that placed him in close contact with both the free colored and white populaces. Michel Fortier, one of the two white militia officers recently appointed by Claiborne to oversee the free colored militia, also served on the Conseil de Ville and was one of the eight men who drafted the resolution to notify Claiborne of the "incendiary address." See the proceedings of the afternoon session, July 7, 1804, New Orleans Conseil de Ville, *Official Proceedings 1803–1829*, vol. 1.

58. William Claiborne to Mayor James Pitot and members of the Conseil Municipal, July 1, 1804, in Rowland, *Official Letter Books*, 2: 232–33; July 10, 1804, New Orleans Conseil Municipal, *Letters, Petitions, and Reports, 1804–1835*, vol. 1, microfilm, New Orleans Public Library, Louisiana Division, AB320.

59. James Pitot ran a successful sugar plantation in Saint Domingue from 1782 until 1792. Present in Saint Domingue at the outset of the Haitian Revolution, he likely knew of the disputes between the free people of color and the colonial administrators that triggered the revolt. In his memoirs, he made clear his feelings toward the free colored caste when he remarked on a public ball held by the free people of color, calling it "the gathering place for the scum of such people and of those slaves who, eluding their owner's surveillance, go there to bring their plunder." James Pitot, *Observations on the Colony of Louisiana from 1796 to 1802*, trans. and ed. Henry C. Pitot (Baton Rouge: Louisiana State University Press, 1979), 181, 29.

60. William Claiborne to James Madison, July 5, 1804, in Rowland, *Official Letter Books*, 2: 236–38; William Claiborne to James Madison, July 12, 1804, in ibid., 244–46.

61. Henry Dearborn to William Claiborne, Feb. 20, 1804, and William Claiborne to James Wilkinson, April 18, 1804, in ibid., 54 and 2: 104.

62. William Claiborne to James Madison, July 12, 1804, in ibid., 244–46.

63. Ibid.

64. From 1803 until April 1812, Claiborne acted as the appointed governor. Yet in

1812, when Louisiana achieved statehood, Claiborne won election to the governorship by a significant majority.

65. James Wilkinson to Henry Dearborn, Jan. 11, 1804, in Carter, *Territorial Papers*, 9: 159–61.

66. Henry Dearborn to William Claiborne, Feb. 20, 1804, and William Claiborne to Henry Dearborn, March 22, 1804, in Rowland, *Official Letter Books*, 2: 54–55, 58–59.

67. The Legislative Council (established 1805) was the territory's first legislative body. Henry Dearborn to William Claiborne, ibid.

68. The new militia law was passed on April 10, 1805, Chapter 28, "An Act for Regulating and Governing the Militia of the Territory of Orleans," *Acts Passed at the First Session of the Legislative Council of the Territory of Orleans* (New Orleans: James M. Bradford, 1805), 202–303.

69. Claiborne noted that the failure to include the free colored militia in the militia law of 1805 "has soured them considerably with the American Government." William Claiborne to James Madison, Jan. 8, 1806, in Carter, *Territorial Papers*, 9: 561; "Speech to the Assembly," Jan. 13, 1807, in Rowland, *Official Letter Books*, 4: 92–93.

70. "Speech to the Assembly," Jan. 13, 1807, in Rowland, *Official Letter Books*, 4: 92–93.

71. Historians and contemporary accounts differ in their estimation of the number of rebels involved in the uprising of 1811. Most agree that the number ranged from one hundred to six hundred individuals. William Claiborne to James Madison, Jan. 9, 1811, in Rowland, *Official Letter Books*, 5: 95–96; Caryn Cossé Bell, *Revolution, Romanticism, and the Afro-Creole Protest Tradition in Louisiana, 1718–1868* (Baton Rouge: Louisiana State University Press, 2004), 46–47; McConnell, *Negro Troops*, 48–49; James Dormon, "The Persistent Specter: Slave Rebellion in Territorial Louisiana," *Louisiana History* 18 (1977): 393–401.

72. William Claiborne to the Legislative Council and the House of Representatives, Feb. 25, 1811, in Rowland, *Official Letter Books*, 5: 163.

73. To qualify, free men of color had to adhere to property, tax, and residency requirements. The act allowed for the creation of a maximum of four companies of free men of color, all of which were to be commanded by white officers appointed by the governor. *Acts Passed at the First Session of the First General Assembly of the State of Louisiana, Begun and Held in the City of New Orleans, on Monday the Twenty-Seventh of July, 1812* (New Orleans: Thierry, 1812), 72.

74. Section 1 of the militia law of 1834 restricted participation to "free white males," while section 102 repealed "all previous laws or parts of laws contrary to the present act." The militia legislation of 1834 was approved on March 6, 1834 in "An act for the organization of the Militia of the State of Louisiana," *Acts Passed at the Second Session of the Eleventh Legislature of the State of Louisiana* (New Orleans: Jerome Bayon, 1834), 143, 167.

6

Dehahuit: An Indian Diplomat on the Louisiana-Texas Frontier, 1804–1815

F. TODD SMITH

In 1800, a young man named Dehahuit became *caddi*, or chief, of the Kadohadacho Indians, a tribe that resided on the banks of Caddo Lake on the Louisiana-Texas frontier (map 6.1). The Kadohadachos were the leaders of various groups—including the Hasinais of East Texas and the Natchitoches of West Louisiana—that made up the Caddo Indian tribe. The Kadohadachos also had influence over other Texas tribes, such as the Wichitas and the Comanches, through their ties with traders from the French town of Natchitoches, located on the Red River in Spanish Louisiana. The acquisition of Louisiana by the United States in late 1803 provided Dehahuit the opportunity to profit materially and diplomatically as the boundary between Texas and Louisiana remained undefined in the various treaty agreements. The Kadohadacho chief quickly established a relationship with the United States and offered his diplomatic services to the Americans in return for ample trade goods and protection from enemy Indians. Acknowledged by the Spaniards and the Americans as the preeminent Indian spokesman of the region, Dehahuit played an important role in the momentous events that occurred soon thereafter: the independence movement in Texas, the Creek Indian uprising, and the British invasion of Louisiana during the War of 1812. Unfortunately, when the border tensions between Spain and the United States decreased after 1815, so did Dehahuit's influence. Despite his declining diplomatic importance, Dehahuit continued to provide leadership for his tribe until his death in 1833. Two years later, the United States forced the rudderless Kadohadachos to sell their lands and join their fellow Caddos in Mexican Texas.

By the time Dehahuit assumed the position of *caddi* at the beginning of the nineteenth century, the Caddo Indians had dealt with Europeans for more than one hundred years. When the French and Spanish first established themselves on the Louisiana-Texas frontier in the late seventeenth century, there were perhaps as many as eight thousand Caddos. The Kadohadacho confed-

Map 6.1. The nineteenth-century Louisiana-Texas border. Map by Tracy Ellen Smith, www.cdrtexas.com.

eracy consisted of four tribes that lived along the bend of the Red River near the Arkansas, Texas, and Oklahoma border. Farther downstream were the Yatasis, Doustionis, and Lower Natchitoches, the three tribes of the Natchitoches confederacy. The Hasinai was the largest Caddo group, living along the upper reaches of the Neches and Angelina rivers in East Texas. Nine principal tribes were included among the Hasinais, and they were arranged in four general groups. The three confederacies shared the same language, Caddoan, and the same impressive culture. They were productive, sedentary agriculturalists who had a well-defined political structure, and a hereditary chief, or *caddi*, governed each individual tribe.[1]

During the eighteenth century, the Caddos welcomed the Europeans and experienced good relations with the French and the Spanish. France claimed the Kadohadachos and Natchitoches as subjects, while Spain claimed the Hasinais. These claims were affirmed through formal ceremonies, in which each tribe accepted the proprietorship of the various European monarchs. In return, the French and Spanish provided their Caddo subjects with official annual presents, as well as gifts and tokens whenever they would meet. The Caddos fully expected and demanded this largesse on the part of the Europeans as a condition of their allegiance. The mercantile French undermined the Spanish claim to the Hasinais by engaging in unofficial trade with the tribe, who then bartered these goods with other Indians in Texas. The Indians provided the French with furs in exchange for European utensils, guns, lead, and powder. The French also used their ties with the Kadohadachos to extend their trade up the Red River to the Caddoan-speaking Wichitas and the Shoshonean Comanches, who were intermittently at war with the Spanish in Texas. The intimate ties with the French enhanced the Caddos' already influential position in the area.[2]

Soon after Spain took full control of Louisiana in 1769, the Kadohadachos, Yatasis, and Natchitoches recognized the Spanish king as their new "father" in a formal ceremony held at the European town of Natchitoches, founded on the Red River by the French in 1714. Later, the Kadohadachos were particularly important in helping the Spanish make peace with the Wichitas and the Comanches. An epidemic spread across the region in 1778–79, and the Caddos lost nearly two-thirds of their population. The declining Spanish neglected them throughout the rest of the eighteenth century by neither providing them protection from the powerful Osage and Choctaw tribes, nor supplying them with enough firearms and ammunition to protect themselves.[3]

Although weakened by war and disease in the final quarter of the eighteenth century, the Caddos retained their pride and maintained their culture in the face of much interference. The tribe proved successful in this effort because the various confederacies gradually aligned themselves more tightly behind the firm leadership of the Kadohadachos and their impressive *caddi*, Dehahuit. By 1800, the Kadohadachos were by far the largest of the Caddo tribes, consisting of about one thousand people, including one hundred warriors. Now reduced to only one remaining tribe, the Kadohadachos had been forced by Osage and Choctaw raiders to move downstream from their former villages to reside on Caddo Lake, thirty-five miles west of the Red River. One contemporary Spanish observer claimed that the Kadohadachos, "of all the Indians, perhaps are the most civilized." An American expressed his belief that the Kadohadacho warriors were "looked upon somewhat like Knights of Malta, or some distinguished military order." The Kadohadachos were predominant over the remaining Caddo tribes, "who look up to them as fathers, visit and intermarry among them, and join them in all their wars."[4]

Among the Indians influenced by the Kadohadachos were the one hundred or so remaining Natchitoches and Yatasi tribesmen, who lived upstream from Natchitoches on Bayou Pierre and the Red River. Three Hasinai tribes—the Hainais, Nabedaches, and Nacogdoches—continued to live in their traditional villages on the Angelina and Neches rivers "in great amity" with the Kadohadachos. The Hasinais, with the Nadacos who lived on the Sabine River northeast of the Spanish town of Nacogdoches, had a population almost as large as the Kadohadachos. Unlike the Kadohadachos, however, all four tribes had experienced a constant turnover of chiefs due to death and disease at the beginning of the nineteenth century, causing them to look toward Dehahuit—described by observers as a "very fine looking man," who was a "remarkably shrewd and sensible" fellow—for direction, especially as he gained prestige from his relationship with the Americans and the Spaniards. During the early nineteenth century, observers noted that nearly all of the Indian tribes of the Louisiana-Texas frontier recognized Dehahuit "as superior."[5]

In addition to the other Caddos, Dehahuit had an influence over the six hundred or so Alabamas and Coushattas, who lived in two villages in the vicinity: one on the Sabine River about eighty miles southwest of Natchitoches, the other on the Red River only about thirty-five miles from the Kadohadachos. The four thousand Wichitas, however, were the most important tribe with whom the Kadohadachos associated. The Taovayas village, located on the Red River a few hundred miles upstream from Natchitoches, constituted the most important native marketplace on the southern Plains. The other two Wichita tribes—the Tawakonis and Kichais—had long conducted trade there with French traders from Louisiana, as did the numerous and powerful Comanches living to the west.[6]

Following the accession of Louisiana by the United States in 1803, the prospects of commerce drew the Caddos, Wichitas, and Comanches toward the young republic. On their part, American traders desired the great amount of horses and furs the three tribes had at their disposal. American officials wanted an alliance with the tribes for reasons other than trade; the manner in which the United States obtained Louisiana placed the Caddoan speakers of the Red River Valley, as well as the Comanches, in the middle of a boundary dispute between the United States and Spain. France had reacquired Louisiana from Spain in 1800, only to sell the huge expanse of territory three years later to the United States without ever taking possession or defining its borders. Thus, the boundary between Louisiana and Texas became subject to various interpretations, the most extreme being that of President Thomas Jefferson, who held that the border was the Rio Grande. Understandably, Spain scoffed at this claim, interpreting the line to be just a few miles west of the Red River, where it had been when France controlled Louisiana before 1763. In reality, the Red River became the focal point of the boundary dispute.[7]

Since the situation was so tenuous, Spanish and American officials understood that the loyalty of the native tribes along the border would be crucial in any boundary determination. The Caddos, Wichitas, and Comanches remained particularly central to this dispute, for the United States held that the tribes formerly allied to France now resided under the jurisdiction of a new "father." Thus, both the United States and Spain claimed the allegiance of the tribes in an attempt to define the border more clearly. In addition, both nations fully expected war with one another and realized that native allies might make the difference. Therefore, the Americans of Louisiana and the Spaniards of Texas both courted the Red River Caddoans and the Comanches, and the representatives of both nations realized the crucial importance of trade to win the tribes' favor. Doctor John Sibley, who became the U.S. Indian agent at Natchitoches, asserted that "whoever furnishes the Indians the Best and Most Satisfactory trade can always control their Politicks [sic]." Manuel Salcedo, the governor of Texas during this period, believed that Spain should establish commercial houses to supply the natives efficiently. In this way, the Spaniards "would be able to get out of [the Indians] anything [the Spanish] proposed to do because the Indians develop and behave like those who trade with them according to the degree of recognized utility, convenience, and advantages that are presented to them." Despite the Spaniards' comprehension of the situation, their lack of resources and general ineffectualness proved no match for the wealthy and energetic Americans in winning the Indians' allegiances.[8]

The Kadohadacho *caddi* Dehahuit understood the situation and adeptly used the boundary dispute to his tribe's advantage. He quickly made the Americans realize his tribe's influential position on the Louisiana-Texas frontier and forced the representatives of the young republic to take measures designed to win his allegiance. Dehahuit made a number of trips to Natchitoches in the fall of 1803 to meet with John Sibley. The Kadohadacho chief impressed the doctor, who tried to gain his favor by promising that the Americans would give the Indians good prices for their furs and provide them with a blacksmith to repair their weapons. Daniel Clark, an Irishman who had been living in New Orleans since 1786, alerted Secretary of State James Madison of the Kadohadachos' great importance and the possibilities of an alliance, stating that "they are the friends of the whites and are esteemed the bravest and most Generous of all the Nations in the vast country." Even before the official transfer of Louisiana, the Kadohadachos and the United States had moved toward establishing friendly relations.[9]

American officials appointed to govern the newly acquired area soon acknowledged the reports from Louisiana about the Kadohadachos' significance. On February 25, 1804, the governor of the territory of Orleans, William C. C.

Claiborne, sent orders to Captain Edward Turner, the civil commandant of the District of Natchitoches, instructing him to receive visiting Kadohadachos "with friendly attention and have regard for their interest." Turner initially arranged, with the assistance of Doctor Sibley, a peace treaty with the Choctaws to gain the friendship of the Kadohadachos. On May 17, 1804, representatives of both tribes arrived in Natchitoches and agreed to lay down their weapons and establish peace. Both tribes also agreed that, in case one group did take up arms against the other, the victimized party would seek retribution through the mediation of agents of the United States rather than obtaining revenge through bloodshed. Whereas the Spaniards had been unable to assist the Kadohadachos in their battles with other tribes, the Americans quickly impressed upon the Indians their willingness to put an end to tribal warfare.[10]

More importantly, the Americans demonstrated their desire to provide ample supplies of trade goods to the Indians of the region. In August 1804, Captain Turner pleased Dehahuit by informing him that the United States would soon establish an official trading house at Natchitoches "for the purpose of supplying their wants on moderate Terms." Two months later Dehahuit notified Turner that he was en route to Natchitoches and expected to receive presents. Turner alerted Governor Claiborne of the impending visit and stated that since the "Spaniards are exerting every means to Induce the Indians to be unfriendly . . . it would not be good policy to let him return [to his village] dissatisfied." Governor Claiborne responded by permitting Turner to award Dehahuit and his principal men gifts worth two hundred dollars. When the Kadohadacho party arrived at Natchitoches, Turner presented them with powder, lead, and tobacco. Now assured that his tribe would receive presents from the Americans, Dehahuit asked Captain Turner for an American flag to fly over his village, for he explained it was "customary to have the Flag of the Nation who claimed his Country in which they lived." Because of the Americans' proven ability to provide the tribe with goods, the Kadohadachos informally recognized their ties with the United States in late 1804.[11]

In response to the measures taken by the United States, Spanish officials in Texas took actions designed to retain their Indian subjects. The Spanish commander at Nacogdoches, Captain José Joaquín Ugarte, grasped the importance of providing the natives with trade; in a letter to Juan Bautista Elguézabal, the governor of Texas, he stressed the necessity of supplying the tribes with clothing and ammunition in order to avoid conflict with them and to keep their friendship. Commandant General Nemesio Salcedo also realized the importance of the alliance with the native tribes of Texas. He instructed the governor of Texas to "try all possible means to see that [the transfer of Louisiana] does not influence the Indian tribes to change the peaceable relations they have hitherto maintained with us." Elguézabal received instructions to "take pains to encourage their loyalty and good will."[12]

As a result of the tension on the Louisiana-Texas frontier, President Jefferson chose John Sibley as part-time Indian agent for the area in December 1804. The position became permanent the following year when the United States established an Indian trading factory at Natchitoches. Upon receiving his appointment, Sibley was instructed by Secretary of War Henry Dearborn to confer with the Indian tribes, win their friendship, and inform them that they must break all connections with the Spanish. Sibley, who appreciated trade as a method for gaining the tribes' allegiance, immediately dispatched men up the Red River to barter with the Kadohadachos and the Taovayas. The Spanish commander at Bayou Pierre, José Manuel de Castro, could not stop the Americans; as a result, he asked Dehahuit to detain the traders at his village. Dehahuit, however, refused to comply with this naive request. A few months later, Castro made a bolder attempt to stop the Kadohadachos' intercourse with the United States. In the spring of 1805, Dehahuit and a few young men were on their way to Natchitoches with furs when they met Castro at Bayou Pierre. Castro warned Dehahuit that if the Kadohadacho party should return from Natchitoches with American goods, he would confiscate them. This warning angered Dehahuit, who threatened to kill the whole Spanish guard. He told Castro that the road to Natchitoches "had always been theirs, and that if the Spanish prevented them from using it as their ancestors had always done, he would soon make it a bloody road." Alarmed by Dehahuit's menacing stance, Castro meekly allowed the group to pass without incident on their return from Natchitoches.[13]

The American trade advantage over the Spaniards increased on May 23, 1805, when Agent Sibley received three thousand dollars' worth of merchandise from the government to distribute to the Indians of the region as presents and trade goods. Secretary Dearborn instructed Sibley to use all means to conciliate the tribes, especially "such natives as might, in case of rupture with Spain, be useful and mischevous [sic] to us." As soon as Sibley obtained the merchandise allocated by Congress he alerted the surrounding tribes. As a result, Taovaya and Tawakoni warriors traveled to Natchitoches in June 1805 and received presents and American flags from Sibley. Dionisio Valle, a Spanish lieutenant at Nacogdoches, noted in the same month that an American trader passed Bayou Pierre on his way from the Wichita and Kadohadacho villages upstream. He reported that it was "openly known that the Caudacho Indians are receiving presents at Natchitoches as subjects of Louisiana," and he had no doubt that the Taovayas were being "stirred up in a similar way."[14]

The Americans also stirred up the Hasinais in East Texas. Through the

Kadohadachos, Agent Sibley had made overtures to the Hasinai tribes, and in June 1805 twenty-five Hainais appeared at the Spanish post at Nacogdoches hinting "at the offers of presents and prospects of trade" with the Americans. Although Lieutenant Valle advised them that it would be improper to accept these offers, Hainai warriors as well as Nadaco, Nacogdoches, Ais, and Adaes men visited the American post at Natchitoches in August. Valle blamed the Kadohadachos for these visits, and he feared that "their instigation may lead those tribes to form a friendship with said Sibley." The American's offers even reached the Comanches; Chief Zoquiné arrived in Nacogdoches on June 27, 1805, intending to go to Natchitoches and sell buffalo skins. Only through Valle's entreaties was Zoquiné convinced to exchange his goods in Nacogdoches and refrain from traveling to Louisiana.[15]

The new governor of Texas, Antonio Cordero, realized that the Spaniards desperately needed to maintain their alliance with the Comanches, for he knew that the Americans planned to increase their involvement with the Indians of the region. Cordero had recently learned that President Jefferson had ordered Major Thomas Freeman and Doctor Peter Custis to ascend to the source of the Red River in an attempt to define the boundary between Louisiana and Texas. In addition, Freeman and Custis were instructed to "court an intercourse with the natives as intensively as you can" and to advise the tribes that they were no longer subjects of Spain but "henceforth [the United States would] become their fathers and friends." Although Spanish officials were unaware of this part of Jefferson's instructions, they certainly understood that the expedition would attempt to win the Indians' allegiances.[16]

For these reasons, Commandant Salcedo considered the American expedition to be an invasion of Spanish territory and was determined to thwart it. On October 8, 1805, he instructed Governor Cordero to post more troops either at Bayou Pierre or at the reinstituted fort of Los Adaes in order to "compel withdrawal of the Red River expedition." He stated that this "object must be facilitated by the Indians who live in those districts," for he recognized that "the accomplishment of the expedition can be completely obstructed by the allied tribes, provided the [natives] are caused to take interest in this matter through the necessary craftiness and compensations." Obviously, Salcedo understood that the Indian tribes of the region held the key to the Red River, and only through their cooperation could the Spanish successfully arrest the American encroachment. Throughout the winter and spring of 1806 the Spaniards tried in vain to win the allegiance of the Texas tribes. Few Indians, however, responded to the Spanish entreaties. Sebastián Rodríguez, the new Spanish commander at Nacogdoches, reported in February 1806 that the "neighboring Indian tribes which have always visited this post are coming here less frequently not so much on account of lack of affection for the Spaniards," but because of the trade advantages and the greater number of presents they received from the Americans at Natchitoches.[17]

In the meantime, the tense situation on the Louisiana-Texas frontier escalated to a point that threatened to bring about the war between Spain and the United States that both sides had been expecting for two years. By the time Freeman and Custis began the expedition in mid-April 1806—when they entered the Red River at its mouth with three boats, twenty-one soldiers and a black servant—most of the East Texas Indians had been swayed by the American presents and trade goods. In response to the launch of the Freeman-Custis expedition, the Spaniards sent out Francisco Viana and troops to stop the American party by force if necessary. As with Rodríguez, Viana tried in vain to induce the region's Indians to join with the Spanish troops to face the encroaching Americans. Although Negrito, the chief of the Aises, pledged his allegiance and claimed that he could enlist one hundred Alabama and Coushatta warriors to the Spanish cause, only seven men from the two emigrant tribes responded to his entreaties. The Spaniards also attempted to enlist the services of Hasinai warriors for battle against the Americans but finally had to admit "that not a single one of them wishes to come." Realizing that few Indians would be joining the Spanish force, Negrito and the Alabama-Coushatta warriors returned home.[18]

The Freeman-Custis expedition reached Natchitoches on May 19 and remained there until June 2. While in Natchitoches, they increased their number to 47 men (including the Kadohadacho interpreter François Grappe) and 7 boats to defend against the Spanish threat. The following day, Viana ordered Lieutenant Juan Ygnacio Ramón and 240 men to intercept the American party at the old Kadohadacho village near the bend of the Red River. Because of his unfamiliarity with the area, Lieutenant Ramón hired a Yatasi man to lead him and his troops to the old Kadohadacho village, but the guide took him to the present town on Caddo Lake by mistake. Dehahuit met Ramón, who asked him accusingly if he "loved the Americans." The *caddi* ambiguously answered that "he loved all men; if the Spaniards had come to fight they must not spill blood on his land." Ramón accepted this vague reply and retreated to the Sabine River. Dehahuit then sent him a defiant message stating that when Freeman and Custis arrived, he planned to supply the Americans with guides to take the party farther upstream.[19]

Dehahuit quickly followed through on his promise to assist the approaching Americans. He sent a courier to the Coushatta village on the Red River to intercept Freeman and Custis and inform them of the presence of Ramón's troops and their intention of stopping the Americans by force. After two weeks of struggling with the logjam known as the Great Raft, Freeman and Custis finally reached the Coushatta village on June 24. Upon receiving Dehahuit's message, Freeman sent the courier back to ask the Kadohadacho chief to meet the Americans at the Coushatta village. While waiting for Dehahuit's arrival, Freeman and Custis visited the Apalache, Alabama, and Coushatta settlements. On June 29 Chief Etienne accepted an American flag from Major Freeman, which he hoisted above the Coushatta village in place of the Spanish flag that had previously flown there. Two days later Dehahuit and forty Kadohadacho warriors arrived on the Red River opposite the Coushatta village and fired their guns in a salute that was returned by the Americans on the other side. As the Indians crossed the river, the members of the American expedition drew themselves up in single file to receive the Kadohadachos "with marked attention." As Dehahuit entered the camp, the Americans fired another salute "with which he seemed well pleased; observing to the Coushatta chief that he never had been so respectfully received by any people before."[20]

Using Grappe as interpreter, the Americans clarified the objective of their mission to the Kadohadachos, telling them that France had sold Louisiana and that "henceforth the People of the United States would be their fathers and friends and would protect them and supply their wants." Dehahuit readily agreed to this, replying that he would now look to the Americans for "protection and support." He said that, although he had no complaints to make against either the Spanish or the French, the Kadohadachos now had an "American father, and in the two years he had known the Americans he liked them also for they too had treated his people well." He was especially pleased by the way the members of the expedition treated "him with respect and candor which the Spaniards did not evince in their conduct." Dehahuit added that he wanted them to proceed and meet his allies, the Panis Piques, who would also be glad to see the Americans.[21]

Major Freeman celebrated this successful meeting by distributing food and liquor to the Kadohadacho warriors. After toasting their alliance, the Americans fell into single file in order to allow each Indian to shake their hands; the Kadohadachos seemed impressed with their new allies, and the principal warrior told the American sergeant that "he was glad to see his new brothers had the faces of men, and looked like men and warriors . . . let us hold fast, and be friends forever." The next day Dehahuit informed Freeman that more Spanish soldiers were en route from Nacogdoches to intercept the Americans "and drive them back or take them prisoners." The Kadohadacho chief promised the major that he would send messengers from his village with information concerning the Spanish troops; he also ordered three other tribesmen to remain with the expedition as guides.[22]

In the meantime, Commandant Salcedo ordered about one thousand troops under the command of Lieutenant Colonel Simón de Herrera to meet Lieutenant Ramón's force at the Kadohadacho village and then proceed to their old village on the Red River to intercept the American expedition. After arriving at Nacogdoches on July 15, Herrera's force set out for the Kadohadacho village. Upon his entrance, Herrera informed Dehahuit that his town was on Spanish soil and that he would have to move eastward if he planned to continue to display the American flag. When the chief hesitated, the Spanish troops boldly cut down the flagstaff. The soldiers then taunted Dehahuit, telling him that they were going after the Americans, "whom they would serve in the same manner, and if resistance was made, either kill them, or carry them off prisoners, in irons." The insulting actions caused some of the Kadohadacho warriors to take up arms, but Dehahuit's cooler head prevailed. If the Kadohadacho chief had had any doubts about allying his tribe with the Americans, Herrera's visit had most certainly put them to rest.[23]

Following Herrera's departure, Dehahuit immediately dispatched three Kadohadacho messengers to find the Americans on the Red River. They met Freeman and Custis high above the Coushatta settlement on July 26, informed the party of the incident at their village, and warned them of the Spanish plan to intercept them. Three days later, an overwhelming Spanish force confronted the Americans, prompting the expedition to retreat. On August 23 Freeman and Custis reached Natchitoches and informed Governor Claiborne of their fate.[24]

The party's return initiated an exchange of letters between Claiborne and Herrera that presented both the Spanish and American claims concerning the Kadohadachos. On August 26 Governor Claiborne protested the fact that the Spanish troops had stopped the American expedition on U.S. soil. By chopping down the American flag in the Kadohadacho village, in his opinion the Spanish had committed "another outrage." Claiborne further argued that while Louisiana had belonged to France, the Kadohadacho tribe had been "under the protection of the French Government . . . hence it follows Sir, that the cession of Louisiana to the United States is sufficient authority for the display of the American flag" in the village. Lieutenant Colonel Herrera, in answering Governor Claiborne two days later, agreed that the United States possessed Louisiana but asserted that the Kadohadacho village was not located on American soil "and on the Contrary the place which they inhabit is very far from it and belongs to Spain." In this way, Herrera justified the removal of the American flag.[25]

Ultimately, the matter remained unresolved, and war was prevented only when Spanish and American representatives signed the "Neutral Ground

Agreement" on November 1, 1806. This document remained in force until 1821 and established a strip of neutral territory between Louisiana and Texas, which, though claimed by both countries, remained ungoverned and unoccupied. Dehahuit's village fell within this neutral ground and thus both countries continued to claim the Kadohadachos as subjects, a situation that proved most profitable for the tribe. In addition, the boundary between Louisiana and Texas was left undefined, allowing American traders the freedom to continue to travel to the Taovaya village.[26]

The Freeman-Custis expedition and Spain's reaction served only to propel the Kadohadachos further toward the Americans. Two weeks after the Spanish repelled the expedition, Dehahuit and a delegation of fourteen warriors met Governor Claiborne, army officers, and leading citizens in Natchitoches. The governor asserted that the Kadohadachos were now subjects of the United States and asked Dehahuit to let his "people hold the Americans by the hand with sincerity and Friendship, and the Chain of peace will be bright and strong." "Our children will smoke together," the governor said, "and the path will never be colored with blood." After smoking the ceremonial pipe, Dehahuit told the governor that the Americans were his "new friends," and he reaffirmed his agreement with Claiborne's claim of jurisdiction by stating, "[If] your nation has purchased what the French formerly possessed, you have purchased the country we occupy and we regard you in the same light as we did them."[27]

Although the United States had formally won over the Kadohadachos, Agent Sibley did not take the alliance for granted and continued to display his gratitude to the tribe. For instance, in January 1807, when Dehahuit's house caught fire and destroyed his family's corn supply, Sibley ordered twenty-three barrels of flour to be distributed to the Kadohadachos as compensation. One month later a party of Kadohadachos arrived in Natchitoches to trade the furs they had acquired during their annual winter hunt. Sibley warmly welcomed them and presented a hat and a blue half-regimental frock coat to Cut Finger, "a particular friend and Companion" of Dehahuit, in return for his being "friendly and attentive" to Major Freeman's party. Dehahuit arrived in Natchitoches on April 14 with fifteen men and pirogues loaded with skins. Sibley presented the delighted Kadohadacho chief with a scarlet regimental coat and gave another tribesman a coat similar to Cut Finger's. All this largesse served to reassure Dehahuit and his men that the Kadohadachos had been correct in siding with the United States.[28]

The Texas Indians and the United States continued to draw even closer in the latter half of 1807. In the summer Dehahuit enhanced his prestigious position on the Louisiana-Texas frontier by arranging a grand council in Natchitoches between Agent Sibley and the Caddos, Wichitas, and Comanches. By August 10 about 300 Indians had arrived in the town, including 80 Kotsoteka Comanches, 26 Tawakonis and Kichais, 90 Kadohadachos, and 119 Hasinais. The following day, Sibley initiated a series of meetings with various tribal leaders, paying particular attention to the Wichitas and the Comanches. On August 12, he addressed a gathering of headmen of the visiting tribes. He told the assembly that although Louisiana had been transferred to the United States, the boundary with Spanish Texas remained undefined. Sibley confirmed that the Indians could be friends with both the Spaniards and the Americans, and he invited the tribes to deposit their goods at Natchitoches and accept American traders in their villages regardless of which side of the border they lived. Then Dehahuit rose and informed Sibley that he had told the western tribes many good things about the agent at Natchitoches, and he expressed "great Satisfaction" with the warm welcome that the American had given his Indian allies. The grand council of 1807 proved mutually beneficial to the United States and the Kadohadachos, and with the aid of Dehahuit, Sibley succeeded in extending his country's influence well into Spanish Texas; likewise, Sibley's graciousness only added to the esteem of the Kadohadacho chief.[29]

Despite the strong alliance with the Americans, the Kadohadachos and Hasinais did not cut their ties with the Spaniards. In November 1807 Dehahuit traveled to Nacogdoches and received food, brandy, tobacco, and a shirt from the Spanish commander during his week-long stay. Two months later another party of Kadohadachos stopped in Nacogdoches following their winter hunt and was presented with gifts as well. In the summer of 1809, Dehahuit represented the Nadacos and Nacogdoches before the governor of Texas, Manuel Salcedo. In August, the chiefs of the two Hasinai tribes traveled to San Antonio with the Kadohadacho *caddi*, "the most important of his nation," to make Salcedo realize the necessity of providing the Texas Indians with a trader. The governor acknowledged Dehahuit's request on behalf of his kinsmen, and he authorized Marcel Soto to establish a trading post in the area. By the end of the first decade of the nineteenth century, it was obvious that Dehahuit had successfully used the Kadohadachos' position on the Louisiana-Texas frontier to gain status, as well as material benefits, for himself and his tribe.[30]

Soto's post, however, failed because of the turmoil created in Texas the following year by the Hidalgo revolt in Mexico, which helped to spark a call for independence from Spain. In Texas, this resulted in a struggle between the royalist forces and the so-called republican revolutionaries. The fact that American filibusters continually crossed the border from Louisiana to aid the republicans clouded the frontier situation. The Kadohadachos thus found themselves at the center of a Euro-American struggle once more, as both sides sought to win an alliance with the border Indians. Dehahuit again expertly manipulated the situation to benefit his tribe. The chaotic situation caused Sibley to take steps to insure the loyalty of the Indian tribes along the Louisiana-Texas frontier. Sibley believed the Kadohadacho *caddi* to be "a man of more importance than Any other ten Chiefs on this Side of the Mississippi" and thus primarily focused his efforts on Dehahuit. Sibley frequently had long conversations "with this Man who has a strong mind" in which they discussed the world situation and its effects on Texas. Throughout Sibley never seriously doubted the chief's fidelity to the United States and stated that Dehahuit "never withdrew . . . his particular Confidence & friendship."[31]

By the end of 1811 the struggle had greatly intensified in Texas, which induced Dehahuit to pay particular attention to the Caddos and Wichitas. Dehahuit used his prestigious rank to counsel the Wichitas; half of the Taovayas had joined the Comanches who wished to enter the fray, while the other half had joined the peaceful Tawakonis. According to Sibley, Dehahuit "was using his interest Among them (which is great) to persuade [the Taovayas] to return & live together as Usual." For the next few years, as the situation heated up along the Louisiana-Texas frontier, this role as counselor and emissary to the Texas tribes remained the most important that Dehahuit and the Kadohadachos would play.[32]

In 1812, the largest filibustering expedition, headed by a refugee Mexican, José Bernardo Gutiérrez de Lara, and a former American army lieutenant, William Magee, crossed into Texas from Louisiana. In response, the Spanish royalists increased their efforts to induce the Indian tribes of Texas to fight for their cause. In May 1812, Dehahuit informed Sibley of the royalist's overtures, and the American agent counseled him "to have nothing to do in their dispute." He furthermore asked Dehahuit to convey his advice to the Texas tribes and expected that "this communicated from the Caddo chief will be conclusive."[33]

A month later, the United States declared war on Great Britain, initiating the War of 1812. Along the Louisiana-Texas frontier, it was fully expected that the war would extend to a struggle with Spain as well and that an official American invasion of Texas would result. This intensified the attempts of both Spain and the United States to win the allegiance of the border tribes. In July, the Spanish royalists sent an agent to the Kadohadacho village to persuade Dehahuit to visit San Antonio and to join their forces. The *caddi* faithfully informed Sibley of this invitation but nevertheless traveled to Nacogdoches to receive presents from the Spanish. Dehahuit and the Nadaco chief subsequently visited Natchitoches, where Sibley found them "unshaken in their Amity & attachment to the United States." He then asked Dehahuit to inform the Texas tribes that any American troops entering Texas "would not enter as enemies of Any Red People." Sibley enjoined the Indians to be neutral; he felt sure the tribes would adhere to this advice because he was "personally well Acquainted with all the Chiefs & Leading Men Amongst them, and the Caddo chief himselfe [sic] being the Bearer who is my particular friend, they will Certainly Receive my tokens & Smoke my tobacco."[34]

Dehahuit complied and was received with great respect by all of the tribes he visited. The Kadohadacho *caddi* even convinced a group of Comanches to break their promise to join the Spanish royalists. Dehahuit returned to Natchitoches in February 1813 and told Sibley that the Indians would remain neutral, but if the United States were attacked, they would join the Americans and fight "as long as there was one Warrior remaining." While Dehahuit was in Natchitoches, he was pressured by agents of the republican forces in Texas who wanted the Kadohadachos to assist their revolution. Sibley did not interfere in these attempts for he "knew the Chief's firmness & that he would do nothing without" consulting him. Dehahuit proved Sibley right in that he gave the revolutionaries a "prompt refusal" to their request for support.[35]

The pressure on the Kadohadachos, however, continued to increase. After suffering a number of defeats, in the summer of 1813 the royalist forces in Texas had turned the tide and crushed the revolutionaries. Many Americans in Natchitoches feared the Spanish would attempt to exact retribution in Louisiana, either by invading or by inciting the Indian tribes. Concurrently, a new threat materialized from east of the Mississippi River in the form of the Creek Indians, who were at war with the United States. They sent emissaries west of the river to gain Indian allies by arguing that the United States was ultimately inimical to all Indians. The Americans responded to these threats by holding a series of meetings with the Kadohadachos aimed at retaining their friendship. On October 15, 1813, Sibley met with the Kadohadachos, Yatasis, and Nadacos, as well as with the Alabama and Coushatta tribes who were related to the Creeks. Sibley told them that the Creeks and Spaniards were telling many lies and assured them that President James Madison "continued his friendly disposition Towards his Red Children, that he wished them all clean Paths, good Crops of Corn, good hunting & happiness." The Alabama chief answered that he deferred to "his Older Brother the Caddo Chief & should always be advised by him." Dehahuit told Sibley that he had heard various reports but had learned to be very cautious in what he believed. He asserted that from the time he "first Took his great Father the President of the United States by the hand," it was "always his Instructions . . . to be kind to white men." He promised Sibley that if the Americans needed assistance, all the warriors under his jurisdiction would enlist. Dehahuit further demonstrated his loyalty to the Americans by suggesting that he personally would reiterate Sibley's desire for peace to "all the Tribes to the West Under his Influence as well as his Own Nation."[36]

Dehahuit returned to Natchitoches a week later to meet with Thomas M. Linnard, the official U.S. trader, who assured the *caddi* that the Creeks and the Spaniards were not to be trusted. Linnard reported that Dehahuit expressed "much satisfaction at the information communicated" and promised that "he was ready and willing to make common [cause] with [the Americans] and that [the Americans'] enemies should be his enemies." The final council with Dehahuit occurred on October 18 when Governor Claiborne met him at Natchitoches. Claiborne recalled their meeting in 1806 and thanked Dehahuit for "the advice you have given to your own people, and to all red men with whom you have influence, [which is like] that of a father to his children." He noted that the Creeks had sent war emissaries to the Indians west of the Mississippi but nevertheless hoped that "all these people will look up to you, as an elder Brother, and hold fast your good advice" of not joining the Creeks in their war against the Americans. In order to express his gratitude, Claiborne gave the *caddi* a sword since "to a Chief, a Man, and a Warrior, nothing could be more acceptable."[37]

The meetings with Dehahuit in 1813 proved successful since none of the tribes influenced by the Kadohadachos joined the Creeks. In fact, Dehahuit's counsel had made the tribes more than willing to join the United States in the war that continued against the British. In August 1814, Nabedache, Hainai, Kichai, and Tawakoni warriors visited Sibley in Natchitoches to offer their services. Noting that the Kadohadacho *caddi* had "an entire Influence over them," Sibley felt that it would be wise to accept their offer in case of a British invasion. When the threat of a British landing in Louisiana materialized in late 1814, the Americans did entreat the Indians to assist them, and under the leadership of the Kadohadachos, the tribes proved true to their word. Governor Claiborne quickly alerted General Andrew Jackson of the Kadohadacho's importance. On October 28 the governor advised Jackson to confer with Dehahuit because he was the "most influential Indian on this side of the River Grande, and his friendship sir, will give much security to the Western Frontier of Louisiana." Although Jackson did not meet with Dehahuit, he nevertheless enlisted the *caddi*'s services. In December, the general gave the order asking the Kadohadachos and their allies to be "mustered into the service of the United States." As promised, the Indians answered the Americans' call, and 150 warriors arrived in Natchitoches ready to aid their allies. Because they arrived too late for the force to travel to New Orleans to intercept the British, they stayed at Natchitoches in readiness just in case they had to secure peace along the Spanish border.[38]

Although the Kadohadachos and their allies did not actually fight alongside the Americans, they had remained stalwart friends of the young republic and had played a large role in helping the United States secure its southwestern border. The Kadohadachos formally tied themselves to the United States in 1806, and throughout the period they used their considerable influence to keep the surrounding tribes friendly to the interests of the Americans. When the boundary was finally established in the Adams-Onís Treaty, effective in 1821, the entire Red River westward to the one hundredth meridian, far above the old Kadohadacho village, was included within the United States.

Assuming the position of *caddi* at the beginning of the nineteenth century, Dehahuit skillfully used the Kadohadachos' position on the disputed Louisiana-Texas frontier to maximize the benefits for his people during the following decade and a half. Following the Louisiana Purchase, he immediately made the Americans realize his tribe's influential position and forced the young republic's representatives to take measures designed to win his allegiance. Due to Dehahuit's diplomatic acumen, the Americans provided the Kadohadachos with protection from the Choctaw and Osage enemies that had been lacking during the era of Spanish control. In addition, the Kadohadachos obtained an abundance of trade goods from the Americans that the Spanish had previously been unable to provide. The respect the Americans, particularly John Sibley, gave to the Kadohadachos and their *caddi*, Dehahuit, helped to secure the tribe's favor. The attention the Kadohadachos received from the United States only added to the eminence of the tribe, and they consolidated their role as leaders of the other Caddo tribes of the region. Acknowledging Dehahuit's brilliant diplomatic skills, all of the Indians living along the Louisiana-Texas frontier ultimately accepted the Kadohadacho *caddi* as their spokesman in discussions with Spanish and American officials.

As soon as the tensions on the Louisiana-Texas frontier subsided after the War of 1812, however, the importance of the Kadohadachos dwindled. No longer necessary to American claims in the region, the tribe was soon regarded as a barrier to white settlement. Agent Sibley was removed from his position in 1815 due to the pressure of Americans in Louisiana who felt that he favored the Kadohadachos' interests. His replacements tended to reflect the government's lack of concern for the tribe's welfare and were unable to assist the Kadohadachos in the problems that plagued them during the next two decades. Among these problems were illegal whiskey traders, American settlers, and emigrant Indian tribes from east of the Mississippi who challenged the tribe's dominant position in the area. When Dehahuit died in 1833, the United States had already formulated plans to make the Kadohadacho lands more accessible to settlers by clearing the Red River of logjams. Two years later, the great *caddi*'s successors succumbed to intense pressure and sold the Kadohadacho's territory to the United States and agreed to move across the border into Mexican Texas. Eventually, all the Caddo tribes came together and settled on a reservation in the Indian Territory. Today, more than four thousand Caddos—nearly twice as many as in Dehahuit's day—reside in southwestern Oklahoma.[39]

Notes

1. For overviews of Caddo history, see F. Todd Smith, *The Caddo Indians: Tribes at the Convergence of Empires, 1542-1854* (College Station: Texas A & M University Press, 1995); Cecile Elkins Carter, *Caddo Indians: Where We Come From* (Norman: University of Oklahoma Press, 1995); David La Vere, *The Caddo Chiefdoms: Caddo Economics and Politics, 700-1835* (Lincoln: University of Nebraska Press, 1998).

2. For overviews of the situation of the Southern Plains in the early eighteenth century, see Elizabeth A. H. John, *Storms Brewed in Other Men's Worlds: The Confrontation of Indians, Spanish, and French in the Southwest, 1540-1795* (Norman: University of Oklahoma Press, 1975); Gary Clayton Anderson, *The Indian Southwest, 1580-1830: Ethnogenesis and Reinvention* (Norman: University of Oklahoma Press, 1999).

3. Agreement Made with the Indian Nations in Assembly, April 21, 1770, in Herbert Eugene Bolton, ed., *Athanase de Mézières and the Louisiana-Texas Frontier, 1768-1780*, 2 vols. (Cleveland: Arthur H. Clark, 1914), 1: 157-58; F. Todd Smith, *From Dominance to Disappearance: The Indians of Texas and the Near Southwest, 1786-1859* (Lincoln: University of Nebraska Press, 2005), 18-66.

4. Smith, *From Dominance to Disappearance*, 75-76; Mattie Austin Hatcher, trans., "Texas in 1820: Report on the Barbarous Indians of the Province of Texas by Juan Antonio Padilla, Made December 27, 1819," *Southwestern Historical Quarterly* 23 (July 1919): 48, hereafter cited as *SWHQ*; John Sibley, "Historical Sketches of the Several Indian Tribes in Louisiana, South of the Arkansas, and between the Mississippi and the River Grande, April 5, 1805," *American State Papers, Class II, Indian Affairs* (Washington: Gales and Seaton, 1832), 721.

5. Smith, *From Dominance to Disappearance*, 76; John Sibley, *A Report from Natchitoches in 1807*, ed. Annie Heloise Abel (New York: Museum of the American Indian Foundation, 1922): 95-96; Sibley to Governor William C. C. Claiborne, Oct. 10, 1803, in Clarence E. Carter, ed., *The Territory of Orleans, 1803-1812*, vol. 9, *The Territorial Papers of the United States*, 28 vols. (Washington: Government Printing Office, 1940), 75-76.

6. Smith, *From Dominance to Disappearance*, 78-79.

7. For background, see Dan L. Flores, ed., *Jefferson and Southwestern Exploration: The Freeman and Custis Accounts of the Red River Expedition of 1806* (Norman: University of Oklahoma Press, 1984), 3-38.

8. Sibley to Secretary of War William Eustis, Nov. 28, 1812, in Julia Kathryn Garrett, ed., "Doctor John Sibley and the Louisiana-Texas Frontier, 1803–1814," *SWHQ* 49 (January 1946): 418; Nettie Lee Benson, ed., "A Governor's Report on Texas in 1809," *SWHQ* 71 (April 1968): 614.

9. Sibley to Claiborne, Oct. 10, 1803, in Carter, *The Territory of Orleans*, 75–76; Daniel Clark to the Secretary of State, Sept. 29, 1803, in ibid., 63.

10. Claiborne to Edward Turner, Feb. 25, 1804, in Dunbar Rowland, ed., *Official Letter Books of W. C. C. Claiborne, 1801–1816*, 6 vols. (Jackson: Press of the Mississippi Historical Society, 1930), 1: 386; Smith, *Caddo Indians*, 88–89.

11. Claiborne to Thomas Jefferson, Aug. 30, 1804, in Rowland, *Official Letter Books*, 2: 287; Turner to Claiborne, Oct. 13, 1804, in ibid., 385; Claiborne to Turner, Nov. 3, 1804, in ibid., 390; Turner to Claiborne, Nov. 21, 1804, in Carter, *The Territory of Orleans*, 336.

12. José Joaquín Ugarte to Juan Bautista de Elguézabal, Nov. 26, 1803, Béxar Archives, Microfilm Copy, Center for American History, University of Texas, Austin, Texas, roll 31 (hereafter cited as BA); Nemesio Salcedo to Elguézabal, May 22, 1804, Béxar Archives Translations, Series 2, Microfilm Copy, University of North Texas Library, Denton, Texas, roll 2 (hereafter cited as BAT).

13. Smith, *From Dominance to Disappearance*, 80; Henry Dearborn to Sibley, Dec. 13, 1804, in Carter, *The Territory of Orleans*, 352–53; Sibley, "Historical Sketches," 721–22.

14. Smith, *Caddo Indians*, 91–92; Dionisio Valle to Elguézabal, June 11, 1805, BAT 7; Valle to Elguézabal, Oct. 3, 1805, ibid.

15. Diary of events at Nacogdoches, June 1805, ibid., 8; Valle to Elguézabal, Aug. 10, 1805, ibid.

16. Quoted in Flores, *Jefferson and Southwestern Exploration*, 55.

17. Nemesio Salcedo to Antonio Cordero, Oct. 8, 1805, BAT 9; Sebastián Rodríguez to Cordero, Feb. 13, 1806, ibid., 11.

18. José María Guadiana to Francisco Viana, May 31, 1806, ibid., 15; Juan Yngacio Ramón to Viana, June 2, 1806, ibid.; Viana to Cordero, June 3, 1806, ibid.; Guadiana to Viana, June 5, 1806, ibid.; Guadiana to Viana, June 20, 1806, ibid., 16.

19. Viana to Cordero, June 3, 1806, ibid., 15; Viana to Cordero, June 6, 1806, ibid.; Ramón to Viana, June 20, 1806, ibid., 16; Flores, *Jefferson and Southwestern Exploration*, 145–46.

20. Flores, *Jefferson and Southwestern Exploration*, 145–67.

21. Ibid., 160–67.

22. Ibid., 166–74.

23. Ibid., 173; Smith, *Caddo Indians*, 95.

24. Flores, *Jefferson and Southwestern Exploration*, 193–207.

25. Claiborne to Simón Herrera, Aug. 26, 1806, in Rowland, *Official Letter Books*, 3: 384; Herrera to Claiborne, Aug. 28, 1806, in ibid., 392.

26. J. Villasana Haggard, "The Neutral Ground between Louisiana and Texas, 1806–1821," *Louisiana Historical Quarterly* 38 (October 1945): 1001–28.

27. Address to the Caddo Chief, Sept. 5, 1806, in Rowland, *Official Letter Books*, 4: 3–5.

28. Sibley, *Report from Natchitoches in 1807*, 20–24; Sibley to Dearborn, July 3, 1807, in Julia Kathryn Garrett, ed., "Doctor John Sibley and the Louisiana-Texas Frontier," *SWHQ* 45 (January 1942): 381.

29. Sibley, *Report from Natchitoches in 1807*, 49–66.

30. Record of goods supplied by William Barr and Samuel Davenport, Nov. 11, 1807, BAT 30; List of Indian Presents, Jan. 11, 1808, ibid., 32; Manuel Salcedo to Guadiana, Aug. 19, 1809, BA 42; Barr and Davenport to Guadiana, Sept. 2, 1809, ibid.

31. Sibley to William Eustis, Jan. 30, 1810, in Julia Kathryn Garrett, ed., "Doctor John Sibley and the Louisiana-Texas Frontier," *SWHQ* 47 (October 1944): 389.

32. Sibley to Eustis, Dec. 31, 1811, in Garrett, "Doctor John Sibley and the Louisiana-Texas Frontier," *SWHQ* 49 (January 1946): 403.

33. Donald E. Chipman, *Spanish Texas, 1519–1821* (Austin: University of Texas Press, 1992), 232–36; Sibley to Eustis, May 18, 1812, *House Reports*, Doc. 1035, 27th Cong., 2nd Sess., 1842 (Serial 411), 106.

34. Sibley to Eustis, Aug. 5, 1812, in Garrett, "Doctor John Sibley and the Louisiana-Texas Frontier," *SWHQ* 49 (January 1946): 414–15.

35. Sibley to Eustis, February 12, 1813, in ibid.: 421–22.

36. Sibley to John Armstrong, Oct. 6, 1813, in ibid.: 602–3.

37. Smith, *From Dominance to Disappearance*, 100; A Talk from W. C. C. Claiborne, Governor of Louisiana, to the Chief of the Caddo, Oct. 18, 1813, in Rowland, *Official Letter Books*, 6: 275–77.

38. Sibley to Armstrong, Aug. 10, 1814, in Garrett, "Doctor John Sibley and the Louisiana-Texas Frontier," *SWHQ* 49 (April 1946): 609; Claiborne to Andrew Jackson, Oct. 28, 1814, in Rowland, *Official Letter Books*, 6: 238–39; Claiborne to James Monroe, Dec. 20, 1814, in ibid., 293–94; Smith, *Caddo Indians*, 102.

39. Smith, *Caddo Indians*, 103–24; F. Todd Smith, *The Caddos, the Wichitas, and the United States, 1846–1901* (College Station: Texas A & M University Press, 1996); Kathleen Du Val, *The Native Ground: Indians and Colonists in the Heart of the Continent* (Philadelphia: University of Pennsylvania Press, 2006), 248.

PART III

Building Fortunes through Family Connections and Local Community

7

The Nature of Loyalty: Antonio Gil Ibarvo and the East Texas Frontier

J. EDWARD TOWNES

In the traditional political-diplomatic interpretation of history, the word "loyalty" equates with allegiance to a sovereign, a country, or an ideology. The historian's bias in favor of or in opposition to these manifestations of power on the part of nation-states has defined patriots and traitors, law-abiding citizens and criminals, heroes and villains. Yet the Spanish borderlands represent a far more complex phenomenon than a traditionally dichotomized, ordered society (map 7.1). Settlers in these remote areas, removed from metropolitan seats of political power and market centralization, relied on kinship and friendship networks, economic interdependence, and ties to the land, initially to survive, and later to prosper. These exigencies, in turn, promoted loyalty at the local and regional levels rather than to the Crown's distant and disconnected government. In the Louisiana-Texas borderlands, these loyalties became part of an engine of self-determination, apart from the concerns of statecraft and national rivalry, which advanced personal and local interests, often in direct opposition to Spanish law and policy, and fostered collusion, resistance, and ultimately civil disobedience against the government of New Spain.

The people of Spanish East Texas differed markedly from those in East and West Florida, and Spanish Louisiana, making the movement toward self-determination even more intriguing. While foreign-born populations, particularly British and Anglo-Americans, dominated the Floridas, and Frenchmen, Acadians, and refugees from revolts in the Caribbean populated Louisiana, the settlers of East Texas came almost exclusively from Mexico. Even by the early nineteenth century, census records for the District of Nacogdoches indicate that foreign-born individuals represented only a small portion of the total population of the area. Spanish subjects throughout their lives, the original settlers of the Texas-Louisiana borderlands had no experience with other governments that might breed discontent. Instead, their dissatisfaction lay in

Map 7.1. The eighteenth-century Louisiana-Texas border. Map by Tracy Ellen Smith, www.cdrtexas.com.

restrictions imposed by a regime in far-off Mexico City that failed to consider conditions on the frontier, and that lacked the flexibility to respond to the needs of its borderland citizens. Pragmatism, rather than legalism, made it possible to survive in the isolation that Texas imposed. Moreover, the people of East Texas, sent there to secure the frontier against French incursion, quickly found that their survival and prosperity depended on cooperation with their Louisiana neighbors.[1]

Until France established a permanent presence at the trading post it named Natchitoches, Spain had no plans for Texas. The vast Northern Province offered no mineral wealth, and virtually nothing to induce settlement to such a remote and inhospitable region. The brief incursion of La Salle's ill-fated colony prompted Spain to establish missions among the Caddo tribes of East Texas and Western Louisiana in the 1690s, but attempts to "missionize" these tribes, bring them under Spanish control, and make them military allies against encroachment by France failed miserably, and the missions closed, leaving Texas again without a Spanish presence.[2]

In the autumn of 1713, the French explorer and trader Louis Juchereau de St. Denis ascended the Mississippi and Red rivers to the heart of the Caddo confederacy in northwestern Louisiana. Under orders from the governor of Louisiana to buy horses, St. Denis struck out overland to the Hasinai villages west of the Sabine River. From there he continued across Texas in an effort to make contact with the Spanish settlements along the Rio Grande. Instead of the welcome St. Denis had hoped for Spanish officials arrested his small expedition at San Juan Bautista in July 1714. Fearing that French traders would flood northern New Spain with contraband and perhaps even invade its mining districts, the viceroy, the Duque de Linares, ordered the reoccupation of East Texas as a buffer.[3]

In April 1716, an expedition under Captain Diego Ramón entered Texas accompanied by St. Denis, who served as a supply officer for the *entrada*. Astonishingly, while nominally under arrest, the Frenchman had learned to speak Spanish, ingratiated himself with his captors, and even courted the presidial commander's granddaughter. Sent on to Mexico City for interrogation, St. Denis persuaded officials that he wished to become a Spanish subject. Rather than suffering incarceration, the fate of many foreign intruders before and after him, St. Denis returned to San Juan Bautista as a Spanish citizen.[4]

St. Denis typifies a pattern of shifting national allegiances that developed in the borderlands; it was a practice that reflected the reality of borderlands life where political affiliations might change when situations dictated. Straddling two worlds, St. Denis's Spanish citizenship allowed him to conduct trade with the Caddoan tribes in Spanish Texas, while as chief official of the French post established at Natchitoches in 1714 he remained free to build a family empire based on commerce and land acquisition in Louisiana. Until the United States imposed its "Factory System" in Natchitoches in 1804, St. Denis's descendants remained firmly in control of the Indian trade in the Texas-Louisiana borderland.

The Spanish built four missions and the presidio of San Francisco de los Dolores in Texas during the summer of 1716. After construction began, Captain Ramón continued eastward to Natchitoches, where he found that Frenchmen had built a stockade on an island in the middle of the Red River. The impetus for a French settlement at Natchitoches came from intelligence supplied by St. Denis. Even while in Spanish custody, the resourceful trader managed to keep the French governor Cadillac informed of the Spaniards' plans. Fearful that eastward-moving Spaniards and westward-moving Englishmen might trap lower Louisiana, Cadillac had ordered the post to establish a French presence beyond the Mississippi.[5]

Natchitoches changed Spain's view of Texas, and officials moved quickly to counter French intentions west of the Red River, which the Spanish considered their eastern border. Lacking sufficient funds for military forces to occupy the region, officials in Mexico City counted on its mission among the Adaes Indians, whose villages lay just west of the new French post, to convert the local tribes and bring them under Spanish control as a buffer against further French encroachment into Texas. When word reached the remote frontier that the War of the Quadruple Alliance had begun, an overly zealous French lieutenant, Philippe Blondel, led a detachment of seven men from Natchitoches to strike the nearest Spanish target; San Miguel de Linares de los Adaes Mission. Finding only a missionary and one soldier there, Blondel and his detail sent them packing. Two years later the Spanish returned, restoring the mission and protecting it with a presidio and a garrison of two hundred men. These initial Spanish settlers, primarily mestizo, mulatto, and Coahuiltecan Indian, entered East Texas at the command of the Crown rather than by choice, serving as pawns in an international chess game.[6]

Unlike Natchitoches, which had a river connection to New Orleans, the presidio and mission at Los Adaes maintained a tenuous link with New Spain. Saltillo, a major source of supply, lay eight hundred miles away. San Antonio de Béxar was three hundred miles distant over little more than a buffalo trace. Under ideal conditions, wagons required a month to travel from Béxar to the remote outpost. Yet conditions seldom approached ideal. Rivers flooded during the rainy season, and in summer and winter draft animals found scant forage. Parties of Indians or bandits often preyed on unprotected or underprotected caravans. Such difficulties endangered cargoes of desperately needed supplies.[7]

Shortages of food and clothing plagued the Spanish at Los Adaes. The worst time for the outpost came during the mid-1730s when a number of circumstances, all aggravated by their remoteness from centers of commerce, combined to create a critical situation. Scarcity of beans, corn, and other dietary staples occurred during the winter of 1734–35, causing famine among the Spanish. In addition, due to a lack of cloth, Spanish clothing consisted mainly of rags, blankets, and buffalo skins. From dire necessity, the presidio turned to the French at Natchitoches for assistance. The imaginary line between imperial claims gave way as the Spanish enclave came to rely on its French Louisiana neighbors for survival.[8]

Spanish law forbade trade with foreign colonies and severely restricted commercial dealings with indigenous tribes. While these mercantile restrictions seemed perfectly logical to a Spanish bureaucrat, they proved unworkable on the frontier. Goods for the frontier trade came through Spain to Vera Cruz, thence to Saltillo, and finally to San Antonio, often at prices far beyond the means of frontier settlers. The French, in contrast, could obtain these goods from New Orleans and Natchez by river at far less cost and sell them at far lower prices than goods arriving overland from Mexico. As a civil settlement and outlying ranches grew up around the presidio of Los Adaes, the area became the center of an elaborate network of illegal trade between Spanish East Texas, local Native American tribes, and the French at Natchitoches.[9]

Family and kinship provided the basic unit in borderlands society. By the mid-eighteenth century, Los Adaes boasted perhaps five hundred residents. Many had family ties to the French in Natchitoches and the local Caddoan tribes. These kinship and friendship networks, and the economy that developed between Los Adaes and French Louisiana, allowed the Spanish settlers to survive so far from the commercial centers of New Spain. A few individuals even became wealthy through networks of clandestine trade that supplied livestock to Louisiana in exchange for food, clothing, and luxury goods.[10]

Antonio Gil Ibarvo prospered in this contraband trade. Born at Los Adaes in 1729, Gil Ibarvo grew up in a society that subordinated ineffectual laws to the good of the community. From his ranch, El Lobanillo, he prospered in the livestock business and illegal trade, and sources suggest that Rancho del Lobanillo had developed to the size of a pueblo by 1772, employing a number of local families and providing contraband goods imported from Louisiana that remained unavailable in other areas of Texas. Even Texas's Spanish governor, Angel Martos y Navarette, who resided at Los Adaes, shared in the profitable "black market" to such an extent that royal officials removed him from his post in 1767 and brought him before the viceroy to answer on charges of smuggling.[11]

Intent on enforcing the law, the Viceroy Marqués de Cruillas sent Don Hugo O'Conor, the *comandante inspector* of *presidios*, to Los Adaes to investigate Martos y Navarette in 1767. An Irishman in the service of Spain, O'Conor had an outstanding military record and powerful friends, including his cousin Alejandro O'Reilly, José de Gálvez, Bernardo de Gálvez, Teodoro de Croix, and Antonio María Bucareli. These men formed a powerful faction in the Spanish court that viewed the Gulf Coast and the lower Mississippi Valley as the key to Spain's empire in the New World. Intractably loyal to the Crown, O'Conor proved a complete juxtaposition to the practical attitude of men such as Gil Ibarvo and Martos y Navarette. When they met, loyalty to the community and loyalty to the government collided.[12]

Insisting on scrupulous adherence to the law, O'Conor resolved to rid

Spain's eastern provinces of illicit trade. His report to the viceroy prompted Martos y Navarette's removal from office, and O'Conor succeeded him as interim governor. O'Conor's insistence on rigid adherence to laws concerning trade quickly made him the enemy of Gil Ibarvo and the community of Adaesaños. O'Conor likewise held the Adaesaños in disdain, seeing their disregard for the law as disloyalty to the Crown. Almost immediately, he focused his contempt on Gil Ibarvo, whom he accused of masterminding the illegal commerce throughout the region. His personal vendetta against the rancher led him to order Gil Ibarvo's arrest in New Orleans on a charge of possessing stolen horses. As a result, Gil Ibarvo remained imprisoned for seven months and gained his release only after the Barón de Ripperdá replaced O'Conor as the governor of Texas. Nevertheless, the clash between Gil Ibarvo's loyalty to the welfare of the community and O'Conor's loyalty to the Crown's law continued.[13]

The circumstances that thrust Antonio Gil Ibarvo to the leadership of the Adaesaños resulted from political changes in Europe. In 1763, France ceded Louisiana to Spain. Since Los Adaes, with a garrison of sixty soldiers, no longer represented the political frontier between French and Spanish imperial claims, Spanish authorities saw no reason to continue to support it. More importantly, a waning treasury and the much more menacing threat posed by the Apache and Comanche to the west necessitated a realignment of resources on the northern frontier of New Spain.[14]

On a midsummer's day in 1772, ministers of the Spanish court met at the home of the Marqués de Croix in Madrid. With Louisiana now in Spanish hands, the committee revisited recommendations made five years earlier by the Marqués de Rubí for a reorganization of defenses along Spain's northern frontier. Their deliberations resulted in the Nuevo Reglamento of 1772, a royal decree to abandon all missions and presidios in Texas except those at Béxar and La Bahía, transfer the capital of Texas from the presidio of Los Adaes to San Antonio, and remove all soldiers and settlers in east Texas to the new capital.[15]

Instructions to carry out this order reached Don Juan María Vicencio, Barón de Ripperdá and governor of Texas, on May 18, 1773. Governor Ripperdá, who was in San Antonio when the order arrived, took personal responsibility for bringing the news to the people of Los Adaes. Arriving on June 6, he ordered the inhabitants to cease work and begin gathering their belongings and livestock, and to prepare to leave for Béxar in two weeks. He explained that once the displaced settlers arrived in San Antonio they could choose new land from unclaimed areas surrounding the new capital. Leaving the aged and infirm Lieutenant José González to carry out the order for the abandonment of East Texas, Ripperdá returned to Béxar.[16]

The citizens of Los Adaes and the vicinity, stunned by this unimaginable order to leave the only home they had ever known and abandon their property, relatives, and friends in Natchitoches, pleaded for time. Such wealth as they possessed lay in their herds of horses and cattle, the mainstay of the illicit trade. They argued that the order should only apply to those living at the presidio and mission, and asked Ripperdá to allow them to remain without the garrison. Coming, as the order had, in early summer, it meant abandoning crops already in the field. With their herds of horses and cattle ranging across open grazing lands, two weeks left no time for a roundup. How, they complained, could they gather their belongings, abandon their crops, and herds, and begin such a long and perilous journey in two weeks? How could they convey all of their household goods without adequate transportation? Their protests fell upon deaf ears.[17]

Upon his departure from Los Adaes Ripperdá wrote to Unzaga y Amézaga, the newly appointed Spanish governor of Louisiana, informing him of the abandonment of the presidio. He expressed hope that the commander at Natchitoches would protect the property of the Adaesaños until the government in San Antonio could arrange to recover what lack of time and means of transportation obliged them to leave behind. It also seems clear from the letter that resistance to forced evacuation, abetted by relatives and friends among the Caddo and in Natchitoches, had already begun. Ripperdá advised Unzaga y Amézaga that several families from Los Adaes had already fled to Natchitoches to avoid removal, directly contrary to the king's order to resettle in San Antonio. He requested the Louisiana governor's help in returning these fugitives.[18]

On June 25, Lieutenant José González, a thirty-seven-year veteran of the garrison of Los Adaes, led those who felt obliged to follow the order to move to San Antonio west along the Camino Real with what few personal belongings they could carry and the livestock they had gathered in the brief time available to them. The caravan made its first stop for rest at Rancho del Lobanillo, where Gil Ibarvo's aged mother received permission to remain at her son's home because of her poor health. She was not the only one. One of Gil Ibarvo's sisters and his sister-in-law, also ill, stayed at the ranch. Since he could not leave the women behind alone, Gil Ibarvo secured permission for several people to stay behind with them. In all, twenty-four individuals abandoned the march at El Lobanillo, adding to the number of those who fled to Natchitoches to avoid removal. There seems little doubt that those who remained behind also kept the ranch operating, a convenient spin of fortune both for them and Gil Ibarvo.[19]

It took the marchers a month to reach the Nacogdoches mission. Along the way, drought and lack of food took their toll. Although the numbers remain uncertain, the historian Herbert Eugene Bolton asserts that at least two women and ten children died between Los Adaes and Nacogdoches. At the mission, old Lieutenant González also fell ill and died, leaving the party without a leader. When the caravan again moved south, Antonio Gil Ibarvo assumed the leadership role.[20]

As the families of Los Adaes left Nacogdoches, the heat and continued drought condemned them to a brutal trek toward San Antonio. Lack of food and water exacted a grim toll. When they reached the Brazos, where a relief party from San Antonio met them with supplies and horses, most of the 167 families felt too ill and weak to go on. Along the way, thirty or more people had simply left the column, apparently intent on making their way back home. After a brief rest, the Adaesaños arrived at Béxar on September 26 exhausted, virtually penniless, and sick at heart for the homes and property they had abandoned. Others, too weak to travel, remained behind at the Brazos.[21]

The day after their arrival in San Antonio, the tired wayfarers from Los Adaes received an order from Governor Ripperdá to proceed at once to the selection of building sites, farmlands, and ranches on unclaimed land within the jurisdiction of the Villa de San Fernando. The former residents of Los Adaes, wanting only to return to their abandoned homes, apparently made little if any effort to comply. Given their months of travel, their exhaustion, and their low morale, this hardly seems strange. Yet it indicates that even among those whose allegiance to the Crown compelled them to comply with the order to abandon their homes, submission had limits; and it appears that they had reached them.[22]

Only eight days after arriving in San Antonio, Gil Ibarvo, who had clearly emerged as the group's leader, called a meeting of the heads of families to draft a petition asking the governor to allow them to relocate to the abandoned mission of the Los Ais, in what is present day San Augustine, Texas. They justified their request by asserting that such a move would place them close enough to Los Adaes to allow them to recover much of their lost property. They further argued that they could not find suitable land for their settlement near the Villa de San Fernando without encroaching upon the rights of others, and that even if they could they did not have the financial means to undertake the construction of an aqueduct for irrigation. Finally, in view of the circumstances in which they found themselves and the sufferings they had endured in obeying the orders of the Crown, they begged permission to found a new settlement near Gil Ibarvo's ranch in East Texas. The petition also stated that, if the governor saw fit to grant their request, the Adaesaños would bear all of the expenses of their return trip.[23]

An analysis of this petition indicates the extent to which community loyalty and cohesion remained paramount. Resistance emerged even among those who obeyed the royal decree to abandon their homes. Although those who remained on the Brazos did not sign the document, the number of signatories still represents more than half of the families who survived the march from Los Adaes. The fact that they had been in San Antonio hardly more than a week and had arrived exhausted from travel suggests that they spent little time or energy looking for suitable land. Finally, how could people so impoverished that they lacked the resources to build an aqueduct for irrigation bear all of the expenses of their return trip to East Texas? Apparently, the petitioners felt that their obedience to the king's will should satisfy the government of New Spain, and they wished to go home.

Despite his part in carrying out the removal, Governor Ripperdá sympathized with the Adaesaños, though his support seems as much political as humanitarian. Motivated by his wish to return with his community to East Texas, Gil Ibarvo repeatedly argued that Spain relied on the good will of the Indians in East Texas, a belief that Ripperdá shared. Though in the minds of Spanish bureaucrats, the acquisition of Louisiana ended the major threat to Spain's northern frontier, both men believed that holding Texas depended on the support of the friendly bands that formed a buffer between the Spanish settlements and the Comanche and Apache to the north and west. Of the East Texas groups, the Tejas, or western bands of the Caddo, and the Bidais represented powerful allies, and the governor concurred with Gil Ibarvo that Spain must maintain their allegiance. In the minds of some tribal leaders, Ibarvo argued, closing the missions and abandoning East Texas sent a dangerous message that Spain had forsaken them in their fight against the more warlike tribes. With limited military strength, Ripperdá also realized that Spain could not stand alone if these previously friendly tribes reached an accommodation with the Comanche and Apache. Maintaining good relations among the tribes of East Texas, the two men agreed, remained paramount in any defensive strategy; and that good will depended on a Spanish presence, which the Adaesaños provided.[24]

Yet the political situation in the province reflected the proverbial two-edged sword. Ripperdá could not contravene a royal decree. Instead, he skillfully avoided a decision by ordering the Adaesaños to try more earnestly to find appropriate lands near San Antonio or along Cibolo Creek to the southeast. Yet this second directive, carefully crafted, included an escape clause for the community. Should the new arrivals fail to find adequate land after making a more diligent effort, the governor authorized them to present their request to settle at the Los Ais mission near Ibarvo's ranch directly to the viceroy. Whether the homesick people of East Texas made more than a token effort to find a suitable site near Béxar the second time remains open to conjecture. During the first week of December, the heads of one hundred and twenty-seven families met with Ripperdá. In his presence, they formally elected Antonio Gil Ibarvo and Gil Flores to present their petition to the viceroy.[25]

With Ripperdá's blessing, Gil Ibarvo and Flores left San Antonio carrying the petition and two letters from the governor; one was to the viceroy, Bucareli, and one was to the *comandante inspector* of *presidios*, Don Hugo O'Conor, Gil Ibarvo's old nemesis, whose position made him responsible for all matters pertaining to the northern frontier of New Spain. Ripperdá's letter to the viceroy strongly endorsed the petition and urged vice regal approval. While Ripperdá admitted that he did not understand all of the reasons for the abandonment of East Texas, he still believed that Spain's security rested in maintaining a presence among the northern Indians. Still, he clearly anticipated a problem with the *comandante inspector*. O'Conor disliked and distrusted Ripperdá, Gil Ibarvo, and anyone connected with Los Adaes, which he considered disloyal to the king and a den of thieves. In addition, politics at the Spanish court affected O'Conor's position. His cousin, Don Alejandro O'Reilly, helped author the Nuevo Reglamento. For O'Conor, the regulations made the status of East Texas clear. To him, obedience superseded all other considerations. Anticipating O'Conor's negative response to the petition, Ripperdá advised the viceroy that the argument against an East Texas settlement based on illicit trade between Texas and Louisiana ignored the fact that, with the Spanish absent, French traders controlled the Indian trade on both sides of the border. Better, he thought, to have the Spanish in control than the French, even if the latter were now Spanish subjects. The governor repeated the same argument in his letter to O'Conor in an effort to solicit his support for the proposed return to East Texas. Doubting that his appeal would move O'Conor, Ripperdá added an alternative suggestion. If O'Conor felt disinclined to recommend the petition to the viceroy as presented, perhaps he would consider allowing the Adaesaños to found a settlement on Gil Ibarvo's ranch. His inclusion of this alternative recommendation certainly must have originated with Ibarvo and implies that those who left the march to San Antonio at El Lobanillo did far more than tend the rancher's sick relatives.[26]

This concern over the Indian trade and the French in Louisiana reflects the disconnected nature of Spain's tenure in Louisiana. With the restructuring of Spanish administration brought about by the acquisition of Louisiana,

Texas became part of the *provincias internas*, falling within the viceroyalty of Mexico, while Louisiana's administration fell under the captain general of Cuba. Despite the close connection between the two provinces, they remained separated administratively and deprived of reciprocal trade privileges. With the absence of Spaniards in East Texas, the Frenchman Athanase de Mézières became Spain's Indian agent on the Louisiana-Texas frontier.

Arriving in Natchitoches in 1742, de Mézières caught the attention of St. Denis, who considered him a capable officer, and made him his protégé. An intelligent and talented young man, De Mézières learned the local Indian languages and customs. He secured an even closer link with the powerful St. Denis family through marriage to his mentor's daughter, Marie Petronille Felicité. By 1763, when Spain acquired Louisiana, de Mézières had become a wealthy trader and planter as well as the commander of the French post at Natchitoches. In 1769, Louisiana's Spanish governor, Alejandro O'Reilly, appointed him as lieutenant governor. Like his mentor, he accepted a new national allegiance, and a position with the Spanish government, for both practical and opportunistic reasons, becoming the major power broker in the borderland until his death a decade later.[27]

In January 1774, Ibarvo and Flores reached Mexico City and presented their petition, along with Governor Ripperdá's letter, to the viceroy and his council. They quickly found allies; particularly José de Areche, the *fiscal*, a former member of the king's royal council and arguably the most influential bureaucrat in Mexico. Areche's persuasive argument in favor of the petition agreed that a settlement in East Texas would serve Spain's interest in retaining the support of the Indians in that region. Further, he suggested that the king's reason for suppressing the missions grew from his majesty's objection to funding a venture that had never successfully converted the local Caddoan peoples, and had nothing to do with civil settlement of the area. It also seems that Areche anticipated O'Conor's opposition to resettling East Texas. Areche suggested that, because of O'Conor's heavy workload, orders for the implementation of the petition should go directly to Governor Ripperdá. With Areche's recommendation in hand the viceroy convened a *junta de guerra y hacienda*, which, after reviewing the petition, Governor Ripperdá's letter, and Areche's opinion, approved the request, effectively overturning the Reglamento of 1772 as respects the abandonment of East Texas. Gil Ibarvo and Flores must certainly have felt elated. Through their determined loyalty to their community and their own self-interest, they had accomplished their goal. The Adaesaños could go home.[28]

Comandante Inspector Hugo O'Conor, a growing political power and a man not to be trifled with, responded in outrage when he received Governor

Ripperdá's letter. Four days after the *junta* approved the petition, Areche received a vitriolic response from O'Conor. O'Conor also replied to Ripperdá's letter in support of the petition, categorically informing the governor that he would not countenance such a request. O'Conor expressed his contempt for Gil Ibarvo and the Adaesaños, and his severe displeasure at Ripperdá's failure to carry out the Nuevo Reglamento to the letter. He peremptorily ordered Ripperdá to bring those persons who remained at Los Adaes, El Lobanillo, Nacogdoches, and Natchitoches, and any other stragglers in East Texas to San Antonio without further delay. O'Conor also dismissed as ridiculous the argument that the Adaesaños could not find suitable lands in or around Béxar. In his mind, their disloyalty to the king seemed clear. His letter to the viceroy accused both Ripperdá and Gil Ibarvo in even more damning terms of attempting to circumvent the matter that he felt lay at the heart of the Nuevo Reglamento—suppression of the contraband trade emanating from Los Adaes. O'Conor believed that Ripperdá, Gil Ibarvo, Flores, and all those promoting the return to East Texas did so in order to profit again from the contraband trade. He expressed regret that the governor of Texas supported and endorsed the petition, and grief that a Spanish official obstructed the execution of the king's orders while he (O'Conor) labored diligently to carry them out. Since his duties made it impossible for him to go to Texas to enforce the king's will, O'Conor demanded that the viceroy instruct Governor Ripperdá in the strictest terms to carry out his orders with respect to the exiles from Los Adaes to the letter.[29]

The Adaesaños' victory over royal policy proved short-lived. Areche knew O'Conor personally. Concerned by his violent opposition to the petition, Areche recommended that the *junta* reconvene to consider O'Conor's argument. The viceroy accepted his advice, and after brief deliberation, the council decided to submit its previous decision to O'Conor for his approval or rejection. Left to O'Conor's resolution, the petition was doomed. Realizing this, Flores and Gil Ibarvo made one final appeal to Viceroy Bucareli, asking permission to relocate to Natchitoches with their families so that they could reclaim the remnants of their herds and property. They promised that they would return and settle in Texas once the government chose a site.[30]

Just as the situation seemed bleakest for the Adaesaños, Viceroy Bucareli unwittingly gave Governor Ripperdá an opportunity to assist them. In a message designed to conform to O'Conor's position the viceroy ordered Ripperdá not to allow the refugees to return to either Natchitoches or El Lobanillo, but to aid them in finding a suitable location "as agreed upon." When the governor questioned the two emissaries on what they and the viceroy had agreed upon, Gil Ibarvo and Flores claimed that the viceroy had given them permission to settle outside San Antonio as long as they chose a site no closer to Natchitoches than one hundred leagues. The governor moved quickly to support the Adaesaños in finding a suitable site for their settlement. Pushing the agreement to its extreme, Gil Ibarvo selected a spot on the Trinity River at Paso Tomás, where the Camino Real crossed the Bahía Road, in what is now Madison County, Texas. The governor agreed, and about seventy families initially traveled north to begin constructing the new settlement. Others followed. They named their new settlement Nuestra Señora del Pilar de Bucareli, echoing the name of their former church, Nuestra Señora del Pilar de los Adaes, and honoring the viceroy. As with most such lofty names, Nuestra Señora del Pilar de Bucareli seldom appears except in official correspondence. Among the inhabitants, the settlement quickly acquired the diminutives Bucareli or La Trinidad, for the river on which it stood.[31]

Although the final decision of the *junta* of May 5 clearly placed the fate of the Adaesaños in the hands of Comandante Inspector O'Conor, fate and quick action by Governor Ripperdá took it away again. For six weeks after O'Conor received the decision he remained too preoccupied with other duties to act on it. When O'Conor finally decided to take charge, Ripperdá replied that the exiles had already established a new settlement in accordance with the instructions communicated to him from the viceroy. O'Conor, furious, severely reprimanded the governor for exceeding his authority in allowing the move to the Trinity. Yet the fact remained that the Adaesaños had taken another step closer to home.[32]

The settlement at Bucareli lasted only five years. Comanche raids, a devastating flood that drowned both crops and livestock, and a fire that destroyed much of the settlement finally forced its abandonment. When the Comanche trouble began, the residents asked Texas's new governor, Domingo Cabello, to allow them to move further east into Caddo territory where they could live in safety. Cabello repeatedly refused their entreaties. In fact, the move to the Trinity, based on the purported verbal agreement between Viceroy Bucareli and the leaders of the Adaesaños, never received official approval in Mexico City. When Teodoro de Croix succeeded O'Conor as the *comandante general*, he asked Governor Cabello for an opinion: "should the unauthorized settlement at Paso Tomás continue, or should it be suppressed?"[33]

Gil Ibarvo and his companions knew that officials in Mexico City favored recalling the settlers to San Antonio in conformance with the Nuevo Reglamento of 1772. When entreaties to the governor proved useless, the people again turned to Gil Ibarvo to lead them back to East Texas. Faced with the decision to ignore Spanish authority and accede to the wishes of his community, Gil Ibarvo ultimately chose loyalty to the community. After several refusals, he agreed to lead the Adaesaños back toward their homes. Still, his decision only ratified what had increasingly become fact. By 1779, when the last settlers left Bucareli, they joined many who had previously filtered back into East Texas. When Gil Ibarvo affirmed the final decision to abandon Bucareli, local leaders rounded up those they could find and moved their settlement to the site of the old Nacogdoches mission, where they founded the pueblo of Nuestra Señora del Pilar de Nacogdoches. This move put the Adaesaños close to their former homes, ranches, and farms, and they quickly proceeded to reoccupy their abandoned ranches or begin new ones.[34]

The choice of the Nacogdoches mission as the center of the new settlement seems, at first glance, odd. Resettlement at Los Adaes, their former home, offered far more protection from the Comanche because it lay even deeper in Caddo country than Nacogdoches. Closer to Natchitoches, Los Adaes also placed those involved in smuggling closer to the Louisiana border. Yet since Spain now controlled Louisiana, Spanish troops from that province might again compel the settlers to leave East Texas and return to San Antonio just as soldiers from Béxar might. Whatever reason compelled Gil Ibarvo to choose Nacogdoches, the location placed him close to his ranch, satisfied the community, and offered more protection from Comanche raids than they had had in Bucareli since it lay within Caddo country.

Still, the potentially volatile move, made by consensus of the community in direct violation of the wishes of the Spanish government, represented a desperate gamble for the Adaesaños. Even the "agreement" made with Viceroy Bucareli specified that the community must remain at least one hundred leagues from Natchitoches. Clearly, they had violated that directive. Spanish officials had removed them once before and might do so again. Nevertheless, their resistance to the forced evacuation of their homes had not waned. Given the opportunity, they chose to defy Spanish authority and return to their homeland.

After the establishment of Nacogdoches, Gil Ibarvo filed a claim against the government for reimbursement of personal funds. He contended that he had expended thousands of pesos to aid the people of Los Adaes during their exile. He further requested arms to defend Nacogdoches, which did not have either a presidio or a garrison. On October 15, 1779, Comandante General Croix granted Gil Ibarvo an annual salary of five hundred pesos and gave him the titles of lieutenant governor and chief justice of Nacogdoches, and captain of the militia. In the following year, Gil Ibarvo also received an appointment as judge of contraband seizures, an interesting position for the man some considered the chief architect of illicit trade in East Texas.[35]

From Nacogdoches, Gil Ibarvo again established friendly relations with the Indians of East Texas. To maintain their good will he asked Governor Cabello to authorize a trading post in Nacogdoches. The governor granted his request. Gil Ibarvo also introduced an informal system of verbal land grants, allowing members of the community to claim individual land that, by law and custom, belonged to the Crown. Unfortunately, his failure to provide written documentation made their legality questionable, and he later received censure for his poor record keeping. He also resumed his questionable business ventures, placing himself in further jeopardy. Despite his position as judge of contraband seizures, a post created to help eliminate smuggling, he continued to engage in clandestine trade with French agents from Louisiana, who in turn traded with Americans east of the Mississippi River.[36]

The last years of Gil Ibarvo's life proved far more difficult than any he had experienced before. He began to tire of his duties as lieutenant governor of Nacogdoches, captain of militia, judge of contraband seizures, and chief justice. In a letter to Governor Manuel Muñoz he described himself as "worn out by my advanced age, which exceeds sixty years." In his request to retire from his duties, he included a petition to the viceroy briefly recounting his services since August 7, 1774, and asking for a pension of one-half his annual salary of five hundred pesos. The government denied his request.[37]

Although Hugo O'Conor left the northern frontier in 1775 and died in 1777, other Spanish officials had begun to take note of Gil Ibarvo's questionable activities. Suspecting him of smuggling and trading in stolen goods, Ramón de Castro, the *comandante general* of the Eastern Provinces, invited Gil Ibarvo to Béxar on a pretext and then had the old man arrested. That he did so suggests strongly that de Castro feared the community's loyalty to Ibarvo enough to avoid a direct confrontation at Nacogdoches. Incarcerated for several months in San Antonio, Gil Ibarvo's case finally went to trial in November 1792. Four years later, the court finally dismissed the case for lack of conclusive evidence. Despite this acquittal, the government placed a heavy penalty on the aging East Texan; he could not return to the city he had founded. Apparently, Spanish officials feared his power over the people of East Texas, where they deemed his presence "contrary to the union and best harmony" of the District of Nacogdoches.[38]

The last years of Gil Ibarvo's life proved taxing for the old man. Legal proceedings deprived him of most of his material possessions. In late 1809 or early 1810, at the age of eighty, Gil Ibarvo died at his home on the west bank of the Attoyac River. Perhaps the most stirring tribute to Don Antonio Gil Ibarvo came from Father José de la Garza, a longtime missionary at Nacogdoches, who recorded that the settlers in East Texas regarded Gil Ibarvo as "the father, protector, and comforter of their recovered homeland."[39]

Until recently, historians have studied the dramatic and tumultuous history of the Spanish borderlands from political, diplomatic, and military points of view. In this context, men such as Hugo O'Conor stand as iconic examples of loyalty. A soldier and bureaucrat devoted to serving the Crown, O'Conor equated loyalty with duty and strict adherence to the law. Yet another type of loyalty existed in the borderlands—a loyalty to family, friends, and community. Though often unnoticed in the larger scope of imperial studies, this type of loyalty motivated common people far more than national allegiance. In the reality of survival and the everyday quest to better their individual existences, a distant government that contributed little to their lives yet expected total obedience seemed far less important than the networks of kinship, friendship, and business on which they relied.

Don Antonio Gil Ibarvo's devotion to his community, his family, and his own success stands in dramatic contrast to the legalistic O'Conor. Placed on the border of Louisiana as pawns in an international chess game, Gil Ibarvo and his Adaesaño neighbors and friends found ways to circumvent laws that hindered their survival and prosperity. They intermarried with their French and Caddoan neighbors, and developed lasting friendships and commercial alliances. When ordered to leave their homes for political expediency, they obeyed the letter of the law as loyal subjects of the Crown. Having done so, they struggled politically to regain the life that they had lost, finally taking matters into their own hands.

Life in the borderlands created a situational ethic, as exemplified in the lives of such men as St. Denis, de Mézières, and Gil Ibarvo. People who lived within this changing geopolitical world developed a pragmatic and opportunistic loyalty to family and an extended community that, for them, superseded adherence to impractical laws and regulations enacted by a distant government with no understanding of their needs. This independent spirit, born of the necessities of life on a frontier far removed from metropolitan centers, led the Adaesaños to resist and ultimately ignore such regulations rather than accept the dissolution of their extended community and their resulting economic ruin. Their fidelity to family and community, and to personal economic prosperity, operated as an independent engine of self-determination apart from the concerns of statecraft and national policy.

In the broader scope of borderlands studies, this episode provides a model for examining the question of loyalty in other areas of the borderlands. For people concerned with the vicissitudes of everyday life, governments seemed far less important than the continuing survival and prosperity of family, friends, and neighbors. Understanding the fluidity of national allegiance lies in the appreciation that loyalty in the borderlands carried many meanings.

Notes

1. James A. Robertson, ed., "A Projected Settlement of English-Speaking Catholics from Maryland in Spanish Louisiana, 1767–1768," *American Historical Review* 16, no. 2 (January 1911): 319–27; Lawrence Kinnaird, "American Penetration into Spanish Louisiana," in George P. Hammond, ed., *New Spain and the Anglo-American West: Historical Contributions Presented to Herbert Eugene Bolton* (1932; repr., New York: Kraus Company, 1969), 2: 211–37; Gilbert C. Din, "Spain's Immigration Policy in Louisiana and the American Penetration, 1792–1803," *Southwestern Historical Quarterly* 76 (January 1973): 255–76; William S. Coker, "The Bruins and the Formulation of Spanish Immigration Policy in the Old Southwest, 1787–88," in John F. McDermott, ed., *The Spanish in the Mississippi Valley, 1762–1803* (Urbana: University of Illinois Press, 1974), 61–71; Light Townsend Cummins, "Oliver Pollock's Plantations: An Early Anglo Landowner on the Lower Mississippi, 1769–1824," *Louisiana History* 29, no. 1 (Winter 1988): 35–48; Cummins, "Anglo Merchants and Capital Migration in Spanish Colonial New Orleans, 1763–1803," *Gulf Coast Historical Review* 4 (1988): 6–27; Cummins, "An Enduring Community: Anglo-American Settlers at Colonial Natchez and in the Felicianas, 1774–1810," *Journal of Mississippi History* 55 (1993): 133–45; and Cummins, "'In Territories So Extensive and Fertile': Spanish and English-Speaking Peoples in Louisiana before the Purchase," in Paul Hoffman, ed., *The Louisiana Purchase and Its Peoples: Perspectives from the New Orleans Conference* (Lafayette: Louisiana Historical Association and University of Louisiana, 2004), 117–25.

2. Herbert Eugene Bolton, *Texas in the Middle Eighteenth Century* (1915; repr., Austin: University of Texas Press, 1970).

3. Accounts of this expedition are based on Spanish sources found in R. C. Clark, *The Beginnings of Texas, 1684–1718* (Austin: n.p., 1907), 49–69; Herbert Eugene Bolton, *The Spanish Borderlands* (New Haven, Conn.: Yale University Press, 1921), 222–25; Carlos E. Castañeda, *Our Catholic Heritage in Texas, 1519–1936* (Austin: Von Boeckmann-Jones, 1936), 2: 26–58

4. Little information exists about St. Denis's wife. St. Denis said her name was Manuela Sánchez. Frequent references to her in the Natchitoches church records identify her as Emmanuela María Sánchez Navarro. Louis de St. Denis, Declaration de D. Luis de San Denis..., in Archivo General de México (hereafter AGM), *Historia,* vol. 27, transcript in the Barker History Center, University of Texas, Austin; Frederic C. Chabot, *With the Makers of San Antonio* (San Antonio: Artes Graficas, 1937), 48; Robert S. Weddle, *San Juan Bautista: Gateway to Spanish Texas* (Austin: University of Texas Press, 1968), 126, 140. 5. St. Denis wrote messages to Cadillac on Feb. 21 and Sept. 7, 1715. See Henry Folmer, *Franco-Spanish Rivalry in North America, 1524–1763* (Glendale, Calif.: Arthur H. Clark Co., 1953), 234–38.

6. Henry E. Chambers, *A History of Louisiana* (Chicago: American Historical Society, 1925); Gary B. Mills, *The Forgotten People: Cane River's Creoles of Color* (Baton Rouge: Louisiana State University Press, 1977); Ross Phares, *Cavalier in the Wilderness: The Story of the Explorer and Trader Louis Juchereau de St. Denis* (Baton Rouge: Louisiana State University, 1952); Germaine Portre-Bobinski and Clara Mildred Smith, *Natchitoches: The Up-to-Date Oldest Town in Louisiana* (New Orleans: Dameron-Pierson Company, 1936); Jean-Baptiste Bernard de La Harpe, *The Historical Journal of the Establishment of the French in Louisiana*, trans. Joan Cain and Virginia Koenig, ed. Glenn R. Conrad (Lafayette: Center for Louisiana Studies, University of Southwestern Louisiana, 1971), 73–86; Herbert Eugene Bolton, *Athanase de Mézières and the Louisiana-Texas Frontier, 1768–1780* (Cleveland: Arthur H. Clark Company, 1914), 1: 44–45; Ralph A. Smith, trans., "Account of the Journey of Bernard de La Harpe: Discovery Made by Him of Several Nations Situated in the West," *Southwestern Historical Quarterly* 62 (July 1958 to April 1959): 75–86; John R. Swanton, *The Indians of the Southeastern United States*, Bureau of American Ethnology Report, Bulletin no. 137 (Washington, D.C.: Government Printing Office, 1946; repr., Washington, D.C.: Smithsonian Institution, 1979), 83–84 (page references are to the reprint edition); Alice Fletcher, *Bureau of American Ethnology Bulletin* 30, in Frederick Webb Hodge, ed., *Handbook of American Indians North of Mexico* (Washington, D.C.: Smithsonian Institution, 1902–10), 1: 37; Peter P. Forrestal, trans., "Peña's Diary of the Aguayo Expedition," *Preliminary Studies of the Texas Catholic Historical Society* 2, no. 7 (January 1935): 53–55; Fray Juan Agustín Morfi, *History of Texas, 1673–1779*, part 2, trans. Carlos E. Castañeda (Albuquerque: The Quivira Society, 1935), 54–56, 219; Eleanor Claire Buckley, "The Aguayo Expedition into Texas and Louisiana, 1719–1722," *The Quarterly of the Texas State Historical Association* 15 (July 1911): 52.

7. Lawrence Kinnaid, trans. *The Frontiers of New Spain: Nicolás de Lafora's Description, 1766–1768* (Berkeley: University of California Press, 1958), 166; Castañeda, *Our Catholic Heritage in Texas, 1519–1936*, 3: 80–81, 2: 175.

8. Oakah L. Jones, Jr., *Los Paisanos: Spanish Settlers on the Northern Frontier of New Spain* (Norman: University of Oklahoma Press, 1969), 61.

9. Castañeda, *Our Catholic Heritage in Texas, 1519–1936*, 2: 144, 178, 265–66, 4: 39; Herbert Eugene Bolton, *Texas in the Middle Eighteenth Century* (Berkeley: University of California Press, 1915), 32.

10. Herbert Eugene Bolton, *Texas in the Middle Eighteenth Century* (1915; repr., New York: Russell and Russell, Inc., 1962), 113. Hiram F. Gregory and James McCorkle, *Los Adaes: Historical and Archaeological Background* (Natchitoches: Northwestern State University, 1980–81), 88–89. See also Odie B. Faulk, *The Last Years of Spanish Texas, 1778–1821* (The Hague: Mouton and Co., 1964), 45; "Captain Antonio Gil Ybarbo of Nacogdoches," unpublished manuscript in the Robert B. Blake Collection, East Texas Research Center, Stephen F. Austin University, vol. 45.

11. Barón de Ripperdá to Viceroy, April 15, May 22, 1773; Viceroy to Ripperdá, June 30, 1773, AGM, Provincias Internas, vol. 100, pt. 2, pp. 456, 466, 468–69; Ripperdá to Viceroy, May 10, May 25, July 11, 1773, AGM, Provincias Internas, vol. 100, pt. 2, pp. 470–72, 489, 493–94.

Despite Antonio Gil Ibarvo's importance in Texas history, his only biography shares a single chapter with the Marqués de Rubí in Donald E. Chipman and Harriett Denise Joseph, *Notable Men and Women of Spanish Texas* (Austin: University of Texas Press, 1999), 178–201.

12. David M. Vigness, "Don Hugo Oconor and New Spain's Northeastern Frontier, 1764–1776," *Journal of the West* 6 (January 1967): 28–35.

13. Juan Agustín Morfi, *Excerpts from the Memorias for the History of the Province of Texas*, trans. and ed. Frederick C. Chabot (San Antonio: The Naylor Press, 1932), 58–59; Morfi, *History of Texas, 1673–1779, part 2*, 151, n. 80.

Hugo O'Conor's name appears in various spellings. Most Spanish documents refer to him as Oconor, and later writers sometimes render the name as O'Connor. Based on documents in the Archivo General de la Nación, J. Ignacio Rubio Mañé asserts that Don Hugo always signed his name "O'Conor." See J. Ignacio Rubio Mañé, "El Teniente Coronel don Hugo O'Conor y la situación en Chihuahua, año de 1771," *Boletín del Archivo General de la Nación* 30, no. 3 (n.d.): 359.

14. Morfi, *History of Texas*, pt. 1, 420–21; Donald E. Chipman, *Spanish Texas, 1519–1821* (Austin: University of Texas Press, 1992), 172–81.

15. David J. Weber, *Spanish Frontier in North America* (New Haven, Conn.: Yale University Press, 1992), 215–20; John L. Kessell, *Spain in the Southwest* (Norman: University of Oklahoma Press, 2002), 268–70; Herbert Eugene Bolton, "The Spanish Abandonment and Re-Occupation of East Texas, 1773–1779," *Quarterly of the Texas State Historical Association* 9, no. 2 (October 1905): 67–137.

16. Barón de Ripperdá to Viceroy, April 15, May 22, 1773; Viceroy to Ripperdá, June 30, 1773, AGM, Provincias Internas, vol. 100, pt. 2, pp. 456, 466, 468–69; and Ripperdá to Viceroy, May 10, May 25, July 11, 1773, AGM, Provincias Internas, vol. 100, pt. 2, pp. 470–72, 489, 493–94.

17. Ripperdá to Governor Unzaga y Amézaga, June 14, 1773, Archivo General de Indies (hereafter AGI), Papeles de Cuba (Dunn Transcripts, 1768–80), 8–10.

18. Ibid.

19. Bolton, "The Spanish Abandonment and Re-Occupation of East Texas," 87. For a discussion of the formation of ranching and the illegal livestock trade between Texas and Louisiana, see Jack Jackson, *Los Mesteños: Spanish Ranching in Texas, 1721–1821* (College Station: Texas A & M University Press, 1986), 116–23, 173–221.

20. Ripperdá to the Viceroy, Sept. 28, 1773; Antonio Gil Ibarvo to Comandante Inspector O'Conor, Jan, 8, 1774; Representation of the settlers of Los Adaes to Ripperdá, Oct. 4, 1774, AGM, Historia, vol. 51, pp. 259–66. Also see Bolton, "The Spanish Abandonment and Occupation of East Texas," 86–89.

21. Ripperdá to the Viceroy, Sept. 28, 1773; Antonio Gil Ibarvo to Comandante Inspector O'Conor, Jan. 8, 1774; Representation of the settlers of Los Adaes to Ripperdá, Oct. 4, 1774, AGM, Historia, vol. 51, pp. 248–51, 253–56, 259–66.

22. Ripperdá to the Viceroy, Sept. 28, 1773; Gil Ibarvo to O'Conor, Jan. 8, 1774, AGM, Historia, vol. 51, pp. 238–51, 259, 266.

23. *Autos que se han introducido por los Vecinos del Presidio de los Adaes*, AGM, Historia, vol. 51, pp. 211–16.

24. *Expediente sobre proposiciones del Gobernador de Texas Barón de Ripperdá*, AGM, Historia, vol. 51, pp. 1–60. The copy of the petition in AGM, Historia, vol. 51 shows seventy-three signatures of heads of families.

25. Ripperdá to the settlers from Los Adaes, Oct. 4, 1773; Document 2 in *Autos que se han introducido . . .* , AGM, Historia, vol. 51, pp. 216–17, 218–21.

26. Ripperdá to the Viceroy, Dec. 10, 1773; Ripperdá to O'Conor, Dec. 11, 1773, AGM, Historia, vol. 51, pp. 218–21, 267–69.

27. The most complete work on De Mézières is Bolton, *Athanase de Mézières and the Louisiana-Texas Frontier, 1768-1780*.

28. Areche, *Dictamen*, March 7, 1774, AGM, Historia, vol. 51, pp. 231–34; *Junta de Guerra y Hacienda*, March 17, *Decreto*, March 23, 1774, AGM, Historia, vol. 51, pp. 235–39.

29. O'Conor to Ripperdá, Feb. 17, 1774; O'Conor to the Viceroy, Feb. 17, 1774, AGM, Historia, vol. 51, pp. 244–47, 274–80.

30. Areche to the Viceroy, March 28, 1774; Junta of May 5, 1774, AGM, Historia, vol. 51, pp. 280–83; 301–4; Petition of Flores and Gil Ibarvo to Viceroy Bucareli, May 10, 1774; *Dictamen Fiscal*, May 12, 1774; *Decreto del Virrey*, May 16, 1774, AGM, Historia, vol. 51, pp. 305–11.

31. Ripperdá to the Viceroy, Sept. 10, 1770, AGM, Historia, vol. 51, pp. 312–14; Ripperdá to the Viceroy, Nov. 15, 1774, AGM, Historia, vol. 51, pp. 315–16.

32. O'Conor to the Viceroy, July 5 and Dec. 31, 1775; the Viceroy to O'Conor, Aug. 30, 1775; O'Conor to Ripperdá, Nov. 20, 1775; Ripperdá to O'Conor, Feb. 5, 1775, AGM, Historia, vol. 51, pp. 323–34.

33. Juan García Botello to Governor Cabello, Dec. 23, 1778; Gil Ibarvo to Governor Cabello, Jan. 12, Jan. 27, 1779, AGM, Historia, vol. 51, pp. 478–82, 490–96. For a detailed discussion of the settlement at Bucareli, see Castañeda, *Our Catholic Heritage in Texas, 1519-1936*, 4: 313–34.

34. Gil Ibarvo to Governor Cabello, Jan. 12, Jan. 27, 1779, AGM, Historia, vol. 51, pp. 490–96; Bolton, *Texas in the Middle Eighteenth Century*, (Berkeley: University of California Press, 1915), 116–19.

35. Order Issued by Governor Domingo Cabello, March 3, 1785, Béxar Archives, Center for American History, University of Texas, Austin.

36. Jackson, *Los Mesteños*, 388–94.

37. [Gil Ibarvo] to Governor Manuel Muñoz, March 22, 1791; Petition to the Viceroy, March 22, 1791, R. B. Blake Collection, vol. 52.

38. AGI, Audiencia de Guadalajara, 59, 94; Pedro de Nava to Manuel Munoz, March 18, 1791, Béxar Archives; R. B. Blake Collection, Supplemental Series, vols. 2–4. The AGI contains documents relating to the investigation of Gil Ibarvo's activities. The Blake supplemental volumes 2–4 are almost entirely composed of materials related to Gil Ibarvo.

39. Father José de la Garza, Statement on the character and service of Gil Ibarvo, Nov. 14, 1787, Béxar Archives.

8

Philip Livingston, Chameleon "Premier" of West Florida

ROBIN F. A. FABEL

If Philip Peter Livingston had died in mid-life, in 1775, colleagues would have mourned him as a colonial servant of unquestioned loyalty to the British Crown. When he in fact died, in 1810, contemporaries remembered him as a Hamiltonian Federalist, a pillar of the young American republic. A common thread that can be found in these otherwise disparate characterizations is Livingston's pursuit of wealth, a passion that did not originate in a poverty-stricken background.

If early identity is molded to advantage by comfort, means, and social position, Livingston would have had little cause to curse his lot. As a scion of colonial New York grandees, he could expect in maturity to enjoy social, economic, and political perquisites, while paying formal respect to the Crown of Great Britain. Every circumstance of his birth breathed privilege. He was born, a first son, in 1740 into one of New York's great landed families. His father, Peter Van Brugh Livingston, one of the Livingston clan's several patriarchs, helped guide the family fortunes through the shifting political and economic currents of eighteenth-century America. His mother, Mary, was an Alexander. Like the Livingstons, the Alexanders shone with exceptional brilliance in the firmament of colonial aristocracy. In it, dynastic marriages were not just common but usual and Mary was a sister to the celebrated Lord Stirling, himself the husband of a Livingston.

A major concern in the social stratum that lodged the Livingstons and their like was the consolidation and augmentation of riches. Except for the De Lanceys the Livingstons were the richest family in New York.[1] At amassing and perpetuating wealth Philip Peter's father and grandfather had tried various means. One was to traffic in slaves. Philip Peter's grandfather, Philip Livingston, Senior, was the second lord of Livingston Manor. During the 1730s he imported slaves first from the Caribbean and, later, directly from West Africa. In 1748, the year before his death, the elder Philip Livingston joined with his sons, one of whom was Peter Van Brugh Livingston, Philip Peter's father, to invest in four African slave ships.[2]

War provided other sources of income for the merchant Peter Van Brugh Livingston. Privateering was one, colonial government another. During the French and Indian War, in partnership with his brother-in-law Lord Stirling, he secured a contract to supply the provincial troops who assaulted Fort Niagara in 1755.[3]

Direct employment in government was another path to secure gold. Philip Peter Livingston would be a prince of pluralism: his shameless accumulation of many simultaneously held government posts would attract hate and envy.

Long before he embarked on his office-filled career came schooling and professional training consistent with parental expectations. That Philip's preparation for maturity should include a college education and apprenticeship in law was suitable for the eldest of fifteen siblings in a family of substance and manifold interests.

It was perhaps for family reasons that Philip attended the College of New Jersey that would later be known as Princeton. His father had attended Yale but became a trustee of the College of New Jersey and a number of Livingstons chose to study there. Although of Presbyterian foundation the college offered what was, for the day, a comparatively secular curriculum based on the ideal of rational piety. Philip may have done well there because a Philip Livingston was chosen from the seniors to give "a handsome Latin oration" in his final year at the college.[4]

Philip graduated in 1758, a hinge year in the French and Indian War, a conflict that involved New York closely. In that year the tide of success turned from the French. British provincial and regular forces for the first time won significant victories. For a gentleman of eighteen, as Philip then was, to have accepted a commission in the army and looked for martial dash would have accorded with eighteenth-century mores. He did no such thing. Instead he read law books.

The basis of law in all British colonies was the English common law. That basis was only one reason to prompt Philip to study in London. A would-be lawyer could read Blackstone anywhere, but only in England could a man on the edge of his career make the social and political contacts that lubricated ascent in colonial hierarchies. "Connexion," as the word was then spelled, was not everything, but it was more important than anything else for appointments and promotion. Personal recommendation, not competitive examinations, decided placement in that world. Patronage ruled.

Philip obtained agreeable chambers at the Middle Temple of London's Inns of Court. He had to attend no lectures because study was self-directed. He

Figure 8.1. Philip Peter Livingston (1783) by Pompeo Girolami Batoni (1708–87). Oil on canvas, purchased with funds from the Marriner S. Eccles Foundation with assistance from Emma Eccles Jones, Museum no. 1991.045.001, from the permanent collection of the Utah Museum of Fine Arts.

worked in the morning. Social life in the afternoon centered on the Turk's Head tavern where he dined regularly with the rich and influential. Life was costly. Philip's father may have winced at the £450 a year that his son asked for, but he perhaps thought the expense worthwhile when he learned that his son had made friends with John and Richard Penn, both of whom would govern Pennsylvania.[5] Other acquaintances from his London years that Livingston knew well enough to cite for recommendations included Staats Long Morris, the husband to the Duchess of Gordon, Richard Jackson, an agent of the Crown for three colonies, James Coutts, who represented Edinburgh in Parliament in 1760, and Henry Drummond, a banker.[6]

Philip lingered in England. He seems to have enjoyed British life to the point of infatuation. To his friend John Penn he would write of Britain as "that dear country . . . all my wishes are centred there, and the height of my ambition is to have it in my power at some future day to become an inhabitant of your island."[7]

In Britain Philip would have known, or at least known of, nabobs. A nabob was a man who had gone to India, then under British domination, made a fortune, and then returned to Britain to buy an estate and live as a gentleman of means. Livingston's letter to Penn suggests that his ultimate ambition was to live like a nabob. No such dream was possible without, in his case, employment as the first step to wealth. When a position in the colonial establishment opened that offered money and influence and a chance to serve his kinsfolk Philip took it. The job was private secretary to Sir Henry Moore.

As Jamaica's lieutenant governor Moore had earned the gratitude of planters, including several Livingstons, when in 1756 he had put down a slave revolt. Impressed, the Crown had rewarded him with a baronetcy. In 1764 it named him governor of New York.[8] To take up his new appointment Moore sailed with his official family, presumably including Philip Peter Livingston, at an unpromising time if he hoped for a tranquil governorship. It was 1765, the year of the detested Stamp Act, and New Yorkers were becoming increasingly restless under British rule.

After arrival the governor took measures to mollify the disgruntled. He dismantled Fort George, where excise stamps had been stored, and even bought a couple of the homespun coats that some New Yorkers wore to flaunt self-reliance. Discontent continued. The Sons of Liberty burned stamps in the streets of the city and in the countryside rioting tenants refused to pay rent.

Although in general the Livingston faction in New York politics approved of Governor Moore, Philip found himself in a delicate position. Moore's duty was to enforce the Stamp Act, which Philip's fellow Livingstons opposed in principle. The Sons of Liberty continued to resist it militantly. To head off further violence Moore, who lacked the power to force the purchase of stamps on unwilling citizens, met with Isaac Sears, a leader of the Sons of Liberty, and agreed to allow the Stamp Act to remain a dead letter in New York.[9]

Anti-British activity, boycotts especially, revived in New York following parliamentary passage of new import duties on tea, glass, lead, and painters' colors in 1767. Known as the Townshend duties, they were a last attempt by a dying chancellor of the exchequer to extract revenue from Britain's American colonies. They did nothing for Governor Moore's popularity. Before the New York assembly elections of 1768 Philip Peter Livingston acted vigorously in his interest and in those of his Livingston allies. He "openly canvassed and made promises in the name of the governor, threatened some with the vengeance of

His Excellency, abused numbers, and coaxed, flattered, and cajoled others."[10] His efforts were in vain. The De Lancey faction, the chief rivals of the Livingstons, gained three of the four available seats in the assembly.

When a riot supporting a boycott of all British imports occurred in November the Livingstons and the governor wrongly assumed that the people, the merchants in particular, did not want the government to endorse the boycott. The De Lanceys thought otherwise and strengthened their political position by backing the rioters' demands.

The supremacy of the De Lanceys was to collapse in 1770 after the Livingstons realized that the key to regaining their influence was to outradicalize the radicals. Meanwhile, in 1769, the Livingstons still fumbled with outworn political issues. Their position was not solid, but Philip Peter's had become downright precarious when in September Sir Henry Moore died.

Lieutenant Governor Cadwallader Colden stepped into Moore's place and promptly fired Livingston from all offices. He lost the private secretaryship and the lucrative offices of principal surrogate and register to the Prerogative Court of New York. His complaint that it was "a severe stroke upon a public officer of government to be removed without any imputation of malconduct" was true but naive.[11] He must have known that there was no hope that Colden, a bitter foe of the Livingstons, would have any use for him. Out of a job, Philip Peter had to decide where to turn.

If loyalty to family had dominated Philip at that time he would have stayed in America and employed his considerable talents to forward Livingston interests, which, in that year, were under stress. Colden opposed them. So did the De Lanceys, who still controlled the New York assembly. Loyalty to the Crown, however, was increasingly unacceptable in New York. The wind of change favored radical Anglophobia. There exist hints that Philip Peter was less willing to bend to it than were other members of his family: "From my education," he wrote to John Penn, "and from the people with whom I have been particularly acquainted [I] have imbibed certain principles and sentiments which will not allow me to associate with such persons and to follow such measures as are absolutely necessary to be pursued in order to acquire more than a bare subsistence by my profession solely in New York."[12] In England, by contrast, not only would Anglophilia and loyalty to the king be respected but, thanks to his contacts, he could hope for an appointment by the Crown. He would not have to depend solely on lawyer's fees.

Philip immediately crossed the Atlantic and badgered the Earl of Hillsborough, the crown minister responsible for the American colonies.[13] During the winter of 1769–70 Livingston obtained several interviews with the earl. He must have impressed. Hillsborough was ready to appoint him to either of two vacant posts. One was private secretary to Lord Dunmore, the new governor of New York. The other was private secretary to Peter Chester, the new governor of West Florida.

It seems there was some uncertainty about Dunmore's interest in Livingston, but not Chester's. In his eagerness Chester promised, in addition to the secretaryship, to nominate Livingston to the positions of chief justice and attorney general in his colony, if they should fall vacant. Hillsborough advised Livingston to accept Chester's offer, rather than Dunmore's, and promised "to pay attention to the recommendation of the governor in case of any vacancy."[14]

Britain had acquired West Florida, a reward for success in war, in 1763. Although the years before Chester's arrival had seen dashed economic hopes, a devastating yellow fever epidemic, quarrels with native Americans, and many changes in its government,[15] the place seemed well-suited to Philip Peter Livingston's needs.

In general a single gentleman in the southern colonies had three routes to wealth: grow plantation staples with cheap slave labor, hold public office, or third, marry an heiress.[16] Because of its position a fourth possibility existed in West Florida—trade with the Spanish Empire. Despite his mercantile background Philip did not pursue that route. Nor did he marry. If he wanted to marry, which is not certain, pioneer West Florida would have been the wrong place to find, or to bring, a suitable wife. Philip believed that for a Livingston to marry without parental approval was a major social sin.[17] His father would have expected him to marry inside the social elite. Eventually he did so marry, but only when his West Florida days were long over.[18] Of the other mentioned routes to wealth he pursued riches through office-holding to supplement his salary of £200 a year as a private secretary much more doggedly than through planting.

Thanks to the absence of a previous holder, James Macpherson, he was able to act as provincial secretary, clerk of the West Florida Council, and register of all grants, patents, and records.[19] West Florida had a small white population but a full complement of law courts. Livingston was clerk to the Court of Ordinary and, as a notary and *tabellion* public, he attended to the processes involved in the making and execution of many legal documents.[20] In addition, he became receiver general of West Florida[21] and in 1776, on the death of the previous holder, collector of Customs at Mobile.[22]

All the while that he lived in Florida Livingston was a member of the West Florida Council as well as its clerk. The council was the upper house of the colony's legislature and, with the governor presiding, its executive body. Well known as Chester's "favourite," Livingston was well-placed to hinder policy that might thwart his personal interests and to forward policies that might help them.

Neither in Britain nor in West Florida was there an official position of prime minister at the time, but thanks to his offices and his influence over Governor Chester, Philip Peter Livingston was de facto premier of the colony. But power did not mean popularity. Although West Floridians had not, and would not, reject the authority of King George III, complaints abounded against his surrogates, both before and during the governorship of Peter Chester. "There is neither man nor woman (except the attorney general) in the place [that] they [Chester and his family] are on any tolerable terms with. And unless the ingenuity and address of Mr. Livingston prevents, I fancy you'll very soon have as many remonstrances as heretofore," wrote an engineer officer.[23]

It is impossible to know how many North American colonists in 1772, the year of that quoted extract, would have expected their complaints to change into armed struggle. When war in 1775 and a separation declaration in 1776 in fact followed, almost all of the Livingston family committed themselves to the Revolution: another Philip Livingston, Philip Peter's uncle, was a signer of the Declaration of Independence.

Philip Peter could have sailed to join his kinsfolk but stayed in West Florida. He must have expected the colony to stay within the imperial system in spite of the war, just as Canada would, because he continued to buy land there.

British West Florida would not, of course, stay in the British Empire. The Spanish would occupy it and listlessly exploit its economic resources. It is therefore possible to scoff at Livingston's land greed, but such scorn would be misplaced.

Land ownership possessed mystique in all pre-industrial societies, but land assumed new weight in the British Empire in the mid-eighteenth century. In the years after 1750 territorialism displaced trade as the dominant imperial motivator, as illustrated by the well-known British preference for unprofitable Canada to the rich sugar island of Guadeloupe in the negotiations for the peace treaty of 1763 that ended the French and Indian War.[24] Livingston's dedicated land acquisition accorded with this trend, although surely personal, not imperial interests moved him.

The West Florida Council approved or vetoed all petitions for land grants in the province. Livingston's dominant position in the council enabled him directly or indirectly to amass vast acreage. His enemies alleged that he acquired one hundred thousand acres as his personal property.[25] As a genuine settler, Livingston was entitled to a limited amount of free land. He did not serve in the French and Indian War, so he could not qualify for other free grants available under the terms of a royal proclamation of October 7, 1763. He compensated for this lack by persuading veterans who could qualify to petition for land that they did not really want, and then to sell him their grants. Thus, for example, from ten members of the 16th infantry regiment he bought six thousand acres.[26]

His vast land acquisitions did not mean Livingston intended permanent residence in West Florida. It was with long-term gain in mind through profitable disposal of his property that he "ventured to combat with a southern climate and . . . banished [him]self to a small corner of the world removed from all . . . friends and almost destitute of society."[27] He seems to have expanded his holdings under the triple delusion that the revolutionary war would not stretch to West Florida, that the material encouragement Chester gave potential immigrants would raise land values in West Florida, and that the Manchac canal project would prosper.

By dredging the Bayou Manchac the envisaged canal would have joined the Mississippi River to Lakes Maurepas and Pontchartrain and thence to the Gulf of Mexico. The produce from the Upper Mississippi that normally went to the Gulf via New Orleans would go by way of the shorter route made possible by the canal. Land on the Comite and Amite rivers that were tributary to the new water route, as well as on the Bayou Manchac itself, would rise in value. It is no coincidence that it was in these places that the bulk of Livingston's holdings lay. It is also not by pure chance that Livingston snapped up thirteen building lots in the proposed town of Harwich that was marked out above the settlement of Manchac. Harwich was never in fact built, but so hopeful was Chester, and surely Livingston too, of its success that Chester suggested to his superior in London that the capital of West Florida be moved from Pensacola to Harwich.[28]

Chester was ready to reserve huge tracts of land for entrepreneurs who promised to bring immigrants to Florida. The most significant of various immigration schemes was that of the Company of Military Adventurers of New England. At his home in Pensacola in March 1773 Livingston entertained its exploring committee before it left for the Mississippi to earmark sites for new townships. In August Livingston sailed to New York where, as the company's West Florida agent, he would have contacted members of the Adventurers. He surely saw his father too, who had his son, just before he sailed, use his influence on the West Florida Council to reserve twenty-five thousand acres as a proposed township for immigrants from New York.[29]

Philip's leave of absence lasted more than a year, during which the march to revolution quickened. The period of his leave saw the destruction of tea in Boston and New York, passage of the Boston Port Act, and the attendance of his uncle at the first Continental Congress. Then, if even minimal revolutionary zeal had gripped him, would have been an excellent time for Philip to declare solidarity with his kinsfolk in their anti-British stance and to resume residence in New York. Instead he boarded the Pensacola-bound schooner *Rose* in October. With him he took his youngest brother, William, who was then seventeen years of age.[30] After stopping at Jamaica the *Rose* wrecked off the Mexican coast, but with new cables, anchors, and fresh water in its barrels, it was able to continue to Pensacola,[31] where Philip resumed his old offices and prepared to receive immigrants.

To encourage immigration was much to Livingston's advantage. He made more money from settler fees than he ever would from selling his lands. Fees were payable for every allegedly free grant. Initially there was a charge for reading and recording every petition for land. Another fee was due if the petition was approved, and a warrant of survey issued. The surveyor general and his assistant had to be paid. Certification and recording of the resultant plot merited another fee. Money also had to be found if the governor then ordered a grant to be written and recorded.[32]

That Governor Chester, Secretary Livingston, and Surveyor General Elias Durnford all collected fees at various stages of this elaborate procedure caused bitterness among settlers. Raising the fees added to their anguish. In 1765 the secretary's fees on the sale of 1,000 acres of land totaled little more than 4 Spanish dollars. Under Livingston they rose in 1772 to 51 dollars, and again in 1778 to 106 dollars.[33]

For investment or, to a lesser extent, his own use, Livingston continued to acquire land after the Revolution was well under way, but his purchases slowed when the expected hordes of immigrants never materialized. In 1775 the king offered generous land bounties for proven loyalism, but war hindered movement. Loyalists could no longer travel overland in safety, while privateers swarmed at sea. Immigrants to West Florida arrived in tens or at best hundreds, not the expected thousands. The best of the immigrant schemes, the Company of Military Adventurers, sent no more than 104 families to West Florida.

The arrival of James Willing of the United States Navy with a boat full of raiders in February 1778 further deterred immigration. It shattered the illusion that the Revolutionary War could not reach to West Florida. Fear and destruction followed his landfall. He found Livingston's plantation on the Amite. After removing its slaves in order to sell them in New Orleans, Willing burned it. The thought of leaving Florida must have begun to press on Livingston, especially as his and Chester's popularity sank to new depths in 1778.

Chester had failed to protect his province against Willing. Moreover, for six years he had ignored demands that he summon a representative assembly.

At last, on orders from London, the governor called for elections in 1778. That West Florida had no militia was one reason for weak resistance to Willing, so it was reasonable that Chester should ask the assembly to pass a bill to institute one. The assemblymen were ready to cooperate but, resentful of Chester's gerrymandering of previous electoral districts, they wanted in return for the militia bill a fairer system of assembly representation. The governor refused to compromise. It fell to Livingston, as Chester's spokesman, to persuade a divided council that it must reject the assembly's representation bill. To do otherwise, he argued, would violate gubernatorial prerogative.[34]

As a result, no bill passed, Chester dissolved the assembly, and its members went home convinced that Chester and Livingston were incorrigibly unjust. A few months later an anti-Chester petition by 132 "gentlemen, freeholders and principal inhabitants of West Florida" included complaints against Livingston. Some were exaggerations, but most contained some truth. For example, Livingston was "an all-ruling favourite . . . a man of suspicious principles, whose father and numerous family are now in active rebellion."[35]

The petition also denounced Livingston's greed for fees and land. The freeholders alleged that Chester approved transfer to Livingston of claims to land of more than fifty military persons "who never existed but in the avaricious imagination of his secretary."[36] No evidence for this charge has survived, although Livingston undoubtedly bought claims from genuine veterans.

Ordered by the secretary of state for American affairs to respond to the freeholders' charges, Chester backed Livingston. The governor insisted his secretary had broken no law and he was certain that Livingston was "as loyal and faithful a subject as any that His Majesty" had in West Florida.[37]

In spite of Chester's support, Livingston's position was invidious. He had been denounced as a traitor to the king, yet his property had been singled out for destruction by a raider armed with a commission from the United States Congress. Any hope he had of staying in Florida, tepidly neutral and getting rich while the Revolution fought itself out elsewhere, was gone. So he too went, abandoning all the landed property sedulously accumulated over nine years. He probably did not even try to sell it. Willing's raid had killed optimism, and immigration, except for penniless refugees, had dried up. After the Revolution some West Florida landowners received some, never very generous, compensation for lost lands from the Loyalist Claims Commission. Livingston was not among them.

Although he sacrificed his landed estates, his quitting West Florida was well-timed. He was able to carry with him the considerable fortune that he amassed from the dedicated taking of fees. It was not lost in the hurly-burly of war, as it might well have been. The secretary took ship in May 1779.[38] On

June 21 Spain declared war on Great Britain and within a week Spanish forces successfully invaded West Florida.

There is not much evidence for Livingston's whereabouts and activities for the next five years. It seems likely that he went first to Jamaica, because that was the destination of his brother William, who left Florida at the same time as Philip. The island was only six days' sail from Pensacola and a number of Livingstons lived there, including his old classmate, Philip Philip Livingston. Along with other nephews Philip Peter had inherited Jamaican property when his uncle Henry died in 1772.[39]

As yet evidence is lacking, but it seems likely that Livingston went from Jamaica to England. His friends in Britain included Richard Penn, who had once been Pennsylvania's lieutenant governor. Penn had left America for Britain in 1775, bearing the so-called Olive Branch Petition. Its purpose was to reconcile the rebellious American colonies with the mother country. It stalled, as did Penn, who never went back to America.

That Livingston went to England after 1779 is unproven. That he was in Italy in 1783 is sure. He sat for the fashionable and expensive portraitist Pompeo Batoni, proof that four years in exile had not impoverished him.

If the Americans had lost the Revolutionary War Livingston, like Penn, might have stayed in Europe. Instead they won and among the victors were Philip Peter's kinsfolk in New York, who from being more moderate than the De Lanceys had triumphed politically by outpacing them in revolutionary fervor. The Livingstons' place at the top of colonial New York's social and political elite was similarly at least as high in the new republic. Once swords were sheathed it seems that the new republican establishment was ready to overlook Philip Peter's record of service to the king.

Livingston renewed landholding, buying land that had been confiscated from a traditional De Lancey rival for the latter's loyalism.[40] Entering politics as a firm Federalist, Livingston voted for the new national constitution at New York's Poughkeepsie Convention. As a Federalist he sat in the New York assembly in 1788 and 1789 before solidifying his position in the state through marriage.[41]

The Van Hornes were a New York family with a strong revolutionary background. On October 7, 1790 Philip Peter Livingston wed Cornelia Van Horne. She and Philip would have four children, of whom two died. Affection for his family showed in their names. The first was christened Philip and another Peter Van Brugh.

In the 1790s Livingston embedded himself in commerce and industry. One of twenty-five directors of the first Bank of the United States, he became president of its New York branch in 1792. He was also a director of the Northern Canal Company and a shareholder in the Society for Establishing Useful Manufactures.[42]

From his farm at Dobbs Ferry north of New York City Philip corresponded with the grandees of the republic. He enjoyed life in the country, but ill health dogged him. On New Year's Day 1800 he complained of a stomach illness and of gout in his hand so severe that he could not write.[43] He died in 1810.

It had been Livingston's luck to be able to choose sides in America's revolutionary era. He threw in his lot with the British, an unfortunate but not a senseless choice: only in the latter stages of the war did American victory become sure.

Livingston was an Anglophile, but he would not have seen himself as English. More likely he saw himself, at least in the 1760s and early 1770s, as an American of the empire, happy, providing that he prospered, in more than one part of it. "I have been brought up from a child with an opinion of inheriting a very good American fortune," he wrote in 1771."[44] At the time cooperation with the British seemed the most sensible way to secure such a fortune. There is nothing to suggest that his voyage to West Florida was dictated by ideology and much to suggest that it was a practical decision: it was the route to riches. He did find wealth there, although less than he expected. Had the Americans lost the Revolutionary War, he would have been much richer and, instead of his family helping him reestablish himself after peace returned, he might have been able to rescue them. His link with his family always seemed firm, even in his loyalist West Florida years. David Taitt was probably correct in writing that he kept corresponding with his family in the north, even at the height of the Revolution. It is tempting to think that he saw his primary role throughout life as a member of the Livingston clan and that he ranked his other roles—Anglophile, servant of the king, opportunist, banker, Hamiltonian Federalist—all of which he filled at different times, as subsidiary.

Philip Peter was the first but not the last Livingston to concern himself with the Gulf region. Robert R. Livingston made a greater impact than Philip, and not just because it is he after whom Livingston Parish in modern Louisiana is named. Robert Livingston's outstanding achievement was his role as minister to France in securing for the United States the vast territories of the Louisiana Purchase in 1803. Another kinsman who greatly influenced Louisiana was Edward Livingston, who, like his brother Robert, and like Philip, was a trained lawyer. As a celebrated jurist and an aide to General Andrew Jackson in thwarting British invasion in 1814 he served Louisiana well. Later he represented the state in both houses of the Congress of the United States.

In spite of their contributions in shaping the Gulf region Philip, Robert, and Edward Livingston did not, and probably never intended to, end their days there. All at last returned to the Livingston homeland of upstate New York.

Philip Peter Livingston goes unmentioned in textbooks on the history of the United States. Even in the history of the Gulf Coast Livingston has no large place because the place of British West Florida itself is small. The colony was an ephemeral experiment. It was there that Livingston used flair to provide stability and effective political management when both were sorely needed, qualities that could have had more lasting effect if he had not lost the bet that he evidently made with himself—that West Florida would remain a British possession.

Notes

1. Leopold S. Launitz-Schurer, *Loyalists, Whigs, and Revolutionaries: The Making of the Revolution in New York, 1765–1776* (New York: New York University Press, 1980), 193.

2. James G. Lydon, "New York and the Slave Trade, 1700–1774," *William and Mary Quarterly*, 3d ser. 35 (1978): 389 n. 42.

3. Paul David Nelson, *The Life of William Alexander, Lord Stirling* (Tuscaloosa, Ala.: University of Alabama Press, 1987), 17.

4. *New York Mercury or Weekly Post Boy*, July 3, 1758. Who orated is ambiguous, because Philip Peter's cousin, Philip Philip [*sic*] Livingston attended the college during the same year.

5. Ruth Corinne Connor, "Gentleman Phil: Eighteenth-Century Opportunist, Philip Peter Livingston, 1740–1810," M.A. thesis, Auburn University, 1982, provided details of Livingston's legal studies. I am indebted to it and to James McLachlan, *Princetonians, 1748–1768: A Biographical Dictionary* (Princeton, N.J.: Princeton University Press, 1976), 232–35, for many useful research leads.

6. E. B. O'Callaghan, *Documents Relating to the Colonial History of the State of New York* (Albany: Weed and Parsons, 1857), 8: 187.

7. Philip Peter Livingston to John Penn, July 20, 1771, Livingston Papers, New York Historical Society.

8. George Metcalf, *Royal Government and Political Conflict in Jamaica, 1729–1783* (London: Longman's, 1965), 152.

9. Alexander C. Flick, *The American Revolution in New York: Its Political, Social, and Economic Consequences* (New York, 1926; repr., Port Washington, N.Y.: Friedman, 1969), 17, 19.

10. Thomas Jones, *History of New York during the Revolutionary War* (New York: New York Historical Society, 1879), 1: 19.

11. Livingston to Lord Hillsborough, Sept. 11, 1769, in O'Callaghan, *Documents*, 8: 187.

12. Livingston to Penn, July 20, 1771, Livingston Papers, New York Historical Society.

13. Wills Hill, the Earl of Hillsborough, was the secretary of state for the American colonies from Jan. 20, 1768 to Aug. 14, 1772.

14. Livingston to Hillsborough, Dec. 12, 1770, C05/578:107, Great Britain, Public Record Office, Kew (hereafter C05).

15. Before Chester's arrival Robert Farmar, George Johnstone, Montfort Browne, and Elias Durnford had governed the province, all within seven years.

16. Kenneth Lockridge discusses these options in "Colonial Self-fashioning Paradoxes and Pathologies in the Construction of Genteel Identity in the Eighteenth Century," in Ronald Hoffman, Mechal Sobel, and Frederic J. Teale, *Through a Glass Darkly: Reflections on Personal Identity* (Williamsburg: University of North Carolina Press, 1997), 300 ff.

17. Livingston to Peter Van Brugh Livingston, April 26, 1770, Livingston Papers, New York Public Library.

18. Philip married Cornelia Van Horne when he was forty years of age.

19. Famous as the translator (or author) of the Ossian poems, Macpherson left one year after his appointment. He deputed his offices to Livingston. Cecil Johnson, "A Note on Absenteeism and Pluralism in British West Florida," *Louisiana Historical Quarterly* 19 (1936): 197.

20. Peter Chester to Hillsborough, Dec. 26, 1770, C05/578:115.

21. John Pownall to John Robinson, Jan. 20, 1772, in K. G. Davies, *Documents of the American Revolution, 1770–1783* (Shannon: Irish Universities Press, 1972–81), 4: 22.

22. Chester to the Earl of Dartmouth, Nov. 11, 1775 in ibid., 10: 134.

23. John Cambel to Tullie(?), Feb. 10, 1772, Great Britain, Public Record Office, Treasury 1/494:61.

24. David S. Shields discusses this displacement in *Oracles of Empire: Poetry, Politics, and Commerce in British America, 1690–1750* (Chicago: University of Chicago Press, 1990).

25. "Petition of the Gentlemen, Freeholders, and Principal Inhabitants of West Florida," n.d., C05/580:156. Exclusive of town lots Ruth Connor identified 40,540 acres; Connor, "Gentleman Phil," 118.

26. Connor, "Gentleman Phil," 99.

27. Livingston to John Penn, July 20, 1771, Livingston Papers, New York Historical Society.

28. Chester to Hillsborough, July 13, 1772, C05/579:135.

29. West Florida Council Minutes, July 10, 1773, C05/630:123.

30. William helped run Philip's plantation on the Amite until he sailed for Jamaica in 1779, after which an American vessel captured him on his way to New York. Jonathan Trumbull to William Livingston, Sr., in *Papers of William Livingston* (New Brunswick, N.J.: Rutgers University Press, 1986), 3: 153.

31. *New York Gazette*, April 10, 1775.

32. Cecil Johnson, *British West Florida, 1763–1783* (New Haven, Conn.: Yale University Press, 1942), 126.

33. Robin F. A. Fabel, *The Economy of British West Florida, 1763-1783* (Tuscaloosa: University of Alabama Press, 1988), 204.

34. Robert R. Rea and Milo B. Howard, Jr., *The Minutes, Journals, and Acts of the General Assembly of British West Florida* (Tuscaloosa: University of Alabama Press, 1979), 276-77.

35. The petition was penned some time before May 10, 1779. On May 23, 1777 David Taitt had written to Thomas Brown that "[Chester's] secretary Livingston (and I believe justly) informs the rebels to the northward of every transaction at Pensacola." Davies, *Documents*, 14: 95.

36. "Petition of the Gentlemen," C05/580:155.

37. "Chester's Answer to the Petition of the Gentlemen et al.," Library of Congress West Florida Papers, micro. no. 24539, Auburn University Library.

38. Chester to Lord George Germain, May 7, 1779, C05/5955:685.

39. *New York Historical Society Collections for 1899* (New York: New York Historical Society, 1900), 180.

40. Alexander Flick, *Loyalism in New York during the American Revolution* (New York: Columbia University Press, 1901), 230, 239.

41. Mary-Jo Kline, ed., *Political Correspondence and Public Papers of Aaron Burr* (Princeton, N.J.: Princeton University Press, 1983), 2: 855.

42. Harold Syrett, ed., *The Papers of Alexander Hamilton* (New York: Columbia University Press, 1966), 1:169.

43. Livingston to William Edgar, Jan. 1, 1800, Livingston Papers, New York Public Library.

44. Livingston to John Penn, July 20, 1778, Livingston Papers, New York Historical Society.

9

Oliver Pollock and the Creation of an American Identity in Spanish Colonial Louisiana

LIGHT TOWNSEND CUMMINS

The economy of Spanish Louisiana experienced a transformation during the last four decades of the eighteenth century. English-speaking merchants played a large part in these profound changes. One of the most successful of these merchants, and also one of the best known to history, was Oliver Pollock, who has long been recognized in the scholarship of the American Revolution. He was a significant source of supply at New Orleans for the rebel cause. Pollock shipped from New Orleans the gunpowder used by the Continental Army at the Battle of Saratoga. He also served as George Rogers Clark's service of supply in the American conquest of the British Illinois country.[1] Important as these accomplishment proved to the course of history, Oliver Pollock also played a larger, more pivotal role in a subtle process that had an equally large historical impact on the region. Pollock, along with other English-speaking merchants in Spanish Louisiana, participated in shifting the fundamental structures of the Louisiana's private economy from what has sometimes been called a "frontier exchange" system, based on barter and localized trade, to a more complex one that involved the colony's meaningful participation in the sophisticated Atlantic market system during the late eighteenth century (map 9.1).[2]

Several historical studies have noted that economic transformations can give rise, as a precondition, to social and cultural changes that in turn foster the formation of a people's identity. This was the case for Americanization along the lower Mississippi Valley at the end of the Spanish colonial era, something about which Spain and her governmental officials remained unaware.[3] This sort of identity formation and the processes that it follows have been noted, for example, in a recent historical study of Confederate Vicksburg during the late antebellum era. The role of economic issues in national identity formation has also been further highlighted by the sociologist Liah Greenfield, who has recently postulated a very clear relationship between economic

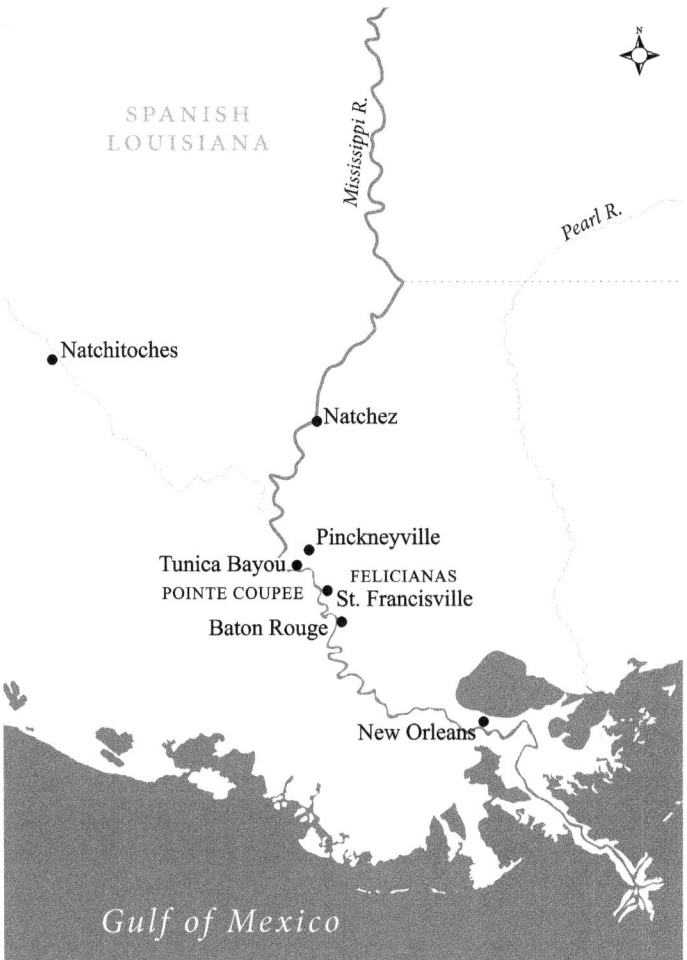

Map 9.1. The Lower Mississippi in the Eighteenth Century. Map by Tracy Ellen Smith, www.cdrtexas.com.

growth and national identity all across modern European history from the fifteenth century to the twentieth, noting that the two phenomenon are closely related in the creation of a people's identity.[4] This was also the case in Spanish Louisiana when American identity formation began in the decade following the Revolution as Spanish Louisiana joined the Atlantic trade networks that had been traditionally dominated by Great Britain, but which shifted to the young United States in the 1780s. The English speakers then living in the lower Mississippi Valley had originally been a diverse group, some of whom passed through the Revolution as British loyalists while some had been American rebels, or at least supported independence. Others were recent arrivals. Whatever their previous identities, the increasing dominance of English speakers in controlling the external trade of Spanish Louisiana within the context of these new commercial affiliations provided an amalgamating force that brought all of them increasingly to adapt an American identity that tied them to the United States. This certainly occurred in the area of staple crop commerce in the 1780s and 1790s. "The swift ascent of sugar and cotton," as Ira Berlin has noted of this process, "moved the lower Mississippi valley from the periphery of the plantation world into its center."[5] A sophisticated market economy had already linked together earlier in the century much of the north Atlantic world into an intricate network that moved staple crops, consumer goods, and slaves through an expanding international commerce that relied upon capital migration and centralized credit as its motive force.[6] Louisiana arrived late when it joined this trade network during the Spanish period. It was Oliver Pollock, and other merchants of his ilk, who brought Louisiana into this system. By that time, the Atlantic market economy had already been crafted and dominated by Great Britain early in the eighteenth century, but after the American Revolution the appearance of the infant United States threw the whole system into open rivalry as Atlantic coast merchants in the newly independent nation quickly became competitors to their British counterparts, especially in the Western Hemisphere.[7]

Oliver Pollock became the first English-speaking merchant to understand the role that Spanish Louisiana would come to play in the Atlantic market economy in the two decades after the American Revolution. Pollock, and others of Louisiana's English-speaking merchants who came after him, provided the mechanism for this trade. This process began when Oliver Pollock arrived in Louisiana early in the Spanish period. His merchant career lasted more than fifty years until he died at Pinckneyville, Mississippi in 1823. His descendants continued to operate plantations in the Felicianas for several generations thereafter.[8] Pollock was born in Northern Ireland, most probably in 1737. His family lived in the linen-drying areas to the south of Derry City, then known by the English name of Londonderry. The Pollock family traced its lineage to the Scottish settlers who came to Northern Ireland during the early waves of immigration from Scotland in the early 1600s. Many of his ancestors settled along the Burn Dennett, a small tributary of the River Foyle north of Strabane. The small village of Pollockstown became their ancestral seat and some of Oliver's ancestors prospered in the rich farming and linen-drying economy of the district. His father, Jaret, however, did not find economic success, most likely because of the mid-eighteenth-century financial crisis in Ulster that resulted in higher land rents and depression in the linen markets. Moving first to the town of Coleraine with several of his children after the death of his wife, the father and several of his sons, including Oliver, eventually departed for America in 1760.⁹ At this time Oliver Pollock clearly defined himself as a Presbyterian and very much as Scotch-Irish.

Once in British North America, Oliver Pollock became an active part of the Scotch-Irish merchant network in Pennsylvania. He, his father, and his brothers initially settled in the Ulster-dominated backcountry near Carlisle. After a year there, Oliver moved to Philadelphia and began to work for major mercantile houses in that city. He became associated with the firm of Willing and Morris, one of the largest commercial houses on the east coast of British America. Pollock traveled to Havana in 1762 as the corresponding agent of Willing and Morris in order to sell supplies to the British army that had occupied the Cuban port during the Seven Years' War. Once a resident of Cuba, Pollock used his background to manipulate his identity in order to become Celtic Irish and Roman Catholic. This gave him better commercial advantages. In so doing, he befriended an Irish priest in the city. He also became part of the circle of loyal acquaintances that evolved around Alejandro O'Reilly, a Spanish general of Irish lineage stationed at Havana. The two men socialized together and eventually enjoyed a warm friendship. Pollock married an Irish girl, Margaret O'Brien, who was then living with her merchant father at Havana.¹⁰

This marriage resulted in Pollock deciding to move his mercantile operations to New Orleans in order to increase his growing fortune. He thus followed Alejandro O'Reilly to New Orleans in 1769 when the general led an expedition there to restore Spanish control in the wake of a local revolt against Governor Antonio de Ulloa in 1768. Oliver Pollock therefore became the first English-speaking merchant O'Reilly allowed in the Spanish-controlled city. O'Reilly awarded Pollock a contract to supply New Orleans with flour since Louisiana lacked that badly needed commodity. The price for flour had risen to the equivalent of thirty dollars a barrel and, partly because of that high price, it remained in short supply. Pollock had arrived on his ship, the *Royal Charlotte*, which carried a cargo of flour bought specially in Baltimore for the New Orleans market. He met with O'Reilly and offered him the cargo of flour at a greatly reduced price. This won the Spanish general to his cause. O'Reilly granted Pollock free trade rights in the city as a result of this. "And I did," Pollock wrote later, "enjoy that privilege so long as I staid [sic] in the country."¹¹

This flour contract provided Pollock with the economic foundation upon which he established a successful merchant house in Louisiana. Pollock prospered quickly and thereafter served as corresponding agent at New Orleans for Willing and Morris in Louisiana and the lower Mississippi Valley. He also became an agent for other Atlantic coast merchant firms. He accordingly reaped great profits, especially as Louisiana and the lower reaches of the river became increasingly a center of trade.[12] He noted: "I was supplied dry goods from London, Negroes from Africa, and flour from Philadelphia to the River Mississippi (for all of which I had not bills protested); and by the correspondence I had with the principal commercial houses in Philadelphia, I became known to the United States."[13] In that regard, Pollock cooperated with other English-speaking merchants, including those in the Illinois region and British West Florida, including George Morgan of the Philadelphia firm Baynton, Wharton, and Morgan. This firm established stores at Kaskaskia, Cahokia, and Vincennes. Starting in 1766, this company began sending flat boats down the Ohio from Fort Pitt. Pollock also served as the agent at New Orleans for David Franks and Company of Philadelphia, a firm represented by William Murray. Pollock and Murray, who eventually settled in the Felicianas district of Spanish Louisiana after the American Revolution, would remain lifelong friends. George Morgan eventually gave up his merchant activities in the Ohio Valley and returned to Philadelphia. He left his unpaid accounts and his unsold stock to Murray. Morgan told his clients to settle their accounts by shipping pelts to Pollock in New Orleans. Pollock, acting as the agent for Baynton, Wharton, and Morgan, shipped the pelts to Philadelphia.[14]

Although Spanish imperial trade laws, in theory, restricted at various times such commerce, in actual practice the province's participation in the larger Atlantic market economy proceeded unabated during the entire Spanish period. In fact, during the final decades of the eighteenth century Spain progressively relaxed her mercantile trade restrictions in order to profit from this commerce. As Arthur P. Whitaker has noted: "Spain was then at the height of its 'Bourbon renaissance' and the court seemed to be making considerable progress in its efforts to adjust its regulations to the needs of colonial commerce."[15] This proved especially the case for Louisiana. As early as 1768, the Spanish permitted Louisiana merchants to have a larger circle of foreign trading partners than those in Spain's other colonies. The Reglamento de Comercio Libre of 1778 expanded these privileges, while additional trade regulations in 1782 further increased the commercial flexibility of merchants in the province. As well, smuggling was often tolerated unofficially as merchants in New Orleans openly conducted a routine trade with Philadelphia and other ports in the United States through French colonies in the Caribbean as way stations, a legal commerce permitted by Spanish mercantile regulations.[16] Boom times for English-speaking merchants and planters of Louisiana arrived definitively in 1788 when a royal order from the Spanish court permitted the shipment of goods from the Ohio and upper Mississippi valleys down the rivers to New Orleans for export, a beneficial situation.[17] Pollock and other merchants tied to the burgeoning Atlantic trade network amassed great fortunes in various aspects of the trade and commerce available to them in Spanish territory.

This certainly proved the case regarding the commerce in staples between New Orleans and ports such as Philadelphia and Baltimore. From 1769 onward, Pollock annually contracted with the Philadelphia firm of Willing and Morris to supply cargoes of badly needed flour; for the rest of the century, a continuing series of Atlantic coast merchants including Robert Dorsey at Baltimore, Robert Smith from Philadelphia, and others shipped cargoes of this foodstuff to their corresponding agents at New Orleans and Natchez.[18] In turn, shipments of indigo and tobacco flowed from the lower Mississippi to the Atlantic coast starting in the 1770s. Then, with the growing preponderance of cotton in the late 1780s, a number of Anglo-American merchants turned to specializing in this staple. One recent study of the New Orleans export trade indicates that between 1793 and 1796 more than 50 percent of all commerce in Louisiana cotton occurred with ports in the United States.[19] The significance of this mercantile activity went far beyond the profits of the trade itself. It also created an important by-product: a lively movement of bills of exchange between Spanish Louisiana and Atlantic coast merchant houses in the United States. This activity provided rudimentary banking and credit services for Spanish Louisiana that by the 1790s had irrevocably tied the lower Mississippi Valley to the United States, while also moving the province further away from participation in Spanish and French trading networks.[20]

Hence, the profits of English-speaking merchants expanded all across the period of Spanish rule in Louisiana.[21] Much of Pollock's personal fortune rested on slave trading. He actively began selling slaves in Spanish New Orleans soon after his arrival in the colony. In 1769, for example, he sold two house servants to a local resident for 265 pesos fuertes. Although these sales might have been in technical violation of Spanish law, since Pollock was not a Louisiana citizen at that time, government complicity for such commerce could be assumed since one of the other eager purchasers was none other than General Alejandro O'Reilly, who bought several slaves.[22] Pollock took full advantage of this situation. He imported an entire boatload of more than eighty African slaves to the lower Mississippi Valley in 1773. He had apparently purchased them in the West Indies, although all of them were native Africans who had come by way of the middle passage to the New World. Pollock's bill of sale described as them "brutish males, females, and children who were not baptized."[23] The following year Pollock sailed to the Atlantic coast, where he purchased another shipment of slaves that he brought back to the lower Mississippi Valley, also selling them at a great profit.

The importation of consumer goods into Louisiana constituted a second category of economic activity for Oliver Pollock, coequal to that of the slave trade, additionally linking Spanish Louisiana to the Atlantic market economy. English-speaking residents all along the river wanted manufactured items and various consumer products, both for domestic and agrarian use, in order to maintain their accustomed lifestyle of daily existence. In large measure, these items served as "cultural markers" around which an American identity formed.[24] Like the slave trade, the networks for furnishing these consumer goods shifted from French to British sources, starting in the late 1760s, and, after the American Revolution, this commerce linked the lower Mississippi Valley to supply centers controlled by merchants in the United States. Oliver Pollock imported large amounts of consumer goods from Atlantic ports during the Spanish period. He regularly sold items such as farm implements, clothing, shoes, coffee, tea, nails, and other manufactured goods to the English speakers who frequented his store at New Orleans. Pollock also opened a store at Tunica Bayou north of Baton Rouge during the early 1770s. He operated this store in partnership with James Willing, the brother of the Philadelphia owner of the merchant house for whom he served as correspondent at New Orleans. The store at Tunica Bayou stocked goods such as premade clothing of the latest American fashion, bridles, saddles, cut saw files, ready-made shoes, and a wide variety of similar dry goods.[25] Pollock and Willing even made concerted efforts to sell supplies to the British for use in the Native American trade. In 1773, James Willing wrote to General Frederick Haldimand, the commandant at Pensacola: "I have taken the Liberty of addressing you to acquaint you of my arrival here with a cargo of goods suitable to the Indian Illinois trade. I propose setting off tomorrow with my goods to Manchac and there to stay with my goods until further hearing from you."[26]

    The importing of consumer goods into Spanish Louisiana followed an established hierarchy of commerce. The larger firms on the Atlantic coast shipped consumer items to the major merchant houses of New Orleans. From there, they went to an increasing number of local stores that had sprung up rapidly all across Louisiana during the late Spanish period. The trading post or small general store came to exist as a fixture of almost every settlement in the region, and after the early 1780s such establishments became equated with English-speaking merchants in every quarter of Spanish territory. These local stores also became social gathering places for the English-speaking settlers in their neighborhoods, thus adding to the growth of a community spirit that had an impact on identity formation. A variety of social interactions that revolved around the English-speaking trading posts and general stores furthered the creation of a new group identity. Drinking, gambling, and the work of entrepreneurial mechanics who plied their trades at such locations also proved to be motivations for group cohesion. As one historian of the Thompson Creek district, north of Baton Rouge, wrote in the 1780s about the settlement that grew up around the Cochran and Rhea Store: "The men loved to visit and frequently met at one another's house to discuss the business of pirating and smuggling that took place on the river. They would remain for several days, drinking, playing cards, and catching up on the news of the world."[27]

The proliferation of smaller, rural stores reflected the expanding commercial grasp of the larger New Orleans firms into the lower Mississippi hinterlands. The significance of these stores increased in the 1780s when the new and expanding English-speaking populations served by this network of stores developed a tendency to remain separate from the Gallic and Hispanophone populations in areas where these groups already resided. That was so because the English-speaking planters who came to Louisiana in the 1780s and 1790s tended to found new communities in areas proximate to the already existing communities. Many of these new, relatively small and—at least initially—very rural communities were located short distances from the established, older settlements such as St. Louis, St. Genevieve, and Natchez, where there had traditionally resided large numbers of non-English speakers.[28] Moreover, the rural store became the social community center for these new settlements. Such places included New Madrid, Bayou Sara, Carondelet, and New Bourbon.

Acquisition of land and the ownership of plantations also became an additional road to wealth for Oliver Pollock as he aggressively pursued the acquisition of land and plantations once he arrived in the lower Mississippi Valley.[29] During the early 1770s, he found himself in the enviable position of holding British citizenship while he enjoyed all of the rights that came with approved residence in Spanish Louisiana. This unique status permitted him to receive land grants and purchase property in both Louisiana and British West Florida. By 1775, Pollock had received several large land grants from the British government in West Florida. His first such acquisition consisted of some four hundred acres along the Tangipahoa River near Pass Manchac. He also received grants of land on the east bank of the Mississippi near Pointe Coupée and at Baton Rouge, the latter being today the partial site of the campus of Louisiana State University.[30] Pollock secured his largest land holding in 1772 when he purchased a large tract at Tunica Bayou from Henry Fairchild, a British settler in West Florida. This plantation, locally known as "Old Tunica," grew indigo along with rice, tobacco, and vegetables. Pollock built a house on the property while he constructed a small boat landing at the point where the bayou entered the Mississippi River. A nephew from Pennsylvania, Hamilton Pollock, arrived at Tunica in the mid-1770s in order to superintend the operation of this plantation.[31] A description of this property noted that "the land in cultivation was of excellent quality" and that there were several fields near the river well-suited for planting crops. Improvements eventually consisted of a large farm house, a warehouse, a log smokehouse, a corn crib, and various cabins.[32] Pollock also purchased town lots at St. Francisville and at New Orleans. He secured property in Spanish Louisiana, including several plantation tracts north of New Orleans all on the east bank of the Mississippi River.[33] Hence, by the mid-1770s, Oliver Pollock owned over a dozen tracts of land in both Louisiana and West Florida, some of which he held for investment and others of which he actively farmed using slave labor.

All of these commercial interests increasingly moved Oliver Pollock toward political, economic, and cultural solidarity with an American identity. The American Revolution served as a catalyst for this significant change in the manner by which Oliver Pollock conceptualized his own identity. To that time in his life, he had variously presented himself as an Ulsterman, a Scotch-Irishman, or a Celtic Irishman, while at times he cast himself as a Presbyterian or a Roman Catholic. The American colonial revolt served as the motivation that helped him to form a permanent identity. Clearly, his being of Irish stock disinclined him to support the British; in overwhelming fashion, however, it was Pollock's career as a merchant in Spanish Louisiana that brought him to an American identity. Although he had apparently never before professed an American colonial viewpoint and had lived in the British North American colonies for less than two years, the events that began at Lexington and Concord marked a significant change in the way he defined his own personal identity. This had become very apparent by the spring of 1776 when a Virginia military officer named George Gibson arrived at Spanish New Orleans. It was Gibson's mission to purchase goods and supplies at New Orleans for use by colonial troops. The Virginia officer quickly made contact with Oliver Pollock, who enthusiastically agreed to intercede with the governor of Louisiana on his behalf. Pollock arranged for a large shipment of gunpowder to be sent by Gibson up the Mississippi and Ohio rivers to Fort Pitt. Captain Gibson also carried with him on his return trip a letter that Pollock wrote to Robert Morris, who, in addition to having been a partner in the firm of Willing and Morris, then served in the Congress as chair of the Secret Committee of Correspondence. Pollock declared unequivocally and absolutely his American identity in this letter to Morris, the man who had been his merchant contact in Philadelphia for almost twenty years. He wrote, "Permit me therefore to make tender my hearty services and to assure you that my conduct shall ever be as to merit the confidence and approbation of the country to whom I owe everything but my birth."[34]

Oliver Pollock had become an American and had largely done so because of his mercantile connections. Over the next four years he engaged in a wide variety of activities in support of the rebel cause. The year following Gibson's visit to New Orleans, Pollock materially assisted in supporting the expedition that the Pennsylvania captain James Willing led to the lower Mississippi Valley. This was, of course, the same James Willing who had lived in British West Florida and who had operated during the early 1770s the store at Tunica in partnership with Pollock. Young Willing had returned to the United States, received an officer's commission, and led an expedition down the Mississippi in the spring of 1778 for the purpose of capturing British West Florida. Willing's expedition caused tremendous discord in British territory along the Mississippi during the spring of 1778. He and his men raided British plantations, took valuable prizes, and arrived at New Orleans where the members of the expedition sought to sell their plunder. During April 1778, Pollock superintended the sale of this property and the slaves who had also been taken during the raid by Willing. Later in that same year, Pollock began assisting George Rogers Clark, who was involved in conquering British territory in the Illinois country. Pollock became the chief source of supplying for George Rogers Clark's troops while they conquered the British territory along the lower Ohio and upper Mississippi rivers. Hence, by the end of the American Revolution, Oliver Pollock had become an American. So too had many of the other English-speaking merchants in the region who had cooperated with him, including Daniel Clark, Thomas Patterson, Alexander Graydon, and several others who were also engaged in the Philadelphia trade from the lower Mississippi Valley.

Many of these English-speaking merchants who had become Americanized, including Pollock, had never lived for substantial amounts of time in the infant United States, or in the British colonies from which the new nation had been born.[35] They nonetheless saw themselves as part of a new, emerging identity in the region: that of being an "American."[36] Peter J. Kastor has noted for the late Spanish period regarding English-speakers in the lower Mississippi Valley and those in the United States: "Americans and Louisianans conceived of citizenship and nationhood in very similar ways." For that reason, "By 1800," he observes, "both groups saw advantages in equality among white male citizens and benefits from broad networks of interest."[37] Although the historian Phillis Whitman Hunter was writing about merchants in Boston during the late eighteenth century, her views have some measure of applicability to the creation of this American identity in Spanish Louisiana. "The privileged status of the mercantile elite was distinctly white . . . ," she writes of Boston, and "whites defined their privileged position by objectifying others."[38] This same process can be seen in the lower Mississippi Valley in the patterns of American identity formation that took place there. This represented a compelling development in Spanish Louisiana because many, if not most, of these English speakers failed to conceptualize themselves as advance agents of United States imperium. Pollock certainly did not when he arrived. Instead, the majority of them lived in the lower Mississippi Valley during the period of Spanish dominion largely for personal reasons, mostly because they wanted the success that mercantile pursuits could bring them and their families. They did not come for reasons of national expansion or geopolitical aggrandizement. Once these people had arrived in Louisiana, they nonetheless engaged in economic practices that fostered group identity formation that made them disposed to a new identity. This American identity should not be confused with nationalism because it was significantly more subtle and operated independently from any individual relationship to the concept of nation. It was instead cultural and social in nature. As Stuart Hall has written of such identity: it was "a sort of collective 'one time self,' hiding inside the many other, superficial and artificially imposed 'selves,' which people with a shared ancestry hold in common." Indeed, it may be that the forging of a perceived cultural identity predates the formation of a national identity historically, as was the case in Spanish Louisiana. "Within the terms of this definition," Hall notes, "our cultural identities reflect the common historical experiences and shared cultural codes which provide us, as 'one people' with stable, unchanging and continuous frames of reference and meaning, beneath the shifting divisions and vicissitudes of our actual history."[39]

The market economy did provide English-speaking merchants in Spanish Louisiana with such a common experience based on tangible manifestations of "shared cultural codes," especially in areas of material culture and lifestyles, upon which an explicit cultural identity formed. This was significant because Pollock and most of the other English-speaking residents who came to live in Spanish territory before the Louisiana Purchase arrived with a wide variety of preexisting and related identities, none of which could initially be styled "American." Some called themselves English, others were Ulster folk, and still others saw themselves as Celtic Irish. Some were Protestant, while some were Roman Catholic. Others saw themselves as British, while others styled themselves as Scottish. They were from Georgia, South Carolina, Pennsylvania, or New Jersey. A few even called themselves Jamaicans or Bahamians. During the American Revolution, some of these settlers remained staunchly Tory, others became committed rebels. They lived during the late eighteenth century in all parts of Spanish Louisiana, but especially in the Old Natchez district and the

Felicianas, as the former British colony of West Florida became known in the Spanish era after the American Revolution.[40]

Indeed, Pollock and these English-speaking merchants had come to represent the colony's most efficient link with the outside world by the late 1780s. On two occasions after disastrous fires at New Orleans in 1788 and 1794, English-speaking merchants played the key role in re-provisioning and rebuilding the city, thus enabling its material recovery and the restoration of its infrastructure. After the conflagration of 1788, Oliver Pollock chartered a special vessel at Philadelphia, loaded it to capacity with needed domestic goods lost in the fire, and sailed it to New Orleans on what turned out to be a particularly profitable voyage. That cargo included, a bit belatedly, a used pump fire engine sold to the Spanish *cabildo* that Pollock had purchased from Benjamin Franklin's Philadelphia Fire Company. Presumably, this first fire engine in Louisiana later saw service in the second major New Orleans fire of 1794, an event that Pollock did not witness.[41]

Oliver Pollock had returned to the United States to live in 1791 and there he remained for the next twenty-eight years. He moved to Pennsylvania, where he operated a tavern and small store at the village of Silver Spring near Carlisle. After the death of his wife, Margaret, he remarried a woman from Baltimore and became a merchant in that city. In partnership with his son, Procopio, who had been born years earlier in Spanish New Orleans, Pollock engaged in maritime trade between Philadelphia, Baltimore, Havana, and New Orleans. Members of his family, however, continued to reside in Spanish Louisiana on the Tunica Bend Plantation, which continued under his ownership as an important asset. His nephew Hamilton looked after Oliver's affairs from his own plantation near Bayou Sara. Pollock's eldest daughter, Mary, and her husband, Dr. Samuel S. Robinson, had settled in present-day Wilkinson County, Mississippi, a few miles north of Tunica Bend, an area that became part of the United States in 1797. The Robinsons made frequent visits to the Old Tunica Plantation from their home in nearby Pinckneyville and, with the passing of Hamilton Pollock in 1814, they began the active management of the plantation.

By the 1790s, cotton dominated this area as the most important staple and, as a result, had become the major crop grown at Tunica Bend. The Pollock family continued to prosper with the arrival of cotton to the area. In so doing, the family reflected the common patterns of landholding and agriculture that had become prevalent among all of these English speakers in Spanish Louisiana. The rise of cotton caused subsistence farming to be replaced all across the lower Mississippi Valley by a reliance on staples during the closing decades of the century. As the historian Roger G. Kennedy has noted of the Mississippi Valley and Gulf Coast for the early decades of the nineteenth century, "The economy of the borderlands was in transition from subsistence agriculture of white and Indian yeoman, growing their own crops and supplementing their diets with meat secured by hunting, to a plantation system, growing cotton and rice for sale to international markets."[42] A recent study of land records from 1760 to the 1800s clearly establishes that many planters who engaged in staple crop production migrated into what would become the Louisiana Purchase territory, bringing their slaves with them.[43] As the historian John Hebron Moore has noted, most of these English-speaking settlers who came "to the lower Mississippi valley were agriculturalists lured away from worn-out farms or plantations in the South Atlantic states by the attraction of easily obtained fertile virgin lands" and, because of them, New Orleans, had become one of the world's leading cotton exporting cities by the time of the Louisiana Purchase.[44] "The province of Louisiana yields very rich produce," John Bonfeld reported to Thomas Jefferson in 1785 from Bordeaux, France, noting that "the two cargoes arrived here will amount to two Million Livres in furs and Indigo."[45] In 1794, the Natchez district produced about 36,000 pounds of cotton. Four years later estimates for the annual amount of cotton production rose to 1.2 million pounds. "We continue to cultivate cotton with very great success," William Dunbar noted of the 1790s. "It is by far the most profitable crop we have ever undertaken in this country."[46] The slave population of the Natchez district grew accordingly, increasing from approximately five hundred bondsmen in 1784 to over two thousand by 1796.[47] Many of the vessels that sailed with cargoes of cotton from Louisiana to Atlantic ports returned to the lower Mississippi with new settlers as passengers. "There is a vessel now laying at Philadelphia," Thomas Jefferson wrote a correspondent in 1791, "advertising to receive immigrants to Louisiana gratis, on account of the Spanish Government."[48]

Susan Garrett Davis has noted of this phase of English-speaking migration: "Coming overland or down the Mississippi on flatboats, these Upland South settlers migrated from the Southern Appalachian and Southern Piedmont areas of eastern Tennessee, Kentucky, West Virginia, and Carolina, northern Georgia, and Alabama."[49] In 1810, one of the English speakers at Bayou Sara wrote to a New Orleans newspaper in order to report that many of these recent settlers were "generally Americans, and many of them purchased lands and settled in Florida since the cession of Louisiana to the United States; fully impressed with the belief that they would soon find themselves under their former laws and government."[50] Not all of these immigrants, however, represented the more upstanding elements of society. As the historian Samuel C.

Hyde, Jr., has observed about some of them, "The region served as a haven for Tories, army deserters, and desperados, all of whom exploited the prevailing instability and absence of American control."[51]

Oliver Pollock returned to the lower Mississippi Valley in 1819 upon the death of his wife and there lived out the remaining years of his life. He maintained his legal residence at the Pinckneyville, Mississippi, home of his daughter, but he often stayed at Tunica Bend, by that time a part of the Florida Parishes of the state of Louisiana. Although a man in his eighties, it seems that Pollock still had the inclinations of an entrepreneur. The increasing volume of steamboat traffic on the river provided him the opportunity for profit. The Pollocks and Robinsons built a levee at the foot of Tunica Bayou and opened a wood yard.[52] This became a popular re-provisioning stop for boats traveling on the river between New Orleans and St. Louis. The success of the wood yard motivated yet other changes. Pollock and some of his children laid elaborate plans for the development of a town on the plantation at the boat landing where Tunica Bayou entered the Mississippi. He laid off street lines, began to sell property, and hoped for the prosperity of this town, which he named Tunicaville. Pollock, however, died on December 17, 1823 before the town could be developed fully. Some of the Pollock children tried to carry forward with promoting Tunicaville. It did eventually receive a post office, but it never grew and the Pollock family realized little profit from the venture. The family eventually sold parcels of the plantation itself to other planters, although family members kept approximately one-half of the original holding for themselves. One grandson, Oliver Pollock Robinson, lived on the Tunica Plantation until the Civil War. Others maintained homes in St. Francisville and at the hamlet of Bayou Sara. As well, in the mid-1830s, the family initiated a series of unsuccessful legal claims that sought to regain titles to some of Pollock's Spanish era land grants that had never been reconfirmed by the government of the United States.[53]

The life story of Oliver Pollock in Spanish Louisiana, and of the family dynasty that he established in the lower Mississippi Valley, may be seen as an example of a process of American identity formation in the region. Indeed, by the 1790s, the existence of an American identity could be clearly seen in the life histories and writings of various merchants whose primary point of contact with the United States had been because of their participation in the Atlantic market economy. Oliver Pollock was chief among them. These merchants and planters, including Daniel Clark, the Jones brothers, James Mather, and many others from the entire English-speaking community of Spanish Louisiana, shared similar life histories that moved them to form an American identity without any prior explicit identification to the United States.

This Americanized identity based on an amalgamation of English-speaking groups in the region thus appeared in tandem with the economic development of Louisiana and its hinterland in the late eighteenth century and the early nineteenth. This identity had an impact greater that the actual number of English-speaking residents in the colony prior to the Louisiana Purchase. Historical estimates, given the lack of accurate or extant census information, hold that approximately fifty thousand persons (exclusive of Native Americans) lived in the purchase territory when it became part of the United States, of whom perhaps as many as one-half were African slaves or free persons of color. These figures exclude the five to seven thousand individuals in the Old Natchez district who became United States citizens in 1797 when that area passed from Spanish control.[54] The net result is that the English-speaking population of Spanish Louisiana constituted no more than several thousand persons, but some of them were individuals who had profitable mercantile businesses. They formed an emerging elite that eventually became a foundation for the subsequent hegemonic Americanization of Louisiana in areas such as culture, economics, and politics. Hence, in some measure, the Louisiana Purchase of 1803 can be seen as the legitimization by territorial acquisition of a preexisting link to the United States created by the presence of an American identity that had been fashioned by joining Spanish Louisiana to the Atlantic market economy and which, in so doing, firmly connected the lower Mississippi Valley to major ports of the East Coast such as Philadelphia and Baltimore. Although the social commentator Hector St. John de Crèvecoeur did not visit Louisiana during his residence in British North America in the early 1780s, his famous essay "Letters from an American Farmer" does have pertinence to the process of identity formation that occurred in the Spanish province. He asked "what is an American" and from "whence came all these people?" Crèvecoeur's answer: "They are a mixture of English, Scotch, Irish, French, Dutch, Germans, and Swedes." "From this promiscuous breed," he observed, "that race now called Americans have arisen."[55] The Americanization of Louisiana was therefore not entirely initiated by the diplomatic events that occurred in 1803 with the Louisiana Purchase. The formation of an American identity in Louisiana was caused in large part by Spanish Louisiana's entrance into the Atlantic market economy of the late eighteenth century, a process set in motion by Oliver Pollock's arrival at New Orleans in 1769.

Notes

1. Light T. Cummins, "Oliver Pollock and George Rogers Clark's Service of Supply: A Case Study in Financial Disaster," in Robert J. Holden, ed., *Selected Papers from the*

1985 and 1986 George Rogers Clark Trans-Appalachian Frontier History Conferences (Vincennes, Ind.: National Park Service, 1988), 1–17.

2. For a full discussion of the frontier exchange economy, see Daniel H. Usner, *Indians, Settlers, and Slaves in a Frontier Exchange Economy: The Lower Mississippi Valley Before 1803* (Chapel Hill: University of North Carolina Press, 1992). As William Cash has noted about the various groups living in this region during the colonial era, "The European explorations, settlements, and international conflicts provide interesting narratives, but more significantly they permitted each of the participants to deposit a portion of their civilization in the area.... Obviously, the English heritage was dominant, as is evident in the enduring legacy of language, political concepts, religion, law, education, and economics." Cash, "European Colonization of Mississippi," in Barbara Carpenter, ed., *Ethnic Heritage In Mississippi* (Jackson: University Presses of Mississippi, 1992), 122–23.

3. The few studies that examine the "Americanization" of Louisiana begin with the purchase of 1803 as the motivating event for the process. This is the case for the only book-length study to deal with this issue: William Lewis Newton, *Americanization of Louisiana: A Study in the Process of Adjustment between French and Anglo-American Populations of Louisiana, 1803–1860* (repr., New York: Arno Press, 1980). In spite of the publication date, Newton's volume is an unrevised Ph.D. dissertation from 1929. Not surprisingly, its focus is very institutional and governmental, giving little notice to more subtle issues such as social, cultural, economic, and race relations. Historians of the Louisiana legal system have begun to pay particular attention to the period of Spanish Louisiana as the formative period of civil procedure as practiced after statehood. See Mark F. Fernandez, "Local Justice in the Territory of Orleans: W. C. C. Claiborne's Courts, Judges, and Justices of the Peace," in Warren M. Billings and Mark F. Fernandez, eds., *A Law Unto Itself: Essays in the New Louisiana Legal History* (Baton Rouge: Louisiana State University Press, 2001), 79; and Fernandez, *From Chaos to Continuity: The Evolution of Louisiana's Judicial System, 1712–1862* (Baton Rouge: Louisiana State University Press, 2001).

4. Christopher Morris, *Becoming Southern: The Evolution of a Way of Life, Warren County and Vicksburg, Mississippi, 1770–1860* (New York: Oxford University Press, 1995); Liah Greenfield, *The Spirit of Capitalism: Nationalism and Economic Growth* (Liverpool, England: Liverpool University Press, 2003). In an earlier seminal publication, Greenfield notes that there are many different definitions of nationalism and national identity based on such factors as territory, language, culture, religion, history, and race. See Liah Greenfield, "In Pursuit of the Ideal Nation: The Unfolding of Nationality in America," in *Nationalism: Five Roads to Modernity* (Cambridge, Mass.: Harvard University Press, 1992), 396–484. There is a burgeoning scholarly literature regarding nationalism and the formation of national identity that offers a wide array of criteria by which it can be defined and how it occurs historically.

5. Ira Berlin, *Many Thousands Gone: The First Two Centuries of Slavery in North America* (Cambridge, Mass.: Harvard University Press, 1998), 325.

6. Spanish Louisiana must be considered by the historian as an emerging part of

the late eighteenth-century Atlantic world in terms of identity formation regarding the various groups that lived along the lower Mississippi River. As Michael J. Braddick has written, "The movement of goods and people around the Atlantic world created a shared material culture which reflected common assumptions about status distinctions. . . . By the eighteenth century these forces had fostered a marked convergence of elite sensibilities across all the territories of the nascent British Empire." Braddick, "Civility and Authority," in David Armitage and Michael J. Braddick, ed., *The British Atlantic World, 1500–1800* (New York: Palgrave Macmillan, 2001), 93. In addition, many historians view the commercial development involved in the creation of the Atlantic world within the context of metropolitan centers and colonial peripheries. "By the time the colonists were numerous enough and wealthy enough to interest the metropole," note Amy Turner Bushnell and Jack P. Greene, "they were also strong enough to resist it and to seize control over their own backcountry." Bushnell and Greene, "Peripheries, Centers, and the Construction of Early Modern American Empires," in Christine Daniels and Michael V. Kennedy, eds., *Negotiated Empires: Centers and Peripheries in the Americas, 1500–1820* (New York: Routledge, 2002), 11. In analogous fashion, such a generic relationship eventually developed in the region between English-speakers and the Spanish governments of Louisiana and West Florida, although the Louisiana Purchase obviated conflict in much of the region, except in the Felicianas where a revolt in 1810 did occur. For a full analysis of Louisiana as part of the Atlantic world complex, see D. W. Meinig, *Atlantic America, 1492–1880*, vol. 1, *The Shaping of America: A Geographical Perspective of 500 Years of History* (New Haven, Conn.: Yale University Press, 1986), 193–202, 416–17, and 424–25; and Alan Taylor, *American Colonies* (New York: Penguin Books), 363–95. See also Ian K. Steele, "Exploding Colonial American History: Amerindian, Atlantic, and Global Perspectives," *Reviews in American History* 26 (1998): 70–95.

7. The best introduction to the Atlantic market economy of the eighteenth century is John J. McCusker and Kenneth Morgan, eds., *The Early Modern Atlantic Economy* (Cambridge: Cambridge University Press, 2000); and William M. Reddy, *The Rise of Market Culture* (Cambridge: Cambridge University Press, 1987).

8. James A. James, *Oliver Pollock: The Life and Times of an Unknown Patriot* (New York: Appleton-Century, 1937); Light T. Cummins, "Oliver Pollock's Plantations: An Early Anglo Landowner on the Lower Mississippi, 1769–1824," *Louisiana History* 29:1(Winter 1988): 35–48.

9. Extensive genealogical information about the Scottish branch of the Pollock family may be found in boxes 40, 68, and 69 of the MacLeod Collection and in box 4 of the Graham Collection, Royal Society of Genealogists, Charterhouse Buildings, London, England.

10. James, *Oliver Pollock*, 4–7.

11. Oliver Pollock to the Captain General of Cuba, June 22, 1796, Archivo General de Indias, Seville, Spain, Papeles de Cuba, Legajo 1469; Pollock to Luis de las Casas, July 14, 1796, ibid.; Pollock's contract was for the supply of flour. For the Cabildo deliberations on the scarcity of this commodity, see Actas del Cabildo, New Orleans,

Oct. 5, 1770, Aug. 2, 1771, and Aug. 16, 1771, vol. 1, pp. 20, 32, 33, WPA Transcripts in Spanish on Microfilm, New Orleans Public Library, New Orleans.

12. The standard book-length studies of Oliver Pollock in the Revolution are James, *Oliver Pollock;* and John A. Caughey, *Bernardo de Gálvez in Louisiana, 1776-1783* (Berkeley: University of California Press, 1934). See also Light T. Cummins, *Spanish Observers and the American Revolution* (Baton Rouge: Louisiana State University Press, 1991).

13. James, *Oliver Pollock*, 54. Pollock to Governor Beverly Randolph of Virginia, Jan. 22, 1791, *Calendar of Virginia State Papers* (Richmond: Willliam Palmer, 1875), 6: 251.

14. James, *Oliver Pollock*, 49-50; Max Savelle, *George Morgan, Colony Builder* (New York: Columbia University, 1932), 52-75.

15. Arthur P. Whitaker, "Reed and Forde: Merchant Adventurers of Philadelphia: Their Trade with Spanish New Orleans," in Gilbert C. Din, ed., *The Spanish Presence in Louisiana, 1763-1803* (1937; repr., Lafayette: Center for Louisiana Studies, 1996), 246.

16. Arthur P. Whitaker, "The Commerce of Louisiana and the Floridas at the End of the Eighteenth Century," *Hispanic American Historical Review* 8 (May 1928): 203-20.

17. Whitaker, "Reed and Forde," 249-50.

18. Firms in the United States and Great Britain included Baynton, Wharton, and Company in Philadelphia; Bridgen and Walker in London; Dennis and Smith in New Haven; Hindley and Needham in London; Walker and Dawson in London; Hugh and Alexander in Philadelphia; and Willing and Morris in Philadelphia.

19. Jesus Lorente Miguel, "Commercial Relations between New Orleans and the United States, 1783-1803," in Jacques Barbier and Allan Kuethe, eds., *The North American Role in the Spanish Imperial Economy* (Manchester, U.K.: Manchester University Press, 1984), 180.

20. Light T. Cummins, "Anglo Merchants and Capital Migration in Spanish Colonial New Orleans, 1763-1803," *Gulf Coast Historical Review* 4 (Fall 1988): 22.

21. Jack D. L. Holmes, "Some Economic Problems of the Governors of Louisiana," *Hispanic American Historical Review* 43 (1972): 877-96; John W. Caughey, "Bernardo de Galvez and the English Smugglers on the Mississippi, 1777," *Hispanic American Historical Review* 7 (1932): 46-58. Most of the periodic attempts to stop contraband trade were usually symbolic actions designed to give the appearance that Spanish governors were vigorously enforcing Spain's mercantile policies. In reality, a succession of Louisiana governors from the 1770s to the 1790s often looked the other way in order to permit the dealings of the Anglo-American merchants, whose mercantile activities were deemed essential to the functioning of the colony. See Caughey, *Bernardo de Gálvez in Louisiana*, and the various biographies of Louisiana governors in Joseph G. Dawson, ed., *The Louisiana Governors: From Iberville to Edwards* (Baton Rouge: Louisiana State University Press, 1990).

22. Acts of Andrés Almonaster y Rojas, vol. 1., Feb. 9, 1770, fol. 9, New Orleans Notary Archives, Civil Courts Building, New Orleans.

23. Acts of Juan Bautista Garic, New Orleans Notary Archives, vol. 4, March 10, 1773.

24. Sociologists postulate that objects of material culture constitute a matrix on which cultural identity forms. In modern times, items such as athletic shoes and CD players serve as "cultural markers" of perceived group identities. One leading sociologist has noted, "Identities are produced, consumed, and regulated within culture—creating meaning through symbolic systems of representation about the identity positions which we might adopt." Kathryn Woodward, ed., *Identity and Difference* (London: Sage Publications, 1997), 2, 12.

25. Account Book of William Dunbar, *Records of Antebellum Plantations*, ed. Kenneth M. Stampp, Microform Collection, Series J, Reel 1.

26. James Willing to James Haldimand, Manchack, Jan. 3, 1772, British Museum, Haldimand Add. Mss., 21,729, f. 280.

27. Virginia Lobdell Jennings, "Narrative of the Settlement at Thompson Creek, 1716–1832," *Louisiana Genealogical Register* 42 (June 1995): 209.

28. Antonio Acosta Rodríguez, *La población de Luisiana española, 1763–1803* (Madrid: Ministerio de Asuntos Exteriores, 1979), 234.

29. Cummins, "Oliver Pollock's Plantations," 42–45.

30. "A Plan of the Coast of Part of West Florida and Louisiana Including the River Mississippi from Its Entrances as High as the River Yazous," Map Library, Louisiana State University School of Geosciences, Baton Rouge.

31. The survey of the Old Tunica Plantation is located in "Undocketed Materials—Natchez," Louisiana Survey Materials, the Historic New Orleans Collection, New Orleans. A description to the plantation is located in "Probate of Oliver Pollock," file no. 81, Clerk of Court Records, West Feliciana Parish Courthouse, St. Francisville, Louisiana.

32. *Alexander Baudin v. G. Davy, Washington White, Widow of W. Roliff, and Samuel Robinson*, April 13, 1821, case no. 2048, box 778, Records of the Supreme Court of Louisiana, Earl K. Long Library, University of New Orleans.

33. Cummins, "Oliver Pollock's Plantations," 38–40.

34. James, "Oliver Pollock, Financier of the Revolution in the West," *Mississippi Valley Historical Review* 16 (1929): 71.

35. Peter Dobson Hall has postulated a clear connection between economic activity and formation of group culture. He has written of this generic process during the twentieth century: "American culture in the twentieth century is characterized by masses of individuals who produce goods and service that they do not consume and consume goods and services that they do not produce—and by institutional mechanisms that coordinate the flow of goods and services as well as the recruitment and training of managers of those institutions on a national basis." Hall, *The Organization of American Culture, 1700–1900: Private Institutions, Elites, and the Origins of American Nationalism* (New York: New York University Press, 1982), 2. In proto-nascent form, the foundations of this twentieth century characterization of culture can be seen in the formation of an American elite identity in Spanish Louisiana.

36. I employ the term American in the strict sentiment of the Spanish term "estadounidense." It is an imprecision of our vernacular English that those persons who are from the United States have no exact and singular popular term by which they are denominated in order to distinguish them with accuracy from other residents of this hemisphere.

37. He further develops this theme by writing: "For settlers of European birth and ancestry in the United States and in Louisiana, the creation of national communities was in large part contingent on white supremacy." Peter J. Kastor, *The Nation's Crucible: The Louisiana Purchase and the Creation of America* (New Haven, Conn.: Yale University Press, 2004), 29.

38. Phillis Whitman Hunter, *Purchasing Identity in the Atlantic World: Massachusetts Merchants, 1670–1780* (Ithaca, N.Y.: Cornell University Press, 2001), 89.

39. Stuart Hall, "Cultural Identity and Diaspora," in Woodward, *Identity and Difference*, 51.

40. The areas known as the Old Natchez district and the Felicianas constitute historically the regions of the lower Mississippi Valley where English-speaking residents dominated territorial space for the longest continuous period of time, from the 1770s until the early antebellum period and beyond. The Natchez district and the Felicianas comprised a common physiographic area along the east bank of the Mississippi River, starting in the south at the Iberville River and running north past Baton Rouge, Bayou Sara, and Natchez to the Big Black River near present-day Grand Gulf. Oriented toward the Mississippi itself, the settled areas sometimes extended only a few miles inland, although settlement eventually went far eastward to Mobile and beyond. Over time, this area experienced complicated territorial shifts of national sovereignty, as various parts of it existed under the shifting domination of Spain, Great Britain, and the United States.

41. For a description of destruction during the fire of 1788, see "Report of the Demands of the Citizens of New Orleans after the Fire, March 21, 1788," E. A. Parsons Collection, Humanities Resource Center, the University of Texas at Austin. Pollock sets forth his intentions to sell goods for the rebuilding of the city in a letter to the Spanish governor; see "Instancia de Olivero Pollock," Feb. 10, 1789, Archivo General de Indias, Seville, Spain, Audiencia de Santo Domingo, 2553, f. 628.

42. Roger G. Kennedy, *Mr. Jefferson's Lost Cause: Land, Farmers, Slavery, and the Louisiana Purchase* (New York: Oxford University Press, 2003), 144.

43. Cummins, "Merchants and Capital Migration," 7–27.

44. John Hebron Moore, *The Emergence of the Cotton Kingdom in the Old Southwest: Mississippi, 1770–1860* (Baton Rouge: Louisiana State University Press, 1988), 5.

45. John Bonfeld to Thomas Jefferson, Bordeaux, Aug. 20, 1785, in Julian P. Boyd, ed., *The Papers of Thomas Jefferson* (Princeton, N.J.: Princeton University Press, 1953), 8: 412.

46. Moore, *The Emergence of the Cotton Kingdom*, 5.

47. Ira Berlin, *Many Thousands Gone*, 341.

48. Thomas Jefferson to William Short, Philadelphia, Aug. 29, 1781, in Boyd, *The Papers of Thomas Jefferson*, 22: 96.

49. Susan Garrett Davis, "The Felicianas," an online chapter in State of Louisiana, *Louisiana's Living Traditions: Virtual Books, Folklife in the Florida Parishes*, http://www.louisianafolklife.org/LT/Virtual_Books/Fla_Parishes/book_florida_feliciana.html, accessed Sept. 24, 2006.

50. Letter signed by "Common Sense," in the *Louisiana Gazette*, New Orleans, July 2, 1810, quoted in Stanley C. Arthur, *The Story of the West Florida Rebellion* (St. Francisville, La.: St. Francisville Democrat, 1935), 39.

51. Samuel C. Hyde, Jr., *Pistols and Politics: The Dilemma of Democracy in Louisiana's Florida Parishes, 1810–1899* (Baton Rouge: Louisiana State University Press, 1996), 2. See also Andrew F. McMichael, "'May God Damn My Soul if I Don't Split Your Brains Out': Cross-Border Crime and Regional Instability in West Florida, 1800–1810," paper presented to the Omohundro Institute of Early American History and Culture, Glasgow, Scotland, July 2001; and Samuel C. Hyde, Jr., ed., *A Fierce and Fractious Frontier: The Curious Development of Louisiana's Florida Parishes, 1699–2000* (Baton Rouge: Louisiana State University Press, 2004), especially the essay by Robin F. A. Fabel, "Boom in the Bayous: Land Speculation and Town Planning in the Florida Parishes Under British Rule," 44–59.

52. *Baudin v. Roliff et. al. Robinson, (1823)*, Case Files, Docket No. 1282, Archives of the Supreme Court of Louisiana, Earl K. Long Memorial Library, University of New Orleans.

53. For records of these claims, see State Land Office, Baton Rouge, *Greensburg Land Claims*, book II, part 2, pp. 9–10.

54. The best population study of Spanish Louisiana remains Acosta Rodríguez, *La población de Luisiana española, 1763–1803*. For other population estimates, see Gilbert C. Din, "Slavery in Louisiana's Florida Parishes under the Spanish Regime, 1779–1803," in Hyde, *A Fierce and Fractious Frontier*, 63–64.

55. J. Hector St. John de Crèvecoeur, *Letters from an American Farmer and Sketches of Eighteenth-Century America*, ed. Albert E. Stone (1782; repr., New York: Penguin Books, 1981), 68.

10

Bordermakers and Landed Women

The Rouquier Sisters of Colonial Natchitoches

BETJE BLACK KLIER AND DIANE M. T. NORTH

By the end of the seventeenth century, France had claimed the heartland of North America. Its territory stretched from the Gulf of Mexico northward encompassing major river systems and reached beyond the Great Lakes and east along the St. Lawrence River to the northern Atlantic. Having successfully established trading operations and missions in present-day Canada, and determined to expand not only its relations with native tribes but also commerce and agriculture from its West Indies colonies to North America, France ordered its agents to begin exploring and settling the southern portion of the entire Mississippi River basin. In 1713, the French governor of Louisiana commanded Louis Juchereau de St. Denis (1674–1744), a Canadian-born explorer and trader, to journey from Mobile to Mexico City and open trade with the Spanish. Eager to thwart threats from Britain, the French then directed St. Denis north from the Gulf of Mexico where, in 1714, he erected Fort St. Jean Baptiste, a trading post beside the Red River in what became Natchitoches, Louisiana. St. Denis purposefully chose the site for a trading hub and guardian of the frontier. This oldest permanent settlement in Louisiana (older than New Orleans) drew newcomers from Europe and Canada who were eager to obtain land grants and trading privileges because Natchitoches held a strategic location as the most westerly river port accessible from western North America.[1]

Throughout the eighteenth century, France, Spain, and Britain competed for empire in the New World at the same time as revolutionists in British America gradually struggled to throw off colonial shackles. Soon after the creation of the United States, revolutionary fever erupted in France and its West Indian colonies, but Napoleon entered the scene and imperial wars commenced on a grander scale. As the Louisiana territory changed hands, an enterprising landed gentry class arose from within the earliest colonists and their descendants. These men and women remained attached to French culture and language until a fourth power, the United States, began to dominate the region.² Spain struggled to hold on to its Mexican provinces, but fame and fortune seekers from many nations descended upon Natchitoches, the point on the map at which the boundaries of imperialism, colonialism, and nationalism played out.

This chapter examines the lives of the Rouquier sisters, daughters of Marie Louise Prudhomme Rouquier (1760–1825) and François Rouquier (1759–1808), the men they chose to marry, and the influence those families exerted on the history of the borderlands.³ The Rouquier sisters were their family's first generation to reach maturity and assimilate as "Americans" after the United States purchased Louisiana in 1803. Marie Louise's grandfather, the French-born Jean Pierre Phillipe Prudhomme (ca. 1690–1739) assisted St. Denis in the construction of the trading post in 1714. In 1732, Jean Pierre married a Parisian who had arrived in 1719. They sent their Natchitoches-born son, Jean Baptiste Prudhomme (1735–86), to France to be educated as a medical doctor. He returned to Louisiana, established a hospital in Natchitoches, and married a Creole from New Orleans.⁴ From this union came the matriarch of the Rouquier girls, Marie Louise, who in 1778 married François Rouquier, a prosperous trader from southwestern France. Marie Louise bore one son and five daughters between 1782 and 1793. In 1795, Spanish administrators granted Rouquier approximately 1,354 acres of land near the post, and his descendants held onto the title through subsequent political regimes as European powers and the United States vied for territory.⁵

In Louisiana, all children divided the inheritance equally. Therefore, the land assured the Rouquiers' daughters and their future families prominent positions in the new American society that emerged following the purchase of the Louisiana Territory by the United States because the women, repeating the example of their mother, avoided local Creole matches, choosing instead to marry well-educated, ambitious, acquisitive border-makers, men from the United States, England, Ireland, and France. The husbands rose to play significant roles in the expansion of the U.S. frontier. This intermingling of nationalities, cultures, languages, and religions represented a microcosm of the assimilation process that created the new American citizen. Even though the marriages resulted in the Rouquier family losing its exclusive connections to the French Creole community, the family benefited socially, economically, and politically through its members' cross-marriages.⁶ These advantageous alliances ultimately formed the backbone of the emerging American society, empowering both the husbands and the wives.

According to the marriage records, when twenty-three-year-old François Rouquier wed the twenty-two-year-old Marie Louise Prudhomme he owned "16,000 livres in silver," or 16,000 pounds sterling. The bride's parents gave the

Figure 10.1. All of the children of Marie Louise (Prudhomme) and François Rouquier lived in the Prudhomme-Rouquier House at 446 Jefferson Street, today the fully restored home of the nonprofit Natchitoches Service League. John and Henriette Carr remodeled the family home during the 1820s, adding the Greek Revival façade. Thanks to Conna Cloutier and Bobby de Blieux, who provided local access. The photo was graciously furnished by Juanita Murphy.

couple one house worth "200 piastres situated in the bourg of this post bordered on one side by the said parents and on the other by [the] Dupain [family]," or in the village located outside the walls of the palisade surrounding Fort St. Jean Baptiste. The Prudhommes offered "one Negritte creolle named Marie," valued at 300 piastres, and a 500 piastre allowance "to purchase a Negress."[7] The young couple's first child and only son, J. François, Jr., was born in 1782. Within the next eleven years, Marie Louise gave birth to five daughters: Anita, who never married; Marianne; Joséphine Aimée; Marie Joséphine, called Marcelite; and Henriette.[8] Thus, by 1795, when the senior Rouquier received the land grant of 1,354 acres, he was blessed with a large family. Between 1799 and 1806 he built what became known as "the grandest house in Natchitoches"; today it remains the largest *bousillage* or wood-frame house filled in with Spanish moss and mud, in Louisiana (fig. 10.1).[9] With parcels of their father's land grant as bait, the Rouquier daughters would select their mates in quick succession.

Joséphine Aimée (or Aimée, 1789–1825) married first. In 1806, she wed the North Carolinian James Bludworth (1779–1852), whose father James Bloodworth, Sr. (1742–99), had served in the American Revolutionary War. Bloodworth's death in 1799 left a large family in financial distress and about 1804 the widow uprooted her brood and sailed to New Orleans. They journeyed northward in search of inexpensive land. When the Bloodworth children arrived in Natchitoches with their persevering mother, they changed the spelling of their family name. In the marriage contract, Bludworth agreed to give his intended wife "the sum of Two thousand Dollars, as her Jointure, or the full value thereof in Land, Tenements, goods or chattels, to be at her own proper disposal, and to be by her received and taken to her own proper use and benefit forever." Jointure, a legal practice derived from the English landed classes in lieu of a dower, served to safeguard a married woman's sustenance and property rights during widowhood. In case his wife died "without issue" in her marriage to Bludworth, "the sum of Two Thousand Dollars shall revert to" the husband, heirs or executors or administrators." Judge John C. Carr officiated at the signing of the marriage contract.[10] Several days after the ceremony, Dr. John Sibley (1757–1837), the U.S. Indian agent whose commission President Thomas Jefferson had recommended, informed his son by letter of Bludworth's marriage to "a French girl." Even though the Rouquier bride's family had lived in the territory for almost one hundred years, Sibley, who settled in Natchitoches in 1803, regarded Joséphine Aimée as "French." Together, Joséphine Aimée and James had nine children, including a set of twins. Part of the land Joséphine Aimée received from her father constitutes the original site of Northwestern State University of Louisiana.[11] Bludworth, an entrepreneur and planter, allied himself with Sibley, who also served as a secret agent and reported on territorial activity for the president. Bludworth led the Eighteenth Regiment of the Louisiana Militia at Natchitoches. Because of Natchitoches's strategic location and the proximity of the U.S.-Spanish border at the Sabine River fifty miles away, Sibley, Bludworth, and some of Bludworth's brothers-in-law took a keen interest in expanding their personal domains as they covertly assisted the president in pushing U.S. control as far west as possible. At one point in 1812–13 during the Gutiérrez-Magee expedition, which left from Natchitoches in an attempt to liberate Mexican Texas from Spain, local Natchitoches notables selected potential new officials of the envisioned republic. Bludworth is recorded as having been selected the commandant of La Bahía, Spain's military outpost located near present-day Goliad, Texas.[12]

Marianne (1788–1831) was the second Rouquier daughter to marry.[13] In 1807, she married Charles Roque Pavie (1777–1838), who arrived from France some time before 1805 after serving as an officer in Napoleon's ill-fated navy. Charles ventured to Louisiana to locate his three uncles, Étienne, Joseph, and Pierre, a priest, who had lost contact with their family in France because of continuous wars on the seas. Étienne, who married Marie Thérèze Buard in 1779, was murdered in 1787.[14] Joseph (b. 1746) arrived from France with his brother, but after spending a few years in Natchitoches, he chose to live in New Orleans with his quadroon companion named Chouteau and their two daughters. The only uncle remaining on the Red River to greet Charles was Father Pierre (b. 1741), who had arrived in the colony as a refugee from the French Revolution and was well known to several generations of Prudhommes and Rouquiers. Because of direct orders from Roman Catholic officials, Pierre Pavie left Natchitoches around 1808. He was generous with his nephew Charles on the eve of his marriage to Marianne.[15]

Charles and Marianne would own two homes—one in town and the other on their plantation located on former Rouquier land along the Red River. In 1804 the United States selected a site in Natchitoches for the first American fort, which it named after William C. C. Claiborne (1775–1817), the territorial governor appointed by Jefferson. However, the federal government did not take into consideration all of the French and Spanish rules for surveying property. Afterward, survey records determined that the Fort Claiborne site encroached upon the private property of Pavie and Bludworth, so they demanded that a fine or "rent" be paid to them.[16] In addition to owning land along the Red River where he successfully cultivated cotton, Pavie purchased land in the Neutral Ground and sought a land grant from the Mexican Republic. These three potential grants represented several land-granting mechanisms of colonial Louisiana and Texas, and reflected the grantors' various agendas. Marianne and Charles Pavie's portion of François Rouquier's grant epitomized Spain's desire to populate the region with loyal Roman Catholic subjects who would produce large families and cultivate the land. In 1813, Charles Pavie and his French-born business partner, Charles Noyrit (also seen as Nayrit, 1782–1853), purchased land in the Neutral Ground from José Antonio Sepúlveda. Ten years later it became incumbent on all to demonstrate that Sepúlveda actually owned the 640 acres at the time he assigned the parcel to them. By law, the transfer must have antedated February 22, 1819, the definitive legal date of the acquisition of the Neutral Ground by the United States. According to Spanish custom practiced in Mexico, witnesses swore that this land was then "inhabited, occupied, and cultivated by his living and growing corn, etc. thereupon, since that time to the present day. . . ."[17]

Following the ratification in 1821 of the Adams-Onís Treaty of 1819, it devolved upon Louisiana notables and the U.S. secretary of the Treasury, William H. Crawford, to settle land claims between the Rio Hondo and the Sabine River. "In default of every kind of authentic or public data," the officials "were compelled to have recourse to the knowledge of individuals of respectability, who from their situation or pursuits, were deemed best capable of throwing lights upon those points of inquiry."[18] Although the claim of Charles Pavie and his partner was affirmed, the men did not develop their parcel; in 1889, fifty years after Pavie's death, a court-appointed curator took over the property.[19]

It appears that Charles Pavie also desired yet another form of land grant west of the Sabine River. In 1823, the newly independent Mexican Republic, after a brief unsuccessful imperial interlude, determined to populate Texas by offering large tracts of land to so-called *empresarios*, such as the well-known Stephen F. Austin. The historian Herbert Eugene Bolton mentions under the rubric "Applications, concessions, and other matters relative to lands in Texas" that in "legajo (bundle or file) 30" in the Saltillo Civil Archives a document exists concerning "Carlos Nogret [*sic*], and Carlos Pavie and Luisa Eufracia Prudhomme." In the same bundle of papers appear documents concerning Frost Thorn (1793–1854) and General Wavell (Arthur Goodall Wavell, 1785–1860), both *empresarios* who received large grants of vacant Texas land, which raises the question: did Charles Pavie wish to colonize Texas?[20]

Throughout his years in Louisiana, Marianne Rouquier's husband, Charles Pavie, worked as a planter managing his large working plantation and as a merchant in town or traveling. Before Louisiana became a state during the turbulent year of 1812, he profited from provisioning the military and represented himself and his colleagues on business trips from "the village" (of Natchitoches) to "the city" (of New Orleans) and overseas when he escorted local products to markets in France. Active in society and noted for his hospitality to visitors, he belonged to the New Orleans' Masonic Lodge.[21]

Charles served as a "sergeant of the grenadiers" during the Battle of New Orleans in 1815. Later he reported that he was "the only Frenchman in [his] little troop." Furthermore, his oral account of the battle adds a rich dimension to our knowledge of the event because his nephew, Theodore, recorded Charles's description during their visit to the Chalmette battlefield in 1830.[22] Pavie discreetly supported American filibustering adventures into Texas. At the time of Pavie's death, the mandatory after-death inventory recorded that David Burnet, the future vice-president of the Republic of Texas, still owed him the money he had borrowed en route to the Texas Revolution.[23]

The Rouquier patriarch died in 1808. That year Marcelite (ca.1787–1878) wed an older widower and educated Frenchman named Juan Cortés/Cortez (or Jacques Cartes d'Artheits) (1748–1829).[24] The following year, the youngest Rouquier sister, Henriette (1793–1878), married Judge John C. Carr (ca. 1777–1834) and they purchased the grand house from her father's estate. Father Pierre Pavie, a priest in Natchitoches, had been removed without being replaced in the flux following the transfer of Catholic Louisiana to the primarily Protestant United States, therefore both of these Rouquier marriages were merely civil unions. On December 23, 1809, a priest visiting from Opelousas sanctified both Henriette's marriage to Judge Carr and her sister Marcelite's earlier marriage to Juan Cortés.[25]

Juan Cortés's Hispanic-sounding name had been changed from Jacques Cartes d'Artheits when he began to serve the interests of Spain in North America. It is uncertain when he arrived, but documents indicate that between 1790 and 1829 he remained in the service of Spain and later Mexico, albeit not always completely agreeing with them. In 1793, he traveled to Matagorda to conduct talks with the Indians and to inspect the coast for French infiltrations. From 1795 to 1798, he was stationed in La Bahía, the presidio in South Texas, as its commandant.[26]

The locus of Cortés's existence remained between Nacogdoches, west of the Sabine in Mexican Texas, and Natchitoches, Louisiana, east of the Sabine, despite the entry of the United States into the southwestern frontier. Once the United States completed the Louisiana Purchase, President Thomas Jefferson directed not one but several expeditions to explore the newly acquired territory. The most famous, the expedition of Meriwether Lewis and William Clark, set out from St. Louis in May 1804, traveled along the Missouri, Snake, and Columbia rivers and reached the Pacific Ocean in November 1805. The following year, Jefferson ordered the Red River expedition, "the first major scientific probe into the American West to be led by civilian scientists." Thomas Freeman, an astronomer and surveyor, Peter Custis, a medical student at the University of Pennsylvania, , and Benjamin Barton Smith, a naturalist, accompanied Captain Richard Sparks and forty-five soldiers who ventured forth into Spanish-held Texas under the pretext of conducting a "purely scientific" expedition. Working as Spain's vice-regal agent in Natchitoches, Cortés observed their preparations and informed Spanish authorities, who dispatched troops from Mexico and Santa Fe. They intercepted the Americans more than six hundred miles up the Red River. Outnumbered, the Americans retreated.[27]

During the spring of 1806, Cortés reported the expected arrival of additional American troops at Natchitoches.[28] He also functioned as the interpreter at the Herrera-Wilkinson negotiations, which created the Neutral Ground late that year. When the lack of a western boundary for the Louisiana Purchase brought the United States and Spain to the brink of conflict, their respective military commanders, General James Wilkinson (1757–1825) and Lieutenant Colonel Simón de Herrera (1754–1813), entered into an agreement on November 5, 1806. The agreement designated the fifty mile disputed territory between the Sabine and Hondo Rivers as the Neutral Ground.[29]

In 1806 Aaron Burr (1756–1836), who served as vice-president during Jefferson's first term, had already launched a scheme, ambitious even by the standards of the time, in partnership with Wilkinson to take part of the territory of Louisiana away from the United States and set up a separate nation. Cortés learned about the plot and informed his friend and colleague Herrera in a letter dated November 14, 1806. In a clear, measured tone, Cortés conveyed what he had heard, even though he thought the intelligence was exaggerated: "Colonel Burr, ex-Vice-President, has placed himself at the head of 20,000 men under the pretext of revolutionizing and separating the States of the West from the rest of the Union. And it is further stated that the members of Congress from Kentucky, Tennessee and Carolina have withdrawn from Congress. Various [United States] officers here with whom I have talked over the matter say that they believe Burr is in conspiracy with [Francisco de] Miranda, who continues to harass the coast of Caracas. Since England is behind him, it is likely they may direct an attack against the Mexican coast, and as Burr is in communication with them he may march to their assistance with the troops under him and many others which he can command." Multilingual Cortés was privy to political reports, which he used to judge gossip and rumors. Although he lived in Natchitoches, it is clear from one of his letters to Herrera that Cortés knew about events unfolding not only in the remote village along the unsettled frontier, but also in London and in Caracas, Venezuela, then struggling for independence from Spain and being led by the Caracas-born Miranda (1750–1816). Once Jefferson found out about the conspiracy, Wilkinson disengaged and professed his patriotism. Burr and a number of his followers were arrested, tried for treason, and acquitted.[30]

During the summer of 1808, Cortés spied for Spain and informed Spanish officials that the United States had commissioned yet another exploratory expedition, this time led by an Anthony Glass, an Indian trader, mustanger, and "semiofficial emissary." Glass left from Natchitoches and explored north and central Texas, illegally trading with Indian tribes who remained under the jurisdiction of Spain. Unlike the Freeman-Custis expedition of 1806, which the Mexican military intercepted and turned back, in 1808, Dr. John Sibley, the Natchitoches Indian agent, planter, and American spy, had devised a scheme to make Glass's expedition appear legal. Using his authority as an Indian agent, he granted licenses to trade with the Indians. Cortés's brother-in-law Judge Carr informed Claiborne, the American governor of the territory, of both Sibley's and Glass's actions. The governor reported to Secretary of State James Madison: "How far Mr. Sibley's conduct has been proper, the President can best determine; I must confess, however, that he seems to me to have gone far beyond his authority." Claiborne told Carr to find someone to enforce the laws, but Glass continued to explore.[31]

After functioning as an interpreter and continuing to work as an Indian trader, Cortés crossed the Sabine from Texas to Natchitoches and, in 1808, married Marcelite Rouquier. He worked as a commercial agent, representing the New Orleans businessman Benjamin Morgan, and owned a barge, the *Marcelette*, which he used to carry goods along the Mississippi.[32] That same year, he petitioned the Spanish government to establish a trading post on the eastern side of the Sabine River at Bayou Pierre as a reward for his spying activities. Spain denied his request in 1809.[33] By 1810, he was working as a merchant in Natchitoches. Having served Spain for many years, Cortés eventually switched allegiance and favored the future independence of Texas.[34] In 1812–13, he acted as the Natchitoches agent for the Gutiérrez-Magee expedition, which his brother-in-law James Bludworth also supported.[35]

The year 1812 signified a watershed in relations among the United States, Great Britain, France, and Spain. Napoleon's empire started to fall apart when his army invaded Russia, and after failing to reach agreement with Britain, the United States declared war during the summer of 1812. In Latin America, French, Spanish, and Portuguese colonists continued to revolt against imperialism. Land-hungry Americans seeking to take over Texas for themselves joined forces with Mexicans eager to declare independence from Spain. After the royalists routed the rebels and captured (and ultimately executed and beheaded) Padre Miguel Hidalgo y Costilla (1753–1811) and Ignacio José de Allende y Unzaga (1769–1811)—the best known of the Mexican *independentistas*—José María Morelos y Pavón took charge of the struggle for independence. A small number of his followers escaped to the North, including José Bernardo Maximiliano Gutiérrez de Lara (1774–1841). Gutiérrez made his way to New Orleans in 1811, upriver to Natchitoches on the *Marcelette*, and then to Washington. There, Secretary of State James Monroe covertly encouraged his activities to free Mexico from Spanish control by paying his transportation back to Natchitoches and providing an advisor in the person of Captain William Shaler, a merchant who had traveled widely throughout the world and who had served recently as the American consul to Cuba. Shaler took up temporary residence in Natchitoches. In April 1812, Governor Claiborne wrote Sibley, Judge Carr, and two other prominent Louisiana officials a letter marked "private": "Do me the favour to receive & to extend to my friend, *Wm. Shaler Esqur.* Your kind attentions.—In the course of his various & honorable pursuits, he has acquired a great fund of information & is esteemed by all who know him, as a Citizen of great worth, & and a Man of strict integrity, . . ."[36]

The next month, Shaler wrote Monroe that he believed "conditions were favorable for an invasion which would overthrow Spanish power and 'open the Internal Provinces to our commerce.'" According to Shaler, since the filibusters were assembling at Natchitoches, Washington needed to decide its position and, if it opposed the venture, take appropriate action. Shaler also acknowledged the explosive conditions along the border in the event of war between Great Britain and the United States. Just as Americans were eager to take over Mexican Texas, Shaler worried that the conflicts between Napoleon and his adversaries could potentially destabilize the borderlands. By 1812, Napoleon had defeated Portugal, whose government fled to Brazil, and Spain, where he installed his brother Joseph as the king. The Spanish royal government, resisting this usurpation, reconstituted itself in Cadiz, northwest of Gibraltar. Shaler posited to Monroe that Spain, assisted by its ally Great Britain, might move the Cadiz government to Mexico and expose the frontier to attack. From Natchitoches, Shaler suggested that the United States respond by organizing five thousand "patriots in the interior of the Mexican provinces."[37]

From this position at the edge of the Neutral Ground and under Shaler's tutelage, Gutiérrez planned his highly publicized invasion of Mexican Texas, which commenced with the participation of many respectable local citizens. Even relatives of U.S. officials joined the filibusters, including James Carr, a brother of Judge John Carr, and James B. Wilkinson, son of the infamous General James Wilkinson, the first governor of the Louisiana Territory, who with W.C.C. Clairborne had accepted the transfer of Louisiana to the United States in 1803 for President Jefferson, who had appointed then removed him from that office. The campaign shifted from success to stalemate, gore, and eventual defeat and rout between 1812 and 1813. All factions lost leaders and Wilkinson's son died in battle. Besides the shameful beheading of the royalist officials Lieutenant Colonel Herrera and Governor Manuel María de Salcedo, the American leader and West Point graduate Augustus William Magee (1789–1813) also died, and his Hispanic substitute, General José Alvarez de Toledo y Dubois (1779–1858), would soon forsake the rebels' cause in favor of a Spanish pardon. The town of Nacogdoches (in Mexican Texas) was abandoned and the independence-seeking survivors returned to Natchitoches to regroup and await a better moment to accomplish militarily what was eventually solved by negotiation.[38]

In 1821, following the ratification of Mexican independence from Spain, Juan Cortés assisted his old friend the royalist Joaquín de Arredondo, a central figure in liberated Mexico, who had defeated the filibusters of the Gutiérrez-Magee expedition at the Battle of Medina on August 18, 1813.[39] Because of his extensive experience trading and negotiating with the Indians—the French achieved greater success than the Spanish or Mexicans in dealing with native tribes—Cortés advised Arredondo about how best to pacify the Comanches and Apaches. Indeed, Cortés used his own money to purchase gifts, which were distributed to the tribes.[40] In 1824, Juan Cortés was among the six Natchitoches residents who were called on to ascertain the validity of land claims in the former Neutral Ground because no written records were available. Under oath Cortés (referred to as John Cortes) swore that "the archives of Nacogdoches were carried off by the royalist authorities at the time of the invasion of Nacogdoches by the Gutiérrez-Magee expedition."[41]

Cortés's brother-in-law John C. Carr, who married Henriette Rouquier, also distinguished himself in the history of the borderlands, most especially by keeping order during the transition from colonial power to statehood. As the first American judge to preside over the newly created Natchitoches District, which functioned as the overland gateway to the West and Mexico, and the river port to the Gulf of Mexico and the Caribbean, Carr ruled on trade, military, and civil disputes in Louisiana. He kept the governor of Louisiana and the presidents of the United States informed of changes in the political climate on this unstable border. His jurisdiction ended at the Neutral Ground, which attracted murderers, thieves, squatters, and riffraff from the United States. After learning of a robbery and murder that took place in the Neutral Ground, Governor Claiborne, who appointed Carr, wrote to him: "I shall have only to express the reliance I place in your efforts to bring offenders to Justice & to request you, to call upon the officer Commanding the Regular Troops for such support as may be necessary to enforce the preservation of good order."[42]

On the other side of the Neutral Ground, across the Sabine River into Spanish Mexico, Mexican law provided a haven for runaway slaves who were the legal property of citizens of Louisiana. On November 6, 1808, the judge reported to the governor about "the successful elopement in one night of more than thirty negroes, the property of Citizens of this Territory."[43] That same day, Claiborne informed Secretary of State Madison: "In the present state of things, the property of many of our frontier fellow Citizens are considered as very insecure, and much uneasiness prevails."[44] Carr continued to relay news about fugitive slaves fleeing to Texas and, even though he chastised Salcedo, the provincial governor in Nacogdoches, for detaining slaves and not returning them, the Spanish official repeated to him "the old story," or how "such measures would be adopted as would tend to perpetuate that harmony . . . so essential to the interests of both Nations." Claiborne told Madison: "The public resentment at Natchitoches is said to be considerable." However, even though Carr did not fear that the Creoles would "commit any extravagance, at least for the present," Claiborne was "not equally sure" of their "Countrymen in that quarter." Claiborne advised Madison of Carr's "serious uneasiness" caused by Salcedo's "countenance and protection" of fugitive slaves and said he would write his Spanish counterpart.[45] In the eyes of Louisianans, Carr was expected to uphold their rights and protect their property despite his legal limitations.

Judge Carr also dealt with American officials, such as Sibley, who exercised a personal interpretation of the law, especially when it came to trade relations with the Indians and diplomatic affairs with the Spanish. Carr suffers a documentary disadvantage in U.S. history. (His name is also erroneously seen as John C. Kerr.) Jefferson's correspondent Sibley, a prolific writer, disliked and disparaged Carr, who enforced existing laws instead of a personal agenda. In turn, both the Spanish and Carr distrusted Sibley.[46] Carr found this judicial position untenable because he lacked the necessary deputies and money to enforce the law he was appointed to uphold. In March 1809, he wrote the governor to explain why he could not post the bond for the parish. "I do not believe I shall be able to pay on half the amount of our Taxes; there is not actually as much specie in the Parish. Last year I advanced 575 dollars out of my pocket to complete the sum, and of which I have not yet been repaid more than 50 or 60."[47] Claiborne supported his appointee with words, commands, admonitions, and ultimately his refusal to accept Carr's resignation. On August 7, 1812, the governor wrote to the judge: "I cannot without considerable inconvenience to the public Interest, asscept [sic] for the present, your resignation . . . and I request you to continue in the functions of that office. . . . [48]

Two days later, as Natchitoches served as the staging ground for one phase of the Gutiérrez-Magee expedition, Claiborne, in a letter to Wilkinson, explained his instructions to the judge: "I have written to the Judge of the parish of Natchitoches, requiring his vigilance in the Maintainance [sic] of Law & good order, & informing him of the provisions of the Statute, which forbids the preparing or seting [sic] on foot within the Jurisdiction of the U:States [sic], a Military expedition against the Dominions at Peace with the U:States."[49] Claiborne issued a proclamation denouncing the pending invasion and warning the filibusters of the consequences of their illegal actions. The governor, who also worried about the involvement of Native Americans in the "Mexican expedition," wrote Carr on August 12: "I confidently expect you will act with promptitude & decision, & that you will cause to be arrested, & bound to their good behaviour all persons concerned, or that you will send them in to New Orleans for trial before the District Court.—Genl. Wilkinson has given the most positive instructions to the officer Commanding at Fort Claiborne, to afford on this occasion, to the Civil Authority all necessary aid."[50]

The natural flow of the Red River made the journey from Natchitoches to New Orleans a swift one. However, Claiborne's strategically vulnerable capital city could be assailed from every direction. Spain inhabited Florida and Cuba to the east and Mexico to the west, and Spain and Great Britain had been allies since Napoleon's usurpation of the Spanish throne, where in 1808 he had installed his brother Joseph as king. British possessions dotted the Gulf of Mexico and the Caribbean. On June 18, 1812, the United States declared war on Britain over long-standing disagreements relating to trade, impressments of American seamen, and boundary violations; and, undeniably, hawks in the U.S. government wanted to conquer Canada. At the same time Claiborne worried about the "Mexican expedition," he issued proclamations and requested munitions because the war had broken out.[51] Natchitoches, a small riverside village, found itself inundated with international issues involving border-making questions.

Four intelligent, brave, and ambitious men—the Englishman John Carr, the American James Bludworth, and the Frenchmen Charles Pavie and Juan Cortés (or Jacques Cartes d'Artheits)—arrived in Natchitoches equipped with innate characteristics that their borderlands experiences forged into the requisite tools for success. They chose wisely when they wed the Rouquier sisters, whose dowries provided parcels of land from their father's extensive Spanish colonial land grant. Because of the remoteness of the frontier, most newcomers were male. This enhanced the attractiveness of daughters, who were a liability in other locations.[52] Except for the French-speaking couple, Charles Pavie and Marianne Rouquier, the three other Rouquier sisters bore children. Some gave birth to twins; in fact, the cause of death listed for Joséphine Aimée was "twins." Charles and Marianne adopted Joséphine Aimée's daughter, Eliza Bludworth.[53] Whereas the French Creoles were entrenched in almost one hundred years of Natchitoches and European traditions, the ambitious Rouquier husbands were not.[54] Had they lived, François Rouquier and Marie Louise Prudhomme Rouquier would not have been able to speak their mother tongue with many of their grandchildren who occupied portions of the original land grant. The price had been paid in linguistic terms for their daughters' cross-marriages to energetic border-makers, but the social, economic, and political dividends enabled their descendants to assume positions of wealth and stature in the emerging new American community. The Rouquier sisters' hard-working husbands matched the wealth of their education and experience to the potential fortune of the land and property strategically situated along the western frontier of the Old Southwest. Carr, Bludworth, Pavie, and Cortés were flexible, decisive, and attentive to the swiftly changing political circumstances, many of which they led or influenced. The rising arc of American nationalism played into their hands.

Notes

1. Louisiana Historical Society, "58th Memorial on Louisiana, Representing the Necessity of Retaining That Colony, in Order to Prevent the English Becoming Masters of Not Only the Whole of North America, but Also of Mexico," Portfolio II, no. 49, in *An Analytical Index of the Whole of the Public Documents Relative to Louisiana, Deposited in the Archives of the Department "de la Marine et des Colonies" et "Bibliothèque du Roi" at Paris* [compiled] by Edmund Forstall. Available at http://memory.loc.gov/cgi-bin/query/r?intldl/ascfr:@field(DOCID+@lit(rbfr0008_0057)) accessed Oct. 9, 2006. According to Forstall, this document, which appears to have been written ca. 1715, confirms that St. Denis led twenty Canadians on an exploring expedition from the Red River to the province of Nuevo León in Mexico—the first of the unauthorized expeditions from Natchitoches into Spanish-held territory and setting the pattern for those that followed with the Louisiana Purchase. Long ignored in Natchitoches historiography, this important record clearly proves the significance of St. Denis's choice of Natchitoches. See also Powell A. Casey, *Encyclopedia of Forts, Posts, Named Camps, and Other Military Installations in Louisiana, 1700–1981* (Baton Rouge: Claitor's Publishing Division, 1983), 194–96. There are numerous insignificant contradictions in the sources—particularly regarding the founding date of 1713, 1714, or 1715; even by the 1720s it was already a question of whose memory was best or whose records had not been lost to hurricanes. Although most historians favor a founding date of late 1713, by general consensus, according to Rick Seale, the manager of the Fort St. Jean Baptiste State Historic Site, 1714 has been and will continue to be cited as the date of inception of "continuous settlement by Europeans." The location of the fort, or in French "poste," changed when the river flooded. Donald E. Chipman and Patricia R. Lemée, "St. Denis, Louis Juchereau de," *The New Handbook of Texas*, ed. Ron Tyler, D. E. Barnet, R. R. Barkley, P. C. Anderson, and M. F. Odintz, 6 vols. (Austin: Texas State Historical Association, 1996), 5: 755–56, hereafter referred to as *The New Handbook of Texas*. See also United States Department of the Interior, National Park Service, *Cane River Louisiana: Special Resource Study, Environmental Assessment* (Denver: National Park Service, Denver Service Center, June, 1993), 9–12, hereafter National Park Service, *Cane River Louisiana*. A replica, the Fort St. Jean Baptiste State Historic Site, was built in 1979.

2. King Louis XIV of France granted Antoine Crozat, Marquis de Chatel, governing and trading rights in Louisiana in 1712 although the king laid out the provisions for land grants. Until 1733, private agents managed the colony, but the following year France established royal control, which it exercised until 1767. At the end of the Seven Years' War in both Europe and America (known in the latter as the French and Indian War), France first ceded to Spain the Louisiana lands located on the west bank of the Mississippi, which included Natchitoches and lands on the east bank below Bayou Manchac. The two nations formalized the transfer in the Treaty of Fontainebleau in 1762, much to the chagrin of French settlers, who revolted against Spanish rule for ten months until Spain sent more than two thousand soldiers to keep order. Formal transfer did not occur until 1768. Under the terms of the Treaty of Paris in 1763, France relinquished all claims to land east of the Mississippi, with the exception of

New Orleans, to Great Britain, who also received Florida from Spain, in exchange for Cuba. By 1800, Spain controlled not only the Louisiana Territory but also East and West Florida. However, Napoleon Bonaparte convinced a weakened Spain to cede the Louisiana Territory to France. In turn, once Bonaparte failed to realize his dream of a French empire in the Caribbean, he sold Louisiana to the United States in 1803. See also National Park Service, *Cane River Louisiana*, 9–12; Elizabeth Shown Mills, "Family and Social Patterns of the Colonial Louisiana Frontier: A Quantitative Analysis" (Master's thesis, University of Alabama, 1981).

3. Records are also taken from Winston de Ville, *Marriage Contracts of Natchitoches, 1739–1803* (Nashville: Benson Printing Co., 1961). Publications of church and civil records are supplemented with a variety of books, including Marie Norris Wise, *Norris-Jones-Crockett-Payne-Blanchard: The Heritage of Marie Norris Wise* (Sulphur, La.: Wise Publications, 1994), 133. Additional primary sources for ecclesiastical records of the diocese of Natchitoches consulted for this chapter include the translations of church records prepared by Elizabeth Shown Mills, *Natchitoches: Abstracts of the Catholic Church Registers of the French and Spanish Post of St. Jean-Baptiste des Natchitoches in Louisiana, 1729–1803*, vol. 2 of the Cane River Creole Series (New Orleans: Polyanthos Press, 1977). Subsequent records also derive from Elizabeth Shown Mills, *Natchitoches: Translated Abstracts of Register Five of the Catholic Church Parish of St. Francois des Natchitoches in Louisiana, 1800–1826*, vol. 4 of the Cane River Creole Series (New Orleans: Polyanthos, 1980), hereafter referred to as Mills, *1800–1826*. Civil marriage booklets, and family sheets come from the scrapbooks and vertical files of the Cammie G. Henry Research Center, Watson Memorial Library, Northwestern State University, Natchitoches, Louisiana. The "research files" include Gladys Lovell Sandefur and Hattie Little Whittington, *Louisiana Ahnentafels, Ancestor Charts and Family Group Sheets* (Natchitoches, La.: Natchitoches Genealogical and Historical Association, 1982), as well as the elaborately decorated oversized "Prudhomme Family Genealogical Chart" prepared in 1975 by the Rouquier-Prudhomme descendant Irma Sompayrac-Willard, hereafter called "Sompayrac-Willard Chart," from the Cammie G. Henry Research Center, Watson Memorial Library, Northwestern State University, Irma Sompayrac-Willard Collection. Note: The French hyphenation of first names such as Jean-Baptiste is dropped to permit indexing by a single set of criteria. The name "Prudhomme" in all cases replaces "Prud'homme, which was favored by Lucile Keator Prud'homme, a genealogist and the author with Fern B. Christensen of *The Natchitoches Cemeteries* (New Orleans: Polyanthos Press, 1977). The Creoles of Natchitoches remained attached to European culture as long as the economy and their language skills permitted. Many historians incorrectly assumed that the core of the settlement was Canadian because Natchitoches was founded by a Canadian, Louis Juchereau de St. Denis, and the next commandant, Athanase de Mézières, had lived in Canada prior to settling on the Red River. But numerous settlers went directly from Europe to New Orleans and on to Natchitoches. "Cajun" and "Creole" are not synonymous. "Cajuns" (from "Acadians") were farmers exiled from Nova Scotia, who settled in South Louisiana, generally far

from New Orleans. This study concerns the northwestern portion of today's state of Louisiana.

4. In relation to this study, the word "Creole" refers to a white person of pure European parentage who was born in a former French colony—Louisiana, Saint-Domingue, or Canada—before 1803. These sophisticated landed gentry either adopted or retained European culture and manners, including language. Jean Pierre Phillipe Prudhomme (ca. 1690–1739) was born in Romans, Dauphine, France. His wife, Mary Catherine Messelier—also seen in documents as Messillier, Melier and Catherinne Miliere—was born in Paris in 1705 and arrived in America aboard *La Baleine* in 1719 as a "cassette" or "casket" girl at the age fourteen, suggesting that she was an orphan as well as the presumed sister of Christine Allorge, the wife of one of the soldiers at the post whose arrival was not recorded. Mary Catherine died in 1781. In 1785, their son, Jean Baptiste Prudhomme (1735–86), married a Creole from New Orleans, Marie Josephine Henrietta Collantin—also seen as Josephe Charlotte Corantin (1738–88). See Donna Rachal Mills, *Biographical and Historical Memoirs of Natchitoches Parish, Louisiana* (Tuscaloosa, Ala.: Heritage Books, Mills Historical Press, 1985), 297. See also http://www.intersurf.com/~bevans/Anita's%20Ancestors/d144.htm, accessed Oct. 16, 2009.

5. François Rouquier emigrated from Puy l'Evêque, a small village located beside the River Lot in the Pyrenees Mountains. His land grant is mentioned in D. Mills, *Biographical and Historical Memoirs of Natchitoches Parish*, 297. Rouquier received 1,600 "arpents" located on Grand Batture Island in Lac Terre Noire, several miles from Natchitoches Post. An "arpent" comprises 0.8463 of an acre and represents a French colonial measure employed in Quebec and Louisiana.

6. Historical studies have pointed out both the gains and losses when marriages are made across language and culture barriers. To examine different interpretations in the study of intermarriage, the transmission of wealth among groups, and cultural adaptation, see Mary Ann Irwin and James F. Brooks, eds., *Women and Gender in the American West* (Albuquerque: University of New Mexico Press, 2004). See also Sarah Deutsch, *No Separate Refuge: Culture, Class, and Gender in the Anglo-Hispanic Frontier in the American Southwest, 1880–1940* (New York: Oxford University Press, 1987).

7. The record from record book 8 at the Natchitoches District Courthouse is reprinted in Wise, *Norris-Jones-Crockett-Payne-Blanchard*, 131. The author is a descendent of the Prudhomme-Rouquier alliance as well as a journalist and professional genealogist. During archeological excavations in 1975, the foundations of the original Rouquier-Prudhomme home were uncovered. This site is located on the west side of LA 1 bypass, on a rise adjacent to the Northwestern State University campus. François Rouquier Homesite, Natchitoches, District 8, Natchitoches Parish, http://www.forttours.com/pages/hmnwla.asp, accessed Oct. 9, 2006.

8. Nardini, Louis Raphael, Sr., *My Historic Natchitoches: Louisiana and Its Environment* (Natchitoches, La.: Nardini Publishing Company, 1963), 209–29. Dr. Klier reconciled information from the book by Nardini, also a descendent of the

Prudhomme-Rouquier alliance, with the Mills records and the Cammie Henry research data files.

9. Robert D. deBlieux, *A Walking Tour of the Historic District* (Natchitoches, La.: Natchitoches Times, 1989), 16. Currently the Service League of Natchitoches owns and operates the "Prud'homme-Rouquier House," which is located at 436 Jefferson Street in the midst of Natchitoches's National Historic Landmark District. Irma Sompayrac-Willard and Robert (Bobby) deBlieux, cousins and Rouquier-Prudhomme descendants, spearheaded the movement to build a replica of the Fort St. Jean Baptiste as it appeared in the plan of 1732 prepared by the French engineer-in-chief Sieur Ignace François Broutin, a plan that "Miss Irma" found on one of her numerous research trips to Paris. Ground was broken in 1973 and the construction completed in 1979. The Louisiana State Parks division continued to develop the site, adding an interpretive center to the complex, located off state highway 6 at 155 Rue Jefferson, Natchitoches, LA 71457. http://www.caneriverheritage.org/main_file.php/fortstjean.php, accessed Oct. 16, 2006.

10. "Documentary History of the Tract of Land" (Bludworth's Hill), a typescript document in the Cammie G. Henry Research Center data files presented by Cora Marshall and Hampton Carver in 1957. Thanks to Chief Archivist Mary Linn Wernet for introducing this document to us. Bludworth Hill used to be the name of the original site of the present-day Northwestern State University, which started as a convent, then became a normal school, later a state college, and now a university. Bludworth's daughter Julia married Judge Charles A. Bullard and they built the mansion where the school started. Today only the columns remain of the original home. The columns are preserved in the university's logo. See also *Natchitoches Times*, July 1921 for the obituary of Julia Bullard Powell.

11. "Documentary History of the Tract of Land"; and Julia Bullard Powell's obituary in the *Natchitoches Times*, July 1921. For Sibley, see Julia Kathryn Garrett, "Doctor John Sibley and the Louisiana-Texas Frontier, 1803-1814," *Southwestern Historical Quarterly Online* 45, no. 3, (January 1942), http://www.tsha.utexas.edu/publications/journals/shq/online/v045/n3/contrib_DIVL5253.html, accessed Oct. 23, 2006; and G. P. Whittington, "Dr. John Sibley of Natchitoches, 1757-1837," *Louisiana Historical Quarterly* 10, no. 4 (October 1927): 463-512. For the letter, see 500-1, a copy of a Letter, John Sibley to Saml. H. Sibley, from Sibley Manuscript Book, vol. 4, Missouri Historical Society.

12. José L. Franco, "Colomera Report, 1812-1813, Document Number 37," in *Documentos para la Historia de Mexico* (La Habana: Publicaciones del Archivo Nacional de Cuba, 1961), lii-liv. Publication pending of Dr. Klier's annotated translation of the report from the original French. René Robert Cavelier, Sieur de La Salle (1643-87) claimed the region for France in 1682, and set up a colony on Matagorda Bay in 1685. When this colony failed, the Spanish planted their presidio on top of the French site to prohibit them from returning. Later, due to Indian depredations, the presidio moved inland but retained the word "bay" in its name, indicative of the place beside which it had been founded.

13. Record preserved in Natchitoches, Louisiana, at the Immaculate Conception Church; copy provided to Dr. Klier by Shelby M. Nealy, the secretary/archivist.

14. Marie Thérèze Buard Pavie was the fourth of ten children of the Swiss-born Gabriel Buard. Buard accompanied his father to the military post at Natchitoches in the early 1700s. He also received a land grant and grew rich; however, the same prosperity did not extend to all of his offspring, as they were too numerous and his wife lacked the ambition of Madame Rouquier in selecting non-Creole mates with promising futures. Only two of his six daughters married well—one to Pavie and the other to François Rouquier's son, when she was thirty-six years old. After Pavie was killed, Marie Thérèze married his best friend, Claude Thomas Pierre Metoyer. Pavie (b. 1740), also called "Esteban Pavia" in Spanish documents, arrived in America in 1775. See Betje Black Klier, *Pavie in the Borderlands: The Journey of Théodore Pavie to Louisiana and Texas, 1829–1830, Including Portions of His Souvenirs Atlantiques* (Baton Rouge: Louisiana State University Press, 2000), 242 n. 6.

15. Pierre's generosity is reflected in his legacy of real estate and slaves to his nephew, who seems to have been even more generous because he manumitted several old slaves who were "gifts" from his uncle. Father Pierre lived with his brother Joseph in New Orleans until the fall of Napoleon in 1814. The Restoration of the Bourbon monarchy permitted him to return to France for the remainder of his life. His return from exile in Louisiana brought veneration in his home parish. Pierre Pavie was honored as the canon at the Cathedral of La Rochelle until his death in 1820. Klier, *Pavie in the Borderlands*, 16–17.

16. See Nardini, *My Historic Natchitoches*, 96, for a copy of the survey of Natchitoches in 1826 that shows the infringement of the fort on private properties. The grand three-story house (two stories plus attic and basement) at the corner of Pavie and Washington with thirteen-foot ceilings, eight fireplaces, generous attic and basement, may or may not be the home Charles purchased for Marianne. Another former owner, Dr. Charles Chauncey Carroll, who died in 1950, prepared a history of the house that has been deposited in the research files at the Watson Memorial Library at Northwestern State University. Major details of Carroll's history are contradicted by deBlieux in his handy walking tour guide *Natchitoches: A Walking Tour of the Historic District*. DeBlieux contends that "architectural details indicate it was not the house you *now* see" at the corner of rue Pavie." Nonetheless, deBlieux adjudges the existing house as "the most significant Greek Revival house in Natchitoches."

17. Carolyn Reeves Erickson, *Natchitoches Neighbors in the Neutral Strip: Land Claims between the Rio Hondo and the Sabine* (Nacogdoches, Tex.: Erickson Books, 1993), for quotation, p. i; see also 1–6, 58–59. Prior to 1806, Texas extended across the Sabine River to the Hondo River. Most of the documents pertaining to that land in the Neutral Ground from 1806 to 1819 were lost during the Gutiérrez-Magee expedition. Credible witnesses were used to verify claims. Noyrit's tombstone reads: "Charles Noyrit, b. Libo [Lille] France, 1782, d. 17 Jan 1853." See Prud'homme, *The Natchitoches Cemeteries*, 35, entry no. 673.

18. Erickson, *Natchitoches Neighbors in the Neutral Strip*, 1; see also Klier, *Pavie in the Borderlands*, 98–99.

19. Klier, *Pavie in the Borderlands*, 25.

20. Herbert Eugene Bolton, *Guide to Materials for the History of the United States in the Principal Archives of Mexico* (Washington, D.C.: Carnegie Institution of Washington, 1913), 440.

21. Powell A. Casey, "Masonic Lodges of New Orleans," *The New Orleans Genesis* (January 1981), 13. This reference was kindly provided by E. Mills.

22. The Pavie Press, owned by his father and grandmother, published the first edition of Theodore Pavie's travel journal, *Souvenirs atlantiques*, in 1831. The enlarged, two-volume second edition containing Charles Pavie's description of the Battle of New Orleans was published in Paris by Roret in 1833.

23. After the death of Marianne Rouquier Pavie in France, it was necessary for Charles's and Marianne's joint property to be inventoried by a notary. This inventory is filed at the Natchitoches District Courthouse. Charles swore that his uncle Pierre's slaves were outside the community property because they had been given to him prior to the marriage.

24. Marcelite (1784–1878) first married Jean Cartes d'Artheits (Juan Cortés), on Jan. 16, 1808. According to Sompayrac-Willard's genealogical chart and Nardini's book, after the death of Cortés, Marcelite then married Jean-François Hertzog; however, this later union falls outside the border-maker considerations explored in this chapter. Nardini, *My Historic Natchitoches*, 12.

25. Mills, *1800–1826*. See also Wise, *Norris-Jones-Crockett-Payne-Blanchard*, 130. It is uncertain if Carr was born in England or Ireland. Carr's date of birth is calculated from the microfilm copy of his death certificate available at the Cammie G. Henry Research Center, Northwestern State University. See "Immaculate Conception Church, Natchitoches, Register No. 5: Funerals, 1793–1796 and 1827–1849." Thanks to Mary Linn Wernet and Sherry Baumgardner for providing this information.

26. Adán Benavides, Jr., comp. and ed., *Béxar Archives, 1717–1836: A Name Guide* (Austin: University of Texas Press, for the University of Texas Institute of Texan Cultures at San Antonio, 1989), 229–30.

27. Dan L. Flores, ed., *Jefferson and Southwestern Exploration: The Freeman and Custis Accounts of the Red River Expedition of 1806* (Norman: University of Oklahoma Press, 1984), 124 n. 2. Salcedo served as the governor of Spanish Louisiana from 1801 to 1803.

28. Benavides, *Béxar Archives*, 230.

29. Even though neither the United States nor Spain entered into a formal treaty, because both countries wanted to avoid war, Wilkinson's and Herrera's agreement remained in force between 1806 and 1819 when it was superseded by the Adams-Onís Treaty of 1819, which was ratified in 1821. Erickson, *Natchitoches Neighbors in the Neutral Strip*, 5; Odie B. Faulk, *The Last Years of Spanish Texas: 1778–1821* (London: Mouton and Co., 1964), 48–49.

30. Walter Flavious McCaleb, *The Aaron Burr Conspiracy*, expanded edition with an introduction by Charles A. Beard (New York: Wilson-Erickson, Inc., 1936), 137–38. McCaleb provides a copy of the letter from Cortés to Herrera, which is also found in Benavides, *Béxar Archives*. Miranda fought in the American and French Revolutions before fighting for independence in Venezuela, but out of jealousy one of his compatriots, Simón Bolívar, betrayed him to the Spanish, who imprisoned him until his death. Venezuelans declared their independence in 1811.

31. Benavides, *Béxar Archives*, [Cortés] Reports Glass's Expedition, Aug. 14, 1808, 230; and Dan L. Flores, ed., *Journal of an Indian Trader: Anthony Glass and the Texas Trading Frontier, 1790–1810* (College Station: Texas A&M University Press, 1985). See also Letter, Claiborne to Madison, New Orleans, Aug. 31, 1808, in Dunbar Rowland, comp. and ed., *Official Letter Books of W. C. C. Claiborne* (Jackson, Miss.: State Department of Archives and History, 1917), 4: 199.

32. Rie Jarratt, *Gutiérrez de Lara: Mexican-Texan, The Story of a Creole Hero* (Austin: Creole Texana, 1949), chapter 5, available online at http://ww.tamu.edu/ccbn/dewitt/delara.htm, accessed Oct. 18, 2006. This spelling might be a transcription error since his wife's name was "Marcelite."

33. Benavides, *Béxar Archives*, 230. The archives note reads: "Denied permission to settle in Texas." See also Rowland, *Official Letter Books of W. C. C. Claiborne*, 6: 158, Letter, New Orleans, Feb. 16, 1808, Claiborne to Governor Folch. Claiborne explains that he now plans to extend the authority of the state of Louisiana over the settlement at Bayou Pierre. See also, 6: 167–68, to the members of the Senate and House of Representatives, Aug. 25, 1812, where Claiborne proposes creating another parish, which would include the post of Bayou Pierre.

34. Flores, *Jefferson and Southwestern Exploration*, 124 n. 2; Jarratt, *Gutiérrez de Lara*.

35. Harris Gaylord Warren, "The Southern Career of Don Juan Mariano Picornell," *The Journal of Southern History* 8, no. 3 (August 1942): 317, see especially n. 25.

36. Rowland, *Official Letter Books of W. C. C. Clairborne*, 6: 75, Letter, New Orleans, April 8, 1812, to "Doct. Sibbley, Judge Carr. Colo Shaumburg, & Judge Claiborne." See also Donald E. Chipman, *Spanish Texas, 1519–1821* (Austin: University of Texas Press, 1994), 216–20; Harris Gaylord Warren, *The Sword Was Their Passport: A History of American Filibustering in the Mexican Revolution* (Baton Rouge: Louisiana State University Press, 1943; repr., Dallas: Kennikat Press and Taylor Publishing Company, 1972).

37. Warren, *The Sword Was Their Passport*, 27. Warren quotes Shaler's letter to Monroe of May 7, 1812, from the Shaler Papers, National Archives, Washington, D.C. Cadiz was the bastion of liberalism in Spain's early nineteenth-century struggle against monarchism. The Peninsular War (1808–14) was fought on the Iberian Peninsula between Napoleon's Imperial Army and an alliance among Spain, Portugal, and Great Britain. Napoleon crowned his brother Joseph "King of Spain and the Indies," and placed Ferdinand VII under house arrest. Spain's government was reconstituted in Cadiz, where a legislative body, called the Cortes, received elected representatives and

adopted the first Constitution in 1812, provoking a civil war. French forces, under the aegis of the restored Bourbon monarch Louis XVIII, pacified Spain and re-enthroned King Ferdinand VII in 1823.

38. Chipman, *Spanish Texas*, 216–20; Harris Gaylord Warren, "José Alvarez de Toledo's Initiation as Filibuster, 1811–1813," *Hispanic American Historic Review* 20, no. 1 (February 1940), 56–82; Julia K. Garrett, *Green Flags over Texas: A Story of the Last Years of Spain in Texas* (Austin: Pemberton Press, 1939); Félix D. Almaráz, *Tragic Cavalier: Governor Manuel Salcedo of Texas, 1808–1813* (Austin: University of Texas Press, 1971). For James, see Benavides, *Béxar Archives*, Letter, Natchitoches, July 22, 1812, James Carr to [the revolutionist] Juan Manuel Zambrano. The general simultaneously was employed as a Spanish agent, often in conflict with his military responsibilities. He rose to power for the last time during the War of 1812. Relieved of his duties he prepared *Memoirs of My Own Times*, 3 vols. (Philadelphia: Abraham Small, 1816); a fourth volume of maps and diagrams appeared the same year. In pursuit of a Texas land grant in 1821, Wilkinson went to Mexico City and died there awaiting Mexican approval of his Texas scheme.

39. Benavides, *Béxar Archives*, 230; Robert H. Thonhoff, "Medina, Battle of," *The New Handbook of Texas*, 4: 601–2. General Toledo led the rebel forces in the "bloodiest battle ever fought on Texas soil."

40. Benavides, *Béxar Archives*, 230.

41. Erickson, *Natchitoches Neighbors in the Neutral Strip*, 1–5.

42. Rowland, *Official Letter Books of W. C. C. Claiborne*, 6: 36, Letter, Jan. 20, 1812, Claiborne to Carr. Carr's jurisdiction, the Natchitoches District, extended over five present day parishes.

43. Ibid., 4: 122, Letter, Nov. 6, 1808, Carr to Claiborne.

44. Ibid., 4: 244, Letter, Nov. 6, 1808, Claiborne to Madison.

45. Ibid., 4: 258, Letter, Nov. 24, 1808, Claiborne to Madison. The governor enclosed copies of his last letter to Judge Carr and another letter to Governor General Salcedo. See also Letter, Jan. 8, 1809, Claiborne to Carr, 4: 285–86.

46. For Sibley, see Garrett, "Doctor John Sibley," and G. Whittington, "Dr. John Sibley."

47. Rowland, *Official Letter Books of W. C. C. Claiborne*, 4: 334, Letter, March 20, 1809, Carr to Claiborne.

48. Ibid., 6: 149, Letter, August 7, 1812, Claiborne to Carr.

49. Ibid., 6: 151–52, Letter, August 9, Claiborne to Wilkinson; see also, 6: 149, Letter, Aug. 7, 1812, Letter, Claiborne to Carr where he mentions a letter he sent to the judge on July 20, 1812. See also 6: 152–53, Letter, Aug. 10, 1812, Claiborne to Diego Murphy.

50. Ibid., 6: 160–61, Letter, Aug. 12, 1812, Claiborne to Judge Carr; and also, 6: 163–64, Letter, Aug. 14, 1812, Claiborne to Judge Carr; 6: 164–65, Letter, Aug. 17, 1812, Claiborne to Judge Steele. For Native Americans, see 6: 153–54, on or about Aug. 9, 1812, "A Talk from William C. C. Claiborne, Governor of the State of Louisiana and Commander in Chief of the Militia thereof, to the Chief Head Men and Warriors of the Chactaw [sic] Nation.

51. Ibid., 6: 161–62, Statement, Aug. 14, 1812, to the Senate and House of Representatives; 6: 162–63, Letter, Aug. 14, 1812, Claiborne to Wilkinson.

52. Younger male members of the Pavie family sought their fortune in Louisiana prior to and during the French Revolution. The Pavie sisters, all of whom became nuns, remained in France and suffered hardships. Their brother Guillaume, the oldest surviving male sibling, inherited the home and Pavie family press in accordance with laws of primogeniture where only the firstborn male could inherit title to land and money. Because he never married, Guillaume was in a position to take charge of his sisters and he brought them back to the family home when French revolutionary leaders closed the convents. Klier, *Pavie in the Borderlands*, 9.

53. When the Pavie-Rouquier nephew, Théodore Pavie, visited from France in the winter of 1829, he fell in love with his Creole cousin, Eliza. Although no marriage occurred, the romance repeats the tendency of the previous generation of Rouquier women to select mates who did not emerge from the local culture. Ibid., 108 n.16.

54. The local circle of eligible spouses was so small that some of the next generation sought dispensation for consanguinity and married their cousins. Within a generation, most of the Prudhomme-Rouquier descendants bore names such as Johnson, Bullard, Smith, Evans, Carver, and Miller. Numerous sources have been cited in this chapter for Prudhomme-Rouquier genealogy. For nineteenth-century family members, Dr. Klier relied on the papers of Irma Sompayrac-Willard because of her research expertise and frequent travels to France, especially Tarn, as well as the reference books of Elizabeth Shown Mills, and on "family sheets" from twentieth-century descendants. All of the volumes and sheets are available in the Cammie G. Henry Research Center at Northwestern State University in Natchitoches, Louisiana, under the Chief Archivist Mary Lin Wernet.

II

Daniel Clark

Merchant Prince of New Orleans

ELIZABETH URBAN ALEXANDER

On December 12, 1803, Daniel Clark, a merchant in New Orleans, wrote an urgent appeal to William Claiborne, the recently appointed commissioner charged by President Jefferson to take possession of the newest acquisition of the United States—the former French province of Louisiana. Clark's letter implored Claiborne to proceed to New Orleans with haste. "Every day," Clark urged, "is a day of fear and suspense for the whole country and . . . you cannot possibly make use of too much expedition to arrive and put an end to it." Clark's warning reflected the fears of the few Americans residing in New Orleans, fears that Spanish resentment at the sale of Louisiana, as well as personal animosity between the former Spanish governor Casa Calvo and the French prefect Pierre Clément de Laussat, would delay or prevent the transfer of the province to its new owner. For weeks Clark had advised a show of military force that would convince the predominantly French and Spanish population of the inevitability of American possession. As the moment of the transfer approached, Clark's apprehension intensified. In the seventeen years since he had left his home in Ireland, Clark had demonstrated a talent for intrigue that allowed him to prosper in a city that lay at the center of one of the world's most vital trade networks. Now, as Louisiana's population prepared to experience a change in nationality for the fourth time in forty years, Clark expected that the province's new identity would offer him an unparalleled opportunity to increase his fortune and political influence. Daniel Clark used his wealth and international connections to encourage the U.S. acquisition of Louisiana, but for him, personal gain prevailed over any possibility of patriotic advantage.[1]

In 1786, at the age of twenty, Clark left his home in the maritime county of Sligo in Ireland, where his prosperous Anglo-Irish family owned considerable property and maintained connections both in England and America. Clark's parents named their eldest son after the most successful member of the family, his father's oldest brother, Daniel Clark, Sr. The elder Clark immigrated to Louisiana in the 1770s and established a thriving mercantile house in New Orleans. After finishing his schooling, the younger Clark joined his uncle, much to the dismay of his parents, who chided their son for his failure to seek his fortune at home.[2]

For an amiable and energetic young man, fortunes were much more easily made in Louisiana. Founded by the French in 1718, New Orleans became a Spanish city in 1763 through the Treaty of Paris, which concluded the Seven Years' War. As the victor, Great Britain had coveted French Louisiana and especially New Orleans as the key to control of the Mississippi River. Fearing an attack on its Mexican provinces, Spain insisted that the settlement provide for Spanish control of New Orleans. The final treaty granted Britain all French territory east of the Mississippi River except the "Isle of New Orleans." This parcel of land, bounded by the Bayou Manchac, the Amite River, and Lakes Maurepas, Pontchartrain, and Borgne, plus the province of Louisiana west of the Mississippi went to Spain.[3]

Louisiana had not prospered under French rule. A chronic food shortage developed because most plantations grew staple crops and relied on imported foodstuffs. Experiments in growing wheat ended when the crop failed to mature in the hot summers of the lower Mississippi Valley. The colony never became self-sufficient in food production, and its principal exports, tobacco and indigo, proved inferior to the products of the French West Indies and brought low prices. Drawn by the prospect of profit, Anglo-American merchants dominated the trade of French Louisiana, smuggling flour into the city from the English colonies on the Atlantic coast and establishing shops in the town. Once in control of the province, Spain considered the presence of English merchants undesirable; Louisiana was to be a strategic barrier between the English colonies in eastern North America and the Spanish possessions in Central America. Early Spanish governors of the province endeavored to bring the colony's trade into compliance with Spanish mercantile regulations by prohibiting Louisiana from trading with non-Spanish ports and expelling English merchants from New Orleans, but the English traders proved too vital to the province's survival to be dislodged.[4]

The first Anglo-American merchant to crack the barrier of Spanish trade restrictions was Oliver Pollock. In 1769, by bringing a desperately needed cargo of flour into New Orleans and selling it at fifteen dollars a barrel when the going rate was thirty dollars, Pollack earned the gratitude of Governor Alejandro O'Reilly and permission to trade with the colony. Following Pollock's success, other English merchants again began to supply flour and other food products and rectify the chronic food shortage in the colony. Although trade between the British colonies and New Orleans was profitable and necessary, much of it was illegal. This did not deter merchants like Pollock or Daniel Clark, Sr., who bought the products of the plantations and the furs shipped downriver and shipped them to contacts in New York, Baltimore, and Philadelphia.[5]

The American Revolution forced Spain to relax its commercial policy. In 1778, in order to "bring relief to the distresses" from which Louisiana suffered, Governor Gálvez announced that the produce of the colony could be shipped to any French or American port. Technically, the governor's order restricted this trade to Spanish ships, but Gálvez overlooked widespread violations, especially after Spain entered the war against Great Britain in 1779. Merchants in New Orleans were equally active in furthering the American cause. Daniel Clark, Sr. turned over forty thousand dollars to Oliver Pollock, who represented the United Colonies in Louisiana. Adding his own fortune to that provided by Clark Sr., and other merchants, Pollock supplied the American colonists with large amounts of arms and ammunition shipped by means of large canoes polled and paddled up the Mississippi and Ohio rivers to Pittsburgh.[6]

In 1782, Spain tried again to incorporate Louisiana into its mercantile system. The Spanish king issued a *cédula* permitting a direct but limited trade between New Orleans and France and French colonies in the West Indies. Louisiana ships owned by Spanish subjects could now sail directly between New Orleans and French St. Domingue (Le Cap). Anglo-American merchants such as Daniel Clark, Sr., Oliver Pollock, and Evan Jones responded by becoming Spanish subjects and expanded this mutually beneficial trade through St. Domingue with merchants in Philadelphia. Since France allowed American ships to trade with the French West Indies, American cargoes could be disguised as French property and transferred to Spanish ships bound for Louisiana. Phineas Bond, the British consul in Philadelphia, estimated that the contraband trade with Louisiana brought "at least $500,000 into this port [Philadelphia] last year."[7]

Dominance of the New Orleans trade by American merchants seemed to threaten Spanish control of the still fragile colony. Much of the produce exported through the port of New Orleans came down the Mississippi River from the growing settlements in the trans-Appalachian west. Although a clause in the Treaty of 1783 declared that the navigation of the Mississippi from its source to the ocean should be forever free to the subjects of England and the citizens of the United States, Spain, not a signatory to the treaty, denied the validity of this clause. By virtue of the victories of Bernardo de Gálvez over the British during the American Revolution, Spain claimed land on both sides of the river and the right to control navigation on the river within Spanish boundaries. In 1784, Spain closed the Mississippi River to all foreign nations, hoping to stifle the frontier settlements whose only practical outlet for their produce was New Orleans. Eager to make the restrictions more palatable for the U.S. government, Spain offered trading concessions for American ships in Spanish ports in Europe. Rumors of this agreement, which would benefit East Coast shippers at the expense of western farmers, roused threats of secession in the west. "If Congress refuses us effectual protection," western settlers wrote in a memorial of 1785, "if it forsakes us, we will adopt the measures which our safety requires, even if they endanger the peace of the Union and our connection with the United States. No protection, no allegiance." As a result of the Spanish action, free navigation of the river and the right to use the port of New Orleans became a principal diplomatic goal of the United States.[8]

Closure of the river trade had an equally devastating effect on the economy of New Orleans. The Spanish intendant Navarro described the "complete stagnation of affairs" existing in the province. "No sales of any kind" occurred, he reported, and "foreigners . . . ceased to make any investments . . . [and] real estate could not be disposed of, even for a mere nominal price." Americans who had attempted to circumvent the trade restrictions and send produce to New Orleans by way of the Mississippi River had their property confiscated, sold, and the proceeds deposited in the provincial treasury. With the loss of their fortunes looming before them, and unwilling to wait for U.S. negotiations with Spain to reopen the river, merchants in New Orleans used the recurrent food shortage to force the Spanish governor to allow American farmers access to the port. In 1787, General James Wilkinson arrived with a cargo consisting of "negroes, cattle, tobacco, flour, bacon, lard, and apples to the amount of 50,000 or 60,000 pesos" from Kentucky. Wilkinson's contact in New Orleans was "Colonel" Daniel Clark, Sr., who convinced the Spanish governor, Esteban Rodríguez Miró, that refusing Wilkinson would anger the Kentuckians and might precipitate an invasion of Louisiana by the outraged westerners.[9]

Although General Wilkinson claimed that the success of his trading venture with Colonel Clark convinced Governor Miró to tolerate American commerce on the river, environmental disasters also provided an important stimulus. Beginning in 1784, cold weather caused crops to fail; on February 13 of that year, fragments of ice measuring from twelve to thirty inches thick filled the Mississippi River, disrupting communication between the banks for five days. Summers were marked by fevers, and in 1787, smallpox "infested the whole province." Early spring in 1788 brought floods, and on Good Friday, fire destroyed much of the city. The Great Fire of 1788 began at the home of Don Vicente José Núñez on the corner of Chartres and Toulouse. A strong south wind carried the flames diagonally across the city squares to the corner of Dauphine and St. Phillip. Within an hour, most of the town was in flames.

The fire destroyed about one-half of the settled area, including 856 houses, the stores of all the merchants, the cathedral, the arsenal, the prison, and other public buildings.[10]

The fire proved a stimulus to trade between New Orleans and Philadelphia. Governor Miró sent three ships to purchase flour and urged the Spanish consul in Philadelphia, Don Diego Gardoqui, to grant permission for other vessels to bring food and provisions to the beleaguered city. Miró also persuaded the Spanish court to relax trade restrictions between western farmers and the province. On December 1, 1788, a royal order announced that Americans could bring raw materials and merchandise into New Orleans subject to an import duty of 15 percent; after further payment of an export duty of 6 percent, the products could be shipped to any of the ports with which Spanish law allowed New Orleans to trade.[11]

Even before the Spanish court acted, the profits generated by Wilkinson's and the senior Clark's trade with the western United States exceeded their expectations. In August 1788, the two men, joined by a third, Isaac Dunn, signed "Articles of Agreement" to begin a three-cornered trade linking Kentucky, New Orleans, and Philadelphia, which was completely illegal at that time according to Spanish policy. Writing to Wilkinson, Clark, Sr., explained that by exploiting loopholes in the Spanish mercantile restrictions products could be smuggled into and out of New Orleans.[12]

Their success was enhanced by the presence of young Daniel Clark, a recent arrival in the town. The younger Clark exhibited a facility with languages that enabled him to obtain a position in the governor's office, where he translated documents from Spanish and French into English. His employment also gave him inside knowledge of Spanish policy, which he used to further his uncle's business. By April 1789, the Pittsburgh *Gazette* confirmed the success of the new trading opportunities: "A general and uninterrupted trade has taken place between the inhabitants of this country and those of the Spanish settlements at New-Orleans. Several boats loaded with goods to a very considerable amount have arrived here, and in return they took large quantities of tobacco, beef, [and] corn." Opening the river to American commerce did not end western demands for duty-free access to the port, but it did attract more Americans to New Orleans and increased their economic domination of its business community. By the beginning of the 1790s, New Orleans combined the functions of frontier marketplace, seaport, military garrison, and provincial capital, and it occupied the center of economic and political life in the Spanish borderlands.[13]

The partnership of Clark, Wilkinson, and Dunn lasted only one year, but its success provided the basis for the successful mercantile house that Colonel

Clark turned over to his nephew a few years later. Daniel Clark made important contacts within the Spanish governor's office, and he learned invaluable lessons about negotiating the labyrinthine Spanish customs regulations. His fluent Spanish and French, gracious manners, and "generally pleasing personality" made a favorable impression on the business community of New Orleans. In the early 1790s the younger Clark took over his uncle's business and began to act as the New Orleans agent for the large Philadelphia firm of Reed and Forde. The Philadelphia merchants sent cargoes of flour, brandy, sherry, pepper, cloth, and furniture to Clark on consignment; in exchange he returned cargoes of "furs, seegars, [and] Indigo." Clark's connections in the custom's office and with the local city government (the *cabildo*) enabled him to circumvent colonial trade regulations for his clients. Adroit bribery could persuade Spanish officials to wink at evasions of the commercial restrictions and allow Clark to obtain permits for the ships of the firm of Reed and Forde to trade in New Orleans.[14]

Clark's clients also valued his shrewd advice on the best way to smuggle specie (gold and silver currency) out of the province. Specie was in short supply in the United States after the Revolution, and New Orleans offered an opportunity to gain hard currency in return for trade goods from producers in the United States. Except when used for the purchase of slaves, the export of specie from New Orleans was subject to an additional duty (above the normal 6 percent export duty). A memorandum from one of his business correspondents in Philadelphia explained that Clark "persuaded" customs officials to enter specie exports on their books as payment for slaves "while in reality it is the return made for merchandise shipped from the United States and for the account of some American House." The large number of advertisements in Philadelphia's papers offering to accept Spanish pesos in payment indicates the extent of specie transfers between the two cities.[15]

In 1793 Clark formed a partnership with Daniel W. Coxe, an active and influential merchant in Philadelphia. Coxe's contacts within the government of the United States complemented Clark's influence in New Orleans, and the partnership served to link Clark's interests with those of the United States. European politics, however, continued to curb the ability of merchants in New Orleans to trade successfully with the ports on the Atlantic coast. Wars, market fluctuations, and hurricanes made travel between New Orleans and the East Coast so dangerous that New Orleans merchants commonly announced that they were going to "hazard an adventure" when setting out on a voyage. The outbreak of war between Spain and France in 1793 resulted in great profits for the firm of Coxe and Clark but also increased the firm's risks. Cancellation of Spanish commercial concessions to France left the United States as the only major neutral carrier and the only available source of supply for Louisiana. Coxe and Clark's ships usually sailed with two sets of papers—American and Spanish—and assumed the guise of Spanish ships when entering the port of New Orleans. The Spanish governor was surely aware of the deception, but the province's need for food and other supplies prevented any vigorous investigation of ownership.[16]

Trading for themselves and acting as agents for other Philadelphia merchants, the firm of Coxe and Clark developed a complex trade route that sent cargoes of Louisiana sugar (after 1795) to Havana, exchanged them for coffee, refined sugar, or cocoa, which was sent to Philadelphia and traded for flour that was subsequently sent back to New Orleans. Another equally intricate routing delivered merchandise from Philadelphia over the mountains to Pittsburgh by wagon or packhorse. There the goods were traded for the bulky farm products of the West and floated down the interior waterways of the Ohio and Mississippi rivers to New Orleans. The firm of Coxe and Clark sold the western produce for specie or sent the products as export goods on to Philadelphia by way of the French West Indies. Western farmers, anxious to reach New Orleans and sell their produce at the "fancy prices" produced by winter's scarcity, engaged in a mad scramble to be the first to reach New Orleans with the spring floods. But the unfamiliar language and laws of Louisiana hampered the "farmer, turned boatman, turned trader" and ensured that he would look to a mercantile house such as Coxe and Clark for storage and assistance. Without the services of a knowledgeable New Orleans agent such as Daniel Clark and a few others, the trade between Philadelphia and New Orleans could not prosper.[17]

The lack of a "deposit" at New Orleans remained a persistent problem for American merchants and a contentious diplomatic issue for Spain and the United States. By allowing produce intended for export to be placed in bond at the port, a deposit would enable merchants to avoid Spanish export taxes. Two things affected Spain's ability to maintain its policy of commercial monopoly: the general European upheaval after the French Revolution, and the fear of an imminent attack by angry western settlers against a "defenseless, weak, and under-populated colony." The declaration of peace between Spain and France in 1795 encouraged Spain to offer concessions to the United States on the right of deposit as an inducement to cling to its neutral status. Fearing that the United States might join Great Britain in an assault on Spanish possessions in the Americas, Spain agreed to the Treaty of San Lorenzo (Pinckney's Treaty) in 1795 granting Americans a place of deposit at New Orleans and recognizing the right of free navigation of the Mississippi River throughout its course. The deposit did not actually open until 1798; when it did the first entry in the books kept by customs officials was for seventy bags of cotton placed in deposit by Daniel Clark. Four months later Clark withdrew the cotton and shipped it to Virginia. He was the single most frequent user of the deposit in 1798; of the fifty-two entries in the records, fifteen are in his name. His shipments sent cotton from Natchez and Nashville, flour from the Ohio Valley, and tobacco from Kentucky to ports on the Atlantic coast; other entries listed occasional exports of furs and skins, lead, iron, hams and bacon, salt pork and beef, and specie.[18]

Although he used the deposit at New Orleans, Clark believed that Spanish taxes on goods imported into the province in American ships—a duty of 21 percent—largely negated any advantage earned through the deposit. In practice the treaty provided only one-way trade: the export of American products through the deposit. For American ships to arrive at New Orleans "in ballast" to take on cargo from the deposit meant total freight charges high enough to deprive the merchants of all profit. Should the ships carry spurious Spanish papers, they would forfeit the right to take American goods from the deposit duty-free, forcing them to pay the tax of 12 percent charged to Spanish shippers.[19]

Soon after the deposit opened Clark presented a memorial to the Spanish intendant Juan Ventura Morales proposing equal taxation of American and Spanish exports through the port of New Orleans. American ships would be allowed to carry Louisiana's products from New Orleans to ports in the United States or other foreign nations after paying the export duty charged Spanish ships. In return, Spanish ships could take cargoes from the American deposit, without payment of export duties, to all ports except those of Spain and her colonies. Clark reminded Morales that Spain's maritime war with Great Britain had deprived the province of necessary shipping, but American shippers were reluctant to export Louisiana's products because of the high tariff. A precedent existed—American ships could export Louisiana's sugar freely—and Clark asked that the principle be extended to all cargoes.[20]

Daniel Clark's wealth and official connections ensured that his proposal received a sympathetic hearing from the intendant. Regardless of the desires of the Spanish court, the colonial government in Louisiana wished to encourage American trade. After other New Orleans merchants enthusiastically endorsed Clark's memorial and Governor Gayoso gave his approval, a formal meeting of the Junta de Real Hacienda (the colonial treasury) not only adopted Clark's recommendations but expanded them. All neutral vessels could trade with New Orleans on the same terms as Spanish ships (payment of a 6 percent duty on both imports and exports); goods exported from New Orleans to the territory of the United States bordering the Mississippi River bore no duty at all.[21]

In Clark's memorial of May 1, 1798, he labeled himself the American vice-consul in New Orleans. This was not entirely accurate. Fearing that foreign consuls might loosen Spain's grip on its lucrative colonial possessions, the Spanish Crown refused to recognize formal representatives of foreign governments in its colonies. Both Presidents Washington and Adams tried to persuade Madrid to change its policy since they believed that consuls were necessary for the protection of American trade and seamen. President Washington made the first consular appointment—Procopio Jacinto Pollock of Pennsylvania, the son of the New Orleans merchant Oliver Pollock, who had been so useful as the financial agent of the Continental Congress in New Orleans. But the colonial government rebuffed Washington's overture, and Procopio Pollock never left Philadelphia, eventually resigning the office.[22]

American merchants in New Orleans agreed that their investments demanded attention. The steady increase of commerce between the United States and Louisiana after the Treaty of San Lorenzo in 1795 prompted them to request that the federal government try again to appoint an official agent to represent the United States and their commercial interests in New Orleans. Daniel Clark was perhaps the richest and certainly the most influential American in New Orleans, and he had already demonstrated his ability to negotiate with Spanish officials. In 1794, when a Spanish ship captured four American vessels and brought three of them into New Orleans for sale, a protest by Clark had succeeded when the government in Washington had failed to move the colonial officials. Using his political and commercial influence, Clark obtained the release of two of the ships to their legitimate owners, and an armed merchantman owned by the firm of Coxe and Clark recaptured the third. Clark's success in representing the interests of the American merchants convinced Captain Isaac Guion, the commander of the U.S. troops at Natchez, and Andrew Ellicott, a member of the commission to establish the boundary between East and West Florida, to request that Clark assume quasi-official status as U.S. consul until one could be selected by the president. Clark's reputation and influence in the merchant community was such that Governor Gayoso acquiesced in this recommendation, and with this authority, Clark had negotiated the reduction in duties paid by American shippers.[23]

Clark hoped to receive a permanent appointment as U.S. consul. In March 1798, he wrote Secretary of State Timothy Pickering, enclosing a copy of Ellicott's and Guion's letter and explaining his negotiations with Morales. Clark was, however, again passed over. Unwilling to appoint a foreign national to represent the interests of the United States, President Adams appointed two vice-consuls, William Emperson Hulings, a physician from Philadelphia who had made a fortune as a merchant in New Orleans, and Evan Jones, who was originally from New York and was also a wealthy member of the merchant community in New Orleans. As before, neither Hulings nor Jones was acceptable to the Spanish Crown. Governor Gayoso permitted Hulings to act unofficially as a consul for eighteen months, but he threatened Jones with arrest for accepting Adams's appointment. Like Daniel Clark's uncle, Evan Jones had become a Spanish citizen during the years when American merchants were not allowed to trade legally in New Orleans, an action probably not known to Adams. He had also served as a captain in the Louisiana militia, and when he was selected by President Adams he was the commandant of the district of Lafourche. Spanish law did not allow a subject of the king to act as the representative of a foreign government.[24]

Although Daniel Clark had been more successful as a representative of American interests than either of the two official appointees, he, too, was not an American citizen in 1798. His uncle, who had a year earlier relinquished all of his business holdings to his nephew, wrote from his plantation in Natchez to urge Clark to join his future to the United States. Following his uncle's advice, Clark journeyed to the Mississippi Territory, where late in December he took an oath of allegiance to his new country.[25]

Two-and-a-half years later Clark received an official appointment as vice-consul to New Orleans from President Jefferson. The New Orleans merchant community, knowing the value of a recognized representative, had continued to petition the president to select a consul that the Spanish government would accept. On July 16, 1801, Jefferson appointed Clark, and the Senate confirmed his nomination the following January. Several members of the Jefferson administration objected to Clark's appointment and questioned his loyalty to the United States. The commission nominating Clark indicated that he was a Spanish subject, but Clark insisted on its correction, declaring that he had "never been a Spanish subject, but had been naturalized, as an American citizen, in the latter part of the year 1798 in Natchez." The most compelling evidence that Clark remained a British subject until his naturalization came from the attitude of the colonial government in New Orleans. The Spanish governor in 1801, the Marquis de Casa Calvo, although prohibited from officially recognizing Clark's position, tacitly accepted his role as a representative of the United States without the friction that had hampered Evan Jones's selection. Nevertheless, the taint of conspiracy still clung to Clark, even after his explanation to Jefferson; one of the most common charges against him in later years insinuated that he switched countries too easily. He was, one political opponent claimed, "a renegade, who had four times changed his allegiance."[26]

Despite lingering doubts of his loyalty, Clark proved to be the most successful appointee to the post of U.S. consul in New Orleans. His ability to untangle Spanish trade regulations allowed him to perform essential services for American merchants and to represent the United States in negotiations with the colonial government. The American presence in New Orleans increased rapidly after 1798. In one year, over two hundred American ships entered New Orleans from the Gulf, and almost four hundred flatboats had come down river. Their crews added over three thousand American sailors and boatmen to the colony's population of eight thousand. The bishop of New Orleans referred to these temporary residents as "godless Americans," but their presence enabled Clark and William Hulings (the other vice-consul) to wring some degree of cooperation from colonial officials. Governor Casa Calvo permitted Clark (and, to a lesser extent, Hulings) to fulfill most of a consul's traditional responsibilities: granting certificates of ownership for cargoes and ships; providing some protection for injured sailors; forcing French privateers to comply with all legal formalities before American ships could be condemned as prizes of war; and furnishing the American government with its only reliable and detailed information on the commerce of the lower Mississippi Valley.[27]

Events in Europe continued to influence the fate of colonial Louisiana and the fortunes of Clark and his business associates. By the secret treaty of San Ildefonso, proposed on March 1, 1801, Napoleon Bonaparte offered to support the claims of the duke of Parma (the husband of the daughter of Charles IV of Spain) to the duchy of Tuscany in return for the restoration of Louisiana to France. The treaty, left unsigned until the Spanish king was certain of his son-in-law's kingdom, was finally completed on October 15, 1802, although the formal transfer of control would not take place for another year. Hints of a secret agreement to return Louisiana to France reached Thomas Jefferson, who responded by instructing Robert Livingston, the U.S. minister to France, to negotiate for the purchase of the "island of New Orleans." French ownership of the port, Jefferson wrote to Livingston, meant that the United States must "marry itself to the British navy." Livingston should make sure that Napoleon understood the consequences for France if it refused to sell the colony.[28]

New Orleans seethed with whispered rumors of a transfer of ownership of the province. In the middle of February 1802, Clark wrote to his New Orleans partners, "There seems to be no doubt that France is to have Louisiana." By March he seemed less certain that the transfer would ever take place. A French informant mentioned the "improbability of France ever taking possession for some time, perhaps never," since Spain "did not like the sacrifice," England would "not look quietly on the measure," and the United States opposed any change in ownership. But by early summer Daniel Coxe informed Clark that business interests in Philadelphia confidently expected to hear confirmations of the cession of Louisiana to France—and American newspapers "from north to south, teem with opposition to the event." Coxe, no supporter of Jefferson, thought that French possession of Louisiana would unfavorably affect Jefferson's political future.[29]

Spanish reluctance to part with Louisiana delayed the transfer of the province to France. Reports of American abuse of the deposit (illegal exportation of specie, smuggling goods disguised as American products) reached the Spanish court. The Peace of Amiens, which temporarily ended the European war, provided an opportune moment for Spain to make one last attempt to integrate Louisiana into the Spanish commercial system in 1802. In June, Daniel Clark warned Secretary of State James Madison that the Spanish intendant Morales would close the American deposit, and his prediction proved remarkably accurate. In October, in response to a secret order received from the Spanish treasury, Morales announced the suspension of the American right of deposit. So well did Morales keep secret the source of his order that even his colleagues in the Louisiana government did not know that he acted under the authority of Madrid. After protests by the government of the United States, both Captain-General Someruelos in Cuba and the Spanish minister Irujo in Washington ordered the intendant to restore the deposit or assign another to the Americans. Morales did not respond to their demands and took extraordinary care to keep secret the orders of the Spanish government because Daniel Clark had so many sources of information among the minor Spanish officials in New Orleans. Clark, however, was under no misapprehension about Morales's authority; his private knowledge of the intendant's character and the inner workings of the provincial government convinced him that Morales had not acted on his own, as Madison and Jefferson originally believed. On March 8, 1803, Clark advised Madison that "informed people" in New Orleans were convinced that Morales "merely executes the order received from his Government." Morales, Clark assured the secretary of state, was "too rich, too sensible, and too cautious" to take such an important step without direct orders from the Spanish court.[30]

News of the closure reached both New Orleans and the East Coast at the same time as the report of the transfer of Louisiana from Spain to France. Americans, not surprisingly, believed that Morales's action was prompted by Napoleon and was only an example of what Americans could expect if France continued to control Louisiana. A decrease in the profitable trade between

New Orleans and the Atlantic ports and in the amount of goods purchased by western settlers from New York City, Philadelphia, and Baltimore was sure to follow.[31]

Closure of the deposit created consternation among the merchants of New Orleans, and business activity halted as merchants waited to see what would happen. Clark's network of informants convinced him that the French government did expect to assume immediate possession of the province, and he took appropriate steps to ensure that the firm of Coxe and Clark did not suffer from any transfer of ownership or the closure of the deposit. Until a changeover actually occurred, he planned that the firm's ships would again assume the disguise of Spanish ships as they entered the port of New Orleans, resuming the flag of the United States before they arrived in Philadelphia with their cargoes from Louisiana. "The moment is big with important events," he wrote to Richard Relf and Beverly Chew, his partners in New Orleans, "and the political horizon is more than usually gloomy." His letter instructed Relf and Chew to sell property, slaves, and ships, "if you can possibly do it," and to call in all debts, including one owed by Governor Casa Calvo.[32]

Clark's concern that a transfer of Louisiana to France would end his privileged position in New Orleans led him to attempt to ingratiate himself with the new French authorities. By November 1802, he was in Paris meeting with the French prefect Pierre Laussat, who had been appointed by Napoleon to accept the transfer of Louisiana from Spain, and General Claud Victor, who had been selected as the captain-general of the province. During separate meetings with the two men, Clark concealed his American citizenship and position as U.S. vice-consul and presented himself only as a merchant from New Orleans who was concerned about future French policy in Louisiana. Clark may have hoped to gain assurances that France would restore the American deposit; if so, he was quickly disappointed. General Victor informed Clark that France regarded the Treaty of San Lorenzo and the American right of deposit in New Orleans as "waste paper." Laussat confirmed that the French government would immediately end that agreement, and merchants in New Orleans could not expect France to continue the Spanish custom of disregarding violations of trade policies. The meetings with the French officials convinced Clark that the French would be even less likely than the Spanish to condone American use of the port and ended any thoughts he might have had about cooperation with the French. His confidential report of the conversations to friends in Louisiana concluded, "Should the French continue in possession of Orleans, such of us here as have fortunes, must become beggars."[33]

Clark's concern that his business ventures in New Orleans would be adversely affected by French possession of Louisiana led him to pressure the

American negotiators. His visits with Victor and Laussat had the approval of Robert Livingston and James Monroe, and the information Clark had obtained contradicted the stated policy of the French government. Talleyrand, the French foreign minister, had verbally assured Livingston that France would honor the American right of deposit but declined to put the promise in writing. Livingston reported both conversations to President Jefferson, urging the president to "draw [his] own inferences."[34]

The influence of Clark's warning on the president's decision to accept the French offer of Louisiana is uncertain. At this point, Jefferson knew little of the merchant of New Orleans, but Clark's earlier prediction that the Spanish would close the deposit in 1802 had proved correct, and Clark seemed equally sure about the duplicity of the French minister. Clark's information must have had an impact, because over the next nine months Jefferson, Secretary of State Madison, and Clark exchanged numerous letters—Jefferson and Madison asking detailed questions about Louisiana and New Orleans, and Clark sending answers, advice, and additional warnings. The American merchant community in New Orleans had little doubt about the importance of Clark's counsel, crediting Clark's information with convincing Jefferson that only the acquisition of New Orleans would ensure American use of the port. "The United States owed the acquisition of Louisiana to Daniel Clark," concluded one prominent resident.[35]

Clark continued to provide confidential information to Jefferson and to use the information for the benefit of his business interests. The first public notice of the purchase of Louisiana appeared in the *New England Palladium*, published in Boston on June 28, 1803. A letter from Rufus King in Paris reached Jefferson on July 3, confirming the cession but mentioning no purchase price. On July 4, 1803, the *National Intelligencer* made the first public announcement of the purchase in Washington, D.C. Two days later, Secretary of State Madison informed Clark of the transfer. Clark, however, had advance knowledge of the agreement. On April 30, the treaty signing date in Paris, an informant urged Clark to buy property in New Orleans before the cession became public knowledge. Such information allowed Clark to reverse his earlier decision to sell out and to buy land and slaves at depressed prices. He emerged from a turbulent year richer than ever.[36]

In the months before the actual transfer of Louisiana to the United States, Daniel Clark demonstrated the extent of his connections in the Spanish government. Requested by Jefferson to ascertain the intentions of Spanish officials (who saw the sale of Louisiana as a betrayal by France), Clark warned that they might try to postpone the delivery of the province to France and thus to the United States. Such delaying tactics might allow "numberless unforeseen and favorable circumstances [to] occur of which they would take advantage." One circumstance appeared especially threatening—the protest lodged by the Spanish minister in Washington against the French sale of Louisiana. Carlos Martínez de Irujo resented Madison's blunt declaration that the Spaniards would have to decide for themselves whether they wanted "a garden of peace or a field of war." Irujo retorted that Louisiana might cost far more than fifteen million dollars if the Americans "undertook a quarrel." Clark worried that if "news of the Protest" reached New Orleans, the Spanish governor might decide to oppose the transfer of the province to the United States. Clark had persuaded Governor Salcedo and Commissioner Casa Calvo, who had been appointed a commissioner by the Spanish Crown after he had served as the governor, that silence on the part of Spain would be "the greatest possible proof she can give of her acquiescence to the Cession made [to] the United States," and he assured, "they begin to place belief in the assertion." To guard against any knowledge of Spanish opposition, Clark bribed local officials to suppress the delivery of all newspapers by post, allowing only those that contained no mention of the Spanish minister's protest to circulate. "I shall endeavor to learn their contents before they are delivered," he promised, "and either suppress or deliver them as the circumstances require." Clark's actions proved successful. The Spanish commissioner Casa Calvo gave up "all idea of opposition," and Clark reported that "no other delay or difficulty will be put in the way of delivery than what may arise from Etiquette or from personal pique between the French and Spanish Commissioners."[37]

Clark's optimism about the possibility of a peaceful transfer for the territory evaporated as problems of "Etiquette" did create friction between the French and Spanish commissioners. When the Spanish governor Salcedo failed to attend a fête held by Madame Laussat, the wife of the French prefect, she denounced the Spaniards as "Souls of Filth," and her husband's explosive temper exacerbated the tense situation. Clark implored Claiborne and Wilkinson to "for God's Sake lose no time in marching this way to put an End to the horrid situation we are in . . . your presence alone can calm the effervescence which the slightest Accident may cause to shew itself in the worst of Forms."[38]

The letters Clark wrote between November 23 and December 19, 1803, depict a steadily worsening situation. He constantly urged the American commissioners, Claiborne and Wilkinson, to make haste to reach New Orleans. Warning that "every delay is a day of fear and suspense," Clark cautioned that New Orleans was "placed over a Mine that may explode from one moment to another [with an] effect . . . dreadful beyond conception." Clark did not explain just what kind of opposition he anticipated. He warned of vague threats to "fire the town," and predicted that Prefect Laussat would "give the lower

Classes a hankering for a French government" and rouse in his fellow countrymen a revolutionary spirit that Clark had "long attempted to subdue."[39]

Despite his urgent recommendation for an American show of force, Clark's own letters to Claiborne and Wilkinson indicate the futility of resistance to the American takeover. The total Spanish and French forces in New Orleans amounted to only three hundred men, of whom seventy-five were in the hospital suffering from dysentery and "nearly as many in arrest or in Prison." Debris clogged the guns placed on the ramparts around the town, and the forts at each corner of the walls were "very slightly and negligently guarded." Nor could any hostile force close the city gates against the American commissioners, since the gates were "incapable of turning on their hinges."[40]

Daniel Clark exaggerated tensions among Spanish, French, and Americans in New Orleans for reasons of his own. Jefferson's appointment of William Claiborne as governor of the new Orleans Territory had disappointed Clark, who had hoped for the position. But, if he could not be governor of Louisiana, he intended to continue the same degree of influence over the American government that he had exercised over the Spanish. Using the uncertain situation in New Orleans to bolster his own position as the only American representative trusted by all sides, Clark promised Claiborne and Wilkinson, "[I will] do all my Endeavors to keep all Parties quiet, as I enjoy the Confidence of all, until you arrive and [I] shall be prepared to give you all possible Assistance." Included in his assistance was the organization of a militia unit "under American colours to preserve and guard the Town." One hundred volunteers drawn from the merchant community elected Clark as their captain and offered their services to Prefect Laussat to keep order in the community during the three weeks between the two transfers.[41]

In spite of Clark's fears, the transfer of Louisiana to the United States proceeded peacefully. Descriptions of the town's reaction to the transfer ceremony vary with the nationality of the viewer. Prefect Laussat described for the French court a sullen populace who by their silence manifested their palpable disappointment at losing their newly regained French citizenship. As the American flag was raised, he reported that it seemed to pause briefly as if "embarrassed to take the place of the glorious French flag." Daniel Clark described a very different reception for Secretary of State Madison and President Jefferson. He emphasized the cheers (from the gathered Americans) that greeted the raising of the American flag. In his opinion, the French populace would support the American government as a welcome alternative to Spanish control, and he anticipated that his connections in the local community would make his aid invaluable to the new governor.[42]

Clark's expectations of honor and influence did not materialize. Animosity between Clark and Governor William Claiborne flared when Claiborne opposed immediate statehood for the new territory, declaring to Jefferson that the new citizens of Louisiana were "uninformed, indolent, luxurious, [and] illy fitted to be useful citizens of a Republic." Of great concern to the new governor, who spoke neither French nor Spanish, was that "not one in fifty . . . appear[ed] to understand the English language." Louisiana Creoles responded by characterizing the governor as "as stranger here, a stranger as far as the soil itself is concerned, its local interests, the customs, habits, and even the language of the inhabitants, who is therefore without even the most absolutely necessary knowledge."[43]

The plan of territorial organization for the newest possession of the United States contained several provisions calculated to create dissension among the citizens of Louisiana. Not only was the promised statehood withheld, the Territory of Orleans would continue to operate under the Spanish commercial policies until the U.S. Congress acted to replace them. This meant that, unlike merchants in other American ports, merchants in New Orleans would pay both import and export taxes. Moreover, although the importation of slaves remained legal in the rest of the country, planters in Louisiana were expressly forbidden to import slaves from outside the United States.[44]

Residents of Louisiana who wished for immediate statehood turned to Clark for leadership. Fifty-five merchants presented a memorial to Congress claiming that the promised "Rights and Privileges" of statehood had not been granted, thus "greatly impeding the Commercial and Agricultural Interests of the Province." Louisiana's uncertain status jeopardized Clark's and the other merchants' commercial activities. With their ships unauthorized to "hoist any Flag whatever" and provided with no proper documentation, with their goods still subject to the Spanish tariffs that had penalized American shippers before the purchase of the territory, Clark and his fellow merchants felt themselves victimized. Other American ports, they complained, carried on "a free, and untaxed Intercourse, and their exports are subject to no Duties whatever."[45]

At another mass meeting in the summer of 1804, merchants and planters of New Orleans presented additional grievances to Congress. This memorial, known as the Louisiana Remonstrance, urged repeal of the congressional prohibition of further importation of slaves into the territory. Such an embargo, the merchants argued, rendered Louisiana plantations "of little or no value." Neither sugar, rice, cotton, nor indigo could be cultivated, nor could the levee be kept in repair without a continued "uninterrupted Trade to Africa," at least until 1808 (when Congress would end the legal importation of slaves into the rest of the United States). The slave trade remained a source of considerable income to Clark, and many of the profits of that trade and his other mercantile interests had been invested in land. In the previous year (1803) Clark had been unusually active as a purchaser of land for himself, jointly with Daniel Coxe, and as a commission agent for others. Limitations on the importation of slaves into Louisiana would decrease his income and the value of his plantation property.

Certain other provisions of the Territorial Act seemed to threaten legal titles to property obtained during the period of Spanish control. The Treaty of 1803 vested the government of the United States with ownership of all land in the Louisiana Purchase not legitimately held by private title. Congressional legislation required that holders of Louisiana land register their titles with a "Register and Recorder of Land Titles" appointed by President Jefferson. Territorial landowners feared this was "a complicated machinery to dispossess them of all their broad and fertile acres," and the beginning of endless litigation and arbitrary decision making by agents with no local background or with ties to one political faction or another. Some claims were questioned. Clark had purchased a large portion of a Spanish grant of land to the Baron de Bastrop, but the federal government refused to recognize the legality of the grant. The land ultimately became part of his estate and was sold by his executors to Daniel Coxe, who vigorously defended his title for several decades.[46]

The turmoil surrounding the acquisition of Louisiana continued to occupy Clark throughout 1803 and 1804, but beginning in 1805 a new scandal of national proportions enmeshed him in charges and countercharges of treason. On the afternoon of June 25, in "an elegant Barge" with "sails, colors and oars" manned by "a sergeant and ten able, faithful hands," Aaron Burr arrived in New Orleans. The ostracized vice-president bore letters of introduction from General Wilkinson to both Clark and Claiborne. Both men entertained Burr, their rivalry prompting them to try to outdo each other. Clark evidently liked Burr. "Pleased with his society," Clark remembered later, "[I] shewed him the civilities usual on such occasions." This meant a banquet that gathered together all the prominent men of the community, including the former Spanish intendant Morales, to meet Burr. Later, Clark lent Burr horses for his journey to Natchez and sent along a servant to bring them back.[47]

The extent of Clark's involvement in Burr's schemes is a matter of conjecture. Wilkinson's letter of introduction to Clark contained the cryptic comment that Burr "would communicate to him many things improper" to write, that "he would not say to any other." When "absurd and wild reports" of a conspiracy to separate the western states from the Union began to circulate in New Orleans, Clark wrote to Wilkinson. "How the devil," he demanded, had he "been lugged into the conspiracy . . . *vous qui savez tout* can best explain this riddle." Clark suggested that Wilkinson amuse Burr with an account of the plot but admonished him not to let Burr's schemes distract him from the business of land acquisition. Clark's letter has been called a "masterpiece of dissembling" by those who link the merchant to Burr's plans. It may be, however, just what it purports to be, a warning to Wilkinson not to let Burr draw him into any foolish schemes.[48]

Eventually Clark learned that what had lugged him into the conspiracy was Burr's freely pledging Clark's credit and naming him the chief financial backer of the venture. The former vice-president had apparently told his supporters that Clark had provided a letter of credit on the house of Chew and Relf (Clark's partners in New Orleans) in the amount of two hundred thousand dollars. Clark later explained that Burr often claimed friendship and support from persons who were unconnected to his designs in order to impress his hearers "with a high idea of his resources." When Burr insinuated that he could draw on Clark for a substantial sum, he did so, Clark wrote in his defense, "[Because] my credit there [in Kentucky], he knew, stood high, and that nothing would impress the public with a better idea of his fiscal operations than a persuasion that I was his banker." When Jefferson's investigator, John Graham, visited New Orleans two years later, Richard Relf convinced him that the firm "never had any funds in their Hands liable to the order of Col. Burr," and Graham reported to Jefferson that rumor had greatly exaggerated Clark's involvement.[49]

Some evidence of Clark's collusion with Burr comes from British archives. Through an intermediary, the former vice-president proposed to the British minister to the United States, Sir Anthony Merry, that British aid would allow Burr to place Louisiana and the Old Southwest into English hands. Merry, convinced that the western states and the Louisiana Territory actually were close to secession, wrote to the British Foreign Office with the suggestion that several British frigates be sent to patrol Gulf waters until "Daniel Clark of New Orleans" should send word that "the revolution had taken place." When this missive reached England it fell into the hands of the new prime minister, Charles James Fox, who had better things for British frigates to do than wait for Clark to "deliver" Louisiana. Merry was promptly recalled.[50]

Clark's actions following Burr's visit to New Orleans only increased suspicions about his involvement in the supposed plot. On September 11, 1805, two months after Burr left New Orleans, Clark set out on an extended journey that took him to several Mexican ports, including Vera Cruz. He returned to New Orleans in late December but left again for Mexico in February 1806. On his return Clark wrote Wilkinson that, surprisingly, he had returned safely from Vera Cruz even though his enemies had told the viceroy that he was "a person dangerous to the Spanish government . . . who had visited that country with no other view than that of acquiring information of its strength & how & when it might be assailed with the greatest probability of success."[51]

The scope of Aaron Burr's schemes in 1805 and 1806 is almost impossible to determine; the former vice-president revealed a different plan to every person he involved. Clark's self-serving defense of his actions, written several years later, casts doubts on his actual participation. "Never," he claimed, would he have "been fool enough to expose a large fortune and a respectable standing to certain destruction on an impractible [sic] scheme." Instead, when Colonel Josef Bellechasse, then the commandant of the territorial militia, told Clark that he, "several members of the territorial legislature, the clerk of the legislative council, and the captain of the port" had been asked to join "an association to undertake some enterprise against Mexico," Clark dissuaded his friends from participating in the venture.[52]

Clark did make a report about Spanish defenses in Vera Cruz to the secretary of war, but business problems provided the primary reason for his trips to Mexico. The commercial contracts he concluded in this "land of promise" proved quite profitable for the firm of Coxe and Clark. Trading Louisiana sugar for a cargo of cochineal (a dye) that was re-exported to England added almost $160,000 to the accounts of the partnership. The infusion of money was desperately needed. The resumption of European hostilities had endangered American trade with foreign ports. The failure of Barclays, one of Coxe and Clark's corresponding brokers in London, put an additional financial strain on the firm. Clark's letters to his Philadelphia partner after his return to New Orleans in April 1806 constantly referred to their precarious financial situation.[53]

Governor Claiborne seized on the reports about Clark's involvement with Burr to discredit the merchant with President Jefferson. "If there be any serious disaffection to the American Government in this Territory," Claiborne promised the president, "it may . . . be attributed to the Intrigues of a few designing, discontented, restless men," of whom Daniel Clark was a "conspicuous and zealous member." Clark's selection (over another candidate favored by Claiborne) as the first territorial representative from Louisiana to Congress prompted Claiborne to denounce Clark as "unprincipled, ambitious, avaricious, and artful." Claiborne's enmity bore fruit. Clark's efforts to persuade Congress and the president of the loyalty of Louisianians and their readiness for statehood failed. The hints of his involvement with Burr, added to the past accusations of changes in his citizenship and his feud with Claiborne, ended any residual hopes Clark might have held about his political future under a Jefferson or Madison administration.[54]

The feud between Clark and Claiborne boiled over upon Clark's return to New Orleans in April 1807. A tumultuous welcome greeted the delegate. Incensed at the "splendid dinner" given Clark, the governor suggested that those who honored him desired a violent return of the "late proceedings here." Not content with their own entertainment, Claiborne fumed, "the Gentlemen propose that their *Wives* should do likewise, and the Ladies, I understand, contemplate giving him a grand fête in a few Days." The extravagant reception of Clark, coupled with the urging of several of the governor's supporters, pushed Claiborne into challenging Clark to a duel.[55]

Although against the law in Spanish Louisiana, duels were common and rarely resulted in criminal penalties. When Louisiana became part of the United States the territorial legislature enacted more stringent anti-dueling laws. No one paid any attention. Until the Civil War almost every man active in Louisiana's public affairs had fought at least one duel; most had engaged in several. A "gentleman" who refused to fight would be "posted" or publicly branded a coward. Daniel Clark had fought several duels and was considered a fine shot. Claiborne had expressed opposition to the practice after his brother-in-law fell in a duel in 1804. But despite his dislike of settling disputes on the "field of honor," Claiborne issued a challenge to Clark.[56]

Claiborne had taken exception to remarks Clark had made before the U.S. House of Representatives the previous December denouncing Claiborne's neglect of the territorial militia. Louisiana citizens, Clark declared, had "offered their services to the United States, and had been disregarded by the man put over them, and a preference given to another corps." The other corps in question was composed of free persons of color, who had received the governor's "Standard" while he supposedly ignored the offers of the white population to be of service to their new country.[57]

When Clark refused to retract or explain his statement, Claiborne demanded satisfaction. Following the prescribed practice, the two named their seconds. Since the governor of the territory should be expected to uphold its laws, the men decided to fight outside the Orleans Territory. To keep the matter secret, Claiborne planned to leave New Orleans on June 3, Clark following three days later. Somehow, news of the projected duel leaked out, and Clark left New Orleans the day after Claiborne, pursued by the sheriff for ninety miles, all the way to the Iberville River, until the duelists had passed out of the territorial jurisdiction. On Monday, June 8, at one o'clock in the afternoon, they met. According to Clark, "We fired almost at the same instant, at 10 paces, and the Governor fell, shot thro' the thigh, and with a most severe contusion on the other." Clark received no injury. Claiborne privately assured General Wilkinson that both "before and after the shot (while on the ground) Mr. Clark and I were mutually polite to each other."[58]

An exultant Clark returned to New Orleans to receive what he termed "the congratulations . . . of the public on the occasion . . . mixed with . . . some bitter reproaches that I should have *dared* to risk [my] life, which they think, ought to be reserved for them." Clark may have overstated the appreciation of the Creoles for his bravery. Claiborne was not as bereft of friends as Clark believed. Moreover, the fortitude with which Claiborne bore the pain of his wounds won the admiration of the citizens of the territory. He did not heal quickly; not until September was Claiborne able to resume his duties as territorial governor.[59]

Although their feud continued, the duel between Clark and Claiborne marked a turning point in the political futures of both men. Claiborne's understanding of the Creole population improved, and his smiling acceptance of his defeat—he felt he had been "sufficiently punished for [his] imprudence"—proved that an American could be as gallant on the field of honor as any Creole. As Claiborne mended his connections with the Creoles of New Orleans, Clark's acceptance as their spokesman diminished. One year later, in the next election for territorial delegate to Congress, his handpicked successor, Dr. John Watkins, the former mayor of New Orleans, failed to defeat Claiborne's candidate, Julien Poydras of Pointe Coupée (one of the wealthiest and most influential Creoles in New Orleans). After 1808, Daniel Clark held no more political offices in Louisiana.[60]

In the years following Clark's duel with Claiborne, the changed political climate in the booming city forced him to acknowledge the loss of his dominance. More and more Americans reached New Orleans, as eager to build fortunes and political influence as Clark had been twenty-five years before. But the newcomers gravitated to Governor Claiborne's councils and shunned Clark, who was too tainted with Burr's plots for their taste. Clark spent his last years attempting to preserve his fortune through the turbulent years preceding the outbreak of war between the United States and Great Britain. His business partners, Richard Relf and Beverly Chew, later claimed that the drop in land values in Louisiana caused by the War of 1812 had bankrupted Clark's estate. Louisiana became a state in 1812, and William Claiborne was elected its first governor. Daniel Clark's intrigues came to an end in 1813. He died suddenly in his home in New Orleans on August 16, and his funeral demonstrated that the community of New Orleans remembered and respected his contributions to the city. Even Governor Claiborne put aside his animosity and walked in the cortege. The funeral procession ended at the St. Louis Cemetery No. 1, where Clark's body was interred in a large stone vault, still visible to visitors to New Orleans. A Latin epitaph placed on the tomb recorded his friends' sentiments:

Here Lies Daniel Clark . . . Consul of the United States, Appointed on account of his Illustrious Virtues. . . . Afterward, by the Unanimous Vote of the People of the Territory of Orleans, He sat as the First Delegate in the Congress of the American People . . . His great Wealth, Accumulated without Fraud, He used in Relieving the Necessities of the Poor; Nevertheless Becoming Richer, By His Liberality. He died, wept of all Good men, August 16, 1813, in the Forty-Seventh year of his Age.[61]

Notes

1. Daniel Clark to William Claiborne, Dec. 12, 1803, in Clarence Edwin Carter, ed., *Territorial Papers of the United States* (Washington D.C.: United States Government Printing Office, 1940), 9: 137.

2. Daniel Clark, *Proofs of the Corruption of General James Wilkinson, and of His Connexion with Aaron Burr* (1809; repr., Freeport, N.Y.: Books for Libraries Press, 1970), 105; Mary Clark to Daniel Clark, Aug. 7, 1794, *E. P. Gaines and Wife v. Relf, Chew, and Others*, General Case Files no. 1765, Record Group 21, National Archives, Southwest Region, Fort Worth, Texas.

3. Joel Gray Taylor, *Louisiana: A Bicentennial History* (New York: Published for the American Association for State and Local History, Nashville, Tenn., by W. W. Norton, 1976), 16–18.

4. John G. Clark, *New Orleans, 1718–1812: An Economic History* (Baton Rouge: Louisiana State University Press, 1970), 152, 164.

5. Raymond J. Martinez, *Pierre George Rousseau, Commanding General of the Galleys of the Mississippi, with Sketches of the Spanish Governors of Louisiana (1777–1803) and Glimpses of Social Life in New Orleans* (New Orleans: Hope, 1965), 36.

6. Charles Gayarré, *History of Louisiana* (New York: William J. Widdleton, 1866), 3: 115; J. Clark, *New Orleans*, 204, 223; Martinez, *Rousseau*, 34; Herbert Asbury, *The French Quarter: An Informal History of the New Orleans Underworld* (New York: Knopf, 1936), 52–53.

7. St. Domingue, now Santo Domingo, was the western portion of the island Columbus called Hispaniola. The main towns in the northern province included Cape Français (Le Cap), Fort Dauphine, Port le Paix, and Cape St. Nicholas. The leading town in the western province was Port-au-Prince. After 1791, slave insurrections left the island with an unstable government, and its value to trade diminished. Carmelo Richard Arena, "Philadelphia-Spanish New Orleans Trade: 1789–1805" (Ph.D. diss., University of Pennsylvania, 1959), 42, 64; Gayarré, *History of Louisiana* 3: 154; Arthur P. Whitaker, *The Spanish Frontier, 1783–1795* (1932; repr., Gloucester, Mass.: Peter Smith, 1962), 198.

8. William McDonald, *Select Charters and Other Documents Illustrative of American History, 1660–1775* (Ann Arbor, Mich.: University Microfilms, 1964), 264; Gayarré, *History of Louisiana*, 3: 157; Carmelo Richard Arena, "Philadelphia-Spanish New Or-

leans Trade in the 1790s," *Louisiana History* 2 (1961): 429–45; Memorial from western settlers quoted in Gayarré, *History of Louisiana*, 3: 457.

9. Gayarré, *History of Louisiana*, 3: 186; Arthur P. Whitaker, "James Wilkinson's First Descent to New Orleans in 1787," *Hispanic American Historical Review* (February 1928): 85; James Wilkinson, *Memoirs of My Own Time* (Philadelphia: Abraham Small, 1816), vol. 2, appendix 6; D. Clark, *Proofs*, 6–9.

10. Gayarré, *History of Louisiana*, 3: 163, 190; Governor Miró's Despatch of April 1, 1788, quoted in ibid., 203.

11. Ibid., 204.

12. Daniel Clark Sr. to James Wilkinson, June 6, 1788, quoted in Wilkinson, *Memoirs*, vol. 2, appendix 13.

13. "Extract from a Memoir Submitted to the Honorable Timothy Pickering, When Secretary of State, by the Honorable Daniel Clark," in D. Clark, *Proofs*, 6–9; *Pittsburg Gazette*, April 18, 1789, from a letter datelined Kentucky, March 2, 1789, quoted in Arena, "Philadelphia-Spanish New Orleans Trade, 1789–1805," 178.

14. Reed and Forde to Coxe and Clark, May 26, 1793, Reed and Forde Letter Book, 1783–94, Reed and Forde Collection, Historical Society of Pennsylvania, Philadelphia. The partnership of Clark, Wilkinson, and Dunn was dissolved by mutual consent on Sept. 8, 1789. D. Clark, *Proofs*, 8–9.

15. Memorandum, undated, Gilpin Family Papers, *Wilkinson v. Clark* Collection, Historical Society of Pennsylvania, Philadelphia; Arena, "Philadelphia-Spanish New Orleans Trade in the 1790s," 435–36.

16. J. Clark, *New Orleans*, 238; Arena, "Philadelphia-Spanish New Orleans Trade, 1789–1805," 90. Daniel Coxe's brother, Tench Coxe, became assistant secretary of the Treasury under Alexander Hamilton on May 10, 1790. Upon his appointment, Tench Coxe transferred all his business holdings to his brother Daniel to avoid the conflict-of-interest charges that had forced the resignation of the previous assistant treasurer, William Durr.

17. J. Clark, *New Orleans*, 272.

18. Arena, "Philadelphia-Spanish New Orleans Trade, 1789–1805," 32; Gayarré, *History of Louisiana*, 3: 357–58; Arthur P. Whitaker, *The Mississippi Question, 1795–1803: A Study in Trade, Politics, and Diplomacy* (Gloucester, Mass.: Peter Smith, 1962), 91; J. Clark, *New Orleans*, 210.

19. Whitaker, *The Mississippi Question*, 93–94.

20. D. Clark, *Proofs*, 106; J. Clark, *New Orleans*, 242–43.

21. Arena, "Philadelphia-Spanish New Orleans Trade, 1789–1805," 116–17; D. Clark, *Proofs*, 106.

22. "Documents: Despatches from the United States Consul in New Orleans, 1801–1803, Part I," *American Historical Review* 32 (1927): 802.

23. Gayarré, *History of Louisiana*, 3: 397; Captain Isaac Guion and Commander Andrew Ellicott to Daniel Clark, March 2, 1798, and Daniel Clark to Guion and Ellicott, March 14, 1798, State Department Consular Despatches, New Orleans, in "Documents, Part I," 801–3; D. Clark, *Proofs*, 106.

24. "Documents, Part I," 803, 805–6.

25. Colonel Daniel Clark, Sr., to Daniel Clark, Nov. 2, 1798, Daniel Clark Papers, Pennsylvania Historical Society, Philadelphia; D. Clark, *Proofs*, 77–78.

26. "Documents, Part I," 807–8; D. Clark, *Proofs*, 142–43; Wilkinson, *Memoirs*, 2: 9.

27. Whitaker, *The Mississippi Question*, 97, 151; J. Clark, *New Orleans*, 242; Arena, "Philadelphia-Spanish New Orleans Trade, 1789–1805," 26, 119.

28. John Kendall, *History of New Orleans* (Chicago: Lewis Press, 1922), 1: 39–40; J. Clark, *New Orleans*, 215.

29. Daniel Clark to Richard Relf and Beverly Chew, Feb. 18, 1802, in *Transcript of Record, Gaines v. Hennen*, comprising case nos. 2619, 2695, 2715, and 2734, in the Circuit Court of the United States, Eastern District of Louisiana, entered in the appeal of *Gaines v. P. H. Monseaux*, case no. 3663, in the United States Circuit Court, Fifth Judicial Circuit and District of Louisiana, to the Supreme Court of the United States (New Orleans: Clerk's Office, United States Circuit Court, Nov. 28, 1877), 894; Clark to Relf and Chew, March 16, 1802, in *Gaines v. Cities of New Orleans and Baltimore*, General Case Files no. 2715, Record Group 21, National Archives, Southwest Region, Fort Worth, Tex.; Daniel W. Coxe to Clark, July 1, 1802, reprinted in *Transcript of Record, Gaines v. Relf, Chew, and Others*, case no. 122, United States Circuit Court, Eastern District of Louisiana, prepared for appeal to the Supreme Court of the United States (New Orleans: Clerk's Office, United States Circuit Court, 1858), 564.

30. Daniel Clark to Secretary of State Madison, June 22, 1802, "Documents, Part I," 815–16; Daniel Clark to Secretary of State Madison, March 8, 1803, "Documents: Despatches from the United States Consul in New Orleans, 1801–1803, Part II," *American Historical Review* 33 (1928): 332. For the text of the Morales decree of Oct. 16, 1802, closing the New Orleans deposit, see *American State Papers, Foreign Relations* (Washington D.C.: Gales and Seaton, 1832), 2: 470.

31. Whitaker, *The Mississippi Question*, 190–96; 200–202.

32. *Frankfurt (Ky.) Palladium*, Jan. 20, 1803, item dated Philadelphia, Dec. 28, 1802, quoted in Whitaker, *The Mississippi Question*, 196; Daniel Clark to Richard Relf and Beverly Chew, Oct. 22, 1802, in *Gaines v. City of New Orleans*, case no. 8835, United States Circuit Court, Fifth Judicial Circuit and District of Louisiana, on appeal to the Supreme Court of the United States (New Orleans: Clerk's Office, United States Circuit Court, October 1883), 2: 1786.

33. Daniel Clark to Secretary of State Madison, April 27, 1803, "Documents, Despatches from the United States Consul in New Orleans, 1801–1803: Part II," *American Historical Review* 33 (1928): 339; Wilkinson, *Memoirs*, 2: appendix 16. Clark's interviews with General Victor and Prefect Laussat are recorded in Robert Livingston's letter to Secretary of State Madison, *American State Papers: Foreign Relations*, 2: 526–27.

34. Livingston quoted in Gayarré, *History of Louisiana*, 3: 471.

35. Josef Bellechasse, deposition of 1837, in *Transcript of Record, Gaines v. City of New Orleans*, 2: 1332.

36. *Territorial Papers of the United States*, 9: 4 n. 4; Secretary of State Madison to

Daniel Clark, July 6, 1803, in *Transcript of Record, Gaines v. City of New Orleans*, 2: 1705–6; Fulwar Skipwith to Clark, April 30, 1803, ibid., 2024; Daniel Coxe to Clark, Aug. 26, 1803, ibid., 1943.

37. Secretary of State Madison to Daniel Clark, Sept. 16, 1803, *Territorial Papers of the United States*, 9: 54–55; Clark to William Claiborne, Nov. 11, 1803, ibid., 102–3; Clark to Claiborne, Nov. 21, 1803, ibid., 115; Clark to Claiborne, Nov. 22, 1803, ibid., 117; Clark to Claiborne, Nov. 23, 1803, ibid., 121.

38. Daniel Clark to William Claiborne, Nov. 23, 1803, ibid., 121; Clark to Claiborne, Nov. 29, 1803, ibid., 125.

39. Daniel Clark to William Claiborne, Nov. 29, 1803, ibid., 125; Daniel Clark to Claiborne and Wilkinson, Dec. 12, 1803, ibid., 137; James Wilkinson to the Secretary of War, Dec. 20, 1803, ibid., 138.

40. Daniel Clark to Secretary of State Madison, Nov. 29, 1803, ibid., 123–24; Clark to William Claiborne, Nov. 22, 1803, ibid., 119.

41. Daniel Clark to William Claiborne and James Wilkinson, Nov. 29, 1803, ibid., 125; Clark to Claiborne and Wilkinson, Nov. 30, 1803, ibid.

42. James A. Robertson, *Louisiana under the Rule of Spain, France, and the United States, 1785–1807: Social, Economic, and Political Conditions of the Territory* (Cleveland: Arthur H. Clark, 1911), 77–78, 81–82.

43. William Claiborne to James Madison, Jan. 2, 1804, quoted in Robertson, *Louisiana*, 2: 233; Claiborne to Thomas Jefferson, Jan. 16, 1804, *Territorial Papers*, 9: 161–62; Étienne Boré, Feb. 10, 1804, and Alexandre Baudin, Feb. 14, 1804, to Jefferson, ibid. 182–88; Joseph Dubreuil de Villars, quoted by George Dargo, *Jefferson's Louisiana: Politics and the Clash of Legal Traditions* (Cambridge, Mass.: Harvard University Press, 1975), 29.

44. William B. Hatcher, *Edward Livingston, Jeffersonian Republican and Jacksonian Democrat* (Baton Rouge: Louisiana State University Press, 1940), 103.

45. "Memorial to Congress from the Merchants of New Orleans," Jan. 9, 1804, *Territorial Papers*, 9: 157–58; Daniel Clark to James Madison, Jan. 23, 1804, Daniel Clark Papers, Historical Society of Pennsylvania, Philadelphia.

46. J. Clark, *New Orleans*, 273; Gayarré, *History of Louisiana*, 4: 6–7; Hatcher, *Edward Livingston*, 103; Joseph G. Tregle, *Louisiana in the Age of Jackson: A Clash of Cultures and Personalities* (Baton Rouge: Louisiana State University Press, 1999), 140.

47. D. Clark, *Proofs*, 94.

48. General James Wilkinson to Daniel Clark, June 9, 1805, Wilkinson, *Memoirs*, 2: appendix 13; Clark to Wilkinson, Sept. 7, 1805, ibid., appendix 14.

49. D. Clark, *Proofs*, 98; John Graham to Daniel Clark, May 13, 1807, Daniel Clark Papers, Historical Society of Pennsylvania, Philadelphia. The historian George Dargo believes that Graham's investigation was too superficial and that Burr's suggestion of financial backing from Clark may have been true. Dargo, *Jefferson's Louisiana*, 63–64.

50. Sir Anthony Merry to Lord Mulgrave, Nov. 25, 1805, MS in British Archives, quoted in Henry Adams, *History of the United States of America during the Second*

Administration of Thomas Jefferson (1893; repr., New York: Charles Scribner's Sons, 1921), 1: 230; Thomas R. Hay, "Charles Wilkinson and the Burr Conspiracy," *Journal of Southern History* 2 (1936): 185–87.

51. Daniel Clark to James Wilkinson, Sept. 7, 1805, Wilkinson, *Memoirs* 2: appendix 14; Clark to Wilkinson, April 14, 1806, ibid., 83–84.

52. D. Clark, *Proofs*, 92–93, 97–98; *Louisiana Gazette*, Apr. 8, 1808, p. 2.

53. Deposition of John Graham, Esq., delivered to the Court of Inquiry in Washington, D.C., 1808, quoted in Wilkinson, *Memoirs* 2: 84–85; D. Clark, *Proofs*, 94–95; Daniel Clark to Daniel W. Coxe, Apr. 3, 1806, in *Transcript of Record, Gaines v. City of New Orleans*, 2: 1539; Clark to Coxe, May 15, 1806, ibid., 1544; Clark to Coxe, June 11, 1806, ibid., 1545.

54. William Claiborne to Thomas Jefferson, June 21, 1806, in Rowland Dunbar, ed., *Official Letter Books of W. C. C. Claiborne, 1801–1816* (1817; repr., Jackson, Miss.: State Department of Archives and History, 1983) 3: 339–40; Claiborne to Jefferson, July 9, 1806, *Territorial Papers*, 9: 67; Claiborne to Jefferson, ibid., 673.

55. William Claiborne to Thomas Jefferson, June 1, 1807, *Territorial Papers*, 9: 742–43.

56. John Kendall, "The Humors of the Duello," *Louisiana Historical Quarterly* 23 (1940): 449.

57. U.S. Congress, *Debates and Proceedings* (Washington, D.C.: U.S. Government Printing Office, 1834–56), 9th Cong., 2nd Sess. (Dec. 24, 1805), 215; *Orleans Gazette*, Feb. 2, 1807, p. 2.

58. J. W. Gurley to Richard Keene, May 31 and June 1, 1807, and Keene to Gurley, May 31 and June 1, 1807, Jefferson Papers, Library of Congress; Daniel Clark to Daniel W. Coxe, June 12, 1807, *Transcript of Record, Gaines v. Relf, Chew, and Others*, 756; William Claiborne to James Wilkinson, June 17, 1807, quoted in Henry C. Castellanos, "Duels and Dueling: The Claiborne-Clark Combat—A Chapter in Louisiana History," *New Orleans Times-Democrat*, Oct. 21, 1894, p. 18.

59. Daniel Clark to Daniel W. Coxe, June 12, 1807, *Transcript of Record, Gaines v. Relf, Chew, and Others*, 756; Clark to Coxe, June 14, 1807, ibid., 758.

60. William Claiborne to Thomas Jefferson, June 28, 1807, *Territorial Papers*, 9: 743.

61. Clark epitaph, trans. in *Transcript of Record, Gaines v. Relf, Chew, and Others*, 1149. Twenty years after Daniel Clark's death, his estate became embroiled in litigation over his rightful heir. Myra Clark Whitney Gaines claimed to be his legitimate daughter by a secret marriage to Zulime Carrière, a young Frenchwoman, and the lawsuit she instigated tied up the Clark estate for the next sixty years. The "Great Gaines Case" was celebrated as the "true-life romance of the American courts," and a justice of the U.S. Supreme Court called it "the most remarkable case" ever brought before that court. See Elizabeth Urban Alexander, *Notorious Woman: The Celebrated Case of Myra Clark Gaines* (Baton Rouge: Louisiana State University Press, 2001).

PART IV

Personal Ambition in Government and Military Service

12

William Dunbar, William Claiborne, and Daniel Clark

Intersections of Loyalty and National Identity on the Florida Frontier

ANDREW MCMICHAEL

When the historian David Potter argued in 1962 that historians tend to focus on people not as individuals but as national groups, and to assume that "the identity of people in terms of their national identity . . . transcend[s] all other identities," he meant to challenge historians to think in new ways about how to study and frame the concept of national loyalty in the historical discourse.[1] And while Potter was concerned with what he called "modern institutional nationalism," its interrelationship with Cold War politics, and historians writing within that framework, his call to move away from "treating nationality as objective rather than subjective" has largely gone unheeded by subsequent historians.[2] Scholarship on the Americas from the late twentieth century and the early twenty-first has contained little critique of the idea of standard political nationalism, national identity, and more importantly national loyalty.[3] Yet when Potter argued that loyalty to other entities besides "nation"—such as self, family, community, religion, or even to more ephemeral ideas such as prosperity or peace—played a part in how people eventually constructed national loyalty, he unwittingly spoke to the situation in West Florida and Louisiana after the United States purchased the territory in 1803.

Given the provenance of the Louisiana territory, an understanding of the components of national loyalty should also include a southward look, where Simon Collier has argued that nationalism did not come naturally in Spanish America, meaning that the revolutionaries of the early nineteenth century would have to create it and then help it to develop.[4] The same would be true for the United States in Louisiana. Collier's discussion of Bolivarian nationalism—in which the ultimate expression of nationalism was political in nature and necessitated by the "absence of a genuine ethnic or cultural dimension"—is instructive.[5] In this he too, unwittingly, spoke to the situation in the newly purchased Louisiana territory, which until recently had been Spanish. That is, in Spanish Louisiana national loyalty rested on the political foundation crucial to Bolivarian nationalism, but came with the caveat that people had different "sub-foundations" upon which they rested their political loyalty. Both South America and the Gulf Coast contained people of diverse ethnicities and nationalities whose loyalties the new government would have to co-opt. For the United States this meant getting residents to subsume their previous national and perhaps ethnic loyalties to the new government.

Recent scholarship on the Louisiana Purchase reminds us how important the Gulf Coast region is to the unfolding of America's economic and political history.[6] However, national loyalty in this region has received less attention. The prominent historian Peter Kastor, who has studied Louisiana during the time of the purchase, makes the cogent argument that "the very weakness of nationalist sentiment" on the borderlands meant that residents of the area did not see themselves as either Spanish or French, but rather held a more localist sentiment that did not fully mature into pro-U.S. nationalism until the War of 1812.[7] Prior to the war, Kastor argues that as elsewhere in the South, a greater attachment to localism prevailed. "Localism" can be an ambiguous term. Does it indicate a loyalty to town? Or does it serve to cover other, more difficult-to-assess forms of loyalty such as economic, political, or social self-interest, or even something less definable such as loyalty to a cause or an idea separate from politics? As of yet, few have attempted to outline the kinds of loyalty that might exist apart from nationalism and to try to discover what form those loyalties might take.

Given that, it makes sense to look at the kinds of loyalty that existed in this subjective and localist universe. That is, a closer study of the Louisiana borderlands reveals something about both the mutability of national loyalty on the borderlands as well as about the ways in which national loyalty developed—and perhaps did not—in the Western Hemisphere in the early nineteenth century. Taking the challenge laid down by David Potter to examine national loyalty in a subjective context, and taking into account Kastor's arguments regarding the plasticity of nationality on the Louisiana borderlands, we can look at the period that transits the Louisiana Purchase, 1798–1804, in a new way. And here Simon Collier's analysis of Bolivia helps guide us. The absence of politically based national loyalty means that we have to look for different kinds of loyalty and the ways in which they surfaced in Louisiana during the period 1798–1804.

When the United States formally took possession of the Louisiana Territory from France in 1804 nobody knew exactly what the United States had acquired. President Thomas Jefferson and others knew that it included a great deal of land—more than a whopping five hundred million acres—but not much about what was in it. National interest and national security required, Jefferson believed, an immediate survey of the interior. What was most immediately clear to the president was the need to send an exploratory group—headed by someone trustworthy and loyal—into the interior, and for that team to report its findings. But Jefferson needed information on more than just Gulf Coast flora and fauna. Aside from the Native American tribes and African slaves, the Louisiana Purchase lay at the intersection of French, Spanish, British, and Russian interests and contained residents from those nations.

Jefferson would need a full accounting of the national loyalty of the people in the new area. Securing the loyalties of anyone living in the territory and forming alliances with the Indians would be critical for the United States in order to help buffer expansionist European nations. More importantly Jefferson needed a frank assessment of whether or not the loyalties of the people in the new territories could be counted upon to align with the United States. In this Jefferson worried most about whether or not the varied inhabitants of the new region could be counted on to support the U.S. government, or if their loyalty was such that French residents might support a French invasion, if Spanish loyalists would work to overturn the Treaty of San Ildefonso of 1800, and whether or not Native Americans would throw their support behind one or the other nation. To explore the interior and report on the natural resources and peoples, Jefferson naturally turned to a longtime friend, someone with whom he had corresponded many times on matters of science, politics, and personal matters. That person was William Dunbar. To discover the nature of loyalty on the borderlands, Jefferson turned to William C. C. Claiborne, the new territorial governor after the purchase, and Daniel Clark, a longtime resident and merchant.

These three men help us to understand a few of the different kinds of loyalty existing in the area and provide a lens through which to understand loyalty in the lower Mississippi Valley and Gulf Coast region. William Dunbar presented a loyalty that sprang not from overt Bolivarian political nationalism, but from a kind of scientific and personal loyalty, as evidenced in his role as explorer for both Spain and the United States, as well as his long chain of correspondence with Thomas Jefferson. William Claiborne exhibited a more traditional kind of institutional nationalism in which he firmly identified with the cause of the United States and its expansion. Finally, Daniel Clark's loyalty was economic and personal, and perhaps situational. He aligned himself with that which would bring the most profit, and demonstrated caution in his attempts to do so. Their stories help us to understand better the nature of loyalty, or perhaps the absence of it, on the Gulf Coast borderlands.

In the first few years after the Louisiana Purchase surveyors under direction from President Jefferson crossed Louisiana, Arkansas, Texas, and West Florida, checking boundaries.[8] But it would be William Dunbar who would provide the United States with its best understanding of the physical geography in the southern parts of the new territory. A Scottish immigrant to Philadelphia, and eventually West Florida and Natchez, Dunbar left a diary rich with the details of everyday life on the Spanish-American frontier. In many ways, Dunbar was a southern Benjamin Franklin who made his fortune in a partnership with an original West Florida settler named John Ross (another Scotsman) growing cotton and indigo, and owning slaves.[9] He then retired to a life of scientific observation, introducing the square-bale style of cotton packing to the Deep South, making astronomical observations, conducting experiments, and exploring the frontiers of what would become Arkansas and Texas, first for Spain and then for the United States.[10] He corresponded with Thomas Jefferson on a number of occasions, and Jefferson recommended Dunbar for membership in the American Philosophical Society. Dunbar eventually wrote twelve entries in that society's publications.[11]

But Dunbar's first job was as a surveyor for the Spanish government, when after the signing of Pinckney's Treaty he took the job of ascertaining the boundary at thirty-one degrees latitude between Spanish West Florida and the United States in 1798. His report to Manuel Gayoso de Lemos, then the governor of Spanish West Florida, depicts a rich land full of potential for Spain—both in terms of profit and danger. The danger came first in the form of "innumerable swarms of Gnats, and a variety of other Stinging and biting insects" that plagued his survey party. But the "inconvenience arising from the Winged insects was easily removed by the smoke of a few fires placed around the encampment and a curtain of gauze secured us . . . from the attack of these minute though troublesome creatures."[12] But while the party saw panthers "of a very ferocious nature," black bears, and wolves, it was "the thundering Crocodile, all of hideous forms," that caused the most fascination for the group.[13] Ever the scientist, Dunbar spent several pages of his diary discussing the mating habits and diet of the alligator.

The American alligator as described by Dunbar provides an excellent symbol for the relationship of Europeans to the Gulf Coast's "unsettled" wilderness environment. On the one hand, the alligator, like the frontier, was "hideous in all its forms"—wild and foreign. On the other hand, settlers could conquer both animal and frontier. Dunbar described the alligator, and his relationship to it, in quasi-military terms, noting, "It has been asserted that their skin (resembling a coat of mail) is impenetrable to a musket ball, but I never found any difficulty in piercing them with small rifle bullets unless the stroke [that is, the shot] was made too obliquely." Dunbar spoke in similar terms of subduing the frontier of Louisiana and Texas, and alligators in some ways symbolize the relationship between Europeans and the Gulf Coast—and the ability of Europeans eventually to tame and alter their environment. Dunbar's crew did begin to affect the frontier land immediately on their arrival, as one of the crew accidentally started a fire that burned out of control for many square miles. However, Dunbar saw his fire as a beneficial precursor to settlement and understood it within the context of taming the land and making it useful for settlers.[14]

Trees provided an initial means of income for settlers, and Dunbar describes more than twenty species, including oaks, ash, and two species of elm tree. Daniel Clark also wrote to Thomas Jefferson describing abundant pecan trees growing wild and the orange trees cultivated by planters.[15] The abundance of trees in West Florida enabled residents to produce a variety of wood products. The rot-resistant cypress tree seemed the most versatile, and residents used it for housing materials in the form of shingles, planks, beams, posts, and rails. Inhabitants also used poplar for boat decking, and deciduous trees provided the raw material for making potash. Residents felled white and black oaks to use in a number of products. The lumber output of the area had been marketed to the West Indies since the 1770s, when a Jamaican newspaper featured an advertisement for barrel staves and headings from West Florida.[16] Residents could also trade wood in a variety of places, but settlers sent a great deal to Havana, where after centuries of deforestation a dire need for wood of all types existed.[17]

The Lewis and Clark expedition remains the most significant of the U.S.-sponsored explorations of the Louisiana Purchase, although it was only one among many. That team certainly gathered a great deal of information on their journey through the northern reaches of the purchased land and beyond. But because Jefferson wanted information not just about the vast territory of Louisiana but also Spanish strength along the western boundaries of the recently acquired land, Spain viewed an exploration as a clear threat to its national sovereignty over lands from Texas west to California.[18] That made William Dunbar the perfect choice for a number of reasons to head an expedition into the lower part of Louisiana known as the Red River area in 1804. A longtime resident of the area who had lived in both Natchez and Baton Rouge, he still owned land in Spanish territory and remained on friendly terms with the Spanish government. While Spain also had an interest in Dunbar surveying the Louisiana-Texas border just after the purchase, Dunbar instead accepted his old friend Jefferson's proposal—though he persuaded Jefferson to confine the initial Anglo-European expedition to the Red River.[19] And while Lewis and Clark could evade Spanish troops by going deep into territory largely unexplored by Europeans, Dunbar could hope to use his connections with Spain and knowledge of Spanish culture to avoid problems.

Departing on October 16, 1804, he worked his way up the Red River, cataloging species of birds, making astronomical observations, taking temperature measurements, sounding the river, and conducting scientific experiments. This "Lewis and Clark of the South" forwarded his information back to Jefferson, who catalogued it with the findings of other expeditions. Dunbar finally returned to Natchez in January 1805, three months after leaving.[20] While he found and reported on many of the same things in 1804–5 that he did on his previous expedition, his observations followed a slightly different track. Many of the basic scientific observations are more precise and detailed, befitting a man with ten years of additional experience. However, Dunbar also paid attention to items of strategic detail for the new nation, such as natural features in the land that might make good defensive positions, people he encountered, and especially military activity.[21] Dunbar also wrote a separate analysis, in late 1805 or early 1806, of the various Indian tribes in Louisiana. Here he described their locations, military prowess and ferocity, and alliances when he knew of them—all pieces of information that would help the United States assess the manner in which it would approach relations with the various Native American groups.[22] Dunbar's language is scientific, and no detail of the adventure seems too small for notice.

The significance of his expedition has long been overlooked. While Lewis and Clark opened the northern area of the continent to American expansion—in essence paving what would become the Oregon Trail—Dunbar's expedition, though much shorter and more limited, nevertheless announced the intention of the United States to continue its southern expansion across Louisiana and Arkansas, thereby directly challenging Spain's holdings in Texas and by extension New Spain out to California. For Dunbar the service he rendered represented a personal one to his correspondent and friend Thomas Jefferson, and more ephemerally to the cause of science. Perhaps reflecting his precarious position as a friend of the Spanish government and resident of convoluted borderlands, his writings contain none of the fawning loyalty seen in that of William Claiborne or certainly Daniel Clark, for whom loyalty took much more concrete forms.

For William C. C. Claiborne, his assessment of Louisiana would come from the much more direct experience of governing the massive province. While one historian describes Claiborne as both a "neglected American statesman" and a "dictator of Louisiana," he came to Louisiana with administrative experience and the favor of Jefferson's administration, having previously served as a congressman from Tennessee and then territorial governor of Mississippi. He also maintained interests in the Gulf Coast region.[23] In late 1803 he found himself the administrator of the largest territory the young United States had known—a territory with unknown boundaries to the north and contested boundaries to the east and west. When he came to New Orleans, Claiborne brought with him a contingent of Mississippi militia under the command of General James Wilkinson—an old business partner of Daniel Clark's from the Kentucky tobacco trade. Seeking to impose stability on New Orleans after the transfer of power, Claiborne begged Washington for troops and weapons. His call became more strident when the black militia, a common sight under the Spaniards, held a parade during the transfer ceremonies. Although the Spanish governor of Louisiana, Vicente Folch, remained in the city during the transfer period to assist with the bureaucratic exchange, no Spanish help would be forthcoming, nor did the Americans want any from Spain.[24]

More specific to the problem of national loyalty, in August 1803, Secretary of State James Madison received a detailed report from Claiborne that answered a number of questions posed in response to the problem of what was included in the purchase. Claiborne told Madison that, first, there existed no dependable large-scale maps of the entire area, though he was working to obtain copies of smaller, detailed maps. The Spaniards had made a few maps, but unfortunately for the Americans they had never published them.[25] Of particular concern was the "West Florida Question" regarding what was included in the purchase. Claiborne informed Madison and Jefferson that according to the Treaty of Paris of 1763, and confirmed by "the authority of the oldest settlers in this territory," "New Orleans was the only tract of Country east of the Mississippi included in the Province of Louisiana as then ceded by France to Spain."[26] From there Claiborne went on to describe the various features of the new territory, as he understood them, the nature of the Spanish militia, the disposition of local Native American tribes, land grant issues, the code of laws and the character of Spanish justice, any system of education that might be found in Louisiana, the monetary and tax system, and the state of trade. In many ways, Claiborne's evaluation of 1803 was an intellectual exploration of the Red River, as he gave a rather frank assessment of the state of Louisiana's civil society.

The next year, conditions with regard to loyalty seemed not to have changed all that much. William Claiborne's assessment in 1804 of Louisiana's loyalty toward the U.S. government was not negative, though it was also not glowing. Most district officials took loyalty oaths without question, while a few Spanish officials "graciously" declined to serve the new government; the United States replaced them without trouble. Claiborne believed that most elites transferred their national loyalty to the United States, especially after U.S. assurances of maintaining the status quo vis-à-vis their local power.[27] But loyalty oaths did not guarantee political loyalty. Under Spain's administration the Crown required a loyalty oath to obtain a grant of land, and even Andrew Jackson, future president of the United States, took an oath of loyalty to the Spanish king in order to obtain land.[28] Possibly with this in mind, Claiborne also noted that Louisianans retained what he called a "great partiality for France as their Mother Country" and as well for the Spanish system.[29] More ominously for the United States, Claiborne could not guarantee that Louisiana Creoles would side with the United States in the event of a war, though he thought it possible. A final problem for the U.S. assessment of residents' loyalty was the state of the free blacks, and the free black militia, about which many others have written.[30]

All of these fears were reinforced by the continuing presence in New Orleans of several high-ranking Spanish officials, despite persistent requests by the United States for them to leave—a seeming echo of the events just after Pinckney's Treaty in 1795 when Spanish troops delayed withdrawal from the Natchez district until 1798 while at the same time stirring up anti-U.S. sentiment among local Indian tribes.[31] In fact, while the French withdrew from Louisiana fairly quickly, Spanish officials remained in the city for years. Part of this may have been, as Philip C. Brooks has argued, because of a perceived need to see to the continued defense of Spain's possessions on the Gulf Coast.[32] Equally likely was that a continued Spanish presence in the area would allow Spain to maintain its protest against American possession of Louisiana, and to keep a close eye on American activities while at the same time interfering with U.S. efforts to establish control over Louisiana. In New Orleans, Claiborne worried that the troops and officials not only "weakened the attachment" of what he called "our Citizens" to the government of the United States, but also that their presence reinforced the belief that the U.S. government was only temporary, and that the area of Louisiana west of the Mississippi would soon be returned to Spain.[33] In the course of discussions with Claiborne, Spanish officials (the Marquis de Casa Calvo of New Orleans and Governor Folch of West Florida) apparently expressed surprise that the United States would try to expand west of the Mississippi. Folch, for his part, neatly played on some of the Federalist debates of previous decades when he "introduced the hackneyed argument that a Republican form of Government could not long exist over extensive territories."[34]

Claiborne also insisted that not all in New Orleans, even two years after the purchase, had moved their loyalties over to the United States, and he worried that Spanish officers in the city might combine with the "many adherents to the Spanish interest" against the United States. These Spanish soldiers also had the potential to stir up discord, at least according to American officials. Claiborne's letter to Madison in February 1804 described a near riot between Spanish troops and residents of New Orleans, but it also contained a warning about the "great share of national pride" evident among the American, French, and Spanish soldiers in the city. Those feelings brought resentment among the various soldiers, and Claiborne saw in those troops the seeds of broader problems for U.S. administration of the territory.[35]

More problematically, the U.S. legal system and legal culture brought concerns to Louisianans and served to slow the development of national loyalty. A pair of lengthy letters from Claiborne to Thomas Jefferson and James Madison designed to educate the U.S. administration on various aspects of Louisiana's political, geographical, cultural, and legal situation dwelled at some length on the court system of French-Spanish-French Louisiana. Claiborne noted that the court system generally favored the wealthy, ironically suggesting that this might make the U.S. system a good replacement. He also noted that the province contained no lawyers in the sense of the way the term was understood in the United States, but rather that the Spanish government employed lawyers as administrators.[36] Madison's enquiry into the state of Louisiana was matched by the residents' musings about the U.S. system. Three years after the purchase residents remained upset by the introduction of the English language that went along with the new government. That might have been expected, yet more vexing for them was the trial by jury and the perceived legal wranglings that went along with it. Claiborne informed Madison that many residents, used to trial by a judge, considered trial by jury as "odious—and the lawyers as serious nuisances."[37]

Claiborne's administrative headaches vis-à-vis national loyalty stretched beyond his dealings with whites, of course. The Louisiana Purchase had a deep effect on slaves and Indian tribes. Longtime actors occupying the "middle ground" in the power struggles among Spain, England, France, and then the United States, Native American tribes used their geographic position, their knowledge of terrain, and their abilities as traders to influence the course of larger nations in what Jane Landers has termed "racial geopolitics."[38] Prior to 1763, when Spain took possession of Louisiana, Indians in Louisiana had been firm allies of the French. Through the 1770s Spain maintained alliances with some Indian groups, while fighting against others. At the same time, Spain encouraged inter-tribal warfare as a means of weakening or at least controlling powerful Indian groups in the lower Mississippi.[39] After Pinckney's Treaty,

General Wilkinson in 1798 accused Spain of trying to stir up anti-American sentiment among the Choctaws in and around Natchez. While Manuel Gayoso de Lemos vehemently denied having any hand in the effort, he did not deny that such efforts had been made.[40]

The following year, rumors percolated out of Natchez that the Marquis de Casa Calvo had told Choctaws who had remained loyal to Spain after the American takeover that they would continue to receive Spanish gifts and protection, despite U.S. control over the area.[41] More threatening was the attendant rumor that Casa Calvo was attempting to arrange a pan-Indian conference with the intent of broadly organizing an alliance among the disparate tribes.[42] The American response to the problem of loyalty here was twofold. There was first the problem of a foreign power trying to subvert so-called Indian loyalty in American territory. But Winthrop Sargent also, paternalistically, seemed just as perturbed that the Spanish offer to clothe the Choctaws as part of the gift-giving portion of the conference amounted to an accusation of negligence on the part of the United States.[43] The Marquis de Casa Calvo and other Spaniards of course denied any attempts to engage in "tampering with the Indians" by organizing the tribes into an anti-American alliance, but local Americans in Mississippi nonetheless remained wary of such a possibility.[44] Meanwhile the fact that some seven hundred Choctaws arrived in New Orleans at the same time that rumors circulated about the beginning of an expedition of Spanish gunboats for what the Spaniards called, but Daniel Clark did not believe was, "exploration" must have also given some pause to Americans in Mississippi.[45] That Americans believed the rumors spoke to continued attempts by the Native tribes themselves to play the two powers off against each other.

The period after the Louisiana Purchase held some promise for Native Americans, and Todd Smith argues that tribes in the western portion of Louisiana favored the purchase of the territory by the United States.[46] Even here, though, Spain held some advantage over the United States, having maintained long-established trade contacts with tribes across the area from the Floridas out to California, and generally having established solid alliances with tribes throughout the region.[47] Though rumors of a Spanish-instigated war with Indians and the United States percolated through Mississippi, Louisiana, and the Floridas, nothing ever materialized.[48] To some extent the rumors and conflicts that occurred in Mississippi after Pinckney's Treaty replayed themselves in 1804, but with Texas as the setting. This time Governor Claiborne and the Marquis de Casa Calvo parried accusations that Spaniards were trying to foment disruption among the tribes along the Louisiana-Texas frontier.[49] Spanish officials, of course, denied the stories, but they came at the same time as news that Indian chiefs and priests had spread rumors of a Louisiana–West Florida trade. Whatever the case, Native Americans' place in between the two European powers certainly gave them some autonomy and power for so long as the two powers needed the tribes as proxies in their battle over the Louisiana frontier.

For slaves, the purchase had a more startling effect. In late 1804 Spanish officials in Nacogdoches, in Spanish Texas, spread news of a royal decree that offered asylum to any slave escaping from American-held Louisiana into the province of Texas. Officials in New Orleans, including Casa Calvo, confirmed its existence.[50] Within weeks rumors of insurrection spread through the lower part of the Louisiana district, and slaves began fleeing American territory for Texas. More frighteningly for whites, some of the slaves took powder and shot with them, raising the specter of armed rebellion. Other slaves told whites that they "knew" that if they fled to Spanish territory the Spaniards would free them, having been told such by Spanish officials and Spanish agents living in and around Nacogdoches.[51] Spain had used this policy to great effect in East Florida in the late seventeenth century and the early eighteenth in an attempt to destabilize the British colony in South Carolina.[52] By late 1804 Claiborne described "a spirit of insurrection" among the slaves at Point Coupée—the site of a rebellion in 1795—and that slaves in that area carried copies of the Spanish proclamation.[53] The decree seemed to have its intended effect as a much-angered Claiborne dispatched troops to Point Coupée, occupied himself with trying to reclaim slaves who had fled to Spanish Nacogdoches, and pleaded with Casa Calvo to rescind the decree. As governor of Louisiana Claiborne could do little but beg. Through 1808 the fugitive slave policy was still in effect, and slaves continued to find refuge in Texas.[54] Perhaps reflecting West Florida's more unstable position with regard to relations between the United States and Spain as well as intercommunity relations between West Floridians and merchants in New Orleans, West Floridians promptly returned fugitive American slaves who had escaped to West Florida.[55]

Of course, the French and Spanish legal systems differed greatly from whatever the Americans would institute, and the same held true for slavery. When the United States took control of Louisiana west of the Mississippi, it at first tried to institute American law in the territory and may have assumed that the Anglo-American forms of race relations would follow. The first territorial legislature, composed mostly of native-born Louisianans, tried to retain most of the Spanish system of law through an act of the legislature. As opposed to French, British, and U.S. law, Spain operated under the principle of civil rather than common law. As noted, Louisianans in 1803 wanted no part of the U.S. courts, or common law, with its system of precedents. The fear among inhabitants was that Jefferson would ban slavery in the new territories, citing as precedent the actions of the Continental Congress with regard to the Northwest Territory. Indeed, the United States had banned new slave importations into the Louisiana territory, and Jefferson endorsed closing the foreign trade into Louisiana altogether.[56]

William Claiborne vetoed the act of the Louisiana legislature, but he agreed to a compromise in 1808 based on Spanish law but that put in place the more stringent measures of the French Code.[57] The compromise solidified Louisiana's Black Code of 1807, which had negated or weakened several components of Spanish law. Slaves could no longer purchase themselves, owners wishing to manumit slaves needed government permission, and removal from a cruel master became next to impossible.[58] So although the code contained a few of the forms of French slave law, it seemed directed toward establishing something similar to the U.S. system of racial and social control that had evolved over the previous two hundred years, and which succeeded in erasing what Americans found as "the objectionable aspects of Spanish slave law."[59]

For Claiborne, then, his loyalty took an institutional form, wedded to his job as administrator of the Louisiana territory. Indeed his economic, personal, and national interests were already tied to the United States before he came to Louisiana, and as governor he did all in his power to assist his nation in the transition from Spanish to French to U.S. territory. As governor of the Louisiana territory, Claiborne had to assess, manage, cultivate, and at times work around the loyalties of a multiplicity of peoples in Louisiana. As an administrator his first loyalty lay to the United States, and so his main task at the time of the Louisiana Purchase involved thinking less about the status of his own loyalty than that of others. In this he was quite unlike Daniel Clark, an entrepreneur and politician whose Gulf Coast story begins in the 1790s.

As noted, assessing national loyalty in the Mississippi Valley in general, and the Gulf Coast in particular, had always been a difficult problem. People such as William Dunbar, Daniel Clark, and, certainly, James Wilkinson, and others frequently worked for both governments, whether as spies, casual informants, explorers, or translators. Their loyalty for the most part hinged on their paychecks, though some did have deeper patriotism toward one or the other government. Clark had been one of the original American merchants to settle in New Orleans, and he first received a land grant of five hundred acres from the British in 1770.[60] He emigrated from Ireland to New Orleans in the 1780s, and at the time of the French transfer served as the U.S. consular agent in New Orleans, and maintained commercial and political connections throughout the United States.[61] Clark's uncle, also named Daniel Clark and often referred to as Daniel Clark, Sr., bought a plantation in Natchez, Mississippi, and maps of West Florida and Feliciana list Daniel Clark, Jr., as a landowner.[62] He counted himself among the aristocracy of New Orleans, having, among other things, introduced the first cotton gin to the city after reading a report of Eli Whitney's design in a local newspaper.[63]

His writing hints at a well-educated and wealthy man who spoke of an annual income of some eight thousand dollars in the 1790s and who littered his prose with Latin phrases when he corresponded with those he thought above his own station.[64] Following a pattern common to New Orleans at the time, Clark did not specialize in any single business, serving as director of at least two banks and owning a cordage factory situated on Royal Street.[65] He also helped General James Wilkinson manage Wilkinson's Spanish-guaranteed monopoly on goods shipped from Kentucky through New Orleans in the 1790s.[66] This potential for conflict of interest, where a man like Clark might find himself on two sides of an international business dispute, remained fairly common through the early American period, and it caused some friction among planters and merchants.[67] Meanwhile, through 1795 and 1796 Clark played both sides off against each other, on the one hand working closely with the Spanish officials Manuel Gayoso de Lemos and the Baron de Carondelet to help maintain the Spanish government in Louisiana and Florida.[68] On the other hand, he encouraged American settlement in Louisiana and West Florida, writing to General James Wilkinson, "I love America, I have long ate her bread: She adopt'd me easily in life as a son—she furnished me with a wife whom my son adores, and I shall ever retain for her a strong national Gratitude."[69]

Aside from the loyalty to state, men such as Daniel Clark developed deep personal friendships with—and, it should be noted, serious animosity toward—men in both governments. Nowhere is that example clearer than in a series of letters from Manuel Gayoso de Lemos, then the governor of the Natchez district, to Daniel Clark in 1796. Writing to Clark after a journey from Pointe Coupée to New Orleans, Gayoso stated that Clark's "effectionate [sic] friendly letter" and its sentiments were "not greater than the attachment" Gayoso had for Clark.[70]

Correspondence between the two men, going back as early as 1792, runs the gamut from the demonstrative assurances of mutual friendship and affection to the more mundane recounting of a demonstration of Clark's cotton gin.[71] Each man also knew that the other might help fulfill private ambitions. In the case of Gayoso it meant that Clark, and through him perhaps Clark's friend Wilkinson, might help Gayoso realize his plans of causing problems for the United States by separating the western United States, including Tennessee and Wilkinson's Kentucky, from the mother country. For Clark Gayoso represented both friendship and a path toward greater wealth through access to

Spanish lands. While Clark gave Gayoso information regarding politics in the lower Mississippi Valley, introduced Gayoso to a more efficient cotton gin, and provided Gayoso's acquaintances with an entrée into American immigrant society, Gayoso reciprocated by resolving legal disputes, helping Clark financially during crop failures, and generally serving as Clark's entrée into Spanish society.[72]

Where, then, was the loyalty—even prior to the Louisiana Purchase when the United States had not yet become a full-fledged power in the Mississippi Valley? The correspondence of the two men suggests a deep sense of mutual personal loyalty that may have transcended national ideology, and Clark's actions in this and later periods more than hint at his lack of anything resembling national loyalty. He was as friendly and devoted to the interests and people of the United States as those of Spain.[73] Gayoso, who worked to cleave the western United States from areas east of the Appalachians, was nothing if not a Spanish patriot. Yet though his first wife was a Spaniard, his next two—married in Louisiana where Spanish women generally did not settle—came from the United States. More importantly, one can see the substance of Gayoso's loyalty in something he once wrote an Indian chief, stating, "If I am anything else than a Spaniard, I am an American as I have married one."[74] Gayoso, unlike Clark, retained a high degree of national loyalty toward Spain. But then he also came from a country with hundreds of years of national history, and where one's position in the government, and therefore one's easiest path to honor, social status, and wealth, depended on loyalty to a sovereign.

Prior to the Louisiana Purchase, in late 1797, Gayoso penned a letter to the king of Spain shortly after taking an extended trip through Tennessee, Kentucky, Virginia, Pennsylvania, Illinois, and Michigan. In letters that made their way to the U.S. government, Gayoso gave a frank assessment of American loyalty on the Tennessee and Kentucky borderlands. The stated purpose of the trip was to allow the Spanish government to follow up on Citizen Genêt's attempts to separate parts of the west from the United States, and allow Spain to assess the loyalty of Americans west of the Appalachians. In the main, Gayoso described the loyalty of Americans in the western frontier as up for grabs.[75]

On the one hand, he spoke against any hopes Spain might have embraced, noting in 1797 that "the dissatisfaction existing among the people four years ago had quieted down" and that Wilkinson felt that western inhabitants had no motive or desire to separate from the United States. Further, Wilkinson declared that Kentuckians had promised to gather an army of some three thousand men to invade Louisiana should the United States and Spain go to war. In part, Wilkinson was engaging in the kind of speculation that permeated documents from this time period. But Wilkinson also told Gayoso that he might be named governor of the new territory around Natchez, and from there he could more effectively execute their shared schemes.[76]

One the other hand, Gayoso presented his king with the observations of Benjamin Sebastian, a judge on the Court of Appeals in Kentucky.[77] Sebastian believed that war with the United States would provide Spain with an "effective way of turning [Kentuckians] against the States of the East." Here Gayoso's opinions and those of Sebastian become indistinguishable, as Gayoso argues that elites in Kentucky, Tennessee, and the Northwest Territory supported Genêt and that given the current climate of hostility between France and the United States, "they are enemies of those that are enemies of the French." Gayoso then outlined three conditions that either he or Sebastian felt might impel the western states to secede from the Union. First, an outbreak of war with France would inflame what he believed to be pro-French sentiment among westerners. Second, any attempt by the United States to either settle in Spanish territory or close navigation of the Mississippi River would raise ire. This last point is fraught with the irony that the closure of the Mississippi River to American navigation by a Spanish official in 1802 was what drove the United States into the Louisiana Purchase, thus destroying any plans Spain might have had with regard to halting American expansion. Finally, Gayoso felt that if the United States forced the issue of tax collection in the west, settlers might respond with force and then be receptive to Spanish overtures. Moreover, the United States maintained negligible forces in the west, and those that did exist were poorly trained and lacked "all the qualities (except bravery) that a good soldier should have."[78]

When Governor Claiborne arrived in New Orleans in 1803, he saw a solution to his militia troubles in the person of Daniel Clark—a man with whom he did not get along, and with whom he would fight a duel in 1807. Claiborne asked Clark to organize the first militia in New Orleans under American control. The force consisted of more than 350 men and included both Americans and French Creoles, but no blacks or resident Spaniards. Clark chose as his militia colonel Reuben Kemper, a resident of New Orleans, a fellow merchant, and a friend, who maintained business connections in New Orleans and, through his brothers Samuel and Nathan, had land interests in the Feliciana district.[79] This connection to the Baton Rouge area (of which the Felicianas were part) was typical. Many people owned land in New Orleans, the Baton Rouge district, across the river in Point Coupée, in Mississippi above the thirty-one-degree mark, and in other parts of Florida such as Mobile or Pensacola. The next task for Clark was to help Jefferson determine what had been included in the purchase, and then set about exploring that territory.

In 1803 Jefferson and Madison began to inquire about a controversy over whether or not West Florida had been included in the Louisiana Purchase. Wanting someone with knowledge about the area, they wrote to Clark—one of the most geographically knowledgeable Americans in the area and lately in the employ of the United States as U.S. consul. Madison's letters, especially, reveal the depth of confusion surrounding the administration's understanding of what was included in the purchase. Asking for "all the information you may be able to give" as to the exact boundaries of Louisiana, Madison also asked Clark to serve as a liaison between French and American officials.[80] With regard to the boundaries, Clark concluded that the line of cession conformed to the Treaty of 1763, in essence telling Jefferson that the boundaries claimed by the Spanish were valid and that West Florida was firmly a Spanish possession. This conclusion made Clark, who owned a great deal of land on both sides of the Spanish-American border, subject to two very different methods of land distribution and administration.[81] Clark had a great deal to gain if West Florida became an American territory. American control of West Florida would certainly open the area up to land speculation, a venture in which he would have no small influence and would be ideally situated to exploit.

At the same time, controversy over the boundaries could bring conflict between the United States and Spain. As a merchant with wide interests in the city Clark could expect to profit handsomely from any problems. He chose, however, to adhere to a strict legal interpretation of the boundaries, while Jefferson chose to ignore him. In all likelihood, Clark was merely hedging his bets, not wishing to alienate either national power until one gained complete control over the borderlands. At the same time, Clark had other personal motivations for his loyalty. When Louisiana became U.S. territory, Clark's office of U.S. consul—and the pay, social status, and access that came with it—came to an end. When Clark found himself without a job in the new government, he seemed to take the situation personally, with much of his ire directed at, among others, William Claiborne.[82]

Yet he also sought to profit. Sometime in 1803, after news of the purchase had reached New Orleans and West Florida, but while the territory was still under French/Spanish control, Clark purchased a tract of 208,000 acres on the Ouachita River in present-day north central Louisiana. Clark capitalized on fear of possible chaos following the change, purchasing as much local land as he possibly could, and quickly turned himself into one of the largest single landholders in the Mississippi Valley. From Thomas Urquhart, Clark purchased nine separate plots in and around the area of Baton Rouge and Feliciana. The land totaled more than 96,000 arpents in size, with the largest plot at 50,000 arpents and the smallest at 602 arpents. These sales placed Clark in a position to capitalize on settlement in West Florida by reselling land to incoming Americans.[83]

It also highlighted the issue of economic loyalty, which can be seen in the actions of both Clark and Juan Ventura Morales, the man who has received the blame for the closure of the port of New Orleans.[84] Given the nature of land sales in West Florida, and the lengths to which Spain seemed to go to ensure an adequate distribution of land, the problems created by Morales struck at the heart of governmental stability in the area in and around the Louisiana Purchase. In 1804 Morales held the titles of paymaster general and intendant pro tempore of West Florida. Described by Claiborne as a man with "more information, but less principle than any Spanish officer," Morales had already been in trouble with his own government for diverting money from the Crown and failing to account for a number of transactions under his responsibility.[85] In light of those actions Claiborne suggested that Spain put Morales on trial under the American court system, though no records exist of this actually ocurring.[86] More interestingly, according to Claiborne, Morales had been at the heart of a plot—along with Daniel Clark—to remove Claiborne from his position as governor, was also rumored to "command in cash five hundred thousand dollars," paid regular bribes to speculators in the city, and was perhaps working with Daniel Clark to further land speculation in West Florida.[87] How much of this is true cannot be known with any certainty, but Claiborne's letters discuss the issue in a manner that suggests that he thought he was reflecting a widespread belief.

What is certain is that sometime before June 1805 Morales set up a land office in New Orleans and began selling large tracts of the Crown's land in eastern West Florida near Pensacola. The rumor in New Orleans was that he had been "instructed by the King of Spain to depose of all the vacant lands in East and West Florida," and therefore acted under the authority of the Spanish government.[88] Given that the Spanish government had been giving away land grants to Americans in West Florida up through 1803 but had then halted them, Morales's actions smacked of profiteering. Additionally, to Americans it must have appeared that the Crown's officials, thinking that the United States and Spain would trade West Florida and Louisiana, were trying to profit from land sales prior to handing over the territory. Finally, as Claiborne asserted to James Madison, rumors that some of the land had been purchased by Spanish officials who intended to engage in speculation began to circulate through New Orleans.[89]

A suspicious Claiborne asked for clarification from Casa Calvo, who initially professed not to know anything about the order, then stated that he believed the Crown had issued the order. Casa Calvo then promised to halt the sales until he could undertake an investigation.[90] More interestingly, the tone of Claiborne's letters indicates a sense of possessiveness regarding East and West Florida, as if the Spanish Crown did not have the right to sell its own land. Claiborne explained this attitude as being consistent with the fact that the United States claimed West Florida as part of the Louisiana Purchase, that Spain and the United States were engaged in negotiations to resolve that dispute, and that selling the disputed land would be improper and would harm relations between the two countries.[91] Casa Calvo, for his part, stated that Morales was acting without authority by misinterpreting a royal order regarding the survey of the Crown's lands in West Florida for new immigrants.[92] Though Morales did claim to be acting on a royal order, no local governors seem to have been informed of it.[93] The land sales, as Morales stated, were an effort by the Crown to gain "all profitable advantages in favor of the Royal Chest" and the order had come straight from the Crown, circumventing the local governors.[94]

Part of Casa Calvo's responses were classic Spanish bureaucratic obfuscation of the type seen everywhere in the empire. But land sales resumed for a time, despite Claiborne's requests that they halt, that Morales's office be closed, and that Morales be expelled from the territory as per the provisions of the treaty of cession.[95] Claiborne reported to James Madison that many leading citizens of New Orleans visited Morales to purchase land.[96] A note in late August from Morales to Claiborne explaining his actions reveals that Morales had taken a rather liberal interpretation of his duties "to regulate and conclude the affairs of interest belonging to Spain in the Province of Louisiana."[97] Under pressure from Spanish and American officials, Morales finally agreed to stop selling the Crown's lands, though he had already sold off more than one million acres in the area east of Baton Rouge out to Mobile. Apparently Morales sold no land in or around Baton Rouge, including the Felicianas.

Some Spaniards—unauthorized or not—selling the Crown's land in West Florida while others were simultaneously buying land had potentially grave effects on the Louisiana–West Florida issue and the development and maintenance of national loyalty in West Florida. On the one hand, Spain's offer to grant land in Matanzas to Floridians wishing to vacate their holdings seemed to confirm the rumor that Spain intended to abandon claims to West Florida, especially given that rumors to this effect were flowing rather freely throughout Louisiana and West Florida already.[98] Claiborne argued such to Madison in August.[99] In fact, the Crown had no intention whatsoever of abandoning its remaining holdings in North America. In the minds of American officials, these problems reinforced the already extant stereotypes regarding Spanish corruption, inefficiency, and inability to control its overseas empire. This issue contributed to the instability in the Gulf region, as residents could not be sure of the long-term tenure of their parent government. On the other hand, Morales was not alone in his efforts to profit from the transfer of power, as elites in New Orleans and West Florida who had bought land from him and each other then turned around and sold their holdings to newcomers, some of whom were intent on becoming the area's new elite.[100]

What do the lives and actions of these disparate men tell us about national loyalty on the Gulf Coast? What we see, most specifically, is the multifaceted nature, as well as the mutability, of national loyalty and identity on the Gulf Coast borderlands and the degree to which political nationalism—inasmuch as it existed—relied on local issues and the promise of prosperity rather than loyalty to any single political entity. For William Dunbar, a Scottish immigrant to British West Florida who then lived under successive Spanish and U.S. governments, his scientific interests and affiliations with scientific societies in the United States and Europe certainly influenced his nationalism and loyalty. He corresponded equally and—as far as the records admit—honestly with Spaniard and American alike, helping further science and exploration for both nations.

William Claiborne's political loyalty, which stretched back to his tenure as governor of the Mississippi Territory, would never seriously be questioned, and he survived the many intrigues aimed at unseating him. Upon his arrival in New Orleans he set about creating an administrative framework that would at once stabilize and then further American interests on the Gulf Coast. His writings reflect his political loyalties.

Daniel Clark, a frontier trader, banker, and land speculator, brought a more personal dimension to the economic aspects of national loyalty. He migrated from Ireland for what one would presume were economic opportunities, and the Gulf Coast presented him with the most promise. His writings and actions, too, reflect his loyalty to self, as he pledged loyalty to Spain and the United States, in turn, and sought to profit from the instability following the Louisiana Purchase.

Of course, this assessment leaves out a great many factors that affect national loyalty. As David Potter points out, "difference" does not equate to "dissent," and white Louisianans ultimately found enough in commonality—fear of French intrigue and of refugees from Saint Domingue, for example—to forge a national loyalty centered on the United States. Perhaps all three men believed there to be something inevitable about U.S. economic, military, and nationalist power, especially given the absence after 1803 of any other strong power. As Simon Collier points out, some unity was required for "greater prosperity and autonomy," and certainly all three men—Dunbar, Claiborne, and Clark—saw that necessity on the Gulf Coast.

Notes

1. Portions of this chapter have previously appeared in Andrew McMichael, *Atlantic Loyalties: Americans in Spanish West Florida, 1785–1810* (Athens: University of Georgia Press, 2008); David M. Potter, "The Historian's Use of Nationalism and Vice Versa," *American Historical Review* 67 (1962): 924.

2. Potter, "The Historian's Use of Nationalism and Vice Versa," 928.

3. Two excellent reassessments of how national loyalty can be created and broken with regard to land and wealth can be found in Leslie Hall, *Land and Allegiance in Revolutionary Georgia* (Athens: University of Georgia Press, 2001); and Woody Holton, *Forced Founders: Indians, Debtors, Slaves, and the Making of the American Revolution in Virginia* (Chapel Hill: University of North Carolina Press, 1999).

4. Simon Bolivar and Simon Collier, "Nationality, Nationalism, and Supranationalism in the Writings of Simón Bolívar," *Hispanic American Historical Review* 63, no. 1 (February 1983): 39.

5. Ibid., 43.

6. See, especially, James G. Cusick, *The Other War of 1812: The Patriot War and the American Invasion of Spanish East Florida* (Gainesville: University Press of Florida, 2003); and Peter J. Kastor, *The Nation's Crucible: The Louisiana Purchase and the Creation of America* (New Haven, Conn.: Yale University Press, 2004).

7. Kastor, *The Nation's Crucible*, 28.

8. Daniel Clark, an American living in New Orleans who had deep ties with the Spanish government, proved especially valuable to Madison in determining the boundaries. See, for example, Madison's continuing requests for information in James Madison to Daniel Clark, Sept. 16, 1803, in *Consular Instructions of the Department of State, 1801–1834*, vol. 1, Oct. 12, 1801–Feb. 26, 1817, microfilm 78, roll 1, National Archives and Records Administration (hereafter NARA); Isaac Joslin Cox, *The West Florida Controversy, 1798–1813: A Study in American Diplomacy* (Baltimore: Johns Hopkins University Press, 1918), 88.

9. Mrs. Dunbar Rowland, ed., *The Life, Letters, and Papers of William Dunbar of Elgin, Moray Shire, Scotland, and Natchez, Mississippi, Pioneer Scientist of the Southern United States* (Jackson: Press of the Mississippi Historical Society, 1930), 9.

10. Ibid., 10.

11. Ibid., 11–12. Dunbar also founded the Mississippi Society for the Acquirement and Dissemination of Useful Knowledge, a society apparently devoted to something along the lines of the American Philosophical Society. *Mississippi Herald and Natchez Gazette*, Nov. 19, 1804, vol. 3 no. 16, p. 4.

12. "Report of William Dunbar to the Spanish Government at the Conclusion of His Services in Locating and Surveying the Thirty-First Degree of Latitude," in Rowland, *The Life, Letters, and Papers of William Dunbar*, 82.

13. Ibid. Dunbar initially labels the reptile a "Crocodile." After the first iteration, however, he uses the word "Alligator."

14. Ibid., quotes, 90, 91, 83. The classic study of the ways in which colonists affected their environment is William Cronon's *Changes in the Land: Indians, Colonists, and the Ecology of New England* (New York: Hill and Wang, 1983). Thomas Vale's *Fire, Native Peoples, and the Natural Landscape* (Washington, D.C.: Island Press, 2002) contains a series of essays examining the role of fire in Native Americans' intentional alteration of the natural landscape. Though the essays focus on the trans-Rockies west, Vale's own essay, "The Pre-European Landscape of the United States: Pristine or Humanized," makes a good case that Indians throughout North America used fire to change the land dramatically. Several excellent studies on the area around Baton Rouge exist, however. In particular, for more on reshaping and commodifying the environment of the lower Mississippi Valley around Baton Rouge and New Orleans in the seventeenth and eighteenth centuries, see Christopher Morris, "Impenetrable but Easy: The French Transformation of the Lower Mississippi Valley and the Founding of New Orleans," in *Transforming New Orleans and Its Environs* (Pittsburgh: University of Pittsburgh Press, 2000). For the environmental problems facing East Floridians during settlement, see James J. Miller, *An Environmental History of Northeast Florida* (Gainesville: University Press of Florida, 1998).

15. Daniel Clark to Thomas Jefferson, Nov. 12, 1799, Library of Congress, Jefferson Papers. On the relationship between settlers and the forest environment, see Timothy Silver, *A New Face on the Countryside: Indians, Colonists, and Slaves in South Atlantic Forests, 1500–1800* (New York: Cambridge University Press, 1990).

16. Robin Fabel, *Colonial Challenges: Britons, Native Americans, and Caribs, 1759–1775* (Gainesville: University Press of Florida, 2000), 120.

17. See Archivo Nacional de Cuba (hereafter ANC), Fondo: Comercio, Legajo 73, no. 2796, for a complete list of all goods exchanged between Spanish ports in the New World and Old in 1803. The commodities traded in New Orleans do not represent the norm for Baton Rouge. In fact, no complete list of goods traded in and out of Baton Rouge exists for any year. In part this is because some residents of West Florida traded through Mobile or Pensacola, while others went through New Orleans, where their produce was probably recorded. Still others smuggled their goods out past customs agents. However, James Cusick's "Across the Border: Commodity Flow and Merchants in Spanish St. Augustine," *Florida Historical Quarterly* 69, no. 3 (January 1991): 277–99 provides excellent detail for another Florida port.

18. A. P. Nasatir, "Anglo-Spanish Rivalry on the Upper Missouri," *Mississippi Valley Historical Review* 16, no. 4. (March 1930): 526.

19. Unknown to William Dunbar, *Miscellaneous Letters Sent by the Secretary of War, 1800–1809*, microfilm, M-370, roll 2, NARA; Thomas Jefferson to William Dunbar, March 13, and April 15, 1804, *The Thomas Jefferson Papers at the Library of Congress*, http://memory.loc.gov/ammem/mtjhtml/mtjhome.html.

20. A full account of this expedition, which had not yet been written about, can be found in Rowland, *The Life, Letters, and Papers of William Dunbar*, 216–320.

21. See, for example, "Tuesday 6th," in ibid., 235–36.

22. "Dunbar on Indians of Louisiana," in ibid., 209–14.

23. Joe Gray Taylor, *Louisiana: A Bicentennial History* (New York: W. W. Norton and Company, 1976), 42, 47. For an analysis of Claiborne's influence on Spanish policy, see Jared Bradley, "W. C. C. Claiborne and Spain: Foreign Affairs under Jefferson and Madison, 1801–1811," *Louisiana History* 12 (Fall 1971): 297–314.

24. A short history of Folch's intendancy in West Florida can be found in David Hart White, *Vicente Folch, Governor in Spanish Florida, 1787–1811* (Washington, D.C.: University Press of America, 1981).

25. William C. C. Claiborne to Unnamed, Aug. 24, 1803 in *State Department Territorial Papers, Orleans Series, 1764–1813: Volume 2, August 19, 1803–December 27, 1803*, in microfilm, T-260, roll 2, NARA.

26. Ibid.

27. Among the many letters outlining the transfer of power and its effects on elite loyalty, see the fifteen-page enclosure in *State Department Territorial Papers, Orleans*, in microfilm, T-260, roll 3, NARA; also John Watkins to William Claiborne, Feb. 2, 1804, enclosure in William Claiborne to James Madison, March 1, 1804, William Claiborne to James Madison, March 1, 1804, in Mary Hackett, ed., *Papers of James Madison: Secretary of State Series* (Charlottesville: University of Virginia Press, 2002), 6: 524–25.

28. Robert Remini, "Andrew Jackson Takes an Oath of Allegiance to Spain," *Tennessee Historical Quarterly* 54, no. 1 (1995): 2–15. On land acquisition, see Light T. Cummins, "Spanish Louisiana Land Policy: Antecedent to the Anglo-American Colonization of East Texas, 1769–1821," *East Texas Historical Journal* 33, no. 1 (1995): 18–26; and Gilbert C. Din, "Proposals and Plans for Colonization in Spanish Louisiana, 1787–1790," *Louisiana History* 11 (Summer 1970): 197–213.

29. William C. C. Claiborne to the Secretary of State, April 29, 1806, *State Department Territorial Papers, Orleans*, microfilm, T-260, roll 8, NARA.

30. See also Kim Hanger, *Bounded Lives, Bounded Places: Free Black Society in Colonial New Orleans, 1769–1803* (Durham, N.C.: Duke University Press, 1997). Hanger's, "Conflicting Loyalties: The French Revolution and Free People of Color in Spanish New Orleans," *Louisiana History* 34, no. 1 (1993): 5–33, provides an excellent analysis of how Spain dealt with the problem of loyalty among free blacks.

31. This was a serious problem for U.S. officials, who suspected the Spaniards of plotting to return New Orleans and Louisiana to Spanish control. Among others, see William Claiborne to the Marquis de Casa Calvo, Aug. 10, 1805, William Claiborne to the Marquis de Casa Calvo, Aug. 17, 1805 in *State Department Territorial Papers, Orleans*, microfilm, T-260, roll 7, NARA; William C. C. Claiborne to James Madison, Jan. 7, 1806, William C. C. Claiborne to James Madison, Jan. 9, 1806, William C. C. Claiborne to Major Porter, Jan. 12, 1806 in *State Department Territorial Papers, Orleans*, microfilm, T-260, roll 8, NARA; Manuel Gayoso de Lemos to General James Wilkinson, March 30, 1798 in *Letters Received by the Secretary of War*, microfilm, M-222, roll

1, NARA. That Spain intentionally delayed its withdrawal is generally recognized, and the Spanish ability to bureaucratically obfuscate is legendary. In specific relation to the issue of boundary lines, see the Baron de Carondelet to Brigadier General James Wilkinson, May 23, 1797, in Ibid., in which Carondelet expresses the concerns of a local commander, Carlos de Hault de Lassus, that without a continuing Spanish presence in Natchez the local Chickasaw tribes might find themselves subject to abuse by former Spanish subjects and incoming American settlers.

32. Philip C. Brooks, "Spain's Farewell to Louisiana, 1803–1821," *Mississippi Valley Historical Review* 27, no. 1 (June 1940): 29.

33. William C. C. Claiborne to James Madison, Jan. 7, 1806, *State Department Territorial Papers, Orleans, 1764–1823*, microfilm, T-260, roll 8, NARA.

34. William C. C. Claiborne to James Madison, April 21, 1805, *State Department Territorial Papers, Orleans*, microfilm, T-260, roll 6, NARA.

35. William C. C. Claiborne to James Madison, Feb. 4, 1804, in Hackett, *Papers of James Madison*, 6: 428.

36. William C. C. Claiborne to Thomas Jefferson, Aug. 24, 1803, *The Thomas Jefferson Papers. Series 1: General Correspondence, 1651–1827*, the Library of Congress, American Memory, http://memory.loc.gov/ammem/collections/jefferson_papers/; "From William C. C. Claiborne" [probably to James Madison] (undated, probably mid-1804), *State Department Territorial Papers, Orleans*, microfilm, T-260, roll 4, NARA.

37. William C. C. Claiborne to James Madison, May 16, 1806, *State Department Territorial Papers, Orleans*, microfilm, T-260, roll 8, NARA. My understanding of the Gulf Coast borderlands during this period is informed by Charles Cutter, *The Legal Culture of Northern New Spain* (Albuquerque: University of New Mexico Press, 1995); and Judith Kelleher Schafer, *Slavery, the Civil Law, and the Supreme Court of Louisiana* (Baton Rouge: Louisiana State University Press, 1994).

38. Fabel, *Colonial Challenges*; Jane Landers, *Black Society in Spanish Florida* (Urbana: University of Illinois Press, 1999), 229; Richard White, *The Middle Ground: Indians, Empires, and Republics in the Great Lakes Region, 1650–1815* (1991; repr., Cambridge: Cambridge University Press, 1995); see also Paul E. Hoffman, *Florida's Frontiers* (Bloomington: Indiana University Press, 2002).

39. David J. Weber, *Bárbaros: Spaniards and Their Savages in the Age of Enlightenment* (New Haven, Conn.: Yale University Press, 2005), 146.

40. Manuel Gayoso de Lemos to General James Wilkinson, March 30, 1798, *Letters Received by the Secretary of War*, microfilm, M-222, roll 1, NARA.

41. Winthrop Sargent to Evan Jones, Nov. 7, 1799, *Despatches from U.S. Consuls in New Orleans*, microfilm, T-225, roll 1, NARA.

42. Ibid; Evan Jones to Timothy Pickering, Nov. 8, 1799, ibid.

43. Winthrop Sargent to Evan Jones, Nov. 7, 1799, ibid.

44. Evan Jones to Timothy Pickering, Nov. 8, 1799, Evan Jones to Winthrop Sargent, Nov. 16, 1799, ibid.

45. Daniel Clark to Evan Pickering, Nov. 18, 1799, ibid.

46. Todd Smith, "Indian Policy in Spanish Louisiana," in Gilbert Din, ed., *The Spanish Presence in Louisiana, 1763-1803* (Lafayette: Center for Louisiana Studies, University of Southwestern Louisiana, 1996), 293.

47. Among the many others, Weber's *Bárbaros* details treaties of friendship, alliance, travel, tribute, and other signs of amity stretching from coast to coast and across the centuries.

48. "Extract of a Letter from Capt. R. S. Blackburn to Lt. Colonel Constant Freeman," April 8, 1802, *Despatches from U.S. Consuls in New Orleans*, microfilm, T-225, roll 1, NARA.

49. William Claiborne to the Marquis de Casa Calvo, Oct. 31, 1804, *State Department Territorial Papers, Orleans*, microfilm, T-260, roll 5, NARA.

50. William Claiborne to James Madison, Sept. 1, 1804; Derbigny to William Claiborne, Sept. 5, 1804; William Claiborne to James Madison, Sept. 8, 1804, in ibid.

51. (Unreadable) to William Claiborne, Oct. 16, 1804, *State Department Territorial Papers, Orleans*, microfilm, T-260, roll 6, NARA; (unreadable) to William Claiborne, Dec. 27, 1804, ibid.

52. Landers, *Black Society in Spanish Florida*, 24-28.

53. William Claiborne to Colonel Butler, Nov. 8, 1804; William Claiborne to the Marquis de Casa Calvo, Nov. 8, 1804; William Claiborne to "The Commandant at Nachitoches [sic]," Nov. 8, 1804, all in *State Department Territorial Papers, Orleans*, microfilm, T-260, roll 5, NARA. For more on the Point Coupée rebellion, see Gwendolyn Midlo Hall, *Africans in Colonial Louisiana: The Development of Afro-Creole Culture in the Eighteenth Century* (Baton Rouge: Louisiana State University Press, 1992).

54. William Claiborne to James Madison, Nov. 20, 1807, *Domestic Letters of the Department of State*, microfilm, M-40, roll 3, NARA; see continued correspondence between Madison and Claiborne during 1808, *State Department Territorial Papers, Orleans*, microfilm, T-260, roll 9, NARA.

55. William Claiborne to Governor Salcedo, March 9, 1808, *State Department Territorial Papers, Orleans*, microfilm, T-260, roll 9, NARA.

56. Schafer, *Slavery, the Civil Law, and the Supreme Court*, 4.

57. Ibid., 5. William C. C. Claiborne is an interesting and complex figure, and because he was the first governor of American Louisiana his feelings on slavery and the slave trade require greater study. In a letter to James Madison of January 31, 1804, he noted the arrival of a slave ship in New Orleans, saying of himself, "Being unwilling to permit so barbarous a traffic, if my powers authorized me to prevent it"; he nonetheless found that Spanish law had allowed the trade and authorized the ship's landing. William Claiborne to James Madison, Jan. 31, 1804, in Hackett, *Papers of James Madison*, 6: 415. A good biography of Claiborne can be found in Joseph Hatfield's *William Claiborne: Jeffersonian Centurion in the American Southwest* (Lafayette: University of Southwestern Louisiana Press, 1976).

58. Schafer, *Slavery*, 6.

59. Stephen Webre, "The Problem of Indian Slavery in Spanish Louisiana, 1769–1803," *Louisiana History* 25, no. 2 (1984): 134.

60. Winston De Ville, *English Land Grants in West Florida: A Register for the States of Alabama, Mississippi, and Parts of Florida and Louisiana, 1766–1776* (Ville Platte, La.: Winston De Ville, 1986), 14.

61. For more on Clark, see Arthur P. Whitaker, "Reed and Forde: Merchant Adventurers of Philadelphia: Their Trade with Spanish New Orleans," in Din, *The Spanish Presence in Louisiana*, 251.

62. John G. Clark, "Economic Life before the Louisiana Purchase," in Din, *The Spanish Presence in Louisiana*, 281; Vicente Pintado, *The Papers of Vicente Sebastián Pintado* (Washington, D.C.: Library of Congress Photoduplication Service, 1979), reel 6, containers 19 and 25.

63. Clark, "Economic Life," 269; Bennett H. Wall, ed., *Louisiana: A History* (Arlington Heights, Ill: Forum Press, 1990), 75.

64. Daniel Clark to General Wilkinson, March 18, 1796, *Letters Received by the Secretary of War, Unregistered Series*, microfilm, M-222, roll 1, NARA.

65. Clark, "Economic Life," 279.

66. Contract between James Wilkinson and Daniel Clark, Aug. 7, 1788, *Letters Received by the Secretary of War*, microfilm, M-222, roll 1, NARA. This contract also contains a list of people to whom Wilkinson sold the goods from Kentucky. For a more detailed list of goods imported and exported by Wilkinson and Clark in 1801, see *State Department Territorial Papers, Orleans*, microfilm, T-260, roll 2, NARA. Historians continue to debate General James Wilkinson's loyalty. For the two most recent sides, see Timothy M. Rusche, "Treachery within the United States Army," *Pennsylvania History* 65, no. 4 (1998): 478–91; and John Thornton Posey, "Rascality Revisited: In Defense of General James Wilkinson," *Filson Club History Quarterly* 74, no. 4 (2000): 309–51.

67. Clark, "Economic Life," 279, 281.

68. Jack D. Holmes, *Gayoso: The Life of a Spanish Governor in the Mississippi Valley, 1789–1799* (Baton Rouge: Louisiana State University Press, 1965).

69. Daniel Clark to Manuel Gayoso de Lemos, Oct. 5, 1796, March 2, 1796, Oct. 18, 1796, Oct. 14, 1796, etc., *Letters Received by the Secretary of War*, microfilm, M-222, roll 1, NARA; Daniel Clark to Major General Wilkinson, March 18, 179[6], ibid.

70. Manuel Gayoso de Lemos to Daniel Clark, March 2, 1796, *Letters Received by the Secretary of War, Unregistered Series, 1789–1861*, microfilm, M-222, roll 1, NARA.

71. Manuel Gayoso de Lemos to Daniel Clark, Oct. 14, 1796, ibid.

72. Manuel Gayoso de Lemos to Daniel Clark, Octobre [sic] 8, 1796, ibid.

73. Daniel Clark to [James Wilkinson], May 30, 1799, in which Clark refers to Wilkinson as a "truly beloved General" and "my Dear General," ibid. By 1806 he was actively trying to have Wilkinson arrested as part of the Burr Conspiracy (for instance, Daniel Clark to James Madison, Nov. 23, 1806, *State Department Territorial Papers, Orleans*, microfilm, T-260, roll 8, NARA).

74. Gayoso to Piomingo, San Fernando de las Barrancas, June 23, 1795, Archivo General de Indias, Papeles de Cuba, Legajo 211, quoted in Holmes, *Gayoso*, 124.

75. Manuel Gayoso de Lemos to the King of Spain, Dec. 5, 1797, *Letters Received by the Secretary of War*, microfilm, M-222, roll 1, NARA.

76. Ibid.

77. Sebastian, too, seems to have been working for both sides on the Spanish American frontier. In 1806, the Select Committee of the Kentucky House of Representatives charged him with having received a pension (as did Wilkinson and probably Clark) from the Spanish government. "The Report of the Select Committee, to whom was referred the Information Communicated to the House of Representatives, charging Benjamin Sebastian, one of the Judges of the Court of Appeals of Kentucky, with having received a Pension from the Spanish Government," Special Collections Research Center, University of Chicago Library, as reproduced in *The First American West: The Ohio River Valley, 1750–1820*, http://lcweb2.10c.gov/ammem/award99/icuhtml/fawhome.html, Library of Congress.

78. Manuel Gayoso de Lemos to the King of Spain, Dec. 5, 1797, *Letters Received by the Secretary of War*, microfilm, M-222, roll 1, NARA, parenthesis in original.

79. John W. Monette, *History of the Discovery and Settlement of the Valley of the Mississippi, by the Three Great European Powers, Spain, France, and Great Britain, and the Subsequent Occupation, Settlement, and Extension of Civil Government by the United States, until the Year 1846* (New York: Harper and Bros., 1846), 2: 560–61. For more on the role of the Kempers and national loyalty, see Andrew McMichael, *Atlantic Loyalties: Americans in Spanish West Florida, 1785–1810* (Athens: University of Georgia Press, 2008).

80. James Madison to Daniel Clark, Sept. 16, 1803, in David B. Mattern, ed., *The Papers of James Madison: Secretary of State Series* (Charlottesville: University Press of Virginia, 2000), 5: 428.

81. Cox, *The West Florida Controversy*, 88.

82. Kastor, *The Nation's Crucible*, 72–73.

83. ANC, Fondo: Realengos, leg. 43, no. 26.

84. Not a great deal has been written about the man who had a great deal of influence on U.S. reasons for purchasing New Orleans. In a short biography Jack Holmes makes the claim that over the course of his career Morales consistently tried to "check the advancing tide of American settlers." However the land sales, many of which went to Americans, seem to belie that claim. Jack D. Holmes, "*Dramatis Personæ* in Spanish Louisiana," *Louisiana Studies* 6, no. 2 (Summer 1967): 155–61.

85. William C. C. Claiborne to James Madison, Aug. 6, 1805, *State Department Territorial Papers, Orleans*, microfilm, T-260, roll 7, NARA.

86. Ibid.

87. Ibid.

88. Ibid.; [Moneau Kelley] to William Claiborne, Aug. 8, 1805, ibid.; William Claiborne to James Madison, Aug. 10, 1805, ibid.

89. William Claiborne to James Madison, May 19, 1805, ibid.

90. William C. C. Claiborne to the Marquis de Casa Calvo, Aug. 3, 1805 and William C. C. Claiborne to James Madison, Aug. 5, 1805, *State Department Territorial Papers, Orleans*, microfilm, T-260, roll 7, NARA.

91. Ibid.

92. The Marquis de Casa Calvo to William C. C. Claiborne, Aug. 8, 1805, ibid.

93. William Claiborne to the Marquis de Casa Calvo, Aug. 17, 1805, ibid.

94. [Moneau Kelley] to William Claiborne, Aug. 8, 1805, ibid.

95. William Claiborne to the Marquis de Casa Calvo, Aug. 10, 1805 and Aug. 17, 1805, ibid.

96. William Claiborne to James Madison, Aug. 6, 1805, ibid.

97. Juan Ventura Morales to William Claiborne, Aug. 19, 1805, ibid.

98. ANC, Fondo: *Realengos*, legajo 43, no. 20.

99. William C. C. Claiborne to James Madison, Aug. 5, 1805, *State Department Territorial Papers, Orleans*, microfilm, T-260, roll 7, NARA.

100. For a list of the amount of land sold, and to whom it went, see the enclosure in William C. C. Claiborne to James Madison, Aug. 15, 1805, ibid.

13

"Motivated Only by the Love of Humanity"

Arsène Lacarrière Latour and the Struggle for the Southwest

GENE ALLEN SMITH

On January 8, 1815, the French-trained engineer Arsène Lacarrière Latour served alongside General Andrew Jackson at New Orleans when the ragtag American army confronted a superior British invasion force of veterans seasoned by long service in the Napoleonic Wars. As the sun burned off the lingering fog that morning, the British general Sir Edward Pakenham confidently ordered his soldiers to make a frontal assault against the American line, expecting that Jackson's troops would flee as had happened some months earlier at Bladensburg, near Washington, D.C. But in this instance the American army had the advantage of terrain, determined leadership, and a strongly constructed, earthen and cotton-bale rampart designed by Major Latour. Within thirty minutes some two thousand British soldiers, including Pakenham himself, lay dead or wounded in front of the American line there on the Plains of Chalmette.[1]

Although the American victory at the Battle of New Orleans marked the last major engagement of the War of 1812, the campaign also determined the future of the northern shore of the Gulf of Mexico.[2] The victory determined conclusively the fate of Louisiana, as Americans strengthened their hold over the polyglot population of the region, slowly transforming them from Spanish and French into a wholly American state. The victory also ended British efforts to establish a toehold along the gulf that could be expanded to link the lower Mississippi Valley to the Great Lakes and Canada, thereby stifling American growth. Yet most importantly, the victory isolated the peninsula of Spanish Florida and moved the western nexus of empire from the lower Mississippi Valley to the Sabine and Red rivers. The Spanish had lost the Baton Rouge district in September 1810 and the Mobile district in April 1813 and in the aftermath of the war, Florida quickly felt the brunt of the expansionist American nation. Army and naval forces of the United States sacked the maroon bastion of Negro Fort along the Apalachicola River in July 1816 (see map

C.1) and Andrew Jackson's forces easily crossed the border and seized Pensacola and St. Marks during the early part of 1818. As John Quincy Adams, the U.S. secretary of state, and Don Luis Onís, the Spanish minister to the United States, negotiated over the Florida question, the on-the-ground contest over land moved west toward Spanish Texas, and with that the old Southwest fell completely within the American orbit. Thereafter, the possibilities of brokering one's national identity and loyalty diminished almost instantly.

In the immediate aftermath of the Battle of New Orleans, although the United States had won the engagement, some uncertainty existed as to the future possibilities for those in the region. Gauging the changing of winds, the Frenchman Arsène Lacarrière Latour attempted to connect his future to the rising fortunes of General Andrew Jackson by writing the important book *Historical Memoir of the War in West Florida and Louisiana in 1814–15, with an Atlas* (1816)—the first historical account of the Battle of New Orleans. The patriot engineer turned historian celebrated Jackson's defense of New Orleans in glowing terms. He related "in detail, with the utmost exactness and precision, the principal events which took place in the course of this campaign." Latour also substantiated his story with copies of original letters, reports, and documents that provided "the vouchers [evidence] of the facts which [he] related." Throughout his memorial, or what Latour called his "inadequate tribute," he insisted that the victory at New Orleans was "due to the energy, ability and courage of a single man." According to Latour, Jackson had preserved the country, and the "voice of the whole nation" acknowledged his selfless sacrifice and service. This patriotic tome told the American people in no uncertain terms that Jackson had saved their country and was their hero (fig. 13.1).[3]

Latour's tribute appears as a nationalistic and patriotic expression of American identity, extolling the virtues of independence and a free government. He concluded his book by insisting that Americans had taught the English that they could not impugn "a nation, which is firmly determined to maintain itself in the enjoyment of FREEDOM and INDEPENDENCE." Moreover, Latour's book does not seem to be a contradictory expression because the Frenchman had served as Jackson's "Principal Engineer" during the battle; rather than betray his adopted country, Latour had joined with Jackson to maintain American independence against the British threat along the gulf. By reading the book one is led to believe that Latour's loyalties lay unquestionably in the American camp, yet that was not necessarily the case.[4]

Géraud-Calixte Jean-Baptiste Arsène LaCarrière Latour was representative of the type of adventurer who flocked to Louisiana during the early nineteenth century (fig. 13.2). Born in October 1778 in the southwestern French village of Aurillac to Guillaume LaCarrière (Seigneur de Latour and Falhiés) and his

Figure 13.1. General Andrew Jackson, from the frontispiece of Latour's book on the Battle of New Orleans. Arsène Lacarrière Latour, *Historical Memoir of the War in West Florida and Louisiana in 1814–15, with an Atlas* (Philadelphia: John Conrad and Co., 1816).

wife, Louise Marguerite Daudin, he would have inherited the family's title and lands had it not been for the French Revolution, which began in May 1789. Unemployment soon became rampant in both cities and countryside. During the summer peasants from across France rose against their manor lords as the price of grain, the grist of ordinary people's diet, soared to prohibitively high levels. A temporary calm had returned to the countryside by the fall, but France soon found itself at war with Austria and Prussia. By 1793 the Reign of Terror was sweeping across the country and the world that Latour had known had disappeared. His uncle Antoine, the priest of Lascalle, was deported during the fall of 1793, and by early 1794 local officials had erected a guillotine in the public square of Aurillac.[5]

While the French Revolution disrupted life for many, Latour gained from the discord. He secured an education in architecture at the Academy of Fine Arts in Paris, but the continuing uncertainty of the French Revolution prompted him to travel to Haiti in 1802 to seek financial security and to recover his wife's family's lands. But when he arrived in Saint Domingue in October 1802, he found an island devastated by twelve years of slave insurrections

Figure 13.2. Portrait of Géraud-Calixte Jean-Baptiste Arsène Lacarrière Latour by an unknown artist. Courtesy of Martine Bardon.

and few opportunities for someone with his education and talents. French attempts to subdue the island had failed, as thousands of soldiers, including the commanding general Charles Leclerc, had succumbed to yellow fever. Latour survived his first sickly season and because of his technical training he soon secured a military appointment in the French Corps of Engineers, attached to General Donatien Rochambeau's command. The appointment fortunately provided the food, housing, and salary that Latour sought.[6]

During the following year, 1803, Rochambeau instituted a policy of terror that drove the island's population to further insurrection. Also compounding French problems on the island, Napoleon broke the Peace of Amiens and renewed his war with Great Britain, which permitted the British to cut off French supplies and reinforcements to the island. The British also supported the insurgents in the southern part of the island who waged a demoralizing guerilla war against French soldiers and the white population. Convinced that the insurgents would exact a horrible revenge, wealthy white refugees began fleeing the island for Cuba and Louisiana aboard privateers, including vessels commanded by the brothers Jean and Pierre Lafitte. In May 1804 Latour informed his father that he had been working in the United States for a few months, which means he escaped the horrors of those last days of French control in Saint Domingue.[7]

Exactly when Latour arrived in Louisiana remains unclear and subject to speculation. Some authors have maintained that he came in 1810, while others have contended that he appeared in Louisiana as early as 1802. One story posits that Latour fled Saint Domingue for Cuba in late 1803 with General Charles François Antoine Lallemand aboard a privateer. He supposedly remained with Lallemand in Havana for a short time before traveling on to Louisiana; the connection between the two men became important after the War of 1812. Even if Latour did not meet the Lafittes prior to his arrival from Saint Domingue, he probably did while in the Cuban city, which had become a hub for privateering activity. He undoubtedly met other French exiles who would soon play important roles in Louisiana, such as the engineer Barthélemy Lafon. In fact, in the introduction to his *Historical Memoir*, Latour declared that he had helped Lafon prepare maps of New Orleans and its Gulf Coast environs for Napoleon's projected occupation of the Louisiana territory in 1803. If so, he certainly fled Saint Domingue and had met Lafon prior to the French surrender.[8]

Regardless of when Latour arrived in Louisiana, his association with Lafon prompts many questions. Appointed a lieutenant in the Louisiana militia, Lafon received votes in 1806 for the territorial House of Representatives and later became the deputy surveyor for Orleans County, Louisiana. But Lafon quickly reshaped his loyalties, as he joined Jean Lafitte's privateers sailing through Louisiana's waters, smuggling slaves into the United States, and flaunting the other American commercial restrictions passed during the Jefferson and Madison administrations. He reportedly participated in the Gutiérrez-Magee filibustering expedition into Texas in 1813, and the following year, on September 1814, was captured when the naval expedition headed by the U.S. master-commandant Daniel Todd Patterson raided Lafitte's Baratarian stronghold at Grand Terre. But Lafon did not remain incarcerated very long as he and many of the other Baratarian prisoners joined the Louisiana militia, serving with Jackson during the British campaign for New Orleans in December 1814–January 1815. Lafon's decision to fight alongside Jackson most likely did not emerge from Lafon's affinity for Americans or for their cause, but rather because he wanted to avoid a prolonged imprisonment on charges of smuggling. After the battle President Madison granted pardons to Lafitte and his associates, providing them with a clean slate to renew their legal and illegal activities; Lafon soon joined with the Lafittes and other filibusters at Galveston. He also later joined with the Lafittes and Latour as a Spanish operative in the southwest during 1817. Obviously Lafon's loyalties moved fluidly from one side to another if and whenever the situation presented itself.[9]

Latour's loyalties have appeared more opaque. In 1804 he and Lafon surrendered to the nefarious U.S. army general James Wilkinson the maps they had prepared. Wilkinson, along with the acting Louisiana governor William C. C. Claiborne, had recently arrived in New Orleans to receive possession of the territory for the United States. But Wilkinson also had other motives for his trip to the Crescent City; he had been on the Spanish payroll for years and the trip to New Orleans provided the chance to renew his connections and request back pay. Wilkinson subsequently delayed his return trip to Washington by at least three weeks, claiming that he had been gathering information for an essay, "Reflections on Louisiana," and a monograph, *The Topography of Louisiana*. Combining hard-to-get reliable information about the territory with excellent maps, supposedly prepared by Latour and Lafon, the essay offered details about the perceived boundaries of the territory, the military situation in the region, and the U.S. government's intentions concerning the Gulf Coast, while the maps illustrated that the Floridas were the key to all American commerce in the gulf. Ultimately, Wilkinson distributed copies to Vicente Folch, the Spanish governor of West Florida—receiving twelve thousand pesos in return—and to Henry Dearborn, the U.S. Secretary of War, who passed the copy along to President Jefferson. Because Wilkinson claimed that he had assembled the report at great personal cost, Jefferson reimbursed him from the presidential contingency fund, which means that the general received money from both the U.S. and Spanish governments for the same report. While Wilkinson obviously worked both sides of the fence, it remains unclear whether Latour and Lafon acted as willing agents in his subterfuge. Yet their activities after the War of 1812 suggest that they complied willingly.[10]

Returning to Louisiana during the summer of 1806 after a failed business relationship in New York, Latour drafted a city plan for Baton Rouge at the insistence of the retired military captain of Spanish Louisiana, Elias Toutant Beauregard. Carlos Grand Pré, the former French commandant who had gained recognition as the fair-minded Spanish governor of Baton Rouge, approved Latour's design and soon thereafter initiated construction. The successful Baton Rouge project provided Latour the entrée he needed to begin potentially profitable business relationships in Louisiana. Soon after the Baton Rouge job, Latour began surveying land for the prominent attorney Edward Livingston, who had become engaged in a series of prolonged land (batture) cases; the association with one of the most influential men in Louisiana placed him in good company and opened doors for future advancement. Latour also spent weeks locating and surveying suitable lands for the Marquis de Lafayette, who had been awarded a sizeable tract for his service in the American

Revolution. In 1808 Latour's father, Guillaume LaCarrière, even asked Lafayette to use his influence to secure for his son the French consulship at New Orleans; although Latour did not receive the position, Lafayette responded that he would speak with his "friends about M. Lacarrière de Latour."[11]

By the fall of 1810 Latour had devoted himself full-time to architecture in New Orleans, opening an engineering and architectural firm with Jean-Hyacinthe Laclotte at the corner of Royal and Orleans Streets; the two men also taught drawing and painting, architecture and carpentry, as well as interior design and decoration in both day and night classes. Their business initially prospered, as they designed Tremoulet's Hotel and began construction on the first Orleans Street Theatre. Latour also designed and constructed the St. Philip Street Theatre, located between Royal and Bourbon streets. In addition, the two designed a house at 619 Bourbon Street, began several other buildings in the city's French Quarter, and managed the renovation of Doctor Yves Lemonnier's house at the corner of Royal and St. Peters streets; for this project they heightened the walls of the first two floors, built a third story, added a roof level of rooms, and installed an ornate iron girded railing, complete with the doctor's monogram, "Y L M," on the third floor balcony.[12]

Latour's architectural skills also won the respect and admiration of Benjamin Henry Latrobe, the famous Washington architect who had designed the U.S. Capitol. Latrobe's son Henry came to New Orleans during the spring of 1811 on business for his father, who had the contract to build the city waterworks. Henry's ability to speak French, as well as his French-sounding name (he styled himself H. Boneval Latrobe), afforded him the chance to meet many of the region's Creole politicians and leading professionals, including Latour, who took the young man under his wing. Latour offered friendship, professional advice, and political connections that helped the young Latrobe deal with the difficulties his father's project faced. And while the waterworks project ultimately failed, Latour had gained another American ally, this one with powerful connections to the American government.[13]

Within only a few years Latour had become one of New Orleans's most successful architects, designing many of the most important buildings in the city. Additionally, he moved easily between the established French Creole elite and the incoming Anglo-American entrepreneurs. Latour possessed the talents to bridge the cultural gaps between the two groups, as well as to gain and maintain their confidence while also promoting his own business interests. Initially Latour seemed very successful doing it all; he spoke multiple languages fluently, took the oath of allegiance as a U.S. citizen during the spring of 1812 (without repudiating his French heritage), and successfully completed jobs that brought money and recognition. In spite of such auspicious beginnings, by May 1813 Latour and Laclotte had filed for bankruptcy—casualties of the economic slowdown brought about by the War of 1812. Such a rapid demise dispirited Latour, but with the war soon moving toward the Gulf Coast new opportunities would present themselves.[14]

After two years of warfare along the Canadian border and in the Chesapeake Bay, the war moved to the Gulf of Mexico. In mid-November 1814 General Andrew Jackson, the commander of the Seventh Military District, verified information via the West Indies that the British intended to attack New Orleans. The city represented the most valuable yet most vulnerable point along the Gulf Coast, and throughout the fall of 1814 Jackson had heard rumors of an impending attack. Yet he believed that the port city of Mobile provided the best British route of attack against the Mississippi Valley, which could permit the British to link the Gulf Coast through the Mississippi Valley and Great Lakes to the Canadian colony in the north. In fact, Jackson felt so assured of his hunch about Mobile that he spent much of the fall of 1814 in that city preparing for a British attack. Even so, Jackson did make preliminary preparations to defend New Orleans. In late November 1814 Edward Livingston strongly recommended Latour as a "man of perfect honor and integrity [who] speaks both French and English fluently." When Jackson arrived in the city a few days later, he appointed Latour as the principal engineer of the Seventh Military District, along with Lewis Livingston—Edward's son—and Henry Latrobe as assistant engineers.[15]

For the French émigré, the war with Britain provided a wonderful opportunity to demonstrate his talents. He had the ability to bridge the linguistic and cultural gaps between the French Louisiana Creoles and the Anglo-Americans. Additionally, Jackson desperately needed Latour's engineering skills because men with such talents were in very short supply, especially along the Gulf Coast. Meeting with Jackson in early December, Latour informed him that there were seven possible water routes for a British attack against New Orleans, including Bayou Lafourche, Barataria Bay, River Aux Chenes and Bayou Terre aux Boeufs, the Mississippi River, and three routes via Lake Borgne. Latour also predicted—correctly so—that Lake Borgne offered the most feasible approach. Ultimately the British advanced through Lake Borgne, using the Bayou Bienvenu, which drained the area east of New Orleans and stretched from Lake Borgne to within a mile of the Mississippi River. From there the British army proceeded north nine miles along the river levee toward New Orleans, arriving within a few miles of the city by December 22, 1814 (fig. 13.3).[16]

Latour spent the early part of December apprising Jackson of the defensive qualities of the region. Fort St. Philip, downriver from New Orleans, ap-

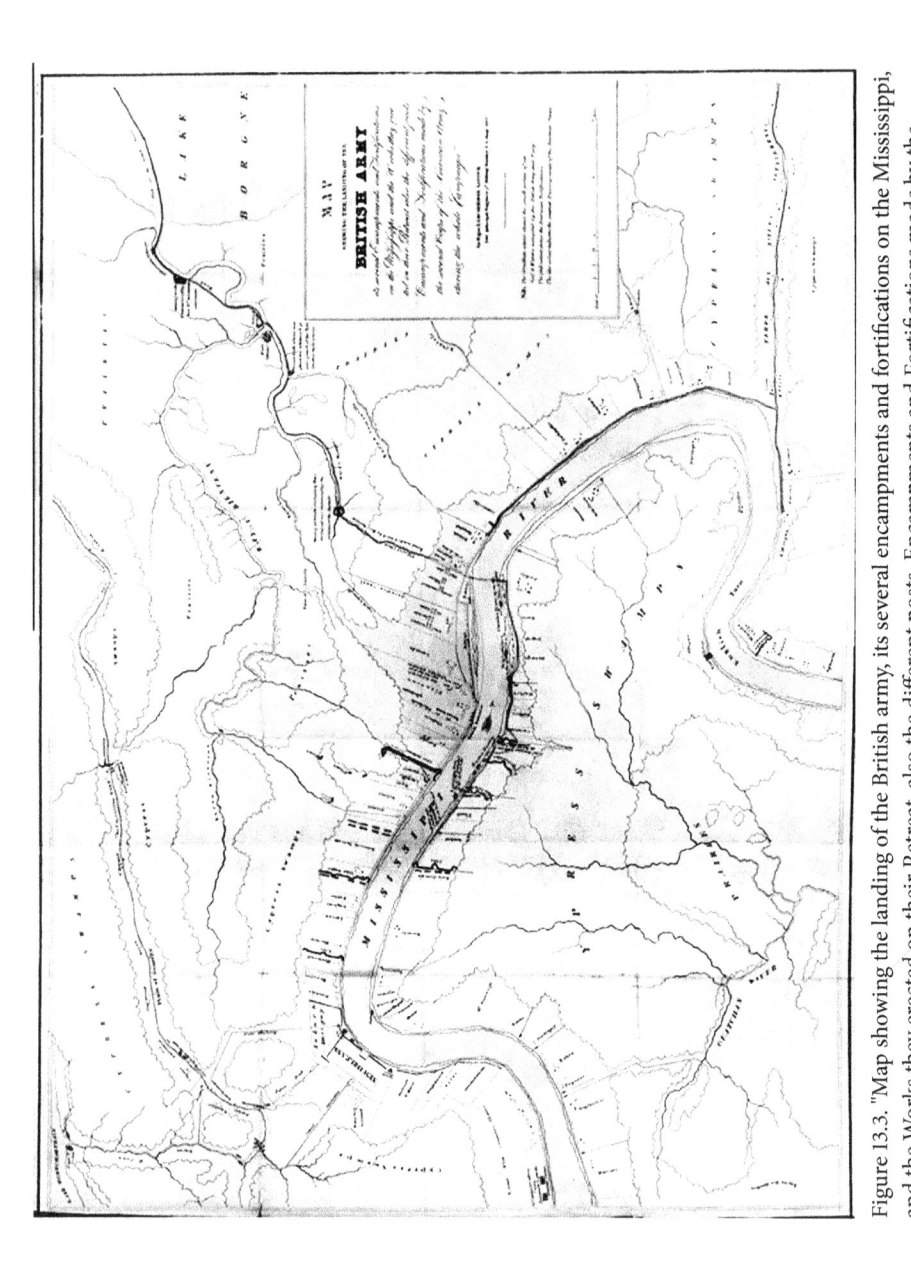

Figure 13.3. "Map showing the landing of the British army, its several encampments and fortifications on the Mississippi, and the Works they erected on their Retreat, also the different posts, Encampments and Fortifications made by the several Corps of the American army during the whole Campaign" by Arsène Lacarrière Latour, *Historical Memoir of the War in West Florida and Louisiana in 1814–15, with an Atlas* (Philadelphia: John Conrad and Co, 1816).

peared in good shape after minor alterations. Latour also showed Jackson that swamps and marshes dominated the southern Louisiana landscape, providing few opportunities for the British to land troops below the city. But to the east of the city lay the Chef Menteur Pass and the Gentilly Road, which Jackson quickly but wrongly concluded offered the most likely route for a British attack. By mid-December Jackson had learned that the American flotilla of gunboats on Lake Borgne, under the command of Lieutenant Thomas ap Catesby Jones, had been overwhelmed by British barges, providing the British with the opportunity to choose their approach of attack.[17]

With but seven hundred troops on paper, and even fewer in reality, Jackson had to resort to desperate measures. He declared martial law on December 16, and accepted the offers of service from Louisiana's free men of color and from Jean Lafitte's "hellish banditti." The Louisiana legislature and a group of influential citizens even petitioned Jackson to secure a pardon for the Lafittes and their associates should they help defend the city. In fact, according to Latour's account of the battle, he helped broker the meeting between Jackson and Jean Lafitte that brought the Baratarians into the service of the United States. Such an arrangement boded well for Jackson, who needed the men and their knowledge and equipment, for the Lafittes and their associates, who needed the pardons for their past offenses, and for Latour, whose ability to broker the alliance benefited him politically and in the future perhaps would do so economically as well.[18]

Latour played a critical role during the preliminary British operations against New Orleans. He reconnoitered British positions on December 22 and provided information that convinced Jackson to launch the important surprise night attack that has been called the turning point in the campaign; the engagement forced the British thereafter to exercise greater caution and to delay their operations until additional troops had been brought up to the line. The extra time permitted Jackson to gain the troops he needed to defend the city and allowed Latour to design and construct defenses that took advantage of the swampy terrain. Latour also gathered information about British activities near the Chef Menteur east of the city, reporting to Jackson that forces south of the city unquestionably represented the main body of the British attack. During the days immediately preceding the battle of January 8, 1815, Latour supervised construction of defensive positions on the west side of the Mississippi River, yet he argued with General David Morgan about where those lines should be positioned. Morgan ultimately preempted Latour's decision, abandoning a nearly finished line and constructing a new longer defensive line that remained uncompleted when the British attacked. Latour considered the American setback on the west bank, which became the most controversial event of the campaign, to have been Morgan's fault, even though when he published his version of the battle he decided to leave the verdict "to the judgment of the reader."[19]

After their defeat on January 8, 1815, the British slowly began evacuating Louisiana. Yet Jackson believed that the British operations represented the advance movements of another planned attack in the region via a different route. This possibility forced Jackson to keep the army ever vigilant and to continue preparing defenses. Latour inspected the bayous around New Orleans and offered an extensive plan for their defense, but those preparations never began, as news arrived along the gulf in mid-February 1815 that the war had ended. The end of the war also brought the end of Latour's tenure with the American army, dated March 17, 1815.[20]

Throughout the spring and summer of 1815 Latour gathered information for his planned book about the New Orleans campaign. Writing to army, navy, and militia officers, as well as to state and federal officials, Latour assembled an impressive collection of documents to verify his account of events. He also interviewed eyewitnesses and sent questionnaires to those who had participated, requesting information on their activities. He wanted to offer a fair assessment of the major participants, but Latour was, first and foremost, a Frenchman who had made his home in Louisiana. His account certainly would not condemn his fellow expatriates serving in the Louisiana militia for David Morgan's failure on the west bank; surprisingly, Andrew Jackson blamed the Kentuckians rather than Morgan or the Louisianans for the debacle on the west bank. Latour's book also included a lengthy appendix as well as copies of the documents that formed the basis of his version of events. Additionally, he prepared a second volume of maps that permitted readers to visualize where the operations occurred. Latour believed that such a thorough and thoughtful book would obviously find patriotic readers, and having spent much of his life trying to find financial security, he also envisioned the profits the book might reap. Yet his *Historical Memoir*, copyrighted on March 6, 1816, did not become a bestseller. In fact, despite a "very favorable review" in Boston's prestigious *North American Review*, it barely grossed any money at all. After paying for production costs, postage, and traveling expenses, Latour decried that he was "absolutely broke." He had spent twelve months "fighting the war at my own expense," he retorted, while earning only the "pitiful sum" that the army had paid him for his services. The country may have been thankful for his service at New Orleans, but he believed that Americans had a peculiar way of showing their gratitude.[21]

Latour had encountered trouble finding a publisher in Philadelphia for his manuscript and that difficulty should have alerted him to the reception that

Map 13.1. The early nineteenth-century southwestern borderlands. Map by Tracy Ellen Smith, www.cdrtexas.com.

the finished book might ultimately receive. Nonetheless, seeking out a publisher in the city during the fall of 1815, the architect-engineer and patriot-historian began making preparations for a third professional life—this time as a Spanish agent in the southwestern borderlands (map 13.1). While in the city Latour also met with his old associate Jean Lafitte, as well as on two occasions with Secretary of State James Monroe, discussing among other things the territorial ambitions of the United States in the Southwest. Latour then passed his information along to the Spanish minister Luis de Onís, who operated an intelligence system that gathered information on the United States, the Caribbean, and Spain's holdings in the New World. Knowing that Spanish Florida and Texas had become the most vulnerable imperial outposts, Onís believed he needed to take proactive steps to prevent the filibustering and rebel movements that embodied the dark underside of American expansionist policy. After all, the United States had used a similar method to annex the Baton Rouge district of West Florida in 1810, and then used the pretext of war to seize the Mobile district in 1813. The Americans would strike again, and Onís knew that engaging agents such as Latour and the Lafitte brothers could provide the Spanish government with the timely and accurate information needed to prevent the immediate loss of further territory.[22]

Onís dispatched Latour and Jean Lafitte on a special expedition into the Internal Provinces to survey the region, gauge the sentiments of the varied inhabitants there, and to determine the extent of American influence. Disguised as a geographic survey of the gold region of Arkansas, the expedition was to pay close attention to American influence in the region, because Arkansas represented where the first wave of American expansion would occur and from where it would inevitably spread toward Santa Fe, Spain's rich fur and mineral outpost and trade-link to California. Onís also hoped to regain some of the lost Louisiana lands and to strengthen Spain's position in the forthcoming border negotiations. Latour's report and maps, based on an exploration of the Red, Sabine, Arkansas, and Colorado rivers, would provide the much-needed information about whether the isolated lands could be reclaimed or defended.[23]

Setting off in the spring of 1816 and traveling under false names—Latour became John Williams, and Lafitte called himself Captain Hillare—the Spanish agents made their first stop at Arkansas Post, a poor agricultural area that prospered by sending meat and pelts downriver to New Orleans. The three hundred or so inhabitants—consisting of Frenchmen, Spaniards, Canadians, and some Americans—indicated to Latour that they would welcome a Spanish return; apparently many of the Creoles had been slow about registering their old French and Spanish lands grants with the Americans and by 1816 they were on the verge of losing their lands. Continuing up the Arkansas, Latour and Lafitte stopped at the Little Rock, Crystal Hill, and Cadron, where they quickly realized that this remote region's isolation was disappearing before their eyes. Major James Pyeatt, one of the area's leading citizens, proclaimed that he did not know of the recent war (War of 1812) with Great Britain until it was well over. Yet by the summer of 1816 Latour noted that U.S. mail carriers rode through Cadron on their way past the Hot Springs on the Ouachita to Natchitoches. Once the mail arrived, citizens, government, and other development would follow closely behind. Additionally, Latour met a trapper who reportedly had made the seven-hundred-mile trip overland to Taos on horseback, arriving in but fifteen days. Latour contended that an army could make the same trip in but a month, descending south seventy miles onto Santa Fe and cutting off the overland route to California. This convinced Latour that should Spain do nothing "the time will come, and unfortunately is not . . . far off, when the Americans . . . will pour in myriads into Mexico."[24]

Returning to New Orleans in November 1816, Latour finished his report, providing a detailed account of "the influence which the southwestern part of the United States will have in the future on the Spanish possession which it borders." The former president Thomas Jefferson, Latour insisted, "was the first author of this plan . . . who gave an impulse to this emigration" by sending expeditions—such as that of Zebulon Pike—to explore lands in the southwest. Latour assured Spanish officials that these reconnaissance expeditions provided the U.S. government with important information about the geography and Indians of the region. Moreover, Pike's published reports, a copy of which Latour had reviewed for the expedition, "succeeded in stiring [sic] up the strong, natural unrest of the people of the west and southwest" and allowed the U.S. government to establish a presence on the southwestern frontier.[25]

Jefferson had expressed concern in the 1780s that Spain "was too feeble to hold [the Gulf Coast region] till [America's] population can be sufficiently advanced to gain it from them piece, by piece." Such had been the case with Louisiana, yet the U.S. government stumbled into possession of that region because of Napoleon Bonaparte and Spanish weaknesses. But there was no certainty in the period after the War of 1812 that lands further west would also fall into American hands. To ensure such a possibility, Latour contended, the United States had encouraged farmers, hunters, and former soldiers to immigrate into disputed lands. He insisted that these self-reliant individuals, accustomed to fighting off "wild beasts" and protecting themselves from the Indians, would provide the necessary manpower to wrest forcibly the region from Spain. Although that possibility may have seemed remote to Spanish officials in Havana, Mexico City, or Madrid, the description of new settlements on the River Poteau near Santa Fe, and on the Arkansas and Red rivers that only a few years earlier had not existed, certainly echoed the probability that Latour had portended.[26]

Latour also suggested that the continued westward movement of Americans would mean the collapse of Spanish control. Farmers seeking fertile lands posed a problem in their own right. But these farmers also forced the Indians to relinquish their lands and move even further west, fragmenting Native American culture and unity. Meanwhile hunters and trappers penetrated deeper into the western and southwestern wilderness, introducing firearms and alcohol to the Pawnee, Kansas, Apache, and Comanche. These tribes, which previously "had only spears and arrows," had constantly harassed Spanish outposts and according to Latour would soon be armed and allied with the United States against Spain. The resulting "consequences would be disastrous."[27]

Latour assured the Spanish government that these Anglo-American frontier settlements would become the center for future expeditions against Mexico. These Americans, according to his observations, were "hardened to fatigue, following the customs of the Indians, and, like them, able to endure privations." They also "have strength of character, courage, . . . skill in the use of their guns, . . . and their eyes fixed on Mexico, like the Jews on the Promised Land." Latour insisted that they would join any expedition against Mexico, even if it had little prospect of success, as "they have everything to gain and nothing to lose."[28]

It appeared inevitable that the expansive Americans would threaten "the future peace of the western possessions of the Spanish crown in the New World." Latour also predicted that while "the Spanish government cannot prevent" American expansion, perhaps it could be postponed. If Spain retained her possessions in the immediate future, Latour insisted that those lands could be held indefinitely, because the United States would not survive forever. Even though the democratic nation had an abundance of land, the American union, he predicted, was precarious at best. Because the United States was facing a host of problems, including the dissatisfaction of many Americans, Latour believed these people would focus their attentions at home before looking outward.[29]

Latour also offered a series of suggestions that he believed would protect the "well being and the tranquility of the peaceful inhabitants" of the Spanish Empire. First, he insisted that Spain should establish a fixed boundary between the two countries—such as Luis Onís negotiated with John Quincy Adams a few years later. Such a demarcation line would provide legitimate authority for the Spanish to drive out the few Americans who had already advanced into Spanish territory without permitting the Americans to use it as a reason to ignite an international crisis. Once the boundaries had been settled, Latour recommended that the Spanish establish military posts on the border. Such installations would impede the progress of Americans, keep the Indians in check, hamper communications between the Indians and Americans—which Latour believed to be very important—and attract traders and hunters, who could augment the Spanish frontier force. Last, Latour suggested that Spain had to restore the allegiance of those who had been marginalized—the "old inhabitants and poor Creoles of Ouachita, of New Madrid, and of the St. Francis, White, Arkansas, and Red rivers." These people had been mistreated by the Americans, their lands had been taken, and their claims ignored. Latour revealed that they "know the Americans and cordially hate them." Moreover, "the Spanish government could count on each one of these men being a faithful and devoted frontier guard" against future American incursions.[30]

Latour concluded that he wanted to "warn the [Spanish] government of the dangers which are coming." Admittedly, he described subjects in his report that did not concern the topography of western lands, but Latour digressed because, as he claimed, he was "motivated only by the love of humanity." He did not want to see Spain's "peaceful inhabitants" threatened by Americans when such dangers could be easily avoided. Although unsure, he hoped that his report would "contribute to the well-being of [his] fellow men." If it aroused the attention of Spanish officials, Latour thought it could be used to postpone "the disastrous consequences which [he] considered inevitable." Americans were going to expand westward, following the setting sun, but Latour believed Spain could delay the inevitable if it acted quickly and decisively.[31]

Latour presented his completed report to Father Antonio Sedella, the head of the Spanish spy network in New Orleans, who read the assessment closely and decided to send the Frenchman-turned-Spanish-agent to Cuba to present the information to his superiors. The Lafittes used Latour's trip to offer information about the Aury and Mina filibustering expedition to the coast of Texas. The Lafittes insisted that Latour should deliver their reports orally and as quickly as possible to Captain General José Cienfuegos, lest their intelligence be intercepted. In fact, Pierre Lafitte reassured Latour that they would be "sufficiently paid by serving humanity's cause"—an idea that resounded in Latour's report. Arriving in Havana in March 1817, Latour, traveling as John Williams, reported to Captain General Cienfuegos, who sent Alejandro Ramírez, the intendant of the army, to meet with the Frenchman. Ramírez knew that Williams was really Latour's alias identity and he was impressed with the Frenchman's talents, reporting favorably that Latour did not immediately seek a reward. Instead Latour provided Ramírez with a copy of his *Historical Memoir* and with two reports on conditions within the Spanish Empire. The first discussed American plans to foment a slave insurrection in the West Indies, which would undermine Spanish rule in the area; supplemented by oral information from the Lafittes, this report included additional materials on pirate and privateer operations in the western Gulf of Mexico. Not surprisingly, this intelligence offered nothing new to Spanish officials as Sedella had reported similar news. Latour's second report, the lengthy account of affairs in the Internal Provinces, warned that should Spain do nothing the Americans would slowly devour southwestern lands. This report made a vivid impression on both Ramírez and Cienfuegos. Moreover, since Latour's information had been substantiated by other agents, they immediately instructed that copies be disseminated to Madrid, to Onís in Washington, to the viceroy of Mexico, and to the provincial governors of Mexico's northern frontier states. And while the report received careful consideration and produced considerable commentary, Spanish officials on the northern frontier did not take it too seriously. Even if they had, they did not have the means to counter the threat Americans presented in this region.[32]

Cienfuegos decided to increase the Spanish presence in New Orleans as a way to keep abreast of the fast-paced machinations in the borderlands. Ramírez, impressed with the thoroughness of Latour's report, offered him the opportunity to serve as the Spanish consul in New Orleans. Latour declined, prompting Cienfuegos to send Felipe Fatio to New Orleans with the money to pay the Lafittes and other Spanish friends for their devoted service to the Crown; undoubtedly Latour also received his due for serving humanity's cause. By 1818 Latour had chosen to relocate to Havana, where he continued his association with the Lafittes and with certain French operatives such as the former French general Charles François Antoine Lallemand, who planned a colony for Napoleonic émigrés in Texas; in fact, this bond endured, for during the early 1830s Lallemand, then the governor of Corsica and a new peer of the Kingdom of France, invited Latour to become his assistant. Latour declined, claiming he wanted to rejoin his family. Latour nonetheless resided in Cuba from 1818 until 1834, longer than he had lived in Louisiana or in any other place. Working as an architect, he operated a firm that built the famous Neptune fountain in Havana, paved roads and squares, constructed a sewer system in Havana, and erected bridges over the Canimar and Almendares rivers. Yet by June 1834 Latour had to liquidate his company to pay debts. Shortly thereafter he returned to Aurillac, France, where three years later Arsène Lacarrière Latour—architect, engineer, soldier, patriot, historian, and foreign agent—succumbed to a flu epidemic that also killed hundreds of others in the region.[33]

Latour's talents and connections had allowed him to move easily throughout the Atlantic world—between Haiti, Louisiana, the eastern United States, and Cuba. His ability to speak French, English, and Spanish also helped him gain the confidence of those in power and of those with whom he dealt. Once he had gained their confidence, his organizational skills and his ability as an architect and engineer opened further doors. During his time along the gulf, 1803–17, Latour had navigated between the various groups vying to determine the fate of Louisiana in the aftermath of the transfer: French Creoles wanted to maintain their identity and power; Spaniards yearned to regain control over an area that had been taken from them; Anglo-Americans wanted to incorporate Louisiana into the United States culturally as well as politically; and slaves and free blacks desired freedom and equality. The seemingly continuous political shifting inspired people to rely on their own abilities and their willingness to negotiate their national identities. And each group carved out its own sphere of power while trying to undermine the influence of their rivals, which provided soldiers-of-fortune like Latour with a chance for advancement, adventure, and success. The War of 1812 and the Napoleonic Wars in Europe also compounded the tension along the Gulf Coast as they uprooted individuals and created a nexus of empire with competing nationalities in Louisiana. After the war, many displaced soldiers and sailors became mercenaries, filibusters, pirates, and patriots searching for adventure in an untamed, ungoverned land, and the Spanish Empire in the Western Hemisphere, including Louisiana, Florida, Texas, and lands further west, acted as a magnet for these restless souls. Moreover, as long as the region remained in flux, the complexities of immigration patterns, social customs, and political regimes of the early southwestern frontiers permitted a fluidity of national identities and loyalties unknown in other regions of North America.[34]

Latour's service with France, the United States, and Spain, and his shifting loyalties reflect vividly the international uncertainty that the gulf borderlands experienced during the late eighteenth century and the early nineteenth. During this tumultuous revolutionary era, a number of flags flew above the North American Gulf of Mexico frontier, leaving the inhabitants of the region to wonder whose colors might be hoisted next. Individuals frequently watched the imperial regime changes, intending to alter their identities and loyalties depending on the outcome. Nationality and loyalty certainly appeared fluid for those not involved directly in the regime change. In fact, individuals could and would change their identity for many different reasons, usually connected with personal gain or self-interest. Yet for governments and communities, national membership and identity embodied collective interests, security, shared values, participation in certain politically controlled advantages, and above all, solidarity in the event of military hostilities; during the Battle of New Orleans—Spaniards, French Creoles, American frontiersmen, Choctaw Indians, free blacks, and slaves—all rallied to the American standard to confront the invading British army. The Frenchman Arsène Lacarrière Latour might have linked his patriotic sentiments to Andrew Jackson and the American cause, but he remained steadfastly loyal to France. That Jackson offered him an army commission, with a salary as well, and a chance to fight against the British—the same enemy that had supported the slave insurgency against General Donatien Rochambeau in 1803—undoubtedly influenced his decision. Latour's later willingness to assist Spain on the southwestern frontier also represented a conscious monetary decision rather than any sense of Franco-Spanish loyalty. When Spain offered Latour the chance to assume a consular post in New

Orleans, he refused, instead choosing to relocate to Havana and practice as a private architect. Apparently his loyalty and patriotism reflected rational and practical matters rather than any abstract concept of national identity or patriotic solidarity.

Competing nationalities combined with political instability in the gulf to provide the chance for legitimate and nefarious activities, which meant that the region could fall under any flag given the right circumstances. Yet shortly after the War of 1812, Anglo-Americans who had incorporated Louisiana into the American union began migrating through western Louisiana and Arkansas—as Latour reported—toward Spanish Texas, settling the Louisiana question and thereby shifting the nexus of empire further to the west. By 1820 the increased flow of American westward expansion had marginalized most French and Spanish influences in the gulf border region, for better or for worse. Latour had recognized the Pax Americana and had told the Spanish government in no uncertain terms. He also understood what such expansion meant to the fragile geopolitical situation in the west; as Americans moved westward, bringing the region under the Stars and Stripes, Spain's tenuous control of that region would be further weakened. Lastly, Latour begrudgingly acknowledged that the ascendancy of the American flag in the gulf borderlands meant that opportunities for adventurers such as himself—those willing to broker their loyalty and divide it between many countries—had vanished forever.

Notes

1. Arsène Lacarrière Latour wrote the first historical account of the Battle of New Orleans and published it in Philadelphia in 1816: Arsène Lacarrière Latour, *Historical Memoir of the War in West Florida and Louisiana, 1814–15, with an Atlas* (Philadelphia: John Conrad and Company, 1816); the most recent full length study of the battle has appeared in Robert V. Remini, *Andrew Jackson and the Course of American Empire* (New York: Harper and Row, Publishers, 1977), 294–95.

2. Joseph C. Tregle, Jr., "Andrew Jackson and the Continuing Battle of New Orleans," *Journal of the Early Republic* 1 (Winter 1984): 373–374.

3. Arsène Lacarrière Latour, *Historical Memoir of the War in West Florida and Louisiana, 1814–15, with an Atlas*, ed. Gene A. Smith (1816; repr., Gainesville: University Press of Florida, 1999), 13, 14, 5.

4. Ibid., 165.

5. Jean Garrigoux, *Un Aventurier Visionnaire: l'étrange parcours d'un Français aux Amériques* (La Haute-Auvergne: Société des lettres, sciences et arts, 1997), 9, 20–22, 28–29.

6. Ibid., 37–40, 57, 68–69, 72–73; Martine Bardon, "Arsène Lacarrière Latour: His

Life in Paris in 1802," pp. 2-3, unpublished manuscript in the holdings of the Historic New Orleans Collection, New Orleans.

7. C. L. R. James, *The Black Jacobins: Toussaint l'Ouverture and the San Domingo Revolution* (New York: Vintage Books, 1963), 358-61, 366-69.

8. Edwin H. Carpenter, Jr., "Latour's Report on Spanish-American Relations in the Southwest," *Louisiana Historical Quarterly* 30 (July 1947): 716; George W. Cullum, *Campaigns of the War of 1812-15 against Great Britain* (New York: James Miller, Publisher, 1879), 310; Garrigoux, *Un Aventurier Visionnaire*, 72-73; Samuel Carter III, *Blaze of Glory: The Fight for New Orleans, 1814-1815* (New York: St. Martin's Press, 1971), 106-7.

9. Militia Returns, Jan. 21, 1806, 4: 633, July 1, 1806, 4: 698, and H. Molier to William C. C. Claiborne, Jan. 21, 1806, 4: 574, all in Clarence Edwin Carter, ed., *The Territorial Papers of the United States: Territory of Orleans* (Washington, D.C.: Government Printing Office, 1940); Frank Lawrence Owsley, Jr., and Gene A. Smith, *Filibusters and Expansionists: Jeffersonian Manifest Destiny, 1800-1821* (Tuscaloosa: University of Alabama Press, 1997), 54-55; Harris Gaylord Warren, *The Sword Was Their Passport: A History of American Filibustering in the Mexican Revolution* (Baton Rouge: Louisiana State University Press, 1943), 19; Stanley Clisby Arthur, *Jean Laffite: Gentleman Rover* (New Orleans: Harmanson, 1952), 81; Robert C. Vogel, "Jean Lafitte, the Baratarians, and the Historical Geography of Piracy in the Gulf of Mexico," *Gulf Coast Historical Review* 5 (1990): 67-68.

10. Royal Ornan Shreve, *The Finished Scoundrel: General James Wilkinson* (Indianapolis, Ind.: Bobbs Merrill Company, 1933), 132-33; Dumas Malone, *Jefferson the President: Second Term, 1805-1809* (Boston: Little, Brown and Company, 1974), 218-19; [James Wilkinson], "Reflections on Louisiana by Vicente Folch," *Louisiana Under the Rule of Spain, France, and the United States, 1785-1807*, ed. James Alexander Robertson (Cleveland: Arthur H. Clark Company, 1911), 325-47, Folch's signature was on the document to protect Wilkinson's identity; David Hart White, *Vicente Folch, Governor in Spanish Florida, 1787-1811* (Washington, D.C.: University Press of America, 1981), 76; William C. C. Claiborne to Post Master General, June 17, 1805, in Dunbar Rowland, ed. *Official Letter Books of W. C. C. Claiborne, 1801-1816* (Jackson: Mississippi Department of Archives and History, 1917), 96-98; Isaac Joslin Cox, "General Wilkinson and His Later Intrigues with the Spaniards," *American Historical Review* 19 (July 1914): 800-801.

11. William B. Hatcher, *Edward Livingston: Jeffersonian Republican and Jacksonian Democrat* (Baton Rouge: Louisiana State University Press, 1940), 106-7, 119, 123, 144-85; Garrigoux, *Un Aventurier Visionnaire*, 82-83; Latour to Mr. Peret, July 10, 1806, Latour to Marquis de Lafayette, without date, both in Marquis de Lafayette Papers, the Henry E. Huntington Library, San Marino, California.

12. *Gazette de la Louisiane*, Sept. 22, 1810; *Louisiana Courrier*, Oct. 17, 1810; Edwin H. Carpenter, Jr., "Arsène Lacarrière Latour," *Hispanic American Historical Review* 18 (May 1938): 222-23; Benjamin Henry Boneval Latrobe, *Impressions Respecting New Orleans*, ed. Samuel W. Wilson, Jr. (New York: Columbia University Press, 19561), 23,

41; Harnett T. Kane, *Queen New Orleans: City by the River* (New York: William Morrow and Company, 1949), 360; Samuel Wilson, Jr., ed., *Southern Travels: Journal of John H. B. Latrobe 1834* (New Orleans: The Historic New Orleans Collection, 1986), 49n., 76n.; Stanley Clisby Arthur, *Old New Orleans* (New Orleans: Harmanson, 1936), 61.

13. Claiborne to Benjamin H. Latrobe, May 24, 1811, in Rowland, *Official Letterbooks of W. C. C. Claiborne*, 5: 255; Talbot Hamlin, *Benjamin Henry Latrobe* (New York: Oxford University Press, 1955), 355–58; Benjamin Henry Latrobe to Latour, Sept. 17, 1811, June 5, 1814, and Latrobe to Andrew Jackson, Sept. 3, 1815, all in Benjamin Henry Latrobe Papers, Maryland Historical Society, Baltimore.

14. Carpenter, "Arsène Lacarrière Latour," 223; Jane Lucas de Grummond, introduction to Arsène Lacarrière Latour, *Historical Memoir* (1816; repr., Gainesville: University of Florida Press, 1964), xxxvi.

15. Remini, *Andrew Jackson*, 236–45; Thomas Butler to Latour, Dec. 17, 1814, file 1, Arsène Lacarrière Latour Archives, Historic New Orleans Collection; Edward Livingston to Andrew Jackson, Nov. 21, 1814, Andrew Jackson Papers, Library of Congress, Washington, D.C.

16. Charles Gayarré, *History of Louisiana* (New York: William J. Widdleton, Publisher, 1866), 4: 385; Remini, *Andrew Jackson* 249–51; Andrew Jackson to William C. C. Claiborne, Sept. 30, 1814, in Horld D. Moser et al., *The Papers of Andrew Jackson* (Knoxville: University of Tennessee Press, 1991), 3: 151–52; Wilburt S. Brown, *The Amphibious Campaign for West Florida and Louisiana, 1814–1815* (Tuscaloosa: University of Alabama Press, 1969), 48, 63; Gene A. Smith, "Floating a Republican Idea: Jefferson's Gunboats at New Orleans," *Military History of the West* 24 (Fall 1994): 104–5.

17. Thomas Butler to Latour, Dec. 7, 1814, file 1, Latour Archives, Historic New Orleans Collection, New Orleans; Remini, *Andrew Jackson*, 251.

18. Andrew Jackson to John Coffee, Dec. 16, 1814, 3: 205–6, and Andrew Jackson to New Orleans Citizens, Dec. 16, 1814, 3: 206–7, in Moser, *The Papers of Andrew Jackson*; Eastern District of Louisiana, New Orleans Division—"N.O. General Minutes," p. 412, RG 21, Records of the District Courts of the United States, National Archives and Records Administration, Southwest Region, Fort Worth, Texas; Latour, *Historical Memoir*, 1999 ed., 57–58.

19. Howell Tatum, *Major H. Tatum's Journal While Acting Topographical Engineer to General Jackson* (Northampton, Mass.: Smith College Studies in History, 1922), 107–10; Robin Reilly, *The British at the Gates: The New Orleans Campaign in the War of 1812* (New York: G. P. Putnam's Sons, 1974), 197, 240; Latour, *Historical Memoir*, 1999 ed., 114–17, 120; Tessier to Latour, April 12, 1815, file 18, Paul Arnaud to Latour, July 27, 1815, file 21, and testimony of Lefebvre concerning work on the fortifications of Camp Jourdan, March 15, 1815, file 3, all in Latour Archive, the Historic New Orleans Collection.

20. Latour, *Historical Memoir*, 1964 ed., 187–97; Henri Chotard to Latour, Jan. 10, 1815, file 2, and March 17, 1815, file 4, and Latour to Andrew Jackson, Jan. 30, 1815, file 33, all in Latour Archives, the Historic New Orleans Collection; John Reid to Howell Tatum and Latour, Jan. 27, 1815, Andrew Jackson Papers, Chicago Historical Society.

21. Questionnaire Regarding Kentucky Troops Movements, n.d. [1815], file 11, Tessier to Latour, April 12, 1815, file 18, Jackson to Latour, May 19, 1815, file 19, Cholester to Morton, Aug. 15, 1815, file 22, Edward Livingston to General Mason, n.d., file 25, Triquer to Latour, Aug. 19, 1815, file 23, Latour to Edward Livingston, Nov. 1, 1816, file 29, Latour to M. Livingston, Nov. 1, 1816, file 29, invoice for Dr. Major A. L. Latour, April 26, 1816, file 30, all in Latour Archives, the Historic New Orleans Collection.

22. Benjamin Henry Latrobe to Latour, May 3, 1816, Latrobe Papers, Maryland Historical Society; Carpenter, "Arsène Lacarrière Latour," 224; Carpenter, "Latour's Report on Spanish-American Relations in the Southwest," 716; Luis de Onís to Pedro de Cevallos, Jan. 29, 1816, Archivo Histórico Nacional (hereafter AHN, Est. Leg. 5559, Exp.), 388; James Monroe to Andrew Jackson, July 3, 1816, Andrew Jackson Papers, Library of Congress; James E. Lewis, *The American Union and the Problem of Neighborhood: The United States and the Collapse of the Spanish Empire, 1783-1829* (Chapel Hill: University of North Carolina Press, 1998), 85-87.

23. Dr. and Mrs. T. L. Hodges, "Jean Lafitte and Major L. Latour in Arkansas Territory," *Arkansas Historical Quarterly* 7 (Winter 1948): 237-56; Carpenter, "Arsène Lacarrière Latour," 224-27; Carpenter, "Latour's Report on Spanish-American Relations in the Southwest," 715-37; William C. Davis, *The Pirates Lafitte: The Treacherous World of the Corsairs of the Gulf* (Orlando: Harcourt, Inc., 2005), 281-90.

24. Carpenter, "Latour's Report on Spanish-American Relations in the Southwest," 715-37; Davis, *The Pirates Lafitte*, 282-85.

25. Carpenter, "Latour's Report on Spanish-American Relations in the Southwest," 735, 724, 722, 723; for Jefferson's interest in expansion, see Owsley and Smith, *Filibusters and Expansionists*, 16-31; for his fulfillment of expansionist desires during his presidency, see Lawrence S. Kaplan, *Thomas Jefferson: Westward the Course of Empire* (Wilmington, Del.: Scholarly Resources, Inc., 1999), 125-52.

26. Jefferson to William Carmichael, May 27, 1788, in H. A. Washington, ed., *Writings of Thomas Jefferson* (Washington, D.C.: Taylor and Maury, 1853), 2: 98; Carpenter, "Latour's Report on Spanish-American Relations in the Southwest," 724-25.

27. Carpenter, "Latour's Report on Spanish-American Relations in the Southwest," 726-28.

28. Ibid., 729.

29. Ibid., 730-31.

30. Ibid., 733-35.

31. Ibid., 735, 732-33.

32. Carpenter, "Arsène Lacarrière Latour," 224-27; Ruíz de Apodaca to the Minister of State, June 3, 1818, AHN, Est., Leg. 5562, Exp. 5, 234-35; José Cienfuegos to León, April 29, 1817, AHN, Est., Leg. 5559, Exp. 26, 427-28; Luis de Onís to Pedro Cevallos, Jan. 29, 1816, AHN, Est., Leg. 5559, Exp. 26, 388; Carpenter, "Latour's Report on Spanish-American Relations in the Southwest," 730; Arthur, *Jean Laffite*, 146-47; Rafe Blaufarb, *Bonapartists in the Borderlands: French Exiles and Refugees on the Gulf Coast, 1815-1835* (Tuscaloosa: University of Alabama Press, 2006), 95; William Earl Weeks, *John Quincy Adams and American Global Empire* (Lexington: University of Kentucky

Press, 1992), 120–22. Weeks makes no reference to the Latour report during Onís's negotiations with Adams over the Transcontinental Treaty.

33. Davis, *The Pirates Lafitte*, 391–92; Carpenter, "Arsène Lacarrière Latour," 224–25; Carpenter, "Latour's Report on Spanish-American Relations in the Southwest," 730; Garrigoux, *Un Aventurier Visionnaire*, 262–66.

34. Owsley and Smith, *Filibusters and Expansionists*, 103–4.

14

Soldier, Expansionist, Politician

Eleazer Wheelock Ripley and the Dance of Ambition in the Early Republic

SAMUEL WATSON

Though forgotten today, Eleazer Ripley was a surprisingly representative American in his time. His ambition, pride, and opportunism were characteristic of men both common and genteel; his adaptability—military, economic, political, and sectional—hints at the open-ended character of life in the early American republic. Often frustrated in ambition, he made change his friend, shifting identities while maintaining pride and public reputation. As he forged new connections while he began to make his way in the new southwest, Ripley's loyalties were not always clear. Unlike his early political career in Massachusetts, where he first made his reputation, or the service in the War of 1812 that brought him fame, Ripley's life in the Gulf borderlands, where he left the army to accept the presidency of a self-proclaimed "Republic of Texas" in 1820, suggests the instability, often ambiguity, of loyalty and identity in this era.

This uncertainty brought Ripley no end of trouble in a culture where men of his class demanded rigid, unwavering loyalty and clear, unambiguous identities as evidence of integrity and the condition of honor. To the gentlemen of the early republic, particularly the military commanders with whom Ripley served on the field of battle, integrity, and being true to one's self, meant being true to a code, of unswerving responsibility for one's actions and how others perceived them. Yet perception and reputation are not natural or self-evident; they are interpretations, in which words often speak louder than actions. They are created by selves, yet each self, each individual, is part of a social, cultural, and often institutional collectivity. Codes of action, responsibility, and honor may be clear in implication and expectation, but the meaning of actions can only be clarified by words, and disputed words muddy meaning, or multiply it, more often than they clarify or cohere. Did integrity mean being true to a code of obligation to others, or did it mean a sense of wholeness for the self, a self-realization or self-satisfaction? Did it mean autonomy or integration? Where did the boundaries between self and society overlap, mix, or fuse together?

Biographies of early American public figures teem with assertions that these men remained true to their vision, whatever its specific, or unspecific, content—unionism, republicanism, or the like—through the many bends in their long careers. Was this the case with Ripley, or was he motivated less by some persistent vision of political ideology, some hoped for shape of things to come, than by the ebb and flow of circumstance, the struggle to sustain the self and seize new opportunities amid the surging sea of change? How and why did this New England Yankee come to adopt the life of a southern planter, this honored soldier to renounce the authority of his commission to return to politics as the president of a conspiracy against national and international law? What can his twists and turns tell us about U.S. policy and the character of American territorial expansion, about intrigue in the Gulf borderlands after the War of 1812, about the motives and careers of American soldiers and filibusters, politicians and public men? What can the story of a national policeman turned international criminal, who then became a respectable businessman and community representative in the halls of the national but increasingly sectionalized Congress, tell us about the interplay of personal ambition, regionalism, nationalism, and international republicanism in the Gulf borderlands and the early American republic?

Detailed research in state and local archives will be necessary to uncover a fuller portrait of Ripley's career before and after his military service. After he graduated from Dartmouth in 1800, his legal skill and eloquence led to his election to the state legislature from a district in Maine in 1807, when he was twenty-five. The most prominent public record of his early views is a Fourth of July address from 1805. Joining a review of the nation's revolutionary struggle with republican platitudes, the young orator applauded American commercial prosperity and praised "the bloodless acquisition of an immense and fertile Territory." For his post-revolutionary generation he claimed the "momentous duty" to defend the nation and its inheritance, "not only from the violence of *foreign aggression*, but the more probable danger of *internal discord* ... the asperities of party spirit."[1] Ripley would spend his entire life confronting the complexities of politics, war, and expansion, negotiating the dilemmas they posed for his fortune and reputation.

After a break out of office, the aspiring public leader returned to the state house of representatives in 1811, serving as its speaker early in 1812.[2] Commissioned a lieutenant colonel that March, Ripley saw no active service in 1812, but he was promoted to colonel and wounded in 1813. The administration needed a Republican general from New England, and in 1814 Ripley became the youngest general in the army save Winfield Scott. Ripley and Scott were then assigned to lead the Regular Army brigades in the Left Division commanded by Jacob Brown, the principal American force on the Niagara front.[3]

Ambitious and diligent, Ripley had risen fast and appeared to be just the sort of fighting commander the nation needed. Space forbids detailing Ripley's part in the Niagara campaign that summer, but he clashed with Brown at every step.[4] Ripley played a crucial role in the Battle of Lundy's Lane; when Brown and Scott were incapacitated, Brown tasked Ripley with organizing the army's return to camp, but demanded he return several hours later to reclaim the battlefield. Ripley left several captured British cannon behind and did not attack the British when he returned to the field; he then pressed Brown to allow the army to withdraw to Fort Erie (where Ripley was later wounded) and across the Niagara. Brown responded by damning Ripley with faint praise.[5]

The Niagara campaign redirected Eleazer Ripley's life and led to his service in the Gulf borderlands, spurring him to question his earlier national allegiance. Brown's imputation that Ripley lacked moral courage set off a battle of reputations from which neither man could easily retreat, and Ripley felt "compelled by a sense of Justice" to his "own reputation," "paramount to all other considerations," to seek a court of inquiry.[6] Republican leaders thought the army's reputation was better served by unity, showering honors throughout the Left Division, than divisive efforts to assign blame for a battle most believed the army had won, and Congress resolved that the president should issue gold medals to all the generals to commemorate their gallantry.[7] Yet Brown refused to concede any credit, and a "Biographical Memoir" of his career published in February 1815 tacitly impugned Ripley's conduct while praising the other brigadiers.[8]

A Republican military hero from New England was more valuable than ever following the sectionalist discussions among regional leaders at the Hartford Convention, and Ripley was retained as one of only six generals in the regular army. President Madison halted the court of inquiry into his conduct after a single witness—Ripley's principal aide—had been heard. Acting Secretary of War Alexander Dallas and Secretary of State James Monroe then persuaded Brown, still Ripley's commander in the army's Northern Division, to sign a partial retraction of the language in his report of the Battle of Lundy's Lane, but Brown only stated that Ripley believed he had to retreat, which was no real concession concerning Ripley's motives.[9]

The letter was supposed to remain private, but Ripley's sense of persecution, his "sense of justice" and reputation, made it impossible to accept a half-hearted confidential remedy to public insult, and he or his friends published their version of the campaign that summer. Appealing to "the justice of the nation," these accounts condemned Brown's conduct of the campaign, implied that he had misrepresented Ripley's conduct, and presented a version of Brown's letter drawn "from recollection." This recollection transformed the letter into an apology, distorting Brown's stated desire "that there should be no misunderstanding of his remarks" into regret that he had "created an impression . . . which I by no means intended." Indeed, Ripley's account ultimately descended to personal slander and an outright lie, claiming that Brown "remained . . . in the rear [during the battle] . . . His wound was a flesh wound." It is surprising the generals did not duel, but there is no written evidence to explain why Brown did not challenge his antagonist.[10]

The quarrel continued in September 1815 with a third account, almost certainly written by Colonel Charles K. Gardner, concluding that Brown "was apprehensive that [Ripley] dreaded responsibility more than danger—that he had a greater stock of physical than moral courage."[11] Ripley responded by impugning Gardner's physical courage because he had missed the battle, leading the colonel to demand personal satisfaction. The challenge was a clear breach of military discipline and subordination, and Ripley arraigned Gardner for court-martial on a variety of charges, particularly cowardice. When Gardner was acquitted, Ripley published a version of the proceedings with Gardner's defense distorted, the verdict left out.[12]

Brown publicly reiterated his stance at a meeting of the officers stationed in Boston that autumn. "[I] believ[e] it due to my own honor to state . . . that I considered [Ripley] as having shrunk from responsibility," he said, claiming that Ripley had broken his word by publishing the contents of Brown's letter. Brown finally drew up court-martial charges against his subordinate, but did not press them, presumably to avoid embarrassing the government. Nevertheless, by the end of 1815 it was clear that the leading lights of the postwar army had united behind Brown's interpretation of Lundy's Lane and the Niagara campaign, so central to the army's reputation and their own. This made it unlikely that Ripley would survive another reduction in force, a possibility that weighed constantly on officers' minds during the half-decade after the war.[13] The battle of the generals was quieted early in 1816, when Ripley was transferred out of Brown's division to command the Eighth Military Department in Andrew Jackson's Southern Division. Ripley protested that "it would be . . . one of the most unpleasant occurrences in the world to be ordered to the westward," but he obeyed rather than resign his commission. Had it not been for this dispute, Ripley would never have been assigned to the Gulf; he would have remained comfortably nested commanding in Boston, and might well have remained in the army after the next reduction in force in 1821.[14]

The controversy that enmeshed Ripley was not unusual for the postwar army, where there were too many distinguished officers with too little to do. Proud, ambitious officers fought verbally, and sometimes literally, to sustain their reputations, refusing submission to any compromise against their claims or any slight against their honor, arraigning peers and arresting subordinates on the slightest pretext. Junior officers responded by demanding time-consuming investigations to justify their conduct, and the officer corps became divided among a complex array of shifting, often overlapping factions. Thus, its value to the army notwithstanding, the contested history of the Niagara campaign fostered intense friction during the years immediately after the war. Ripley and Brown were the highest-ranking of the antagonists; indeed Ripley seems to have absorbed much of the dissension and anger that might otherwise have been directed at Brown and Scott for their deficient reporting of subordinates' achievements.

Given the army's reduction and the opportunities that preceded the panic of 1819, many officers were willing, even eager, to resign from national service. Yet Ripley tried to hold on to his prestigious national position rather than returning to state politics like his brother (a militia general during the war), persisting for several years despite the animosity of his fellow generals and senior subordinates. Moving to the Southern Division put Ripley at a distance from most officers of the Left Division, but he seemed unable, and as a man of reputation was probably unwilling, to avoid controversy. Andrew Jackson, the major general commanding the Southern Division, foresaw this and tried to prevent Ripley's transfer, noting a strong feeling against the brigadier— more by reputation than personal acquaintance—among the officers of his command. Indeed, Jackson vowed that any officer who charged another with cowardice "and fails in the proof," as Ripley had at Gardner's court-martial, "ought to be dismissed for lying." Jackson eventually became reconciled to Ripley's transfer, praising him at a public dinner in Nashville that November, but the pervasive presence of Left Division veterans, the core of the officers retained in 1815, meant he could not escape controversy.[15]

Arriving in New Orleans as the most powerful American military commander in the southwest, Ripley was quickly drawn into intrigues over the future of the Spanish colonies to his east and west. His actions on the southern frontier eventually combined every dimension of the army's response to Spain's American collapse. Late in 1816 he received a proposal for the seizure of Pensacola from Jean Joseph Amable Humbert, a French Napoleonic exile and a prominent figure among the "Patriot" adventurers against Spanish rule concentrated at New Orleans. ("Patriot" was a term used by and for virtually anyone rebelling against Spanish colonial rule in the Western Hemisphere during the period 1808–25, and was often assumed by Anglo-Americans fighting the Spanish, whether in support of indigenous rebels or as filibusters, freebooters, or pirates pursuing self-aggrandizement.) Ripley advised the War Department that Humbert "has very little weight," enclosing his response to the filibuster: "In a State of Peace . . . I think it my duty to apprise you, that no act will be done on my part, or allowed of by any forces under my command, which will in any manner compromit the neutrality of the United States." Ripley was clearly torn between patriotisms, between values of republican liberty and accountability to civilian political authority: "I consider myself as a soldier bound to support the Government & Laws of my Country. . . . I view with the liveliest sympathy the struggles of the American Spaniards for their Independence. All the feelings of a man attached to free institutions prompt me to wish them unlimited success, while my duty as a Soldier requires me to refrain from assisting them without the orders of my Government. Such orders you may rest assured will not be given unless the Congress of the Nation assume openly and avowedly a belligerent attitude [toward Spain]." Ripley seemed clearly committed to the constitutional separation of powers, civilian control of the military, and accountability to national and international law.

Ripley hoped his inner tensions would be resolved through decisive American policy: "It is one of our principles of national policy to do nothing insidiously. While we remain apparently at peace with Spain, every duty which such a state requires will be enforced and practiced on the part of the government. Should aggressions finally arise to such a point as no longer bear toleration, the remedy would be found not simply in secret assistance to the Patriots, but . . . in again developing those moral and physical qualities which render the people of this Country invincible in Arms." A state of war would provide moral, ethical, and legal clarity and satisfy his sense of national pride and honor. Yet Ripley did not wholly disavow the entanglement into which he was being drawn. Though he declared that he would not trouble himself about the Patriots, he instructed the secretary of war, "Keep Humbert's name a secret. I shall make the old man useful." Doing so might be valuable for keeping tabs on the filibusters and preventing violations of American neutrality, and avoiding crises that could escalate into war with Spain and even Britain, but Ripley was entering a shadowy world of lures and snares, a fateful choice for his future.[16]

Ripley was a cautious, responsible, and insightful commander, and the danger that filibusters would cause war with Spain led him to ponder the defensive needs of his department. Indeed, he sent the War Department a five-page letter detailing Spanish troop strengths in Mexico and outlining the probable military strategy of the Patriots, "to seize strong positions on the Gulf of Mexico, of which their privateers give them the control, and to carry on a partisan warfare on the continent." "Hence," he wrote, "I apprehend a system of war which may . . . involve us in the contest, unless we have a force sufficiently powerful at this point" (the New Orleans region). Such depth of analysis, attempting to assess the character of a conflict and anticipate its second- and third-order effects, was rare among American generals during that period. Ripley observed that the Patriot forces were recruited largely from the United States, and he expressed concern that an offensive against Pensacola, perhaps under Francisco Xavier Mina, an authentic liberal revolutionary, would entice Americans into violations of the neutrality laws. Threats to the Spanish position on the Caribbean, and American involvement therein, might produce an unexpectedly powerful reaction. In Mexico the Spanish were "scattered through an almost indefinite extent of country and could not be concentrated," but Ripley believed that the Spanish would retake Pensacola from any Patriot force and "instantly possess themselves of Mobile," unless the Americans had "an imposing force to cover it."[17]

Ripley had much to worry about: the "heterogeneous" population of Louisiana and West Florida, the lack of effective militia in those regions, the shortage of regular officers and soldiers, many of whom had enlisted in 1812 and would soon leave the army unless funds became available to reenlist them, and the poor location of many defensive positions. Always thinking of the worst case in his military estimates, Ripley believed that the only means by which they could preserve themselves "quiet and tranquil (should such be the national policy)" was "an efficient force . . . sufficient for any contingency," and he requested two or three regiments "from the north" to bring his force to four thousand men. This meant nearly half the army's infantry, and it meant taking troops from the Canadian border, from Jacob Brown's Northern Division. It would almost certainly weaken or delay Edmund Gaines's operations against the Creeks and Seminoles, much more active antagonists—much more immediately threatened by American expansionism—than the Spanish. Ripley would not receive such reinforcements.[18]

The administration's fears of Ripley's expansionism may have been another reason why his pleas were ignored. His fears of a Spanish counteroffensive against Mobile notwithstanding, Ripley considered Havana vulnerable to U.S. and Patriot forces. He did not explain why he thought the Patriots would seize Pensacola rather than Havana, or why Spain would launch so powerful a counteroffensive to recover West Florida, but not Cuba, a much more valuable province. Nor did he address the potential for British or other European intervention should the United States assault Cuba. Following the path laid out by Jesup the preceding summer, Ripley asserted that he could seize Havana with three thousand U.S. troops, though he made it clear, unlike Jesup, that he would not try to do so unless Spain and the United States actually went to war.[19]

Meanwhile, unable to get a clear commitment from Ripley, the Patriots—or more precisely the New Orleans Associates, a group of American businessmen who hoped to profit from the colonial revolutions—turned to Colonel William King, the commander of the Fourth Infantry temporarily acting in Ripley's stead, for a loan of arms. King "indignantly refused," reporting their plans for a foray from Galveston to Adjutant General Daniel Parker along with his intention to forcibly disperse any filibuster—"or more properly speaking . . . *brigand*"—expedition entering the Eighth Department. King doubted such aggressive action would meet with the approval of his superiors but worried that the governor of Pensacola would be compelled to call on him for assistance to protect the inhabitants from "slaughter & desolation" at the hands of the invaders. Like Ripley, King advocated a clear-cut solution: "permit the '*Star Spangled Banner*' to wave o'er the works of the Barrancas [Pensacola] & St. Augustine & the Troops of the U.S. to occupy those posts subject to the future arrangement of the two governments."[20]

Unsure how far King might go, Adjutant General Parker felt compelled to affirm Ripley's republican internationalism while prohibiting U.S. military intervention, whatever the motive. Parker's words to King encapsulated the neutral stance officially taken by the U.S. government, as well as the antagonism many officers felt toward Spanish rule: "It is the policy of our government to have nothing to do with the Patriots or the authorities of Florida. I have no doubt the Patriots will not only win possession of Florida but that all South America will soon be independent of old Spain. I wish success to the Patriots but it is determined that we shall do nothing in favor of either party." Unfortunately, King got the impression that Parker thought he intended to assail Pensacola on his own initiative, and demanded to know, "[How] in the name of all the Gods . . . can it be possible that the President of the U.S. . . . believes that I am so dam'd a fool as to think seriously of entering the Spanish dominions with a military force, without the orders of my government?" Clearly King was not privy to Jesup's proposals to invade Cuba, nor to his threat to attack Pensacola to liberate Americans held prisoner there during the autumn of 1816. Nor does he seem to have reflected on Lieutenant Colonel Duncan Clinch's operations, initiated by Edmund Gaines with the support of Jackson contrary to the intent of the War Department, which culminated in the bombardment and destruction of the "Negro Fort," at Prospect Bluffs on the Apalachicola River, sixty miles deep in Spanish territory that July (see map C.1).[21]

Gaines, in contrast, felt no qualms about warning a Spanish officer visiting his headquarters that he would occupy Pensacola if the Patriots seized it, much as the United States had done with West Florida in 1810, and would do with Amelia Island in 1818.[22] Few officers stationed in the borderlands truly "wish[ed] success" to the Patriots in Florida. To do so would imply recognizing the legitimacy of autonomous, self-created polities that might continue to obstruct U.S. expansion, and the experience of the War of 1812 combined with the expansion of plantation agriculture had determined southern whites not to allow any nation save the United States to control Florida. Republican ideology demanded virtuous citizens, and army officers found few virtuous Patriots. But there was a fine line between the self-restraint of civic republican virtue and the martial self-assertion of territorial expansion; officers' sense of American national virtue could easily feed veterans' hard-won confidence in their martial prowess, their nation's natural title to land apparently wasted by dissolute Spaniards. Conduct that officers labeled banditry among Latin Patriots and private citizens might seem reasonable if undertaken by commanders serving the United States, a course they must have believed destined, if not manifest. In a world of expansive nationalism and popular expansionism, in the absence of unambiguous legal boundaries, the course of national growth and glory could easily take military officers beyond the constitutional bounds of accountability and subordination to civil authority, their transgressions not infrequently sanctioned by those very civil authorities or their inaction in the face of military adventurism.

Perhaps fortunately for American relations with Spain, Ripley was often absent from his command, lobbying in Washington during the first half of 1818 for money to build barracks and fortifications, leaving William Trimble in command of the district. This trip had been approved well before Gaines and Jackson escalated tensions along the Florida frontier into invasion and the First Seminole War, though it is reasonable to assume these generals were happy to see Ripley out of the way during active operations.[23] Trimble was often stationed or stationed himself at Fort Selden near Natchitoches, and tended to look west for threats and opportunities, giving a great deal of thought to possible operations in Texas during 1817 and 1818, repeatedly seeking intelligence on the Indians and Spanish forces while offering to explore the province. This implied an American military expedition across the Neutral Ground agreed upon by U.S. and Spanish military commanders to resolve the Sabine frontier crisis in 1806; it implied armed intrusion on land the Spanish considered their own—an invasion. Trimble shared Jesup's belief that war with Spain would be justified, reporting that Spanish officials were stirring up the Indians and trying to stimulate revolt among the French in western Louisiana. Sounding much like Jesup, Trimble boasted to his brother that he could raise enough volunteers "to march to the Rio del Norte" (the Rio Grande), seizing "valuable mines" en route. Yet by December 1817 he thought war less likely, advising Andrew Jackson—who was about to invade Florida—that the Spanish posed no threat from Texas. This did not mean that Trimble had lost interest in the future Lone Star State: he soon remarked that "were it not for a doubt that the [U.S.] government might abandon their claims to that country, there would in a few years be a sufficient American population to defend"—he initially wrote "hold"—the Spanish province.[24]

Ripley's trip to Washington also enabled him to continue his campaign for vindication while counteracting a resurgence of animosity from Brown (who was still commanding the Northern Division) early in 1818. Ripley may have provoked Brown's resumption of the dispute by some new act, though he does not appear to have published any further memoirs; the dearth of personal papers makes it impossible to say. Most threatening, of course, was the specter that Congress would further reduce the army: given the army's politics, dominated by Brown and Jackson, and Ripley's declining political significance, he would surely be the first general to be discharged. In the reduction of 1821 Brown was made the army's sole major general, with Scott and Gaines the only brigadiers, while Alexander Macomb accepted reduction to colonel. Jackson and Ripley had already left, or were leaving, the army. These developments were easy to foresee in 1818.

That spring, Brown labeled Ripley "depraved" and "unworthy" of "the gallant and honorable men" who served under Brown's command, accusing his antagonist of "efforts . . . to give falsehood the air of truth, & create a reputation which was not acquired in the field." Brown then sought a copy of his confidential letter from April 1815, along with certificates from Alexander Dallas and William H. Crawford, former secretaries of war, and Benjamin Crowninshield, a former secretary of the navy, that the letter had been intended to remain confidential, and asked that they be placed in the public War Department files. President Monroe rejected this appeal, and the documents were put away, to remain unopened, for the remainder of Monroe's term in office. Nevertheless, Brown seized the opportunity to present his version of the controversy to Jackson and John C. Calhoun, the incoming secretary of war, and the antagonists continued to collect evidence and advance their claims well into the next decade, long after Ripley had left the army. Ripley focused on absolving himself, or criticizing Brown, to influential officers like Jesup and potential historians of the campaign. Brown used his position as commanding general, which he retained until his death in 1828, and his connections supporting John Quincy Adams, to push his account directly to the new president, perhaps to forestall any attempt by Ripley to return to the army in case Brown died of complications from a stroke he had suffered in the autumn of 1821.[25]

Meanwhile, returning to the southwest in the summer of 1818, Ripley shared his subordinates' desire for military preparedness along the Texan frontier. Yet his work in Washington did little to remedy recruiting shortfalls during the postwar economic boom, and he soon found his command in much the same state as before. That October, facing "a black population so strong as continually to excite alarm," his total force, supposedly three to four regiments, amounted to no more than 630 soldiers, less than a single full regiment. Yet, "with the Spaniards [supposedly 500 in number] moving up to [the] frontier," spying in Natchitoches, "and already menacing [the] thin population," troops had been transferred from his department to Gaines's force watching Florida. The Eighth Infantry had only 144 of the more than 800 soldiers authorized by law, and Ripley warned that "this Regt. will be struck virtually from the rolls of the Army unless it be concentrated[,] organized and disciplined." Nor was there any "disposable [meaning deployable] militia force of any kind," and Ripley reported that the New Orleans branch of the Bank of the United States was demanding an unusually high discount on his official drafts. Ripley made his demoralization clear: "I actually am sickened with a State of service where every hope is defeated and every calculation disappointed."[26]

Yet the combination of Spain's inability to resist American advances in Florida and widespread public approval for Jackson's incursion may have also encouraged a new confidence and belligerence in the usually cautious Ripley, who sought funding for posts on the Red and Sabine rivers—positions within the demilitarized Neutral Ground agreed upon by U.S. and Spanish commanders in 1806. Reporting that "the Government & Inhabitants of Louisiana are greatly alarmed" by Spanish movements and the lack of troops, Ripley deployed the First Infantry, 360 soldiers, to the Sabine, within the Neutral Ground, at the end of October, and requested a loan of the Fourth Infantry, then occupying Pensacola, from Gaines's department. Indeed, Ripley may have begun planning his own thrust against Spain: in November he advocated building a road from the Mississippi River to Natchitoches, advising that it would "turn a pretty strong current of population towards the Sabine & up Red river and would do more than Posts and fortifications to cover that portion" of what he called "our country."[27]

Early in 1819 rumors appeared in northern newspapers that Ripley was concentrating a force at Baton Rouge to invade Texas. The political climate was not favorable for these plans or for Ripley's future: the economy was entering a depression and Congress was debating Jackson's invasion of Florida, encouraging talk that the army would be reduced in strength, pressure that grew following the Transcontinental Treaty with Spain. That summer Ripley incurred Jackson's enmity because he had failed to complete a road he had been ordered to build from Bay St. Louis, on the Gulf Coast west of Mobile, back in 1817. Ripley had put less than a hundred troops to work on the project; lack of supplies reduced them to "a state of starvation" and they raided private cornfields to eat. After two years no more than seventy miles of road had been cut. Ripley repeatedly failed to respond to Jackson's demands for information, and Jackson vowed that "there must be some neglect [a court-martial offense] somewhere." Under these circumstances Ripley's request for a furlough to settle his accounts was considered, probably correctly, a prelude to resignation. Whatever his motives, Robert Butler, the adjutant general of the Southern Division, gave Ripley the final push that July, indicating that he would accept Ripley's resignation, which he had not yet offered. Complaining that "this command has been difficult[,] laborious and embarrassing," Ripley sent a letter of resignation in August, a step he told Secretary of War Calhoun he had "contemplated for a long period." In September he was ordered to Washington to settle his accounts; his resignation was formally accepted in December, taking effect February 1, 1820.[28]

Meanwhile, Dr. James Long of Natchez organized two armed expeditions without government sanction—illegal invasions by forces not organized by government, of the sort later termed filibusters—from Louisiana into East Texas, declaring that region—and implicitly Texas as a whole—an independent republic.[29] The army chain of command responded carefully, in language full of constitutional precision. The delicate political situation that followed Jackson's invasion of Florida was one reason: "You will act in all cases in subordination to the civil authority . . . without their calls . . . make no military movement," read Ripley's order to Captain William Beard, the commander on the Sabine, on July 9, 1819. The only exception would be in case of an invasion of U.S. territory, presumably by Spanish troops attempting to preempt or pursue the filibusters. Caught between congressional criticism and his unwillingness to jeopardize U.S. chances for securing Florida, Jackson approved Ripley's instructions: "the military being subordinate to the civil power [they] cannot act in the present case, unless their services are required" by the appropriate civil officials. Filibuster sympathies among civil officials in Natchitoches prevented Beard from acting decisively, but an attempt was made to arrest Long at his headquarters in Natchez, army officers impounded a supply vessel in Louisiana, and a group of filibuster recruits was later arrested outside New Orleans.[30]

Ripley's actions toward the Long filibusters were not limited to defensive reinforcements and official neutrality, however. Early in 1817 he expressed antipathy for smugglers operating along the Gulf Coast—a view common among military commanders serving in the nation's borderlands—but his personal interests and connections seem to have evolved as he became more familiar with the opportunities available on the southwestern frontier. He had missed the First Seminole War while lobbying in Washington, and August 1818 found him lamenting that there was no "prospect of kicking up a dust. . . ." "Under these circumstances," he wrote, "we have nothing left but simply to vegetate." Unable to win glory in the nation's regular army, Ripley claimed to have disrobed himself "of all views of ambition," but worked to develop personal and financial contacts with filibuster financiers, the New Orleans Associates, in Louisiana. By June 1820 he had become sufficiently tired of "the repose and quiet" he now enjoyed as a citizen to accept election by Long's "Supreme Council" as president of the Republic of Texas. This supposedly carried a magnificent salary of twenty-five thousand dollars per year, far in excess of that paid to any general in the army, as well as a substantial land grant. Ripley then worked to facilitate Long's second invasion of Texas, raising funds and gathering supplies through his extensive network of connections—developed as a U.S. military commander—in Louisiana and the Southwest. Yet Ripley followed a cautious path even as a filibuster, remaining in New Orleans while advising Long to delay his advance against San Antonio.[31]

The departing brigadier left a bad taste among his fellow officers.[32] Even Perrin Willis, Ripley's assistant adjutant general, reported to Adjutant General Parker on the "loose manner in which General Ripley conducted . . . the business of the Department," charging that "from some cause, perhaps to conceal his own conduct, [he] preferred moving in turbid water." Indeed, the government sued Ripley for thousands of dollars in expenses, further discouraging action on the congressional resolution of 1814 thanking him for his service on the Niagara. Yet military accountability to law only went so far; I have found no military criticism of Ripley's ties to the filibusters who violated American neutrality laws. When it came to military hierarchy and civilian control, form apparently trumped motive—or some motives were so widely shared that only deviations from form raised military eyebrows.[33]

Ripley's aid did little good for James Long; despite some Mexican support the filibuster's second expedition never got far off the ground, and his force remained isolated at Bolivar Point opposite Galveston for nearly two years after its defeat in 1819. There is no evidence that Ripley ever physically joined the ragtag group. Long finally moved to seize La Bahía in September 1821, but surrendered to Spanish forces two weeks later, ending whatever remained of Ripley's limited exposure to filibustering. Meanwhile, Ripley's first wife had died of cholera, cutting another of the cords that bound him to New England. Yet association with Long may have done Ripley some good, demonstrating that the national military hero identified with expansionist regional objectives, for he was not long without a military role, accepting command of the Sixth Division of the Louisiana state militia as a major general.

Ripley was unable to kick up any more dust there than he had as a regular, and he resigned his militia commission in January 1822. Within six months he turned to state politics, gaining nomination for a seat in the state House of Representatives from New Orleans. This choice of venue proved mistaken: newspapers reported that "the French ticket prevailed by a great majority," and Ripley was defeated.[34] He then turned his back on these public careers for several years, reentering the legal profession, where he seems to have specialized in disputes over land claims. He also sent at least one letter to Mexican officials in support of a group of Americans who wanted to settle in Texas. Displaying more politesse than at any point since 1812, the former filibuster assured his correspondent that "they will conform to your language and political institutions, they would defend your territory [against "the Caddo and other Indians"], and . . . be of vast service to yourself individually and to the nation of Mexico." The Mexicans might be forgiven for suspecting these men of patriotism for the United States, rather than the land Ripley had so recently endeavored to absorb.[35]

Neither the national crime of filibustering nor political defeat diminished Ripley's public reputation in Louisiana, and he was appointed to the state Board of Commissioners for Internal Improvements. Having done well financially, and maintained his public visibility, the veteran campaigner returned to politics in the Jackson movement, authoring the formal address to the people of Louisiana by the Jackson state convention at New Orleans in February 1828. He secured his finances through marriage to a wealthy Natchez widow, the sister-in-law of Jefferson Davis, in 1830. He was rumored a candidate for the Senate the following year, though this turned out to mean the Louisiana Senate, to which he was elected. Perhaps embittered by his difficulties with banks in the army, Ripley voted for resolutions opposing the recharter of the Bank of the United States, and against state support for banks in Louisiana. He also spoke against nullification and advocated the constitutionality of the Tariff of 1828, but sought compromise through modifications to the law.[36]

Newspaper accounts of his political career, particularly his congressional campaign of 1834, provide a case study in the excesses of Jacksonian communications and the uncertainties of partisan identity in the early years of Jackson's administration: newspapers on both sides of the partisan divide repeatedly claimed Ripley as one of their own, sometimes with no regard for his record. The *Louisiana Whig*, for example, asserted his support for "a judicious protective tariff, a national bank, the supremacy of the laws and Constitution, as interpreted by the judiciary, and the duty of the Executive to enforce obedience to the Constitution and laws, when so interpreted." In reality, Ripley rejected protectionism; he had avoided taking a stance on Jackson's refusal to enforce the Supreme Court's decision in *Worcester v. Georgia*; and he gave no sign whatsoever of support for a national bank.[37]

Ripley worked in the Florida parishes of Louisiana to rally support for Edward Livingston's selection as U.S. senator, and he was rewarded with nomination and election as a representative in the Twenty-fourth Congress in 1834. His reemergence on the national political scene came alongside five crucial personal events. The first child of his second marriage died a year (1834) after her birth, and in 1835 he was beaten "in the most atrocious and cruel manner" by three men in New Orleans. (They apparently escaped capture, their motives unknown, though probably mere robbery.) That summer the government's attempt to recover losses it attributed to Ripley during his military service ended in a substantial victory for the former general, the U.S. District Court at New Orleans granting him a settlement of twenty thousand dollars. Bad news soon followed, however: Ripley's son, Henry Dearborn Ripley, was murdered in the massacre following the Texan surrender at Goliad the following March. These sorrows created sympathy for the aging congressman, and the court decision opened the way for the administration to reward his loyalty with the medal promised by Congress in 1814. Partisanship now helped reassert Ripley's military reputation: the *Washington Globe*, the administration newspaper, seized the opportunity to contrast the "noble daring" of the "gallant and gifted" Ripley, "so gloriously won in the day of danger," to the wartime performance of the Whig presidential candidate William Henry Harrison, "continually preparing for retreats—burning or burying provisions." Jacob Brown, dead since 1828, might have argued the point, but Winfield Scott did not, at least in public.[38]

Ripley's Jacksonian credentials were born out during the first session of the Twenty-fourth Congress, the only one he attended at any length. Yet his recorded utterances are more policy-oriented, and national or sectional, than overtly partisan in tone. Indeed, he at one point supported calls for reconsidering "the reeligibility . . . term, and patronage of the Chief Executive," a constitutional amendment aimed at Jackson by the Whigs. Most significant, Ripley had become a strong southern sectionalist, perhaps, according to an otherwise sympathetic biographer, "one of the most inexorable and ardent pro-slavery men of his time." In December 1835 the former New Englander spoke against petitions against slavery in the District of Columbia, declaring that there was no subject more important to his constituents than its defense, that he had been elected for just that purpose. Though he did not deny the right of petition per se, Ripley asked the support of northern representatives to allay southern fears; jointly rejecting abolitionist petitions would break down "the double wall of partition" between the sections and deter the "fanatics" who irritated the body politic. He was later quoted vowing that "he did not intend to sit here deliberating upon the question of receiving petitions from SLAVES," that "if it had come to that, he was for taking a course adequate to the crisis," rather threatening language when taken in context.[39]

Ripley was as much a western as a southern representative, however, easily linking the regions in his speeches. In April 1836 he "addressed the House at some length in reference to the exposed state of the sparsely-settled population on the western and southwestern frontier, the formidable . . . tribes of Indians" there, and the "necessity of providing for the permanent defense" of that frontier by raising a second regiment of dragoons. Two weeks later he expressed his surprise at John Quincy Adams's criticism of U.S. troops entering Texas, citing Adams's efforts to justify Jackson's seizure of Pensacola while secretary of state, "the principle of which [to prevent hostilities by the Indians] was identical with the present exigency" on the Louisiana border.[40]

Ripley's expansionism took commercial, populist, and agrarian form, mingling many of the varied elements of Jacksonian political economy. Worried by speculation and inflation during the land boom of the mid-1830s, he favored restricting preemption rights to public lands to actual settlers, rather than the "capitalists and speculators" he accused of buying "floating" rights to the most valuable land at great cost to potential public revenue. Settlement was more important than revenue, however: Ripley suggested granting the land to actual occupants free of any charge, the principle embodied in the Homestead Act twenty years later. The owner of several plantations, he supported the establishment of a first-rate naval station at Pensacola to protect U.S. and foreign commerce in the Gulf of Mexico. His expectation of harmonious growth, and his willingness to use government to promote and regulate it, was best demonstrated in his advocacy of public land grants to railroads. "Railroads were now the order of the day in the South," he proclaimed, enhancing land values and revenues in land once "comparatively worthless." Congress could forestall instability and corruption by prohibiting the development of towns and other speculative ventures within the bounds laid off for the railroads, while all the surrounding areas would benefit from easier access to markets.[41]

Ripley never lost sight of the vast bounty beyond the Sabine River; in July 1836 he addressed a public dinner in New York City for "some of the distinguished friends of Texas." Yet he had little opportunity to press for further American expansion, for he was struck with paralysis during the second session of the Twenty-fourth Congress, early in 1837. Though reelected to the Twenty-fifth Congress the preceding autumn, he was compelled to return home and remained there, his "precarious health" attributed to "a general derangement of the nervous system, occasioned in part by the bullet wound received through his neck at the sortie from Fort Erie," nearly a quarter-century before, "and partly from a *sun-stroke*." By the spring of 1838 he was rumored to be mentally incapacitated or insane, and he died a year later. He was buried in St. Francisville, the center of the West Florida rebellion against Spanish rule in 1810 and the short-lived West Florida Republic that followed: like that rebellion, a symbol of American expansionism and the paradoxical blend of liberalism and republicanism, the potential for liberty, opportunity, and slavery, expansionism carried west.[42]

Memory and reputation are tricky things, particularly in the court of public opinion. Whatever the merits of their positions, both Brown and Ripley conducted themselves poorly in their dispute. Ripley pressed his case more aggressively in public, through courts of inquiry that virtually had to find in his favor, while Brown attempted to confine the dispute to officers' private meetings and War Department letters that few Americans would ever see. At the same time, Brown's ability to exile Ripley to New Orleans severely limited Ripley's influence in debates over the army's structure and made it clear that Ripley would be vulnerable to discharge during any reduction in force, effectively denying him the chance for an extended military career. Brown's death in 1828 removed the leading obstacle to Ripley's redemption in the court of national public opinion; the District Court's decision in his favor, and the consequent award of his congressional medal, created an opportunity for wholesale revisionism at Brown's expense. An article reprinted in the *Army and Navy Chronicle*, the army's professional journal, shows that Ripley retained supporters, however confused, in the army community, asserting that Lundy's Lane "was fought upon Gen. Ripley's own responsibility," that he captured sixty British cannon—about ten times the actual number present—and that Brown ordered him to retreat across the Niagara, leaving the guns to be recaptured! Indeed, the article conveyed the impression that Ripley had commanded the battle; Scott was not mentioned at all, and Brown appeared only momentarily, as Ripley's "commander-in-chief" ordering the retreat. Ripley was in such extreme ill health, and the claims of the article were so extreme, that it seems unlikely that he was the author, but it is astounding that no rebuttal from Scott or his supporters can be found within the army's sole professional journal. Presumably no former or serving officer took it seriously.[43]

Lauded as "the patriot, the statesman, the hero" in epitaphs by newspapers in Louisiana, Ripley's star soon faded amid the tumult of sectional strife. The principal national papers, both Democratic and Whig, appear to have missed his death. A biography of Zebulon Pike in 1860 included sections on Ripley and Jacob Brown but hardly referred to their dispute. Nicholas Baylies's biography, published in 1890, concentrates on Ripley's wartime record and constitutional views, never mentioning his southern command or Long's expeditions. Ripley could have done far worse. Lundy's Lane should be seen as his shining moment, and he led capably at Fort Erie, but his postwar record was undistinguished and not infrequently disingenuous: resigning his commission to join private citizens invading a country with which the United States was at peace merits the harshest criticism.[44]

Yet Ripley recovered from the enmity of his former comrades in arms and returned to regional prominence—albeit in a different region than before the war—as a successful lawyer, planter, and politician. He was not alone in making such a transition in location, loyalty, and identity, as the large wartime officer corps faced a deep postwar reduction in force amid a surging export market, particularly in southern cotton. Their positions and careers threatened by republican antagonism toward a costly national force, which was no longer essential given Anglo-American rapprochement and Spain's withdrawal from North America, the years around 1820 became a sorting out period for the army, as men less certain or committed to a military future departed for greener pastures. For many, these pastures were political; the road to politics was often paved through law, and in the South through plantations. Serving a national institution, posted less according to sectional origin than by institutional circumstance and the demands of national security, numerous officers born in the North spent their careers, military and post-military, in the South. Ripley was not the first Massachusetts man to settle in Louisiana after he left the army, nor was he the first to command militia, practice law, and serve in local and state office. Several of the military officers who directed the occupation and initial government of Louisiana in 1804 and 1805 settled there, most notably Edward Turner and Bartholomew Shaumburgh in Natchitoches and Henry Hopkins in Attakapas. Nor was this pattern limited to Louisiana: several of the commanders who led the occupation of Mississippi in 1798 settled there, Isaac Guion as a planter and Andrew Marschalk as a printer, when discharged in 1802. Nor were all these men Republican expansionists like Ripley: Guion, Turner, and Shaumburgh had all been accused, with good reason, of Federalist sympathies.

This transition from national military officer to southern man of affairs—planter, lawyer, and sometime land speculator—was much more pronounced after the War of 1812, when a much larger officer corps faced a much deeper reduction in force. A fair number of these commanders had added reason to leave the army because of their dissatisfaction with its leaders over credit for their service in the Niagara campaign. Thus the rigidity of genteel, and especially military, conceptions of honor, the zero-sum clash of reputations, spurred capable men, full of pride and ambition, to reenter civilian life in search of wider horizons than would be available in the small army retained in 1821. These men had the initiative, and in many cases the connections, to go far regardless of their military careers and reputations, as Ripley had already done before the war, and their demonstrated courage in military service garnered them fame, much less disputed in civilian quarters than among jealous fellow commanders. Their military assignments took them far from the regions of their nativity, introducing them to the full opportunities of the expanding nation, drawing men like Ripley from the settled shore to the far frontiers of commercial enterprise.

Not a few of these men turned to politics, territorial, state, and national. Frustrated in his quest for justice from Edmund Gaines, William Trimble resigned in 1819 and almost immediately became a U.S. senator from Ohio, serving until his death in 1821 from complications of the wound he suffered at Fort Erie. Robert Carter Nicholas, Trimble's predecessor as lieutenant colonel of the First Infantry, was blamed for his regiment's disordered rebuff at Lundy's Lane but was promoted to colonel by seniority shortly thereafter and retained command of the Eighth Infantry (with Trimble as his subordinate) in 1815; he ultimately preferred tending to his plantations in Virginia and Kentucky and left the army four years later. His Virginia connections secured him a lucrative post as U.S. agent to the Chickasaw in 1821, but his principal interest became his sugar plantation in Louisiana; he served as a U.S. senator from Louisiana from 1836 to 1841, while Ripley was serving in the House of Representatives: half of the state's small congressional delegation were disgruntled veterans of the Left Division.

This transition from military command to civilian leadership was equally apparent in the other trans-Mississippi frontier territories and states, particularly Arkansas and Missouri, half of whose congressional delegation of 1837 had been regiment commanders in the War of 1812, and in Florida, where Andrew Jackson served as the first territorial governor and drew on many former subordinates, his "military family" of aides and staff officers, for his administration. For these men, like James Miller of the Twenty-First Infantry who served as the civilian territorial governor of Arkansas between 1819 and

1825, departure from the army was usually more a matter of choice than compulsion, and federal office smoothed their transition to civil life.[45]

The clash of reputations, combined with the shortage of institutional opportunities despite distinguished service, made continued military careers a dubious option for many veterans of the War of 1812. In the short term this led many to the private sector, from republicanism to liberalism, and, along with the Panic of 1819 and debates over the role of government, may have encouraged growing cynicism and the decline of public authority during the Jacksonian era. During the 1810s Ripley was brought low by his anger and frustration, achieving rapid early success, rising quickly, and souring on public service when his motives were questioned by men who were determined that no possible obstacle obscure the reputation of American arms. Yet he returned to public life and service, for public and private life can be distinguished but not severed, as Americans have repeatedly learned to our cost. Whether from ambition, pride—which, with identity, we gain in the eyes of the public, as well as our own—or a resurgent vision of public service, Ripley ultimately recognized that republicanism was essential to liberalism, that citizenship requires the obligation of loyalty to something larger than one's self.

Notes

1. Eleazar Wheelock Ripley, *An Oration Pronounced at Hallowell* (Portland, Me.: Willis, 1805), Early American Imprints, S9264, pp. 7–12. Neither the National Union Catalog of Manuscript Collections nor the electronic database Archives USA reveal major collections of Ripley's private papers; there is one box of papers associated with his first wife, Love Allen Ripley, in the Forbes Library, Northampton, Massachusetts.

2. Charles R. Corning, "General Eleazar Wheelock Ripley," *Granite Monthly* 17 (July 1894): 1.

3. *Life of General Jacob Brown, to Which Are Added Memoirs of Generals Ripley and Pike* (New York: P. J. Cozans, 1860); Donald Graves, *Field of Glory: The Battle of Crysler's Farm, 1813* (Toronto: Robin Brass, 1999), 218–27.

4. Robert S. Quimby, *The U.S. Army in the War of 1812: An Operational and Command Study*, 2 vols. (East Lansing: Michigan State University Press, 1997), 518; Richard V. Barbuto, *Niagara 1814: America Invades Canada* (Lawrence: University Press of Kansas, 2000), 163, 170; G. Auchinleck, *A History of the War between Great Britain and the United States of America during the Years 1812, 1813, and 1814* (1855; repr. London: Arms and Armour Press, 1972), 313; Statement by Major Darby Noon, March 18, 1815, in *Facts Relative to the Campaign on the Niagara in 1814* (Boston: Patriot-Office, 1815), 5. The Niagara Campaign has been examined in numerous works; the best are by Robert S. Quimby, Richard V. Barbuto, and Donald E. Graves, *Where Right and Glory*

Lead! The Battle of Lundy's Lane, 1814, 2nd ed. (Toronto: Robin Brass, 1997); see also John D. Morris, *Sword of the Border: Major General Jacob Jennings Brown, 1775–1828* (Kent, Ohio: Kent State University Press, 2000).

5. Ripley, Sept. 4, 1814, file R-77, Office of the Secretary of War, Letters Received, Registered Series, Record Group 107, National Archives (hereafter, SWLR: Reg., without providing addressee, unless it was not the secretary of war); Brown to Secretary of War John Armstrong, July 7, 1814, in E. Cruikshank, ed., *The Documentary History of the Campaign upon the Niagara Frontier*, 9 vols. (Welland, Ont.: Lundy's Lane Historical Society, 1896–1908) (also available in the *Library of American Civilization* microfiche collection, LAC 23870–73), 2: 38–41; Brown to Secretary of War John Armstrong, Aug. 7, 1814, file B-82, SWLR: Reg.

6. Ripley, Aug. 29 and 31 (quotations), Sept. 15, and Nov. 21, 1814, files R-47, 35, 51, and 83, SWLR: Reg.

7. Senate Journal, Nov. 2, 1814; Francis B. Heitman, comp., *Historical Registry and Dictionary of the United States Army, from Its Organization, September 29, 1789 to March 2, 1903*, 2 vols. (Washington, D.C.: Government Printing Office, 1903), 1: 47–48.

8. "A Biographical Memoir of Jacob Brown, Major General in the Army of the United States," *Port-Folio* (February 1815): final page.

9. Brown, April 28, 1815, file B-274, SWLR: Reg. Some accounts date the letter April 30, but that was the date noted on the cover sheet. This letter is actually enclosed in Brown, May 16, 1818, file B-218, SWLR: Reg., rather than the files from 1815.

10. *Facts Relative to the Campaign on the Niagara in 1814*, v, vi, 5–8, 16, 44, 24–27, 29, 40, appendix, and 46. The "Biographical Memoir" of Ripley that appeared in the August *Port-Folio* contained the same ideas, in softer language.

11. Quotation from "Battle of the Falls," *Port-Folio* (September 1815): final page; "Memorandum of Occurrences and Some Important Facts Attending to the Campaign on the Niagara" (undated draft), and "Remarks on the Military Memoir of Major General Ripley, published in the *Portfolio*" (undated draft), Gardner Papers, New York State Library (hereafter NYSL).

12. Morris, *Sword of the Border*, 190–91; Gardner to Ripley, Sept. 14, and to Brown, Sept. 25, 1815, and memorandum of the court-martial, in Gardner's handwriting, Feb. 6, 1816, Gardner Papers, NYSL; "Proceedings of a General Court Martial, etc." (Boston, 1816), in *Early American Imprints*, second series (Shaw-Shoemaker), no. 38714.

13. Brown to Dallas, Nov. 20 and Dec. 23, 1815, encls. to Brown, May 16, 1818, file B-218, SWLR: Reg.; committee of officers, Boston, undated note, Brown Papers, LC; draft court-martial charges, December 1815, Jacob Brown Papers, American Antiquarian Society.

14. Harold D. Moser, David R. Hoth, and George H. Hoemann, eds., *The Papers of Andrew Jackson*, 6 vols. to date (Knoxville: University of Tennessee Press, 1994) (hereafter, *PAJ*) 4: 25; Ripley, May 27 and June 29, 1816, files R-80 and 101, SWLR: Reg.; Secretary of War William H. Crawford to Andrew Jackson, March 15, 1816, Office of the Secretary of War, Letters Sent, Record Group 107, National Archives.

15. Jackson to Secretary of War Crawford, April 24, 1816, *PAJ* 4: 26.

16. Jan. 6, 1817, file R-28, SWLR: Reg., enclosing Ripley to Humbert, Jan. 2, 1817. See also Harris Gaylord Warren, "Pensacola and the Filibusters, 1816-1817," *Louisiana Historical Quarterly* 21 (July 1938): 806-22.

17. Jan. 18, 1817, file R-73, SWLR: Reg. See William C. Davis, *The Pirates Laffite: The Treacherous World of the Corsairs of the Gulf* (New York: Harcourt, 2005); Harris Gaylord Warren, "The Origin of General Mina's Invasion of Mexico," *Southwestern Historical Quarterly* 42 (July 1938): 1-20; and Warren, ed., "Documents Relating to the Establishment of Privateers at Galveston, 1816-1817," *Louisiana Historical Quarterly* 21 (October 1938): 1086-1109.

Mina's expedition did attract several former officers discharged after the War of 1812, but Warren exaggerates their number. In "Pensacola and the Filibusters," 817, he asserts that Mina's expedition was "largely made up of former American army officers," a statement that takes the logic out of "largely." In "Xavier Mina's Invasion of Mexico," *Hispanic American Historical Review* 23 (February 1943): 53, Warren maintains that "many adventurous young men . . . [who] had held commissions in the United States army," joined Mina, but he does not present any more substantial evidence to support this assertion. Only three such men have been identified who actually served in the regular army as commissioned officers; like the former officers who joined the Gutiérrez-Magee expedition, these men were short-timers, averaging two to three years' service. Indeed, only one, ex-major Ross Bird, had served more than two years, and only he had served during peacetime. Two were from the Northeast (one of whom had served in New Orleans) and one was from Louisiana, proportions, however small the absolute numbers, akin to those of the former officers involved in the Gutiérrez-Magee expedition. The Louisianan, Henry D. Peire, had served as a volunteer aide-de-camp to James Wilkinson in 1812 and 1813, leading to his commission as a major in the Forty-fourth Regiment that retook Grand Terre from the Baratarians. Peire commanded the Seventh Infantry in the battles around New Orleans, winning a brevet for gallantry in combat, but like most officers commissioned during the war he had been discharged in 1815. Several other filibuster leaders have been labeled army officers but were actually New Orleans businessmen and community leaders who had served as temporary volunteer aides or supply contractors with Jackson during the New Orleans campaign. These civilians exaggerated their status through association with the masculinity of military service and the connections implied in a federal commission; some scholars have unintentionally exaggerated the expansionism of postbellum army officers by lumping such civilians among them.

18. Feb. 5, 1817, file R-47, SWLR: Reg.

19. Jan. 18, 1817, file R-73, SWLR: Reg. See Jesup to Jackson, Aug. 18, and Monroe, Sept. 8, and Jackson to Jesup, Aug. 1, 1816, Jesup Papers, LC; Jesup to Claiborne, Aug. 10, 1816, Jesup Papers, William L. Perkins Library, Duke University.

20. King to Parker, Jan. 25, 1817, Parker Papers, Historical Society of Pennsylvania (hereafter HSP).

21. Jeanne T. Heidler and David S. Heidler, *Old Hickory's War: Andrew Jackson and*

the Quest for Empire (Mechanicsburg, Pa.: Stackpole Books, 1996), 78; Parker to King, Feb. 23, 1817, file P-32, SWLR: Reg.; King to Parker, April 2, 1817, Parker Papers, HSP.

22. Warren, "Pensacola and the Filibusters," 816–17.

23. Capt. Alexander Gray to Lt. Col. William A. Trimble, Jan. 8, 1818, William Allen Trimble Papers, Ohio Historical Society (hereafter OHS); Ripley to Jackson, Dec. 30, 1817 and June 11, 1818, *PAJ* 4: 480 and 502.

24. Trimble to Jesup, May 6, 18, and 20, 1817, Jesup Papers, LC; Jesup to Trimble, April 1, Trimble to Major (assistant adjutant general) Reynolds M. Kirby, March 17, to Ripley, March 17, April 2, and June 4, to Jackson, Dec. 13, 1817, and unaddressed draft, Jan. 26, 1818, William Allen Trimble Papers, OHS; William Trimble to Allen Trimble (his brother), March 17, 1817, William Allen Trimble Papers, Western Reserve Historical Society. See also Calhoun to Trimble, Oct. 16, 1818, Office of the Secretary of War, Confidential Letters Sent, Record Group 107, National Archives.

25. Brown, May 16, 1818, file B-218, SWLR: Reg.; Brown, memorandum of the Niagara campaign, Brown Papers, LC; Ripley to Jesup, Oct. 3, 1818, encl. in Jesup to Brown, Dec. 20, 1818, and Ripley to Henry Lee, Jan. 23, 1826, Brown Papers, Massachusetts Historical Society; Ripley to McNeil, April 30, 1827, Miscellaneous Manuscripts, New York Historical Society; Morris, *Sword of the Border*, 191–92.

26. Ripley to Trimble, March 15 and April 16, 1818, William Allen Trimble Papers, OHS; Oct. 31 (two letters) and Sept. 9, 1818, files R-46, 48, and 30, SWLR: Reg.

27. Oct. 31 and Nov. 31, 1818, files R-48 and 72, SWLR: Reg.

28. *New Hampshire Sentinel*, Jan. 9, and *American Advocate and Kennebec Advertiser*, Feb. 13, 1819, Readex Early American Newspapers website (hereafter, REANPS); Ripley to Butler, June 6, Jackson to Ripley, July 31, Butler to Ripley, July 16 and Sept. 11, and Parker to Butler, Dec. 22, 1819, *PAJ* 4: 536, 305, 539, 545, and 554; Ripley to Calhoun, Aug. 20, 1819, in Robert L. Meriwether and W. Edwin Hemphill, eds., *The Papers of John C. Calhoun*, 28 vols. (Columbia: University of South Carolina Press, 1969) (hereafter *PJCC*), 4: 260.

29. Captain William C. Beard to Natchitoches district judge Henry Adams Ballard, June 14, 1819, to U.S. Marshal John C. Carr, June 18, 1819, and to Ripley, June 22, 1819, all encls. to Jackson, July 24, 1819, file J-55, SWLR: Reg. Ballard had been a leader in the Gutiérrez-Magee expedition; as Natchitoches district judge in 1812, Carr had done little to discourage violations of the neutrality law. The filibusters also included Edmund Gaines's brother James, a civilian businessman; their backers included usual suspects like Bernardo Gutiérrez and the Kemper brothers. See Edward A. Bradley, "Fighting for Texas: Filibuster James Long, the Adams-Onís Treaty, and the Monroe Administration," *Southwestern Historical Quarterly* 102 (January 1999): 336–37; Bradley, "Forgotten Filibusters: Private Hostile Expeditions from the United States into Spanish Texas, 1812–1821" (Ph.D. diss., University of Illinois at Urbana-Champaign, 1999); Davis, *The Pirates Laffite*, 393–436 passim (which does not cite Ripley); and from the Spanish perspective, Alfred B. Thomas, "The Yellowstone River, James Long, and Spanish Reaction to American Intrusion into Spanish Dominions, 1818–1819," *New Mexico Historical Review* 4 (1929): 164–87.

30. Ripley to Beard, July 7, 1819, and Jackson to Ripley, July 24, 1819, both encls. to Jackson, July 24, 1819, file J-55, SWLR: Reg. (which contains much of Beard's correspondence on the incident); Bradley, "Fighting for Texas," 338. See also Beard to the Officer Commanding, Eighth Military Department (Ripley), Oct. 10, 1819, and Beard, October 2, encl. in Jackson, Oct. 10, 1819, SWLR: Reg. Other military commanders reacted more energetically: remembering the trouble Aaron Burr had caused him more than a decade before, brevet Brigadier General Daniel Bissell, commanding the Ninth Military Department from St. Louis, immediately dispatched Captain Robert Coombs into the Neutral Ground to Crow's Ferry on the Sabine River, with orders to prevent anyone crossing from the American side (Coombs, June 9, 1819, SWLR: Reg.). See also the letter of an officer of the army to the editor of the New Orleans *Gazette*, Oct. 8, 1819, excerpted in the *Daily National Intelligencer*, Nov. 22, 1819.

31. Ripley to Jesup, Feb. 28, 1817, Jesup Papers, LC; Ripley to Christopher Van Deventer, "Private," Aug. 15, 1818, Christopher Van Deventer Papers, William L. Clements Library, University of Michigan; and November 14, 1819, *PJCC* 4: 408 (second and third quotations); Harris Gaylord Warren, *The Sword Was Their Passport: A History of American Filibustering in the Mexican Revolution* (Baton Rouge: Louisiana State University Press, 1943), 250–51; Charles A. Gulick, Jr., et al., eds., *The Papers of Mirabeau B. Lamar: Edited from the Original Papers in the Texas State Library*, 6 vols. (1920–27; repr., Austin: Pemberton Press, 1968), 2: 94–98 and 103–4. In 1818 the longtime filibuster leader Fulwar Skipwith wrote to Secretary of War Calhoun that Ripley said the United States would purchase land from him to build an arsenal (July 24, 1818, *PJCC* 2: 423).

Information about Ripley's role in the Long expeditions is very difficult to come by. There are no overt references in the *PAJ* or *PJCC*, the American State Papers, the Jacob Brown Papers at the Massachusetts Historical Society and the Clements Library, or in the voluminous letters received by Adjutant and Inspector General Daniel Parker in the Historical Society of Pennsylvania, nor have I found any in my National Archives research in Southern Division correspondence, the SWLR: Reg., SWLR: Unregistered, War Department Letters Sent, and Adjutant General's Office Letters Sent. Nor did I find any in the electronic databases Early American Newspapers, Early American Imprints, Nineteenth-Century U.S. Newspapers, Sabin Americana (which contains a number of mid-nineteenth-century histories of Texas and Louisiana), or the American Periodicals Series. Neither Henry S. Foote, *Texas and the Texans, or, Advance of the Anglo-Americans to the South-West* (Philadelphia: Thomas, Cowperthwait, 1841); Henderson K. Yoakum, *History of Texas from Its First Settlement* (New York: Redfield, 1855); nor Charles E. A. Gayarré, *History of Louisiana* (New York: W. J. Widdleton, 1867) mention Ripley in connection with Long.

32. Jackson, Jan. 17, 1820, file J-178, SWLR: Reg.; Jackson to Calhoun, Sept. 7, 1819, *PJCC* 4: 306; Calhoun to Jackson, Jan. 22 and Feb. 5, 1820, *PJCC* 4: 591 and 635–36.

33. Taylor to Jesup, April 20, 1820, Zachary Taylor Papers, LC; Willis to Parker, Aug. 23, 1820, Eighth Military Department, Letters Sent, Record Group 98, Entry 75, National Archives.

34. New Orleans *Eastern Argus*, Feb. 1, *Baltimore Patriot*, July 15, *Salem* (Mass.) *Gazette*, Aug. 9, 1822, all in REANPS. See also "General Ripley—Not Dead!" *American Beacon and Norfolk and Portsmouth Daily Advertiser*, Dec. 30, 1820.

35. For example, G. Davis to George Graham, Feb. 4, 1826, in *American State Papers: Documents, Legislative and Executive, of the Congress of the United States, Class VIII, Public Lands*, 8 vols. (Washington, D.C.: Gales and Seaton, 1832-61), 4: 946; Ripley, Au[gust?] 1823, no addressee, at www.tamu.edu/ccbn/dewitt/adp/archives/documents/ripley_emigrate.html. Further discussion of Ripley's finances, and his role in Louisiana state politics, must await examination of the manuscript census and sources in Louisiana. A document of 1820 placed an Eleazer W. Ripley in possession of a tract east of the Pearl River (Mobile), based on a claim derived from a squatter; *American State Papers: Public Lands*, 3: 444. The census schedule for 1830 (reel 43, p. 211) has an "El W Ripley" in East Feliciana Parish but does not enumerate any members of the household.

36. Nicholas Baylies, *Eleazer Wheelock Ripley and the War of 1812* (Des Moines, Iowa: Brewster and Co., 1890), 90, 94, 97, and 101; *New Hampshire Patriot and State Gazette*, March 3, 1828; *Baltimore Patriot*, Jan. 21, and *Rhode Island American and Gazette*, Dec. 1 and 6, 1831; *Richmond Enquirer*, July 31, 1832, all in REANPS.

37. *National Intelligencer*, July 17 (in *Salem Gazette*, Aug. 5), *New Hampshire Patriot and State Gazette*, Aug. 4, *Rhode Island Republican*, Aug. 6, *Louisiana Whig*, Aug. 25 (in *Baltimore Patriot*, Sept. 20, quoted), 1834, REANPS; Baylies, *Eleazer Wheelock Ripley and the War of 1812*, 101-12. The "General Ripley" cited in several newspaper accounts of a disputed election in Maine ca. 1830 was Ripley's brother James.

38. Baylies, *Eleazer Wheelock Ripley and the War of 1812*, 100; *New Hampshire Patriot and State Gazette*, Jan. 26, and *New Bedford Mercury*, June 26, 1835; Sen. Henry Hubbard (N.H.), "General Ripley," *U.S. Senate, Register of Debates*, 24th Congress, 1st sess., June 3, 1836 (Washington, D.C.: Gales and Seaton), 1676-86; *Washington Globe*, quoted in the *Macon* (Georgia) *Telegraph*, June 9, 1836, REANPS; Winfield Scott, *Memoirs* (New York: Sheldon and Co., 1864), 142-46.

39. *Niles' Weekly Register*, Jan. 7, 1837; *Congressional Globe*, March 30, 1836, 307; *New Hampshire Patriot and State Gazette*, Aug. 9, 1836, REANPS; Corning, "General Eleazar Wheelock Ripley," 7-8; *Globe*, Dec. 18, 1835, 31-32; "The Slaveholder's Heart," *Antislavery Record* 3 (March 1837): 7.

40. *Globe*, April 22 and May 7, 1836, 386 and 434.

41. Baylies, *Eleazer Wheelock Ripley and the War of 1812*, 109-10 and 121; *Globe*, Jan. 7, April 7, and March 26, 1836, 82, 333, and 294.

42. *Niles' Weekly Register*, July 23, 1836, 345, and September 2, 1837, 2; *Rhode Island Republican*, April 4, 1838; Baylies, *Eleazer Wheelock Ripley and the War of 1812*, 137 and 146.

43. "Presentation of the Medal Awarded by Congress to Gen. Ripley," reprinted from the *Madisonian* (March 22, 1838), *Army and Navy Chronicle* 6 (April 5, 1838): 213.

44. *Clinton Louisianan*, quoted in the *New Hampshire Patriot and State Gazette*,

April 1, 1839, REANPS. It does not appear that the *Globe, Niles' Weekly Register*, or the *National Intelligencer* published epitaphs for Ripley.

45. We can also recognize a transition, and growing differentiation, between civil and military leadership roles in the frontier and the borderlands. The territories of Indiana, Mississippi, Orleans, and Louisiana were all initially governed, at least outside their capitals, by regular army commanders or men temporarily clothed in military rank. Even after the transfer of sovereignty to the United States, and occupation by U.S. military forces escorting federal civil officials, William Henry Harrison and William Hull, the first governors of the Indiana and Michigan territories were former army officers, as were most of the major territorial civil officials of Arkansas and Florida during the 1820s. Note that the Northwest Territory had a substantial cadre of civil officials, though many were Continental Army veterans, and "military rule" was limited to outposts in Indiana—particularly Vincennes in the late 1780s. This was also true in the Southwest Territory, which became Tennessee in 1796. Orleans (Louisiana) Territory had sufficient population, and Mississippi Territory was so limited in space actually available to white settlers, that military and regular army veteran influence in civil governance and officeholding seems to have diminished rapidly after being very significant in 1798 (in Mississippi) and 1804–5 (in Louisiana). I have not investigated the civil officership of Alabama and Mississippi territories during the late 1810s: though there were probably many veterans of the War of 1812, population growth was so rapid, and the transition to statehood so quick, that overt military influence and connections probably dissipated with equal speed. Thus, by the 1820s, active duty military officers no longer held territorial civil offices, and the role of former officers was decreasing in the more thickly populated territories. Nevertheless, we should remember that between 1804 and 1832, military men governed Missouri directly until 1807, and former regular army officers did so between 1807 and 1809, 1813 and 1820, and 1828 and 1832. Similarly, a large proportion of the civilian Indian agents were former regular army officers.

Conclusion

GENE ALLEN SMITH AND SYLVIA L. HILTON

Throughout their lives individuals negotiate complex entanglements of multiple identities and loyalties. Identity is a socially constructed sense of self. All individual human beings function in the world with several (or even many) personal identities. Gender, age, family, marital status, race, ethnicity, nationality, local community, religion, language, education, political ideology, profession, and economic status immediately spring to mind as significant elements of individual identities. All of these criteria (and many others) lend themselves to constantly variable combinations and interpretations. Different personal identities may remain stable or change over time in response to new circumstances. Identities may be perceived by individuals and communities as compatible and complementary, or conflictive. Identities express a person's sense of self in relation to society as a whole and to recognized social groups within the community. This means that membership in any one group depends on both the individual's acceptance of that identity, and the group's recognition of that person as a member. However, groups and communities may apply selective criteria to distinguish different "levels" of membership so that an individual might be seen, for example, as a fully fledged member, or one with only partial rights and duties, or a provisional, conditional, or temporary member. Finally, it is in the collective interest of any community to try to know and exert some control over the different personal identities of its members, but individuals may reject socially assigned identities, and sometimes they can also try to keep one or more identities partially or wholly hidden.

Loyalty is generally understood to be both an ethical principle and a voluntary personal commitment, and it must express a relation with at least one other person, although it is most highly valued as applicable to larger social and political connections. Different social groups expect their members to be loyal to the group, and to express that loyalty actively in the practical defense and promotion of collective interests. This may represent no problem in a large social or political community when the essential interests of its constituent groups converge or coincide, or when there is a broad consensus on the need to subordinate particular group and individual interests to the larger general interest. Yet groups and individuals may experience inner tensions or manifest open conflict when perceiving that their different identities and loyalties are, or have become, incompatible. Many historians, compelled by the quest for "intellectual order," now work on the assumption that individuals have many identities and related loyalties, and that sometimes these are conflicted.[1]

In trying to understand revolutionary upheavals, historiographical explanations that tend to concentrate on structures and processes can easily lose sight of the individual human being. This book has purposefully focused on individuals who lived in the Gulf borderlands of North America (from West Florida to Texas) between the 1760s and the 1820s (maps I.1 and C.1). Their lives offer concrete examples of how people dealt with issues of identity and loyalty in a time and place in which nothing was certain except constant change.

The period may be defined in many ways, but whichever interpretive model one prefers—crisis of the *ancien régime*, the era of liberal bourgeois revolutions, of Atlantic revolutions, of western democratic revolutions—that sixty-year span was the historical cradle of modern nation-states. Consequently, some older historiographical traditions emphasized ethnocentric and nationalistic interpretations. By contrast, more recent work holds that people living in the Americas actually exhibited strong patriotic sentiments rooted in their local and imperial identities and loyalties. This was true in both the Spanish and the British empires.[2] Strong imperial loyalties are represented in this book by Robin Fabel's study of Philip Livingston, Ed Townes's profile of Hugo O'Conor, and Sylvia Hilton's examination of Spanish officials. Chapters by Ed Townes, Betje Black Klier and Diane North, and Sophie Burton indicate that Antonio Gil Ibarvo, the husbands of the four Rouquier sisters, and Marie Thérèze dit Coincoin clearly felt bound by strong ties, albeit for different reasons and in different ways, to their local communities.

Whether one chooses to adopt the perspectives of the Hispanic monarchy, of the British Empire, or of the nascent U.S. republic; whether one focuses on political, social, economic, or cultural processes; whether one's primary concern centers on the struggles of migrants, Native Americans, blacks, or women, one of the significant keys to understanding this historical period resides in the revolutionary redefinition of the relations between individuals, their local and national communities, and their local and national governments. In that process of redefinition, one of the central political debates revolved around the renegotiation of reciprocal rights and obligations.

The governments interested in the Gulf borderlands knew well that coercion was not an option. Indeed, contrary to theories of imperialism that

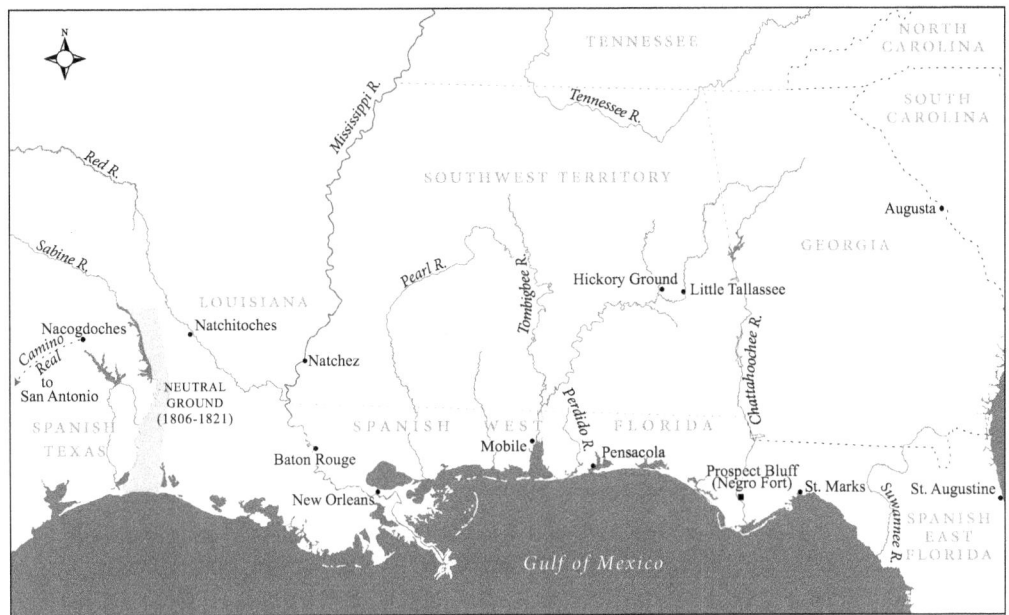

Map C.1. The Gulf Coast borderlands, 1783–1821. Map by Tracy Ellen Smith, www.cdrtexas.com.

envision power emanating only from the center to the peripheries, theories of imperial rule explain that the inability of empires to exert directly the full force of central government authority in their distant peripheries meant that responsibility must be delegated to cooperative local elites. Thus, according to Herfried Münkler, "the interesting question is . . . how the loyalty of local decision-makers can be ensured."[3]

In the United States, Fisher Ames thought that the answer was "for the government to follow, rather than to control the general sentiment."[4] Pondering the political limitations facing early U.S. governments, one British historian explains that they understood the necessity of "careful and sensitive statecraft well attuned to the sensitivities of constituent communities."[5] The chapter by Sylvia Hilton illustrates that this judgment could just as easily apply to Spanish analyses of the situation in Spain's far-flung imperial frontiers on the Gulf Coast of North America. In short, it meant that metropolitan or central government authority remained weak in these North American borderlands, and consequently individuals enjoyed greater freedom to define and pursue their own interests and priorities as circumstances changed or opportunities arose.

When the first American civil commandant of Upper Louisiana, Amos Stoddard, addressed the people of that territory in 1804, his words showed that he understood the complexities of the situation. Speaking of "the actual or implied compact between society and its members," and the "reciprocal duties" of citizens and governments, Stoddard spelled out the familiar arguments designed to win the loyalty of the region's inhabitants and to encourage the acceptance of their new national identity as Americans. He affirmed that "the constituted authorities of the Union" would protect not only citizens' rights of liberty, property, and religion, but also "their feelings, and all the tender felicities and sympathies so dear to rational and intelligent natures." In turn, citizens must obey and help to uphold the laws, repel any invasion, and defend public liberty through inexcusable militia service. He did not doubt that, thus far, the inhabitants of Spanish "Luisiana" had been loyal to Spain. In fact, he took it for granted, and in that assumption found justification for his expectations regarding their loyalty to the Union: "It is confidently expected that you will not be less faithful to the United States than you have been to his Catholic Majesty." Stoddard's references to "feelings," "tender felicities and sympathies," in tandem with "rational and intelligent natures" suggest that he appreciated the importance of recognizing the intervention of both emotion and reason in human motivations. Like Esteban Miró and others before him, he understood that patriotic sentiments could not be improvised, and that they might spring from many different sources, but he placed the highest value on patriotism inspired by knowledge and reason. "Patriotism will gradually warm your breasts and stamp its features on your future actions," he predicted, but he then stressed that "to be useful, it must be enlightened—not the effect of passion, local prejudice or blind impulse."[6] Evidently, he feared that the emotional components of patriotism would tend to sustain loyalties rooted in long-standing local and imperial identities, which might continue to compete advantageously with the nascent and as yet weak American nationalism.

The racial, national, and cultural diversity of the population inhabiting and moving within the Gulf borderlands is clearly a common thread weaving throughout the chapters in this volume. At the same time, all of the people studied here were imbued with a palpable sense of political instability created by the changing sovereignties and governmental regimes in this region. Consequently, the individuals presented in this volume are seen to be adopting attitudes, making decisions, and acting in accordance with different personal interests, and a few even seem to be bent on reinventing themselves.

Some individuals and social groups obviously had greater freedom than others to move smoothly from one public identity to another. This is so because human endeavors in social contexts result from the convergence of capacity, will, and opportunity, and the absence of an opposing force. Many human beings have similar capacity, but the will to act depends more on each individual's temperament. In these Gulf Coast borderlands of the revolutionary era, opportunities definitely favored some more than others, but the crucial factor was probably the existence or absence of social opposition to suggestions or aspirations that certain groups or individuals might recast their identities.

Since identities are perceptions of self in social contexts, individuals tend to value membership of local and, sometimes, national communities. Indeed, many if not most people find the greatest self-interest and satisfaction (whether rationally or emotionally defined) not in the individual freedom and independence that might result from retreat or exclusion from social relations, but in the recognition of their status as members of one or more social groups, that is, in inclusion. The enjoyment of diverse advantages linked to these memberships meant that favored individuals who inhabited the Gulf Coast borderlands amid the turmoil of the revolutionary era were expected to show their loyalty often.

The ways and degrees in which individuals embrace imperial, national, and other political loyalties are not so easy to discern. Government and military service may be taken to indicate a conscious commitment of loyalty, and this criteria plays a significant part in the ideas and lives of Esteban Miró, Martín Navarro, Hugo O'Conor, and other Spanish colonial officials mentioned in different chapters, Philip Livingston (who served as the governor of British West Florida in the 1770s), Oliver Pollock, Daniel Clark, William C. C. Claiborne, William Dunbar, Arsène Lacarrière Latour, and Eleazer Wheelock Ripley, all of whom served the U.S. government, as well as Louisiana's black militiamen, whose frustrated aspiration to make the transition from Spanish to American service is reflected in the chapter by Erin M. Greenwald.

Immigration requires a different kind of commitment. Deliberate, personal decisions lay behind the movements and actions of emigrants from Europe such as Oliver Pollock, Daniel Clark, François Tastanegy, Arsène Lacarrière Latour, and two of the Rouquier sisters' husbands. In these cases, expressions of loyalty were simply necessary to enable their personal pursuit of private fortunes.

By contrast, choice and commitment played a much smaller part in the imperial or national "identities" imposed on the Native American and African inhabitants of the Gulf borderlands by France, Spain, England, and the United States. While imperial rivalries lasted, the Creeks, Dehahuit of the Caddos, the black militia of Louisiana, and Coincoin might be considered to have had discrete if decreasing margins for maneuvering, but on being transferred with the territory into U.S. hands, all became obliged to accept U.S. sovereignty yet without recognized benefits of nationality. Their ethnic identities, based on their own constructions of communities of descent, cultural heritage, and (perhaps) solidarity in the face of their experience of marginalization, could provide a sense of membership of and loyalty to larger social groups. However, white prejudices and pressures meant that Native Americans and people of African parentage faced daunting odds that made any attempt to negotiate their racial identities very difficult.

F. Todd Smith's analysis of Native American acceptance of Spanish and U.S. flags in their villages illustrates how symbols can be differently construed. For the Americans, putting the U.S. flag in place of the Spanish flag represented Caddo recognition of U.S. national sovereignty and political jurisdiction. For the Caddos, it meant that the Americans were now their suppliers, friends, protectors, and fathers, and as such could expect a conditional Caddo loyalty. But the Caddos wanted to maintain friendly diplomatic relations and trade simultaneously with the Spaniards, and the U.S. flag was not deemed to express any aspect of Caddo identity. In short, as relatively weak but independent polities that aspired to maintain their neutrality, and in order to maximize advantages and reduce risks to their own integrity, both the Caddo and the Creek peoples studied by Kathryn Braund sought peace, friendship, and trade with all nations, enmity and war with none.

Economic interests, too, clearly drove individuals to pursue their personal fortunes wherever and by whatever means they could. The Gulf borderlands offered ample opportunities for profitable investments in land cultivation and speculation or in commercial ventures. Thus, several of the individuals studied in this book sought mercantile connections and engaged in economic activities and financial commitments that tied them to larger, sometimes transnational, networks. Philip Livingston, Antonio Gil Ibarvo, Oliver Pollock, Daniel Clark, the Rouquier husbands, and even Dehahuit, and Coincoin, as shown in the respective chapters, all bent their talents and energies to the pursuit of material wealth.

Finally, family ties provided a major criterion for the studies of the identities and loyalties of Coincoin, Livingston, and the husbands of the four Rouquier sisters. Coincoin's parentage put her at a disadvantage, but as a free black woman, she succeeded in maximizing the opportunities she had, despite the fact that her options were limited. Livingston's impressive social advantages gave him far greater freedom of action to exploit a wide range of opportunities. Marital alliances provided the routes to personal advancement for the Rouquier spouses. For these individuals, it was their families that anchored their identities and claimed their first and most enduring loyalties.

The almost sixty years of uncertainty and changing flags of the revolutionary era in the Gulf region led people—out of choice or necessity—to rely on their own abilities to redefine or negotiate their local community and national identities. Individuals often traded their loyalty in order to secure personal advancement and economic gain. Moreover, the constant pressures generated by imperial and national rivalries in the Gulf borderlands meant that identities and loyalties could change easily as long as the region remained in political flux. By the early 1820s the region no longer represented a nexus for imperial competition, as migrants from the United States swarmed across the area and established what would prove to be a lasting political union. In doing so, a new U.S. national identity and loyalty began to crystallize, reducing significantly the earlier fluidity that had created certain kinds of opportunities for individual initiative and enterprise. This book illustrates some of the ways in which people adjusted their attitudes, choices, and conduct amid myriad complexities, as they lived their daily lives in a land where little could be taken for granted except the changing times.

Notes

1. Ian K. Steele, "Exploding Colonial American History: Amerindian, Atlantic, and Global Perspectives," in Louis P. Masur, ed., *The Challenge of American History* (Baltimore: Johns Hopkins University Press, 1999), 70–95, at 78, explains: "People's thoughts and actions could be affected by attachment to their colony, their 'nation,' their monarch, their religious faith, or their perception of civilization. Then, as now, individuals usually stacked several loyalties together quite comfortably; different aspects of life simply evoked different mental boundaries. Naturally, historians are particularly interested in examining moments when loyalties collide . . . it would be helpful, though difficult, to learn the relative importance of each of these 'imaginary communities' in less trying times."

2. See, for example, John H. Elliott, *Empires of the Atlantic World: Britain and Spain in America, 1492–1830* (New Haven, Conn.: Yale University Press, 2006). On Anglo-Americans, see John Murrin, "A Roof without Walls: The Dilemma of American National Identity," in Richard Beeman, et al., eds., *Beyond Confederation: Origins of the Constitution and American National Identity* (Chapel Hill: University of North Carolina Press, 1987), 333–48, 338–39.

3. Herfried Münkler, *Empires: The Logic of World Domination from Ancient Rome to the United States* (Cambridge: Polity Press, 2007), 23.

4. Fisher Ames to William Tudor, April 25, 1789, in Charlene Bangs Bickford and Kenneth R. Bowling, *The Birth of the Nation: The First Federal Congress, 1789–1791* (Madison, Wis.: Madison House, 1989), 1.

5. Colin C. Bonwick, "American Nationalism, American Citizenship, and the Limits of Authority, 1776–1800," in Cornelis A. van Minnen and Sylvia L. Hilton, eds., *Federalism, Citizenship, and Collective Identities in U.S. History* (Amsterdam: VU University Press, 2000), 34, explains: "Shared interests and common values are of themselves unlikely to guarantee the survival of a complex and extended political

system; patriotic fervor can fade under stressful circumstances to a point at which national commitment comes to be questioned and then replaced by an alternative allegiance. Careful and sensitive statecraft well attuned to the sensitivities of constituent communities is also an essential ingredient if long-term cohesion is to be sustained."

6. Amos Stoddard, "Address to the People of the Territory of Upper Louisiana, St. Louis, March 10, 1804," repr. in Louis Houck, *A History of Missouri from the Earliest Explorations and Settlements until the Admission of the State into the Union* (Chicago: R. R. Donnelley and Sons Co., 1908), 2: 370–72.

About the Contributors

Elizabeth Urban Alexander is associate professor of history at Texas Wesleyan University. She is the author of the award-winning biography *Notorious Woman: The Celebrated Case Of Myra Clark Gaines* (2001).

Kathryn Holland Braund is professor of history at Auburn University. Her research focuses on the ethnohistory of the Creek and Seminole Indians in the eighteenth and early nineteenth centuries. Her first book was *Deerskins and Duffels: The Creek Indian Trade with Anglo-America, 1685–1815* (1993). She is also the coauthor, with Gregory A. Waselkov, of *William Bartram on the Southeastern Indians* (1995) and editor of an annotated version of Bernard Romans's *A Concise Natural History of East and West Florida* (1999) and an annotated edition of James Adair's 1775 classic: *History of the American Indians* (2005).

H. Sophie Burton is an independent scholar who has written numerous articles about the Louisiana-Texas frontier as well as a book, coauthored with F. Todd Smith, entitled *Colonial Natchitoches: A Creole Community on the Louisiana-Texas Frontier* (2008).

Light Townsend Cummins holds the Guy M. Bryan, Jr., Chair of American History at Austin College in Sherman, Texas. He is interested in the late eighteenth and early nineteenth century southeastern Spanish Borderlands, specializing in Anglo-American migration into the lower Mississippi River valley and Texas. He is the author or editor of seven books, including *Spanish Observers and the American Revolution*, *A Guide to the History of Louisiana*, and *Louisiana: A History*. He has recently completed a biography of Emily Austin, the sister of Stephen F. Austin.

Gilbert C. Din taught at Fort Lewis College for many years. He is the author of numerous publications on colonial Louisiana and Latin American history, including the award-winning *Spaniards, Planters, and Slaves: The*

Spanish Regulation of Slavery in Louisiana, 1763–1803, *The Canary Islanders of Louisiana*, *Francisco Bouligny: A Bourbon Soldier in Spanish Louisiana*, and *The New Orleans Cabildo: Colonial Louisiana's First City Government, 1769–1803* (with John E. Harkins).

Robin F. A. Fabel is professor emeritus of history from Auburn University. He is the author of *Bombast and Broadsides: The Lives of George Johnstone* (1987), *The Economy of British West Florida, 1763–1783* (1988), *Shipwreck and Adventures of Monsieur Pierre Viaud* (1990), and *Colonial Challenges: Britons, Native Americans, and Caribs, 1759–1775* (University Press of Florida, 2000).

Erin M. Greenwald is a Ph.D. candidate in history at Ohio State University. Her dissertation is entitled "Company Towns and Tropical Baptisms: From Lorient to New Orleans on a French Atlantic Circuit." She is currently the exhibitions editor for the Historic New Orleans Collection.

Sylvia L. Hilton is head of the Department of History of the Americas at the Complutense University of Madrid, Spain. She has published extensively on Spanish-Indian-Angloamerican interactions and international relations in early modern North America. Her books include, with coeditor Cornelis van Minnen, *Political Repression in U.S. History*, *Frontiers and Boundaries in United States History*, *Nation on the Move: Mobility in U.S. History*, and *Federalism, Citizenship, and Collective Identities in U.S. History*.

Betje Black Klier has written numerous books and articles in English and French on the Sabine Borderlands and French travelers in Texas. The former Auburn University professor often journeyed across the Borderlands to her home in Austin, where she discovered a key French travel journal at the University of Texas. Her history of the Pavie family in France and Louisiana and translation of the travel narrative *Pavie in the Borderlands: The Journey of Theodore Pavie to Louisiana and Texas, 1829–1830, Including Portions of His Souvenirs Atlantiques* won the Best Book in Texas History award from the East Texas Historical Association as well as the prestigious nonfictional prize of the Dallas Public Library for Outstanding Contribution to New Knowledge. Klier, a historian and art historian, is completing books on the art and music of the 1818 Bonapartist colony at Champ d'Asile.

Andrew McMichael is associate professor of history at Western Kentucky University. Interested in the colonial American Atlantic World—focusing on British colonial North America and its connections with Latin America—he is author of *Atlantic Loyalties: Americans in Spanish West Florida, 1785–1810* (2007). He is currently examining the Atlantic dimensions of the Seven Years' War.

Diane M. T. North, Ph.D., an award-winning history professor, teaches historical writing and U.S. and Western history for the University of Maryland University College. Although born and educated in the nation's capital, she has lived throughout the United States and worked as an art historian and historic preservation specialist before turning her attention westward. A scholar of the western expansion of the United States, North edited Klier's prize-winning volume on the Sabine Borderlands. Her other publications include *Samuel Peter Heintzelman and the Sonora Exploring & Mining Company*, as well as the cartographic history of explorer-adventurer Herman Ehrenberg, and various scholarly articles on preterritorial Arizona and California history.

F. Todd Smith is professor of history at the University of North Texas. He has written four books on Indians of the Louisiana-Texas frontier, the most recent of which is entitled *From Dominance to Disappearance: The Indians of Texas and the Near Southwest, 1786–1859* (2005). His latest book, *Colonial Natchitoches: A Creole Community on the Louisiana-Texas Frontier* coauthored with H. Sophie Burton, was published in 2008.

Gene Allen Smith is professor of history, director of the Center for Texas Studies at Texas Christian University, and curator of history at the Fort Worth Museum of Science and History. He has written, edited, or coauthored several books on aspects of naval and maritime history, the War of 1812, and early American territorial expansion in the Gulf South, including *Filibusters and Expansionists: Jeffersonian Manifest Destiny, 1800–1821* (1997) and *Thomas ap Catesby Jones: Commodore of Manifest Destiny* (2000).

J. Edward Townes teaches in the history department at Texas Christian University. His research interests include comparative North American frontiers in the eighteenth and nineteenth centuries, with particular emphasis on the Spanish Borderlands.

Samuel Watson is associate professor of history at the United States Military Academy, teaching courses on American frontiers and the U.S. Army through 1900. He is the editor of *Warfare in the USA, 1784–1861* (2005) and the author of the forthcoming *Frontier Diplomats: The Army Officer Corps at Work in the Borderlands of the Early American Republic, 1814–1846*.

Index

Acadians, 9, 16, 65, 163
Adams, John, 249–50
Adams, John Quincy, 299, 312, 331, 336
Adams-Onís Treaty (Transcontinental Treaty), 5, 156, 223, 332
Adelman, Jeremy, 4, 24
Ailhaud St. Anne, Jean Baptiste, 104
Alabama, 39, 63, 210
Alexander, Mary, 183
Allegiance: within political flux, 5–6, pledges to the Spanish Crown, 8; loyalty oaths and immigration, 12–15; influence of membership, 24–25; of Upper Creeks to the British Empire, 48; of New Orleans Free Colored Battalion to Spain, 124; of New Orleans Free Colored Battalion to the United States, 125; Caddo relationship with French and Spanish, 142; the United States and Spain influence Indian allegiances, 144; Spanish and Americans compete for Red River tribes, 146–48; Spain and the United States during the War of 1812, 153; Kadohadacho importance, 156; local leaders vs. Crowns, 163; in borderlands, 165; borderlands limit of, 170–71; Athanase de Mézières pledges to Spain, 173; importance of family and community loyalty, 178–79; Juan Cortés changes, 227; western farmers and navigation of Mississippi for, 244; concerns regarding Clark, 250–51; Latour takes oath of allegiance to U.S., 304; Spain restore allegiance of marginalized, 312; Ripley and his national allegiance, 323
Allende y Unzaga, Ignacio José de, 227
Alliot, Paul, 19
Alvarez de Toledo y Dubois, Gen. José, 228

Amelia Island, 329
American Philosophical Society, 274
American War for Independence, 202; reshaped boundaries, 4; afterward Loyalists remained in West Florida, 9; Creek loyalty during, 39–41; Milford departed France after, 6; Livingston family supported, 189, 193–94; events led to, 191; Livingston acquire land during 192; reached West Florida, 192; and Oliver Pollock, 198; Louisiana identity changed after, 199–200; Louisiana's economic role after, 200; U.S. controlled commerce after, 204; shaped identity, 206–9; Bloodworth served in 222; forced Spain to change policy, 243; specie short afterward, 246; Lafayette award land for service in, 303–34
Ames, Fisher, 349
Amite River, 190–91, 242
Andry, Manuel, 132
Angelina River, 141, 143
Apalachicola River, 298, 329
Apatana Ajoo (Mad Frog), 74
Ardennes, 65, 80
Areche, José de, 173–74
Arkansas, 141, 274, 276, 310, 316, 339
Arkansas Post, 310
Arkansas River, 310–12
Aron, Stephen, 4
Arredondo, Joaquín de, 228
Atlantic market system, 198–202, 204, 211–12
Atlantic World, 12, 14, 23, 314
Attoyac River, 177
Augusta, Ga., 43–47, 52
Augustin, Nicolas, 90–91
Aurillac, France, 299–300, 314
Austin, Stephen F., 224

Badin, Pierre, 98
Bahamas, 67
Bahia Road, 175
Baltimore, 201, 203, 209, 212, 243, 253
Bank of the United States, 193, 331, 334
Barataria Bay, 302, 305
Barclays, 260
Barnard, Timothy, 47
Bastrop, Baron de, 17, 258
Batoni, Pompeo Girolami, 185, 193
Baton Rouge, 204; Anglo-American militiamen in, 19; Pollock's land grant in, 205; Dunbar lived in, 275; part of the Felicianas, 285; Clark purchased land in, 286; land not sold in, 288; 1810 revolution, 298, 310; Latour drafted city plan, 303; forces concentrated in, 331
Battalion of Orleans Volunteers, 126
Battle of Lundy's Lane, 323–24, 337–39
Battle of Medina, 228
Battle of New Orleans, 224, 298–99, 302, 315
Battle of Saratoga, 198
Baylies, Nicholas, 338
Baynton, Wharton, and Morgan, 202
Bayou Bienvenu, 305
Bayou Lafourche, 305
Bayou Manchac, 190, 204–5, 242
Bayou Pierre, 143, 146–47, 227
Bayou Sara, 205, 209–11
Bayou Terre aux Boeufs, 305
Bay St. Louis, 332
Beard, Capt. William, 332
Beauregard, Elias Toutant, 303
Beckley, John, 114
Bega, Marie-Anne, 80
Bellechasse, Col. Josef, 260
Bergeron, Antoine, 104
Berlin, Ira, 200
Bermúdez y de Soto, Antoine Manuel, 89
Bernarde, Ursule, 103
Bladensburg, 298
Blondel, Lt. Phillipe, 166
Bloodworth, James, Sr., 221–22
Bludworth, Eliza, 231
Bludworth, James, 221–23, 227, 231
Bolivar Point, 333
Bolivia, 272

Bolton, Herbert Eugene, 170, 224
Bonaparte, Napoleon, 222; sold Louisiana, 4; First Consul, 79; and imperial wars, 219, 227–28; usurped Spanish throne, 231; Treaty of San Ildefonso, 251; and Louisiana, 252–53, 302, 311; Peace of Amiens, 301
Bond, Phineas, 243
Bonfeld, John, 210
Bonwick, Colin, 4
Boone, Daniel, 10, 11
Bordeaux, France, 210
Boston, 42; American success at, 46; Tea Party, 190; merchants in 207; newspaper, 254, 308; U.S. officers stationed in, 324–25
Boston Port Act, 190
Bourke, Father Carlos, 20
Bowles, William Augustus, 67–69, 71–72, 81
Braund, Kathryn, 352
Brazil, 228
Brazos River, 170–71
Brooks, Philip C., 278
Brown, Jacob, 323–25, 327, 330–31, 334, 337–38
Brown, John, 15
Bruin, Peter Bryan, 17
Bryan, Jonathan, 47
Buard, Jean Baptiste, 98
Buard, Marie Thérèze, 99, 223
Bucareli, Antonio María, 167, 172, 174–76
Buchet, Christian, 65–66
Burn Dennet, 200
Burnet, David, 224
Burr, Aaron, 3, 115, 225–26, 258–60, 262
Burton, Sophie, 348
Butler, Robert, 332

Cabello, Gov. Domingo, 175, 177
Caddi (hereditary chief), 140–42, 144, 148, 152–57
Caddo Lake, 140, 142, 148
Cadillac, Gov. Antoine Laumet de La Mothe, sieur de, 165–66
Cadiz, 228
Cadron, Ark., 310
Cahokia, 202
Calhiche, 96
Calhoun, John C., 330, 332

California, 275–76, 280, 310–11
Cameron, Alexander, 41, 48–49, 51, 53–54
Camino Real, 169, 175
Canada, 189, 219, 231, 298
Cane River, 90, 103
Captain Allick, 46
Capuran, Joseph, 98
Caracas, Venezuela, 226
Caribbean, 3, 9, 163, 183, 202, 229, 231, 309, 327
Carondelet, 205
Carondelet, Gov. Francisco Luis Héctor, Barón de, 123; distrust of migrants, 11–12, 16; and settler loyalty, 17–18; ruled Louisiana and West Florida, 65; and Milford, 70–71, 73, 75–78; feared invasion, 76–78; worked with Clark, 283
Carr, James, 228
Carr, Judge John C., 222, 224–31
Cartes d'Artheits, Jacques, 224–25, 231
Casa Calvo, Gov. Marquis de: concerned about patriotism, 22; at Louisiana transfer, 123, 255; animosity toward Laussat, 241; Spanish governor of Louisiana, 250–51, 253; worried about American expansion, 278; and Indians, 280–81; affirmed Spanish policy, 281, 287–88
Casas, Luis de Las, 20
Castro, José Manuel de, 146
Castro, Ramón de, 177
Catt (Indian thief), 67
Caughey, John W., 71
Cayton, Andrew, 4
Chaise, Louis de la, 99
Chalmette Battlefield, 224, 298
Charleston, S.C., 52, 78
Chase, Jeanne, 6
Chattahoochee River, 45
Chef Menteur Pass, 307
Chesapeake Bay, 305
Chester, Peter, 188–92
Chew, Beverly, 253, 259, 262
Chief Etienne, 149
Chief Small Prince, 77
Chief Zoquiné, 147
Chota, 45
Chouteau, 223
Cibolo Creek, 171
Cienfuegos, Cap. Gen. José, 313–14
Claiborne, Nathaniel, 114
Claiborne, William C. C.: Indians and New Orleans free blacks, 113–33; arranges meeting between Turner and Kadohadachos, 144–45; claims American influence over Kadohadacho, 150–51; meets with Dehahuit, 154–55; Natchitoches name for, 223; communications regarding Shibley and Glass's explorations, 226–27; concerns regarding the Neutral Ground, 229–30; receives Clark's New Orleans letter, 241; transfer of Louisiana, 255–58; feud with Clark, 260–62; appointment to territorial governor, 273; loyalty as territorial governor, 276–77; dealings with Indians and slaves, 280–82; intrigues during his tenure as territorial governor, 286–90; arrives in New Orleans, 303; loyalty of, 351
Clark, Daniel: New Orleans and loyalty: 18; becomes U.S. consul in New Orleans, 122–23; and Kadohadachos, 144; becomes American, 207; the American identity of, 211; life history of, 241; economic and political ventures in New Orleans, 245–62; loyalty of, 273; ideas regarding loyalty, 276; suspicious of the Spanish, 280; political characteristics of, 282–87; interest in personal gain, 289; questions regarding loyalty, 351
Clark, Daniel, Sr., 241–46, 282
Clark, George Rogers, 10, 13, 77, 198, 207
Clark, William, 225
Clarke, Elijah, 77
Clinch, Lt. Col. Duncan, 328
Coartación (self-purchase), 95–97, 99–102
Cochran and Rhea Store, 205
Code Noir, 91–92
Coincoin, Dominique, 90
Coincoin, François, 89, 90
Coincoin, François (child), 90
Coincoin, Françoise, 89
Coincoin, Jean Joseph, 89
Coincoin, Joseph Antoine, 90
Coincoin, Louis, 90
Coincoin, Marie Eulalie, 90

Coincoin, Marie Françoise (mother), 89
Coincoin, Marie Françoise (daughter), 90, 98
Coincoin, Marie Louise, 89, 91, 104
Coincoin, Marie Thérèze dit: and the free black population of Natchitoches, 89–97; and manumission, 99–103; loyalty to community, 248; problems with identity, 351–52
Coincoin, Minette, 98
Coincoin, Pierre, 90, 100
Coincoin, Roselie, 90
Coincoin, Thérèze, 89
Colden, Lt. Gov. Cadwallader, 187
Coleraine, Northern Ireland, 200
Collell, Francisco, 20
Collier, Simon, 271–72, 289
Collot, Gen. George Victor, 79
Colorado River, 310
Columbia River, 225
Comite River, 190
Company of Military Adventurers of New England, 190–91
Company of the Indies, 121
Continental Congress: planning meetings with Creek and Cherokee Indians, 41–42; Creeks attend talk sent by, 46; receiving Creek peace tokens, 57; Philip's uncle attends, 190; Robert Morris as chair of Secret Committee of Correspondence, 206; Pollock as financial agent of, 249; setting precedent for slavery in the new territories, 282
Cordero, Antonio, 147
Corkran, David, 56
Cornell, Joseph, 74
Cortés (Cortez), Juan, 224–29, 231
Cossacks, 80
Coutts, James, 185
Coweta, 41, 46–47, 50–52, 54–55 74
Cowkeeper of Latchoway, 47
Cox, Isaac Joslin, 10
Coxe, Daniel W., 246, 252, 258
Coxe and Clark, 246–47, 249, 253, 260
Crawford, William H., 223, 330
Crèvecoeur, Hector St. John de, 212
Croix, Teodoro de, 167–68, 175–76
Crook, Ben, 78

Crowninshield, Benjamin, 330
Cruillas, Viceroy Marqués de, 167
Crystal Hill, Ark., 310
Cuba: arrival of Marquis de Casa Calvo from, 123; Louisiana and captain general of, 173; Pollock traveled to, 201; Shaler as American consul to, 227; Spanish control of, 231; protests by Captain-General Someruelos in, 252; Saint Domingue refugees fleeing to, 301; Latour sent to, 313; Latour lived in, 314; Ripley's plan to take Cuba, 327–28
Cummins, Light Townsend, 23
Custis, Dr. Peter, 147, 225
Cut Finger, 151
Cutthroat Bob, 67

Dallas, Alexander, 323, 330
Dartigaux, Jean Baptiste, 104
Dartmouth, 322
Daudin, Louise Marguerite, 300
Dauphiné, France, 104
David Franks and Company, 202
Davis, Jefferson, 334
Davis, Susan Garrett, 210
Dearborn, Henry, 117–18, 124–6, 131, 146, 303
Declaration of Independence, 125, 189
Declaration of the Rights of Man, 121, 125
DeConde, Alexander, 23
Dehahuit, 140, 142–46, 148–57, 351–52
Delacroix de Constant, Charles, 79
De Lanceys, 183, 187, 193
Delassus, Lt. Gov. Charles Dehault, 11
De Mézières, Athanase, 90, 173, 178
Derbanne, Pierre, 103
Derbigny, Pierre, 127
Deslonde, Charles, 132
Din, Gilbert, 23
Dobbs Ferry, 194
Dooly, Capt. John, 52
Dooly, Capt. Thomas, 52
Dorsey, Robert, 203
Douglas, Marie Ann, 99
Drummond, Henry, 185
Duchess of Gordon, 185
Duels, 66, 261–62, 285, 324
Dunbar, William, 210, 273–76, 282, 289–90, 351

Dunmore, Earl of, 67–68, 188
Dunn, Isaac, 245
Durnford, Elias, 191

East Florida: Lower Creeks negotiating issues related to, 39; Georgia and South Carolina threat to invade, 45; Loyalist supported by Creeks in, 47–48; Seminole warriors planned an attack from, 53; Juan Nepomuceno de Quesada, governor of, 65, 70; British merchants, 67; Genet and Clark plotting an attack on, 77; Spanish East Texas different from, 163; Spanish policy against British colonies, 281
Eighteenth Regiment of the Louisiana Militia, 222
Elbert, Col. Samuel, 52
Elguézabal, Juan Bautista, 145–46
Ellicott, Andrew, 249
Elliott, John, 24
Emisteseguo, 41, 44–46, 48–49, 53–57
Escochabey, 46–47
Ezpeleta, Lt. Col. José de, 65

Fabel, Robin, 348
Factory Trading System, 146, 165
Fairchild, Henry, 205
Fatio, Felipe, 314
Fauchet, Jean Antoine Joseph, 78
Favrot, Cap. Pierre, 65
Federalists, 115, 193–94
Fee, Thomas, 47
Feliciana: Anglo-American militiamen in, 19; Pollock's family plantations in, 200; Pollock and Murray settled in, 202; settlers in, 209; Clark owned land in, 283; connection to Louisiana Purchase, 285; Morales unable to sell lands in, 288
Felicité, Marie Petronille, 173
Filhiol, Juan, 12, 17
Filibusters: crossing Louisiana into Spanish Texas, 152; and Pavie's support of going into Texas, 224; and Mexican Texas, 227–28; Claiborne denounces Gutiérrez-Magee expedition, 230; Lafon involved in, 302; after the War of 1812, a rise in, 315; Ripley typical of, 322; patriots as, 326; Long's expedition and definition of, 332–33
First Seminole War, 329, 333
Flint River, 68–69, 72
Flores, Gil, 172–75
Floridablanca, Count (Francisco de Goya), 9
Floridas, 3, 4, 39, 42, 63, 78; British rule, 9; Military defense, 12; Spanish policy, 8, 9; U.S. acquisition, 4
Folch, Gov. Vicente, 277–78, 303
Fontenot, Louis, 96
Fort Claiborne, 223, 230
Fort Erie, 323, 337–39
Fort George, 186
Fort Niagara, 184
Fort Pitt, 202, 206
Fort Rosalie, 121
Fort San Marco de Apalache, 66, 69
Fort St. Jean Baptiste, 219, 221
Fort St. Philip, 305
Fort Selden, 329
Fortier, Michel, 126
Fox, Charles James, 259
France: 65; Ardennes, 65; Canada, 9; expansion, 3–4, 19, 63, 219; identity, 20; Revolution, 4, 78–79, 247, 300; West Indies, 9; Louisiana cession, 18; recovery of Louisiana, 65, 78–79; Napoleonic Wars, 80; Code Noir, 91–92; Rights of Man, 121, 125; National Assembly, 122; control over Louisiana, 123, 143; sold Louisiana, 149, 254, 272–73; established Natchitoches, 164; ceded Louisiana to Spain, 168, 242; acquires Louisiana from Spain, 251, 253; war with United States, 285; Reign of Terror, 300
Françoise, Marie, 98
Franklin, Benjamin, 209, 274
Free Colored Battalion, 123–27, 131–32
Freeman, Maj. Thomas, 147, 149, 225
Freeman-Custis Expedition, 147–51, 226
French and Indian War. *See* Seven Years' War
French National Assembly, 122
Friendship, 6, 56, 163, 178, 283
Frontier Exchange, 198
Fuero military, 121
Fulton, Robert, 79

Gage, Gen. Thomas, 42
Gaines, Edward, 327–31, 339
Gainesville, Fla., 45
Galphin, George, 41–53, 55–57
Galphin, George (Son), 43
Galphin, John, 43, 72, 74
Gálvez, Gen. Bernardo de, 65, 121, 167, 243
Gálvez, José de, 167
Galveztown (Galveston), Texas, 20, 302, 328, 333
Gardner, Col. Charles K., 324–25
Gardoquí, Don Diego, 13, 21, 245
Garza, Father José de la, 178
Garzón, Antonio, 74
Gayoso de Lemos, Gov. Manuel Luis: and American settlers at Natchez, 12; opinion of Anglo settlers, 16–18; wish to Hispanicize New Orleans, 22–23; trade and official relations with U.S.A., 248–50; receives survey of U.S.-Spanish West Florida border, 274; denied agitating Indians, 280; loyalty of, 283–85
Genêt, Edmond, 18, 77, 284–85
Gentilly Road, 307
Georgia: Natchez immigrants from, 12; expansionist ambitions of, 18; and Creeks during the American War for Independence, 39; actions of the Creek during the American War for Independence, 42–57; Milford's arrival in, 63; Milford supplying Creeks in, 68; relations between Americans and Creeks in, 71–72; Creeks and Americans fight in, 74; Genêt and Clark's involvement with Creek in, 77–78; Creek dispute American land claims in, 116; people from settling in Spanish Louisiana, 208; settlers going to Florida and Louisiana, 210
Gibraltar, 228
Gibson, George, 206–7
Gil Ibarvo, Antonio, 167–78, 348, 352
Glass, Anthony, 226
Godoy, Manuel, 9, 79
González, Lt. José, 169–70
Graciosa (notarized act to emancipate slave), 95–102

Graham, John, 259
Grande Terre, La., 302
Grand Pré, Carlos, 303
Grappe, François, 98, 148–49
Grappe, Jean Baptiste, 96
Graydon, Alexander, 207
Great Britain: identity, 20; military commanders, 3; expansion, 4, 219; attack of New Orleans, 4–5, 140, 155, 299, 305–8; support of Indians, 43–46, 48; trade, 50–51; loss of Mobile, 65; ceded Floridas, 67; war with the United States, 153, 155, 227, 231; Spain declared war on, 193; Atlantic market economy, 200; coveted Louisiana and New Orleans, 242; Merry's support for Burr, 259
Great Fire of 1788, 244–45
Great Lakes, 4, 219, 298, 305
Great Raft, 149
Greenfield, Liah, 198–99
Greenwald, Erin M., 351
Guadeloupe, 189
Guichard, Antoine, 103
Guion, Capt. Isaac, 249, 338
Gulf Borderlands: political disaffection in, 3; questions of identity and allegiance in, 5–6; competing nationalities in, 315–16; Ripley's career and opportunities in, 321–22; challenges of people living in, 348; diverse identities in, 350–53
Gulf Coast: competition and tensions between peoples and nations along the, 3–5; foreign immigrants, 8; free black population, 93; and Lower Mississippi Valley important to Spanish New World Empire, 167; Livingston in the history of the, 195; economic transition of, 210; definition of national loyalty in the, 272–75; American and Spanish claims for the, 277–78; Clark's ventures in the, 282; assertions regarding national loyalty in the, 289–90; Latour and Lafon's activities in the, 302–3; Jefferson's opinion regarding Spanish control of the, 311; War of 1812 and Napoleonic War, 305, 315; Ripley and smugglers, 332–33; individual opportunities and

demands in, 349–51; historiography, few studies on, 4; loyalty, 8; economic transition, 210; few studies on national loyalty in the, 272
Gulf of Mexico: canal to, 190; French control, 219; Natchitoches district port to, 229; British possessions, 231; Battle of New Orleans, 298; War of 1812, 305; pirate and privateers in, 313; various national rulers, 315; Spanish privateers in, 327; commerce, 336
Gutiérrez de Lara, José Bernardo Maximiliano, 153, 222, 227, 228
Gutiérrez-Magee Expedition, 222, 227–30, 302

Haiti, 80, 105, 300–301, 314; Revolution, 122, 130–31
Haldimand, Gen. Frederick, 204
Hall, Stuart, 208
Handsome Fellow (Hobbythacco), 44, 46, 50–53, 57
Hanger, Kimberly, 92
Harrison, William Henry, 335
Hartford Convention, 323
Harwich, 190
Havana, Cuba: Pollock traveled to, 201; trade, 209; Coxe and Clark trade routes, 247; wood trade, 275; Latour in, 302; mentioned, 311; Latour living in, 313–14; Latour architect in, 316; Ripley plotted an assault on, 327–28
Herrera, Lt. Col. Simón de, 150, 225–26, 228
Herzog, Tamar, 12, 20, 24
Hidalgo Revolt, 152
Hidalgo y Costilla, Padre Miguel, 227
Hillsborough, Earl of, 187–88
Hilton, Sylvia, 348–49
Historical Memoir of the War in West Florida and Louisiana, 1814–15, with an Atlas, 299, 302, 306–9, 313
Holmes, Jack D. L., 23
Hopkins, Henry, 338
Horseshoe Bend, 4
Hothlitiaga, 74
Hot Springs, Ark., 310
House of Representatives, 114, 116, 132, 261, 339
Howe, Gen. William, 51
Hulings, William Emperson, 250–51
Humbert, Jean Joseph Amable, 325–26
Hunter, Phillis Whitman, 207
Hyde, Samuel C. 210–11

Iberville River, 261
Identity: definitions of, 5–6; social and personal, 15; development of national, 19–20; and patriotism, 26; of free blacks, 92; free blacks and whites, 103; restricting free blacks, 106; mentioned, 183; formation of, 198–201; consumerism and market economy, 204; formation of Pollock's national, 206–8; formation of an American, 211–12; Louisiana's national, 241; in relation to national loyalty, 271; on the Gulf Coast borderlands, 289; and Latour's description of American virtues, 299; based on practical and rational reasons, 313–16; instability of in Gulf Borderlands, 321; Ripley changes, 338; mentioned, 340; explanations of and changes in, 347–53
Illinois, 198, 202, 204, 207, 284
Ireland, 220, 241, 282, 289
Irujo, Carlos Martínez de, 17, 20, 22, 252 255
Ishenpoaphe, 47, 51
Isle Breville, 91, 102, 105–6
Istillicha, "Manslayer," 67
Italy, 20, 193

Jackson, Andrew: 18, military victories, 4; enlisting Kadohadachos aid, 155; Philip an aid to, 194; oath of loyalty to Spain, 278; Battle of New Orleans and aftermath, 298–99; preparing for British attack, 305; end of the War of 1812, 308; relations with Latour, 315; Southern Division and relations with Ripley, 324–25; and army, 330; partisan identities during administration of, 335; as territorial governor, 339
Jackson, Richard, 185
Jacobs, James R., 13
Jamaica, 186, 191, 193

Jefferson, Thomas, 228, selecting a territorial governor, 113–17; selecting Claiborne, 119, concerns about free black population, 122–24; policy in Louisiana, 130–31; border dispute, 143, defining boundary, 146–47; trade and immigrants, 210; selecting U.S. representatives for Louisiana, 222–23; Wilkinson conspiracy, 225–26; appointed Claiborne, 241; purchasing Louisiana, 250–52; negations regarding Louisiana, 254; Burr conspiracy, 256–60; transfer of power, 273–77; geography and politics of Louisiana, 279; and slavery in territories, 282; negotiating Louisiana Purchase boundary, 284–86; commercial restriction, 302–3; encouraging expeditions, 311
Jesup, Thomas, 328–30
Jones, Evan, 211, 243, 250
Jones, Thomas ap Catesby, 307

Kaskaskia, 202
Kastor, Peter J., 207, 272
Kemper, Nathan, 285
Kemper, Reuben, 285
Kemper, Samuel, 285
Kemper Brothers, 19
Kennedy, Roger G., 210
Kentucky, 339; plans to invade Spanish territory, 13; emigrants to Spanish territory, 17; French and Creek activity, 76–78; migration from, 210; Wilkinson and, 244–45; trade, 248; Burr and Clark interests in, 259; Wilkinson from, 277; Wilkinson and Spanish trade in, 283–85
Kerr, John C., 230
Kerr, Lewis, 126
King, Rufus, 254
King, William, 328
King Charles IV, 251
King George III, 189
King Joseph of Portugal, 228, 231
Kinship, 6, 104, 163, 167, 178
Kirkland, Col. Moses, 67
Klier, Betje Black, 348
Kukla, Jon, 13

La Bahía (Goliad, Texas), 168, 222, 225, 334
LaCarrière, Guillaume, Seigneur de Latour and Falhiés, 299, 304
Laclotte, Jean-Hyacinthe, 304–5
Lafayette, Marquis de, 303–4
Laffite, Jean, 301–2, 307, 309–10, 313–14
Lafitte, Pierre, 301–2, 307, 310, 313–14
Lafon, Barthélemy, 302–3
Lake Borgne, 242, 305, 307
Lake Maurepas, 190, 242
Lake Pontchartrain, 190, 242
Lallemand, Gen. Charles François Antoine, 302, 314
Landers, Jane, 279
LaSalle, Rene Robert de, 164
Latour, Arsène Lacarrière, 298–316, 351
Latrobe, Benjamin Henry, 304
Latrobe, Henry Boneval, 304–5
Laurens, Gov. Henry, 51
Laussat, Madame, 255
Laussat, Pierre Clément, 123, 124, 241, 253–56
LeClerc, Gen. Charles, 301
LeClerc, Jean-Antoine, 65
LeComte, Margueritte, 105
LeComte, Marie Perine, 105
LeComte, Widow, 100
LeCour (LaCour), Marie Pelagie, 105
LeCourt (LaCourt), Pelagie, 103
Lemonnier, Dr. Yves, 304
Lennan, Father Francis, 17
Leonard, Gilberto, 17
Leslie, John, 9, 25
Leslie, Robert, 70
Lewis, Meriwether, 225
Lewis and Clark Expedition, 275–76
Lexington and Concord, 206
Libres (Free people of color), 90–106, 120
Linares, Duque de, 165
Linnard, Thomas M., 155
Little Rock, 310
Little Tallassee, 41, 44, 50, 54–55, 78
Livingston, Edward, 194, 303, 305, 335
Livingston, Henry, 193
Livingston, Lewis, 305
Livingston, Peter (son), 193
Livingston, Peter Van Brugh, 183–84

Livingston, Peter Van Brugh (son), 193
Livingston, Philip, 183–84
Livingston, Philip (signer of the Declaration), 189
Livingston, Philip Peter, 183–95, 348, 351–52
Livingston, Philip Peter (nephew), 193
Livingston, Philip Philip, 193
Livingston, Robert R., 194, 251, 254
Livingston, William, 191, 193
Localism, 272
London: Milford traveling to, 78; Philip's life in, 184–85; Chester's communication with, 190; orders from, 192; trade, 202; mentioned, 226; Clark's brokers in, 260
Londonderry, 200
Long, Dr. James, 332–34, 338
López y Angulo, Ramón, 17, 25
Lord Stirling, 183–84
Los Adaes, 147, 166–72, 174, 176
Louisiana: Creoles, 9; immigration into, 8, 9, 16, 18, 20, 23–25, 210–11, 283; political uncertainty, 3, 219; Purchase, 3, 94, 119, 156, 194, 208, 210, 212, 258, 280, 284, 285–87; military defense, 12–13, 75; Spanish policy, 21, 23; Spanish governor, 65; French creoles, 76; Clark's plan for attack, 77; ceded to France, 78; defense of, 79; sale to the United States, 80, 140, 220, 272; slaves and Code Noir, 92; libre population in, 93, 104, 120, 278; frontier, 101–2, 104–5, 140; militia, 121, 132–33, 277–78, 285; French control over, 123, 254; transfer, 124, 143, 152, 256, 272; Memorial to Congress, 127–28; Claiborne's policies in, 130; 1811 slave rebellion, 132–33; Spain takes control, 142; Neutral Ground, 150–51; British attack against, 155; ceded to Spain, 168; illicit trade with Texas, 172; market economy, 200–205, 208; Pollock owned land, 206; inheritance, 220; government encouraged American trade, 248; desire for statehood, 257; Burr Conspiracy, 258–60; loyalty of inhabitants, 3, 260, 271–73, 277–78, 282, 284; historiography, 272; flora and fauna, 274–75; exploring expeditions, 275–76; geographic location, 277; Spanish interference after Purchase, 278–79; American policy, 279; Indians, 279–81; purchase and slaves, 281; legal system, 281–82; geographical defenses during War of 1812, 305–7; incorporated into the U.S., 316; threat of slave uprising, 331
Louisiana Remonstrance, 257
Louisiana State University, 205
Louis XV, 80
Loyalist Claims Commission, 192
Loyalists, 9, 20, 53–54, 191, 199
Loyalty: along the Gulf Coast borderlands, 5–6; Spanish loyalty oaths 11–19; weakened Spanish, 22; in exchange for rights, 24; rule and concepts of, 26; divisions among the Creeks, 44; land bounties for, 191; questions about, 163; to government and community, 167; and community, 175; motivations for, 178–79; land bounties for, 191; Louisianians and, 260; historical discourse, 271; Louisiana and national, 277–78; and Claiborne 282; personal, 284; transfer of, 286; restrictions of, 299; and Latour, 302–3; fluidity of, 315–16; definitions of, 347–53

Macarty, Agustín, 13, 16
Macomb, Alexander, 330
Macpherson, James, 188
Mad Dog, 71–72, 75–76
Madison, James, 127; Claiborne writing to, 116; directing Claiborne, 117; Free Colored Battalion, 124; communication with Claiborne, 129; importance of Kadohadachos, 144; relation with Indians, 154; reports about Sibley and Carr, 226; warned about Spanish movements, 252; and Louisiana Purchase, 254–56; Clark's ambitions under, 260; correspondence about Louisiana, 277; tensions in New Orleans, 279; border dispute, 285–88; commercial restrictions, 302; and Ripley's retreat, 323
Madrid, Spain, 16, 21, 79, 168, 249, 252, 311, 313
Mad Turkey, 47
Magee, Augustus William, 153, 228

Maine, 322
Manumission, 90–92, 94–103, 105–6, 121
Mariotte, Marie Louise dit, 89, 91, 104
Maroon communities, 4, 298
Marschalk, Andrew, 338
Martos y Navarette, Gov. Angel, 167–68
Massachusetts, 42, 321, 338
Matagorda, 225
Matanzas, 288
Mather, James, 211
McDermott, John Francis, 63
McGillivray, Alexander, 53–57, 66–73, 78
McGillivray, Jeanette, 66
McGillivray, Lachlan, 53, 66,
McIntosh, Gen. Lachlan, 48
McIntosh, William, 46, 49–51, 54–55
McLatchy, Charles, 66
McMichael, Andrew, 19
McMurphy, Daniel, 53
Mercier, Charlotte, 98
Merry, Sir Anthony, 259
Metoyer, Claude-Thomas-Pierre: Coincoin's relationship with, 89–91; frees Coincoin, 95; giving Coincoin land, 97; the will of, 99; Coincoin's reliance on, 101–3; legacy of Coincoin's relationship with, 105–6
Metoyer, Dominique, 105
Metoyer, Joseph Antoine, 90, 105
Metoyer, Nicolas Augustin, 90–91, 105
Metoyer, Pierre, 105
Mexico: independence, 5; Hidalgo Revolt, 152; East Texas settlers from, 163; trade, 167; Viceroyalty of, 173; Neutral Ground, 223; Cortés's activities in, 225; independence and Napoleonic War, 227–29; War of 1812, 231; Burr and Clark's interest in, 259–60; Latour warning of Anglo settlers, 311–15; Spanish troops in, 327; American settlers in Texas, 334
Mexico City, 164–66, 173, 175, 219, 311
Michigan, 284
Middle Temple (Inns of Court), 184
Milford, Louis LeClerc de, 63–81
Militia: Spanish foreign-born, 12–13; free black, 102; Claiborne and ill-equipped, 117; New Orleans Free Colored, 120–27; Claiborne's respect for black militia, 131–33; lack of one in Florida, 192; activities of Louisiana Militia, 222, Jones captain of Louisiana, 250; Clark organizing, 256; Clark's plans to organize a, 260–61; during transfer of Louisiana, 277–78; Clark organized Louisiana, 285; Lafon's service in, 302; problems with, 327; Ripley's warnings regarding, 331; and loyalty, 350
Miller, Bonnamy and Company, 67–68
Miller, James, 339
Mina, Francisco Xavier, 313, 327
Miranda, Francisco de, 226
Miró, Gov. Eteban Rodriguez: immigrant policy, 10; loyalty oaths, 13; Wilkinson and Spanish policy, 15–16; creating loyalty, 21–22; gained Milford's attention, 65; American commerce, 244–45; importance of patriotism and loyalty, 350–51
Mississippi River: changing control, 4–5; Americans wanting to settle west of, 17; defense of, 48; Milford's trip up, 65; Milford's opinion regarding U.S. control of, 76; American trade on, 79; mentioned, 89; Indians, 153–56; French and Spanish influence, 165–66; trade, 177; proposed canals, 190; Pollock's trade along, 202–3; growth of New Orleans, 205–7; social and economic transitions, 210–11; French exploration, 219; trading posts, 227; history of, 242–44; Coxe and Clark trading along, 247; American duties, 249; U.S. interest west of, 277–78; U.S.A. taking control, 281; U.S. navigation of, 285; War 1812, 305–7; road from Natchitoches to, 331
Mississippi Territory: Claiborne governor of, 114; conditions in, 116–19; concerns regarding free blacks in, 122–24; Clark traveling to, 250; mentioned, 277; Americans in, 280; Claiborne and loyalty, 289
Mississippi Valley: under different flags, 5; Americans and Indians in, 117; as key to Spanish empire, 167; Americanization and economics in, 198–205; trade, 207–12;

French in 242; importance of American settlers in, 251; loyalty in, 273; assessing national loyalty in, 282; loyalty in, 284; Clark's landholdings in, 286; U.S. control of, 298; possible British attack, 305
Missouri River, 225
Missouri Territory, 339
Mobile, Ala.: Creeks, 52; Milford in, 65; Milford leaves, 78; free black population in, 93; Livingston becomes collector of Customs at, 188; St. Denis travels through, 219; mentioned, 285; Morales sold land in, 288; Spanish loss of, 298; Jackson's thoughts on, 305; American seizure of, 310; Spanish threat, 327; Ripley's failed road through, 332
Moniac, Jacob, 54
Monroe, James, 227–28, 254, 309, 323, 330
Moore, Henry, 186–87
Moore, John Hebron, 210
Moore, Sam, 53
Morales, Juan Ventura, 16, 17, 248–49, 252, 258, 287–89
Morelos y Pavón, José María, 227
Morenos, 89, 96–99, 102–4, 121
Morgan, Benjamin, 227
Morgan, Gen. David, 307–8
Morgan, George, 10, 13, 16, 21, 65, 202
Morris, Robert, 206
Morris, Staats Long, 185
Mulon, Jean Lebrun dit, 104
Mulon, Jeannot, 100
Münkler, Herfried, 349
Muñoz, Gov. Manuel, 177
Murray, William, 202
Muskogee Indian State, 69

Nabob, 186
Nacogdoches, Texas: Hainais tribes, 143; trade, 145–47; Spanish forces in, 149–50; Dehahuit in, 152–53; census records, 163; mission in, 170; Nuevo Reglamento and, 174; establishment of Nuestra Señora del Pilar de Nacogdoches, 176–78; Cortés around, 225; abandoned and land claims in, 228–29; asylum to slaves, 281

Nashville, 248, 325
Nassau, Bahamas, 67–69
Natchez, Miss.: American settlers in, 12; questions regarding Americans in, 17–18; thefts in, 116; Choctaw and Claiborne relations, 118–19; military action, 121; French trade, 167; commerce, 203; non-English-speaking settlers, 205; slave population, 208; cotton production, 210; Old Natchez district, 212; Clark's success in, 248–50; Burr in, 258; Dunbar's description of, 274–76; Spanish withdrawal from, 278; Choctaws, 280; Clark's activities in, 282–83; Wilkinson in, 285; Long from, 332; Ripley marries woman from, 334
Natchitoches, La.: Coincoin's life in, 89–106; Natives around, 140–48; American and Native relations, 150–56; French presence in, 164–67; Spanish and French in, 173–76; history of, 219–31; mentioned, 310; Trimble at Fort Selden, 329; 331–32, occupational government in, 338
Nationality: in regards to indentify, 5–6; Wilkinson and, 14; ethnic and cultural parts of, 21; Louisiana, 241; U.S. control of Louisiana, 256; on the Louisiana borderlands, 271–72; fluidity of in Gulf Coast region, 315; and personal identity, 347; of marginalized peoples, 351
Native American tribes: Adaes, 147, 166; Ais, 147–48; Alabamas, 143, 148–49, 154; Apache, 168, 170–71, 228, 311; Apalache, 149; Bidaís, 171; Chickasaw, 71, 75–76, 121, 339; Coahuiltecan, 166; Coushattas, 143, 148–50, 154; Doustionis, 141; Hasinais, 140–43, 146–48, 152, 155, 165; Kadohadachos, 140–57; Kansas, 311; Kichai, 143, 152, 155; Lower Natchitoches, 141; Nabedaches, 143, 155; Nacogdoches, 143, 147, 152; Nadaco, 143, 147, 152–54; Natchitoches, 140–42; Osage, 142, 156; Panis Piques, 149; Pawnee, 311; Stockbridge, 42; Taovayas, 143, 146, 151, 153; Tawakonis, 143, 146, 152–53, 155; Tejas, 171; Wichitas, 140, 142–44, 146, 152–53; Yatasis, 141–42, 148, 154

—Caddo: history and relations with Europeans, 140–44; and Dehahuit, 152–54; influence of U.S.A. on, 156–57; St. Denis and, 164–65; ties with French, 167; aiding those in Los Adaes, 169; mentioned, 171; Spanish want support of, 173; Texans moving into land of, 175–76; relations with the French, 178; Ripley's opinion of, 334; Caddo relations with the U.S.A., 351–52

—Cherokee: relations with British, 41; trade, 45; attacks during War for Independence, 47–50; and British attack of Georgia, 53–55; Seagrove leave for, 72; possible confederation, 75; Claiborne and, 116

—Choctaw: Creek-Choctaw War, 44; role along the Mississippi, 48; Cherokee flee to towns of, 54; Spanish and, 71; possible confederation, 75; Claiborne and, 116; meeting with Claiborne, 118–19; growing power, 142; peace treaty, 145; mentioned, 156; Spain and anti-American sentiment, 280; Battle of New Orleans, 315

—Comanche: Kadohadacho influence on, 140; trade, 142–44; Spanish alliance with, 147; meetings with Sibley, 152–54; threat to west, 168; mentioned, 171; raids of, 175–76; pacifying, 228; trade with American trappers, 311

—Creek: Horseshoe Bend, 4; during American War of Independence, 39–57; Milford's relations with, 63–81; Claiborne and, 116; uprising of, 140; threat to the United States, 154–55; Gaines's operation against, 327; negotiating with the United States, 351–52

—Seminole, 333; in Florida, 39; raids against Georgia, 46–47; preparing to attack Georgia, 53; trade, 67–69; Gaines's operation against, 327; First Seminole War, 329

Navarro, Martín, 13, 15, 21–22, 25, 244, 351
Navy, U.S., 191
Neches River, 141, 143
Negrito, 148
Negro Fort, 298, 329
Neutral Ground, 150–51, 223, 225, 228–29, 329, 331
Neutrality Act of 1794, 77

Nueva Bourbon, 205
Nuevo Reglamento of 1772, 168, 172–75
New Jersey, 184, 208
New Madrid, 65, 205, 312
New Orleans, 3, 4, 22–23, 70, 72, 77, 89, 91–93; Jackson's defense 4; manumission in 96–98, 100–101; *libres* in 102, 104, 118, 120; in 1803, 113; composition of population 114; transfer to U.S., 119; colored militia, 122, 124–25, 133; Conseil de Ville, 128; 1811 slave rebellion, 132–33; British attack, 156; trade from 167; 168; commerce, 190, 201–2; 191; James Willing's raid, 207; fires 209; Masonic Lodge, 224; trip via red river, 230; Clark establishes mercantile house, 242; English merchants in 242; fire in 244–45; borderland town, 245; right of deposit at, 247–48; American merchants in 249; closed to American commerce, 252; geographic location, 277; mentioned, 281; Clark's business interests, 283; closure of port, 288; battle of 298–99, 305–8; Associates, 328, 333
New Purchase Cession, 43, 45
New Spain: Texas in, 5; U.S. and British expansion toward, 9; problems with Texas-Louisiana borderlands, 163; threat of French traders, 165–68; governing of, 171–72; U.S. threat to, 276
New York: McGillivray travels to, 68; New York agreement, 70; William left for, 114; Livingston's history in, 183–84; lead-up to the American War for Independence, 186–88; Philip's connections to, 190–91; mentioned, 193; Livingston's return to, 195, Jones from, 250; Latour in, 303
New York City, 194, 243, 253, 337
Niagara Campaign, 323–25, 339
Nicholas, Robert Carter, 339
North, Diane, 348
North Carolina, 41
Northern Canal Company, 193–94
Northern Ireland, 200
Northwestern State University of Louisiana, 222
Northwest Territory, 282, 285
Noyrit (Nayrit or Nogret), Charles, 223–24

Nuestra Señora del Pilar de Bucareli, 175, 176
Nuestra Señora del Pilar de los Adaes, 175
Nuñez, Don Vincente José, 244

O'Brien, Margaret, 201
Ocfuskee, 74, 76–77
Ochlockonee River, 69
Oconee River, 72, 77
O'Conor, Don Hugo, 167–68, 172–75, 177–78, 348, 351
Ogeechee River, 47, 50, 68
O'Hara, Capt. Remigio, 20
Ohio, 339
Ohio River: Anglo-French rivalry in, 4; Spanish policy in, 10; Americans settling in, 16; Sevier representing the, 114; trade, 202; Clark conquering, 206–7; Pollock supplying Americans in, 243; commerce 247
Ohio Valley, 202, 248
Oklahoma, 141, 157
Old Tallassee King, 49–50
Olive Branch Petition, 193
Olivier, Don Pedro, 70–75, 78
O'Neill Col. Arturo, 65, 69–70, 72
Onís, Don Luis de, 299, 309, 312–13
Oregon Trail, 276
O'Reilly, Gov. Alejandro: attracting American settlers, 9; general rules of, 16; mentioned, 167; and the *Nuevo Reglamento*, 172–73; friends with Pollock, 201; buying slaves 203; allowed Pollock to trade, 242
Orleans Territory: Claiborne governor, 114; Claiborne travels to, 119; political climate in, 122; Claiborne's policies in, 130; Indians in, 144; organization of, 256–57; Clark and Claiborne duel, 261; mentioned, 263
Ouachita River, 11, 12, 17, 286, 310, 312

Pacific Ocean, 9, 225
Pakenham, Gen. Sir Edward Michael, 298
Panic of 1819, 325, 340
Panton, Leslie and Company, 25, 66, 68, 69, 78
Panton, William, 9, 25, 66, 69–71, 74, 78
Pardos, 90–91, 96–98, 100, 102–5, 121
Paris, France, 78, 80, 253–54, 300

Parker, Daniel, 328, 333
Patriotism: in Spanish frontier, 9; of birth nation, 14; definitions of, 19–23; and Spanish officials and policy, 25–26; Wilkinson's, 226; and commerce, 282; Latour and practical, 316; Ripley's, 326; Mexican concerns about Anglo, 334; Miró and, 350
Patriots, 326–29
Patterson, Daniel Todd, 302
Patterson, Thomas, 207
Pavie, Charles Roque, 222–24, 231
Pavie, Étienne, 89, 222–23
Pavie, Father Pierre, 222–24
Pavie, Joseph, 222–23
Pavie, Theodore, 224
Peace of Amiens, 252, 301
Peñalver, Luis de, 22
Penn, John, 185–87
Penn, Richard, 185, 193
Pennsylvania, 185; Penn as lieutenant governor of, 193; Scotch-Irish merchant network in, 201; Hamilton Pollock from, 205; immigrants from, 207–9; Procopio Jacinto Pollock from, 249; Gayoso's trip through, 284
Pensacola, Fla.: 193; Congress of Pensacola, 44–45; Creeks and British in, 48–50; threatened, 52; Cameron and Taitt flee to, 54; defense of, 57; officials at, 65; Creeks and Milford in, 67–78; free blacks in, 94; Livingston in, 190–91; Haldimand as commandant of, 204; land in, 285; Morales selling land near, 287; Jackson and, 299; Ripley and, 325; Ripley's concern regarding attacks on, 327–29; Fourth Infantry in, 331; Adams and Jackson's seizure of, 336
Philadelphia: Milford travel to, 78; Claiborne's connections in, 114–15; trade, 201–4; commerce, 206–7; Pollock trade through, 209–10; connected to Mississippi Valley ports, 212; merchants, 243; trade with New Orleans, 245–47; U.S. representatives from, 249–50; business interests in New Orleans, 252–53; Clark's letters to, 260; Dunbar from, 274; Latour and publishers in, 308; Philbrick, Francis, 10, 13
Pickering, Timothy, 249

Piernas, Joseph, 20
Pierre, Jean, 104
Pike, Zebulon, 311, 338
Pinckneyville, Miss., 200, 209, 211
Piquery, Nicolas, 102
Pitot, James, 129
Pittsburgh, 243, 245, 247
Place d'Armes, 113, 126
Pointe Coupée, 205, 262, 281 283
Poissot, Agnes, 105
Poissot, Athanase, 103
Poissot, Marie Agnes, 100, 103
Poissot, Remy, 103
Pollock, Hamilton, 205, 209
Pollock, Jaret, 200
Pollock, Margaret O'Brien, 201, 209
Pollock, Oliver, 198, 200–11, 242–43, 351, 352
Pollock, Procopio Jacinto, 209, 249
Pollockstown, 200
Porter, Roy, 15
Portugal, 228
Posey, John Thornton, 14
Potter, David, 271–72, 289
Poughkeepsie Convention, 193
Poydras, Julien, 262
Princeton University, 184
Prudhomme, Jean Baptiste, 220
Prudhomme, Jean Pierre Phillipe, 220
Prudhomme, Luisa Eufracia, 224
Prudhomme, Marie Louise, 220
Pyeatt, Maj. James, 310

Quebec, 46
Quesada, Juan Nepomuceno de, 65, 70
Quintanilla, Father Luis de, 90

Rachal, Jean Baptiste, 100, 103
Rae, John, 44
Rae, Robert, 41, 42, 44, 46, 53
Ramírez, Alejandro, 313–14
Ramón, Capt. Diego, 165
Ramón, Lt. Juan Ygnacio, 148, 150
Rancho del Lobanillo, 167, 169, 172, 174
Red River: Coincoin, 89–90; Caddoans of, 140–44; U.S. and Spanish interests, 146–50; U.S. control of, 156–57; St. Denis in, 165–66; French trading post, 219; French settlers, 223; Red River expedition, 225; travel on, 230; Dunbar leading expedition, 275–77; after War of 1812, 298, settlers along, 311–12; Ripley's interest in, 331
Reed and Forde Company, 246
Regiment of City (New Orleans) Militia, 126–27
Reglamento de Comercio Libre of 1778, 202
Relf, Richard, 253, 259, 262
Republic of Texas, 224, 321, 333. *See also* Texas
Richmond, John, 68
Rio Grande, 143, 155, 165, 330
Rio Hondo, 223, 225
Ripley, Eleazer Wheelock, 321–40, 351
Ripley, Henry Dearborn, 335
Ripperdá, Barón de, 168–75
River Foyle, 200
River Poteau, 311
Rivière aux Cannes (River Aux Chenes), 105, 305
Robinson, Dr. Samuel S., 209, 211
Robinson, Mary, 209, 211
Rochambeau, Gen. Donatien, 301, 315
Rodríguez, Sebastián, 147–48
Romain, 68
Rose (schooner), 191
Ross, John, 274
Rouquier, Anita, 221
Rouquier, François, 220, 223, 231
Rouquier, Henriette, 221, 224–25, 229
Rouquier, J. François, Jr., 221
Rouquier, Joséphine Aimée, 221, 222, 231
Rouquier, Marianne, 221–24, 231
Rouquier, Marie Louise Prudhome, 221, 231
Rouquier, Marie (Marcelite) Joséphine, 221, 224–25, 227
Rousseau, Marie Ann, 98
Royal Charlotte, 201
Rubí, Marqués de, 168
Russia, 227, 273
Rutledge, John 52

Sabine River: 229; Hasinais living on, 143; Ramón retreating to, 148; St. Denis in, 165; U.S. expansion to, 222–25; Cortéz crossing, 227; impact of War of 1812 on, 298; Latour's exploration of, 310; 1806 frontier crises, 329; Ripley wants posts along, 331–32; Ripley's interest in, 337

Saint Domingue: revolt in, 121–23; influence on New Orleans free blacks, 125; Claiborne's concerns regarding blacks in Louisiana, 127–28; Claiborne avoid repetition of, 130–32; Spanish trade, 243; refugees from and loyalty, 289; Latour in, 300–302

Salcedo, Gov. Manuel María de, 114, 152, 228–29, 255

Salcedo, Nemesio, 145, 147, 150

Saltillo, Mexico, 166–67

Saltillo Civil Archives, 224

San Antonio de Bexar, 152–53, 166–72, 174–77, 333

San Augustine, Texas, 170

San Juan Bautista, 165

San Miguel de Linares de los Adaes Mission, 166

Santa Fe, 225, 310–11

Sargent, Winthrop, 116, 280

Savannah, Ga., 40, 48, 57

Scotland, 200

Scott, Winfield, 323, 325, 330, 335, 337

Seagrove, James, 71–72, 74–76, 78

Seagrove, Robert, 72

Sears, Isaac, 186

Sebastian, Benjamin, 285

Sedella, Father Antonio, 313

Sepúlveda, José Antonio, 223

Seven Years' War (French and Indian War), 45, 184, 189, 201, 242

Sevier, John, 10, 18, 114

Shaler, Capt. William, 227–28

Shaumburgh, Bartholomew, 338

Shaw, Capt. John, 3,

Sibley, Dr. John, 144–47, 151–56, 222, 226–27, 230

Silver Spring, Pa., 209

Smith, Benjamin Barton, 225

Smith, F. Todd, 280, 352

Smith, Robert, 203

Snake River, 225

Society for Establishing Useful Manufactures, 194

Someruelos, Marqués de, 252

Sons of Liberty, 186

Soto, Marcel, 152

South Carolina, 52; Creek problems in, 39; during American War for Independence, 41–45; Natives visit Galphin in, 48; Creek attack on, 55; American settlers from, 208; Spanish plots against, 281

Spain: Bourbon Reforms, 12, 21, 202; loyalty oaths, 8, 11–17, 19, 21; protesting Louisiana Purchase, 3, 255; expansion, 4, 12; diplomacy, 5; identity, 20, 284; immigration Policy, 9–11, 17, 23–25, ; defensive policy, 9–10, 23, 172–73, 312–13; military service, 13; tolerance, 10; land policy, 11, 16, 17, 18, 21; acquired Florida, 67; cede Louisiana, 78, 251; slave laws, 91; blacks in society, 102; boundary dispute, 143, 286, 312; claimed Indian allegiance, 144; acted to retain Indian allegiance, 145; acquired Louisiana from France, 168; declared War on Britain, 193; competed for Empire, 219; English merchants in New Orleans, 242; mercantile system, 243; navigation of Mississippi River, 243–44; closes Mississippi River, 252; Louisiana national loyalty, 272; Indian policy, 280–81, 311–12; Louisiana Purchase and slaves, 281; corruption, 287–89; land sales, 287–89; Latour report on American expansion, 313–14; warned of the Pax Americana, 316; stirring up Indians, 329–30; threat in Texas, 330–31

Sparks, Capt. Richard, 225

St. Augustine, 41, 45, 49, 50, 328

St. Denis, Louis Juchereau, 89, 165, 173, 178

St. Denis, Marie des Nieges de, 89–90

St. Denis, Pierre Antoine Juchereau, 89, 219–20,

St. Francis River, 312

St. Francisville, 206, 211, 337

St. Genevieve, 205

St. Lawrence River, 4, 219

St. Louis, 11, 205, 211, 225

St. Louis Cemetery No. 1, 262

St. Marks, Fla., 299

St. Marys River, 71–72, 74

Stamp Act, 186

Steuben, William Frederick von, 13, 16
Stoddard, Amos, 349–50
Strabane, 200
Stuart, John, 41–51, 53, 56
Sussex County, Va., 114

Taitt, David, 41, 43, 45, 54, 57, 194
Tallapoosa River, 54, 77
Talleyrand-Périgord, Charles Maurice de, 254
Tangipahoa River, 205
Taos, N.M., 310–11
Tastanegy, Gen. François, 66–67, 79, 351
Tennessee, 114, 116, 210, 226, 277, 283–85
Teute, Fredika, 4
Texas: 3, 4, 5, 18, 89–90, 93; Louisiana frontier, 101–2, 104–5, 140; border, 141; Neutral Ground, 150–51; royalist regain control, 154; isolation of 164; illicit trade with Louisiana, 172; lands in, 224; revolution, 224; agreement, 225; independence of 227; slaves fleeing to, 229, 281; vulnerable Spanish outpost, 309–10; magnet for illicit activity, 315. *See also* Republic of Texas
Thomas, Samuel, 46
Thompson Creek, 205
Thorn, Frost, 224
Tignon ordinance, 120
Tonyn, Gov. Patrick, 45, 47, 49
Townes, Ed, 348
Townshend Act, 186
Transcontinental Treaty (Adams-Onís Treaty), 5, 156, 223, 332
Treaty of 1783, 67, 243
Treaty of Nogales, 75
Treaty of Paris (1763), 242, 277, 286
Treaty of San Ildefonso, 251, 273
Treaty of San Lorenzo (Pinckney's Treaty), 79, 247, 249, 253, 274, 278–80
Treaty of Tellico, 116
Trimble, William, 329–30, 339
Trinity River, 175
Tuckabatche, Fla., 72, 74, 75, 76
Tuckabatchee, 40, 50, 51,
Tunica Bayou, 204–5, 211
Tunica Bend, 207, 209, 211
Tunicaville, 211

Turk's Head Tavern, 185
Turner, Cap. Edward, 145, 338

Ugarte, Cap. José Joaquin, 145
Ulloa, Gov. Antonio de, 201
Ulster, 200, 201, 206, 208
United States, 4, 5, 13, 14, 17, 18, 140; acquired Louisiana, 143, 152, 194; claimed Indian allegiance, 144; alliance with Kodohadachos, 145, 151, 156; war with Britain, 153, 227; war against Creeks, 154; trade 204; purchased Louisiana, 220; war with France, 285; boundary dispute with Spain, 286; expansion across the southwest, 310–12; Goliad, 222, 335–37
Unzaga y Amézaga, Gov. Luis de, 169
Urquhart, Thomas, 286

Valle, Lt. Dionisio, 146–47
Van Horne, Cornelia, 193
Vera Cruz, Mexico, 167, 259–60
Viana, Francisco, 148
Vicencio, Don Juan María, 168
Victor, Gen. Claude Perrin, 79, 253–54
Villa de San Fernando, 170
Villebeuvre, Cap. Juan de la, 76
Villevallier, France, 80
Villiers, Lt. Luis de, 76–78
Vincennes, 202
Virginia, 114, 206, 248, 284, 339

Wakulla River, 66, 69
War of 1812: U.S. expansion after, 5; British invasion of Louisiana during, 140; start of, 153; Kadohadochos' importance lessens after, 156; drop in land values after, 262; U.S. nationalism and, 272; impact on Gulf of Mexico, 298; Latour's actions, 302–3; economic problems after, 305; U.S. westward expansion, 310–11, tensions and loyalties after, 315–16; Ripley and, 321–23; changes in the U.S.A. after, 329; U.S. military after, 339–40
War of the Quadruple Alliance, 166
Washington, George, 249
Washington, D.C.: Gutiérrez in, 227–28; Spanish minister in, 252; announce-

ment of Louisiana Purchase in, 254–55; Claiborne wanted troops from, 277; mentioned, 298; Wilkinson in, 303–4; Onís in, 313; Ripley's lobbying in, 329–333; *Washington Globe* and Ripley, 335
Watkins, John, 262
Wavell, Gen. Arthur Goodall, 224
Weber, David, 15
Wellbank, George, 69–70
West Florida: loyalty oaths in, 8; Loyalists in, 9; loyalty of American settlers in, 17–21; historiography of loyalty in, 23; Spanish immigration policy, 25; loyalists trade, 41–43; Stuart and deerskin trade, 45; Choctaw defense of, 48; liquor from, 50; British trade in, 66–67; Treaty of Nogales, 75; U.S. boundary, 79; different from Spanish Texas, 163; Chester, governor of, 188; Livingston in, 190; no militia, 192; Livingston travels to, 194–95; Pollock land in, 205–6; Felicianas, 209; loyalty in, 271; U.S. surveyors to, 274–75; Native American trade, 281; Clark's land in, 283; border dispute, 285–89; American filibustering in, 310
West Indies: refugees from, 9; trade, 48; illegal immigration from, 127; slaves from, 203; French trade with, 219; French and Spanish trade with, 242–43; Philadelphia and, 247; lumber trade, 275; Jackson informed from, 305; rumors of a slave revolt in, 313

West Virginia, 210
Whitaker, Arthur P., 8, 10, 23, 202
White, Col. Enrique, 65, 70, 72–74, 76–78
White, Richard, 4
White Lieutenant of Ocfuskee, 74, 77–78
White River, 312
Whitney, Eli, 283
Widow Buard, 98
Wilkinson, Gen. James: as colonizer, 10; 1788 colonizing effort, 12; questions of honor and allegiance, 13–17; and national identity, 20–21; thoughts on the Mississippi Territory, 117; commissioner to Louisiana, 119; transfer of Louisiana Territory, 123; gave Claiborne flags, 127; thoughts on free black militia, 131; Burr Conspiracy, 225–26; Neutral Ground, 228–29; trade, 244–45; transfer of power in Louisiana, 255–56; relationship with Clark and Burr, 258–59; Clark-Claiborne duel, 261; Mississippi militia, 277; accusations against Spain, 280; loyalty of, 282–84; commerce, 303
Wilkinson, James B., 228
Willing, James, 191–92, 204, 207
Willing and Morris, 201, 203, 206
Willis, Perrin, 333
Worcester v. Georgia, 335

Yale University, 184
Yazoo River, 75

www.ingramcontent.com/pod-product-compliance
Lightning Source LLC
Chambersburg PA
CBHW051803230426
43672CB00012B/2615